Understanding
ECONOMICS
A Contemporary Perspective

Seventh Edition

MARK LOVEWELL

Ryerson University
Toronto, Ontario

McGraw-Hill
Ryerson

McGraw-Hill
Ryerson

Understanding Economics: A Contemporary Perspective
Seventh Edition

The Internet addresses listed in the text were accurate at the time of publication. The inclusion of a website does not indicate an endorsement by the authors or McGraw-Hill Ryerson, and McGraw-Hill Ryerson does not guarantee the accuracy of information presented at these sites.

ISBN-13: 978-1-25-903080-2
ISBN-10: 1-25-903080-6

2 3 4 5 6 7 8 9 0   TCP   1 9 8 7 6 5

Printed and bound in Canada.

Care has been taken to trace ownership of copyright material contained in this text; however, the publisher will welcome any information that enables it to rectify any reference or credit for subsequent editions.

DIRECTOR OF PRODUCT MANAGEMENT: Rhondda McNabb
SENIOR PRODUCT MANAGER: James Booty
MARKETING MANAGER: Jeremy Guimond
PRODUCT DEVELOPER: Kamilah Reid-Burrell
PHOTO/PERMISSIONS RESEARCH: Robyn Craig
SENIOR PRODUCT TEAM ASSOCIATE: Stephanie Giles
SUPERVISING EDITOR: Joanne Limebeer
COPY EDITOR: Janice Dyer
PLANT PRODUCTION COORDINATOR: Scott Morrison
MANUFACTURING PRODUCTION COORDINATOR: Emily Hickey
COVER DESIGN: Claude Poulin
COVER IMAGE: ICHORO/Getty Images
INTERIOR DESIGN: Lightbox Visual Communications Inc.
PAGE LAYOUT: Laserwords Prviate Limited
PRINTER: Transcontinental Printing Group

Library and Archives Canada Cataloguing in Publication

Lovewell, Mark A., author
     Understanding economics : a contemporary perspective / Mark Lovewell,
Ryerson University – Seventh edition.
Includes bibliographical references and index.
ISBN 978-1-25-903080-2 (pbk.)

     1. Economics–Textbooks. 2. Canada–Economic conditions–Textbooks. 3. Canada–Commerce–Textbooks. I. Title.
HB171.5.L78 2015   330   C2014-903641-8

This book is dedicated to my students.

Mark Lovewell grew up in various communities of his birth province, Newfoundland. He also lived in Bermuda before moving to Alberta as a teenager. He attended high school in the city of Red Deer, and studied undergraduate economics at the University of Alberta in Edmonton. Moving to Ontario, he completed his M.A. in Economics at the University of Toronto. He spent several years at Balliol College, Oxford University, before returning to Toronto. In 1981, he began his career at Ryerson University. His long-time experience teaching Ryerson's introductory microeconomics and macroeconomics courses led him to write *Understanding Economics.*

During part of his time at Ryerson, Mark served as senior tutor for the University's distance education arm, Open College. He also worked intermittently as a broadcaster on Toronto's classical, jazz, and education radio station (now JAZZ-FM). More recently, he helped develop Ryerson's International Economics degree program, and for several years served as the program's coordinator. Between 2003 and 2007, he was founding director of Ryerson's humanities-based Arts and Contemporary Studies program. Since then, he worked as an academic administrator.

In addition to his career-related activities, Mark is interested in literature, the arts, and public policy. He is a contributing editor and former co-publisher of the national book review magazine, the *Literary Review of Canada.* More information on Mark is available at his personal website, marklovewell.com.

BRIEF CONTENTS

CONTENTS

PREFACE

This edition has the same purpose as its predecessors–namely, to combine economic theory and application in an up-to-date, accessible, and appealing way. When I first decided to write *Understanding Economics: A Contemporary Perspective*, my aim was to use my years of undergraduate teaching to create a text that would engage first-year students and help them realize the power of economic theory in explaining the practical aspects of their lives. I hope this new edition is as successful as the first six in accomplishing this goal.

What's New in the Seventh Edition?

The favourable reception of the previous editions led several instructors and students to make valuable criticisms and suggestions for change. I have incorporated many of these suggestions in this new edition. For example, extra material has been added to Chapter 1 on the production possibilities curve and its interpretation, as well as on the environment and concerns over climate change. In Chapter 3, new problems allow students to explicitly compare answers found using percentage change calculations with those using average prices and average quantities. New material has been added to Chapter 5 to make it clear why the book's examples of perfect competition are from a relatively narrow range of products. In Chapter 7, the concepts of consumer surplus, producer surplus, deadweight loss, and excess benefit have been used to extend and clarify the discussion of spillover effects, excise taxes, and price controls.

Chapter 13 includes a newly updated and expanded Sideline, *A Crisis Too Far*, to provide a detailed discussion of the 2008 financial crisis and its aftermath, and the innovative central banking career of former Bank of Canada governor Mark Carney is explored in a new Advancing Economic Thought article. A new discussion has been provided in Chapter 15 on the rise of emerging countries in the global economy, and a new Advancing Economic Thought article highlights the economic impact of the digital revolution by introducing the ideas of American economist Tyler Cowen.

The book's organization is comparable with that of the sixth edition, with several exceptions.

Specific Changes in the Seventh Edition

Throughout the text, the majority of questions at the end of each part and chapter have been recast into auto-gradeable problems to align with the new online versions available on Connect. In several chapters, material has been restructured so that every chapter part is associated with a distinct learning objective and a corresponding set of practice problems.

Specific chapter-by-chapter changes include:

PART 1

Chapter 1's discussion of the production possibilities model has been extended with a new Thinking About Economics text box and new practice and end-of-chapter problems. The chapter's circular flow diagram has been added to enhance its clarity, and the material on the global response to the threat of climate change has been updated to reflect recent developments.

In Chapter 2, a further emphasis is placed on shifts on demand and supply and the effects of these shifts on equilibrium through a range of new practice and end-of-chapter problems.

Chapter 3 has been extended with new problems that ask students to compare answers found using percentage change calculations with elasticity calculations involving average prices and average quantities. The material on excise taxes and price controls has been moved to Chapter 7 to allow for a more comprehensive treatment of these topics.

PART 2

In Chapter 5, a new discussion has been added to explain why the book's examples of perfectly competitive markets are from a limited range of products, while new end-of-chapter problems provide extra examples of real-world markets illustrating each of the four market structures.

In Chapter 7, the concepts of consumer surplus, producer surplus, deadweight loss, and excess benefit have been incorporated in the treatment of spillover effects, excise taxes, and price controls, now all in this chapter. One of the chapter's Thinking About Economics text boxes has been extended to cover intergenerational income mobility and details about the top 1 percent of income earners.

PART 3

Chapter 8 incorporates recent changes in the way Statistics Canada calculates the income-based components of GDP. Previous material on GNP and its calculation has been replaced with Statistics Canada's new specification of GNI. In Chapter 9, a discussion on the prevalence of youth unemployment has been added.

Chapter 11 has been extended with an updated discussion of recent shifts in fiscal policy in Canada in the aftermath of the 2008–2009 recession, as well as a new chart comparing Canada's government debt as a percentage of GDP with that of other major industrial countries. In Chapter 12, the highlighted definitions of the money supply have been reformulated to reflect the Bank of Canada's ongoing shifts in its key money supply figures. The Advancing Economic Thought Movement article on Milton Friedman, previously in Chapter 13, has been moved to the end of this chapter.

Chapter 13 now includes an updated and expanded Sideline, *A Crisis Too Far*, on the 2008 financial crisis and its aftermath. Additional content has been added on the theoretical context associated with the interpretation of the Phillips Curve. A new Advancing Economic Thought article at the end of this chapter focusses on former Bank of Canada governor Mark Carney and his path-breaking central banking career.

PART 4

Chapter 15 incorporates a new discussion on the rise of emerging countries in the global economy, including pie charts on the shifting distribution of world income using PPP-adjusted GDP. A new Advancing Economic Thought article deals with the ideas of economist Tyler Cowen on the economic impact of today's digital revolution.

Current Issues

As did its predecessors, this edition explores important current issues. After all, economics is part of daily life–in the choices we make, in the decisions of communities, governments, and businesses, and in the media. While developing the theoretical framework of economics, *Understanding Economics* offers real-world examples and explores current economic issues. Articles, essays, and interviews stimulate critical thinking, research, application, and more. By providing a balanced and wide range of perspectives, these elements encourage students to evaluate and debate economic issues for themselves.

Within each chapter, an **Advancing Economic Thought** feature details the ideas of an influential thinker of the past or the present, and allows students to judge their contemporary relevance. So, for example, Adam Smith's defence of private markets, Karl Marx's theory of capitalist exploitation, and Thomas Malthus's treatment of population growth are featured, as well as David Foot's treatment of demographic change, Paul Romer's innovative view of economic growth, and Tyler Cowen's analysis of the economic impact of the digital revolution.

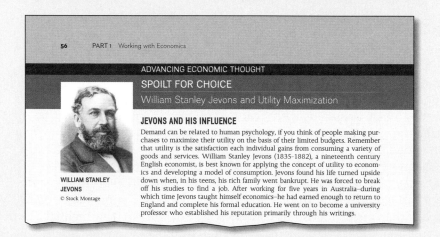

In addition, each chapter includes several points for discussion called **Thinking about Economics**–many with a contemporary focus on new technologies and the Internet–to help students interpret and apply the concepts they are learning through a question-and-answer format.

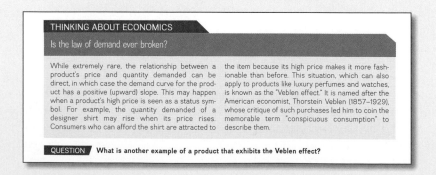

Emphasis on Skills

Application is the key to effective learning. Overall, the text emphasizes skills so that students have ample opportunity to apply the knowledge they acquire. As an initial review and a resource to return to for direction and hints, the **Graphing Module** reviews interpreting and creating tables and graphs. A separate **Skills Resource** focuses on the basics of critical thinking, the use of economic language and visual materials, research, and ways of presenting findings. Both the Graphing Module and Skills Resource are located on Connect.

In the body of each chapter, issues relating to the use of **Economics as a second language** are highlighted.

The Demand Curve

demand schedule: a table that shows possible combinations of prices and quantities demanded of a product

demand curve: a graph that expresses possible combinations of prices and quantities demanded of a product

change in quantity demanded: the effect of a price

The quantities demanded of a product at various prices can be expressed in a demand schedule like the one in Figure 2.1. Expressing the schedule on a graph, as shown on the right in Figure 2.1, gives the consumer's demand curve (D) for strawberries. The demand curve is drawn by placing the price of strawberries on the vertical axis and the quantity demanded per month on the horizontal axis. Note that the independent variable (price) is on the vertical axis, while the dependent variable (quantity demanded) is on the horizontal axis. This choice that economists have made differs from the convention in mathematics, in which the independent variable (x) is on the horizontal axis and the dependent variable (y) is on the vertical axis.

The demand curve's negative (downward) slope reflects the law of demand: an increase in the product's price decreases the quantity demanded, and vice versa. Changes such as these are examples of a change in quantity demanded and produce a movement *along* the demand curve. For example, an increase in

At the end of each part and each chapter are problems with complementary auto-gradeable Connect versions and questions with instructor gradeable Connect versions. These also appear at the end of all supplementary articles. **Policy Discussion Questions,** at the end of most chapters, deal with practical issues in the application of economic thinking to day-to-day policies. **Internet Application Questions,** occurring in many chapters and located on Connect, allow students to practise accessing and manipulating online data.

Study Aids

To make *Understanding Economics* inviting and engaging for students, care has been taken to present the text in a clear and readable style and to use an appealing design. At the same time, a variety of features make this text user-friendly.

Demand and Supply

Each day, we buy an assortment of goods and services—a meal, a snack, maybe a magazine. What determines the price of the pizza slice we buy at lunchtime? the selection of chocolate bars we find at our local variety store? the types of software apps available for our phone? The answer to all these questions is demand and supply. These two powerful forces are the economic equivalents of gravity—never seen, but always exerting their influence in the most visible ways. In this chapter, we will study the impact of these two forces on our daily lives by seeing how they operate in individual markets. We will also gain a better appreciation of how the "invisible hand" of competition coordinates the plans of buyers and sellers, nudged along by the interaction of demand and supply.

Teach a parrot to say demand and supply, and you've created an economist.

—OLD JOKE

LEARNING OBJECTIVES After reading this chapter, you will be able to

LO 1
Describe the nature of demand, changes in quantity demanded, changes in demand, and the factors that affect demand

LO 2
Summarize the nature of supply, changes in quantity supplied, changes in supply, and the factors that affect supply

LO 3
Explain how markets reach equilibrium—the point at which demand and supply meet

2.1 | The Role of Demand

A product market exists wherever households and businesses buy and sell consumer products—either face-to-face, or indirectly by mail, telephone, or online. Some markets, such as the market for crude oil, are global in scope. Others, such as the market for hot dogs at a local baseball game, are tiny by comparison.

LO1

2.2 | The Role of Supply

What Is Supply?

In product markets, supply is related to the selling activity of businesses. The role of supply is most easily analyzed in competitive markets, where the "invisible hand" of competition, identified by Adam Smith, operates. Because the actions of sellers are independent from those of buyers in these markets, the role of supply can be studied separately. In any competitive market, supply is the relationship between the various possible prices of a product and the quantities of the product that businesses are willing to put on the market. While the inde-

LO2

supply: the relationship the various possible pric product and the quantitie

Every chapter begins with **Learning Objectives,** which introduce the content students are to learn and which are reinforced with an icon throughout the body of the text where concepts are covered.

Then, each **Brief Review** summarizes key ideas, while margin notes define key terms highlighted in the text. These terms are defined again in a consolidated **Glossary** at the end of the book for easy reference. Following each Brief Review are **Practice Problems** whose answers appear on Connect. Because interpreting graphs is a challenge for many students, virtually all graphs are paired with tables so that it is possible to see at a glance how they are plotted. This technique not only makes graphs easier to interpret, but also helps students appreciate the usefulness of visual aids in presenting economic information. Lastly, the **Index** helps students access the text in a variety of ways.

connect

McGraw-Hill Connect™ is a web-based assignment and assessment platform that gives students the means to better connect with their coursework, with their instructors, and with the important concepts that they will need to know for success now and in the future.

With Connect, instructors can deliver assignments, quizzes, and tests online. Nearly all the problems from the text are presented in an auto-gradeable format and tied to the text's learning objectives. Instructors can edit existing questions and author entirely new ones. Track individual student performance–by question, by assignment, or in relation to the class overall–with detailed grade reports. Easily integrate grade reports with Learning Management Systems (LMS).

By choosing Connect, instructors are providing their students with a powerful tool for improving academic performance and truly mastering course material. Connect allows students to practise important skills at their own pace and on their own schedule. Importantly, students' assessment results and instructors' feedback are all saved online–so students can continually review their progress and plot their course to success.

Connect also provides 24/7 online access to an eBook–an online edition of the text–to help them successfully complete their work wherever and whenever they choose.

Key Features

SIMPLE ASSIGNMENT MANAGEMENT

With Connect, creating assignments is easier than ever, so you can spend more time teaching and less time managing.

- Create and deliver assignments easily with selectable end-of-chapter questions and testbank material to assign online.
- Streamline lesson planning, student progress reporting, and assignment grading to make classroom management more efficient than ever.
- Go paperless with the eBook and online submission and grading of student assignments.

SMART GRADING

When it comes to studying, time is precious. Connect helps students learn more efficiently by providing feedback and practice material when they need it, where they need it.

- Automatically score assignments to give students immediate feedback on their work and side-by-side comparisons with correct answers.
- Access and review each response; manually change grades or leave comments for students to review.
- Reinforce classroom concepts with practice tests and instant quizzes.
- Provide help with graphing; some problems include video-based feedback that gives step-by-step guidance for how to graph the answers.

INSTRUCTOR LIBRARY

The Connect Instructor Library is your course creation hub. It provides all the critical resources you'll need to build your course, just how you want to teach it.

- Assign eBook readings and draw from a rich collection of textbook-specific assignments.
- Access instructor resources, including ready-made PowerPoint presentations and media to use in your lectures.
- View assignments and resources created for past sections.
- Post your own resources for students to use.

eBOOK

Connect reinvents the textbook learning experience for the modern student. Every Connect subject area is seamlessly integrated with Connect eBooks, which are designed to keep students focused on the concepts key to their success.

- Provide students with a Connect eBook, allowing for anytime, anywhere access to the textbook.
- Merge media, animation, and assessments with the text's narrative to engage students and improve learning and retention.
- Pinpoint and connect key concepts in a snap using the powerful eBook search engine.
- Manage notes, highlights, and bookmarks in one place for simple, comprehensive review.

▓|LEARNSMART°

No two students are alike. Why should their learning paths be? LearnSmart uses revolutionary adaptive technology to build a learning experience unique to each student's individual needs. It starts by identifying the topics a student knows and does not know. As the student progresses, LearnSmart adapts and adjusts the content based on individual strengths, weaknesses, and confidence, ensuring that every minute spent studying with LearnSmart is the most efficient and productive study time possible.

▓|SMARTBOOK°

As the first and only adaptive reading experience, SmartBook is changing the way students read and learn. SmartBook creates a personalized reading experience by highlighting the most important concepts a student needs to learn at that moment in time. As a student engages with SmartBook, the reading experience continuously adapts by highlighting content based on what each student knows and doesn't know. This ensures that the individual is focused on the content needed to close specific knowledge gaps, while it simultaneously promotes long-term learning.

connectINSIGHT

New to the Seventh edition! Visualized data tailored to your needs as an instructor make it possible to quickly confirm early signals of success, or identify early warning signs regarding student performance or concept mastery—even while on the go.

INSTRUCTOR RESOURCES

- **Instructor's Manual** Written by the author, this useful manual offers a range of teaching and testing aids and provides answers to all problems and questions in the book itself.

- **Computerized Test Bank** Written by the author, the test bank contains more than 900 multiple-choice questions categorized by level, type, and topic. The computerized test bank uses EZ Test—a flexible and easy-to-use electronic testing program—which allows instructors to create tests from book-specific items. EZ Test accommodates a wide range of question types and allows instructors to add their own questions. Test items are also available in Word format (Rich text format). For secure online testing, exams created in EZ Test can be exported to WebCT, Blackboard, and EZ Test Online. EZ Test comes with a Quick Start Guide. Once the program is installed, users have access to a User's Manual and Flash tutorials. Additional help is available online at www.mhhe.com/eztest.

- **Microsoft® PowerPoint® Lecture Slides** Created by the author, these slides contain animated illustrations along with a detailed, chapter-by-chapter review of the important concepts presented in the book.

SUPERIOR LEARNING SOLUTIONS AND SUPPORT

The McGraw-Hill Ryerson team is ready to help you assess and integrate any of our products, technology, and services into your course for optimal teaching and learning performance. Whether it's helping your students improve their grades, or putting your entire course online, the McGraw-Hill Ryerson team is here to help you do it. Contact your Learning Solutions Consultant today to learn how to maximize all of McGraw-Hill Ryerson's resources!

For more information on the latest technology and Learning Solutions offered by McGraw-Hill Ryerson and its partners, please visit us online at **www.mcgrawhill.ca/he/solutions.**

ACKNOWLEDGEMENTS

I am indebted to Kamilah Reid-Burrell, James Booty, Joanne Limebeer, and Janice Dyer for their innumerable editorial contributions in casting this seventh edition in its final form. Special thanks are owed as well to Sonya Dann for overseeing the preparation of the Connect platform that accompanies the book. Her technical wizardry and insightful suggestions have added immeasurably to all aspects of this edition's assessment resources. Others have played a significant editorial role in the previous six editions: Maria Chu, Andrea Crozier, Ron Doleman, Laura Edlund, Lynn Fisher, Joan Levack, and Brenda Hutchinson. I am also grateful to the reviewers of this edition for their perceptive comments and criticisms. They include

Aurelia Best, Centennial College

Percy Christon-Quao, Kwantlen Polytechnic University

Bruno Fullone, George Brown College

Eric Moon, University of Toronto

Mike Tucker, Fanshawe College

Franc A. Weissenhorn, Nova Scotia Community College

Encouragement has come from past and present members of Ryerson's Economics Department, especially Ingrid Bryan, John Isbister, Eric Kam, Harry Pope, Eric Wright, and Augustus Zaks, as well as my former associates at CJRT-Open College. Brenda Gayle-Anyiwe and Ibrahim Hayani, both of Seneca College, have made valuable suggestions which I have incorporated in various editions. At the Literary Review of Canada, I would like to thank my associates Alastair Cheng, Bronwyn Drainie, Madeline Koch, James Harbeck, and Helen Walsh for their continuing endeavours to help me improve my writing style. On a personal note, I wish to thank my parents, Patricia and David Lovewell, my sister Rachael Lovewell, as well as my friends Chalo Barrueta, Deborah Brown, Johnny Simeonakis, Dorothy Salusbury, and Marina Vitkin. Without their good-humoured support, writing this book would not have been possible.

Mark Lovewell

The Age of Chivalry is gone—that of sophisters, economists, and calculators has succeeded.

—EDMUND BURKE, BRITISH POLITICAL WRITER

Working with Economics

Economics is important for everyone who votes or participates in the marketplace. Is it possible to quantify happiness? What options do Canadians have when deciding how to operate our economy? As consumers, how do we go about selecting the products we buy? How do businesses decide how much of their product they wish to sell? And how are these decisions brought together in the marketplace? The first three chapters explore the principles that can help us answer such questions.

CHAPTER 1
The Economic Problem

CHAPTER 2
Demand and Supply

CHAPTER 3
Elasticity

The Economic Problem

Economics is about making choices. We face countless choices in everyday life. Similarly, we face choices as an entire society. Some choices are minor, such as which pair of shoes to buy or whether to have pizza or a hamburger for lunch. Others are more important, such as where to live and what career to pursue. Our resources are limited, so every one of our choices has a price. This basic fact of human existence applies equally to individuals and societies. Individuals must decide how to use their limited time and budgets. Societies must decide how to employ a fixed supply of resources. The insights of economics help us understand how individuals and societies can make the best possible decisions given these constraints.

> Economy is the art of making the most out of life.
>
> —GEORGE BERNARD SHAW, IRISH PLAYWRIGHT

LEARNING OBJECTIVES   After reading this chapter, you will be able to

LO 1

Describe the economic problem—the problem of having unlimited wants, but limited resources—that underlies the definition of economics

LO 2

Explain how economists specify economic choice, including the production choices an entire economy faces, as demonstrated by the production possibilities model

LO 3

Identify the three basic economic questions and how various economic systems answer them

satisfying unlimited wants with limited means.

1.1 | How Economists Think

The Economic Problem

LO1

A fundamental goal of this book is to introduce the economic way of thinking. What distinguishes economists' methods from how others view the world? As social scientists, economists seek objective ways to analyze how humans act in social settings. What sets economists apart from other social scientists is the extent to which they focus on the logic that underpins human behaviour. Economists assume that people customarily engage in **rational behaviour**, meaning that each one of us makes choices by logically weighing the personal benefits and costs of every available action, then selects the most attractive option based on our individual wants. This does not imply that we always act in commendable ways: rational behaviour is not necessarily right or ethical. But the assumption of rationality is nonetheless significant. As long as it is met, human behaviour can be fruitfully analyzed and predicted.[1]

rational behaviour: making choices by logically weighing the personal benefits and costs of available actions, then selecting the most attractive option

The choices we'll study in this chapter include everyday decisions to satisfy individual wants. Wants vary widely from person to person: we may have a special preference for ice-cream sundaes or chocolate cake, rock concerts or classical recitals, video games or digital music players. Because we face so many choices, the sum total of wants is virtually unlimited. Our resources, however, are not. Thus, we have the **economic problem**.

economic problem: having unlimited wants but limited resources with which to satisfy them

THINKING ABOUT ECONOMICS

The famous Indian statesman M.K. (Mahatma) Gandhi once said, "There is enough for the needy, but not for the greedy." What are the implications of this statement for the economic problem?

Gandhi's statement reveals a way the economic problem can be solved without the help of economics—by curbing our selfish wants. Is such a scenario feasible? In some cultures, and for idealistic individuals or small groups, it can be. However, attempts to control the wants of large groups of people have tended to be spectacular failures.

QUESTION   What are some examples of societies that have tried to curb individual wants?

The limited nature of resources–or scarcity–requires that we make choices based on both non-economic factors, such as the need for security, and economic factors. For many individuals, time and money are most scarce. For societies as a whole, it is the basic items used in all types of production, known as economic resources, that are scarce. These resources come not only from nature, but also from human effort and ingenuity. **Economic resources** are often categorized as natural resources, capital resources, and human resources.

economic resources: basic items used in all types of production, including natural, capital, and human resources

---

[1] In those special cases in which the rationality assumption appears not to be met, economists are keen to analyze the reasons why. Indeed, an entire new field, known as *behavioural economics*, has recently emerged to help explain just how the assumption of rationality, and instances in which it is broken, play out in real-life situations.

NATURAL RESOURCES

natural resources: the resources from nature that are used in production, including land, raw materials, and natural processes

Natural resources represent nature's contribution to production. These resources include not only land–used for farms, roads, and buildings–but also raw materials, such as minerals and forests. As well, natural resources include useful natural processes, such as sunlight and water power.

CAPITAL RESOURCES

capital resources: the processed materials, equipment, and buildings used in production; also known as capital

In economics, the term **capital resources**, or capital, refers to the real assets of an economy–the processed materials, equipment, and buildings that are used in production. An example is a newspaper printing plant and its printing presses, as well as the processed inputs–paper and ink–used to make newspapers. **Therefore, the term "capital" has a special meaning in economics. As economic resources, capital resources do not include financial capital, such as stocks and bonds. A person's shares in Bombardier, for example, do not add to the economy's stock of real capital. Similarly, the bonds issued by a company, such as Bell Canada, are viewed as financial capital by their holders, but not as real capital by economists.**

HUMAN RESOURCES

labour: human effort employed directly in production

Two main types of human resources are used in production. **Labour** represents human effort employed directly in production, such as the work of a computer programmer, store clerk, factory supervisor, or brain surgeon. On the other hand, **entrepreneurship** is the initiative, risk-taking, and innovation necessary for production. It includes the efforts of the inventor who brings a new product to the market, the head of a multimillion-dollar corporation, the owner of a small variety store, and the student who starts a summer house-painting business. Entrepreneurship is often difficult to pinpoint, but it brings together natural resources, capital resources, and labour to produce a good or service.

entrepreneurship: initiative, risk-taking, and innovation necessary for production

RESOURCE INCOMES

Economic resources have corresponding incomes, which reflect their contributions to production. When a natural resource is employed, its owner receives a rent, which is the payment for supplying the resource. Similarly, providers of capital resources (as well as providers of financial capital, such as bonds) receive an income in the form of interest. Finally, people are paid wages for their labour and profit for their entrepreneurship.

Economics Defined

economics: the study of how to distribute scarce resources to make choices

Arising from unlimited wants and scarce resources, economics is the study of how to distribute limited resources to make choices. **Economics** is divided into two branches, which are studied separately: microeconomics and macroeconomics.

MICROECONOMICS

microeconomics: the branch of economics that focuses on the behaviour of individual participants in various markets

Microeconomics focuses on the behaviour of individual participants in various markets. How do people decide on the quantity of a particular product they will consume? How do businesses decide on the quantity of a particular product they will produce? How are prices set within markets? What determines how incomes are distributed to the various participants in an economy? These are the sorts of questions studied in microeconomics.

MACROECONOMICS

In contrast, **macroeconomics** takes a more wide-ranging view of the economy. It is concerned with entire economic sectors, which are treated as separate entities. The four important sectors in the economy are households, businesses, government, and foreign markets. How these sectors interact determines a country's unemployment rate, general level of prices, and total economic output. Explaining these larger economic forces is the central task of macroeconomics.

macroeconomics: the branch of economics that takes a wide-ranging view of the economy, studying the behaviour of economic sectors

Economic Models

Economists use models to help them understand economic behaviour. **Economic models**–also known as laws, principles, or theories–are generalizations or simplifications of economic reality. As an example, think about the Canadian economy, in which literally millions of separate transactions–sales and purchases–are made each day. Trying to keep track of every sale and purchase for the purpose of understanding economic activity would be impossible. Instead, economists build useful abstractions of reality that allow them to see the basic workings of the economy. In other words, a good economic model allows economists to see the forest instead of the trees.

economic models: generalizations about or simplifications of economic reality; also known as laws, principles, or theories

Without even realizing it, we regularly use models. When driving in unfamiliar territory, for example, we often depend on maps. Although an aerial photograph of our route, which is the most realistic representation, may be useful in some circumstances, it is not the most popular driving guide. A road map, however, gives exactly the detail needed to find the way. Similarly, a good economic model can help us understand some facet of economic behaviour without overwhelming us with details.

CAUSE AND EFFECT

How can economic models help explain economic trends and behaviour? Usually, by including two or more **variables**, or factors that have measurable values. For example, the price of an item and the quantity that is purchased of that item are two variables. In a model, variables are connected by a causal relationship, meaning that one variable is assumed to affect another. Suppose a model states that a rise in the price of cell phones reduces the number of cell phones purchased. In this case, the variable that is causing the other to change–known as the **independent variable**–is the price of cell phones. The variable that is being affected–called the **dependent variable**–is the number of cell phones purchased.

variables: factors that have measurable values

independent variable: the variable in a causal relationship that causes change in another variable

dependent variable: the variable in a causal relationship that is affected by another variable

INVERSE AND DIRECT RELATIONSHIPS

A model proposes what effect one variable will have on another. If the value of one variable is expected to increase as the value of another variable decreases, the variables have an **inverse relationship**. An increase in cell phone prices that reduces the number of phones sold is an example of an inverse relationship. Two variables can also have a **direct relationship**, meaning that when the independent variable rises or falls, the dependent variable moves in the same direction. A rise in the hourly wage of café baristas that causes a corresponding rise in the number of people who wish to work in this occupation is an example of a direct relationship.

inverse relationship: a change in the independent variable causes a change in the opposite direction of the dependent variable

direct relationship: a change in the independent variable causes a change in the same direction of the dependent variable

THE NEED FOR ASSUMPTIONS

In order to focus on the relationship between two variables, economists must make assumptions to temporarily simplify the real world. Let us return to the relationship that states that the quantity of cell phones purchased is inversely related to their price. Economists must assume that another factor—such as consumer incomes—is not affecting purchases of cell phones. Assuming that all other factors affecting a dependent variable remain constant is common in economics. This assumption is known as ***ceteris paribus*** (pronounced kay'-teh-rees pah'-ri-bus), which is the Latin expression for "all other things remaining the same." The *ceteris paribus* assumption, as well as any other assumptions that are made, should be outlined explicitly in an economic model.

ceteris paribus: the assumption that all other things remain the same

POSITIVE AND NORMATIVE ECONOMICS

When using economic models, we need to distinguish between two types of economic enquiry: positive and normative economics.

positive economics: the study of economic facts and why the economy operates as it does

Positive economics (sometimes called *descriptive economics*) is the study of economic reality and why the economy operates as it does. It is based purely on economic facts rather than on opinions. This type of economics is made up of positive statements, which can be accepted or rejected through applying the scientific method. "Canadians bought five million high definition televisions last year" is a positive statement—a simple declaration of fact. A positive statement can also take the form of a condition that asserts that if one thing happens, then so will another: "If rent controls are eliminated, then the number of available rental units will increase." Both declarations of fact and conditional statements can be verified or disproved using economic data. Though this process is rarely straightforward, it is often easier to make generalizations about the behaviour of large groups than it is to predict what a certain individual will do on a particular occasion; individual behaviour is sometimes swayed by random factors, which largely cancel each other out when looking at large groups.

normative economics: the study of how the economy ought to operate

In contrast, **normative economics** (also called *policy economics*) deals with how the world ought to be. In this type of economics, opinions or value judgments—known as normative statements—are common. "We should reduce taxes" is an example of a normative statement. So is "A 1 percent rise in unemployment is worse than a 1 percent rise in inflation." Even people who agree on the facts can have different opinions regarding a normative statement, since the statement relates to questions of ethical values.

BRIEF REVIEW

1. Economists assume that virtually all human behaviour is rational, which means that people make choices by logically weighing the benefits and costs of available actions, subject to individual wants.

2. The basic economic problem faced by both individuals and societies is that while human wants are virtually unlimited, the resources to fulfill them are limited or scarce.

3. Economic resources can be categorized as natural resources, capital resources, and human resources. Each resource has a corresponding income or incomes.

4. Whereas microeconomics concentrates on the ways consumers and businesses interact in various markets, macroeconomics takes a broader look at the economy as a whole and highlights such variables as unemployment, inflation, and total output.

5. Economic models include causal relationships between variables and are based on simplifying assumptions.

1.1 | PRACTICE PROBLEMS

1. a. Would you say that a smoker who wants to quit, yet still continues to smoke two packs a day, is behaving rationally? Why or why not?
   b. Economists argue that it is sometimes possible to overcome instances of irrationality through a system of rewards and punishments designed to change an individual's behaviour. Provide an illustration of a system a cigarette smoker who wants to quit might devise.
2. Analyze the following statement: "The economic welfare of a country's citizens falls if there is a reduction in the quantity of the country's economic resources."
   a. The statement refers to two variables. What are they? Which is the independent variable and which is the dependent variable?
   b. Is the relationship between these variables direct or inverse?
   c. Is the statement positive or normative?
   d. How is the statement related to the economic problem?
3. List the four types of resource income.

1.2 | Economic Choice

How do people make economic choices? They do so by effectively using the scarce resources they have, which means comparing an action's costs and benefits. This decision-making process, which is at the heart of the economic way of thinking, involves two main factors: utility and cost.

Utility Maximization

Economists assume that whenever you make an economic choice, you are trying to maximize your own utility. **Utility** can be defined as the satisfaction or pleasure you derive from any action. Let us examine utility maximization with the illustration of you and your lunch. Economists assume first the **self-interest motive**—that is, that you are primarily concerned with your own welfare. So, when deciding among lunch options that cost the same amount of money, you pick the one that gives the most utility. For example, suppose you have $2 to spend at a fast-food restaurant. Two options are available: a pizza slice or a low-calorie veggieburger. How do you make a choice? According to economists, you decide by making a rational comparison of the utility gained from either product. If the satisfaction from a pizza slice outweighs the pleasure of a veggieburger, you will buy the pizza. If the opposite applies, the veggieburger will win out.

utility: the satisfaction gained from any action

self-interest motive: the assumption that people act to maximize their own welfare

Opportunity Cost

Maximizing utility is only one part of making economic decisions. Acquiring anything prevents someone from pursuing an alternative. Instead of measuring cost in terms of money, economists use a concept that accounts for the tradeoffs

Does the fact that many individuals give part of their income to charities go against the self-interest motive?

Not necessarily. Economists contend that when people give to charities, they do so because of the personal satisfaction they gain from their donation. Only when the satisfaction derived from a donation exceeds the satisfaction that could be gained from spending the same amount in other ways will an individual make the donation. Charitable organizations recognize the importance of the self-interest motive by doing all they can to increase the attractiveness to potential donors of making a donation.

QUESTION   **What strategy do charitable organizations use to enhance the satisfaction their donors experience when giving to their cause? Explain.**

opportunity cost: the utility that could have been gained by choosing an action's best alternative

resulting from any economic choice: opportunity cost. The **opportunity cost** of any action is the utility that could have been gained by choosing the best possible alternative.

The notion of opportunity cost involves more than money. To illustrate, the person who spends $2 to buy a pizza slice at the fast-food restaurant faces an opportunity cost equal to the utility that could have been gained by eating a low-calorie veggieburger instead. If the person chooses the veggieburger, the opportunity cost is the sacrificed pleasure of eating a pizza slice. For a weight-conscious consumer, for example, the utility gained from eating the veggie-burger probably exceeds the pleasure from eating the pizza slice. This means that the veggieburger's opportunity cost is lower than the opportunity cost of the pizza slice (even though both have the same monetary price), making the veggieburger the preferred choice for this individual.

The concept of opportunity cost also relates to how we spend time, since time passed in one activity means less devoted to another. Suppose a student is deciding whether to spend a free hour keeping up with friends on a social networking website or watching a TV program. The opportunity cost of keeping up with friends online is the pleasure that could have been gained from watching the TV program. Likewise, the opportunity cost of watching the TV program is the benefit sacrificed by not keeping up with friends online.

Because utility is subjective and differs for each individual, it is difficult to quantify. Therefore, economists often use a simpler method for measuring opportunity cost. Using this more straightforward approach, the opportunity cost of any action is the number of units of the next best alternative that are sacrificed when choosing this action. This approach gives a rough (though not exact) estimate of the utility that could have been gained by choosing an action's best alternative.

The Production Possibilities Curve

The production possibilities model illustrates the tradeoffs that society faces in using its scarce resources. Like all models, it is an abstraction of the real world based on various simplifications. In this case, we make the following assumptions: only two items are produced, resources and technology are fixed, and all economic resources are employed to their full potential.

TWO PRODUCTS

An immense range of goods and services are produced in any nation's economy. The production possibilities model, however, narrows the list to only two: computers and hamburgers, for example.

FIXED RESOURCES AND TECHNOLOGY

The model assumes that there is a set amount of available economic resources and that technology remains constant. However, resources can be moved from the production of one product to the other. Workers who make hamburgers, for example, can be shifted to the assembly of computers.

FULL PRODUCTION

In the production possibilities model, all economic resources are employed; that is, there is no excess. Also, resources are used to their greatest capacity, no matter which product they are producing—in this case, computers and hamburgers.

THE PRODUCTION POSSIBILITIES CURVE

To maximize the welfare of its citizens, a society must make economic choices. How much of each product should be produced in a certain year, given the resources at the society's disposal? A choice is necessary because producing more of one item means making do with less of the other. This choice is illustrated in Figure 1.1. On the left is the economy's **production possibilities schedule**, a table outlining, in this case, the possible combinations of computers and hamburgers. Expressing the schedule in a graph gives us the economy's **production possibilities curve**. Because making more of one product means making less of the other, there is an inverse relationship between the quantities of computers and hamburgers produced. Therefore, the curve has a negative slope—from left to right, the curve falls.

As Figure 1.1 demonstrates, it might be possible for the economy to make 900 hamburgers and assemble one computer in a given year (point *b*). If the output of hamburgers is reduced to 600, it might also be feasible for the economy to produce two computers (point *c*). The extreme cases serve as useful reference points: when all the economy's resources are devoted to the making of hamburgers, a total of 1000 can be produced annually (point *a*); but when the economy devotes all its resources to making only computers, three can be made (point *d*).

THE ROLE OF SCARCITY

As well as depicting the economic choices a society faces, the production possibilities curve highlights the scarcity of economic resources. The curve is a boundary between all those output combinations that are within the reach of an economy and all those combinations that are unattainable. Anywhere on or inside the curve, such as point *e* in Figure 1.1, represents a feasible combination of the two products. At point *e*, for example, 500 hamburgers and one computer can be produced. The production of both hamburgers and computers could be increased by moving toward point *c* on the curve. At any point, such as *e*, some of an economy's resources are not being fully employed or used to their greatest capacity. Hence, all the points inside the curve represent situations where resources are not being fully used.

production possibilities schedule: a table that shows the possible output combinations for an economy

production possibilities curve: a graph that illustrates the possible output combinations for an economy

FIGURE 1.1	The Production Possibilities Model

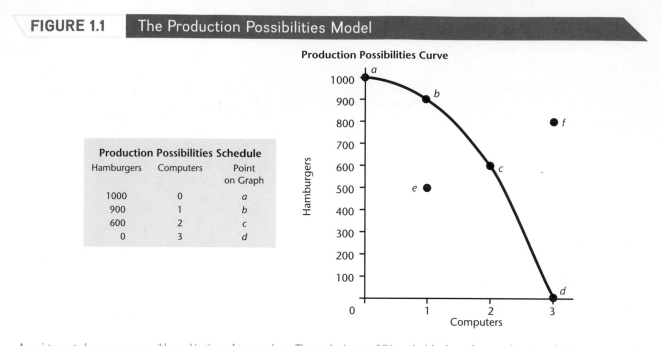

A society must choose among possible combinations of two products. The production possibilities schedule shows these combinations, which are represented by points on the production possibilities curve. Both the schedule and the curve show that more computers can be assembled only if fewer hamburgers are produced. Any points on or within the curve, as illustrated by *e*, are feasible. Those outside the curve, like *f*, are not.

In contrast, point *f* in Figure 1.1 is outside the curve. In this case, the economy would be producing 800 hamburgers and three computers annually. As long as the economy's resources remain constant, this point cannot be reached. More of both hamburgers and computers could be made if point *f* were attainable, but the economy's resources are already being fully used at point *c*.

INCREASING OPPORTUNITY COSTS

The notion of opportunity cost is best seen when moving from one point to another on the production possibilities curve. Notice that the curve in Figure 1.1 bows out to the right. This shape reflects what is called the **law of increasing opportunity costs**, which states that as more of one product is produced, its opportunity cost in terms of the other product increases. This law arises from the fact that economic resources do not transfer perfectly from one use to another. For example, because of training and experience, some workers are better at making hamburgers than assembling computers. When the first computer is assembled, it is made using resources suited to computer assembly rather than to making hamburgers. Hence, the number of hamburgers sacrificed is relatively small. But if further computers are assembled, resources that are not as well suited to this new task must be shifted from making hamburgers. Therefore, more and more hamburgers have to be given up to gain each new computer.

Figure 1.2 illustrates the law of increasing opportunity costs. Assume that society begins by producing only hamburgers (point *a* on the curve) and then

law of increasing opportunity costs: the concept that as more of one item is produced by an economy, the opportunity cost of additional units of that product rises

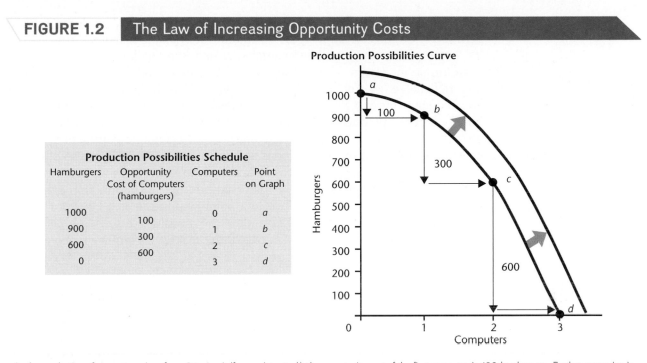

FIGURE 1.2 The Law of Increasing Opportunity Costs

Production Possibilities Curve

Production Possibilities Schedule			
Hamburgers	Opportunity Cost of Computers (hamburgers)	Computers	Point on Graph
1000		0	a
	100		
900		1	b
	300		
600		2	c
	600		
0		3	d

As the production of computers rises from 0 to 1 unit (from point *a* to *b*), the opportunity cost of the first computer is 100 hamburgers. Further expansion in the output of computers comes at higher opportunity costs: 300 hamburgers for the second computer (from point *b* to *c*), and 600 hamburgers for the third computer (from point *c* to *d*).

decides that one computer should be assembled (point *b*). The opportunity cost of this first computer is the number of hamburgers that must be given up. Since hamburger production falls from 1000 to 900, the new computer costs 100 hamburgers. This is shown on the schedule, and appears as the height of the triangle connecting points *a* and *b* on the curve. The same reasoning can be applied in moving from point *b* to *c*–as a second computer is added, hamburger production drops from 900 to 600. The opportunity cost of this extra computer is, therefore, 300 hamburgers. Finally, in moving from point *c* to *d*, hamburger production drops another 600 to zero, meaning that the opportunity cost of the third computer is 600 hamburgers. The opportunity cost of each new computer, in terms of hamburgers, therefore, rises from 100, to 300, and then to 600.

ECONOMIC GROWTH

In the long run, this society may experience **economic growth**, or an increase in the total output of goods and services, either due to a rise in the amount or quality of available resources or an improvement in technology. Both trends cause an outward shift in the production possibilities curve, as shown by the outer curve in Figure 1.2, which means that the area of feasible output combinations expands. As a result, a society can choose output combinations that were previously unattainable–more of both items can now be produced.

If computers are considered a capital product and hamburgers a consumption product, then society's choice between the two products affects the position of its future production possibilities curve. By choosing to produce more

economic growth: an increase in an economy's total output of goods and services

capital products, such as computers, and fewer consumption products, such as hamburgers, a society can increase its amount of available resources, shifting out its future production possibilities curve. Indeed, the focus on capital resources is an important reason why high-income countries–Canada included–have been able to achieve healthy rates of economic growth in the past.

Economic growth also occurs when an economy moves from within the area bounded by the production possibilities curve to the curve itself. Just as economic growth is possible, so too is the opposite case of economic contraction. In this case, a society's total output of goods and services falls, either because of a drop in the amount of available resources, which leads to an inward shift in the production possibilities curve, or because the assumption of full production is broken, which causes the economy to move to a point within the area bounded by the production possibilities curve. Explaining the possible reasons for economic growth and economic contraction is one of the main topics in macroeconomics.

THINKING ABOUT ECONOMICS

Which factors that can cause economic growth are most significant today?

At one time, economic growth was seen primarily as the result of a society choosing to produce fewer consumption products so that it could increase its output of capital products. Such choices are important, but just as significant are society's actions to improve technology. This may allow more output to be produced from the same amount of resources, or even create completely new types of products. Such technological change has been crucial in recent decades, not just in Canada but around the world, due to the information revolution caused by computers.

QUESTION   How is the information revolution, including the increased use of computer-based capital products, affecting rates of economic growth in countries such as Canada?

BRIEF REVIEW

 1. Economists assume that individuals make economic choices among scarce items by maximizing their own utility while minimizing opportunity cost.

2. The production possibilities curve shows the range of choices faced by an economy. It assumes only two products, fixed resources and technology, and full production.

3. Points inside the production possibilities curve are feasible, but indicate that not all resources are being used effectively. Conversely, points outside the curve cannot be reached unless resources increase or technology improves.

4. The fact that economic resources are specialized leads to the law of increasing opportunity costs: as the economy's production of any item is expanded, that item's opportunity cost rises.

5. Economic growth is associated with an outward shift of the production possibilities curve or a movement from within the area bounded by the curve to the curve itself. Economic contraction occurs when the production possibilities curve shifts inward or when the economy moves from the curve itself to within the area bounded by the curve.

1.2 | PRACTICE PROBLEMS

1. An island castaway spends eight hours each day acquiring two items—coconuts and fish—based on the following production possibilities schedule.

Production Scenario	Coconuts	Fish
A	24	0
B	20	1
C	12	2
D	0	3

   a. From a starting point of production shown by scenario A, what is the castaway's opportunity of catching the first fish (scenario A to B)? the second (scenario B to C)? the third (scenario C to D)?

   b. Do these results conform to the law of increasing opportunity costs?

   c. If you drew a graph showing the castaway's production possibilities curve, what shape would it have?

   d. What assumptions must be met for the castaway to operate on his production possibilities curve?

   e. What happens to the castaway's production possibilities curve if he works for 12 hours, instead of eight hours, each day? six hours each day?

   f. What happens to the castaway's production possibilities curve if he manages to make a fishing rod, which he then uses successfully to catch fish?

2. The graph below shows the production possibilities curve for an economy that produces only two goods—hotdogs and smartphones.

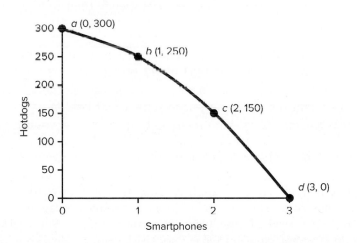

   a. What is the opportunity cost of producing the first smartphone (point *a* to *b*) in terms of the number of hotdogs sacrificed? the cost of the second smartphone (point *b* to *c*)? the cost of the third smartphone (point *c* to *d*)?

   b. Do these results illustrate the law of increasing opportunity costs? Why or why not?

3. If an economy is subject to constant opportunity costs instead of exhibiting increasing opportunity costs, what would its production possibilities curve look like?

1.3 | Economic Systems

LO3   Basic Economic Questions

Because of the basic economic problem of scarcity, every country, no matter how it chooses to conduct its economic affairs, must answer three basic economic questions: what to produce, how to produce, and for whom to produce.

WHAT TO PRODUCE

Countries face economic choices when trying to decide what items to produce, as depicted by the production possibilities curve; for example, making more hamburgers means assembling fewer computers. Somehow, a country must decide how much of each possible good and service to supply. Should these decisions be based on past practice, the individual choices of consumers, or government planning?

HOW TO PRODUCE

Once the question of what to produce has been answered, a country must then decide how these items should be produced. Which resources should be employed and in what combinations? For example, should farmers use horse-drawn plows and large amounts of labour to produce wheat, or should they use sophisticated farm machinery and very little labour? And how should these decisions be made? Should the farmers follow tradition and use price signals provided by markets, or should government planners specify their production methods?

FOR WHOM TO PRODUCE

Each country must also determine how to distribute its total output of goods and services. How output is divided might be based on custom. Alternatively, each person's ownership of economic resources may be the key factor. Or, the government might distribute output in some other fashion.

  To answer these three basic economic questions, a country organizes its economy. The result is an **economic system**, which represents the country's distinct set of social customs, political institutions, and economic practices. We will look at three main economic systems: traditional economy, market economy, and command economy. Each of these is a pure or theoretical system, so few economies come close to them. Most economies today are mixed; that is, they combine aspects of the main economic systems. These systems are all founded on different views of what a society's primary aims should be.

Traditional Economy

In a **traditional economy**, economic decisions depend on custom, such as a traditional division of work between women and men. The mix of outputs, the organization of production, and the way in which outputs are distributed are passed on relatively unchanged from generation to generation. Religion and culture tend to be considered at least as important as material welfare. As recently as a century ago, most people lived in traditional economies; today, these economies exist only in isolated pockets. For example, many farmers in

economic system: the organization of an economy, which represents a country's distinct set of social customs, political institutions, and economic practices

traditional economy: an economic system in which economic decisions are made on the basis of custom

the remote country of Nepal still use traditional methods that have existed for generations. Since they are based on tight social constraints, traditional economies are resistant to change. Even in countries that are witnessing profound economic change, such as China and India, there remain regions–especially in rural areas–whose economies are run along traditional lines. Still, the long-term outlook for these economies seems clear: they are increasingly being broken down by expanding consumer wants and the inability of traditional production methods to meet these wants.

Supporters of traditional economies suggest that they offer the advantage of stability. These economies can also be viewed as beneficial because they emphasize the spiritual and cultural aspects of life. However, critics argue that traditional economies' widespread poverty and tightly defined social roles restrain human potential; people must follow the dictates of custom rather than having the freedom to make their own economic choices.

Market Economy

In a **market economy**, individuals are free to pursue their own self-interest. This type of economy is based on the private ownership of economic resources and the use of markets in making economic decisions. In this system–often referred to as capitalism–households use incomes earned from their economic resources by saving some and spending the rest on consumer products. Businesses buy resources from households and employ these resources to provide the consumer products demanded by households. Government performs only the political functions of upholding the legal system and maintaining public security.

The circular flow diagram in Figure 1.3 illustrates the transactions between households and businesses in a market economy. This diagram includes not only households and businesses, but also two markets. A **market** is a set of arrangements between buyers and sellers that allows them to trade items for set prices. **Product markets** are those in which consumer products are traded. **Resource markets** are those in which economic resources–natural resources, capital resources, and human resources–are traded.

market economy: an economic system based on private ownership and the use of markets in economic decision-making

market: a set of arrangements between buyers and sellers of a certain item

product markets: markets in which consumer products are traded

resource markets: markets in which economic resources are traded

FIGURE 1.3   The Circular Flow Diagram

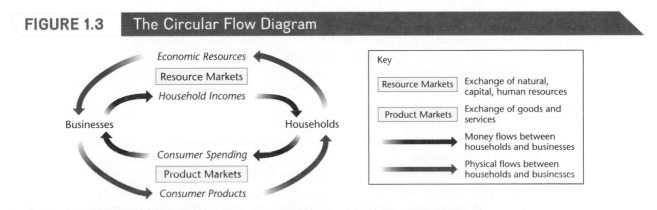

Households and businesses participate in two main markets, one involving consumer products and the other economic resources. The red arrows in the diagram represent monetary flows of incomes and consumer spending, while the blue arrows represent the physical flows of resources and products.

Households and businesses face each other in both sets of markets. In product markets, households are the buyers of consumer products such as food and clothing, while businesses are the sellers. In resource markets, the roles are reversed: households sell resources–such as labour–that businesses purchase so that they can produce goods and services. Households and businesses are connected by two circular flows. The inner loop in Figure 1.3 shows the circulation of payments–both household incomes and consumer spending. The outer loop shows the circulation of consumer products and economic resources in the opposite direction.

BENEFITS OF A MARKET ECONOMY

Placing markets at the centre of economic activity can have benefits. The main benefits are associated with consumer sovereignty and innovation.

Consumer Sovereignty

consumer sovereignty: the effect of consumer needs and wants on production decisions

Market economies are characterized by **consumer sovereignty**, meaning that the decision of what to produce is ultimately guided by the needs and wants of households in their role as consumers. In other words, consumers use their dollars to "vote" on what types of goods and services should be produced, based on the role of prices as a crucial signaling device. Prices play this role by coordinating the activities of buyers and sellers to stop either too much or too little of an item from being produced.

For example, if households wish to switch some of their consumption dollars from the purchase of video game consoles to flat-screen monitors, a chain reaction will occur in the product and resource markets. In product markets, the extra demand for monitors pushes up monitor prices, while the lower demand for consoles pushes down console prices. The higher monitor prices provide businesses lured by the chance to make higher profits with an incentive to supply more monitors. Meanwhile, a price drop for consoles causes businesses to cut their console production. These shifts in production also result in changes in the employment of economic resources, with more resources being used to make monitors and fewer being used to make consoles.

Innovation

The incentive to make a profit in a market economy encourages innovation and entrepreneurship, which help foster advances in technology. For example, it was the lure of profits that drove the invention of new products such as digital music players and computer tablets by entrepreneur Steve Jobs. Consumers benefit through improvements to existing products and the introduction of completely new products.

DRAWBACKS OF A MARKET ECONOMY

The main drawbacks of a market economy are associated with income distribution, possible market problems, and potential instability of total output.

Income Distribution

Without intervention by governments, the distribution of income in a market economy can create significant inequities. If household incomes are based solely on the ability to supply economic resources, then some individuals in the economy might not earn enough to provide even for their basic needs.

Market Problems

Other deficiencies of market economies arise because private markets do not always operate in a way that benefits society as a whole. Negative external effects of economic activity–such as pollution–may require intervention by governments to prevent harm to society. Negative internal effects may also cause governments to step in, for example when one or a few companies control a certain product market, thus depriving consumers of the advantages of competition.

Instability

Finally, market economies can display considerable instability in the total output produced from year to year. Such fluctuations can harm the economy's participants through substantial variations in prices or employment levels.

As a result of these deficiencies, there are very few real-world examples of pure capitalism. The closest approximations have occurred in the past–in particular, during the first half of the nineteenth century in Great Britain.

Command Economy

Opposite to a market economy is a **command economy**, in which all productive property–natural resources and capital–is in the hands of government, and markets are largely replaced by central planning. Rather than being based on consumer sovereignty and individual decision-making, command economies rely on planners to decide what should be produced, how production should be carried out, and how the output should be distributed. For example, in a market economy, decisions made by households about how much to consume and how much to save determine the split between consumer and capital products. In a command economy, however, central planners determine the split on the basis of their judgment of the future needs of the entire economy.

command economy: an economic system based on public ownership and central planning

BENEFITS OF A COMMAND ECONOMY

The reliance on planning rather than markets gives command economies some possible benefits related to income distribution and economic growth.

Income Distribution

A country that adopts a command system can choose to distribute income among its citizens on the basis of considerations other than purely economic ones. In these economies, an attempt is usually made to distribute income more equally than would be the case with market economies.

Economic Growth

Central planners can focus on promoting the rate of economic growth by devoting more resources to capital products than would be the case in a market economy. This strategy can be particularly effective when an economy is first building a manufacturing sector. During this stage of development, economic growth is closely tied to the quantity of capital products, such as machines and factories, that an economy possesses.

DRAWBACKS OF A COMMAND ECONOMY

Command economies also have serious drawbacks related to planning, efficiency, and individual freedom. Because of these deficiencies, pure command economies are almost as rare as pure market economies; the closest approximation in contemporary times is North Korea.

Planning Difficulties

Trying to plan an entire economy is a difficult task requiring a tremendous amount of information that is unlikely to be at the planners' disposal. Incorrect estimates of future conditions are all too easy to make, leading to overproduction of some items and underproduction of others.

Inefficiencies

Government ownership of productive property can lead to waste and inefficiency, since command economies cannot depend on the lure of profit to promote the efficient use of resources. Without markets to control individual self-interest, corruption of government officials is also a frequent problem, and it is possible for this corruption to be so extreme that incomes in command economies are highly unequal. As well, because planners emphasize quantity by setting production quotas, the quality of goods and services can suffer.

Lack of Freedom

Opponents of command economies also suggest that putting so much power into the hands of government stifles individual freedom. Because central planners are responsible for so many economic decisions, people living in command economies have limited economic choices. All too often, critics contend, command economies are associated with a lack of political freedom as well.

Mixed Economies

modern mixed economy: an economic system that combines aspects of a market economy and a command economy; production decisions are made both in private markets and by government

Most countries fall between the extremes of traditional, market, and command economies. A **modern mixed economy** is one that combines both the use of markets and a significant government presence in economic decision-making. Modern mixed economies are now the norm and take a variety of forms, depending on the relative importance given to private markets and to the economic functions of government. In some countries, such as Canada and the United States, markets play the dominant economic role. In other countries, such as Sweden, the government's economic role is more important. Figure 1.4 illustrates all three types of economic systems, showing the range of possible modern mixed economies (along the top edge of the triangle) that exist between the two poles of pure market and command economies.

While modern mixed economies vary widely, they have some common attributes. Each one includes a private sector in which economic activity is dominated by markets, and there is private ownership of productive resources. Each of these economies also includes a public sector in which governments conduct economic activity–often without the use of markets–and own productive resources.

In most modern mixed economies, the distinction between the private and public sectors is not clear-cut. Governments can intervene in the private sector by levying taxes or providing subsidies to some industries. In Canada, for example, the federal government plays a part in the private sector through personal and corporate taxes and the subsidies it provides to business. Government also intervenes in the private sector by imposing regulations, such as environmental laws, on businesses. In addition, government owns some companies, such as Canada Post.

Countries with entirely traditional economies are rare. However, some countries still possess a significant traditional sector in which economic activity is

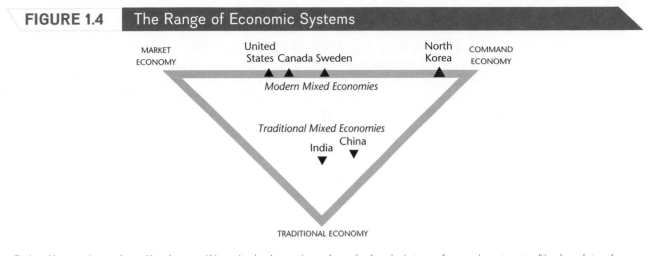

FIGURE 1.4   The Range of Economic Systems

Real-world economies can be positioned on or within a triangle whose points make up the three basic types of economic systems: traditional, market, and command. Countries with surviving traditional sectors combine them with emerging private and public sectors.

based on custom and traditional production methods. Economies that possess a traditional sector alongside more modern sectors are known as **traditional mixed economies**. All three sectors coexist in these economies, as in the case of China and India. As shown in Figure 1.4, traditional mixed economies appear below the top of the triangle.

traditional mixed economies: economic systems in which a traditional sector coexists with modern sectors

CONFLICTS AND OPPORTUNITIES

Mixed economies must deal with inevitable conflicts among their component sectors. Each sector emphasizes a distinct view of society's underlying aims—the focus on self-interest in a private sector, wider national objectives in a public sector, and continuity in a traditional sector. As the sectors interact, differences in these views are sure to cause friction. But such friction can also provide creative opportunities for those living in mixed economies, especially when the relative importance of various sectors is undergoing rapid change.

Three major countries, which together account for over a third of the world's population, give ample illustration of these benefits and drawbacks. China, India, and Brazil are examples of **emerging economies**, exhibiting high rates of economic growth and rising average incomes. As recently as several decades ago, these nations—as well as other emerging economies—faced widespread poverty and lacklustre growth, with governments in each playing a dominant role. In China, the bulk of economic activity was managed via a tightly controlled central planning process. In India and Brazil, planning was less widespread, but the private sectors in each country were heavily constrained by laws and regulations. However, conditions in these countries are rapidly changing, with major effects beyond their borders as economic power and financial clout become less concentrated in the rich economies of the West and spread more widely across the globe.

emerging economies: economies that have recently exhibited high rates of economic growth and rising average incomes

China

In China, major changes began with rural reforms in the late 1970s. Before this time, the country's communist regime had outlawed private ownership of land, forcing farmers to work in large collectives. Rural reforms meant that individual families were able to rent land and keep farming proceeds for themselves. The result was a sharp rise in agricultural output, matched by the mid-1980s in the rest of the economy once state-owned producers in other sectors were allowed to keep a portion of their profits. After 1990, private businesses started to become common and the country's economic growth rate accelerated further. So spectacular were the results of this embrace of private markets that by 2010, the Chinese economy was well over five times as large as it had been in 1978–much of the expansion due to China's emergence as the prime global exporter of manufactured goods.

Average incomes have risen for millions in China's new middle class. Between 1981 and 2009, for example, the proportion of China's population living in extreme poverty–i.e., on less than (US)$1.25 per day–plummeted from 84 to 12 percent. Despite this remarkable shift, not all the country's citizens have shared in this new prosperity. As the gap between rich and poor continues to widen, political tensions have been on the rise. But so, too, has the justifiable sense of pride felt by many Chinese in their country's accomplishments. Besides improving the living standards of most of its citizens, China has succeeded in transforming its role on the world stage. The country has already achieved super-power status rivalling that of traditional Western powers. If current trends continue, the size of the Chinese economy will overtake that of the current world economic leader, the United States, sometime in the next few decades–probably before 2030.

India

India's transformation is more recent. In the early 1990s, government reforms freed private business to operate in key areas of the economy. The growth that followed was first evident in the country's service-based industries, whose global sales benefited from the widespread knowledge of English in India's workforce. This growth later spread to manufacturing. Whereas the Chinese economy has steadily grown by 10 percent or more each year, India's economy regularly achieves annual growth rates of 8 percent. Average living standards have visibly risen, and a middle class has come into existence. Between 1981 and 2009, for example, the proportion of India's population living on less than (US)$1.25 a day dropped from 60 to 33 percent. But India's "economic miracle" still faces considerable challenges. Extreme poverty remains the lot of hundreds of millions of the country's citizens, as many of the poor migrate from rural to urban areas in search of a better life–a trend at work in China's economy as well.

Brazil

For decades, Brazil was seen as a nation of largely untapped economic potential. Starting in the mid-1990s, when a new stable economic environment was forged with the aid of market reforms, sustained rates of high economic growth finally became a reality. Unlike China and India, where the drivers of growth have been manufacturing and services, Brazil's abundant supplies of natural resources, such as oil, minerals, and fresh water, are key to its economic growth. Historically, the country has exhibited significant disparities between its richest and poorest citizens. Though these disparities remain, extreme poverty is quickly receding, with the proportion of Brazil's population living on less than (US)$1.25 a day falling by over half, from 17 to 6 percent between 1981 and 2009. As these trends continue, the country is joining China and India as a new entrant among the world's largest economies. But Brazil's growth potential has been bedevilled by a variety of challenges, including a costly pension scheme for public sector workers and significant underinvestment in key amenities such as sanitation and public transport. Its growth has also brought significant costs, including environmental damage created by its rapid resource exploitation as well as its expanding manufacturing sector. Like China and India, the country has joined the ranks of the largest Western economies as a major global polluter.

Economic Goals

Choosing economic goals is an issue of normative economics and depends on the political and moral constraints set by society. In other words, it requires making value judgments. Because of these moral and political considerations, not all countries will necessarily choose to emphasize particular economic goals to the same degree. Nonetheless, the economic goals that various countries strive for are often similar. In 1964, the Economic Council of Canada–formerly a federal "think tank" on economic issues–listed what it considered to be the five main goals of the Canadian economy: income equity, price stability, full employment, a viable balance of payments, and economic growth. Most Canadians would add economic efficiency and environmental sustainability to the list. For now, we will briefly summarize the significance of all but the last of these goals. Because of growing concerns over the goal of environmental sustainability in Canada, the significance of this goal will be sketched in greater detail, using climate change as an illustration.

INCOME EQUITY

Income equity is achieved when a country's total output is distributed fairly. This prompts the question, "What is fair?" Is it fair that the salary of a bank executive is hundreds of times higher than the year's wages of a part-time gardener? Because value judgments come into play, defining and satisfying the goal of income equity is controversial.

PRICE STABILITY

Government policy-makers try to minimize the country's rate of **inflation**, which is a rise in the general level of prices. As the average price level in the economy increases, households must pay more to buy the same items. In other words, the purchasing power of a single dollar falls. Meanwhile, people's incomes do not necessarily increase along with these higher prices. Those households whose incomes stay the same or grow only slightly are hurt by inflation because they can buy fewer goods and services than they could before.

inflation: a rise in the general level of prices

FULL EMPLOYMENT

The Canadian government endeavours to minimize involuntary unemployment in the labour force. The labour force can be defined as those people who are working plus those who are involuntarily unemployed and actively seeking employment. The **unemployment rate** is the percentage of the country's labour force that is involuntarily unemployed.

The costs of involuntary unemployment are significant, both to the jobless and to the entire economy. Being without work represents a waste of personal potential and can bring economic hardship to the unemployed and their families.

unemployment rate: the percentage of a labour force that is involuntarily unemployed

For the Canadian economy, a high unemployment rate means a lower total output than could otherwise be produced. In terms of the country's production possibilities curve, economic activity takes place within the curve, where resources are not used to their full potential.

VIABLE BALANCE OF PAYMENTS

balance-of-payments accounts: a summary of all transactions between Canadians and foreigners that involve exchanging Canadian dollars for other currencies

Canadians engage in a constant flow of imports, exports, and financial dealings with other countries. These international flows–including importing, exporting, borrowing, and lending–are of great significance to the Canadian economy. The **balance-of-payments accounts** summarize all transactions between Canadians and foreigners that involve exchanging Canadian dollars for other currencies, such as American dollars or British pounds. Because of Canada's dependence on foreign markets, it is important that Canadian imports and exports roughly balance one another. Similarly, financial flows in and out of the country need to be more or less evenly matched. As long as these conditions are met, then Canada exhibits a viable balance of payments.

ECONOMIC GROWTH

Economic growth, as we have seen, is depicted by an outward shift in the production possibilities curve. Economic growth is an important national goal because it helps to raise the average standard of living for Canadians. Thus, over recent decades, the entire Canadian economy has expanded considerably, and individual Canadians are better off than they were in previous decades. For example, average Canadian workers in the 2010s can buy over three and a half times as much with their income as could average workers in the early 1920s. Maintaining a healthy rate of growth in the Canadian economy will ensure that future generations achieve even higher living standards. For the global economy as a whole, economic growth is equally important–especially for emerging economies that are keen to eradicate the extreme poverty still faced by many of their citizens. In recent years, most emerging economies have maintained rates of economic growth higher than rich nations such as Canada. When lumped together as a group, the world's emerging economies are in the process of overtaking the combined size of rich Western economies. But individual Canadians–like their counterparts in other rich countries–will likely continue to enjoy high average living standards (at least when viewed in global terms) for decades to come.

ECONOMIC EFFICIENCY

economic efficiency: employing scarce resources in a way that derives the highest benefit

In general, **economic efficiency** means getting the highest benefit from an economy's scarce resources. In other words, efficiency requires that scarce economic resources be employed in a way that maximizes utility.

ENVIRONMENTAL SUSTAINABILITY

Economic activity must be carried out so that the quality of our physical environment can be sustained without significant harm. In recent centuries–especially the last one–the world's air, water, and land resources have seriously deteriorated, so much so that there are signs that irreversible damage has occurred. To eliminate, or at least minimize, these problems in the future requires adjustments in the way economic activity is now conducted, especially in industrialized countries such as Canada, as well as in emerging economies such as China, India, and Brazil that are undergoing rapid industrialization. In recent years, many Canadians have become increasingly focused on the challenges related to the goal of environmental sustainability, particularly the reduction of the most harmful forms of air pollution. Concern over climate change is a major reason for the prominence of environmental sustainability. The complexities involved in accomplishing economic goals can be illustrated by taking a closer look at the issues relating to climate change.

Climate Change

Worries over possible warming of the world's climate led to the signing of the international agreement known as the Kyoto Protocol in 1997. The agreement aimed to reduce emissions of carbon-based greenhouse gases, in particular carbon dioxide. The protocol's motivation was the consensus within the scientific community (with some scientists dissenting) that carbon emissions are causing a global rise in average temperatures. Not all areas of the planet are being affected to the same extent, and estimates of the overall predicted increase vary widely. But the general view is that average temperatures will climb somewhere between 1.5 and 6 degrees centigrade by 2100, unless emissions are substantially reduced in upcoming years. An increase of even a few degrees will have profound consequences, not least because of the partial melting of polar icecaps it will cause. Such melting (at least of icecaps atop land) will raise ocean levels, potentially flooding coastal areas that include the most heavily populated parts of the planet.

Over 170 countries signed the Kyoto Protocol. Participating countries fell into two groups: rich nations that historically have been major carbon emitters, and less rich countries that until recently were not. Nation members of the first group were required to reduce their carbon emissions between 2008 and 2012 so that their average rates would be 5 percent below what they were in 1990. Members of the second group were not expected to cut emissions until after 2012. Any member of the first group that did not satisfy its cutback requirements could purchase "carbon credits" to cover the excess, either from other members of the first group that surpassed their targets, or from members of the second group that chose to cut their emissions.

It was a complicated arrangement and one that has caused considerable controversy, in part because the second group of countries includes some of the world's major polluters. For example, thanks to its skyrocketing economic growth, China now is by far the largest carbon emitter on the planet, having surpassed the total emissions of the United States, whose government signed the Kyoto Protocol but did not end up ratifying it. Non-Western countries now account for over half of the world's carbon emissions, though their rates of emission per person are far lower than in rich nations. Still, when considering past history, rich Western nations have accounted for a large majority of the carbon pumped into the atmosphere since 1850.

In 2009, an international conference was convened in Copenhagen in an attempt to forge a new agreement to extend the Kyoto Protocol commitments after 2012. However, the conference was a failure, in large part because of the growing divide between Western nations and their non-Western counterparts. Subsequent international conferences have seen little progress to rectify this divide. While rich nations are most interested in extending targets on total carbon emissions and argue that the targets this time should include emerging economies, non-Western nations are more interested in setting per capita emissions targets. There remains a deep disagreement over how much rich nations should pay poorer countries to help them meet any new emission goals and to reimburse citizens in poorer countries for the high costs they are expected to bear as a result of global warming.

In the meantime, as the time span since the Kyoto Protocol was signed lengthens, there is a growing realization that it, too, has been unsuccessful. Rich Western countries that ratified the protocol committed to reduce their greenhouse emissions, each by a different percentage in relation to their emissions before the protocol came into effect. But, despite some national success stories, global carbon emissions have risen significantly since 1997 when the protocol was signed.

Canada is one of the countries that did not deliver on its promises. Until its formal withdrawal from the protocol, it was one of several countries vying for the dubious title of having exceeded its Kyoto commitments by the widest proportion. Many Canadians see this as a source of profound embarrassment. Some are calling for more serious attempts to cut carbon emissions. Others, especially those not persuaded by the science surrounding climate change, blame what they see as the unrealistic expectations that surrounded the protocol and the guiding assumptions behind its implementation.

The issues Canadians face in settling this debate are complicated. The costs of even a noticeable reduction in the gap between Canada's actual performance and its Kyoto commitments would have been extremely high. Because of the country's large geographic size, its relatively cold climate, and its large manufacturing base, Canadians are major users of polluting energy sources such as coal, gas, and oil. To what extent will Canadians choose to tackle this problem? If a decision is made to make major cutbacks, what ways can be found to minimize the costs and to share these costs fairly among Canadians? As we will see in later chapters, economists have a great deal to say about such questions.

COMPLEMENTARY GOALS

In some cases, success in reaching one economic goal makes another goal easier to achieve. Goals that are related in this way simplify the task of those in charge of government economic policy and are said to be complementary. Full employment and economic growth, for example, are considered to be complementary goals, since government policies that help to push up employment levels in an economy also lead to expanded national output.

CONFLICTING GOALS

Some economic goals, however, are bound to conflict so that attaining one goal makes another goal more difficult to achieve. For example, price stability and full employment frequently clash because government measures that bring down the rate of inflation often restrain the level of production in an economy, thus raising the unemployment rate. Similarly, income equity and economic efficiency often clash, since efforts to make the distribution of income fairer can reduce incentives for households to supply their resources. This can mean that an economy's resources are used less efficiently than before. Conflicts like these mean that government policy-makers must set priorities, and this can result in one goal being achieved at the cost of another.

BRIEF REVIEW

1. Every country must answer three basic economic questions: what to produce, how to produce, and for whom to produce.

2. Traditional economies stress the role of custom and tradition. Market economies rely on private property and the operation of markets. Command economies depend on publicly-owned property and central planning.

3. Modern mixed economies combine features of both market and command economics in different degrees. Traditional mixed economies include both traditional and modern sectors. China, India, and Brazil are high-profile illustrations of emerging economies exhibiting high rates of economic growth and rising average incomes.

4. The difficulties Canada faces in achieving the goal of environmental sustainability are of considerable concern to many citizens. This is especially true given the country's lack of success in meeting the carbon emission targets set by the Canadian government under the Kyoto Protocol, as well as the wider failure of the 2009 Copenhagen conference and the 2010 conference in Cancun, Mexico to extend the Kyoto Protocol commitments.

5. The main goals of the Canadian economy are economic efficiency, income equity, price stability, full employment, a viable balance of payments, economic growth, and environmental sustainability. Some of these goals are complementary, while others are conflicting.

1.3 | PRACTICE PROBLEMS

1. Countries Alpha and Beta each have traditional, private, and public sectors. The traditional and public sectors each make up a larger proportion of Alpha's economy than their proportions in Beta. On the other hand, the private sector is relatively larger in Beta than in Alpha.
   a. Which country will tend to have more economic freedom?
   b. Which country's economy will tend to have greater stability?
   c. In which country will there be the greatest conflict between traditional culture and national planners?
   d. If the two countries' systems are plotted in the triangle shown in Figure 1.4, will Alpha be northwest, southwest, northeast, or southeast of Beta?
2. Full employment and economic growth are seen as complementary goals, while price stability and full employment are considered to be conflicting goals. What does this suggest about the relationship between economic growth and price stability?

LAST WORD

In this chapter, we saw how individuals make choices on the basis of their calculation of utility and the opportunity cost of scarce personal resources. We also saw how societies make economic choices on the basis of normative goals and the opportunity cost of scarce social resources. We will return to the ways that individuals make choices in the next two chapters of Part 1. Meanwhile, later parts of the book focus on how society meets its goals: economic efficiency and income equity in Part 2, price stability and full employment in Part 3, and a viable balance of payments and economic growth in Part 4.

PROBLEMS

1. You have been going to a health club two or three times a month for the past 10 years, paying per visit. You recently decided you want to improve your physical fitness and you intend to start visiting the club twice per week. You can pay $60 per month for unlimited visits if you sign a one-year contract, or continue paying $10 per visit. You know that you don't always follow through with your intentions to improve yourself.
   a. Which payment scheme is most rational for you?
   b. Does your past behaviour of not always following through with plans affect your choice?

2. Your friend wishes to begin saving, but he finds he continually spends the amount he plans to save each month on impulse purchases.
   a. Would you say your friend is being rational? Why or why not?
   b. Is there any plan you could suggest to your friend to help him adjust his behaviour to better meet his goals?

3. Specify which of the two variables is the independent variable and which is the dependent variable.
   a. The quantity of CDs purchased is reduced due to a drop in the price of digitally streamed music.
   b. A reduction in Canadian household incomes leads to the government spending more on transfer payments to households.
   c. The number of people seeking a career in computer programming expands due to a rise in the average salary of computer programmers.
   d. A fall in the price of wheat fertilizer increases the amount of wheat planted by farmers.
   e. Canada's rate of economic growth drops because of a fall in output per worker in the Canadian economy.

4. Specify whether the following relationships are direct or inverse.
   a. An increase in income tax rates paid by households reduces consumption spending in the economy.
   b. The quantity of smartphone apps purchased increases due to a rise in the number of consumers using smartphones.
   c. An increase in the price of online advertising results in an increase of the hours of TV advertising time bought.
   d. The rate of inflation rises because of an increase in spending in the economy.
   e. A larger money supply in Canada leads to a drop in the interest rate on loans.

5. Specify whether the following statements deal with a topic in microeconomics or macroeconomics.
   a. An increase in prices paid on online auction websites expands the quantity of collectibles offered for sale.
   b. The quantity of high fashion clothing purchased is pushed up by a rise in consumer incomes.
   c. An increase in household wealth in Canada prompts greater consumer spending.
   d. The quantity purchased of a brand name painkiller falls as a result of a drop in the price of a no-name painkiller.
   e. Investment spending is boosted by a drop in the interest rate on loans.

6. Identify the following statements as positive or normative. In each case, explain your answer.
   a. To stimulate economic growth, the Canadian economy should produce more capital goods and fewer consumer goods.
   b. Inflation in Canada is currently lower than in most other countries.
   c. If economic efficiency drops, citizens of the country will see a decrease in their living standards.
   d. The Canadian government should be more concerned with ensuring environmental sustainability and less concerned with achieving low inflation.

7. A consumer would gain more utility from purchasing a video game console than from purchasing a flat-screen TV, even though both products have the same price of $600.
   a. If the consumer is rational, will she choose to purchase the console or the TV?
   b. Does utility relate to the concept of opportunity cost in deciding what to purchase?

8. The graph below shows a production possibilities curve for an economy that produces only two goods—skateboards and bicycles.

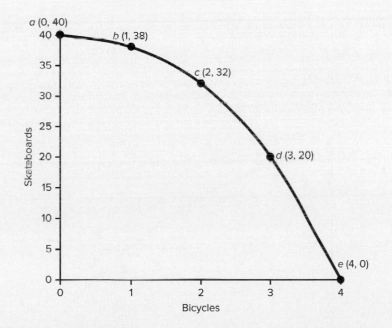

   a. Calculate the opportunity cost of bicycles in terms of skateboards when the economy moves from point *b* to c. What is the new opportunity cost for bicycles when the economy moves from point c to *d*? Do your answers illustrate the law of increasing opportunity costs?
   b. Can the economy produce 38 skateboards and two bicycles? Why or why not?
   c. If 32 skateboards and one bicycle are produced, how would you describe production in this economy?
   d. Describe how a technological improvement in the assembly of bicycles would affect the production possibilities curve.
   e. Describe how an increase in the economy's supply of labour would affect the production possibilities curve.

9. The diagram below shows the size of the private, public, and traditional sectors in three hypothetical countries.

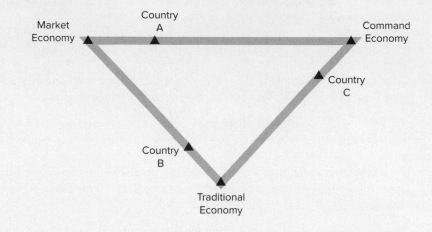

a. Which of these countries likely has the most stable culture? the most equal distribution of income? the greatest economic freedom?

b. Traditional sectors in emerging economies are continually shrinking. Using the diagram, describe the movement caused by an increase in the private sector in Country B and an increase in the public sector in Country C.

10. (Advanced Problem)

The production possibilities curve below applies to an economy that produces only ice-cream sodas and industrial robots.

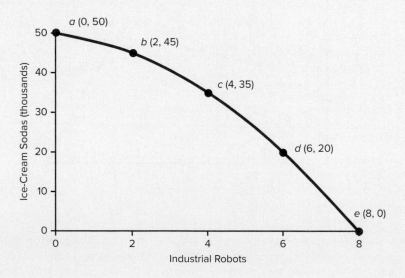

a. What is the opportunity cost of industrial robots in terms of ice-cream sodas when the economy moves from point *a* to *b*? from point *b* to *c*? What is the opportunity cost of ice-cream sodas in terms of industrial robots when the economy moves from point *e* to *d*? from point *d* to *c*? Do your answers in each case illustrate the law of increasing opportunity costs?

b. Describe how a technological improvement in the assembly of industrial robots would affect the production possibilities curve.

c. If industrial robots can be viewed as a capital good, then describe in words how this economy's decision to produce more industrial robots will affect its future production possibilities curve.

11. To promote income equity, the federal government decides to tax away all household incomes above $60 000 per year. What will be the likely effect of this policy on economic efficiency?

12. (Advanced Problem)
http://www5.statcan.gc.ca/cansim/
   a. Calculate Canada's misery index, which is the sum of a country's inflation and unemployment rates expressed as percentages, for the years shown in the table below. Construct a table showing your results.

Annual Inflation and Unemployment Rates in Canada, 1990–2010

	Inflation (%)	Unemployment (%)		Inflation (%)	Unemployment (%)
1990	4.8	8.1	2000	2.7	6.8
1991	5.6	10.3	2001	2.5	7.2
1992	1.4	11.2	2002	2.2	7.7
1993	1.9	11.4	2003	2.8	7.6
1994	0.1	10.4	2004	1.8	7.2
1995	2.2	9.5	2005	2.2	6.8
1996	1.5	9.6	2006	2.0	6.3
1997	1.7	9.1	2007	2.2	6.0
1998	1.0	8.3	2008	2.3	6.1
1999	1.8	7.6	2009	0.3	8.3
			2010	1.8	8.0

Source: Statistics Canada, CANSIM database http://www5.statcan.gc.ca/cansim/, Tables 282-0086 and 326-0021 (retrieved March 16, 2014).

   b. What was the average value of the misery index during the years 1990–2010? In which years was the index greater than the average value? In which years was it less?
   c. What does the misery index indicate? How are the inflation rate and the unemployment rate weighted in this index? Would everyone agree with this weighting? Explain.

13. (Policy Discussion Question)
   There is currently a debate in Canada over the relative advantages of having health care provided by the public sector or the private sector.
   a. What are the main advantages associated with health care provided by the public sector? by the private sector?
   b. Do you believe more of Canada's health care services should be available privately? Why or why not?

THE FOUNDER OF MODERN ECONOMICS
Adam Smith and the Invisible Hand

ADAM SMITH

© Library of Congress Prints and Photographs Division (LC-USZ62-17407)

SMITH AND HIS INFLUENCE

Adam Smith (1723–1790) is known as the father of present-day economics. Indeed, Smith is often seen as having launched the entire discipline, though he employed ideas developed by earlier thinkers. While he deserves his reputation as a trailblazer, his greatest talent was in combining innovative ideas—many conceived by others—into a theory that had a profound influence on economic thinking, not only in his own time but ever since.

The son of a middle class Scottish family, he was an avid student, attending universities in both England and Scotland. At the University of Glasgow, he gained a reputation as the stereotypical absent-minded professor who, when distracted by some difficult theoretical problem, would walk for hours, oblivious to his surroundings.

Smith first made a name for himself through his writings in philosophy. He then turned his attention to economic issues. In 1776, after years of research, he published his classic work, *An Inquiry Into the Nature and Causes of the Wealth of Nations*, which brought him both fame and a modest fortune. For generations, the book was a standard in economics, and it can still be read profitably today.

THE INDUSTRIAL REVOLUTION

Smith lived at the beginning of the Industrial Revolution. In the latter half of the 1700s and early 1800s, agriculture lost its central role in the British economy. Through a host of technological innovations, a powerful new manufacturing sector based on labour-saving machinery and steam power took its place. By transforming the lives of common people, this revolution had a profound social and economic impact in many countries, but first in Britain:

> The Industrial Revolution marks the most fundamental transformation of human life in the history of the world recorded in written documents. For a brief period, it coincided with the history of a single country, Great Britain. An entire world economy was thus built on, or rather around, Britain, and this country therefore temporarily rose to a position of global influence and power unparalleled by any state of its relative size before or since, and unlikely to be paralleled by any state in the foreseeable future.[1]

THE DIVISION OF LABOUR

When Adam Smith was writing *The Wealth of Nations*, these great changes in the British economy were just beginning. As the title of his book suggests, he wished to explain why some countries become more wealthy than others. Smith viewed the division of labour—the degree to which the job of each worker is a specialized task—as the most significant single cause of economic progress. To support this claim, he provided his famous illustration from the trade of pin-making:

> The greatest improvement in the productive powers of labour, and the greater part of the skill, dexterity, and judgement with which it is anywhere directed, or applied, seem to have been the effects of the division of labour. . . .

To take an example, . . . the trade of the pin-maker; a workman not educated to this business, . . . nor acquainted with the use of the machinery employed in it, . . . could scarce, perhaps, with his utmost industry, make one pin in a day, and certainly could not make twenty. But in the way in which this business is now carried on, not only the whole work is a peculiar [i.e., particular] trade, but it is divided into a number of branches, of which the greater part are likewise peculiar trades. One man draws out the wire, another straight[en]s it, a third cuts it, a fourth points it, a fifth grinds it at the top for receiving the head; to make the head requires three distinct operations; to put it on is a peculiar business, to whiten the pins is another; it is even a trade by itself to put them into the paper; and the important business of making a pin is, in this manner, divided into about eighteen distinct operations, which, in some manufactories, are all performed by distinct hands, though in others the same man will sometimes perform two or three of them.[2]

Smith mentioned that he visited a small factory where, through the division of labour, 10 employees produced a total of 48 000 pins a day—4800 times the estimated product of one pin per worker when the division of labour was not used!

THE INVISIBLE HAND

The benefits associated with the division of labour are not the only reason why some nations are better off than others, according to Smith. Economic progress is also spurred by the self-interest motive or the desire individuals have to increase their own happiness. "It is not from the benevolence of the butcher, the brewer, or the baker that we expect our dinner," Smith stated, "but from their regard to their own interest. We address ourselves, not to their humanity but to their self-love, and never talk to them of our own necessities but of their advantages."[3] In other words, if people are free to pursue their own private interests, they act in a way that aids the economy as a whole. What causes this is competition. As long as there are many businesses selling a product, the product's price will be driven down to a point where it covers only the businesses' costs, including a reasonable profit for the owners. If the price of the product were any higher, others would enter the industry to gain excess profits. Because consumers can buy the product at the lowest possible price, they reap the ultimate rewards of competition.

In more general terms, the forces of individual self-interest and competition ensure that resources are used in ways that promote economic growth and national prosperity. To explain his theory, Smith used a term that has become part of everyday language. He said that the forces of market competition act like an "invisible hand" so that self-interested behaviour can work to the benefit of all society.

THE PRINCIPLE OF LAISSEZ FAIRE

Although Adam Smith pointed out the potential benefits of people's selfish actions, he was not merely acting as a mouthpiece for the business class. As he was quick to point out, individual self-interest ceases to benefit society when competition is lacking. In the case of a monopoly, where a single producer controls an entire market, the business class's selfish motives cause prices to be driven to the highest value that the market will bear, meaning that consumers suffer.

Often, it is governments that cause monopolies to flourish, said Smith, by offering privileges to a chosen firm. In fact, governments themselves can be considered a type of monopoly. All too frequently, Smith argued, public officials engage in political favouritism or misuse their power for private ends. In doing so, they illustrate how selfish behaviour, when unimpeded by private competition, harms rather than helps society.

Given his skeptical view of government actions, Smith asserted the principle of laissez faire, the French term for "let things be"–meaning that, in general, governments should interfere as little as possible in the day-to-day operations of private markets.

RELEVANCE FOR TODAY

While modern economists, as a rule, express admiration for Smith's achievements, some question the suitability of his theories in contemporary times. They suggest that Smith's "invisible hand" only operates when an economy is made up of many small businesses. However, most modern markets do not meet these requirements. A contemporary American economist named Robert Heilbroner upholds this view:

> Today's market mechanism is characterized by the huge size of its participants: giant corporations and equally giant labor unions obviously do not behave as if they were individual proprietors and workers. Their very bulk enables them to stand out against the pressures of competition, to disregard price signals, and to consider what their self-interest shall be in the long run rather than in the immediate press of each day's buying and selling.[4]

Other economists claim that Smith's conclusions are just as relevant today as they were over 200 years ago. Although huge corporations are an important factor in contemporary economies, so are small businesses. And, as various nations become integrated into a single global economy, international competition among companies–both large and small–is playing a greater role than ever before.

Supporters of Smith's relevance also point to the recent growth of markets in emerging economies, including in formerly communist and socialist ones. They argue that now, more than ever before, private competition is preferred over government intervention–a testament to Smith's farseeing insight into economic activity and its motivations. Smith may have died well over two centuries ago, but his ideas are as alive today as they ever were.

1. What is the main reason why the division of labour can lead to increased output in a production process such as pin-making?

2. In each of the following cases, use Adam Smith's concept of the invisible hand to explain the events that occur if the relevant markets are competitive and operate without government intervention. In your answers, identify the self-interested behaviour that causes beneficial results.
   a. Because of Good W's sudden popularity, suppliers of this good presently make exorbitant profits.
   b. A new innovation reduces the cost of producing Good X.
   c. Two neighbouring countries, A and B, agree for the first time to allow goods to flow freely between them.

3. Explain why the absence of the invisible hand of competition in the following situations can lead to harmful results for consumers.
   a. A catering company wins the exclusive right to sell food in a stadium.
   b. By keeping out potential rivals, a few large corporations control sales of Good Y.
   c. A labour union, which, by law, includes all workers involved in the production of Good Z, manages on the basis of a strike threat to gain a significant wage increase from employers.

Notes

1 *From Industry and Empire: From 1750 to the Present Day* by E.J. Hobsbawm (Harmondsworth: Penguin, 1969), p. 13, copyright © E.J. Hobsbawm, 1968, 1969. Reprinted by permission of Simon & Schuster, Inc.

2 Adam Smith, *The wealth of nations* (Harmondsworth: Penguin, 1983), pp.109–10.

3 *Ibid.,* p. 119.

4 *The Worldly Philosophers,* 6th ed. (New York: Simon and Schuster, 1986), p. 59. Copyright © 1953, 1961, 1967, 1972, 1980, 1986, 1992 by Robert L. Heilbroner. Copyright renewed © 1981, 1989 by Robert L. Heilbroner. Reprinted by permission of Simon & Schuster, Inc.

CHAPTER 2

Demand and Supply

Each day, we buy an assortment of goods and services—a meal, a snack, maybe a magazine. What determines the price of the pizza slice we buy at lunchtime? the selection of chocolate bars we find at our local variety store? the types of software apps available for our phone? The answer to all these questions is demand and supply. These two powerful forces are the economic equivalents of gravity—never seen, but always exerting their influence in the most visible ways. In this chapter, we will study the impact of these two forces on our daily lives by seeing how they operate in individual markets. We will also gain a better appreciation of how the "invisible hand" of competition coordinates the plans of buyers and sellers, nudged along by the interaction of demand and supply.

> Teach a parrot to say demand and supply, and you've created an economist.
>
> —OLD JOKE

LEARNING OBJECTIVES   After reading this chapter, you will be able to

LO 1

Describe the nature of demand, changes in quantity demanded, changes in demand, and the factors that affect demand

LO 2

Summarize the nature of supply, changes in quantity supplied, changes in supply, and the factors that affect supply

LO 3

Explain how markets reach equilibrium—the point at which demand and supply meet

2.1 | The Role of Demand

A product market exists wherever households and businesses buy and sell consumer products—either face-to-face, or indirectly by mail, telephone, or online. Some markets, such as the market for crude oil, are global in scope. Others, such as the market for hot dogs at a local baseball game, are tiny by comparison.

What Is Demand?

Because households are buyers in product markets, their behaviour can be analyzed using the concept of **demand**, which is the relationship between the various possible prices of a product and the quantities consumers will purchase at each price. In this relationship, price is the independent variable. **Quantity demanded**—the amount of the product that consumers are willing to purchase at each price—is the dependent variable. To isolate the relationship between these two variables, all other factors affecting price and quantity demanded are assumed to remain constant. Recall that this is the assumption of *ceteris paribus*— "all other things remaining the same."

demand: the relationship between the various possible prices of a product and the quantities of that product consumers are willing to purchase

quantity demanded: the amount of a product consumers are willing to purchase at each price

The Law of Demand

Is the relationship between price and quantity demanded direct or inverse? To answer this question, consider the example of the amount of strawberries you might eat during a month. As shown in the table in Figure 2.1, you might buy two kilograms per month when each kilogram is priced at $2. If the price rises to $2.50, you will likely purchase fewer strawberries, perhaps one kilogram per month at this new price. Conversely, if the price falls to $1.50, you will probably buy more strawberries per month. At this lower price, strawberries become a better deal in terms of the satisfaction you get from each dollar spent. Thus, you

FIGURE 2.1   An Individual's Demand Schedule and Curve

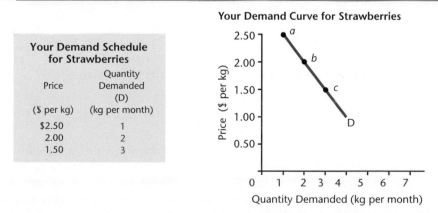

Your Demand Schedule for Strawberries

Price ($ per kg)	Quantity Demanded (D) (kg per month)
$2.50	1
2.00	2
1.50	3

The demand schedule shows that as the price of strawberries falls, you are willing to purchase more strawberries. The demand curve D depicts this same inverse relationship between price and quantity demanded. For example, a fall in price from $2 to $1.50 causes quantity demanded to rise from 2 kg (point *b*) to 3 kg (point *c*).

law of demand: states that there is an inverse relationship between a product's quantity demanded and its price

may decide to increase your purchases to three kilograms per month. This inverse relationship between price and quantity demanded, when all other factors are kept constant, is known as the **law of demand**.

The Demand Curve

demand schedule: a table that shows possible combinations of prices and quantities demanded of a product

demand curve: a graph that expresses possible combinations of prices and quantities demanded of a product

The quantities demanded of a product at various prices can be expressed in a **demand schedule** like the one in Figure 2.1. Expressing the schedule on a graph, as shown on the right in Figure 2.1, gives the consumer's demand curve (D) for strawberries. The **demand curve** is drawn by placing the price of strawberries on the vertical axis and the quantity demanded per month on the horizontal axis. Note that the independent variable (price) is on the vertical axis, while the dependent variable (quantity demanded) is on the horizontal axis. This choice that economists have made differs from the convention in mathematics, in which the independent variable (x) is on the horizontal axis and the dependent variable (y) is on the vertical axis.

change in quantity demanded: the effect of a price change on quantity demanded

The demand curve's negative (downward) slope reflects the law of demand: an increase in the product's price decreases the quantity demanded, and vice versa. Changes such as these are examples of a **change in quantity demanded** and produce a movement *along* the demand curve. For example, an increase in the price of strawberries from $1.50 to $2 decreases the quantity demanded per month from three kilograms (point c on the demand curve) to two kilograms (point b).

THINKING ABOUT ECONOMICS

Is the law of demand ever broken?

While extremely rare, the relationship between a product's price and quantity demanded can be direct, in which case the demand curve for the product has a positive (upward) slope. This may happen when a product's high price is seen as a status symbol. For example, the quantity demanded of a designer shirt may rise when its price rises. Consumers who can afford the shirt are attracted to the item because its high price makes it more fashionable than before. This situation, which can also apply to products like luxury perfumes and watches, is known as the "Veblen effect." It is named after the American economist, Thorstein Veblen (1857–1929), whose critique of such purchases led him to coin the memorable term "conspicuous consumption" to describe them.

QUESTION **What is another example of a product that exhibits the Veblen effect?**

Market Demand

market demand: the sum of all consumers' quantity demanded for a product at each price

Market demand, which can again be shown as a schedule or a curve, is the sum of all consumers' purchases, or quantity demanded, at each price. This is illustrated in Figure 2.2 in the unlikely case that there are just two consumers in the strawberry market–you and a friend–with individual demand curves D_0 (yours) and D_1 (your friend's). While you purchase two kilograms per month at a $2 price, your strawberry-loving friend purchases three kilograms per month at this same price. These amounts are based on what each of you is able and willing to pay for strawberries. The total quantity demanded in the market is,

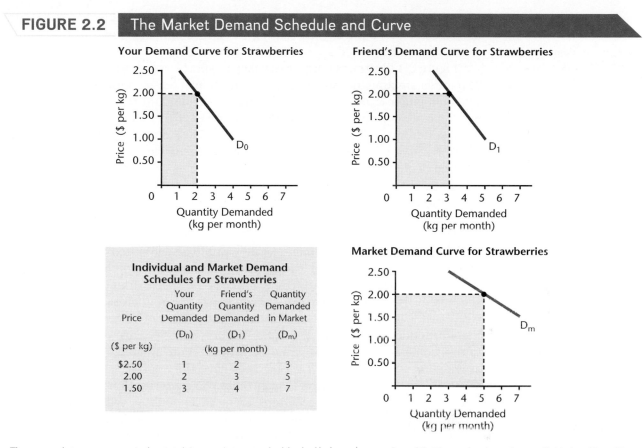

FIGURE 2.2   The Market Demand Schedule and Curve

There are only two consumers in the strawberry market, you and a friend, with demand curves D_0 and D_1. The market demand curve (D_m) is found by adding the number of kilograms purchased by both consumers at each possible price. For example, at a price of $2, you buy 2 kg and your friend buys 3 kg, giving a quantity demanded in the market of 5 kg at this price.

therefore, five kilograms. Repeating this procedure at every possible price gives the market demand curve (D_m) on the lower right in Figure 2.2.

Changes in Demand

Earlier, we stated that to study the relationship between price and quantity demanded, all other factors affecting these variables must be assumed constant. Now, let us examine these other factors, which are known as **demand factors**. These factors can cause the entire market demand curve to shift. The five main demand factors are the number of buyers in a market, their average income, the prices of other products, consumer preferences, and consumer expectations about future prices and incomes. With each factor, it must be assumed that all other factors remain constant.

demand factors: factors that can cause an increase or a decrease in a product's demand

NUMBER OF BUYERS

When the number of buyers for a certain product increases, more purchases are made. Thus, the amount of the product demanded increases, whatever its price. The result is called an **increase in demand**. On a graph, an increase in demand is shown as a shift of the entire demand curve to the right. When the number

increase in demand: an increase in the quantity demanded of a product at all prices

decrease in demand: a decrease in the quantity demanded of a product at all prices

of buyers in a market decreases, the amount of the product demanded also decreases at every price, thus causing the entire demand curve to shift to the left. This result is called a **decrease in demand**.

Figure 2.3 illustrates both cases using a hypothetical market for strawberries. The initial amounts demanded per year in the market are shown in the demand schedule under D_0. When demand increases, the amount demanded increases at every possible price. For example, at a price of $2, the amount demanded increases from 9 to 11 million kilograms. Thus, on the graph, the original demand curve (D_0) shifts to the right, giving a new demand curve (D_1). When demand decreases, the amount demanded decreases at every price. For example, at a price of $2, the amount demanded decreases from 9 to 7 million kilograms. Thus, the demand curve shifts to the left, from D_0 to D_2.

INCOME

normal products: products whose demand changes directly with income

inferior products: products whose demand changes inversely with income

When consumers' incomes increase, they purchase more luxury products, such as expensive jewellery and caviar, with their luxury purchases rising more rapidly than the increase in income. Purchases of necessities, such as milk and shoes, also rise, but by a smaller proportion than the increase in income. But, whether for luxury products or for necessities, demand increases, thus shifting the entire demand curve to the right. Products whose demand changes directly with income are known as **normal products**. There are a few products, known as **inferior products**, for which incomes have the opposite effect. Turnips and second-hand suits are examples. As incomes rise, consumption of these products falls, as buyers switch from turnips to more expensive vegetables and from second-hand suits to new ones. The result is a decrease in demand for these products, reflected in a shift of the entire demand curve to the left.

FIGURE 2.3   Changes in Demand

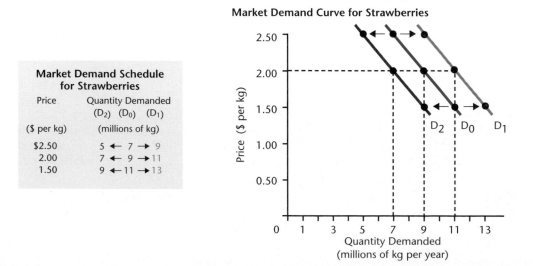

Market Demand Schedule for Strawberries			
Price	Quantity Demanded		
	(D_2)	(D_0)	(D_1)
($ per kg)	(millions of kg)		
$2.50	5 ←	7 →	9
2.00	7 ←	9 →	11
1.50	9 ←	11 →	13

When the number of buyers in a market increases, the amount of strawberries demanded increases at every possible price. Each point on the demand curve, therefore, shifts to the right, from D_0 to D_1. Similarly, a decrease in the number of buyers pushes down the amount demanded at every price, shifting the demand curve to the left, from D_0 to D_2.

PRICES OF OTHER PRODUCTS

Substitute products are products that can be consumed in place of one another, such as butter and margarine, or cell phones and landline phones. When the price of a product rises, consumers choose to purchase more of any reasonable substitute available, thus shifting the substitute product's demand curve to the right. For example, a higher price for butter causes some consumers to switch to margarine, increasing the demand for margarine. If the price of cell phones falls, however, there will be a decrease in the demand for landline phones.

substitute products: products that can be consumed in place of one another

Complementary products are products that are consumed together, such as cars and gasoline, or video games and video game consoles. In the case of complementary products, an increase in the price of one product causes a decrease in demand for its complement. For example, if the price of cars rises, the demand for gasoline falls. The reverse is also true: a fall in the price of video games leads to a rise in demand for video game consoles.

complementary products: products that are consumed together

CONSUMER PREFERENCES

People's preferences also affect buying patterns. A significant uptick in consumer concerns over nutrition, for example, causes an increase in the demand for nutritious foods. Consumer preferences are also influenced by current fashion or advertising, as in the case of clothing. This is illustrated by a sudden fad for a particular brand of athletic shoes, which increases their demand and shifts this product's demand curve to the right.

CONSUMER EXPECTATIONS

The expectations that consumers have about future changes in prices and their own incomes affect their current purchases. For example, if a majority of consumers expect the price of laptop computers to fall, the current demand for laptops decreases. This is because consumers will delay their purchases of laptops until the expected drop in price occurs. Alternatively, if consumers expect their incomes to grow and the prices of products they buy to remain constant—in other words, if they expect their standard of living to rise—their current demand for normal products will increase, and their current demand for inferior products will decrease.

Change in Quantity Demanded versus Change in Demand

The terms *change in quantity demanded* and *change in demand* have special meanings in economics. Figure 2.4 shows both types of change. As we have seen, a change in quantity demanded results from a change in the product's own price. For example, the number of skis purchased per month will increase when the price of skis decreases, as shown on the graph on the left in Figure 2.4. Here, a movement (from point *a* to point *b*) occurs along demand curve D_0, since varying the product's own price does not alter the position of the curve. An increase or decrease in demand, however, results from a change in a demand factor. For example, a change in consumer preferences or in consumer incomes can cause the entire demand curve to shift. This is because the amount of the product demanded changes at every possible price for the product. The graph on the right shows how an increase in incomes increases the demand for skis, which are a normal product, causing a shift of the entire demand curve for skis from D_0 to D_1.

FIGURE 2.4   Change in Quantity Demanded and Change in Demand

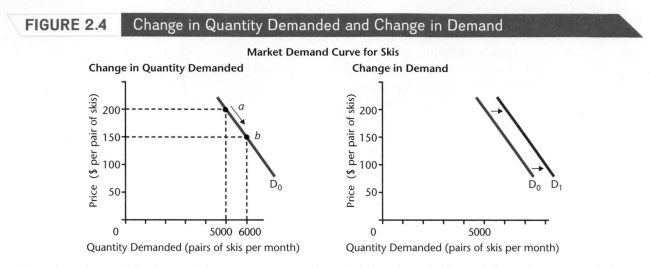

Market Demand Curve for Skis

A change in quantity demanded is shown on the left graph as a movement along a single demand curve (D₀) that results from a change in the product's own price. There is a rise in quantity demanded when the price of skis drops, causing a movement from point *a* to point *b*. The graph on the right shows a change in demand as a shift in the entire demand curve to the right, from D₀ to D₁. This shift results from a change in a demand factor, such as consumer incomes.

BRIEF REVIEW

 1. In product markets, demand represents the decisions of households purchasing consumer items.

2. The demand curve for a particular product shows the relationship between its price and the quantity demanded, either by an individual consumer or in the market as a whole. According to the law of demand, price and quantity demanded are inversely related.

3. A change in quantity demanded is shown by a movement along a product's demand curve and is caused by a change in the product's own price.

4. A change in demand is shown by a shift of the entire demand curve and is caused by a change in a demand factor: the number of buyers, their average income, the prices of other products, consumer preferences, or consumer expectations about future prices and incomes.

5. Demand shifts to the right with an increase in the number of buyers, an increase in income for a normal product, a decrease in income for an inferior product, an increase in the price of a substitute product, or a decrease in the price of a complementary product.

2.1 │ PRACTICE PROBLEMS

1. During a given week, Student 1 demands four milkshakes at a price of $2, five at $1.80, six at $1.60, and seven at $1.40. Student 2 demands five milkshakes at a price per milkshake of $2, seven at $1.80, nine at $1.60, and 11 at $1.40.
   a. Is the law of demand satisfied for each student as the price of milkshakes falls? Why or why not?
   b. How is the market demand curve derived if these two students are the only two consumers in the market?

   c. What are four points on the market demand curve D$_m$?

   d. Draw a graph showing the demand curves for Student 1 and Student 2, D$_1$ and D$_2$, as well as the market demand curve D$_m$. Plot four points for each of the demand curves, for a total of twelve points.

2. How will the demand for eBooks be affected in each of the following situations?

   a. consumer incomes rise

   b. the price of eBook readers decreases

   c. there is a sudden expectation by consumers that the price of eBooks will soon drop

   d. the price of print books rises

3. A decrease in the price of coffee affects both the market for coffee and the market for tea.

   a. Is the change in the coffee market a change in quantity demanded or in demand? Why?

   b. Is the change in the tea market a change in quantity demanded or in demand? Why?

2.2 | The Role of Supply

What Is Supply?

In product markets, supply is related to the selling activity of businesses. The role of supply is most easily analyzed in competitive markets, where the "invisible hand" of competition, identified by Adam Smith, operates. Because the actions of sellers are independent from those of buyers in these markets, the role of supply can be studied separately. In any competitive market, **supply** is the relationship between the various possible prices of a product and the quantities of the product that businesses are willing to put on the market. While the independent variable is again price, the dependent variable is now **quantity supplied**–the amount of the product that businesses are willing to supply at each price. Once again, we can consider both individuals (in this case, individual businesses) and groups (in this case, all businesses producing the same product). **Market supply** is the sum of all producers' quantities supplied at each price. As before, all other factors that affect supply are assumed to be constant.

The Law of Supply

When price changes, quantity supplied changes in the same direction. If the price of strawberries rises, for example, farmers find it desirable to increase the quantity of strawberries they supply because the higher price provides the lure of increased earnings for every unit produced. This direct relationship between price and quantity supplied, when all other factors are kept constant, is called the **law of supply**.

The Supply Curve

The law of supply can be illustrated in a **supply schedule**, such as that for the strawberry market in Figure 2.5. Expressing the schedule on a graph gives us the

LO2

supply: the relationship between the various possible prices of a product and the quantities of the product that businesses are willing to supply

quantity supplied: the amount of a product businesses are willing to supply at each price

market supply: the sum of all producers' quantities supplied at each price

law of supply: states that there is a direct relationship between a product's quantity supplied and its price

supply schedule: a table that shows possible combinations of prices and quantities supplied of a product

FIGURE 2.5   The Market Supply Schedule and Curve

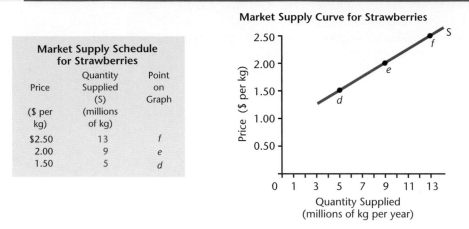

Market Supply Schedule for Strawberries		
Price	Quantity Supplied (S)	Point on Graph
($ per kg)	(millions of kg)	
$2.50	13	f
2.00	9	e
1.50	5	d

The supply schedule shows that when the price of strawberries falls, as from $2 to $1.50 per kg, then quantity supplied also falls, from 9 million (point *e*) to 5 million kg (point *d*), as farmers find it profitable to produce fewer units. The positively sloped supply curve S indicates a direct relationship between price and quantity supplied.

---

supply curve: a graph that expresses possible combinations of prices and quantities supplied of a product

change in quantity supplied: the effect of a price change on quantity supplied

supply curve for the strawberry market. As with the demand curve, a change in a product's price causes a movement *along* the supply curve, thus a **change in quantity supplied**. This is illustrated in Figure 2.5 by the movement from point *f* to point *e* on the supply curve. Because of a drop in the price of strawberries from $2.50 to $2 per kilogram, the quantity supplied by farmers per year drops from 13 to 9 million kilograms. The positive (upward) slope of the supply curve illustrates the direct relationship between price and quantity supplied.

Changes in Supply

supply factors: factors that can cause an increase or a decrease in a product's supply

While price changes will cause changes in quantity supplied, other factors cause supply to change. These factors, which cause the entire supply curve to shift, are known as **supply factors**. The six main supply factors are the number of producers, resource prices, the state of technology, changes in nature, the prices of related products, and producer expectations. Once again, with each factor, we must assume that all other factors remain constant.

NUMBER OF PRODUCERS

increase in supply: an increase in the quantity supplied of a product at all prices

decrease in supply: a decrease in the quantity supplied of a product at all prices

An increase in the number of businesses in an industry causes an **increase in supply**, thus giving a higher quantity supplied at each price and shifting the supply curve to the right. In contrast, a decrease in the number of businesses in the industry creates a **decrease in supply** and a corresponding shift of the supply curve to the left. Figure 2.6 illustrates both cases for the strawberry market. The column marked S_0 in the supply schedule gives the quantity supplied per year by the original number of producers. When the number of producers increases, so does the quantity supplied (indicated by column S_1) at every possible price–for example, from 9 to 11 million kilograms per year at a price of $2. Thus, the supply curve shifts to the right, from S_0 to S_1. Conversely, a decrease in the supply of the product causes the quantities supplied (indicated by column S_2) to decrease at each possible price, for

| FIGURE 2.6 | Changes in Supply |

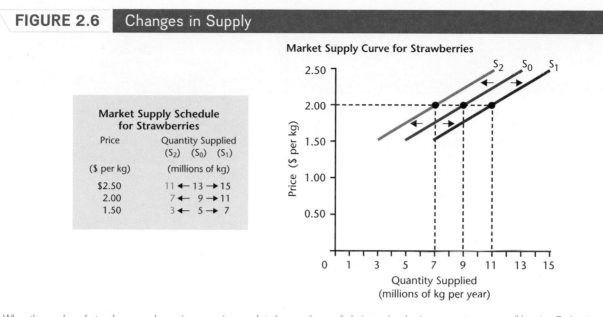

Market Supply Schedule for Strawberries

Price	Quantity Supplied (S_2) (S_0) (S_1)
($ per kg)	(millions of kg)
$2.50	11 ← 13 → 15
2.00	7 ← 9 → 11
1.50	3 ← 5 → 7

When the number of strawberry producers increases in a market, the quantity supplied of strawberries increases at every possible price. Each point on the supply curve shifts to the right from S_0 to S_1. In contrast, a decrease in the number of producers decreases the quantity supplied of strawberries at every price, shifting the supply curve to the left from S_0 to S_2.

example, from 9 to 7 million kilograms per year at a price of $2. The supply curve, therefore, shifts to the left, from S_0 to S_2.

RESOURCE PRICES

As discussed in Chapter 1, businesses buy various resources, such as capital resources and natural resources, to produce goods. If there is a price increase for a resource used in a particular industry, costs for businesses in that industry increase. As a result, fewer units of the product can be produced for the same expenditure. Thus, businesses will tend to cut back on production, causing the supply curve to shift to the left. For example, an increase in the wages of workers in the apple industry causes a decrease in the supply of apples.

STATE OF TECHNOLOGY

Technological progress affects the supply curve by allowing businesses to use more efficient production methods. With increased efficiency, more units can be produced at every price, so supply will increase. Use of a better grain fertilizer, for instance, causes the supply of barley to increase, shifting the supply curve to the right.

CHANGES IN NATURE

Changes in nature–for example, an early frost, record high temperatures, a flood, or an earthquake–can affect the supply of many products, especially agricultural products. A cold, rainy summer in Canada's prairies, for example, will decrease the supply of grains, such as wheat. As a result, the market supply curve for wheat will shift to the left.

THINKING ABOUT ECONOMICS

Is the expanded use of the Internet for business-to-business (B2B) and business-to-consumer (B2C) commerce having an impact on the levels of competition in national markets?

E-commerce is making at least some markets more competitive. For example, in B2C commerce, the supply of computer software, telecommunication services, music, financial services, newspapers, magazines, eBooks, and information databases are being most affected, since consumers are able to buy and directly consume these services in digital form over the Internet. In some parts of the world, cell phones are being increasingly used for this purpose (personal banking in particular). This fast-growing trend, known as m-commerce, first took off in emerging economies in Africa and parts of Asia (where its introduction allowed consumers in these countries to leapfrog

older payment systems) and in Europe. It is now spreading to North America, with new m-payment systems extending the types of phone-based transactions that consumers can complete, including financial services such as buying and selling stocks and bonds, purchasing concert tickets and travel, and downloading paid entertainment content. In B2C markets such as the selling of print books, the Internet is being used to order and purchase products, which are then shipped through traditional delivery methods. The basic result in all these cases is the same: consumers can access businesses globally rather than just locally, thereby increasing competition.

www.mobilecommercedaily.com/

QUESTION   **As e-commerce and m-commerce become more common, what should happen to the large price spreads currently found for many products when bought in a common currency (e.g., the American dollar) in various national markets?**

PRICES OF RELATED PRODUCTS

A product's supply can be influenced by changes in the prices of other products. For example, declines in the price of tobacco have caused some Ontario farmers to switch to ginseng, a medicinal root. As a result, the supply for ginseng has increased, resulting in a shift to the right of the supply curve.

PRODUCER EXPECTATIONS

If producers expect the price of the item they sell to change in the near future, this affects the product's current supply. For example, barley farmers may anticipate barley prices will soon fall. In this case, they provide as much of the product as possible now, raising its current supply. In contrast, an expected rise in the price of beef means beef producers hold back on the amounts they make available to the market, immediately reducing the supply of beef.

Change in Quantity Supplied versus Change in Supply

As in the case of demand, it is important to distinguish between a *change in quantity supplied* and a *change in supply*, both of which are shown in Figure 2.7. An increase or decrease in quantity supplied is the effect of a change in a product's price and is illustrated by a movement along the supply curve. As shown on the graph on the left, a rise in the price of ginseng, which raises the quantity of ginseng produced, is a change in quantity supplied. In contrast, a change in supply is caused by a change in a supply factor, such as a resource price or a

FIGURE 2.7   Change in Quantity Supplied and Change in Supply

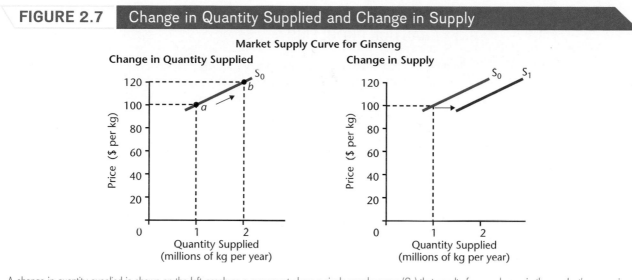

A change in quantity supplied is shown on the left graph as a movement along a single supply curve (S₀) that results from a change in the product's own price. There is a rise in quantity supplied when the price of ginseng rises, causing a movement from point *a* to point *b*. A change in supply is shown on the right graph as a shift in the entire supply curve to the right, from S₀ to S₁. This shift results from a change in a supply factor—for example, a drop in the price of a related product, such as corn.

technological innovation. Because the amount of the product supplied is altered at every possible price for the product, a change in supply shifts the *entire* supply curve. As shown on the graph on the right, a decrease in the price of corn increases the supply of ginseng, causing a shift in the entire supply curve to the right.

BRIEF REVIEW

1. In product markets, supply is the relationship between the various possible prices of a consumer item and the quantities of the item that businesses are willing to put on the market.

2. The law of supply states that there is a direct relationship between the two variables of price and quantity supplied.

3. A change in quantity supplied is caused by a change in price and is shown as a movement along the supply curve.

4. A change in supply is caused by a change in a supply factor and is shown as a shift of the *entire* supply curve. The six supply factors are the number of producers in a market, resource prices, the state of technology, changes in nature, the prices of related products, and producer expectations.

5. Supply shifts to the right with an increase in the number of producers in the market, a decrease in resource prices, technological progress, or an expectation by producers that the price of the product will soon fall. The effects of a change in nature or a change in the price of a related product on supply are determined on a case-by-case basis.

2.2 | PRACTICE PROBLEMS

1. In a certain tomato market, 5 million kg are supplied annually at a price of $1 per kg, 7 million kg at a price of $2, and 9 million kg at a price of $3.
   a. Does this supply curve satisfy the law of supply? Why or why not?
   b. Draw a graph showing this market supply curve S_0. Plot three points to draw this curve.
   c. What will happen to the supply of tomatoes if (i) wages paid to farm workers rise; (ii) there is a drop in the price of corn, which can be cultivated instead of tomatoes; (iii) there is a sudden early autumn frost before the tomatoes are harvested; (iv) a new mechanized tomato-picker is introduced that raises efficiency; (v) producers anticipate that the price of tomatoes will soon fall.
   d. If the quantity supplied of tomatoes doubles at every price, what will be the effect on the market supply curve? Draw this new market supply curve, S_1, on your graph. Plot three points to draw this curve.
2. A drop in the price of corn affects both the market for tomatoes and for corn.
   a. Is the change in the corn market a change in quantity supplied or in supply? Why?
   b. Is the change in the tomato market a change in quantity supplied or in supply? Why?

2.3 | How Competitive Markets Operate

Market Equilibrium

market equilibrium: the stable point at which demand and supply curves intersect

In competitive markets, demand and supply play a key role in coordinating the decisions of consumers and producers. Changes in price drive quantities demanded and supplied to a point of stability, known as **market equilibrium**, where the demand and supply curves intersect. Whenever the market is out of equilibrium—quantity supplied cannot keep up with quantity demanded, for example—the market tries to right itself and achieve equilibrium. To see how equilibrium is reached, consider the example of the strawberry market shown in Figure 2.8.

EFFECTS OF A SURPLUS

At a price of $2.50 per kilogram, the quantities demanded and supplied of strawberries per year are 7 and 11 million kilograms, respectively. The quantity supplied exceeds the quantity demanded, so there are 4 million more kilograms of strawberries for sale than consumers wish to purchase. This excess is called a **surplus**. As a result of this surplus, producers are holding unwanted inventories.

surplus: an excess of quantity supplied over quantity demanded

The pressures produced by a surplus in a competitive market cause the price to fall. As the surplus appears and inventories rise, some producers respond by reducing their prices, and all others soon follow. As the price falls, two adjustments take place. First, consumers buy more at the lower price so that the quantity demanded rises. This increase in quantity demanded is shown as a move down the demand curve in Figure 2.8 (from point *a* to *e*). Second, producers offer less for sale so that the quantity supplied drops. This decrease in quantity supplied is shown as a move down the supply curve in Figure 2.8 (from point *a* to *e*). Both responses reduce the surplus until price comes to rest where quantity supplied matches quantity demanded. Once this happens, the market has reached a stable

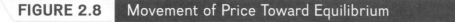

FIGURE 2.8	Movement of Price Toward Equilibrium

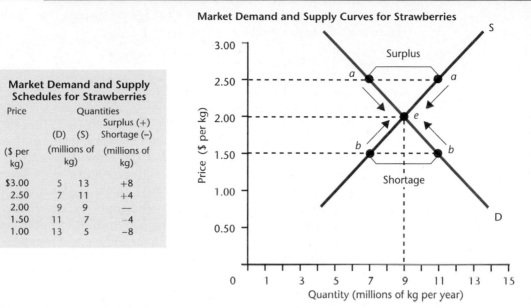

As shown both in the schedule and on the graph, when price (at points *a*) is above its equilibrium level of $2, the quantity of strawberries supplied exceeds the quantity demanded, creating a surplus. This causes price to fall until both quantities demanded and supplied are equal at the equilibrium point (point *e*). If price (at points *b*) is below equilibrium, a shortage results. Price is forced higher until its equilibrium level (point *e*) is again reached.

equilibrium point—at a price of $2 in the case of the strawberry market. At this point, the amount of the product exchanged (9 million kilograms) is simply called "quantity" and can refer to either quantity demanded or quantity supplied.

EFFECTS OF A SHORTAGE

When price is below equilibrium, the quantity of strawberries that consumers wish to purchase exceeds the quantity supplied. This excess of quantity demanded over quantity supplied is called a **shortage**. Because of this shortage, some consumers are unable to purchase strawberries. For example, at a price of $1.50, the quantities demanded and supplied per year in the strawberry market are 11 and 7 million kilograms, respectively, giving a shortage of 4 million kilograms.

shortage: an excess of quantity demanded over quantity supplied

A shortage in a competitive market pushes the price higher. Once it becomes apparent that producers do not have enough to satisfy the prevailing quantity demanded, the demand of consumers who are determined to purchase strawberries causes some producers to raise their prices, and soon all others do the same. Both consumers and producers respond to the price increase. Consumers purchase less, decreasing quantity demanded from point *b* to *e* on the demand curve. At the same time, producers provide more for sale, raising quantity supplied from point *b* to *e* on the supply curve. As a result of these movements up the demand and supply curves in Figure 2.8, the shortage shrinks until the quantities demanded and supplied are again equal at the equilibrium point.

The Role of Price

Notice that if there is either a shortage or a surplus, the price in a competitive market changes until equilibrium is attained. Only at this point is the pressure for further adjustments eliminated. The market then remains at equilibrium until changes in some demand or supply factor cause demand or supply to change. Whenever this happens, the shortage or surplus that results will force the market to a new equilibrium point.

Changes in Demand

Consider the case in which the demand for strawberries increases because of a price increase for a substitute product, such as cherries. As a result, as shown in Figure 2.9, the demand curve shifts to the right, from D_0 to D_1. From an equilibrium price of $2 and a quantity of 9 million kilograms, quantity demanded shifts to 13 million kilograms. Quantity supplied lags behind, at 9 million kilograms, thus creating a shortage of 4 million kilograms per year in the market (13 million versus 9 million). For the market to right itself, price and quantity supplied both push up to a new equilibrium price of $2.50 and quantity of 11 million kilograms. So, with an increase in demand, the equilibrium values of both price and quantity rise. A decrease in demand would have the opposite effect, causing the equilibrium values of both price and quantity to fall.

Changes in Supply

The effects of a change in supply can be outlined in a similar fashion. For example, the supply of strawberries may increase because new producers enter the industry. As a result, as shown in Figure 2.10, the supply curve shifts to the right, from S_0 to S_1. From an equilibrium price of $2 and quantity of 9 million kilograms, quantity supplied becomes 13 million kilograms. Quantity demanded lags behind at 9 million kilograms, thus causing a surplus of 4 million kilograms per year in the market (13 million versus 9 million). For the market to right

FIGURE 2.9   Effects of Changes in Demand on Equilibrium

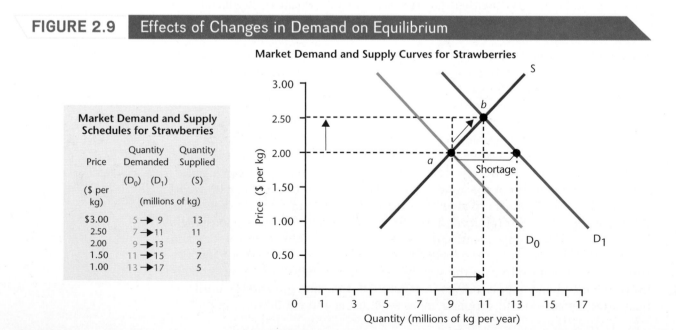

Market Demand and Supply Schedules for Strawberries

Price	Quantity Demanded		Quantity Supplied
	(D_0)	(D_1)	(S)
($ per kg)	(millions of kg)		
$3.00	5 → 9		13
2.50	7 → 11		11
2.00	9 → 13		9
1.50	11 → 15		7
1.00	13 → 17		5

When the demand curve shifts to the right, from D_0 to D_1, there is a shortage of 4 million kg at the original equilibrium price (point *a*). As a result, price rises until a new equilibrium point of demand and supply is reached, at point *b*. Both equilibrium price and equilibrium quantity rise from their original values.

| FIGURE 2.10 | Effects of Changes in Supply on Equilibrium |

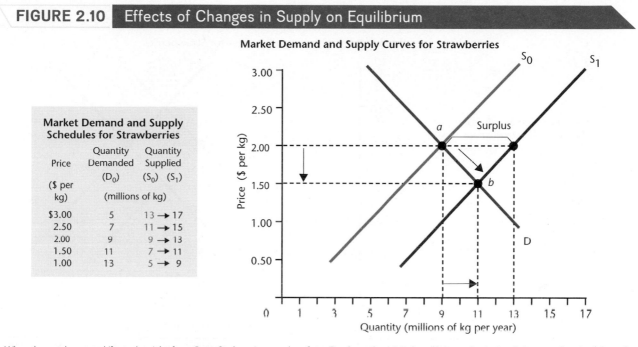

Market Demand and Supply Curves for Strawberries

Market Demand and Supply Schedules for Strawberries

Price ($ per kg)	Quantity Demanded (D_0)	Quantity Supplied (S_0) (S_1)
	(millions of kg)	
$3.00	5	13 → 17
2.50	7	11 → 15
2.00	9	9 → 13
1.50	11	7 → 11
1.00	13	5 → 9

When the supply curve shifts to the right, from S_0 to S_1, there is a surplus of 4 million kg at the original equilibrium price (point a). As a result, price falls until a new equilibrium point of demand and supply is reached at point b. In this case, the equilibrium values for price and quantity move in opposite directions, with price falling and quantity rising.

itself, price is driven down until it reaches a new equilibrium value of $1.50, and quantity demanded is driven up to a new equilibrium value of 11 million kilograms. So, with an increase in supply, the equilibrium values of price and quantity move in opposite directions, with price falling and quantity rising. A decrease in supply would have the opposite effects: price would rise and quantity would fall to reach a new equilibrium point.

Changes in Both Demand and Supply

When both demand and supply shift simultaneously, a range of possibilities can occur. When both demand and supply move in a given direction, so too does equilibrium quantity, but the direction and extent of the change in equilibrium price depend on how large the shift in the demand curve is in relation to the shift in the supply curve. For example, Figure 2.11 shows the case where both demand and supply in the strawberry market increase–demand shifting to the right from D_0 to D_1 and the supply curve shifting right from S_0 to S_1. From the initial equilibrium price and quantity of $2 and 9 million kilograms at point a, the market moves without any intermediate surplus or shortage to point b. Quantity is pushed upward by the movement in both demand and supply, to a new equilibrium value of 13 million kilograms. But in this case, the shifts in demand and supply curves counteract each other's influence on price, so that equilibrium price stays the same at $2. If the demand curve had shifted by less than the supply curve–to anywhere between D_0 to D_1–then equilibrium price would have fallen instead. Alternatively, if the demand curve shifted more than supply, to anywhere to the right of D_1–then equilibrium price would have risen.

| FIGURE 2.11 | Effects of Increases in Demand and Supply on Equilibrium |

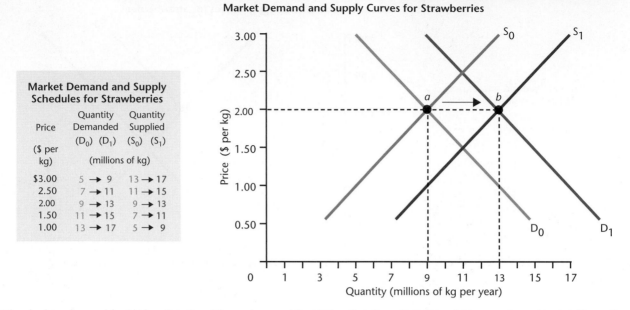

Market Demand and Supply Curves for Strawberries

Market Demand and Supply Schedules for Strawberries

Price	Quantity Demanded		Quantity Supplied	
	(D_0)	(D_1)	(S_0)	(S_1)
($ per kg)	(millions of kg)			
$3.00	5 → 9		13 → 17	
2.50	7 → 11		11 → 15	
2.00	9 → 13		9 → 13	
1.50	11 → 15		7 → 11	
1.00	13 → 17		5 → 9	

When the demand curve shifts right from D_0 to D_1 and the supply curve shifts right from S_0 to S_1, equilibrium immediately moves from point *a* to *b*. The equilibrium value for quantity necessarily increases, but given the identical counteracting shifts in the demand and supply curves, equilibrium price stays constant. On the other hand, if the shift in the demand curve (to anywhere between D_0 and D_1) is less than the shift in supply, then equilibrium price falls. Alternatively, if the demand curve shifts more than supply (to anywhere to the right of D_1), then equilibrium price rises.

THINKING ABOUT ECONOMICS

Does a change in demand affect quantity supplied, or does a change in supply affect quantity demanded?

Both situations apply. A shift in the demand curve has an impact on quantity supplied. Notice in Figure 2.9, for example, that an increase in demand causes movement to the right along the supply curve, meaning that quantity supplied rises as well. Thus, a change in demand pushes quantity supplied in the same direction. With an increase in supply, as depicted in Figure 2.10, there is a movement to the right along the demand curve, which causes an increase in quantity demanded. A change in supply, therefore, drives quantity demanded in the same direction.

QUESTION   **How does a decrease in supply affect quantity demanded?**

Demand and supply can also move in opposite directions. Then the change in equilibrium price becomes definite, while the direction and extent of the change in equilibrium quantity depend on how large the shifts in demand and supply are in relation to one another. Figure 2.12 depicts the case where demand increases and supply decreases. When the demand curve shifts right from D_0 to D_1 and the supply curve shifts left from S_0 to S_1, equilibrium immediately moves from point *a* to *b*. The equilibrium value for price necessarily increases, but identical counteracting shifts in the demand and supply curves mean that

FIGURE 2.12   Effects of Demand Increase and Supply Decrease on Equilibrium

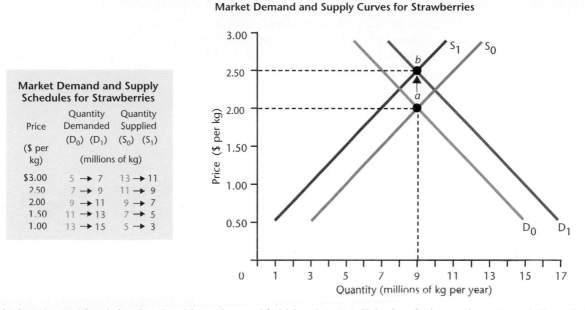

Market Demand and Supply Curves for Strawberries

Market Demand and Supply Schedules for Strawberries

Price ($ per kg)	Quantity Demanded (D_0) (D_1)		Quantity Supplied (S_0) (S_1)	
	(millions of kg)			
$3.00	5 → 7		13 → 11	
2.50	7 → 9		11 → 9	
2.00	9 → 11		9 → 7	
1.50	11 → 13		7 → 5	
1.00	13 → 15		5 → 3	

When the demand curve shifts right from D_0 to D_1, and the supply curve shifts left from S_0 to S_1, equilibrium immediately moves from point *a* to *b*. The equilibrium value for price necessarily increases, but identical counteracting shifts in the demand and supply curves mean that equilibrium quantity stays constant. In contrast, if the shift in the demand curve (to anywhere between D_0 and D_1) is less than the shift in supply, then equilibrium quantity falls. Alternatively, when the demand curve shifts more than supply (to anywhere to the right of D_1), then equilibrium quantity rises.

equilibrium quantity stays constant. In contrast, if the shift in the demand curve (to anywhere between D_0 and D_1) is less than the shift in supply, then equilibrium quantity falls. Alternatively, when the demand curve shifts more than supply (to anywhere to the right of D_1), then equilibrium quantity rises

BRIEF REVIEW

1. In a competitive market, the appearance of either surpluses or shortages forces price and quantity toward the intersection of the demand and supply curves. This point represents market equilibrium.

2. An increase in demand—with the demand curve shifting to the right—causes the equilibrium values for both price and quantity to rise. A decrease in demand—with the demand curve shifting to the left—causes the equilibrium values for both price and quantity to fall.

3. An increase in supply—with the supply curve shifting to the right—causes the equilibrium price to decrease and the equilibrium quantity to increase. A decrease in supply—with the supply curve shifting to the left—causes the equilibrium price to increase and the equilibrium quantity to decrease.

4. Changes in both demand and supply affect both equilibrium price and equilibrium quantity. Increases in both demand and supply cause equilibrium quantity to rise, with the change in equilibrium price dependent on the relative sizes of the two shifts. An increase in demand and a decrease in supply, on the other hand, cause a rise in equilibrium price, with the change in equilibrium quantity dependent on the two shifts' relative sizes.

2.3 | PRACTICE PROBLEMS

1. In a particular competitive market, initial equilibrium occurs at a price of $3 and a quantity of 4 million units. Then a shift in supply causes equilibrium price to rise.
   a. Which way has supply shifted?
   b. Has equilibrium quantity undergone an increase or decrease?
   c. Immediately after the change in supply, is it a temporary shortage or surplus in the market that pushes price to its new equilibrium value?

2. In the same competitive market as in question 1, initial equilibrium occurs at a price of $3 and a quantity of 4 million units. Now a shift in demand causes equilibrium price to rise.
   a. Which way has demand shifted?
   b. Has equilibrium quantity undergone an increase or decrease?
   c. Will the changes in equilibrium price and quantity be driven by a temporary shortage or temporary surplus in the market?

LAST WORD

In this chapter, we examined how the forces of demand and supply can influence competitive markets and how these markets find equilibrium through the interplay of buyers and sellers. But our examination of demand and supply is far from over. In the next chapter, we will use what we have learned so far to examine how it is possible to quantify responses of both buyers and sellers to changes in price. Then, repeatedly throughout the rest of the book, demand and supply will reappear, making it clear that they are two of the most basic tools of economic thinking.

PROBLEMS

1. Kate buys three chocolate bars per week at a price of $1.25, five at a price of $1, and seven at a price of 75 cents. Her friend Carlo buys five chocolate bars at a price of $1.25, eight at a price of $1, and 11 at a price of 75 cents.
   a. If these two friends are the only consumers in the market for chocolate bars, what are three points on the market demand curve?
   b. Does this market demand curve satisfy the law of demand? Why or why not?
   c. Draw a graph showing Kate's and Carlo's demand curves D_K and D_C and market demand curve D_{mo}. Plot three points for each of the three curves.
   d. If Kate and Carlo both double their purchases of chocolate bars per week at every price, what will be the effect on the market demand curve you drew in part c? How would you describe this change? Draw this new demand curve D_{m1} on your graph. Plot three points on this curve.

2. In a certain apple market, 70 000 kilograms are offered for sale each week at a price per kilogram of $2, 150 000 at $3, and 230 000 at $4.
   a. Is the law of supply satisfied as the price of apples rises? Why or why not?
   b. Outline what happens if the amount of apples offered for sale each week increases by 50 000 kilograms at each possible price.

c. What are three points on the new market supply curve after the increase in the amount of apples offered for sale?

d. Draw a graph showing the market supply curves S_o and S_1. Plot three points to draw each curve.

3. For each market whose product is highlighted in italics, identify whether demand or supply is increasing or decreasing. In each case, identify the demand or supply factor causing the change. In which direction does the demand or supply curve shift?

a. Medical researchers discover that consumption of *blueberries* reduces the risk of cancer.

b. New automated equipment is introduced in the production of *tea*.

c. A significant rise in the price of game consoles affects the market for *computer games*.

d. Higher prices for grazing land have an impact on the production of *wool*.

4. For each market whose product is highlighted in italics, identify whether each of the following trends represents an increase or decrease in demand or an increase or decrease in quantity demanded. How would you describe each change in graphical terms?

a. The drop in the monthly subscription rate changes the number of subscribers to a *cable TV* provider.

b. The quantity of *canned milk* purchased adjusts due to a decrease in consumer incomes.

c. The price of a particular brand of *perfume* rises, leading to a change in sales.

d. A rise in the popularity of free online games changes how many *computer games* consumers choose to purchase.

5. For each market whose product is highlighted in italics, identify whether each of the following trends represents an increase or decrease in supply or an increase or decrease in quantity supplied. How would you describe this change in graphical terms?

a. The price of *tomatoes* increases, leading to change in how many are offered for sale.

b. An oil spill on the Pacific coast has an impact on the stock of *salmon*.

c. There is a decrease in the price of *cranberries*, affecting how many farmers supply.

d. More sophisticated boring equipment causes a change in the production of *iron*.

6. a. Fill in the appropriate numerical values in the table below for the surplus or shortage of baseball caps in the fourth column and the effect on price in the fifth column.

Market Demand and Supply Schedules for Baseball Caps

Price ($ per cap)	Quantity Demanded (caps per week)	Quantity Supplied (caps per week)	Surplus (+) or Shortage (−)	Effect on Price (up or down)
$25.00	8 000	14 000	___	___
20.00	9 000	12 000	___	___
15.00	10 000	10 000	___	___
10.00	11 000	8 000	___	___
5.00	12 000	6 000	___	___

b. Draw a graph showing the demand and supply curves D_o and S. Plot only the endpoints of the two curves for a total of four points.

c. Identify the equilibrium quantity and price. Why could no other price represent the equilibrium value?

d. Suppose the demand schedule in this market changes so that 11 000 caps are demanded at a price of $25, 12 000 are demanded at $20, 13 000 at $15, 14 000 at $10, and 15 000 at $5. Is this an increase or decrease in demand? How would this change be shown on a graph?

e. Create a new table like the one in part a to show the demand and supply schedules in this market after the change in demand and draw the new demand curve D_1 in your graph. Plot only the endpoints of the new curve. Identify the new equilibrium price.

7. The table below provides information on the market demand and supply for inline skates.

Market Demand and Supply Schedules for Inline Skates

Price ($ per pair)	Quantity Demanded (thousands of pairs per week)			Quantity Supplied (thousands of pairs per week)		
	D_0		D_1	S_0		S_1
$200	40	→	20	80	→	60
175	50	→	30	70	→	50
150	60	→	40	60	→	40
125	70	→	50	50	→	30
100	80	→	60	40	→	20

a. Draw a graph showing the demand and supply curves D_0, D_1, S_0, and S_1. Plot only the endpoints of each curve for a total of eight points.

b. If the initial demand and supply curves are D_0 and S_0, what are the initial equilibrium price and quantity?

c. Because of heightened concerns over injuries, the demand for inline skates changes from D_0 to D_1. What are the new equilibrium price and quantity associated with D_1 and S_0? How do these equilibrium values compare with those in part b?

d. Now, due to a rise in wages, the supply of inline skates changes from S_0 to S_1 while demand stays at D_1. What are the new equilibrium price and quantity associated with D_1 and S_1? How do these equilibrium values compare with those found in part c?

8. How will the following events affect equilibrium price and quantity for the product highlighted in italics? In each case, identify how the supply or demand curve shifts.

a. A drop in consumer incomes influences the demand for *dry cleaning*.

b. Declining numbers of law school graduates affect the supply of *legal services*.

c. Consumer expectations that the price of turkeys will soon rise affect the current demand for *turkeys*.

d. A cost-saving technological innovation influences the supply of *rice*.

9. How will the following sets of events affect equilibrium price and quantity for the product highlighted in italics? In each case, identify how both the demand and supply curves shift.

a. Consumer income falls at the same time as the price of combine harvesters drops, affecting the demand and supply of *wheat*.

b. There is a particularly severe flu season at the same time as the price of the ingredients of a *herbal flu remedy* rise, affecting the demand and supply of this product.

c. Consumer preferences for spicy food increase at the same time as the wages paid to farmworkers drop, affecting the demand and supply of *jalapeno peppers*.

d. There is a widespread consumer expectation that the price of *tuna* will rise at the same time as the number of tuna fishers drops.

10. (Policy Discussion Question)

In an attempt to curb the use of illegal drugs, such as marijuana or cocaine, or the use of harmful legal substances, such as tobacco, governments can use two basic options: decrease demand through public education or decrease supply through legal restrictions or taxes.

a. Using two graphs, explain how each type of policy reduces quantity in affected markets. What is the result on the price as seen by consumers for each type of policy?

b. Which of these two types of policies is likely to have more long-term success? Why?

For more information on the resources available from McGraw-Hill Ryerson, go to **www.mcgrawhill.ca/he/solutions**.

SPOILT FOR CHOICE

William Stanley Jevons and Utility Maximization

WILLIAM STANLEY JEVONS

© Stock Montage

JEVONS AND HIS INFLUENCE

Demand can be related to human psychology, if you think of people making purchases to maximize their utility on the basis of their limited budgets. Remember that utility is the satisfaction each individual gains from consuming a variety of goods and services. William Stanley Jevons (1835-1882), a nineteenth century English economist, is best known for applying the concept of utility to economics and developing a model of consumption. Jevons found his life turned upside down when, in his teens, his rich family went bankrupt. He was forced to break off his studies to find a job. After working for five years in Australia–during which time Jevons taught himself economics–he had earned enough to return to England and complete his formal education. He went on to become a university professor who established his reputation primarily through his writings.

THE LAW OF DIMINISHING MARGINAL UTILITY

Jevons based his model of consumption on the utilitarian views of the British philosophers Jeremy Bentham and James Mill. These philosophers assumed that utility can be measured in units, which they called "utils." According to Jevons, a consumer's total utility–or overall satisfaction gained from consuming a particular product–depends on the number of units he or she purchases. Consider the example of a student drinking cups of cappuccino at a sidewalk café on a summer afternoon. As shown in Figure A, the student's total utility increases with every additional cup he drinks, but each new cup gives him less extra pleasure than the one before. This is illustrated on the top graph by the increases in total utility between *ab* and *bc*, and then *cd* and *de*: the shaded areas get steadily smaller. These shrinking areas are highlighted on the marginal utility graph. For each extra cup he drinks, the student's marginal–or extra–satisfaction is less.

The fall in marginal utility at higher consumption levels led Jevons to state what has become a general rule in economics. The *law of diminishing marginal utility* states that as a consumer purchases more units of a particular product in a given time period, that consumer's extra satisfaction from each additional unit falls. According to Jevons, common sense suggests that this law applies to the consumption of virtually all products. Other economists developed their own versions of the law of diminishing marginal utility, but Jevons' version has remained the most influential.

CHOOSING ONE PRODUCT OVER ANOTHER

One of the most important uses of the law of diminishing marginal utility is in helping to understand how much consumers choose to spend on various products. Consider again the student visiting a sidewalk café one afternoon. He arrives with $4 in his pocket and plans to spend it all on $1 cappuccinos and $2 Danish pastries. To get the most out of his $4, the student should use it in a way that gives him the greatest added satisfaction from each new dollar. In other words, he should make each purchase on the basis of which item gives him the highest marginal utility per dollar. These figures can be found by dividing the student's marginal utilities for cappuccinos and pastries by their prices.

FIGURE A   Total and Marginal Utility

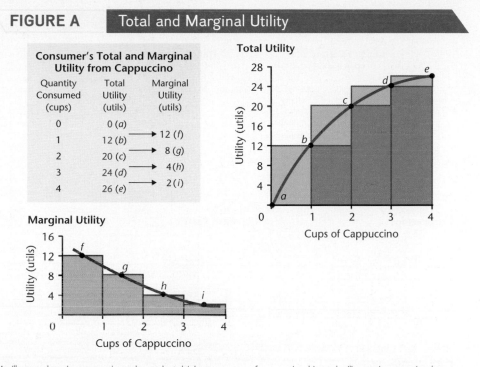

Consumer's Total and Marginal Utility from Cappuccino

Quantity Consumed (cups)	Total Utility (utils)	Marginal Utility (utils)
0	0 (a)	
1	12 (b)	12 (f)
2	20 (c)	8 (g)
3	24 (d)	4 (h)
4	26 (e)	2 (i)

As illustrated on the top graph, as the student drinks more cups of cappuccino, his total utility continues to rise, but at a decreasing rate. Each new cup provides less added satisfaction than the one before. The bottom graph also illustrates that each additional cup provides less marginal utility.

When making his first purchase, the student can choose either 12 utils in extra satisfaction from a cappuccino or 16 utils from a pastry, as shown in columns 2 and 5 of the schedule in Figure B. His marginal utilities per dollar are shown in columns 3 and 6, and on the graphs. Because the 12 utils (= 12 ÷ $1) per dollar spent on cappuccinos exceeds the 8 utils (= 16 ÷ $2) per dollar spent on pastries, the student buys a cappuccino. For his second purchase, the student compares the 8 utils (= 8 ÷ $1) per dollar he could spend on the second cappuccino with the 8 utils per dollar he could spend on his first pastry. Since these marginal utilities per dollar are equal, he buys both items, exhausting his $4.

THE UTILITY-MAXIMIZING RULE

According to the utility-maximizing rule, the student keeps buying both products until the marginal utility per dollar from both cappuccinos and pastries is the same ($MU_1 \div P_1 = MU_2 \div P_2$). This economic law, which Jevons developed, applies no matter how many items are being bought. By following the rule, consumers maximize their overall satisfaction, or total utility, from a whole range of products.

RELEVANCE FOR TODAY

Jevons' model rests on the assumption that utility is measurable in set units. While his critics suggested that this assumption is unrealistic, others argued that

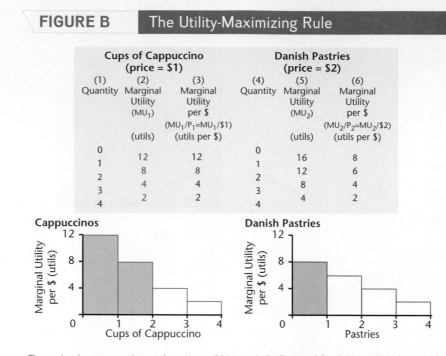

FIGURE B — The Utility-Maximizing Rule

The student buys cappuccinos and pastries until his marginal utility per dollar (MU ÷ P) is the same for both items. Given his $4 budget, he buys two cappuccinos and one pastry (the highlighted figures in the table and shaded bars on the two graphs). With these purchases, the student's marginal utility per dollar for each product equals 8 utils. The utility-maximizing rule ($MU_1 \div P_1 = MU_2 \div P_2$) is therefore satisfied.

it is a legitimate way to simplify reality. By assuming that utility could be measured, Jevons made a verifiable conclusion concerning the relationship between two observable variables–the quantity of a product that individuals wish to consume and the price they pay–and the result is unaffected by how this satisfaction is measured. More recently, economists have adapted utility theory without needing to assume measurable units of satisfaction. As long as consumers can say they prefer one set of products to another (without having to state exactly how much more they prefer it), conclusions like those drawn from the law of diminishing marginal utility and the utility-maximizing rule can still be reached.

1.   **a.** Complete the table below, showing the utility Consumer X gains from products A and B.

Consumer X's Utility Maximization Table

Consumption of A (price = $2)				Consumption of B (price = $4)			
Units of A	Total Utility (utils)	Marginal Utility (utils)	Marginal Utility per $ (utils per $)	Units of B	Total Utility (utils)	Marginal Utility (utils)	Marginal Utility per $ (utils per $)
0	0	—	—	0	0	—	—
1	22	—	—	1	20	—	—
2	40	—	—	2	36	—	—
3	54	—	—	3	48	—	—
4	64	—	—	4	56	—	—
5	70	—	—	5	60	—	—

b. Using the utility-maximizing rule, find the combination of A and B that maximizes Consumer X's utility if her total expenditure on these two products is $22.

c. If Consumer X's total expenditure on products A and B falls to $12 while the prices of A and B remain unchanged, what is her new utility-maximizing combination of A and B?

2. As a guest at a party, you perceive the price of root beer provided by your host as being very close to zero. How will your consumption of root beer at the party differ from consumption of your own root beer at home? Use the utility-maximizing rule and the law of diminishing utility to explain your answer.

CHAPTER 3

Elasticity

Usually, when we wish to acquire goods and services—a new digital music player, a pair of shoes in the right size and style, a last-minute holiday package to a Caribbean island—we can buy them quickly and conveniently. In this chapter, we will analyze in more detail the ways in which markets accomplish this task. In particular, we will look at the concept of elasticity and how this crucial concept helps us measure in quantitative terms the impact of the interplay of demand and supply in competitive markets.

> There is no resting place for an enterprise in a competitive economy.
>
> -ALFRED P. SLOAN, AMERICAN BUSINESSMAN

LEARNING OBJECTIVES   After reading this chapter, you will be able to:

LO 1

Describe price elasticity of demand, its relation to other demand elasticities, and its impact on sellers' revenues

LO 2

Define price elasticity of supply and identify the links between production periods and supply

3.1 | Price Elasticity of Demand

How can we refine our analysis of the role of demand and its impact in particular markets? One of the most important ways is by studying the numerical relationship between changes in price and quantity demanded. For example, from Chapter 2 we know that if the price of a computer game falls, then the number of games purchased rises. But by how much? If price is reduced by half, will quantity demanded double or triple, or will it rise by a smaller proportion, such as 10 percent or 20 percent? To answer these questions, we need to understand the **price elasticity of demand** (also called demand elasticity). Price elasticity of demand is the extent to which consumers, and the quantity they demand, respond to a change in price.

LO1

price elasticity of demand: the responsiveness of a product's quantity demanded to a change in its price

Elastic and Inelastic Demand

Consumers can be very responsive or very unresponsive to price changes. Consider Figure 3.1, which shows the demand curves for a sidewalk vendor selling ice-cream cones in two seasons. During the winter, the vendor raises her price from $2 to $2.40, which is an increase of 20 percent [= (($2.40 − $2.00)/$2.00) × 100%]. The result is that monthly quantity demanded drops from 1000 to 500 cones, which is a decrease of 50 percent [= ((500 − 1000)/1000) × 100%]. If a given percentage change in price causes a *larger* percentage change in a product's quantity demanded, the product has **elastic demand**. Thus, the vendor faces elastic demand in the winter, as shown on the graph on the left. In the summer, greater demand for ice-cream cones pushes demand to the right. In addition, when the vendor increases her price in the summer by 20 percent, from $2 to $2.40, monthly quantity demanded only decreases from 2000 to 1800 cones, or by 10 percent. If a given percentage change in price causes a *smaller* percentage change in quantity demanded, the product has **inelastic demand**. The graph on the right shows an inelastic demand for ice-cream cones.

elastic demand: demand for which a percentage change in a product's price causes a larger percentage change in quantity demanded

inelastic demand: demand for which a percentage change in a product's price causes a smaller percentage change in quantity demanded

FIGURE 3.1   Elastic and Inelastic Demand Curves

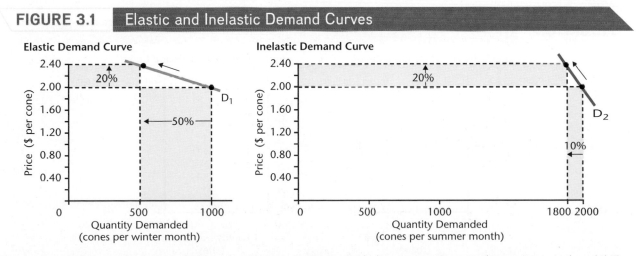

For the elastic demand curve (D₁) shown on the left graph, a 20 percent increase in price leads to a greater 50 percent decrease in quantity demanded. The graph on the right shows an inelastic demand curve (D₂). The same 20 percent increase in price now leads to a smaller 10 percent decrease in quantity demanded.

Perfectly Elastic and Perfectly Inelastic Demand

perfectly elastic demand: demand for which a product's price remains constant regardless of quantity demanded

There are two extreme cases of demand elasticity. When a product has **perfectly elastic demand**, its price remains constant whatever quantities are demanded. Because price never varies, the demand curve is horizontal, as shown in Figure 3.2, on the left. Consider the example of an individual producer, a soybean farmer, who is a *price-taker*. **This means that the farmer has no influence over the market price of soybeans, since the farmer's operations are too insignificant to affect the market.** This farmer would face demand as illustrated by the demand curve D_3. Because the same price of $100 per tonne of soybeans applies at all possible amounts demanded, the farmer faces a perfectly elastic demand curve. In contrast, when a product has **perfectly inelastic demand**, its quantity demanded is completely unaffected by price. This situation creates a vertical demand curve, as shown in Figure 3.2, on the right. An example is the demand for insulin: since this product is essential to people who have diabetes, they are willing to pay any price for a certain quantity of insulin. This means that the market demand curve for insulin (D_4) is vertical at a given quantity demanded, such as 1000 litres.

perfectly inelastic demand: demand for which a product's quantity demanded remains constant regardless of price

Price Elasticity of Demand and Total Revenue

total revenue: the total income earned from a product, calculated by multiplying the product's price by its quantity demanded

Demand elasticity plays a role in determining what effect a price change has on **total revenue** (TR). Total revenue is defined, either for an individual business or for all businesses producing the same product, as the price of a product multiplied by its quantity demanded:

$$TR = P \times Q_d$$

For example, if the price of a certain product is $4 and 1000 units are purchased, then the total revenue generated is $4000 (= $4 × 1000).

Consider how a rise in a product's price affects the total revenue of businesses selling the product. The higher price, by itself, increases the revenue pocketed by the sellers, but the accompanying decrease in quantity demanded

---

FIGURE 3.2   Perfectly Elastic and Perfectly Inelastic Demand

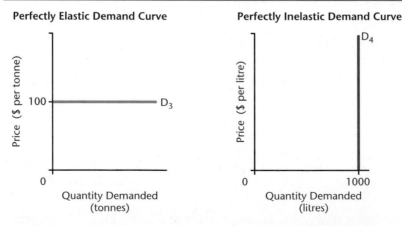

A single soybean farmer might face a perfectly elastic demand curve, as shown on the left graph, with a constant price. In contrast, a producer of insulin might face a vertical or perfectly inelastic demand curve, as shown on the right graph, with the quantity demanded constant.

has the opposite effect. The price elasticity of demand determines which of these two effects–the increase in price or the decrease in quantity demanded–has the greater influence on the sellers' total revenue.

ELASTIC DEMAND

If demand for a product is elastic, price changes cause large variations in quantity demanded. Since a price increase of a certain percentage causes an even bigger percentage decrease in quantity demanded, the sellers' total revenue is reduced. Likewise, a price decrease of a certain percentage causes an even bigger percentage increase in quantity demanded, thus raising total revenue for the sellers. So, when demand is elastic, total revenue and price have an inverse relationship total revenue changes in the opposite direction to the change in price.

Consider an example. A hotdog street vendor faces an elastic demand for hotdogs, as shown in Figure 3.3. At a price of $5 per hotdog, the vendor sells 500 hotdogs each day. The vendor's total revenue at this point on the demand curve is $2500 (= $5 × 500 hotdogs). This total revenue is represented by the

FIGURE 3.3   Revenue Changes with Elastic Demand

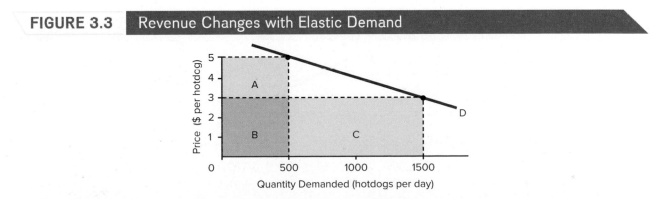

With elastic demand, a 40 percent decrease in the hotdog price from $5 to $3 causes a larger 200 percent increase in daily sales. Total revenue for the business increases from the area AB to the area BC. Thus, the changes in price and total revenue are in opposite directions. (Note that area C is greater than area A.)

area of the shaded rectangle AB. At a price of $3 per hotdog, the vendor sells 1500 hotdogs each day, pushing up total revenue to $4500 (= $3 × 1500 hotdogs), which is represented by the shaded area BC. Therefore, a decrease in price raises the vendor's total revenue because the effect of the price decrease is outweighed by the effect of the increased quantity demanded.

INELASTIC DEMAND

When the demand for a product is inelastic, changes in price have less effect on quantity demanded. Since an increase in price leads to a smaller percentage decrease in quantity demanded, the sellers' total revenue increases. Similarly, a decrease in price causes a smaller percentage increase in quantity demanded, thus causing total revenue to fall. Therefore, when demand is inelastic, price and total revenue have a direct relationship–total revenue shifts in the same direction as the change in price. Take, for example, a ride at an amusement park that has inelastic demand, as shown in Figure 3.4. With a price of $2, there are 10 000 riders a day. Total revenue for the ride's operator, therefore, is $20 000, as shown by the shaded area FG. If the price increases to $3, there are 8000 riders a day and a total revenue of $24 000, as shown by the shaded area EF. Therefore, an increase in price adds to the total revenue because the price increase more than compensates for the reduced quantity demanded.

UNIT-ELASTIC DEMAND

unit-elastic demand: demand for which a percentage change in price causes an equal change in quantity demanded

In the case of **unit-elastic demand**, a percentage change in price causes an equal percentage change in quantity demanded. Thus, when demand is unit-elastic, a price change leaves total revenue unchanged. This is because the revenue gain caused by a price increase is precisely offset by the lost revenue due to the decrease in quantity demanded. Figure 3.5 summarizes the effect of a price change on total revenue in this case, along with all other possible cases.

Factors That Affect Price Elasticity of Demand

Four factors affect a product's price elasticity of demand: the portion of consumer incomes devoted to buying the product, consumer access to substitutes, whether the product is a necessity or a luxury, and the time consumers have to adjust to price changes.

FIGURE 3.4   Revenue Changes with Inelastic Demand

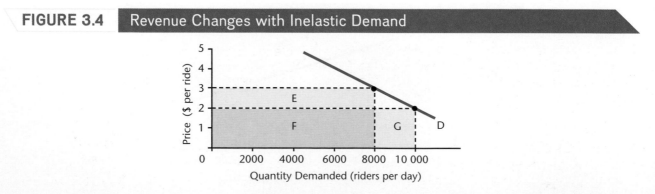

Because demand is inelastic, a 50 percent rise in the price of the ride causes a smaller 20 percent drop in daily ridership. As a result, total revenue for the ride's operator grows from area FG to area EF. The changes in price and total revenue are, therefore, in the same direction. (Note that area E is greater than area G.)

FIGURE 3.5	Price Elasticity of Demand and Changes in Total Revenue

	Price Change	**Change in Total Revenue**
Elastic Demand	up	down
	down	up
Inelastic Demand	up	up
	down	down
Unit-Elastic Demand	up	unchanged
	down	unchanged

PORTION OF CONSUMER INCOMES

If the price of a product represents a hefty portion of consumer incomes, consumers will be more responsive to price changes. For consumers who are deciding whether or not to buy a flat-screen TV, for example, a price change can often determine whether or not they make the purchase. If prices of flat-screen TVs are cut in half, quantity demanded will rise by a considerably higher percentage—an important reason why flat-screen TVs are such a popular Boxing Day sale item. In contrast, consumers who are deciding how much sugar to buy pay little attention to price; a 50 percent drop in the price will cause a much smaller percentage increase in the amount of sugar purchased. The demand for big purchases, therefore, tends to be more elastic than the demand for smaller purchases.

ACCESS TO SUBSTITUTES

If there are many close substitutes for a product, consumers will be more responsive to changes in the product's price because they have more options and can easily change their buying patterns. The demand for a particular brand of low top athletic shoes, for example, will be more elastic than the demand for athletic shoes in general. If only one brand becomes more expensive, its quantity demanded will plummet as consumers substitute cheaper brands. A rise in the price of all athletic shoes, however, will not radically affect quantities purchased. As this example illustrates, the more narrowly a product is defined, the more elastic its demand will be.

NECESSITIES VERSUS LUXURIES

Recall that necessities are essential items—such as bread and milk—that satisfy basic wants. Consumers tend to buy similar amounts of necessities, regardless of their price; thus, necessities tend to have inelastic demand. In contrast, such products as tourist travel, expensive sports cars, and yachts are luxuries that buyers can easily live without. Because these items are expendable, their demand is more likely to be elastic.

TIME

Demand tends to become elastic over time. In the short run, consumers tend not to be strongly responsive to price. For example, immediately after a price increase, consumers of nachos will not modify their buying habits significantly, and users of furnace oil will continue to purchase furnace oil, regardless of price. Over time, however, consumers change their habits and needs: nacho-eaters reduce their consumption, and homeowners change their furnaces to use less fuel.

Calculating Price Elasticity of Demand

It is possible to quantify elasticity–that is, give it a numerical value. The larger this numerical value (e_d), the greater the price sensitivity–or price elasticity–of the product's demand. If e_d is greater than 1, then quantity demanded is sensitive to price changes, and demand is elastic. If e_d is less than 1, the quantity demanded is comparatively unresponsive to price changes, and demand is inelastic. If e_d is 1, then the product is unit-elastic.

Recall the case of the hotdog vendor (Figure 3.3), who sells 500 hotdogs a day at a price of $5 each and 1500 hotdogs when the price drops to $3. The vendor can use the following formula to calculate the price elasticity of demand. In the formula, Q_d stands for quantity demanded, and Δ stands for change. (The symbol Δ is the Greek capital letter "delta," which signifies a change in some variable.)

$$e_d = \frac{\Delta Q_d \div \text{average } Q_d}{\Delta \text{ price} \div \text{average price}}$$

$$= \frac{(1500 - 500) \div [(1500 + 500) \div 2]}{(\$3 - \$5) \div [(\$3 + \$5) \div 2]}$$

$$= \frac{1000 \div 1000}{-\$2 \div \$4}$$

$$= \frac{1}{\dfrac{-1}{2}}$$

$$= (-)2$$

Recall that we identified whether demand curves were elastic or inelastic by comparing percentage changes in quantity demanded and price. To calculate these percentage changes, we divided the absolute changes in both quantity demanded and in price by their respective initial values. While this is the simplest procedure, it is not sufficiently exact when calculating numerical values for elasticity. Instead of using the initial values for quantity demanded and price, we incorporate the average values of these two variables in our formula. Over a given range of a demand curve, these average values are the same no matter whether we are moving up or down the demand curve. This useful property does not apply to the initial values of either quantity demanded or price, which are different depending on where we start on the demand curve.

So, in the numerator and denominator of this formula, the changes in quantity demanded and price, respectively, are divided by each variable's average value. The average quantity demanded is the value at the midpoint between the old and new quantities demanded, and is found by adding together the new and old quantities demanded and then dividing by 2. The same method is used to derive the average price, which is the value at the midpoint between the old and new prices, and is the sum of the new and the old prices divided by 2. Therefore, in the example of the hotdog vendor, e_d is 2, which means that a certain percentage change in price (calculated using average price) causes twice that percentage change in quantity demanded (calculated using average quantity demanded). Note that the answer is a pure number with no units attached. Also, it always has a negative sign, because its formula's numerator and denominator necessarily have different signs. Because it is customary to define the numerical value of the price elasticity of demand in terms of the number's absolute value, this negative sign is usually cancelled out of the final answer; the negative sign is ignored, so the number is always considered to be positive.

Elasticity and Linear Demand Curves

It is possible to calculate the price elasticity for various ranges along a linear demand curve. A linear demand curve's slope is constant, given the definition of slope as the change in price over change in quantity demanded–the "rise" over the "run." We can see this in Figure 3.6, which shows a hypothetical market demand curve for sports drinks. Anywhere along this curve, quantity demanded rises by 1 million drinks for each $1 drop in price, giving a slope of –1 millionth. But the curve's elasticity coefficient, which is the ratio of the relative changes in quantity demanded and price, varies as we move along the curve. Between prices $5 and $4, the coefficient has a value of (–)9. Then, for each new lower pair of prices, the coefficient drops–to 2.33 (between $4 and $3), 1 (between $3 and $2), 0.43 (between $2 and $1), and finally 0.11 (between $1 and $0).

The reason for the varying values of price elasticity is that at high prices (such as $5 and $4), the $1 price change is made smaller when dividing by average price ($4.50). At the same time, the change in quantity demanded (1 million drinks) is made larger when compared with average quantity demanded (500 000). The result is an elasticity coefficient greater than 1, with the curve being elastic in its upper range. But further down the demand curve, the relationship between price and quantity is reversed. At low values of price (such as $1 and $0), the same $1 price change is made larger when compared with average price ($0.50), while the high values for quantity demanded (4 million and 5 million drinks) mean the change in quantity demanded of 1 million drinks is made smaller relative to the average quantity (4.5 million drinks). The elasticity coefficient is, therefore, less than 1, and the curve is

---

FIGURE 3.6   Elasticity and a Linear Demand Curve

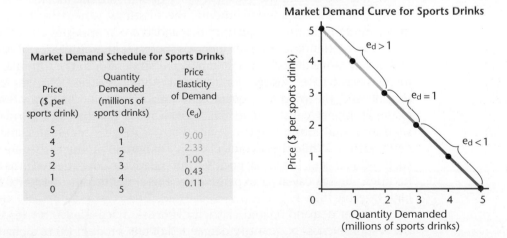

Market Demand Schedule for Sports Drinks

Price ($ per sports drink)	Quantity Demanded (millions of sports drinks)	Price Elasticity of Demand (e_d)
5	0	
4	1	9.00
3	2	2.33
2	3	1.00
1	4	0.43
0	5	0.11

Market Demand Curve for Sports Drinks

The slope of this linear demand curve is always −1 millionth. But at any price range above $3, this linear demand curve is elastic, with a price elasticity (e_d) greater than 1. Between prices $3 and $2, the curve is unit-elastic, with an e_d equal to 1. Finally, at any price range below $2, the curve is inelastic, and e_d is less than 1.

inelastic in its lower range. Finally, in the curve's middle range, the relative changes in price and quantity demanded just balance one another so that the curve in this range is unit-elastic.

The implication of this illustration is clear: it is best to be careful when referring to a linear demand curve as either elastic or inelastic.

Income and Cross-Price Elasticities

The price elasticity of demand is not the only elasticity concept relating to demand. We can also measure the extent to which a product's quantity demanded varies with changes in consumer income or the price of another product.

income elasticity: the responsiveness of a product's quantity demanded to a change in average consumer income

Income elasticity (e_i) is defined as the responsiveness of a product's quantity demanded to an adjustment in consumer income. It is calculated as the ratio of the changes in quantity demanded and consumer income, with each change divided by its respective average value. The formula for income elasticity is, therefore, similar to the mathematical expression for the price elasticity of demand. It is the ratio of the change in quantity demanded (ΔQ_d) divided by its average value, over the change in consumer income (ΔI) divided by its average value. For example, if an increase in average consumer income from \$20 000 to \$40 000 causes the quantity demanded of computer tablets to rise from 1000 to 2000, then income elasticity of computer tablets is 1.

$$e_i = \frac{\Delta Q_d \div \text{average } Q_d}{\Delta I \div \text{average } I}$$

$$= \frac{(2000 - 1000) \div [(2000 + 1000)/2]}{(\$40\ 000 - \$20\ 000) \div [(\$40\ 000 + \$20\ 000)/2]}$$

$$= \frac{1000 \div 1500}{\$20\ 000 \div \$30\ 000}$$

$$= \frac{1/1.5}{2/3}$$

$$= 1$$

Unlike the case of the price elasticity of demand, the income elasticity's sign is important. For an inferior product, this elasticity is negative because changes in consumer incomes and quantity demanded are in opposite directions. To illustrate, a reduction in consumer incomes increases the purchases of canned meat, giving a negative denominator and positive numerator in the formula. In contrast, income elasticity is positive for a normal product because changes in consumer income and the product's quantity demanded are in the same direction. For example, higher consumer incomes mean more purchases of normal products, such as digital music players, giving both a positive numerator and a positive denominator. While the income elasticity of normal products that are necessities, such as milk and bread, is positive but relatively low (between 0 and 1), for luxuries, such as caviar or expensive jewellery, the income elasticity is relatively high (greater than 1).

cross-price elasticity: the responsiveness of a product's quantity demanded to a change in the price of another product

Another demand-related elasticity is **cross-price elasticity** (e_{xy}), defined as the responsiveness of quantity demanded of one product (x) to a change in price of another (y). In mathematical terms, the formula for cross-price elasticity is the ratio of the changes in quantity demanded of product x (ΔQ_d) and the price of product y (ΔPy), with each change divided by the respective average value. For example, if a drop in the price of computer tablets from $1000 to $500 causes the quantity demanded of laptop computers to fall from 5000 to 3000, then cross-price elasticity of these two products is 0.75.

$$e_{xy} = \frac{\Delta Q_d \div \text{average } Q_d}{\Delta P_y \div \text{average } P_y}$$

$$= \frac{(3000 - 5000) \div [(3000 + 5000)/2]}{(\$500 - \$1000) \div [(\$500 + \$1000)/2]}$$

$$= \frac{-2000 \div 4000}{-\$500 \div \$750}$$

$$= \frac{-1/2}{-2/3}$$

$$= 0.75$$

The cross-price elasticity's sign differs, depending on whether products x and y are substitutes or complementary. When one product is a substitute for the other, as in the case of computer tablets and laptops, the cross-price elasticity is positive. This is because the changes in both x's quantity demanded and y's price are in the same direction. On the other hand, the cross price elasticity for complementary products is negative. An increase in the quantity demanded of video game consoles, for example, might be caused by a fall in the price of video games.

BRIEF REVIEW

1. Price elasticity of demand is the responsiveness of a product's quantity demanded to changes in the product's price. When demand is elastic, a given percentage change in price causes a larger percentage change in quantity demanded. When demand is inelastic, a given percentage change in price causes a smaller percentage change in quantity demanded.

2. Demand is perfectly elastic when the price of a product is constant at all quantities demanded. Demand is perfectly inelastic when the quantity demanded of a product is constant at all prices. Demand is unit-elastic when a percentage change in price causes an equal percentage change in quantity demanded.

3. Price and total revenue have an inverse relationship when demand is elastic, but a direct relationship when demand is inelastic. When demand is unit-elastic, total revenue is constant, regardless of price.

4. Four factors affect the price elasticity of demand of a product: the portion of consumer incomes the product accounts for, access to substitute products, whether the product is a luxury or a necessity, and the amount of time that elapses after a price change.

5. Other demand-related elasticity concepts include income elasticity, which measures the sensitivity of a product's quantity demanded to a change in consumer income, and cross-price elasticity, which measures the sensitivity of a product's quantity demanded to a change in another product's price.

3.1 | PRACTICE PROBLEMS

1. Annual purchases of laptop computers in a certain market are 10 000 at a price of $3000, 20 000 at a price of $2000, and 30 000 at a price of $1000.
   a. Draw a graph showing this demand curve. Plot three points to draw the curve.
   b. Find sellers' total revenue at each price.
   c. On the basis of your answer to part b, is the market demand curve for laptop computers elastic or inelastic in the price range $3000 to $2000? in the price range $2000 to $1000?
   d. Calculate the numerical values of demand elasticity in the two relevant price ranges.
   e. Are your answers to parts c and d consistent?
2. Calculate the appropriate elasticity coefficient in each of the following cases.
   a. A drop in the price of hydrogen-powered cars from $25 000 to $20 000 causes purchases of gasoline-powered cars to fall from 1 million to 750 000 per year.
   b. Monthly purchases of smartphones rise from 15 000 to 17 500 when the average price of smartphones decreases from $500 to $400.
   c. A fall in average consumer incomes from $80 000 to $50 000 raises weekly purchases of canned sardines from 2000 to 3000 cans.

3.2 | Price Elasticity of Supply

price elasticity of supply: the responsiveness of a product's quantity supplied to a change in price

Just as the price elasticity of demand measures the responsiveness of consumers to a change in a product's price, the **price elasticity of supply** (also called supply elasticity) measures the responsiveness of producers (and the quantities they supply) to changes in the product's own price.

Elastic and Inelastic Supply

elastic supply: supply for which a percentage change in a product's price causes a larger percentage change in quantity supplied

In the case of **elastic supply**, a certain percentage change in the product's price leads to a larger percentage change in its quantity supplied. In other words, the quantity that producers are willing to offer for sale is very responsive to price changes. Consider the example of a tomato producer, as in Figure 3.7. As shown on the graph on the left, if the price of tomatoes increases by 50 percent, from $2 to $3 per kilogram, the quantity of tomatoes supplied annually increases from 100 000 to 200 000 kilograms—a 100 percent increase. If, as shown on the graph on the right, the identical 50 percent price increase for tomatoes causes a much smaller 20 percent increase in quantity supplied—from 100 000 to 120 000 kilograms—then we have **inelastic supply**. In other words, if a product has inelastic supply, a given percentage change in price results in a smaller percentage change in quantity supplied.

inelastic supply: supply for which the percentage change in a product's price causes a smaller percentage change in quantity supplied

As in the case of the price elasticity of demand, the price elasticity of supply is not the same as the slope of the supply curve. However, when two supply curves are drawn on the same set of axes, as in Figure 3.7, then—over a certain price range—the flatter curve (S_1) is more likely to be elastic than the steeper curve (S_2).

Factors That Affect Price Elasticity of Supply

The main factor that affects the price elasticity of supply is the passage of time. In competitive markets, three production periods can be distinguished: the

| **FIGURE 3.7** | Elastic and Inelastic Supply |

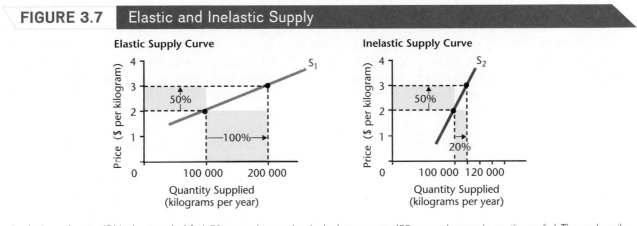

An elastic supply curve (S_1) is shown on the left. A 50 percent increase in price leads to a greater 100 percent increase in quantity supplied. The graph on the right shows an inelastic demand curve (S_2). The same 50 percent increase in price now leads to a smaller 20 percent increase in quantity supplied.

immediate run, the short run, and the long run. The price elasticity of supply differs in each period. Figure 3.8 illustrates elasticity for each of the three production periods in the market for strawberries.

THE IMMEDIATE RUN

The **immediate run** is the period during which businesses in a certain industry can make no changes in the quantities of resources they use. In the case of strawberry farming, the immediate run may be a month. For example, if the price of strawberries suddenly jumps as a result of an increase in demand, then during the immediate run, farmers are unable to increase their production. Because quantity supplied is constant, the supply curve (S_1), shown on the left, is vertical at a given quantity, such as 750 000 kilograms. Thus, for the immediate run, the supply is said to be **perfectly inelastic**.

immediate run: the production period during which none of the resources required to make a product can be varied

perfectly inelastic supply: supply for which a product's quantity supplied remains constant regardless of price

| **FIGURE 3.8** | Time and Price Elasticity of Supply |

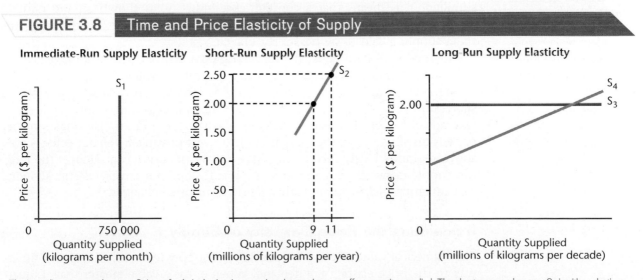

The immediate-run supply curve S_1 is perfectly inelastic, since a price change does not affect quantity supplied. The short-run supply curve S_2 is either elastic or inelastic, with quantity supplied varying in the same direction as price. The long-run supply curve S_3 shows the case of a constant-cost industry, where supply is perfectly elastic, since price is constant for every possible quantity supplied. The long-run supply curve S_4 shows the case of an increasing-cost industry, where price rises as quantity supplied expands.

THE SHORT RUN

short run: the production period during which at least one of the resources required to make a product cannot be varied

The **short run** is the period during which the quantity of at least one of the resources used by businesses in an industry cannot be varied. In the case of strawberry farming, a period of less than a single growing season is bound to be short run. If there is a rise in the price of strawberries from $2 to $2.50, then during the short run, farmers can increase their production by, for example, using more labour and maximizing the crop with mulch or fertilizers, but they cannot bring more land into production until the next growing season. In this case, illustrated on the middle graph of Figure 3.8, the price rise causes an increase in quantity supplied from 9 to 11 million kilograms. The supply curve (S_2) for the short run may be either elastic or inelastic. This depends on whether a given percentage change in price causes a bigger or smaller percentage variation in quantity supplied.

THE LONG RUN

long run: the production period during which all resources required to make a product can be varied, and businesses may either enter or leave the industry

In the **long run**, the quantities of all resources used in an industry can be varied. Also, businesses may enter or leave the industry. In the case of strawberry farming, the long run is a period longer than a single growing season–perhaps as long as a decade. Over this period, a rise in the price of strawberries will cause a temporary increase in strawberry farmers' earnings beyond what they have been in the past. The lure of these greater earnings leads to more resources being devoted to strawberry production. Not only will existing farmers expand their operations, but new farmers will enter the market. Both these changes increase the quantity supplied of strawberries. Two results are then possible, depending on what happens to price in the long run at the new, higher production levels.

constant-cost industry: an industry that is not a major user of any single resource

If strawberry farming is a **constant-cost industry**, one that is not a major user of any resource, the increase in quantity supplied following a short-run rise in the price of strawberries has no effect on resource prices. The lure of extra earnings keeps production expanding and the price of strawberries falling, until this price is finally driven back to its original level. Thus, the price of strawberries always returns to the same level in the long run, regardless of quantity supplied. This means that a constant-cost industry, as shown on the right in Figure 3.8, exhibits a horizontal long-run supply curve (S_3). For the long run, then, supply is said to be **perfectly elastic**.

perfectly elastic supply: supply for which a product's price remains constant, regardless of quantity supplied

increasing-cost industry: an industry that is a major user of at least one resource

If strawberry farming is an **increasing-cost industry**, it is a major user of at least one resource. Therefore, a greater quantity supplied leads to an increase in the price of this single resource, such as land or farm machinery. Again, a short-run rise in the price of strawberries causes production to grow as farmers take advantage of extra earnings. As long as the lure of extra earnings remains, price is driven down in the long run to its lowest possible level, but price is now above its initial level, since farmers face higher per-unit costs. Hence, the long-run supply curve (S_4) has a positive (upward) slope but is very elastic, showing that quantities supplied are highly sensitive to price changes.

Calculating the Price Elasticity of Supply

The numerical value of the price elasticity of supply (e_s) is calculated in a similar way to the price elasticity of demand. When e_s has a value greater than 1, quantity supplied is sensitive to price changes, and supply is elastic. If e_s is less than 1, quantity supplied is comparatively unresponsive to price changes, and supply is inelastic.

Consider the case of the tomato industry with an elastic supply curve (Figure 3.7). When the price of tomatoes rises from $2 to $3 a kilogram, the quantity supplied by farmers increases from 100 000 to 200 000 kilograms. The value of the price elasticity of supply for this industry can be found using the following formula, in which Q_s stands for quantity supplied.

$$e_d = \frac{\Delta Q_s \div \text{average } Q_s}{\Delta \text{ price} \div \text{average price}}$$

$$= \frac{(200\ 000 - 100\ 000) \div [(200\ 000 + 100\ 000) \div 2]}{(\$3 - \$2) \div [(\$3 + \$2) \div 2]}$$

$$= \frac{100\ 000 \div 150\ 000}{\$1 \div \$2.50}$$

$$= \frac{0.667}{0.4}$$

$$= 1.67$$

Therefore, the tomato suppliers face a price elasticity of supply of 1.67, which means that a certain percentage change in price causes a percentage change in quantity supplied that is 1.67 times as large (when both percentage changes are calculated using average values). Because there is a direct relationship between price and quantity supplied, the changes in these two variables are always in the same direction. Thus, the numerator and the denominator of the supply elasticity formula are either both positive or both negative, giving a final answer that is always positive. Like the numerical value of demand elasticity, this is a pure number with no units attached.

THINKING ABOUT ECONOMICS

Do decreasing-cost industries exist?

Yes, they do. For example, some industries in the information technology sector have witnessed a marked decrease in product costs as the industries have expanded. The example of computer chips is particularly telling. According to Moore's Law, developed in 1965 by one of the founders of chipmaker Intel, the processing power of computer chips doubles every 12 months. So far, Moore's Law has been correct, reducing the real price of processing power since the 1960s by 99.9999 percent, and making innovations such as laptops, tablets, and digital music players a reality. With continued advances in computing, there is no reason why this pace of growth cannot continue.

Similar trends are emerging in the biotechnology industry, especially in the fast-rising field of genetics. For example, the cost of DNA sequencing is estimated to have fallen to a hundred-thousandth of what it was as recently as 1999, and predictions are that this staggering reduction of costs could continue on the same path in decades to come. However, the problem in extending the analysis of long-run supply elasticity to such scenarios is that industries with a pattern of decreasing costs will probably not be perfectly competitive; the advantages of "bigness" for the leading businesses in the industry are simply too large to be ignored.

QUESTION   **Presuming a decreasing-cost industry is competitive, what would the slope of its long-run supply curve be?**

BRIEF REVIEW

1. Price elasticity of supply is the responsiveness of a product's quantity supplied to changes in the product's price.

2. When supply is elastic, a given percentage change in price causes a larger percentage change in quantity supplied. When supply is inelastic, a given percentage change in price causes a smaller percentage change in quantity supplied.

3. Price elasticity of supply is dependent mainly on the production period. In the immediate run, supply is perfectly inelastic, meaning a change in price has no effect on quantity supplied. In the short run, supply may be elastic or inelastic.

4. In the long run, price elasticity of supply depends on the industry's use of resources. In a constant-cost industry (not a major user of any one resource), supply in the long run is perfectly elastic, with a constant price at all possible quantities supplied. In an increasing-cost industry (a major user of at least one resource), the long-run supply is very elastic, with price rising gradually at higher quantities supplied.

3.2 | PRACTICE PROBLEM

1. In a certain lettuce market, the price rises from $1 to $1.20 per head. For each case below, determine the value of e_s.

   a. In the immediate run, monthly quantity supplied remains constant at 80 000 heads.
   b. In the short run, annual quantity supplied rises from 1 million to 1.2 million heads.
   c. In the long run, the price of lettuce returns to $1 as quantity supplied continues to expand.
   d. Based on your answer to part c, is this a constant-cost or increasing-cost industry? Why?
   e. Draw a graph showing the three supply curves. For each graph, plot only the two endpoints, the first and last points, of the supply curve.

LAST WORD

This chapter extended the basics of demand and supply studied in Chapter 2 to examine in more detail how buyers and sellers interact in private markets. The concept of elasticity allowed us to see how consumer decisions affect the sellers' total revenue, and how supply factors affect price and quantity in various production periods. In the following chapters, we will further explore the ways in which businesses and consumers interact in particular markets, and examine various forms of intervention that governments use to amend market outcomes.

PROBLEMS

1. Calculate the percentage change of the variable in each of the following cases. Then calculate the percentage change if the movement is occurring in the opposite direction, with what was the final value now the initial value and vice versa. Now calculate a comparable percentage change using the average of the initial and ending values.

a. A fast food restaurant, which originally sold hamburgers at a price of $3, increases their price to $6.

b. The number of autos sold monthly at a car dealership drops from 250 to 150.

c. The monthly fee for unlimited texting charged by a cellphone service provider falls from $12 to $4.

d. The number of copies of a small town newspaper purchased weekly rises from 1500 to 2000.

2. Identify whether demand in the case of each of the following products is likely to be inelastic, elastic, or unit-elastic.

   a. a luxury item with many close substitutes

   b. an item that represents a large portion of consumers' incomes and has many close substitutes

   c. a necessity whose demand is being viewed in a short-run time frame

   d. a luxury item that represents a large portion of consumers' incomes

3. In each case below, determine the effect on the sellers' total revenue and identify whether the demand curve in this particular market is elastic, inelastic, or unit-elastic in the relevant price range.

   a. When the price per package of a brand of chocolate chip cookies increases from $4 to $5, monthly quantity demanded decreases from 20 000 to 15 000.

   b. A fall in the price of sugar from $4 to $3 per carton raises weekly quantity demanded from 20 000 to 25 000 cartons.

   c. A rise in the quantity demanded of a monthly fashion magazine from 35 000 to 40 000 copies occurs when its newsstand price is reduced from $10 to $9.

   d. Daily quantity demanded of a particular model of digital music player rises from 5000 to 6000 players if its price drops from $60 to $50.

4. The table below shows demand and supply schedules for leather jackets.

Market Demand and Supply Schedules for Leather Jackets

Price ($ per jacket)	Quantity Demanded (jackets per year) (D)	Quantity Supplied (jackets per year) (S$_0$)
$300	70 000	100 000
250	80 000	80 000
200	90 000	60 000
150	100 000	40 000
100	110 000	20 000

   a. Draw a graph showing the demand and supply curves D and S$_0$, and the associated equilibrium point. Plot only the two endpoints of each curve.

   b. What are the equilibrium price and quantity in this market?

   c. Due to an increase in the number of producers, the annual quantity supplied in this market increases by 60 000 jackets at every price. What will the new equilibrium price and quantity be?

   d. Draw the new market supply curve (S$_1$) on the graph from part a and indicate the new equilibrium.

   e. Due to the change in supply conditions, how has the sellers' total revenue changed when compared with the initial equilibrium price and quantity? Is demand elastic, inelastic or unit-elastic in this price range?

5. The table below shows a market demand schedule for canoes.

Market Demand Schedule for Canoes

Price ($ per canoe)	Quantity Demanded (canoes per month)
$800	400
600	800
400	1200
200	1600

   a. Draw a graph showing the demand curve D. Plot only the two endpoints of the curve.
   b. What is sellers' total revenue at each price?
   c. On the basis of your answers to parts a and b, state whether the market demand for canoes is elastic, inelastic, or unit-elastic in the three price ranges $800 to $600, $600 to $400, and $400 to $200.
   d. Compute the value of the coefficient of the price elasticity of demand, e_d, in the three relevant price ranges.
   e. Are your answers to parts c and d consistent? Why or why not?
   f. What is the numerical value of the slope of this demand curve? Does a demand curve with a constant slope have a constant numerical elasticity? Why or why not?

6. Calculate the absolute value of the coefficient of the price elasticity of demand in each of the following situations.
   a. Consumer A's purchases of romance novels fall from 4 to 3 per month when their price increases from $10 to $12.
   b. Weekly purchases of packs of chewing gum rise from 1.2 million to 1.3 million packs when their price declines from $1 to 80 cents.
   c. A rise in the price of a health supplement from $25 to $30 per bottle reduces the number of bottles sold from 85 000 to 80 000.
   d. The annual quantity demanded of tablet computers rises from 200 000 to 300 000 when the price of tablets falls from $700 to $600.

7. Calculate the coefficient of cross-price elasticity in each of the following situations. In each case, identify whether the two products in italics are substitute or complementary products.
   a. The price Consumer X pays each month for access to the *Internet* decreases from $20 to $10, causing the quantity demanded of *e-magazines* he reads on his computer to rise from 3 to 5.
   b. The quantity demanded of *do-it-yourself hair-cutting sets* increases from 5000 to 10 000 when the average price of a *hairstylist's cut* rises from $40 to $60 per hour.
   c. A fall in the average price of *smartphones* from $300 to $200 increases purchases of *smartphone apps* from 1 million to 3 million per month.

8. Calculate the coefficient of income elasticity in each of the following situations. In each case, identify whether the relevant product is normal or inferior.
   a. Purchases of automobiles rise from 2 million to 3 million when average consumer incomes per year increase from $50 000 to $70 000.
   b. A rise in average consumer incomes per year from $30 000 to $40 000 causes the quantity demanded of powdered milk to fall from 100 000 to 50 000 kilograms.
   c. A fall in average consumer incomes per month from $3000 to $2800 leads to a drop in visits to massage therapists from 120 000 to 100 000.

9. Calculate the absolute value of the coefficient of the price elasticity of supply in each of the following cases.
   a. A rise in the price of wheat from $300 to $350 per metric tonne increases the amount supplied by wheat farmers from 8 million to 9 million tonnes.
   b. The amount of farmed salmon sold annually drops from 2 million to 1 million kilograms when the price of salmon falls from $8 to $7.50.
   c. When the price of oranges rises from $2 to $3 per kilogram, the annual amount supplied rises from 2 million to 4 million kilograms.

10. In the silver market, 1 million ounces are offered for sale each month by producers at the initial price of $6 per ounce. The price then rises to $8.
   a. Given the new $8 price for silver, what happens to quantity supplied in the immediate run? If you drew the associated supply curve, what would it look like?
   b. Given the new price for silver, what happens to quantity supplied in the short run? If you drew the associated supply curve, what would it look like?
   c. If silver mining is a constant-cost industry, how will the price of silver change in the long run? What if it were an increasing-cost industry? If you drew the associated supply curves, what would they look like?

11. a. A market supply curve has three prices—$1.50, $2, and $2.50—with a quantity supplied of 5 tonnes at the price of $1.50, 9 tonnes at $2, and 13 tonnes at $2.50. Is this supply curve linear? Why or why not?
   b. What is the numerical value of the price elasticity of supply between prices $1.50 and $2 and between prices $2 and $2.50?
   c. Based on your answers to parts a and b, must a supply curve with a constant slope have a constant numerical elasticity?

12. The total annual revenue for producers of a given product called widgets is always $10 million, regardless of the price.
   a. On the basis of this information, plot the market demand curve for widgets on a graph.
   b. How would you describe the elasticity of this demand curve? Explain.

PROPHET OF CAPITALISM'S DOOM

The Economic Theories of Karl Marx

KARL MARX

©Library of Congress Prints
and Photographs Division
(LC-USZ62-16530)

MARX AND HIS INFLUENCE

Karl Marx (1818–1883) is best known as the founder of the international socialist and communist movements. He was born in the German state of Prussia, studied philosophy, and worked as a journalist before beginning his career as a political activist. Exiled from both Germany and France, he moved to England where, with his close friend Friedrich Engels (1820–1895), he applied his revolutionary views to the fields of philosophy, history, and economics.

Of these three subjects, it was what he called "the confounded ramifications of political economy" that gave him the most headaches. In his mammoth three-volume work, *Das Kapital*, Marx developed his theory of economics. He concluded that capitalism, by its very nature, was unjust.

MARX'S VIEW OF CAPITALISM

Marx's years in England allowed him to witness first-hand the effects of the British Industrial Revolution. By the mid-1800s, manufacturing was the mainstay of Britain's economy, and a large portion of the population had moved from rural areas to the burgeoning new cities in the hope of finding jobs in manufacturing. In the long run, the industrial transformation experienced in Britain enhanced the economic well-being of the majority of citizens of industrialized countries. But in Marx's day, the benefits of the Industrial Revolution seemed to be limited to the wealthier members of society. Living conditions were horrendous for the labouring classes in the rapidly expanding urban areas:

> And what cities! It was not merely that smoke hung over them and filth impregnated them, that the elementary public services—water-supply, sanitation, street-cleaning, open spaces, and so on—could not keep pace with the mass migration of men into cities, thus producing, especially after 1830, epidemics of cholera, typhoid and an appalling constant toll [from] air pollution and water pollution . . . The new city populations . . . [were] pressed into overcrowded and bleak slums, whose very sight froze the heart of the observer.[1]

MARX'S THEORY OF CAPITALISM

The Labour Theory of Value   Marx blamed these conditions on capitalism itself. His attack was based on his "labour theory of value," in which prices of products depend on how much labour goes into producing them. According to this theory, only company owners (whom Marx called capitalists) have the financial resources to hire workers and sell the resulting output. By paying wages that are less than the value workers contribute to production, company owners are able to skim off a portion of value for themselves. By doing this, they engage in capitalist exploitation of their workforce.

The Theory of Exploitation An example will help explain Marx's theory. It may take a worker four hours to make a shirt and eight hours to make a suit. According to Marx, the price of the shirt should then be half that of the suit; say, the prices of the two products are $40 and $80, respectively. If so, workers

FIGURE A   Marx's Theory of Exploitation

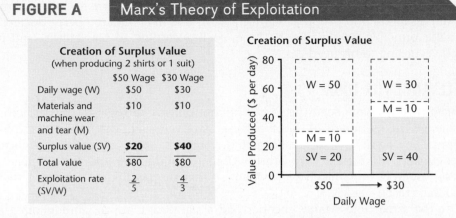

Creation of Surplus Value (when producing 2 shirts or 1 suit)		
	$50 Wage	$30 Wage
Daily wage (W)	$50	$30
Materials and machine wear and tear (M)	$10	$10
Surplus value (SV)	**$20**	**$40**
Total value	$80	$80
Exploitation rate (SV/W)	$\frac{2}{5}$	$\frac{4}{3}$

If daily wages are reduced from $50 to $30, daily surplus value extracted from each worker is increased (the shaded portions on the bar graphs). As a result, surplus value as a proportion of daily wages also increases.

Source: Brue. *Evolution of Economic Thought*, 6th ed. © 2000. South-Western, a part of Cengage Learning, Inc. Reproduced by permission. www.cengage.com/permissions.

producing either two shirts or one suit in an eight-hour day create $80 of value. Let us assume that daily wages in the textile trade are $50 and that the cost of materials plus daily wear and tear on the machines each worker uses is $10. The portion of value kept by the capitalist, or each worker's "surplus value," is, therefore, $20 [= $80 − ($50 + $10)] as shown in Figure A, while the size of surplus value can also be specified as a proportion of daily wages, giving a ratio known as the rate of exploitation which plays a key role in Marx's theory.

DYNAMICS OF CAPITALISM

With time, Marx argued, the rate of exploitation by capitalists would worsen, meaning surplus value would increase as a proportion of the daily wage. This could happen either through further decreases in wages or a lengthening of the workday.

Decreased Wages   Capitalists try to slash wages as much as possible. The daily wage in our example could drop from $50 to $30, while the cost of materials, plus the wear and tear on machines, remains constant at $10. As a result, surplus value would rise to $40 [= $80 − ($30 + $10)]. Surplus value as a proportion of the daily wage would then increase from $20/$50 to $40/$30.

Lengthening of the Workday   Capitalists also have an incentive to raise the number of hours workers put in each day. This expands the daily value created by each worker. As long as the daily wage remains the same, surplus value as a proportion of this wage would again rise.

COMMUNIST REVOLUTION

Marx believed that capitalist exploitation would worsen the living standards of workers until, finally, workers would violently revolt, first in the nations of Western Europe, which were most industrialized at the time Marx was writing, and later in other parts of the world. The overthrow of capitalism would usher in a socialist age based on common ownership of property. Once socialist ownership had been consolidated, true communism would arrive. Governments would disappear and people would be able to live in complete liberty. Society's guiding principle would then be "from each according to his abilities, and to each according to his needs."[2]

RELEVANCE FOR TODAY

Marx's theories have been the source of continuing controversy. His detractors challenge the usefulness of the labour theory of value and the notion of surplus value. They argue that other economic resources, such as capital and entrepreneurship, make their own contributions to production and that owners of these resources must receive a payment so that they will keep supplying their resources to businesses.

At the same time, Marx's theories had a significant impact throughout the twentieth century. Socialists–who advocate that the community as a whole own and control the means of production, distribution, and exchange–have held power in many parts of the world. Among socialists, communists accepted the bulk of Marx's theories and applied them in countries subject to communist rule. In a country such as China, which is still officially communist, the influence of Marxist theory can be seen in the major role that government plays in regulating the economy and controlling many sectors through state-owned firms. In most nations, however, any influence Marx has had is less direct. Labour movements, for example, owe much to Marx's theories of capitalist exploitation. Through gradual reform, rather than revolution, socialists in such countries as Canada have played a major part in social reform and in creating modern mixed economies in which governments are much more important than they were a century or more ago.

1. In a particular industry, workers produce $120 of value in an eight-hour day and the costs of materials plus the daily wear and tear on machines each worker uses is $30.
   a. If workers' wages are $50 per day, what is the surplus value per worker per day?
   b. If workers' wages are $60 per day, what is the surplus value per worker per day?
   c. As a result of the increase in wages, what happens to the rate of exploitation?

2. Workers in a certain industry produce $120 of value in an eight-hour day, workers' daily wages are $50, and the cost of materials plus the daily wear and tear on machines each worker uses is $20.
   a. If the working day increases from 8 to 12 hours, what is the daily value each worker produces? the daily wear on tear on machines per worker? the surplus value per worker?
   b. As a result of the lengthening of the workday, what happens to the rate of exploitation?

Notes

[1] Adapted from *Industry and Empire: From 1750 to the Present Day* by E.J. Hobsbawm (Penguin Books, 1969). Copyright © E.J. Hobsbawm, 1968, 1969. Reprinted by permission.

[2] Karl Marx, *Critique of the Gotha Program*, 1875.

> **That action is best which procures the greatest happiness for the greatest numbers.**
>
> — FRANCIS HUTCHINSON, BRITISH PHILOSOPHER

Efficiency and Equity

All societies must weigh the importance of gaining the most benefits from the economy's scarce resources (efficiency) against the importance of distributing the country's total fairly (equity). So too must individual citizens as they participate in the political arena. Given their significance, these two goals, which lie at the heart of microeconomics, are often in high-profile conflict. In modern mixed economies, such as Canada's, the private sector has traditionally stressed the goal of efficiency, while the public sector—especially in the decades since World War II—has tended to focus on the goal of income equity. In the next four chapters, we will examine the impact of each goal and how they are related. We will also examine the impact of an important third goal: environmental sustainability.

CHAPTER 4

Costs of Production

There is an old saying you've probably often heard: "There's no such thing as a free lunch." Its meaning? Everything has a cost. This chapter highlights one of the most important types of cost—how production creates expenses for businesses. In the future, if not already, most of us will have a close connection with a business as an employee or owner. All of us have a connection to businesses by virtue of being consumers. For now, we will ignore the selling side of business to look at how businesses make decisions about production processes and how they deal with production costs. In later chapters, we will complete the picture by looking again at sales revenues to see the crucial role production costs play in determining the profits that companies earn.

> Knowledge is the only instrument of production that is not subject to diminishing returns.
>
> -J.M. CLARK,
> AMERICAN ECONOMIST

LEARNING OBJECTIVES   After reading this chapter, you will be able to:

LO 1

Identify economic costs (explicit and implicit) of production and economic profit

LO 2

Describe short-run (total, average, and marginal) products and explain the law of diminishing marginal returns

LO 3

Derive short-run (total, average, and marginal) costs

LO 4

Explain the long-run results of production (increasing returns to scale, constant returns to scale, and decreasing returns to scale) and long-run costs

4.1 | Production, Costs, and Profit

A **business** is an enterprise that brings individuals, financial resources, and economic resources together to produce a good or service for economic gain. **Production** is the process of transforming a set of resources into a good or service that has economic value. The resources used in production are known as **inputs**. Recall that natural resources, capital resources, and human resources are the three economic resources used in production. Inputs for most businesses include all three of these *factors of production*. **Output** is the result of this production, the quantity of a good or service that is produced.

Businesses and the industries in which they operate fall into one of three sectors depending on the type of production: primary, secondary, or service (also known as tertiary). The primary sector includes industries that extract or cultivate natural resources, such as mining, forestry, fishing, and agriculture. The secondary sector involves fabricating or processing goods and includes, among other industries, manufacturing and construction. Finally, the service sector includes trade industries (both retail and wholesale), such as banking and insurance, and the new information industries. Despite the differences among these three sectors, they all follow the same production principles.

Productive Efficiency

In producing a certain good or service, businesses can typically choose from several processes, each using a different combination of inputs. A **labour-intensive process** is one that employs more labour and less capital than do other processes to produce a certain quantity of output. Conversely, a **capital-intensive process** uses more capital and less labour to produce the same quantity of output.

Suppose you have started a small clothing company, Pure 'n' Simple T-Shirts, with a $100 000 inheritance. You rent a building to use as a factory, and buy a supply of materials. Before you hire workers or buy sewing machines, you discover that you can make 250 T-shirts a day by using one of two possible production processes, each involving a different combination of workers and machines. Figure 4.1 shows the combinations of labour and capital employed in each process. Process A is labour-intensive, since it requires more workers and fewer machines than does Process B to produce 250 T-shirts per day. Process B is capital-intensive, since it requires more machines and fewer workers than does Process A.

How does a business decide which production process to use? Owners who want to earn as much profit as possible should try to maximize the business's

business: an enterprise that brings individuals, financial resources, and economic resources together to produce a good or service for economic gain

production: the process of transforming a set of resources into a good or service that has economic value

inputs: the resources used in production

output: the quantity of a good or service that results from production

labour-intensive process: a production process that employs more labour and less capital

capital-intensive process: a production process that employs more capital and less labour

---

FIGURE 4.1	Choosing a Production Process	
	Workers (labour)	**Sewing Machines (capital)**
Process A	4	2
Process B	3	3

Pure 'n' Simple T-Shirts can produce a daily output of 250 T-shirts with one of two possible combinations of workers and sewing machines—A, a more labour-intensive process, or B, a more capital-intensive process.

productive efficiency:
making a given quantity of output at the lowest cost

productive efficiency, which means making a given quantity of output with the least costly mix of inputs. Selecting the most efficient process, therefore, depends both on the quantity of each input used and on the prices of these inputs. Consider again the example of Pure 'n' Simple T-Shirts. As the owner, you can maximize your business's productive efficiency by using the lowest-priced combination of workers and sewing machines needed to turn out the daily output of 250 T-shirts. You find that the daily cost of a worker (hourly wage plus employee benefits) is $100, while the daily cost of a sewing machine (including wear and tear on the machine, use of electricity, and maintenance) is $25. All other costs for the business (for example, rent of the building) remain constant no matter which process is used, so they can be ignored in making this decision. With Process A, the daily costs of employing four workers and two machines come to $450 [= ($100 × 4 workers) + ($25 × 2 machines)]. In contrast, the daily costs of employing three workers and three machines with Process B are $375 [= ($100 × 3 workers) + ($25 × 3 machines)]. In this case, productive efficiency is maximized by using the capital-intensive Process B.

THINKING ABOUT ECONOMICS

Which industries are part of Canada's "new economy"?

The new economy is made up of industries experiencing rapid innovation and technological change—in particular, those associated with advanced information and communications technologies (ICTs). According to Industry Canada, the country's new economy includes industries connected with computers and peripherals, home electronics, telecommunications equipment and related activities, as well as computer and telecommunication services. Together, these industries represent about 5 percent of the entire economy, and their significance is bound to grow in coming years.

www.ic.gc.ca/eic/site/ict-tic.nsf/eng/h_it07229.html

QUESTION   **Are there other industries that might be considered part of Canada's new economy?**

Economic Costs

explicit costs: payments made by a business to businesses or people outside of it

Businesses face two types of costs: explicit costs and implicit costs. **Explicit costs** are payments made by a business to businesses or people outside of it. Explicit costs are also referred to as "accounting costs" because they include all the costs that appear in the business accounting records. These costs include such items as payments made for wages, buildings, machinery, and materials. For Pure 'n' Simple T-Shirts, for example, the explicit costs of producing 250 T-shirts a day using Process B include $375 for labour and machinery. The business may face a whole range of other accounting costs that add up to $675 per day. The daily explicit costs are, therefore, $1050 (= $375 + $675).

implicit costs: the owner's opportunity costs of being involved with a business

In contrast, **implicit costs** are estimates of what owners give up by being involved with a business–the owner's own opportunity cost, in other words, of pursuing this course of action over another. Implicit costs relate to the resources provided by the owners. One implicit cost is **normal profit**, or the minimum return that owners must receive to keep their funds and their entrepreneurial skills tied up in their business. To calculate normal profit, owners must determine the highest possible return they could have received by using their funds and entrepreneurial skills in another way. Consider again the T-shirt company. You might estimate that rather than making T-shirts, you could use your $100 000 to purchase a partnership in your friend's catering business, which would provide you with a return of $50 a day.

> **normal profit:** the minimum return necessary for owners to keep funds and their entrepreneurial skills in their business

Another implicit cost is the wages that owners sacrifice by providing labour to the business. If, for example, you provide labour by working as the manager of Pure 'n' Simple T-Shirts, you might estimate the value of your work as $150 a day, which is what you could earn by working for someone else. The sum of these two costs means that the implicit costs for Pure 'n' Simple T-Shirts are $200 (= $50 + $150) per day.

Recall from Chapter 1 that economists define "cost" as opportunity cost, which includes any sacrificed opportunity that results from some course of action, even if no outright monetary payment is made. Thus, the **economic costs** encountered by a business are all the opportunity costs involved in production and include both explicit and implicit costs. So, for Pure 'n' Simple T-Shirts, the explicit costs of producing 250 T-shirts per day are $1050, and the implicit costs are $200. The total economic costs faced by the business are, therefore, $1250:

> **economic costs:** a business's total explicit and implicit costs

$$\text{Economic costs} = \text{explicit costs} + \text{implicit costs}$$
$$\$1250 = \$1050 + \$200$$

Economic Profit

In accounting, profit is found by deducting explicit costs from total revenue to find **accounting profit**. A different approach is used in economics.

When economic costs are subtracted from total revenue, the excess is known as **economic profit**. If this gives a negative figure, the business faces a negative economic profit or a loss. To find the daily economic profit of Pure 'n' Simple T-Shirts, calculate total revenue and subtract economic costs. If the company sells 250 T-shirts at a price of $6 each, then the total revenue gained by producing 250 T-shirts is $1500 (= $6 × 250 shirts). When the economic costs of $1250 are deducted, we get an economic profit of $250 (= $1500 − $1250):

> **accounting profit:** the excess of a business's total revenue over its explicit costs

> **economic profit:** the excess of a business's total revenue over its economic costs

$$\text{Economic profit} = \text{total revenue} - \text{economic costs}$$
$$\$250 = \$1500 - \$1250$$

When a business's economic profit is positive, as it is for Pure 'n' Simple T-Shirts, the business has reason to continue operating, since it is reaping a positive amount after both explicit and implicit costs have been accounted for. But if economic profit is negative over an extended time period, the business's owners should consider closing down because they are unable to cover all of their explicit and implicit costs.

BRIEF REVIEW

1. Production processes may be labour-intensive or capital-intensive. To achieve productive efficiency, a business must choose the production process that is the cheapest way to produce a certain quantity of output.

2. Economic costs, as opposed to accounting costs, include both explicit costs (payments to those outside the business) and implicit costs (opportunity costs owners sustain by running the business).

3. Economists measure profitability using economic profit, which is found by deducting both explicit and implicit costs from a business's sales revenue.

4.1 | PRACTICE PROBLEM

1. A photocopy shop can produce its daily output of 10 000 copies with either of two processes. Process A uses two workers and six photocopy machines. Process B uses three workers and three photocopy machines.
    a. If each worker's daily wage is $80, and the daily rental (as well as wear and tear) of a photocopy machine is $40, will the shop's owner choose Process A or B? What are the total daily costs of employing capital and labour in Process A? Process B?
    b. Besides the costs of labour and capital, the owner daily pays $30 in building rent and $10 in business taxes. What are the shop's daily explicit costs?
    c. If the shop's price per photocopy is $0.06 (6 cents), what is the daily accounting profit?
    d. The owner estimates that she could earn $150 a day if she managed another shop instead of her own shop, and the $150 000 she invested in her business could earn $30 a day if she put it into her friend's business venture. What are the shop's daily implicit costs? daily economic costs?
    e. What is the shop's daily economic profit?
    f. Should the owner consider closing down her business? Why or why not?

4.2 | Production in the Short Run

Recall from Chapter 3 that the short run is the period during which quantities of one or more of a business's inputs cannot be varied. In manufacturing, companies usually cannot adjust the quantity of machinery they use or the size of their factories on short notice. In agriculture, there is typically an additional quantity that cannot be varied–the land available for cultivation. Inputs that cannot be adjusted in the short run are known as **fixed inputs**. Inputs that can be adjusted are known as **variable inputs**. Typically, variable inputs in the short run include the labour and materials a business uses in production. For example, as owner of Pure 'n' Simple T-Shirts, you are considering adjusting your current production of 250 shirts a day. You have already bought three sewing machines and cannot acquire more without a considerable delay. Hence, the three machines represent a fixed input for your business in the short run. But you can change the number of workers you employ, so labour represents a variable input in the short run.

fixed inputs: inputs whose quantities cannot be adjusted in the short run

variable inputs: inputs whose quantities can be adjusted in the short run

Total, Average, and Marginal Products

To increase production of a certain good or service, a business must employ more of all variable inputs, including workers. The result is a rise in **total product**, which is the overall quantity (q) of output associated with a given workforce. The employment of labour is a convenient measure of a company's scale of production, since labour is a variable input in making virtually all products. But businesses also use other variable inputs, such as natural resources or semi-processed goods.

total product: the overall quantity of output produced with a given workforce

Once again, let's look at Pure 'n' Simple T-Shirts. Suppose you conduct a few experiments to see what happens to total product for your business when the number of workers employed is changed but the number of sewing machines—three—remains constant. As shown in columns 1 and 2 of Figure 4.2, an increase in workers from three to four, for example, causes an increase in total production from 250 to 270 shirts per day.

In addition to total product, two other concepts are important when analyzing production in the short run. **Average product** is the quantity of output produced per worker and is found by dividing total product (q) by the quantity of labour (L) employed. **Marginal product**, in contrast, is the extra output produced when an additional worker is hired. To calculate marginal product, divide the change in total product (Δq) by the change in the amount of labour employed (ΔL). (The symbol Δ is the Greek capital letter "delta," which signifies a change in some variable.)

average product: the quantity of output produced per worker

marginal product: the extra output produced by an additional worker

Columns 3 and 4 of Figure 4.2 list the marginal and average products for Pure 'n' Simple T-Shirts. When employing three workers, the workforce's average product is 83.3 shirts per day (= 250 shirts ÷ 3 workers). If a fourth worker is added, the marginal product of this worker is 20 shirts, which comes from subtracting the old total product (250 shirts) from the new total product (270 shirts) and dividing the difference by the change in the workforce from three to four:

$$\text{Average product} = \frac{\text{total product (q)}}{\text{number of workers (L)}}$$

$$83.3 \text{ shirts} = 250/3$$

$$\text{Marginal product} = \frac{\text{change in total product } (\Delta q)}{\text{number of workers } (\Delta L)}$$

$$20 \text{ shirts} = \frac{270 - 250}{4 - 3}$$

FIGURE 4.2   Production in the Short Run

(1) Labour (L) (workers per day)	(2) Total Product (q) (T-shirts per day)	(3) Marginal Product (Δq/ΔL) (T-shirts per day)	(4) Average Product (q/L) (T-shirts per day)
0	0		–
		80	
1	80		80
		120	
2	200		100
		50	
3	250		83.3
		20	
4	270		67.5
		10	
5	280		56
		−10	
6	270		45

As the number of workers increases, total product increases when each of the first five workers is hired. Marginal product peaks when the second worker is hired, and becomes negative at the same point that total product begins to drop. Average product peaks at two workers.

In a table such as Figure 4.2, marginal product is shown halfway between the values for total and average products. This is because marginal product is defined as a change from one employment level to another. So, for example, in column 3 the marginal product of 20 shirts for the fourth worker is shown between the rows for three and four workers. The same principle also applies to expressing the marginal product on a graph; the marginal product of 20 shirts for the fourth worker will be plotted halfway between the horizontal coordinates for three and four workers.

Diminishing Marginal Returns

law of diminishing marginal returns: at some point, as more units of a variable input are added to a fixed input, the marginal product will start to decrease

The marginal product values in Figure 4.2 reflect a law that applies to production in the short run. According to the **law of diminishing marginal returns**, at some point—as more units of a variable input are added to a fixed input—the marginal product will start to decrease, since the new units of the variable input (for example, workers) are being added to an increasingly scarce fixed input (for example, land). It is possible to prove the law of diminishing returns through a type of argument known by the Latin term *reductio ad absurdum* (pronounced *re-dook'-shio ad ab-surd'-um*). This type of argument verifies a statement by showing that its opposite leads to absurdity. For the law of diminishing marginal returns, consider what would happen if you used a flower pot to grow food. If the law of diminishing marginal returns were false, then as you used more labour, the total product of food grown in the flower pot would rise at a faster and faster rate, until the world's entire food supply could be provided from this single pot. Since this conclusion is obviously absurd, the law of diminishing marginal returns must be true.

In the case of Pure 'n' Simple T-Shirts, where the main fixed input is sewing machines rather than land, the law of diminishing marginal returns can be best understood by thinking of what happens to the use of these machines as the number of workers employed rises. Sooner or later, workers find their access to sewing machines lessened as the labour force expands. As a result, after some point, each newly hired worker contributes a lower marginal product than the one before.

Three Stages of Production

The top graph of Figure 4.3 shows Pure 'n' Simple T-Shirts' total product, and the bottom graph shows its marginal product and average product. We can divide both graphs into three ranges. On the bottom graph's first range, marginal product rises as more workers are added. On the top graph's first range, total product rises at a higher and higher rate, giving the curve a positive slope that gets steeper. Businesses will never limit production in this range, given the prospect of producing additional units of output that each add more to total product than the units before. During the second range, marginal product begins to fall but is still positive. Total product in this second range continues to rise, but at a lower rate so that the curve becomes flatter. The business will end up selecting its production level somewhere in this range since points in the final range, where marginal product falls below zero and total product decreases, will never be chosen by the business.

Average versus Marginal Product

The shape of the average product curve reflects an important series of rules governing the relationship between average and marginal values. The average

FIGURE 4.3 | Total, Marginal, and Average Products

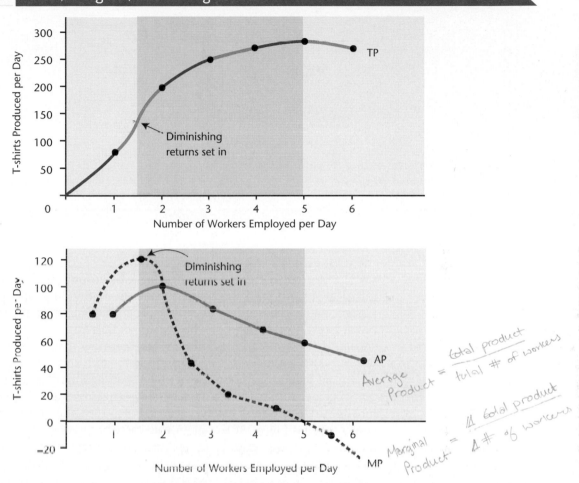

Pure 'n' Simple T-Shirts' total product curve is hill-shaped, with its peak at five workers and its slope dependent on the behaviour of marginal product. The first range, where marginal product rises, applies during the hiring of the first and second workers. In the second range, during the hiring of the third, fourth, and fifth workers, marginal product falls and is positive. In the last range, from the sixth worker onward, marginal product falls and is negative. The shape of the average product curve can be linked to marginal product, since average product reaches a maximum where it crosses the marginal product curve at two workers.

rises if the marginal value is above the average value. The average value stays constant if it equals the corresponding marginal value. Finally, the average value falls if the marginal value is below the average value.

These rules are borne out by the bottom graph in Figure 4.3. At first, marginal product is above average product so that average product must be rising. At two workers, average product crosses the marginal product curve so that values for both must be equal. Here, average product is constant, meaning it has a zero slope. Beyond this point, marginal product is below average product, causing average product to fall.

The rules that connect marginal and average values apply in a variety of situations. To help explain these rules, we will use an illustration every student is familiar with—marks. Suppose there are two tests in a course, each worth 50 marks, with a student's final grade calculated as the sum of the two marks. A student's *marginal mark* is the mark on each test, while her *average mark* is

FIGURE 4.4	A Student's Marginal and Average Marks

		Marginal Mark	Average Mark
Test 1		$\dfrac{36}{50}$	$\dfrac{36}{1} = 36$
Test 2	(Case A)	$\dfrac{34}{50}$	$\dfrac{(36 + 34)}{2} = 35$
	(Case B)	$\dfrac{36}{50}$	$\dfrac{(36 + 36)}{2} = 36$
	(Case C)	$\dfrac{38}{50}$	$\dfrac{(36 + 38)}{2} = 37$

On the first test, the student receives a mark of 36, which represents both her marginal and average marks. In Case A, the marginal mark on the second test is below the previous average, so the average mark falls. In Case B, the marginal mark on the second test equals the previous average, so the average stays the same. In Case C, the marginal mark on the second test is above the previous average, so the average mark rises.

the total earned so far divided by the number of completed tests. For example, say the student receives a marginal mark of 36 out of 50 on the first test. Her initial average is also 36, which comes from dividing 36 by 1, as shown in Figure 4.4. If the student receives a marginal mark of 34 out of 50 on the second test, her average on the two tests falls to 35 [= (36 + 34) ÷ 2]. The student's average mark declines because her new marginal mark of 34 is below her previous average of 36. On the other hand, she may get another mark of 36 on the second test. Because her new marginal mark is the same as her previous average, this student's average stays the same at 36 [= (36 + 36) ÷ 2]. Finally, if the student receives a mark of 38 on the second test, her average rises to 37 [= (36 + 38) ÷ 2]. In this case, her average rises because her new marginal mark is greater than her previous average. Figure 4.4 shows all three of these cases.

BRIEF REVIEW

1. In the short run, production is governed by the law of diminishing marginal returns, which states that as more units of a variable input are added to a fixed input, at some point the marginal product will start to decrease.

2. Because of the law of diminishing marginal returns, the marginal product curve is hill-shaped. The total and average product curves are also hill-shaped because of their connections with changes in marginal product.

4.2 | PRACTICE PROBLEMS

1. You are an NBA team manager who wishes to increase the average height of players on your team. As you draft new players, you should adopt a rule that involves the marginal heights of new players. What is the rule?

2. Weekly production for a potter varies with the number of workers employed, as shown in the table on the next page.

Short-Run Production for Pot-Works

(1) Labour (workers per day)	(2) Total Product (pots per day)	(3) Marginal Product (pots per day)	(4) Average Product (pots per day)
0	0		
1	50	____	____
2	200	____	____
3	270	____	____
4	300	____	____
5	240	____	____

a. Fill in column 3 in the table.

b. Identify the ranges where marginal product rises, where it falls, and where it is negative.

c. Fill in column 4 in the table.

d. In which employment range is marginal product equal to average product? greater than average product? less than average product?

e. Explain how in this case average product varies based on its relation to marginal product.

4.3 | Costs in the Short Run

In the short run, just as businesses use fixed and variable inputs, they face corresponding fixed and variable costs. **Fixed costs** (FC) do not change when a business changes its quantity of output, since these costs relate to fixed inputs, such as machinery and land. **Variable costs** (VC), in contrast, relate to variable inputs, which change when a business adjusts the quantity produced. The most important variable costs are wages and payments for materials used in production. **Total cost** (TC) is the sum of the costs of all inputs, both fixed and variable, and is found by adding fixed and variable costs at each quantity of output.

Figure 4.5 shows the short-run costs for Pure 'n' Simple T-Shirts. The company's fixed costs (column 4) reflect its expenditures on such inputs as factory rent and machinery and are a constant $825, regardless of how many shirts are produced. In contrast, variable costs (column 5) rise along with output, reflecting a wage of $100 per worker and a cost of materials of $0.50 per T shirt. Therefore, at the level of three workers, total cost (column 6) is $1250 (= $825 + $425):

$$\text{Total cost (TC)} = \text{fixed cost (FC)} + \text{variable cost (VC)}$$
$$\$1250 = \$825 + \$425$$

with the $425 variable cost found by adding the $300 in total wages paid to the three workers (= 3 workers × $100) and the $125 cost of materials to produce 250 T-shirts (= 250 T-shirts × $0.50 per T-shirt).

Marginal Cost

"Marginal" has a different interpretation when referring to cost rather than product. While marginal product is defined in terms of each new unit of labour, with cost the focus instead switches to new units of output.

LO3

fixed costs: economic costs for inputs that remain fixed at all quantities of output

variable costs: economic costs for inputs that vary at each quantity of output

total cost: the sum of all fixed and variable costs at each quantity of output

FIGURE 4.5   Short-Run Costs for Pure 'n' Simple T-Shirts

(1) Labour (L)	(2) Total Product (q)	(3) Marginal Product (MP)	(4) Fixed Costs (FC)	(5) Variable Costs (VC)	(6) Total Cost (TC) (FC + VC)		(7) Marginal Cost (MC) ($\Delta TC/\Delta q$)	(8) Average Fixed Cost (AFC) (FC/q)	(9) Average Variable Cost (AVC) (VC/q)	(10) Average Cost (AC) (AFC + AVC)
0	0		$825	$0	$825					
		→80				→140	$1.75			
1	80		825	140	965			$10.31	$1.75	$12.06
		→120				→160	1.33			
2	200		825	300	1125			4.13	1.50	5.63
		→50				→125	2.50			
3	250		825	425	1250			3.30	1.70	5.00
		→20				→110	5.50			
4	270		825	535	1360			3.06	1.98	5.04
		→10				→105	10.50			
5	280		825	640	1465			2.95	2.29	5.24

Columns 1 and 2 are from Figure 4.2, while columns 4 and 5 represent possible fixed and variable costs for the business. The remaining columns are based on calculations shown in the table. Total cost in column 6 is the sum of the fixed and variable costs. Marginal cost in column 7 is found by dividing the changes in total cost by the changes in total product. Columns 8 and 9 are derived by dividing fixed and variable costs by total product. Average cost in column 10 is the sum of the average fixed and average variable costs.

marginal cost: the extra cost of producing an additional unit of output

Marginal cost (MC), or the extra cost of producing an additional unit of output, is the most important cost concept in economics. Marginal cost is found by calculating the change in total cost (ΔTC) that results whenever a new worker is hired, and then dividing this change by the change in total product (Δq) that results from employing another worker. So, for example, column 7 of Figure 4.5 shows the marginal costs for Pure 'n' Simple T-Shirts at each output level. When the fourth worker is hired, total cost in column 6 rises by $110 (= \$1360 − \$1250), and marginal product, in column 3, is 20 shirts (= 270 − 250). Therefore, the marginal cost of each of these additional 20 shirts is $5.50 (= \$110.00 ÷ 20 shirts):

$$\text{Marginal cost (MC)} = \frac{\text{change in total cost } (\Delta TC)}{\text{change in total product } (\Delta q)}$$

$$\$5.50 = \frac{\$110.00}{20 \text{ shirts}}$$

Figure 4.6 shows that the marginal cost curve is shaped like the letter "J" (or the Nike "swoosh"). Note that, corresponding to the graph of marginal product in Figure 4.3, each point on the marginal cost curve is plotted halfway between the two relevant horizontal coordinates. For example, the first marginal cost value ($1.75) is plotted halfway between the two associated output levels, 0 and 80 shirts. This halfway value is 40 shirts, which can be found by adding the two output levels and then dividing by two [40 = (0 + 80) ÷ 2]. Early in the process of adding labour, the addition of each new worker produces a proportionally greater increase in output than in the existing labour. So, the marginal cost connected with each new worker falls for each extra unit of output as long as marginal product keeps increasing. But at some point, marginal product starts to decline. From this point, each new worker contributes fewer extra units of output than the previous worker, and the marginal cost connected with adding a new worker is greater for each extra unit of output. Marginal cost, therefore, rises as long as marginal product continues to fall.

FIGURE 4.6	The Marginal Cost Curve

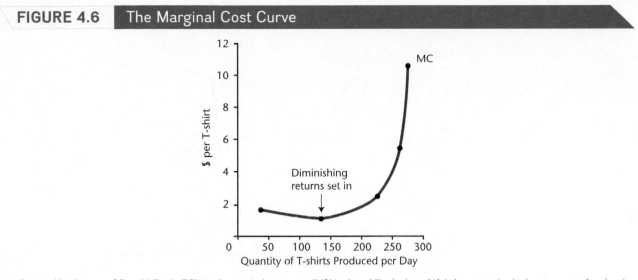

As illustrated by the case of Pure 'n' Simple T-Shirts, the marginal cost curve (MC) is shaped like the letter "J." At low output levels, the extra cost of each unit produced falls. Marginal cost starts to rise when marginal product begins to fall.

Per-Unit Costs

While marginal cost is based on changes in a business's total product, per-unit costs are expressed in terms of a single level of output. These costs are related to a business's fixed costs, variable costs, and total costs. As a result, there are three separate types of per-unit costs: average fixed cost, average variable cost, and average cost.

AVERAGE FIXED AND AVERAGE VARIABLE COSTS

Average fixed cost (AFC) is the fixed cost per unit of output and is calculated by dividing the business's fixed costs (FC) by its total product (q). Similarly, **average variable cost** (AVC) is the variable cost per unit of output and is calculated by dividing the business's variable costs (VC) by total product (q). For example, for Pure 'n' Simple T-Shirts, columns 8 and 9 of Figure 4.5 show the average fixed and average variable costs. When three workers are employed, the business's fixed costs of $825 are divided by the total product of 250 shirts, giving an average fixed cost of $3.30. Similarly, the $425 variable costs at this employment level are divided by 250 shirts, resulting in an average variable cost of $1.70.

average fixed cost: the fixed cost per unit of output

average variable cost: the variable cost per unit of output

$$\text{Average fixed cost (AFC)} = \frac{\text{fixed costs (FC)}}{\text{total product (q)}}$$

$$\$3.30 \text{ per shirt} = \frac{\$825}{250 \text{ shirts}}$$

$$\text{Average variable cost (AVC)} = \frac{\text{variable costs (VC)}}{\text{total product (q)}}$$

$$\$1.70 \text{ per shirt} = \frac{\$425}{250 \text{ shirts}}$$

Figure 4.7 shows the average fixed cost for Pure 'n' Simple T-Shirts on a graph. When no shirts are produced, the denominator of the average fixed cost formula

FIGURE 4.7   The Family of Short-Run Cost Curves

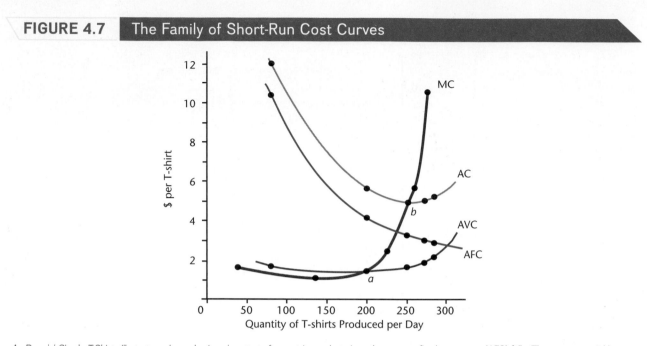

As Pure 'n' Simple T-Shirts illustrates, when a business's output of a certain product rises, the average fixed cost curve (AFC) falls. The average variable cost curve (AVC) declines until it reaches point *a*, where it meets the marginal cost curve (MC), after which the AVC curve rises. The average cost curve (AC) also falls and then rises. It reaches a minimum at point *b*, where it meets the MC curve.

is zero, meaning that average fixed cost is an infinitely high number. Average fixed cost then falls as the business's total product increases, since the denominator in the formula rises. Therefore, the average fixed cost curve has a negative (downward) slope, and becomes flatter as output rises.

In contrast, the average variable cost curve shown in Figure 4.7 is saucer-shaped, reflecting its connection with the associated marginal cost curve. At the initial quantities of output, marginal cost is below average variable cost, causing average variable cost to decline. (In terms of our previous example in Section 4.2, this is the case where a student's marginal mark is below her initial average, causing her average mark to fall.) Once the two curves meet (at point *a*)–where the marginal and average values are equal–the average variable cost curve has a zero slope and reaches its minimum. At higher output levels, marginal cost is above average variable cost, causing average variable cost to rise (just as a student's marginal mark that is higher than her initial average leads to a rise in her average mark).

AVERAGE COST

average cost: the sum of average fixed cost and average variable cost at each quantity of output

Average total cost, or simply **average cost** (AC), is the business's total cost per unit of output. Average cost is the sum of average fixed cost and average variable cost at each quantity of output. So, for example, in column 10 of Figure 4.5, when Pure 'n' Simple T-Shirts produces 250 shirts, average fixed cost is $3.30 and average variable cost is $1.70, giving an average cost of $5 (= $3.30 + $1.70):

Average cost (AC) = average fixed cost (AFC) + average variable cost (AVC)

$5 per shirt = $3.30 + $1.70

Like the average variable cost curve, the average cost curve in Figure 4.7 is saucer-shaped. It represents the sum of the values plotted for the average fixed cost curve and the average variable cost curve. At an output level of 250 shirts, for example, the $5 average cost is the sum of the heights of the average fixed cost curve ($3.30) and the average variable cost curve ($1.70). At lower output levels, average cost is high because of average fixed cost. Once average cost has passed its lowest point, its rise is due to the impact of expanding average variable cost. The average cost curve reaches its minimum at point *b*, where it intersects the marginal cost curve. This relationship parallels the relationship between average variable cost and marginal cost. Therefore, marginal cost provides the minimum values for both the average variable cost curve and the average cost curve. In each case, an average value remains constant when it equals its associated marginal value.

BRIEF REVIEW

1. Marginal cost, or the extra cost of producing another unit of output, is inversely related to marginal product. The marginal cost curve is shaped like the letter "J."

2. Average fixed cost represents fixed costs per unit of output. Its curve has a negative slope and is flatter at higher output levels. Average variable cost, or variable costs per unit of output, has a saucer-shaped curve that reaches its minimum where it crosses the marginal cost curve.

3. Average cost, or total cost per unit of output, is the sum of average fixed and average variable costs at given output levels. The curve for average cost is saucer-shaped and reaches a minimum where it intersects the marginal cost curve.

4.3 | PRACTICE PROBLEM

1. The daily short-run costs for a flowerpot maker, Pot-Works, are shown in the table below.

(1) Labour (workers per day)	(2) Total Product (pots per day)	(3) Fixed Cost	(4) Variable Cost	(5) Total Cost	(6) Marginal Cost	(7) Average Fixed Cost	(8) Average Variable Cost	(9) Average Cost
0	0	$100	$ 0	$_____				
1	50	_____	100	_____	$_____	$_____	$_____	$_____
2	160	_____	200	_____	_____	_____	_____	_____
3	230	_____	300	_____	_____	_____	_____	_____
4	280	_____	400	_____				

a. Fill in the table.

b. How are marginal values described in relation to output? When graphed, how are these marginal values plotted?

c. Briefly describe the shape of the average fixed cost curve, the average variable cost curve, and the average cost curve, including any key points where these curves intersect with the marginal cost curve.

d. Draw a graph showing the marginal cost, average variable cost, and average cost curves. Plot four points for the marginal cost curve, four points for the average variable cost curve, and three points for the average cost curve, for a total of 11 points. Remember to plot the marginal values halfway between the two relevant quantity levels on the horizontal axis.

THINKING ABOUT ECONOMICS

Is production in knowledge-based industries different from that found in more conventional parts of the economy?

The use of knowledge does differ from the use of other inputs, since knowledge is not necessarily used up when employed in production. For example, when a software company produces a new program, it can keep on making it at virtually no marginal cost, especially when software is sold online. This means that almost all costs are the fixed ones connected with software development. Variable costs, meanwhile, are virtually zero. The same applies for many other products that are sold on the Internet. An online retailer such as Apple iTunes, for example, faces considerable fixed costs when buying rights to the entertainment products it sells. Once these rights are bought, the marginal cost of each song, film, or book it distributes is virtually zero. In the extreme case, if all costs for a business like iTunes were fixed, then the business's average cost curve would become identical with its average fixed cost curve, and average costs would always fall as output increased.

www.apple.com/itunes

QUESTION   Instead of keeping down prices for the entertainment products it sells through iTunes, Apple prices these online products significantly above cost, while keeping the prices of related hardware such as iPods and iPads at attractively low levels. Why?

4.4 | Production and Costs in the Long Run

LO4   As we discussed in Chapter 3, the long run is the period in which quantities of all resources used in an industry can be adjusted. So, even those inputs that had been fixed in the short run–such as machinery, buildings, and cultivated land–can be adjusted in the long run. Because all inputs can vary in the long run, the law of diminishing marginal returns no longer applies as in the short run. Instead, new questions arise. If a business expands all inputs used to produce a certain product, how will the output of the product vary, and what effect will these changes have on costs? There are three possible results: increasing, constant, and decreasing returns to scale.

Increasing Returns to Scale

increasing returns to scale: a situation in which a percentage increase in all inputs causes a larger percentage increase in output

Increasing returns to scale (also known as economies of scale) occur when a business expands all inputs for a certain product by a given percentage and the output rises by an even higher percentage. For example, if a car manufacturer doubles all inputs used to make a certain car model (that is, expands all inputs by 100 percent) and the total output of the car more than doubles (rising by, for example, 150 percent), the manufacturer enjoys increasing returns to scale. Virtually all businesses experience increasing returns to scale over the initial range of output. There are three basic causes: division of labour, specialized capital, and specialized management.

DIVISION OF LABOUR

As Adam Smith illustrated with the pin-making factory over two centuries ago, increases in the scale of production and worker specialization can go hand in hand. Performing fewer tasks allows workers to become more efficient at their jobs. As a result, Smith concluded, quantities of output tend to rise more quickly than the number of workers producing them. The impact of the division of labour is just as prevalent today in labour-intensive production. For example, if a very small restaurant where workers do everything expands, then workers can begin to specialize in either food preparation or service, thus making both sets of workers more efficient in the tasks they do.

SPECIALIZED CAPITAL

In most manufacturing industries, a greater scale of production is associated with the use of specialized machinery. If a car manufacturer raises the quantity of all its inputs, for example, capital equipment can have more specialized functions so that it performs fewer tasks more efficiently than before.

SPECIALIZED MANAGEMENT

The same principle that underlies the division of labour applies to management. When the scale of production is small, there are few managers. Each is forced to deal with a wide range of duties, some of which they are better at performing than others. An accounting expert may need to devise a marketing strategy, or a production manager may have to deal with personnel problems. Along with an enlarged scale of production, more managers are hired and are assigned to the area in which they have the most expertise.

Constant Returns to Scale

In contrast to increasing returns to scale, in the case of **constant returns to scale**, a business that expands inputs by a given percentage will see output rise by the same percentage. This may be the case for an artisan making pottery, doubling her input also doubles her output. Constant returns to scale usually result when making more of an item requires repeating exactly the same tasks used to produce previous units of output.

constant returns to scale: a situation in which a percentage increase in all inputs results in an equal percentage increase in output

Decreasing Returns to Scale

The last possible case is **decreasing returns to scale**, or diseconomies of scale, in which a business that expands inputs to a product's production by a certain percentage sees output rise by a smaller percentage. For example, a 100 percent expansion in all inputs used by a copy shop may lead to its output rising by only 75 percent. There are two major reasons for decreasing returns to scale: management difficulties and limited natural resources.

decreasing returns to scale: a situation in which a percentage increase in all inputs causes a smaller percentage increase in output

MANAGEMENT DIFFICULTIES

Continual expansion in the scale of production will eventually make a business so cumbersome to administer that managers will face problems in coordinating operations to ensure efficient production. Virtually all businesses reach an output level above which management difficulties cause decreasing returns to scale to become dominant.

LIMITED NATURAL RESOURCES

In primary industries, such as fishing or forestry, a business may be able to acquire only a limited supply of easily available natural resources, even in the long run. In this case, an output level is reached above which further increases in all inputs lead to a smaller rise in output, resulting in decreasing returns to scale.

Returns to Scale and Long-Run Costs

The concept of returns to scale is useful in analyzing the effect on a business's costs when inputs that are fixed in the short run become variable. Figure 4.8 shows the case of a magazine publishing company that expands its printing plant three times and faces a different short-run average cost curve for each plant size. With each expansion of the plant, the curve shifts to the right, demonstrating the effects of the increased output.

When the plant is first expanded, the short-run average cost curve falls from AC_1 to AC_2. This shift results from increasing returns to scale. Recall that average cost is found by dividing total cost by the quantity of output. With increasing returns to scale, output rises more rapidly than the total cost of inputs so that average cost falls as the scale of production expands.

With the second plant expansion, the shift of the short-run average cost curve (from AC_2 to AC_3) reflects constant returns to scale. Output and the total costs of inputs rise at the same rate when the plant is expanded this second time, so the average cost curve moves horizontally as the output of magazines rises.

With the final plant expansion, the company's short-run average cost curve not only shifts to the right, but also rises (from AC_3 to AC_4). This shift reflects decreasing returns to scale. Since the printing plant's output is rising less rapidly than the total cost of input costs, the average cost curve rises as the production of magazines continues to increase.

Long-Run Average Cost

long-run average cost: the minimum short-run average cost at each possible level of output

A business's **long-run average cost** in producing a certain product is the lowest short-run average cost curve at each possible level of output. Figure 4.8 shows that the long-run average cost curve is made up of points from the lowest short-run average cost curve at each output level. Notice, from Figure 4.8, that this does not necessarily mean that the lowest point on any short-run average cost curve is chosen by the business in the long run. For AC_1 and AC_4, the selected

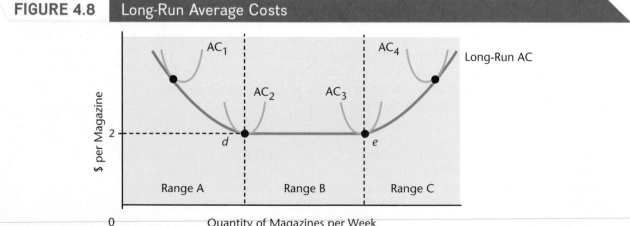

FIGURE 4.8 Long-Run Average Costs

With many possible plant sizes, the long-run average cost curve for producing a product, such as magazines, is drawn by finding the lowest possible short-run average cost at every quantity. This results in a single point being included from each short-run curve. The long-run AC curve has three ranges. Range A has a negative slope, reflecting increasing returns to scale. Range B is horizontal, at a constant cost per unit (e.g., $2), indicating constant returns to scale. Range C has a positive slope, showing decreasing returns to scale.

points are to the left (in the case of AC_1) and to the right (in the case of AC_4) of the lowest point on the short-run average cost curves. What distinguishes these selected points is that each is the lowest possible point from *any short-run average cost curve* at that given level of output. Given a wide range of possible plant sizes, the long-run AC curve is smooth and saucer-shaped, with only one point represented from each short-run curve. As depicted in Figure 4.8, long-run average cost falls in the initial output Range A because of increasing returns to scale, remains the same in Range B at a constant cost per unit of $2 due to constant returns to scale, and rises in Range C because of decreasing returns to scale.

Industry Differences

While virtually all businesses face a saucer-shaped long-run average cost curve, these curves are not necessarily symmetrical for all industries. In a particular industry, one range (or portion of the curve) will often dominate the long run average cost. Figure 4.9 illustrates long-run average cost curves characteristic of manufacturing industries, craft industries, and primary industries.

MANUFACTURING INDUSTRIES

Manufacturing industries tend to exhibit an extended range of increasing returns to scale due to the degree to which specialization is possible in the use of both labour and capital. This is particularly true of companies in which assembly-line techniques are used. It is not until output is very large that the conditions leading to constant returns to scale and decreasing returns to scale become relevant. The left graph of Figure 4.9 shows the long-run average cost curve faced by businesses in most manufacturing industries. In this case, the curve falls over a wide range of output levels before briefly levelling out and then rising.

CRAFT INDUSTRIES

In contrast, craft industries are dominated by constant returns to scale. Because raising output levels of crafts tends to depend on repeating exactly the method of production, an increase in input usually results in an equal increase in output.

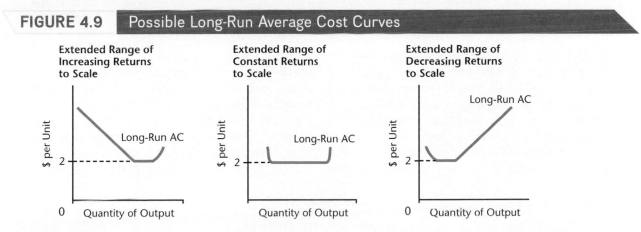

FIGURE 4.9 Possible Long-Run Average Cost Curves

On the left graph, the long-run AC curve's negative slope dominates, illustrating a wide range of increasing returns to scale, as usually occurs in assembly-line manufacturing. The middle graph shows the long-run AC curve when the horizontal range of constant returns to scale at a constant cost of $2 per unit dominates, which is characteristic of craft industries. On the right graph, the positive slope dominates, illustrating the range of decreasing returns to scale, as is common in primary industries.

As a result, except at very low or very high levels of output, the long-run average cost curves for producers of such items as handmade pottery are horizontal, at a constant cost per unit of $2, as in the middle graph of Figure 4.9.

PRIMARY INDUSTRIES

Decreasing returns to scale, meanwhile, are most prevalent for businesses in primary industries, as in some types of fishing, where the limits of resource supplies are particularly acute. In this case, the slope of the long-run average cost curve becomes positive at a relatively low level of output, as shown on the right in Figure 4.9.

Business Size and Returns to Scale

The predominance of increasing returns to scale in an industry raises the chances that businesses in the industry are large. Because of their lower long-run average costs, big companies have a competitive advantage over smaller rivals. It is increasing returns to scale, for example, that helps explain the gigantic size of most companies in the automobile industry. In contrast, smaller companies tend to prevail in industries characterized by constant or decreasing returns to scale because there is no cost disadvantage associated with low output levels. Another factor that helps explain the large size of businesses in markets such as the automobile industry is a concept that has parallels to increasing returns to scale. **Economies of scope** refers to the cost advantage associated with a single business producing different products—such as a variety of car models made by an automobile company. Because many aspects of production—from knowledge of car design to marketing and other affiliated functions—can be shared among the company's various products, so too can the costs of these inputs. For many large companies with a wide range of products, this provides another competitive edge over smaller rivals.

economies of scope: the cost advantage related to a single business producing different products

---

THINKING ABOUT ECONOMICS

How is technological change affecting returns to scale?

Computers and robotics, including 3D printers (so-called fabricators or "fabbers") that use digital blueprints to construct a vast array of products, are rapidly making manufacturing smarter and more flexible. This results in less need for complicated assembly lines and specialized equipment in many manufacturing industries. In these industries, the range of increasing returns to scale ends at comparatively low quantities of output so that businesses can customize their products in small batches—an option that was not available in the past. Also, electronic commerce is making it easier to supply these small batches to niche markets, with such innovations as online auctions and search-based advertising and marketing through sites such as eBay, Craigslist, and Facebook, while lowering of transaction costs for sales and distribution.

www.appaut.com

www.ennex.com/~fabbers/

QUESTION   Do manufacturing businesses that use customized production methods need to be as large as those employing traditional assembly lines?

BRIEF REVIEW

1. When, in the long run, all inputs can be varied, there are three possible results for a business: increasing, constant, and decreasing returns to scale.

2. Increasing returns to scale exist when a given percentage change in inputs causes an even greater percentage change in output. Division of labour, specialized capital, and specialized management are the major causes.

3. Constant returns to scale exist when a given percentage change in inputs causes an equal percentage change in output. When production of any additional unit of a product depends on repeating exactly the tasks used to produce the previous unit of the product, constant returns prevail.

4. Decreasing returns to scale exist when a given percentage change in inputs causes a lower percentage change in output. Management difficulties and limited natural resources are the major causes.

5. The long-run average cost curve is saucer-shaped, reflecting ranges first of increasing, then constant, and finally decreasing returns to scale.

6. In general, increasing returns to scale dominate in manufacturing industries, constant returns to scale dominate in craft industries, and decreasing returns to scale dominate in primary industries.

4.4 PRACTICE PROBLEM

1. A business whose only inputs are labour and capital expands its employment level in the long run from six to nine workers and its capital from two to three machines. Assuming that the daily wage of $100 and the daily upkeep (including wear and tear) of each machine of $20 remain constant in the long run, identify the relevant returns to scale and the change in long-run average cost if daily output were to expand in each of the following possible ways:
   a. from 120 to 240 units
   b. from 120 to 180 units
   c. from 120 to 160 units

LAST WORD

In this chapter, we explored how the view of cost in economics differs from that in accounting. This is because economists emphasize productive efficiency, while also recognizing the subjective implicit costs that accountants ignore. The chapter examined how economic costs for any business fit a set pattern in the short run, due to the law of diminishing marginal returns and its effect on both marginal product and marginal cost. A different pattern emerges in the long run, based on the variability of all inputs and the three possible returns to scale. In the next two chapters we will turn our attention from production to the selling side of business activity, and see how the revenue conditions that exist in various markets can be combined with the cost concepts outlined in this chapter to determine how businesses maximize economic profit.

PROBLEMS

1. Process A uses four workers and two sewing machines to produce a certain number of T-shirts, while Process B uses three workers and three machines to produce the same quantity. Which production process maximizes productive efficiency in the following cases?
   a. The daily cost of a worker is $20 and the daily cost of a sewing machine is $25.
   b. The daily cost of a worker is $100 and the daily cost of a sewing machine is $150.

2. Rodriguez operates a variety store with an annual revenue of $480 000. Each year, he pays $25 000 in rent for the store, $15 000 in business taxes, and $350 000 on products to sell. He estimates he could put the $80 000 he has invested in the store into his friend's restaurant business instead and earn an annual 20 percent profit on his funds. He also estimates that he and his family could earn a total annual wage of $90 000 if they worked somewhere other than the store.
   a. Calculate the total explicit costs and total implicit costs of running the variety store.
   b. What are the accounting profit and economic profit of the variety store?
   c. Should Rodriguez consider closing down this business? Why or why not?

3. Identify each of the following short-run costs as either variable or fixed:
   a. depreciation charges for a construction firm
   b. employee health benefits for an automobile-parts manufacturer
   c. lumber costs for a pulp-and-paper producer
   d. property insurance for a restaurant
   e. gasoline bills for a taxi company

4. Daily production for Pot-Works, a flowerpot maker, varies with the number of workers employed, as shown in the table below.

Short-Run Production for Pot-Works

(1) Labour (workers per day)	(2) Total Product (pots per day)	(3) Marginal Product (pots per day)	(4) Average Product (pots per day)
0	0		
1	100	_____	_____
2	280	_____	_____
3	510	_____	_____
4	560	_____	_____
5	550	_____	_____

   a. Fill in the table.
   b. In which employment range is marginal product rising? falling and positive? negative?
   c. Draw the total product curve on one set of axes and the average product and marginal product curves on another set of axes. For the total product curve, plot six points in total including the origin point (0, 0). For the average product and marginal product curves, draw five points each for a total of ten points (exclude the origin point for both curves). Remember to plot marginal values such as marginal product halfway between the two relevant employment levels on the horizontal axis.

5. The table below shows the hourly short-run costs for a parking lot.

Short-Run Cost for a Parking Lot

(1) Labour (workers per day)	(2) Total Product(cars parked per day)	(3) Marginal Product (cars parked per day)	(4) Fixed Costs	(5) Variable Costs	(6) Total Cost	(7) Marginal Cost	(8) Average Fixed Cost	(9) Average Variable Cost	(10) Average Cost
0	0	_____	$25	$ 0	$_____				
1	40	_____	25	20	_____	$_____	$_____	$_____	$_____
2	92	_____	25	40	_____	_____	_____	_____	_____
3	132	_____	25	60	_____	_____	_____	_____	_____
4	160	_____	25	80	_____	_____	_____	_____	_____
5	180	_____	25	100	_____	_____	_____	_____	_____

a. Fill in the table.
b. Draw the graph showing the marginal cost, average variable cost, and average cost curves. Plot five points for each of the three curves for a total of 15 points. Remember to plot marginal values such as marginal cost halfway between the two relevant quantity levels on the horizontal axis.
c. At which employment level do diminishing returns set in? How is this point related to the behaviour of marginal cost in column 7?
d. Referring to the quantities in column 2, at what quantity do average variable cost and marginal cost have the same value? Again referring to the quantities in column 2, at what quantity do average cost and marginal cost have the same value?

6. For the following industries, state whether the long-run average cost curve has an extended range with a negative slope, a positive slope, or a zero slope, and whether decreasing, constant, or increasing returns to scale dominates in this industry.
a. handcrafted pottery
b. manufacturing of smartphones
c. a particular high-quality variety of coffee
d. e-book publishing

7. Pot-Works, a flowerpot maker, has $500 in daily fixed costs and a single variable input (labour), with each worker paid a daily wage of $150. The first worker produces 100 pots, and each new worker adds 100 pots to the business's total output, up to a total of 500 pots per day. The first graph below shows Pot-Works' fixed cost, variable cost, and total cost. The second graph at the top of the next page shows the associated marginal cost curve.

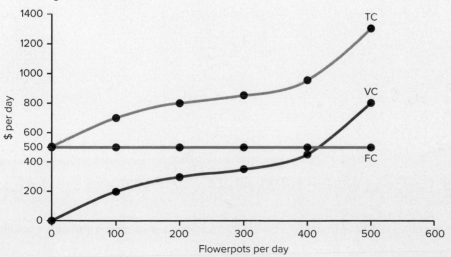

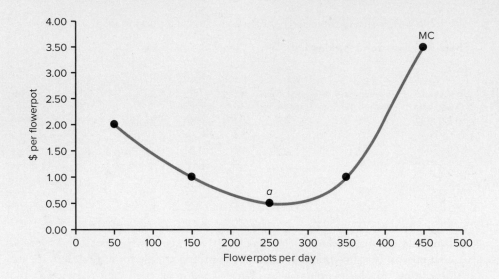

a. Based on these graphs, as quantity increases, what happens to total cost, variable cost, and fixed cost?

b. As quantity increases, what happens to marginal cost?

c. Outline how the changes in total and variable cost are related to marginal cost as quantity increases.

8. For each of the five points highlighted on the MC curve in Figure 4.6, identify the associated level of T-shirt output on the graph's horizontal axis, and explain how to derive each of these horizontal coordinates.

9. (Policy Discussion Question)
   How can governments play a role in promoting knowledge-based industries in which fixed costs are high and marginal costs are close to zero?

ADVANCING ECONOMIC THOUGHT

CRITIC OF THE MODERN CORPORATION

John Kenneth Galbraith and the Role of Management

**JOHN KENNETH
GALBRAITH**
© Bettman/CORBIS

GALBRAITH AND HIS INFLUENCE

John Kenneth Galbraith (1908-2006) was one of Canada's most notable intellectual exports. Born near Port Talbot, Ontario, he studied agricultural economics at what is now the University of Guelph. He then immigrated to the United States where, as a professor at Harvard University, he became one of the most widely-known economists in the latter half of the twentieth century.

A prolific writer, Galbraith caused considerable debate in the 1960s and 1970s about the role of the modern corporation. He popularized the view that corporate managers possess the real decision-making power in modern capitalist economies. These managers, according to Galbraith, are more interested in their own prestige and income than they are in making profit for their employers.

FINANCING CORPORATE ACTIVITY

To follow Galbraith's argument, we must first consider how corporations finance their operations. Unlike other types of businesses, corporations have a legal status independent of their owners, who have the advantage of limited liability. This means they can lose only what they put into the business. Corporations can acquire funds by issuing stocks and bonds.

Stocks Corporations sell stocks (also known as shares) through the stock market to buyers, who are known as shareholders. Stockbrokers act as go-betweens in this market, buying and selling stocks on behalf of their customers. People who purchase stocks of a certain corporation do so because they expect to receive dividends, which are periodic payments by the corporation to its shareholders. Shareholders may also expect the price, or resale value, of a company's stock to increase as its profit outlook improves. However, there are no guarantees to shareholders—the company may not perform as expected, and dividends may not be declared (corporations are not required to pay dividends). Also, changing conditions in the stock market can cause price fluctuations for a wide range of stocks.

Bonds Corporations can also raise funds by selling bonds. A bond is a type of loan governed by a formal contract that sets out when the borrower will provide interest payments and also when the original amount of the loan (known as the principal) will be paid back to the bondholder. Bonds differ from most other loan contracts in that they can be bought and sold. To convert a bond into cash, the bondholder does not return the bond to the borrower, but rather sells it to an interested buyer. Unlike shareholders, bondholders are considered to be lenders to the corporation, rather than its owners. Unless a corporation becomes insolvent, bondholders have no say in the company's operations.

SEPARATION OF OWNERSHIP AND CONTROL

According to Galbraith, the ways that corporations raise funds can cause a separation of ownership and control. Most large corporations have no single shareholder owning a significant portion of the shares, but are owned and managed by different groups. On the one hand, the owners are the corporation's shareholders who receive income through dividends and higher stock prices. On the other hand, the corporation's managers are, strictly speaking, employees. The interests of these two groups, according to Galbraith, do not coincide. A corporation's managers may be more interested in maximizing the company's sales revenue rather than its profit, since as the corporation expands, so will the managers' salaries and power in the organization. Managers may also siphon off profit by providing themselves with generous perks and rewards. While such actions go against shareholder interests, managers do not have to fear reprisals as long as the stake of each shareholder in the company is small enough to rule out a costly examination of management actions.

RELEVANCE FOR TODAY

Galbraith's outlook has been influential with the general public and with some economists. His critics suggest that recent developments in stock markets have tended to increase the power of shareholders over management. Since the 1980s, much attention has been focused on the frequency of corporate takeovers, in which one company buys a sufficiently large portion of another company's shares to control its operations. Corporate takeovers can either be friendly or hostile, depending on how those taking over a company view its current managers. When a takeover is hostile, managers are often turfed out, especially if they have been looking after their own interests rather than maximizing the company's profit. According to Galbraith's critics, the ever-present threat of a hostile takeover helps to ensure that managers act in the shareholders' interests. Galbraith and his supporters have replied that this possible check on inefficient or corrupt managerial performance is often negated by the ability of managers to control the flow of information about the corporation.

In recent years, high-profile bankruptcies in the US and several other countries have renewed interest in Galbraith's theories, as have the spate of revelations of misdoings by corporate managers, especially in the financial sector, in the aftermath of the 2008 credit meltdown. As these examples show, self-interested managers can use questionable accounting practices to hide their corporation's true financial situation, which makes it difficult, and at times impossible, for current and prospective shareholders to adequately judge the corporation's performance.

1. a. Are payments made by corporations to shareholders fixed or variable? Are payments made on bonds fixed or variable?
   b. For a wealth holder, what is one possible advantage of holding shares? What is one possible disadvantage of holding bonds?

2. What attributes make a corporation a likely object for a hostile takeover bid? Explain what makes these attributes significant.

3. What are some possible ways that corrupt corporate management could mask a company's financial troubles in their public accounting statements?

CHAPTER 5

Perfect Competition

How does a giant company like Bell Canada differ from a small-town restaurant or a single farmer who grows broccoli? From an economist's perspective, the main distinction is the type of market in which each producer does business. In this chapter, we will introduce the four market structures: perfect competition, monopolistic competition, oligopoly, and monopoly. We will then focus on the first of these structures, perfect competition. We will see that though perfect competition is not the most common market structure, it is an ideal against which all other markets are compared.

> Under perfect competition, the business dodoes, dinosaurs, and great ground sloths are in for a bad time—as they should be.
>
> -R.H. BORK AND
> W.S. BOWMAN JR.,
> AMERICAN LEGAL SCHOLARS

LEARNING OBJECTIVES After reading this chapter, you will be able to:

LO 1

Identify the four market structures and the main differences among them

LO 2

Describe the profit-maximizing output rule and explain how perfect competitors use it in the short run

LO 3

Identify how perfectly competitive markets adjust in the long run and the benefits they provide to consumers

5.1 | Market Structures

LO1 While product markets come in all shapes and sizes, each has one of four structures: perfect competition, monopolistic competition, oligopoly, or monopoly. The number of businesses involved in the market, whether or not a standard product is being sold, and the ease with which businesses can enter and exit the industry, all determine the market structure.

Perfect Competition

perfect competition: a market structure characterized by many buyers and sellers of a standard product and easy entry to and exit from the industry

The ideal form of competition, which we will focus on in this chapter, allows for the unobstructed operation of demand and supply forces. **Perfect competition** has three main characteristics: many buyers and sellers, a standard product, and easy entry to and exit from the industry. In a perfectly competitive market, businesses consider the price of the product they sell to be determined by the forces of demand and supply. While common in primary industries, such as agriculture, and in markets for financial assets, such as stocks, bonds, and foreign currencies, perfectly competitive markets are not common in most other sectors of the economy. It is for this reason that in Chapter 2, as well as in this chapter, the examples used to illustrate the dynamics of perfect competition are from this relatively narrow range of products. As we will see in Chapter 6, many real-world markets *approximate* perfect competition, but do not meet its ideal conditions exactly.

MANY BUYERS AND SELLERS
The most important feature of perfectly competitive industries is that there are large numbers of buyers and sellers. For example, in the Canadian broccoli market, there are many consumers and many farmers. As a result, no single participant is large enough to affect the prevailing price in the industry.

STANDARD PRODUCT
In a perfectly competitive market, each business supplies a product that is indistinguishable from that of other businesses. One farmer's crop of broccoli, for example, is not noticeably different from that same variety of broccoli produced by other farmers.

EASY ENTRY AND EXIT
Finally, for a market to be perfectly competitive, businesses must be free to enter or exit the industry. Compared with most other industries, for example, it is relatively easy for farmers to transfer resources from the production of other crops to the growing of broccoli, since agricultural land has a wide variety of uses. Similarly, farmers can leave the broccoli market with little difficulty by devoting resources to alternative agricultural uses.

Monopolistic Competition

monopolistic competition: a market structure characterized by many buyers and sellers of slightly different products, and easy entry to and exit from the industry

Monopolistic competition is the structure most prevalent in the service sector, for example the restaurant industry. This market structure is characterized by a large number of businesses (though not as many as in a perfectly competitive industry), perceptible differences among the products of competitors, and easy entry and exit of businesses. Product differences can be related to location, quality, or the image consumers have of each business's product.

Oligopoly

An **oligopoly** is a market in which there are only a few businesses, and entry to the industry is restricted. Oligopolies are extremely common in the Canadian economy (as in most other economies), as illustrated by the steel, automobile, and insurance industries. The products sold in oligopolies may or may not vary, depending on the particular market. For example, the steel industry produces a standard product, whereas the automobile and insurance industries offer some variety among their products.

oligopoly: a market structure characterized by only a few businesses offering standard or similar products and restricted entry to the industry

Monopoly

A **monopoly** is an industry in which a single business supplies a product with no close substitutes. This market structure is the exact opposite of perfect competition. Monopolies are quite common in the Canadian economy. Electrical power companies, for example, often have a monopoly in particular regions of the country. High-profile monopolies include Canada Post and Via Rail. Small companies, such as a caterer with exclusive rights to sell food at a particular sports stadium, can be monopolies as well.

monopoly: a market structure characterized by only one business supplying a product with no close substitutes and restricted entry to the industry

Entry Barriers

Markets that are oligopolies and monopolies require entry barriers to continue as such. **Entry barriers** are economic or institutional obstacles that stop potential competitors from setting up in an industry where economic profits are being made. There are six main entry barriers: increasing returns to scale, market experience, restricted ownership of resources, legal obstacles, market abuses, and advertising.

entry barriers: economic or institutional obstacles to businesses entering an industry

INCREASING RETURNS TO SCALE
In industries where established companies benefit from increasing returns to scale, and therefore decreasing average costs when output increases in the long run, small companies just entering the market will be unable to charge as low a price. This is because small companies find it difficult to raise sufficient funds to take full advantage of increasing returns to scale. Such obstacles arise because financial investments are often irreversible, increasing the risks associated with entering an industry.

In the extreme case, known as a **natural monopoly**, increasing returns to scale mean that it makes sense to have only one supplier of a product, given the size of the market. This applies to public utilities, which provide such products as water and such services as public transit. Having more than one company would require a large-scale duplication of inputs, thus leading to high per-unit costs and product prices.

natural monopoly: a market in which only one business is economically viable because of increasing returns to scale

While the concept is applicable to some markets, the term "natural monopoly" can be misleading, since there is nothing "natural" about this concept. For example, the telephone industry was once considered a natural monopoly, until recent technological innovations—such as cell phones and Internet phone services—made it possible to have

competition. Similarly, cable television companies that were once regional monopolies are gradually losing this status because of new forms of satellite delivery. In the market for electrical power, the emergence of alternate means of generating electricity, such as solar and wind power, means that this industry's natural monopoly features are now limited to power transmission, not power generation.

MARKET EXPERIENCE

Even in cases where increasing returns to scale are not predominant, well-established businesses may have a cost advantage over potential rivals, simply because of their experience. A business can learn from experience how to supply a product more efficiently, thus decreasing its per-unit costs at all possible output levels.

RESTRICTED OWNERSHIP OF RESOURCES

When one or a few businesses control supplies of a resource to make a product, they effectively bar other businesses from entering the industry. One example of such control has been the South African company De Beers, which until recently owned or controlled over 75 percent of the world's supply of diamonds.

LEGAL OBSTACLES

Legislation regarding, for example, patents or licences can act as a barrier to entry. A patent gives the exclusive right to produce, use, or sell an invention for a given period (now 20 years in Canada). This exclusive right allows individuals and companies to reap some rewards of their innovations. Companies can become monopolies with patented products, as the patent-holder for the artificial sweetener aspartame, known as Nutrasweet, did for many years. Government licensing, too, can create closed or regulated markets. For instance, only Canada Post has the legal right to provide regular mail service, making it a monopoly in this industry. Similarly, only a certain number of Canadian television or radio stations have broadcast rights within different regions of the country, thus making these broadcasting industries oligopolies.

MARKET ABUSES

predatory pricing: an unfair business practice of temporarily lowering prices to drive out competitors in an industry

Established businesses in an industry may use unfair practices to maintain their dominant positions. A business might, for example, temporarily drop the price of its product below average cost to drive a new competitor out of business. This illegal strategy (a criminal offence in Canada) is known as **predatory pricing**. At one time, predatory pricing was used in the international airline industry; some large companies cut fares only to increase them once upstart competitors had gone into bankruptcy.

ADVERTISING

The use of advertising as an entry barrier is most common in oligopolies, such as the beer and soft-drink industries. Because consumer preference for these products is so dependent on promotion, established companies with large advertising budgets can often stop small competitors from gaining a significant toehold in these markets. For example, the two beer companies with the largest presence in Canada, Molson Coors and AB-Inbev (seller of Labatt), use advertising to help them maintain sales of their various brands, which represent about 80 percent of the total quantity demanded in the Canadian beer market.

Do "new economy" industries exhibit entry barriers?

Some important markets in the new economy are oligopolies or even monopolies, suggesting the existence of entry barriers. In new economy industries, new types of entry barriers often appear alongside more traditional barriers, such as increasing returns to scale. For example, the network effect refers to the fact that some information products (for example, software such as a word-processing program, web resources such as a social networking site, or telecommunications services such as a text-messaging protocol) become more valuable when they are used by many people. Similarly, the lock-in effect refers to consumers' reluctance to buy a new information product (such as a particular brand of software) once they have already invested the time in learning or applying a similar product. In the case of Apple's iTunes, for example, consumers who use this software for buying music and movies soon acquire digital libraries configured using the provider's software. Users are therefore reluctant to switch to a competitor provider, especially if they are uncomfortable with the technical demands of converting digital files from one format to another. The lock-in effect can also be related to innovations in hardware design. For example, the oligopolistic nature of the e-book market—in which Amazon is a dominant player—is partly tied to the particular types of e-book readers that consumers choose to buy, since in many cases e-book readers are formatted to accept content from only one distributor. Once consumers have bought one of these readers, those uncomfortable with the technical demands of converting digital file formats are effectively limited in which content they can purchase, helping create a powerful barrier to entry. Similarly, in the closely connected market for electronic tablets, such as the iPad, consumers can typically buy digital products from a range of providers, but find it most convenient to make purchases from the tablet's manufacturer.

www.the-ebook-reader.com/ebook-reader.html

QUESTION What are some examples of new economy industries, besides e-books, in which network and lock-in effects have helped create oligopolies or monopolies?

Market Power

Businesses in perfectly competitive markets–or perfect competitors, as they may be called–are price-takers because they are forced to take the price for their product that is set by the market forces of demand and supply. In contrast, businesses in the remaining three types of markets have some influence over a product's price, so they are price-makers. In other words, these businesses have some measure of **market power**, or the ability to affect the price they charge. A business's market power depends on how easy it is for buyers to find substitutes for the business's output.

market power: a business's ability to affect the price of the product it sells

As a rule, a business in a monopoly (a monopolist) has the most market power. It deals with no competitors and has the largest possible size in relation to the industry. Because the monopolist sells a product with no close substitutes, the product's demand curve tends to be less elastic than for other products. A company in an oligopoly (an oligopolist) commonly has substantial market power because of the small number of competitors and the company's large size relative to the industry. A business in a monopolistically competitive market (a monopolistic competitor) has less market power because it faces many competitors and is small in relation to its market. Moreover, because it sells a product with close substitutes, its demand curve is relatively elastic. Finally, a perfect competitor has no market power because of its role as a price-taker. Figure 5.1 summarizes the attributes of different market structures.

FIGURE 5.1 | Attributes of Market Structures

	Perfect Competition	Monopolistic Competition	Oligopoly	Monopoly
Number of Businesses	very many	many	few	one
Type of Product	standard	differentiated	standard or differentiated	not applicable
Entry and Exit of New Businesses	very easy	fairly easy	difficult	very difficult
Market Power	none	some	some	great
Example	farming	restaurants	automobile manufacturing	public utilities

While perfect competitors have no market power due to the large number of businesses selling a standard product, a monopolist has a great deal of market power because it is the only seller of a product with few substitutes. Monopolistic competitors have some market power due to the differentiated products they sell, and oligopolists have even more, depending on the number of businesses in a particular industry.

BRIEF REVIEW

1. Product markets have one of four structures: perfect competition, monopolistic competition, oligopoly, or monopoly.

2. Market structure is determined by the number of buyers and sellers in the market, whether or not a standard product is being sold, and the ease with which businesses can enter or exit the market.

3. In monopolies and oligopolies, potential competitors face the entry barriers of increasing returns to scale, market experience, restricted ownership of resources, legal obstacles, market abuses, and advertising.

4. A business's market power, or ability to be a price-maker, tends to be greater for monopolists than for oligopolists, and greater for oligopolists than for monopolistic competitors. Perfect competitors possess no market power.

5.1 | PRACTICE PROBLEMS

1. Identify the market structure in which each of the following sellers operates:
   a. a café in a busy commercial district of a city
   b. a public transit company in a large metropolitan area
   c. a corporation that makes a popular brand of breakfast cereal
   d. an individual share-owner who sells 100 shares of RBC on the Toronto Stock Exchange
   e. a chartered bank that takes deposits and makes loans to businesses and households
   f. a creator of software apps for a popular brand of smartphone

2. Razor manufacturers often sell razor handles at relatively low prices while charging higher prices for razor blades, because consumers who have bought a razor handle at a low price are willing to pay a relatively high price for blades. What type of barrier to entry is this?

5.2 | Perfect Competition in the Short Run

How do businesses make operating decisions? They do so by comparing a range of potential revenues and costs. All businesses–whether they are perfect competitors, monopolistic competitors, oligopolists, or monopolists, and whatever their product–use the same general methods in pursuing maximum profit. However, each business must apply the methods differently according to the market structure in which it operates. To examine profit-maximizing decisions and actions, we will look first at a perfect competitor in the short run.

LO2

Business's Demand Curve

Because a perfect competitor is a price-taker, it must accept the price dictated by the market forces of demand and supply. Thus, the individual **business's demand curve** is different from the market demand curve. Recall that the market demand curve (D_m) has a negative slope, given that price and quantity demanded are inversely related. Because a perfect competitor is one of many businesses in a market, the quantity it chooses to supply has no effect on equilibrium price and quantity in the market. See the graph for the T-shirt market in Figure 5.2. (We chose a basic item such as plain T-shirts because they are exchanged in a market that approximates perfect competition.) On the left, the intersection of the market demand and supply curves (D_m and S_m) provides the equilibrium price of $6 per T-shirt. No matter how many shirts Pure 'n' Simple T-Shirts supplies, it will sell all it produces at a price of $6 per shirt. Thus, the individual business's demand curve (D_b) is horizontal, or perfectly elastic, at a price of $6 (as shown on the right in Figure 5.2).

business's demand curve: the demand curve faced by an individual business, as opposed to an entire market

Revenue Conditions

On the basis of the horizontal demand curve the business faces, the perfect competitor's total revenue (TR), or the overall earnings from selling a

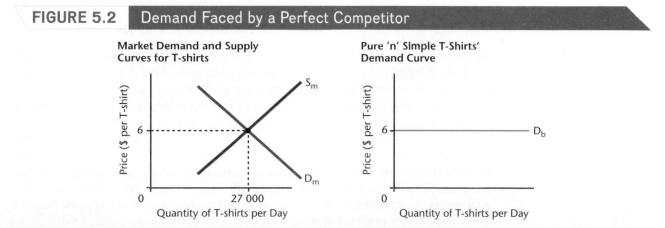

FIGURE 5.2 | Demand Faced by a Perfect Competitor

Market Demand and Supply Curves for T-shirts

Pure 'n' Simple T-Shirts' Demand Curve

Equilibrium occurs where the market demand and supply curves, (D_m and S_m) meet as shown on the graph on the left. The equilibrium price ($6) sets the position of the business's demand curve (on the graph on the right).

product, is calculated by multiplying the product's price by each potential quantity of output (q). For example, if Pure 'n' Simple T-Shirts sells 250 shirts at a price of $6, then its total revenue is $1500 (= $6 × 250). In addition to total revenue, the perfect competitor can examine two other revenue concepts to help make operating decisions: average revenue and marginal revenue.

AVERAGE REVENUE

average revenue: a business's total revenue per unit of output

Average revenue (AR) is the business's total revenue per unit of output (q). When Pure 'n' Simple T-Shirts sells 250 shirts and its total revenue is $1500, its average revenue equals $6 per unit of the product:

$$\text{Average revenue (AR)} = \frac{\text{total revenue (TR)}}{\text{quantity of output (q)}}$$

$$\$6 \text{ per shirt} = \frac{\$1500}{250 \text{ shirts}}$$

Note that average revenue for Pure 'n' Simple T-Shirts equals each shirt's $6 price. For all businesses, regardless of the market structure in which they operate, price will equal average revenue. This is because price can be defined in the same way as average revenue–as the business's total revenue per unit of output. The only exception to this rule occurs when a business practises price discrimination (or charges different prices to different customers for exactly the same product).

MARGINAL REVENUE

marginal revenue: the extra total revenue earned from an additional unit of output

Marginal revenue is the extra total revenue (ΔTR) earned when the business sells another unit of output (Δq). For example, if Pure 'n' Simple T-Shirts has an increase in total revenue from $1500 to $1620 when it increases its output from 250 to 270 shirts, then the marginal revenue of each of these last 20 shirts is $6:

$$\text{Marginal revenue (MR)} = \frac{\Delta TR}{\Delta q}$$

$$\$6 \text{ per shirt} = \frac{\$120}{20 \text{ shirts}}$$

Relationship between Revenue Conditions and Demand

As the case of Pure 'n' Simple T-Shirts illustrates, average and marginal revenues are always equal for a perfectly competitive business. This follows from the fact that average revenue (or price) is constant at each possible quantity of output. Recall that when an average value, such as average revenue, is constant, it equals its related marginal value–which, in this case, is marginal revenue.

Figure 5.3 illustrates the relationships among price, average revenue, and marginal revenue for our example of Pure 'n' Simple T-Shirts. In the table, the values for price (column 1), marginal revenue (column 4), and average revenue (column 5) are identical. The demand curve this perfect competitor faces also represents the business's average revenue and marginal revenue curves. Because the business is a price-taker, this combined curve shows a constant value at all quantities of output. Thus, for a perfectly competitive business:

Price (P) = Average revenue (AR) = Marginal revenue (MR)

FIGURE 5.3   Revenues for a Perfect Competitor

Revenue Schedules for Pure 'n' Simple T-Shirts

(1) Price (P) ($ per T-shirt)	(2) Quantity (q) (T-shirts per day)	(3) Total Revenue (TR) (P x q)	(4) Marginal Revenue (MR) (ΔTC/Δq)	(5) Average Revenue (AR) (TR/q)
$—	$ 0	$ 0		—
6	80	480	480/80 = $6	480/80 = $6
6	200	1200	720/120 = 6	1200/200 = 6
6	250	1500	300/50 = 6	1500/250 = 6
6	270	1620	120/20 = 6	1620/270 = 6
6	280	1680	60/10 = 6	1680/280 = 6

Revenue Curves for Pure 'n' Simple T-Shirts

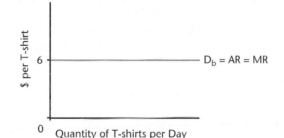

The business's demand schedule is shown in columns 1 and 2 of the table, which also shows that the constant values of price (P), average revenue (AR), and marginal revenue (MR) are identical. On the graph, the business's horizontal demand curve also represents its AR and MR curves.

Profit Maximization

Regardless of the market it operates in, any business can maximize its profit by following a single **profit-maximizing output rule**: produce the quantity of output (q) at which marginal revenue and marginal cost intersect.

Profit maximizing output rule: **Marginal revenue (MR) = Marginal cost (MC)**

Of course, this may result in an awkward quantity, such as 5.73 units, in which case the producer would choose the closest whole number, such as 6 units.

What happens if the condition MR = MC is not met? If each new unit of output is still providing more extra revenue to the business than it adds in cost, output should be increased to maximize profit. So, for example, if a business has a marginal revenue of $3 at its current output level, but the marginal cost of producing this unit is $2, the business is wise to increase its output. Recall that profit is the difference between total revenue and total cost. In this case, an additional unit of output is adding more revenue ($3) than it is costing ($2), so the profit added by this unit is $1. Profit-adding units such as these should be produced, no matter how small the contribution to profit. Once output is raised to the level at which marginal revenue and marginal cost are equal, any further increase in output would cause the business's profit to fall. So, for example, if a business produces beyond the output level at which marginal revenue and marginal cost are both $3, the business will soon find the marginal revenue of $3 surpassed by a marginal cost of $4. Hence, each additional unit is subtracting from profit, and output should be returned to the point at which marginal revenue and marginal cost are equal.

So, perfect competitors, like all other businesses, must determine their profit-maximizing output by looking at the business's cost and revenue figures. Pure

profit-maximizing output rule: produce at the level of output where marginal revenue and marginal cost intersect

'n' Simple T-Shirts, for example, would examine the data in Figure 5.4 and ask: "At what output level does marginal revenue intersect with marginal cost?" If the marginal revenue and marginal cost figures are graphed, as shown, we can see that the profit-maximizing point occurs at point *a*. As the closest associated whole number is 270, Pure 'n' Simple T-Shirts should choose a quantity of 270 T-shirts. Note that, at this point, marginal cost is rising (i.e., upsloping). This condition is essential to make the intersection of the MR and MC curves a profit-maximizing point. If marginal cost were instead falling (i.e., downsloping), then the point would not be a desired one. Units of output to the left of such a point, when seen on a graph, would provide a loss. Meanwhile the business would be sacrificing profitable units that could be gained by expanding output.

We can check this point against the table in Figure 5.4. The figures for marginal revenue (column 3) and marginal cost (column 4) pass through the same values nearest the output of 270 T-shirts (column 1). As can be seen in both the table and graph of Figure 5.4, the marginal cost of $5.50 falls short of the $6 marginal revenue between the output levels of 250 and 270 T-shirts. In

| FIGURE 5.4 | Profit Maximization for a Perfect Competitor |

Profit Maximization Table for Pure 'n' Simple T-Shirts

(1) Total Product (q)	(2) Price (P) (=AR)	(3) Marginal Revenue (MR)	(4) Marginal Cost (MC) ($\Delta TC/\Delta q$)	(5) Average Variable Cost (AVC) (VC/q)	(6) Average Cost (AC) (TC/q)	(7) Total Revenue (TR)	(8) Total Cost (TC)	(9) Total Profit (TR − TC)
0		$6	$1.75			0	$ 825	−$825
80	$6	6	1.33	$1.75	$12.06	$ 480	965	−485
200	6	6	2.50	1.50	5.63	1200	1125	75
250	6	6	5.50	1.70	5.00	1500	1250	250
270	**6**	**6**	10.50	**1.98**	**5.04**	**1620**	**1360**	**260**
280	6			2.29	5.24	1680	1465	215

Profit Maximization Graph for Pure 'n' Simple T-Shirts

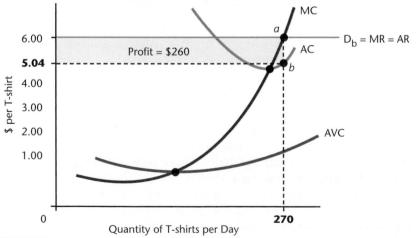

We can use either a graph or a table to find the quantity of output at which the business maximizes its short-run profit or minimizes its short-run loss. On the graph, the profit-maximizing output is found where the MR and MC curves intersect at point *a*. Total profit is the area of the shaded rectangle, the width of which is the profit-maximizing output (q) and the height of which is the average revenue (AR) minus average cost (AC) at points *a* and *b*. In the table, this profit-maximizing output occurs where marginal cost (MC) in column 4 passes through the same values as the constant marginal revenue (MR) in column 3. To verify the answer, calculate total profit at every output level, as in column 9, and then find the output level at which the highest positive (or lowest negative) profit is possible.

THINKING ABOUT ECONOMICS

Does the profit-maximizing output rule also apply when a business is making a loss at all possible quantities of output?

Yes. In this case, the profit-maximizing output rule is used to determine the quantity at which the business makes the minimum possible loss. Since a loss is simply a negative profit, this means finding the output level with a negative profit that is closest to zero.

QUESTION   **If a loss-making business is choosing between two output levels that provide negative profits of −$100 and −$300, which output level minimizes its loss?**

contrast, between 270 and 280 T-shirts, marginal cost (now $10.50) is greater than the constant $6 marginal revenue. (Remember that marginal revenue and marginal cost are defined as changes that occur when moving from one output to another.) This means that marginal revenue and marginal cost cross closest to 270 T-shirts. To verify this result, the business's owners might calculate the total profit they would make at every possible quantity of output. The highest positive (or lowest negative) profit figure in this column corresponds to the profit-maximizing quantity. In the case of Pure 'n' Simple T-Shirts, the owner would subtract total cost (column 8) from total revenue (column 7), to get total profit (column 9). So, scanning column 9, it is clear that the best choice is again at 270 shirts, where total profit reaches its highest value of $260 (= $1620 − $1360).

While the profit-maximizing point can be verified with the table, using a graph to find this point has a bonus: the graph immediately shows whether or not the business is earning an economic profit. When price (P) exceeds average cost (AC) at the profit-maximizing output, the business enjoys a short-run economic profit. If price is less than average cost, the business suffers a loss, or negative profit. If the business is at a profit-maximizing output where price and average cost are equal, the business is making no economic profit and is said to be at its **breakeven point**. Note, however, that at this point the business is still making a normal profit so that the owners are paid a sufficient amount to keep their funds and entrepreneurial skills tied up in the business.

breakeven point: the profit-maximizing output where price (or average revenue) equals average cost

Business's breakeven point:

Price (P) = Average Cost (AC) at the profit-maximizing output

Because the breakeven point is associated with a profit-maximizing output, this term has a special meaning in economics. Only at a single possible price will a business choose to break even. For a perfect competitor, this price equals minimum average cost. At higher prices, positive profits can be made, while at lower prices, the business can only make a loss.

Using a graph to show the profit-maximizing point has another bonus: with a graph, you can see immediately the relationship of a business's profit to its revenue and costs. The "revenue rectangle" has a height that is equal to price and a width that is equal to the quantity of output. The "cost rectangle" has a height that is equal to average cost and a width that is again equal to the quantity of output.

The "profit rectangle" is the area of the revenue rectangle less the area of the cost rectangle. So, for example, in Figure 5.4, the marginal cost curve and marginal revenue curve for Pure 'n' Simple T-Shirts intersect at the profit-maximizing point. As we also know from the table, this point is closest to an output level of 270 shirts and a price of $6 per shirt. Thus, the company's revenue rectangle has an area of $1620 (= $6 price × 270 quantity). The cost rectangle has an area of $1360 (= $5.04 average cost × 270 quantity). The profit rectangle, then, is the shaded area of $260 profit (= $1620 − $1360).

WHEN SHOULD A BUSINESS CLOSE?

Would Pure 'n' Simple T-Shirts remain in business if it were making a loss? In the short run, the business would likely continue to operate as long as it earned sufficient revenue to pay its variable costs. The remaining fixed costs would have to be paid in the short run, whether or not the company stayed in business. As long as a business's total revenue more than covers its variable costs, it is better off remaining in business rather than shutting down and still having to pay its fixed costs. If total revenue were to fall below variable costs, however, the business would not be able to fund even its day-to-day operations, and it would have no choice but to close down.

Recall that total revenue for a business is found by multiplying price by the quantity of output (TR = P × q). Recall also that the sum of variable costs (VC) and fixed costs (FC) equals total cost (TC), so that variable costs can be found by subtracting fixed costs from total cost at any given output level (VC = TC − FC), and average variable cost is variable costs divided by quantity (AVC = VC ÷ q). To consider the question of whether or not a business should continue to operate, take a look at average variable cost in another way: variable costs equal average variable cost multiplied by quantity (VC = AVC × q). Now we can establish a relationship between price and average variable cost by looking at the formula for total revenue (TR = P × q) and the formula for variable costs (VC = AVC × q). Recall that as long as variable costs do not exceed total revenue, the company should stay in business; if the variable costs begin to exceed total revenue, the company should shut down. Cancelling the quantity of output (q)–because it is a common element in both these expressions–means that total revenue exceeds variable costs as long as price is greater than average variable cost. Variable costs exceed total revenue when average variable cost exceeds price. At the profit-maximizing output where total revenue and variable costs (or average variable cost and price) are equal, the business reaches its **shutdown point**, which occurs at the point of minimum average variable cost:

shutdown point: the level of output where price (or average revenue) equals minimum average variable cost

Business's shutdown point: Total Revenue (TR) = Variable Cost (VC)

$$(P \times q) = (AVC \times q)$$

$$P = \text{minimum AVC}$$

Why does the shutdown point occur where price equals the minimum point on the average variable cost curve? Because at this point, the profit-maximizing output rule, MR = MC, is met at the same time as total revenue equals variable costs.

Consider our example of Pure 'n' Simple T-Shirts in Figure 5.5. When receiving a price of $6 per T-shirt (at point *a*), the company is maintaining a positive economic profit. If, for some reason, the price drops to $5, the business reaches its breakeven point (point *b*). At the lowest point on the average variable cost

FIGURE 5.5   Supply Curve for a Perfect Competitor

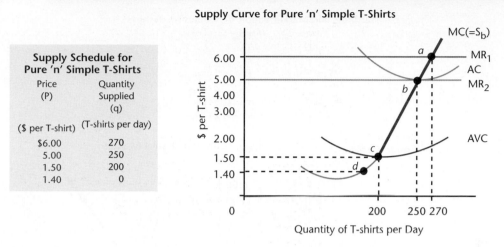

Supply Schedule for Pure 'n' Simple T-Shirts	
Price (P)	Quantity Supplied (q)
($ per T-shirt)	(T-shirts per day)
$6.00	270
5.00	250
1.50	200
1.40	0

At point *a* on the graph, price exceeds average cost (AC), and positive economic profits are made. Point *b* is the breakeven point, where price equals AC. At lower prices, the business makes a loss. Point *c* is the business's shutdown point, where price equals average variable costs (AVC). Below the shutdown point—for example, at point *d*—average variable costs would exceed price. The marginal cost curve (MC) above point *c* is the business's supply curve (S_b), the highlighted part of the curve.

curve, at $1.50 (point *c*), average variable cost equals price, thus variable costs equal total revenue.

Pure 'n' Simple T-Shirts' shutdown point:

$$\text{TR (\$300)} = \text{Variable Cost (VC)}$$
$$\text{P} \times \text{q (\$1.50} \times 200) = \text{AVC} \times \text{q (\$1.50} \times 200)$$
$$\text{P (\$1.50)} = \text{minimum AVC (\$1.50)}$$

Point *c* in Figure 5.5 is Pure 'n' Simple T-Shirts' shutdown point. If the price falls further, to a price such as $1.40 (point *d*), the company closes down its operations, since total revenue, which at 200 units of output would now be $280 (= $1.40 × 200), no longer covers variable costs ($300).

BUSINESS'S SUPPLY CURVE

Figure 5.5 also sheds light on how a change in price influences the operations of a perfectly competitive business. For example, if price falls from $6 to $5, the profit-maximizing output for Pure 'n' Simple T-Shirts changes from 270 to 250 shirts. At the same time, the business's economic profit falls to zero, since point *b* is the breakeven point. Notice that the effect of this price change on the business's quantity supplied is shown as a movement along the marginal cost curve (MC). Because the various profit-maximizing points for the business are all on the marginal cost curve, at least a portion of it represents the **business's supply curve** (S_b). The business's supply curve shows the quantity of output supplied by the business at every possible price. If price moves below the shutdown point (point *c*), Pure 'n' Simple T-Shirts will no longer be in business, and its output will fall to zero. Therefore, only that part of the marginal cost curve above this point is the business's supply curve (the highlighted part of the MC curve).

business's supply curve: a curve that shows the quantity of output supplied by a business at every possible price

FIGURE 5.6 — Supply Curves for a Perfectly Competitive Business and Market

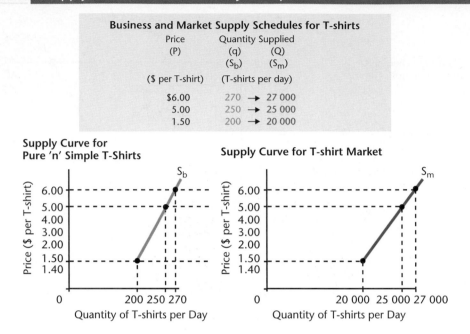

Business and Market Supply Schedules for T-shirts

Price (P)	Quantity Supplied	
	(q) (S_b)	(Q) (S_m)
($ per T-shirt)	(T-shirts per day)	
$6.00	270 →	27 000
5.00	250 →	25 000
1.50	200 →	20 000

Supply Curve for Pure 'n' Simple T-Shirts

Supply Curve for T-shirt Market

If the T-shirt industry is made up of 100 identical businesses, then find the market supply curve (S_m) by multiplying each output level on Pure 'n' Simple T-Shirts' supply curve (S_b) by 100.

MARKET SUPPLY CURVE

The market supply curve (S_m) for a perfectly competitive industry is created using the supply curves for all businesses in the market. So, for the T-shirt market in which Pure 'n' Simple T-Shirts operates, we have the supply curve S_m as illustrated in Figure 5.6. If there are 100 businesses all identical to Pure 'n' Simple T-Shirts in the industry, then find the market supply curve for T-shirts by adding the profit-maximizing outputs produced by all 100 businesses at each possible price. Thus, at a price of $6, the quantity supplied in the market (Q) would be 27 000 shirts (= 270 shirts × 100 businesses), given that each business's output is 270 shirts.

BRIEF REVIEW

1. All businesses—whatever market structures they operate in—maximize profits by finding the output level at which marginal revenue intersects marginal cost.

2. At the profit-maximizing output, a business's economic profit is positive if price is greater than average cost. When price and average cost are equal at the profit-maximizing output, the business is at its breakeven point, with economic profit at zero. If price is lower than average cost, then the business is operating at a loss, with negative economic profit.

3. For a perfect competitor, the breakeven point occurs when price equals minimum average cost. At lower prices, a perfect competitor will continue in business until the shutdown point, where price equals minimum average variable cost. A perfectly competitive business's supply curve is only the portion of its marginal cost curve that is above the shutdown point.

4. To find the supply for the entire perfectly competitive market, add the profit-maximizing outputs of all businesses in the market at each possible price.

5.2 | PRACTICE PROBLEMS

1. A fisher sells salmon in a perfectly competitive market and faces a price of $5 per kg at possible weekly outputs of between 0 and 5000 kg.
   a. What is the fisher's marginal revenue in this output range?
   b. Because the fisher operates in a perfectly competitive market, how are marginal revenue and price related?
   c. Draw the fisher's marginal revenue curve on a graph. Plot only the endpoints at 0 and 5000 kg to draw the curve.
2. A salmon fisher faces a price of $5 per kg and produces a weekly output of 4000 kg. The fisher's marginal cost is $4.95 between the possible outputs of 3800 and 4000 kg and $5.05 between the possible outputs of 4000 and 4200 kg. Assume that salmon fishing is a perfectly competitive industry.
   a. Is the fisher producing at the profit-maximizing point?
   b. If the average cost at an output of 4000 kg is $5.20, what is the fisher's total profit or loss?
   c. If the average variable cost at 4000 kg is $4.80, should the fisher stay in business in the short run?
   d. Draw the marginal revenue and marginal cost curves, a single point from the average cost and average variable costs curves, and the area representing the fisher's total profit or loss on a graph. Plot the endpoints at 0 and 5000 kg to draw the marginal revenue curve, two points for the marginal cost curve, one point for average variable cost, and one point for average cost, for a total of six points. Identify the area of profit or loss. Remember to plot marginal values such as marginal cost halfway between the relevant quantities on the horizontal axis.

5.3 | Perfect Competition in the Long Run

In the long run, ease of entry into and exit from a perfectly competitive market becomes a crucial factor. Short-run profits and losses cause perfectly competitive markets to move toward a point of long-run equilibrium. Entrepreneurs enter industries where an economic profit can be expected and leave those industries where there are losses. Movement to and from the industry continues until all the businesses in the market reach long-run equilibrium, at which point they are just breaking even, with price equalling average cost and a normal profit being made.

Figure 5.7 illustrates the operation of these long-run competitive forces for the T-shirt market. Assume that this is a constant-cost industry of the sort described in Chapter 3, in which input prices are fixed regardless of the quantity of T-shirts produced. As a representative business in this industry, Pure 'n' Simple T-Shirts is originally in long-run equilibrium at a price of $5 (point *a* on the left), which is determined by the intersection of the market demand and supply curves (D₀ and S₀) at point *c* on the graph on the right. At this price, Pure 'n' Simple T-Shirts produces 250 shirts per day. Since price equals average cost, it is breaking even, or making zero economic profit. If the market demand for

FIGURE 5.7   Long-Run Equilibrium for a Perfectly Competitive Business

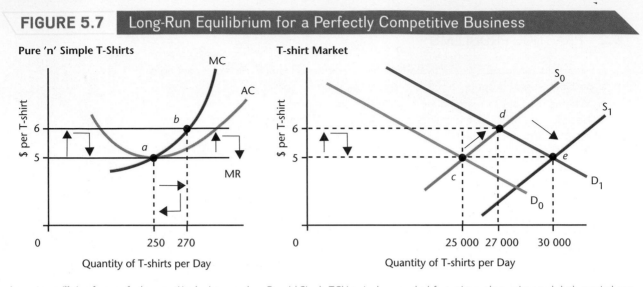

Long-run equilibrium for a perfectly competitive business, such as Pure 'n' Simple T-Shirts, is shown on the left at point *a*, where price equals both marginal cost and minimum average cost. Associated with this point is the equilibrium point *c* for the entire market on the graph on the right. An increase in market demand for T-shirts from D_0 to D_1 shifts equilibrium to point *d*. At the new profit-maximizing point for the business (point *b* on the left graph), a positive profit is being made. The lure of economic profit causes new businesses to enter the market. Assuming that this is a constant-cost industry, the market supply curve shifts to the right, from S_0 to S_1, until price is driven back down to its original level at point *e*. On the left graph, Pure 'n' Simple T-Shirts returns to its long-run equilibrium point *a* because of these competitive forces.

T-shirts increases from D_0 to D_1, the conditions of long-run equilibrium are temporarily broken. The new price in the market is $6, found at the intersection of D_1 and S_0 (point *d*). At this new price, Pure 'n' Simple T-Shirts makes a short-run economic profit, as shown on the graph on the left, since price (point *b*) exceeds average cost. This economic profit acts as a lure to new companies, who enter the industry and cause a shift in the market supply curve to the right, from S_0 to S_1. As a result, price returns to $5. With long-run equilibrium restored (point *e*), businesses in the market are again breaking even with a price equal to average cost, as exemplified by Pure 'n' Simple T-Shirts.

Benefits of Perfect Competition

The long-run equilibrium shown in Figure 5.7 illustrates the advantages of perfectly competitive markets for buyers. It also helps explain how, through the "invisible hand" of competition, consumers ultimately benefit when competitive producers act in their own self-interest. This is because a perfectly competitive market in long-run equilibrium meets two requirements known as minimum-cost pricing and marginal-cost pricing.

MINIMUM-COST PRICING

minimum-cost pricing: the practice of setting price where it equals minimum average cost

By operating at the breakeven point, where price equals minimum average cost, perfectly competitive businesses in long-run equilibrium satisfy the condition of **minimum-cost pricing**. If the price businesses are charging is above the minimum possible average cost, they can change the scale of production and reduce average costs further to maximize profit. By charging the minimum-cost price of $5 when it is in long-run equilibrium, Pure 'n' Simple T-Shirts, for example, chooses the least costly combination of inputs. Moreover, it is making zero economic profit, so that all these cost savings are passed on to T-shirt buyers. As long as this condition is met, the purchasing power of consumers' incomes when acquiring T-shirts is maximized.

MARGINAL-COST PRICING

In long-run equilibrium, perfectly competitive businesses also practise **marginal-cost pricing**, meaning they produce at an output level where the price that consumers are willing to pay equals marginal cost. The fact that they do so follows from the equality of marginal revenue and price for perfectly competitive firms. The profit-maximizing output rule means that perfect competitors choose the quantity of output at which marginal revenue and marginal cost intersect. Since marginal revenue and price are identical for individual perfectly competitive businesses, the profit-maximizing output rule can also be expressed as the condition that price equals marginal cost.

If each business's marginal cost incorporates all possible costs to society, then a perfectly competitive market in long-run equilibrium operates at a price that fully reflects the product's opportunity cost. Furthermore, if all markets in an economy are close to being perfectly competitive, society's scarce resources are distributed among industries in a way that maximizes the overall satisfaction of consumers. This is because the prices of various products accurately reflect the extra costs of producing them.

Considering again the example of T-shirts, if they are priced at $6, while the marginal cost of an additional T-shirt is $3, then more of society's resources should be devoted to T-shirt production. Otherwise, consumers who derive satisfaction (measured in dollar terms) worth less than $6 from an extra unit of this product are not purchasing it, even though many of them would be willing to pay more than the product's marginal cost. Production in this market should, therefore, be increased until marginal cost equals $6. In contrast, if T-shirts are priced at $6 but the marginal cost of an additional T-shirt is $9, then less of society's resources should be employed in T-shirt production, since some units are being produced for which the extra cost is greater than the satisfaction (measured in dollar terms) that consumers gain from these units. Only if marginal cost and equilibrium are the same will resources be distributed to this industry in a way that maximizes the satisfaction of consumers.

marginal-cost pricing: the practice of setting the price that consumers are willing to pay as equal to marginal cost

BRIEF REVIEW

1. In the long run, perfectly competitive markets reach an equilibrium at which businesses are at their breakeven point.

2. In long-run equilibrium, perfectly competitive businesses operate at the minimum-cost and marginal-cost prices, thereby benefiting consumers.

5.3 | PRACTICE PROBLEM

1. A perfectly competitive market is in short-run equilibrium with price at $50 and the average cost of businesses in the market at $40.
   a. Are businesses in this market making a loss or profit? Will businesses enter or leave the industry? What happens to the market supply curve and the profits or losses of businesses in the industry?
   b. At the initial price of $50, is the minimum-cost pricing rule being met?
   c. At the initial price of $50, is the marginal-cost pricing rule being met?

LAST WORD

In this chapter, we examined the main differences between market structures in terms of how many businesses there are in each market, whether or not their products are standard, and how easy it is to enter and exit the industry. We also examined how businesses can maximize economic profit by following the profit-maximizing output rule. We took the case of a perfectly competitive business to analyze how it maximizes profit in the short run and long run. Because perfect competitors are price-takers, they have to make only one decision when maximizing profit—how much quantity of output to produce. In the next chapter, when we switch our attention to businesses in the other market structures, we will see that they must choose from among various possible quantities and prices when maximizing their economic profit.

PROBLEMS

1. Categorize each seller below on the basis of the type of market it operates in:
   a. a cattle farmer
   b. a big-box retailer
   c. a picture-framing shop in a large metropolitan area
   d. a seller of Canadian dollars in foreign currency markets

2. The profit-maximization table below applies to a vegetable gardener who sells carrots at a local farmer's market.

Profit-Maximization Table for a Vegetable Gardener

(1) Price ($ per kilogram)	(2) Quantity (kilograms per month)	(3) Total Revenue ($)	(4) Total Cost ($)	(5) Marginal Revenue ($ per kilogram)	(6) Marginal Cost ($ per kilogram)	(7) Average Cost ($ per kilogram)	(8) Profit ($)
$_____	0	$ 0	$ 18				$_____
_____	100	49	41	$_____	$_____	$_____	_____
_____	200	98	57	_____	_____	_____	_____
_____	300	147	76	_____	_____	_____	_____
_____	400	196	112	_____	_____	_____	_____
_____	500	245	175	_____	_____	_____	_____
_____	600	294	330	_____	_____	_____	_____

a. Fill in the table.

b. What type of market does the gardener operate in?

c. Draw the gardener's marginal revenue, marginal cost, and average cost curves on a graph. Plot the endpoints at 0 and 600 kilograms to draw the marginal revenue curve, and plot six points each for the marginal cost and average cost curves, for a total of 14 points. Remember to plot marginal values such as marginal cost half-way between the two relevant quantities on the horizontal axis.

d. Identify the gardener's profit-maximizing or loss-minimizing quantity of output (rounded to the nearest 100 kilograms). At this quantity, what is the gardener's profit or loss?

e. Using your graph, at what price and quantity of output (rounded to the nearest 100 kilograms) would the gardener reach his breakeven point?

3. A fisher who sells mackerel in a perfectly competitive market faces revenues and costs shown in the table below.

(1) Price ($ per kilogram)	(2) Quantity (kilograms per day)	(3) Total Revenue ($)	(4) Fixed Costs ($)	(5) Variable Costs ($)	(6) Total Cost ($)	(7) Average Fixed Cost ($ per kilogram)	(8) Average Variable Cost ($ per kilogram)	(9) Average Cost ($ per kilogram)	(10) Marginal Cost ($ per kilogram)
	0	$ ____	$ 254	$ 0	$ ____				$ ____
$ 0.70	90	____	254	50	____	$ ____	$ ____	$ ____	____
0.70	170	____	254	70	____	____	____	____	____
0.70	260	____	254	117	____	____	____	____	____
0.70	300	____	254	149	____	____	____	____	____
0.70	340	____	254	238	____	____	____	____	____

a. Fill in the table.

b. Draw the marginal revenue, marginal cost and average cost curves in a graph. Plot only the two endpoints at 0 and 340 kilograms for the marginal revenue curve and plot five points each for the marginal cost and average cost curves, for a total of 12 points. Remember to plot marginal values such as marginal cost half-way between the two relevant quantities on the horizontal axis.

c. What is this fisher's profit-maximizing or loss-minimizing quantity of output? At this quantity, what is the fisher's profit or loss?

d. Identify the quantities associated business's breakeven point and its shutdown point.

e. What is the business's supply curve?

f. If price remains at 70 cents in the long run and the total costs shown in the table still apply, what action will this fisher take? Explain.

4. How do the conditions of minimum-cost and marginal-cost pricing correspond to Adam Smith's notion of the "invisible hand"?

Appendix | How Resource Markets Operate

Recall that in resource markets, households sell economic resources to businesses and households receive incomes in return. So, for their contribution of natural resources (including land), capital resources, and human resources (in particular labour and entrepreneurship), households receive incomes in the form of rent, interest, wages, and profit.

When analyzing resource markets, economists are especially interested in the way that resource prices are set, since these prices play a crucial role in determining people's incomes. For example, the relevant price in a labour market is the wage, which is the amount earned by a worker for providing labour for a certain period. **While a wage is usually thought of as a worker's income paid on an hourly basis, the term is used more broadly in economics to include workers' incomes (often known as salaries) paid by the day, month, or year.** It is important to remember that resource markets are affected by a wide array of factors. While social customs, governments, and labour unions play a part in determining resource prices, the interaction of demand and supply remains the central feature in these markets. Indeed, demand and supply conditions often influence resource markets *despite* outside intervention.

The Demand for Resources

Unlike the demand for consumer items, the demand for resources is determined indirectly. Since resources are used to produce final goods and services, it is the demand for these products that ultimately determines the demand for resources. For example, the number of printing presses demanded by a newspaper publishing company depends on the demand for the company's product. If the newspaper attracts more readers, the company will respond by increasing production and, therefore, buying more printing presses. Similarly, the number of workers hired by a car manufacturer depends on demand in the car market. A drop in the demand for cars will lower the demand for workers, resulting in hiring freezes, and perhaps even layoffs.

marginal productivity theory: the theory that businesses use resources on the basis of how much extra profit these resources provide

To calculate resource demand, economists use **marginal productivity theory**, which states that businesses use resources on the basis of how much extra profit these resources provide. Therefore, when deciding whether or not it is profitable to buy one more unit of a resource, businesses consider three factors: the resource's marginal cost, its marginal product, and the marginal revenue provided by each new unit of output produced.

First consider the example of a strawberry farm. Assume that the strawberry market is perfectly competitive, that the farmer hires labour in a perfectly competitive resource market, and that factors other than output and labour remain constant. So, the farmer hires workers in a market with many buyers and sellers, each of them having no effect on the prevailing price of the resource—namely, the hourly wage for farm workers. Therefore, the strawberry farm is a price-taker in both its product and resource markets.

According to the marginal productivity theory, a business decides how much of a resource to use on the basis of the resource's marginal product and marginal revenue, in addition to the resource's marginal cost to the business.

MARGINAL PRODUCT

The strawberry farmer must first estimate how much output will be added by hiring each new worker, while all other factors remain constant. In other words, the farmer must determine each worker's marginal product. Columns 1, 2, and 3 of the table in Figure A show the results. For the sake of simplicity, assume that the marginal product of labour starts to decline with the very first worker. At harvest time, the farmer hires more labour, and the total quantity of strawberries picked per hour increases, as shown in column 2; however, the marginal product of labour, shown in column 3, declines. For example, when the second worker is hired, the total product of strawberries rises from 10 to 18 kg, giving a marginal product for the second worker of 8 kg (= 18 − 10). With the third worker, the total product rises from 18 to 24 kg, giving a marginal product for the third worker of only 6 kg (= 24 − 18).

MARGINAL REVENUE

Once the marginal product of each worker is determined, the farmer must calculate the marginal revenue gained by selling the additional strawberries. Because the farmer is a price-taker in the perfectly competitive strawberry market, the price of strawberries is constant, and the price and marginal revenue for strawberries are equal. As a result, the farmer needs to know only the price of strawberries

---

FIGURE A   Labour Demand and Supply for a Product and Resource Price-Taker

Labour Demand and Supply Schedules for a Strawberry Farm

(1) Labour (L) (no. of workers)	(2) Total Product (q) (kilograms)	(3) Marginal Product (MP) (Δq/ΔL) (kilograms)	(4) Output Price (P) ($ per kilogram)	(5) Total Revenue (TR) (P × q)	(6) Marginal Revenue Product (MRP = ΔTR/ΔL)	(7) Marginal Resource Cost (MRC = W) ($ per hour)
0	0		$2	$ 0		
1	10	10	2	20	$20 (a)	$10
2	18	8	2	36	16 (b)	10
3	24	6	2	48	12 (c)	10
4	28	4	2	56	8 (e)	10 >(d)
5	30	2	2	60	4 (f)	10

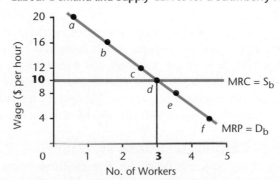

Labour Demand and Supply Curves for a Strawberry Farm

To find the price-taking business's demand for labour D_b, calculate the marginal revenue product (MRP), or the change in the business's total revenue from hiring each new worker. The business's supply curve S_b is the marginal resource cost (MRC) of each new worker. Since the business can hire workers at a constant wage, S_b is a horizontal line, and the business's profit-maximizing employment level of labour is at point d.

to find marginal revenue. Figure A shows the price of strawberries in column 4 as $2 per kilogram.

MARGINAL REVENUE PRODUCT

marginal revenue product: the change in total revenue associated with employing each new unit of a resource

The effects of marginal product and marginal revenue on the business's demand for labour are summarized by the concept of **marginal revenue product** (MRP), which is the change in total revenue associated with employing each new unit of a resource–in this case, each new worker. Because it represents the *extra* revenue provided by the *extra* units of output produced by each new worker, marginal revenue product incorporates both marginal revenue and marginal product. The table in Figure A shows total revenue in column 5 (found by multiplying each total product value by price), and the marginal revenue product (the change in total revenue) in column 6. Expressing the marginal revenue product on the graph gives us the marginal revenue product curve. So, in the strawberry farm example, total revenue is $20 (= 10 × $2) when employing one worker and $36 (= 18 × $2) when employing two workers. Therefore, the marginal revenue product of the second worker is the difference between the two amounts, or $16 (= $36 − $20), shown on the graph at point *b*.

BUSINESS'S LABOUR DEMAND AND SUPPLY

marginal resource cost: the extra cost of each additional unit of a resource

Given this information, it is a straightforward task for the strawberry farmer to find the profit-maximizing employment of labour. The extra cost of each additional unit of a resource for the business is referred to as **marginal resource cost** (MRC). In the case of the strawberry farmer, who is a price-taker in the labour market, and therefore a "wage-taker," marginal resource cost is simply the prevailing wage paid to farm workers. In our example, the wage is $10 per hour. According to the marginal productivity theory, the employer will use additional resources as long as marginal resource cost does not exceed marginal revenue product. Therefore, our strawberry farmer will hire three workers because each of the first three workers adds revenue ($20, $16, and $12, respectively) greater than the $10 cost per worker. Beyond this point, it is not profitable to hire more workers, since the extra revenue that each worker will provide the business will be less than the extra cost of that worker.

business's labour demand curve: a graph showing the possible combinations of workers demanded by a business at each possible wage

Expressed on the graph in Figure A, the marginal revenue product curve represents the **business's labour demand curve** (D_b). The business's labour demand curve shows how many workers are demanded by a business at each possible wage. The demand curve has a negative (downward) slope because businesses find it profitable to employ more workers at lower wages. The marginal resource cost curve represents the **business's labour supply curve** (S_b). This curve shows how many workers are supplied to a business at each possible wage. Because the business is a price-taker in the resource market, this curve is horizontal. No matter what action the strawberry farmer takes, the wage is fixed at the equilibrium wage determined by the entire market.

business's labour supply curve: a graph showing the possible combinations of workers supplied to a business at each possible wage

PROFIT-MAXIMIZING EMPLOYMENT RULE

profit-maximizing employment rule: a business should use a resource up to the point where the resource's marginal revenue product equals its marginal resource cost

The profit-maximizing point for the business occurs at the intersection of its demand and supply curves for labour (D_b and S_b). In other words, the business will hire workers up to the point where marginal revenue product and marginal resource cost are the same. This result provides a general **profit-maximizing employment rule** for resources. No matter what market a business operates in, it should use a resource up to the point where the resource's marginal revenue product equals its marginal resource cost.

Profit-maximizing employment rule:

$$\text{Marginal revenue} = \text{Marginal resource}$$
$$\text{product (MRP)} \qquad \text{cost (MRC)}$$

Note that the profit-maximizing employment rule parallels the profit-maximizing output rule outlined in the chapter, which is used by businesses to decide levels of output. Recall that the profit-maximizing output rule states that to maximize profits, a business should produce the quantity of output at which marginal revenue and marginal cost intersect, since up to this point, every unit of output has a marginal revenue that exceeds its marginal cost. Similarly, a business can maximize its profits by using a resource up to the point at which marginal revenue product equals marginal resource cost. By doing so, the business employs all units that give more extra revenue than they add to the business's costs.

MARKET DEMAND AND SUPPLY

Now, if we assume that all 1000 employers of farm workers in the region have marginal revenue product curves identical to the one shown in Figure A, we can derive the **labour market demand curve** (D_m). The labour market demand curve shows how many workers are demanded in a competitive labour market at each possible wage. By adding the labour demand curves of all businesses in this market, we have the labour market demand schedule and curve shown in Figure B. For example, at an hourly wage of $14, each of the 1000 farmers demands two workers, which gives a total labour demand of 2000. If the wage were to drop to $10, each farmer would demand three workers, raising total labour demanded in the market to 3000.

Corresponding to this market demand for farm workers is a **labour market supply curve** (S_m), which shows the total supply of workers offering their services in a certain labour market at each wage. This curve has a positive

labour market demand curve: a graph showing the possible combinations of workers demanded in a certain labour market at each possible wage

labour market supply curve: a graph showing the possible combinations of workers supplying their labour in a certain labour market at each possible wage

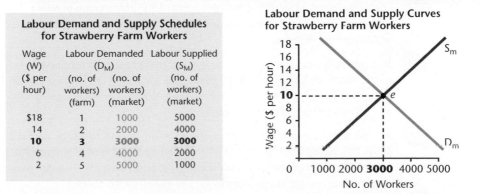

| **FIGURE B** | Demand and Supply in a Competitive Labour Market |

Labour Demand and Supply Schedules for Strawberry Farm Workers

Wage (W) ($ per hour)	Labour Demanded (D_M) (no. of workers) (farm)	Labour Demanded (D_M) (no. of workers) (market)	Labour Supplied (S_M) (no. of workers) (market)
$18	1	1000	5000
14	2	2000	4000
10	**3**	**3000**	**3000**
6	4	4000	2000
2	5	5000	1000

Labour Demand and Supply Curves for Strawberry Farm Workers

The market demand curve for strawberry farm workers (D_m) is found by adding together the workers demanded by each farm at various wages. In a competitive labour market, this demand curve and the market supply curve (S_m) intersect at equilibrium point *e*.

(upward) slope because, in general, higher wages in a given market encourage more workers to offer their labour in that market. Suppose that for our strawberry market, wages increase from $10 per hour to $14 per hour. Figure B shows that this wage increase would increase the quantity of farm workers supplied from 3000 to 4000. Figure B also demonstrates another feature of resource markets that is similar to that in product markets: equilibrium occurs at the intersection of the labour market supply and demand curves.

MARKETS FOR OTHER RESOURCES

While marginal productivity theory can be employed in analyzing labour markets, this theory is not always applicable to other resources. In theory, a business should make choices about all economic resources on the basis of each resource's marginal revenue product and marginal resource cost. In practice, however, marginal revenue product tends to be calculated for labour and for natural resources, but not for the other economic resources. This is because both labour and natural resources can be measured in standardized units–for example, an hour of a certain type of labour or a hectare of a certain grade of land. In contrast, it is usually harder to calculate marginal revenue product for capital goods. While it is possible to calculate the marginal revenue product of a particular material or type of machine used by a business, this cannot be done for an entire investment project, such as when a business contemplates building a factory. One investment project differs so much from another that it is impossible to measure them in standardized units. Because they are physically indivisible, they must be counted in monetary terms–the number of dollars a business needs to undertake a certain investment project.

BRIEF REVIEW

1. Resource markets, like product markets, are governed by the forces of demand and supply. However, the demand for resources is determined indirectly.

2. On the basis of the profit-maximizing employment rule, businesses decide how much of a resource to use by equating the resource's MRP (the change in total revenue associated with each new unit of resource) and MRC (the extra cost to the business of employing each additional unit of resource).

3. In a perfectly competitive resource market, the business is a price-taker; therefore, the business's resource supply (or MRC) curve is a horizontal line. In this market, the profit-maximizing employment level occurs where the business's resource demand (or MRP) curve and its resource supply curve intersect.

4. In a perfectly competitive resource market, the market's resource demand is the sum of the individual businesses' resource demand. The market's resource supply is the sum of all the individual resource owners' resource supply. Equilibrium is the point at which the market demand and market supply curves for the resource intersect.

5. Marginal productivity theory is commonly employed in analyzing markets and natural resources, but not for capital goods and entrepreneurship because of difficulties in measurement.

PRACTICE PROBLEM

1. A farmer whose revenue and costs data are shown in the table below sells pumpkins in a perfectly competitive product market at a price of $1 per kg and hires workers in a perfectly competitive labour market at an hourly wage of $7.50.

Marginal Revenue Product for a Pumpkin Farmer

(1) Labour (no. of workers)	(2) Total Product (kilograms per hour)	(3) Marginal Product (kilograms per hour)	(4) Product Price ($ per kilogram)	(5) Total Rev- enue ($ per hour)	(6) Marginal Revenue Product ($ per hour)
0	0	$ _____	$1	$ _____	$ _____
1	15	_____	1	_____	
2	27	_____	1	_____	_____
3	36	_____	1	_____	_____
4	42	_____	1	_____	_____
5	45	_____	1	_____	_____

a. Fill in the table.
b. What is the farmer's profit-maximizing employment level?
c. Draw a graph showing the marginal revenue product and marginal resource cost curves, as well as the profit-maximizing employment level. Plot only the endpoints of the marginal revenue product and marginal resource cost curves, for a total of four points. Remember to plot marginal values halfway between the two relevant employment levels on the horizontal axis.
d. If there are 10 000 identical employers of farm workers in this region, then how many farm workers will be demanded in the market at a wage of $7.50?

PROBLEMS

1. The table below gives short-run production conditions for Ham-It-Up, a company that makes radios.

Production Conditions for Ham-It-Up Radios

(1) Labour (number of workers)	(2) Total Product (radios per week)	(3) Marginal Product (radios per worker)	(4) Average Product (radios per worker)
0	0		
1	140	_____	_____
2	240	_____	_____
3	300	_____	_____
4	320	_____	_____
5	300	_____	_____

a. Fill in the table.
b. Describe how marginal product behaves as each new worker is hired.
c. How are marginal product and average product related at each employment level?
d. As employment is increased, does production for Ham-It-Up Radios exhibit ranges of increasing, decreasing, and negative returns?

e. Draw one graph showing the total product curve and another graph showing the marginal product and average product curves. In the first graph, plot points for the total product curve at each employment level up to five workers, including the point (0, 0), for a total of six points. In the second graph, plot only the end-points of the marginal product and average product curves, for a total of four points. (Exclude the origin point for both curves.) Remember to plot marginal values such as marginal product halfway between the two relevant employment levels on the horizontal axis.

2. The table below shows production and revenue data for a salmon fisher who sells his catch for $2.50 per kilogram in a perfectly competitive product market, and hires boat-hands in a perfectly competitive labour market at an hourly wage of $15.

Marginal Revenue Product for a Salmon Fisher

(1) Labour (no. of workers)	(2) Total Product (kilograms per hour)	(3) Marginal Product (kilo- grams per hour)	(4) Product Price ($ per kilo- gram)	(5) Total Revenue ($ per hour)	(6) Marginal Revenue Product ($ per hour)
0	0	$_____	$2.50	$_____	$_____
1	20	_____	2.50	_____	_____
2	36	_____	2.50	_____	_____
3	48	_____	2.50	_____	_____
4	56	_____	2.50	_____	_____
5	60		2.50	_____	

a. Fill in the table.
b. At an hourly wage of $15, how many boat-hands should this fisher employ?
c. Draw a graph showing the marginal revenue product and marginal resource cost curves, and identify the profit-maximizing employment level. Plot only the end-points of the marginal revenue product and marginal resource cost curves, for a total of four points. Remember to plot marginal values halfway between the two relevant employment levels on the horizontal axis.
d. If the price of salmon falls from $2.50 to $1.50, the values of total revenue and marginal revenue product change at every employment level in the table. What are these new values? At the same hourly wage of $15, how many boat-hands should this fisher now employ?
e. Add the new marginal revenue product curve and profit-maximizing employment level to the graph you drew in part c. Plot only the endpoints of the marginal revenue product curve.

CAN CAPITALISM SURVIVE?

Joseph Schumpeter and the Prospects for Capitalism

Joseph Schumpeter (1883–1950) is one of the most famous economists of the twentieth century. The originality of his ideas and the breadth of his learning have been matched by few others. Born into a middle-class business family, he enjoyed an aristocratic upbringing after his father died and his mother married a high-ranking military commander in the Austrian army. Schumpeter studied law and economics at the prestigious University of Vienna. After working as a lawyer, he took up a career as a professor of economics. For a brief period after World War I, he served as the Minister of Finance in the Austrian government. In the 1930s, the political turmoil surrounding the rise of the Nazis in Germany caused him to move to the United States, where he taught for many years at Harvard University.

JOSEPH SCHUMPETER
© Bettman/CORBIS

SCHUMPETER AND HIS INFLUENCE

Schumpeter's work is fascinating because of his ability to combine seemingly contradictory ideas. Although he was a strong supporter of capitalism and private markets, he devised a theory of capitalist development that has interesting parallels with the work of Karl Marx. Like Marx, Schumpeter used not only the tools of economics, but also the other social sciences. He was, therefore, able to highlight the role played by politics and culture in affecting economic conditions.

The crucial player in Schumpeter's theory of capitalism is the entrepreneur. For Schumpeter, entrepreneurs are much more than risk-takers—they are innovators who, through imagination and creativity, supply new products or adopt new types of technology. While not necessarily inventors, they are able to bring fresh ideas to the marketplace. As Schumpeter noted:

> To carry any improvement into effect is a task entirely different from the inventing of it, and a task, moreover, requiring entirely different kinds of aptitudes. Although entrepreneurs, of course, may be inventors just as they may be capitalists, they are inventors not by nature of their function but by coincidence and vice versa.[1]

Schumpeter saw entrepreneurs as the driving forces of economic progress. He believed that a capitalist system would ensure the fastest possible pace of technological change because capitalism allows entrepreneurs to keep the profits resulting from their innovations.

According to Schumpeter, the importance of perfectly competitive markets is overrated in economic theory. In real capitalist economies, he said, competition usually takes place between a few rivals in oligopolistic markets. In pursuit of profit and market power, the rivals introduce new products and production methods, which, in turn, lead to economic growth and revitalize the capitalist system. Schumpeter called this process "creative destruction," since it destroys parts of the economy at the same time as it creates new industries and products.

PREDICTIONS FOR THE FUTURE

Given Schumpeter's opposition to socialism and his strong support for capitalism, we might expect that he would predict the downfall of socialism and the final victory of capitalism throughout the world. On the contrary, he believed that in the long run, capitalism was doomed, not because of its internal economic contradictions, but because of cultural and political trends flowing from its success. Hence, in answer to the question, "Can capitalism survive?" he gave the straightforward answer, "No. I do not think it can."[2]

According to Schumpeter, because of the advantages they possess, giant companies will gradually take over most industries. In the process, the innovative spirit that once guided them will be crushed, as the imaginative entrepreneur is replaced by the cautious professional manager at the helm of business. Without the entrepreneur, there will no longer be a force in society to support the institution of private property.

At the same time, the growing class of intellectuals–professors, writers, and journalists–who live well off the prosperity provided by the capitalist system, will use their persuasive powers to turn others against capitalism. Therefore, a majority of people will also become opposed to property rights. Why are so many intellectuals hostile to capitalism? Because, stated Schumpeter, most of them are outsiders who are much more competent at criticizing the system than they are at working within it.

Schumpeter predicted that the elimination of the entrepreneur and the new popular hostility toward capitalism would lead to more government involvement in the economy. Attempts would be made by government bureaucrats to smooth out economic fluctuations, as well as reduce inequalities in the distribution of incomes. Gradually, the role of private property would shrink, and capitalist societies would turn toward socialism–of either the democratic or the authoritarian variety.

RELEVANCE FOR TODAY

It is important to note that Schumpeter developed his theories before and during World War II, before the massive expansion in government activity that took place in developed capitalist countries, such as Canada. As criticism of capitalist institutions became common in Canada and other countries in the 1960s and 1970s, many commentators suggested that Schumpeter's forecasts contained a good deal of truth. Are his predictions still as applicable in the 2010s as they were in previous decades? Some would argue that there has been a resurgence in entrepreneurship and popular support for capitalism that now makes Schumpeter's theories less relevant than they once were:

> During the late 1960s . . . Schumpeter's predictions seemed to be coming true. Third World nations, newly liberated from Europe, turned to socialism. By the early 1970s, Ph.D.s were driving taxicabs and blasting the establishment. But what did the 1980s bring us? Yuppies, short hair, striped shirts, and a parade of underdeveloped nations trading *Das Kapital* in for *Dress for Success*. . . . Nobody urges centralized planning anymore. . . . Even if a return to market mechanisms does not magically turn poverty into wealth, at least governments have jettisoned rigid, ideological abhorrence of market economic systems.[3]

In the aftermath of the 2008 credit meltdown, criticism of capitalist institutions, especially in the financial sector, came under renewed scrutiny and criticism, though it is not clear whether this shift in attitudes will be long-lasting. But, right or wrong, Schumpeter's work provides a classic example of how economic theorizing can be made to include not only economic factors, but also political and social trends. Meanwhile, his emphasis on entrepreneurship and innovation as drivers of growth has become an integral element of mainstream economic theory, as has his view of the potential competition to be found in oligopolistic markets.

1. Outline one possible reason why Schumpeter's predictions about capitalism have not been borne out since the 1980s.

2. If alive today, Schumpeter would doubtless argue that the process of creative destruction continues in capitalism. What might be a contemporary example from the Canadian economy?

Notes

[1] Joseph A. Schumpeter, *The Theory of Economic Development* (New York: Oxford University Press, 1961), pp. 88-89.

[2] Joseph A. Schumpeter, *Capitalism, Socialism and Democracy* (New York: Harper & Row, 1976), p. 61, as quoted in *New Ideas From Dead Economists* by Todd G. Buchholz. Copyright © 1989 by Todd G. Buchholz. Used by permission of Dutton Signet, a division of Penguin Books USA Inc.

[3] Todd G. Buchholz, *New Ideas From Dead Economists*. Copyright © 1989 by Todd G. Buchholz. Used by permission of Dutton Signet, a division of Penguin Books USA Inc.

CHAPTER 6

Monopoly and Imperfect Competition

Monopolies are a notable part of the Canadian economy, as illustrated by businesses as large as a public transit system in any of Canada's major cities, or as modest as a small-town newspaper. Pricing decisions in all such cases are analyzed with the same set of tools. Monopolistic competition and oligopoly—often grouped together and called imperfect competition—are even more common. We will see how the market forces facing each of these types of firms differ from those facing perfect competitors, and that Adam Smith's invisible hand of competition does not necessarily apply in all real-world markets.

> The biggest things are always the easiest to do because there is no competition.
>
> -SIR WILLIAM VAN HORNE,
> CANADIAN CAPITALIST

LEARNING OBJECTIVES   After reading this chapter, you will be able to:

LO 1

Outline the demand conditions faced by monopolists, monopolistic competitors, and oligopolists

LO 2

Explain how monopolists maximize profits

LO 3

Explain how monopolistic competitors and oligopolists maximize profits

LO 4

Describe non-price competition and the arguments over industrial concentration

6.1 | Demand Differences

While perfectly competitive markets do exist, they are by no means the most common market structure. Actual markets are more likely to exhibit features of either monopoly or imperfect competition—a category that includes both monopolistic competition and oligopoly. We will look first at the demand conditions faced by businesses in each of these market structures, and then at how businesses in each of these markets maximize profit.

Monopoly

As sole supplier of a product, a monopolist faces the same demand curve as that for the entire market—a curve with a negative slope. Therefore, the monopolist has considerable ability to influence price. Figure 6.1 gives the example of Megacomp, the only seller of large supercomputers.

Monopolistic Competition

Because it has some ability to influence the price it charges, a monopolistic competitor faces a different type of demand curve. Consider the example of Jaded Palate, a restaurant that serves highly spiced Cajun food. Customers of this restaurant view its food as distinct from that of nearby restaurants, none of which specializes in this cuisine. If Jaded Palate raises the average price of its meals from $10 to $11, as shown in Figure 6.2, it will lose some, but not all, of its customers. Quantity demanded will fall from 200 to 100 meals a day. If the restaurant lowers the average price of meals from $10 to $9, there will be an increase in quantity demanded, from 200 to 300. Hence, the restaurant faces the demand curve D. Since customers see other restaurants as possible substitutes, a given percentage change in the price of a meal causes an even greater percentage change in quantity demanded. In other words, the monopolistic competitor's demand curve is elastic. As a general rule, the demand curves for monopolistic competitors are more elastic than the demand curves for monopolists.

FIGURE 6.1   Demand Faced by a Monopolist

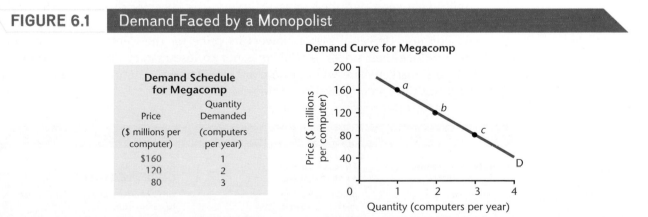

The demand curve for the individual business is identical to the market demand curve (D). As D shows, if Megacomp increases its price, quantity demanded decreases.

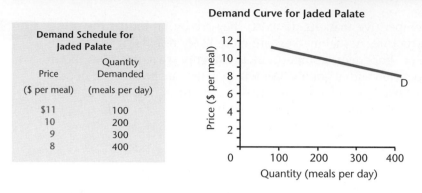

FIGURE 6.2	Demand Faced by a Monopolistic Competitor

Demand Schedule for Jaded Palate

Price	Quantity Demanded
($ per meal)	(meals per day)
$11	100
10	200
9	300
8	400

Demand Curve for Jaded Palate

The restaurant's demand curve (D) has a negative slope so that a change in price causes an opposite change in quantity demanded. Since demand is elastic, the change in quantity demanded is relatively large compared with the initial change in price.

Oligopoly

mutual interdependence: the relationship among oligopolists in which the actions of each business affect the other businesses

In the case of an oligopoly, the fact that each business makes up a considerable part of the market leads to **mutual interdependence**. This is a situation where businesses in the industry cannot afford to ignore their competitors' actions that might indirectly affect sales. Because of mutual interdependence, businesses in an oligopoly can operate in either of two ways: as rivals or as fellow players who cooperate to increase combined profits.

RIVALRY AMONG BUSINESSES

market share: a business's proportion of total market sales

Businesses in an oligopoly where rivalry prevails are concerned with maintaining their **market share**, or the proportion of total market sales they control. Because their actions influence their rivals, these businesses must take into account the reactions of competitors whenever they consider a price change. They must then predict how the responses of other businesses will influence their own market share.

Consider the hypothetical situation of Universal Motors and its luxury car, the Centaur. If Universal Motors increases its price for the Centaur, competitors will likely keep the prices of their luxury cars constant to increase their sales. Thus, Universal Motors will lose some of its market share to its competitors. If, in contrast, Universal Motors lowers its price for the Centaur, its competitors will reduce their prices as well so as not to lose market share. Thus, Universal Motors' market share will remain constant. Figure 6.3 summarizes these actions and reactions among rival companies in an oligopoly.

FIGURE 6.3	Actions and Reactions Among Rivals in an Oligopoly

Action of Company A	Probable Response of Competitors	Effect on Company A's Market Share	Company A's Quantity Demanded
Raise price	keep prices constant	product now high-priced, so market share falls	large decrease as market share lost to competitors
Lower price	match price drop	since all companies selling at lower price, Company A's market share stays constant	small increase as lower prices for all companies attract new buyers

Now, let us continue the example of Universal Motors in Figure 6.4. If the original price of the Centaur is $30 000, a price increase to $35 000 will cause competitors to keep their prices constant, and the market share for the Centaur will drop from 20 000 to 10 000 cars. The change in quantity demanded (from point *b* to point *a*) causes the demand curve for this price range to be fairly flat. If Universal Motors lowers the price of the Centaur from $30 000 to $20 000, competitors will lower the prices of their cars. Sales of Centaur cars will increase–from 20 000 to 25 000–but not in equal proportion to the price drop. Thus, the demand curve for this price range (from point *b* to point *c*) is steep. As shown on the graph in Figure 6.4, the result is a **kinked demand curve**–a demand curve with two segments, one fairly flat and one steep, with the kink or bend at the original price of $30 000 (point *b*). This kinked demand curve is typical of oligopolies in which businesses jostle one another for profit and market dominance.

kinked demand curve: a demand curve with two segments, one fairly flat and one steep, that is typical of rival oligopolists

COOPERATION AMONG BUSINESSES

Oligopolists can also cooperate in ways that are against the interests of consumers. In an oligopoly, for example, there may be an unspoken understanding that one company–usually the largest–acts as the price leader. In a case of **price leadership**, other companies will follow any price change initiated by the price leader and adjust their output accordingly. In the past, price leadership has occurred in the automobile and farm-machinery industries. Oligopolies may take their cooperation even further. When oligopolists band together–either secretly or openly–to act as much as possible as if they were a monopoly, they are practising **collusion**. In this case, they act jointly to maximize total profits. To do so, the businesses must first estimate the most profitable output level and then agree to maintain this total market output and its associated price. When this sort of agreement among producers is a formal one, the oligopolists together are known as a **cartel**. The best-known example of a cartel is the Organization of Petroleum Exporting Countries (OPEC).

price leadership: an understanding among oligopolists that one business will initiate all price changes in the market and the others will follow by adjusting their prices and output accordingly

collusion: oligopolists acting together as if they are a monopoly

cartel: a union of oligopolists who have a formal market-sharing agreement

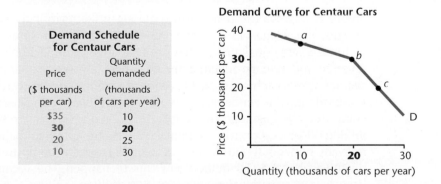

FIGURE 6.4	Demand Faced Among Rivals in an Oligopoly

Demand Schedule for Centaur Cars

Price ($ thousands per car)	Quantity Demanded (thousands of cars per year)
$35	10
30	**20**
20	25
10	30

The demand curve for Centaur cars is shown as two differently sloped segments. When Universal Motors raises the price above $30 000, competitors keep their prices constant to raise their sales. The results are a substantial drop in the quantity demanded of Centaur cars, and a flat demand curve (from point *b* to point *a*). If price moves below $30 000, competitors are forced to drop their prices as well. Thus, quantity demanded for Centaur cars increases by only a minor amount, producing a steep demand curve (from point *b* to point *c*).

BRIEF REVIEW

1. Monopolists face the demand curve of the entire market—a downward-sloping curve.

2. A monopolistic competitor faces an elastic demand curve with a negative slope.

3. Oligopolies are characterized by mutual interdependence. Rivalry among oligopolists creates a kinked demand curve because of competitors' responses to price changes.

4. Cooperation among oligopolists may lead to price leadership or collusion. If collusion is formal and explicit, the companies make up a cartel.

6.1 | PRACTICE PROBLEM

1. Consider the following demand curves facing a business: (i) relatively inelastic, (ii) perfectly elastic, (iii) kinked, and (iv) relatively elastic. Identify which one best describes:
   a. a perfect competitor
   b. a monopolistic competitor
   c. a monopolist
   d. an oligopolist in a market where rivalry exists

6.2 | Monopoly

LO2 How does a monopolist choose to maximize its profit? Because it is a price-maker, the monopolist must establish both a level of output and a price when attempting to maximize profit. Thus, the monopolist applies the profit-maximizing output rule in a different way from that used by perfectly competitive businesses.

Revenue Conditions

Figure 6.5 shows the relationships among price, marginal revenue, and average revenue for Megacomp. In the table, price (column 1) and average revenue (column 5) are equal, just as they are for perfect competitors. However, marginal revenue and average revenue are no longer always the same. Recall that if an average value, such as average revenue, declines, then its corresponding marginal value (marginal revenue) is below it. For example, when Megacomp sells its first computer, the business's average and marginal revenues are both equal to $160 million. (Remember that marginal values are graphed halfway between the relevant horizontal coordinates). But once the next computer is added, average revenue falls to $120 million. For this to happen, the second computer must have a lower marginal revenue of $80 million. Selling the second computer requires that the price of *both* computers sold be lowered. Therefore, the extra $120 million from selling the second computer must be adjusted down by the $40 million drop in price on the first computer, giving the marginal revenue of $80 million (= $120 million − $40 million).

FIGURE 6.5	Revenues for a Monopolist

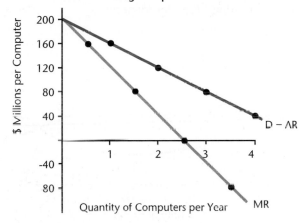

Revenue Schedules for Megacomp

(1) Price (P) ($ millions per computer)	(2) Quantity (Q) (computers per year)	(3) Total Revenue (TR) (P × Q) ($ millions)	(4) Marginal Revenue (MR) (ΔTR/ΔQ) ($ millions per computer)	(5) Average Revenue (AR) (TR/Q) ($ millions per computer)
	0	$ 0		
$160	1	160	$160	$160/1 = 160
120	2	240	80	240/2 = 120
80	3	240	0	240/3 = 80
40	4	160	–80	160/4 = 40

Revenue Curves for Megacomp

Megacomp's demand schedule is shown in columns 1 and 2. Though the values for average revenue (AR) in column 5 are the same as for price (P), Megacomp's marginal revenue (MR) in column 4 equals P and AR only at their initial values. Beyond this point, MR falls more quickly than price when quantity rises, as shown on the graph.

On the graph shown in Figure 6.5, the demand (D) and average revenue (AR) curves for Megacomp are identical, but the demand and marginal revenue (MR) curves intersect only at their initial points. As the quantity of output for the business rises, marginal revenue drops below price.

Profit Maximization

Given its ability to choose price, the monopolist maximizes profit by first finding the appropriate quantity of output, and then using this quantity level to determine the highest possible price it can charge. Figure 6.6 illustrates this profit-making procedure. In addition to the business's demand and marginal revenue curves, the graph shows the relevant curves for marginal cost and average cost. To maximize profit, the business must find the point at which marginal revenue and marginal cost intersect. This occurs at point *a*, which is at the profit-maximizing quantity of two computers. Price is then set at $120 million by drawing a vertical line up to the business's demand curve at point *b*, and then across to the price axis.

The table shows the same results: marginal revenue (column 4) and marginal cost (column 5) pass through the same values nearest the quantity of two computers and price of $120 million.

FIGURE 6.6	Profit Maximization for a Monopolist

Profit Maximization Table for Megacomp

(1) Price (P) (AR)	(2) Quantity (Q)	(3) Total Revenue (TR) (P × Q)	(4) Marginal Revenue (MR) (ΔTR/ΔQ)	(5) Marginal Cost (MC)	(6) Average Cost (AC)
($ millions per computer)	(computers per year)	($ millions)	($ millions per computer)	($ millions per computer)	($ millions per computer)
	0	$ 0			
$ 160	1	160	$160	$60	$140
120	**2**	**240**	80	40	**90**
80	3	240	0	70	83
40	4	160	−80	150	100

Profit Maximization Graph for Megacomp

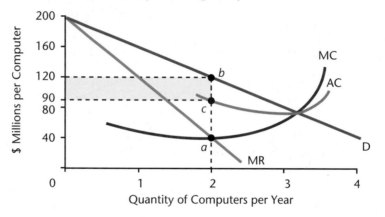

On the graph, the profit-maximizing output is found at the intersection of the marginal revenue (MR) and marginal cost (MC) curves (at point *a*). At this output, the demand curve gives a price (at point *b*) of $120 million (determined by drawing a vertical line to the demand curve, then across to the price axis). The table also shows that marginal revenue and marginal cost pass through the same values around an output of two computers and a price of $120 million. On the graph, Megacomp's profit is the area of the shaded rectangle, with a height equal to the difference between price (point *b*) and average cost (point *c*), and with a width equal to quantity.

The monopolist may be making an economic profit or a loss, or it may be breaking even, depending on whether the business's average cost is above, below, or equal to price. Because, in our example, Megacomp has an average cost of $90 million (at point *c*) that is below the $120 million price (point *b*), it is making a positive economic profit. The business's profit rectangle has a height equal to the distance between points *b* and *c* ($30 million = $120 million − $90 million) and a width of two computers, giving a total economic profit of $60 million.

Notice that a monopolist satisfies neither of the conditions for consumer benefit: minimum-cost pricing and marginal-cost pricing. Because the monopolist has no competitors due to entry barriers, it can keep its price constant in the long run. In the case of Megacomp, this price would be $120 million, as shown in Figure 6.6. Since price does not equal the lowest possible average cost, the minimum-cost pricing condition is not met. Similarly, this price is not equal to the business's marginal cost, meaning the marginal-cost pricing condition is not met either.

Monopoly versus Perfect Competition

To see the impact on price and quantity of a monopoly, compare them with price and quantity in a perfectly competitive market. To do this, consider what would happen if a perfectly competitive market in long-run equilibrium were transformed into a monopoly.

Figure 6.7 shows the market demand and supply curves for the T-shirt industry. Equilibrium for a competitive market occurs at the intersection of these curves (point *a*), with a price of $4 and a quantity of 22 000 shirts. If the industry becomes one large company, the market demand curve remains the same, despite the change in the market structure. With the transformation to a monopoly, the demand curve for the entire market simply becomes the business's demand curve. There is a significant change, however. Now that the business is a monopolist, its price (given by the demand curve) and its marginal revenue are no longer equal. Instead, the marginal revenue curve falls below the demand curve, as was the case for Megacomp.

Next, consider supply. Recall that a perfect competitor's supply curve shows the quantity of output supplied by the business at each possible price and is represented by a portion of the marginal cost curve. In turn, the market supply curve is the sum of all the supply curves of the businesses in the market. After the change to a monopoly, production facilities remain the same as before, with inputs originally owned by the perfectly competitive producers now in the hands of one business. When the monopolist combines the cost figures for these various facilities, it finds a marginal cost curve that is merely an extension of the perfectly competitive supply curve, shown in Figure 6.7.

EFFECTS ON PRICE AND QUANTITY

The T-shirt monopoly's profit-maximizing output is 18 000, where the new marginal revenue and marginal cost curves intersect (point *b*). At this output level, the price is $7 (point *c*), as found on the demand curve. Thus, with the

---

FIGURE 6.7   Monopoly Versus Perfect Competition

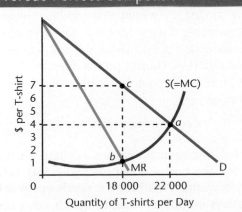

When the T-shirt industry is perfectly competitive, equilibrium occurs at the meeting point (*a*) of the market demand and supply curves (D and S). If the industry becomes a monopoly, the profit-maximizing output for the single seller decreases, where marginal revenue (MR) and marginal cost (MC) meet (point *b*). The new price is found on the demand curve (point *c*).

THINKING ABOUT ECONOMICS

How easy is it for a monopolist, such as Megacomp, to estimate the profit-maximizing values for price and quantity?

The task requires estimating both demand and costs. Whereas the perfect competitor has an easy time estimating demand conditions (because market price is the only factor to be determined), monopolists (as well as imperfectly competitive businesses) have a harder task estimating how much consumers will buy at each possible price. As far as cost estimates are concerned, all businesses must estimate how much the explicit and implicit costs would be at each possible output level. When a business sells more than one item, it must also distribute its costs among these various products.

QUESTION   **How easy is it for perfect competitors to estimate costs at each possible output level?**

transformation from perfect competition to monopoly, T-shirts become more expensive, and fewer of them are produced.

Regulation of Natural Monopolies

When an industry is a natural monopoly, increasing returns to scale mean that the single business can produce a product at a significantly lower per-unit cost than could several companies. To ensure that these cost savings are passed on to the consumer, governments usually intervene in natural monopolies. Either they provide the service through a government-owned corporation (as in the case of Canada Post), or they regulate the single private company in the market (just as the Canadian Radio-television and Telecommunications Commission regulates cable television businesses).

AVERAGE-COST PRICE

average-cost pricing: the practice of setting price where it equals average cost

Public agencies that regulate monopolies have a difficult task. Not only must regulators estimate each business's costs, they must also try to choose the "best" possible price for the monopolist to charge. Usually, regulators use **average-cost pricing** so that the monopolist can break even without public funds. As a practical matter, regulators applying the average-cost price do not undertake the cumbersome task of estimating the cost and demand curves of the regulated business. Instead, they control profits directly. A business's **accounting-profit rate**, or rate of return, is its accounting profit divided by owner's equity, expressed as a percentage:

accounting-profit rate: a measure of a business's profitability, calculated as its accounting profit divided by owner's equity

$$\text{Accounting-profit rate} = \frac{\text{accounting profit}}{\text{owner's equity}} \times 100\%$$

fair rate of return: the maximum accounting-profit rate allowed for a regulated monopoly

The regulating agency imposes a ceiling, such as 8 percent or 9 percent, on the profit rate the business can earn. This **fair rate of return** is arrived at by estimating how much the business needs to cover both explicit costs (such as wages and outlays on materials) and implicit costs (in particular, the business's normal profits).

While it is often the only viable method of regulation, setting a fair rate of return leads to inefficiencies. Because of profit controls, there is little incentive for the company's managers to control costs. Indeed, the easiest way for the business to raise its price is by inflating costs. Generous perks, bloated payrolls, and plush offices are then paid for by consumers in the form of higher prices. Regulators try to overcome such problems by imposing performance standards on the business, but these standards are difficult to implement. Alternatively, governments often deal with natural monopolies by creating publicly-owned companies to take on the monopolist's role, with the understanding that these companies will charge a fair rate of return. This option has been commonly used in Canada. At the federal level, Crown corporations such as Canada Post and Via Rail act as monopolists in their respective markets. Publicly-owned monopolists are also found at provincial and municipal levels, as in the case of urban transit systems. The effectiveness of this option is the subject of considerable debate. Supporters argue that administering monopolies in the public sector ensures that bloated costs can be constrained by political oversight. Opponents argue that the same lack of cost control is found in both publicly-owned and private monopolies.

BRIEF REVIEW

1. The monopolist faces a demand curve that is equal to marginal revenue only at its initial value. Marginal revenue drops more quickly than price as output rises.

2. A monopolist can make a positive economic profit in both the short run and the long run, and meets neither of the minimum-cost and marginal-cost pricing conditions.

3. A monopolist necessarily charges a higher price and produces a lower quantity than would a perfectly competitive industry in the same market.

4. Regulators usually force natural monopolies to charge an average-cost price, where the businesses are just breaking even.

6.2 | PRACTICE PROBLEMS

1. A monopolistic pharmaceuticals company produces a patented drug. In one year, it could sell 400 000 prescriptions at a price of $20, or instead it could sell 500 000 prescriptions at a price of $15.
   a. Identify the marginal revenue associated with this range of the business's demand curve.
   b. Since this company is a monopolist, what shape does its demand curve have? How is the marginal revenue curve positioned relative to the demand curve?
   c. Draw the relevant range of this business's demand curve and identify a point on its marginal revenue curve. Plot two points on the demand curve and one point on the marginal revenue curve. Remember to plot marginal values such as marginal revenue halfway between the two relevant quantities on the horizontal axis.
2. A monopolist produces at a daily output of 100 000 units, with marginal cost and marginal revenue at this output both equal to $4 and price equal to $6.
   a. Is the monopolist operating at its profit-maximizing output? Why or why not?
   b. If the government turns this monopolist into a perfectly competitive market, will output be less than or greater than 100 000 units? Will price be less than or greater than $6?

6.3 | Imperfect Competition

LO3 Because of the similarities they share, monopolistic competition and oligopoly are often lumped together in a general category, known as imperfect competition. Like monopolists, businesses in both these markets are price-makers, which means that they must decide on both price and quantity when choosing a profit-maximizing point. However, there are important differences in how each type of market operates. Monopolistically competitive industries blend elements of monopoly and competition in ways that clearly highlight the distinction between the short run and the long run. As a rule, government policy-makers are content to let monopolistic competitors operate with minimal public oversight. Oligopolies, on the other hand, can behave in a multitude of ways, depending on the specific conditions in which they operate. Partly because of such variety, deriving a standard economic model of oligopolistic behaviour has proven to be extremely difficult.

Given this complexity, few other areas in microeconomics are currently receiving as much attention as the study of oligopolies.

Monopolistic Competition

REVENUE CONDITIONS

Figure 6.8 shows the relationships among price, marginal revenue, and average revenue for a monopolisitic competitor, the Jaded Palate restaurant. As in the

---

FIGURE 6.8   Revenues for a Monopolistic Competitor

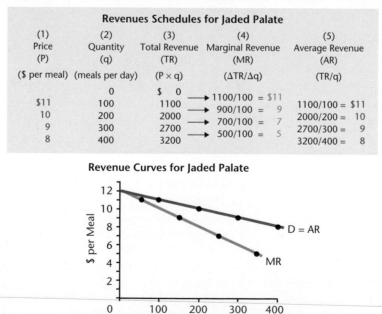

Revenues Schedules for Jaded Palate

(1) Price (P)	(2) Quantity (q)	(3) Total Revenue (TR)	(4) Marginal Revenue (MR)	(5) Average Revenue (AR)
($ per meal)	(meals per day)	(P × q)	(ΔTR/Δq)	(TR/q)
	0	$ 0		
$11	100	1100	1100/100 = $11	1100/100 = $11
10	200	2000	900/100 = 9	2000/200 = 10
9	300	2700	700/100 = 7	2700/300 = 9
8	400	3200	500/100 = 5	3200/400 = 8

The business's demand schedule is shown in columns 1 and 2. The values for price (P) and average revenue (AR) in columns 1 and 5 are equal, while marginal revenue (MR) in column 4 is the same as P and AR only at their initial values. After this, MR falls more quickly than price, as the graph shows.

case of a monopolist, price and average revenue are the same, but marginal revenue is below average revenue due to the fact that average revenue is declining. For example, the first 100 meals sold by Jaded Palate have an average and marginal revenue both equal to $11. With the addition of the next 100 meals, however, average revenue declines to $10, while marginal revenue is lower still at $9. As shown on the accompanying graph in Figure 6.8, Jaded Palate's demand and marginal revenue curves intersect at their initial points, and from then on the marginal revenue (MR) curve declines more rapidly than the demand (D) curve.

THE SHORT RUN

Given its ability to choose price, the monopolistic competitor maximizes its short-run profit by first finding the appropriate quantity of output and then using this quantity level to determine the highest possible price it can charge. This profit-making procedure is illustrated on the left in Figure 6.9. In addition to the business's demand and marginal revenue curves, the graph shows the relevant curves for marginal cost and average cost. Once again, to maximize profit, the business must find the point at which marginal revenue and marginal cost intersect. This is point *a*, which is at the profit-maximizing quantity of 200 meals. Price is then set at $10 by drawing a vertical line up to the business's demand curve at point *b* and then across to the price axis.

Jaded Palate could be making an economic profit or loss in the short run, or it could be breaking even. As in the case of perfect competitors, the answer can be found by comparing price and average cost at the profit-maximizing quantity. Because the price of $10 is above the $8 average cost at a quantity of 200 meals (point *c*), Jaded Palate is making a positive economic profit. On the graph, the revenue rectangle equals price multiplied by the quantity of output ($10 × 200 meals = $2000), and the cost rectangle equals average cost

FIGURE 6.9   Profit Maximization for a Monopolistic Competitor

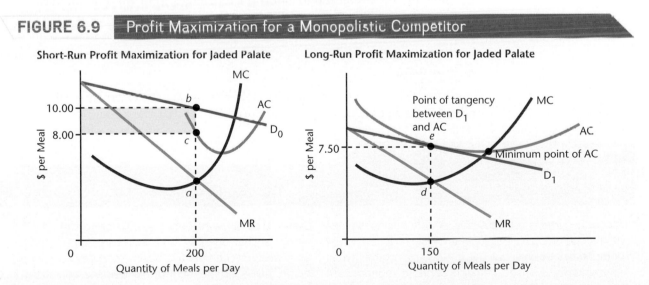

On the left, the business's short-run profit is maximized at point *a*, where the marginal revenue (MR) and marginal cost (MC) curves intersect. The price is found by drawing a vertical line up to point *b* on the business's demand curve (D₀) and then across to the price axis. The shaded rectangle shows the business's total profit. On the right, the long-run profit-maximizing output of 150 meals occurs at the point where MR and MC are equal (point *d*). The price of $7.50—which equals long-run AC—is point *e* on the business's long-run demand curve (D₁).

multiplied by the quantity of output ($8 × 200 meals = $1600). Therefore, the profit rectangle equals $400 (= $2000 − $1600) and is shown as the shaded rectangle on the short-run graph.

THE LONG RUN

The competitive elements of monopolistic competition become evident in the long run. Because short-run economic profits are being made in the restaurant industry, new businesses enter the market in the long run. The graph on the right in Figure 6.9 shows how the increase in competition shifts demand (from D_0 to the new D_1 curve) for established restaurants, such as Jaded Palate. The entry of new competitors causes demand for Jaded Palate to shift to the left because there are now fewer customers at each possible price that the restaurant can charge. The new demand curve (D_1) is also more elastic than D_0, since there are more close substitutes available for Jaded Palate's product. Once again, the market adjusts: profits go down, and eventually, long-run equilibrium is reached at point e. Besides showing Jaded Palate's demand and marginal revenue curves, the graph on the right shows the marginal cost and average cost curves in the long run. The profit-maximizing point where marginal revenue equals marginal cost now occurs at a quantity of 150 meals (point d). The new price is $7.50, which is found at point e on the long-run demand curve (D_1).

Note that monopolistic competitors reach neither the minimum-cost nor the marginal-cost pricing conditions in long-run equilibrium. Since average cost and price are equal at point e in Figure 6.9, the business is breaking even in the long run. However, this price does *not* equal the minimum point on the average cost curve. This minimum-cost price could only be achieved at a higher output for each business. Figure 6.9 also illustrates that in the long run, for monopolistic competitors, price (point e) is greater than marginal cost. This means that too few units of output are produced for price to reflect the product's full opportunity cost. Still, the amounts by which the long-run price diverges from the minimum-cost and marginal-cost conditions are usually not all that large for monopolistic competitors; policy-makers rarely intervene to counteract discrepancies in this type of market.

Oligopoly

We have already seen how an oligopoly that is characterized by rivalry among competitors faces a kinked demand curve. Recall that the kinked demand curve

THINKING ABOUT ECONOMICS

Why are there no supply curves for businesses in imperfectly competitive markets?

A supply curve is relevant only when a business plans how much output to produce at various prices. Perfect competitors do this, but not the sellers in other types of markets. Given its demand curve, a monopolistic competitor or oligopolist chooses one output level and then charges the highest possible price the demand allows at that quantity. It is, therefore, impossible for an imperfectly competitive business to devise a supply curve that is independent of the demand conditions it faces.

QUESTION   **Is it possible for a monopolist to derive a supply curve?**

is based on the different responses of competitors when the business either raises or reduces its price. In Figure 6.10, when Universal Motors increases the price of its Centaur car, rivals do not increase their prices. Thus, the quantity demanded of Centaur cars decreases sharply, giving the flatter segment of the demand curve. Were Universal Motors to decrease its price on the Centaur, rivals would follow suit, so the change in quantity demanded would be small, giving the steeper segment of the demand curve.

REVENUE CONDITIONS

The table and graph in Figure 6.10 show the marginal revenue for Centaur cars. Just as with the demand curve, the marginal revenue curve has two distinct segments. In this case, however, the flatter segment and the steeper segment do not meet, but must be joined by a vertical line at the quantity of 20 000 cars, the quantity associated with the $30 000 price.

| FIGURE 6.10 | Profit Maximization for an Oligopolist |

Profit Maximization Table for Centaur Cars

(1) Price (P) (=AR)	(2) Quantity (q)	(3) Total Revenue (TR) (P × q)	(4) Marginal Revenue (MR) (ΔTR/Δq)	(5) Marginal Cost (MC)	(6) Average Cost (AC)
($ thousands per car)	(thousands of cars per year)	($ millions)	($ thousands per car)	($ thousands per car)	($ thousands per car)
	0	$ 0			
$35	10	350	$ 35	$13	$30
30	**20**	**600**	25	10	**20**
20	25	500	−20	15	19
10	30	300	−40	25	20

Profit Maximization Graph for Centaur Cars

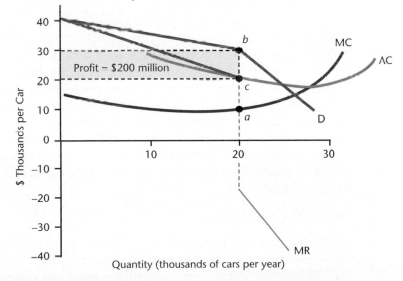

In an oligopoly characterized by rivalry, a business faces a kinked demand curve (D) with two segments. The marginal revenue curve also has two segments, however the segments are separate, so they must be joined with a vertical line. On the graph, the marginal revenue (MR) and marginal cost (MC) curves meet at point *a*, giving the profit-maximizing output level. To determine price, we must look to the demand curve; at the relevant quantity, the price should be $30 000 (point *b*). According to the table also, the values of marginal revenue (column 4) and marginal cost (column 5) pass through the same values around the same output as on the graph.

PROFIT MAXIMIZATION

To maximize profit, the oligopolist, like all businesses, must follow the profit-maximizing output rule. Therefore, Universal Motors should produce at the output level where the marginal revenue and marginal cost curves intersect, at point *a* in Figure 6.10, or 20 000 cars. According to the demand curve, this quantity of cars should be sold at a price of $30 000 (found by extending a vertical line from a quantity of 20 000 to the demand curve, at point *b*, which aligns on the price axis with a $30 000 price). Looking at the table in Figure 6.10, we can see that marginal cost and marginal revenue pass through the same values closest to an output of 20 000 cars.

At the profit-maximizing point, an oligopolist may make a positive, negative, or zero economic profit in the short run. When average cost is below price at the business's profit-maximizing output, the business makes a positive economic profit. When average cost is above price at the profit-maximizing quantity, the business makes an economic loss. When average cost and price are equal at the profit-maximizing point, the business breaks even. In the case of Universal Motors, at the output level of 20 000 cars and the price of $30 000 (point *b* in Figure 6.10), the average cost is $20 000 (point *c*). Therefore, the company makes an economic profit on Centaur cars equal to quantity multiplied by the difference between price and average cost, or $200 million [= 20 000 × ($30 000 − $20 000)].

The kinked demand curve–which applies equally in both the short run and the long run–explains why rival oligopolists tend to keep prices constant even as costs change. In the case of the Centaur illustrated in Figure 6.10, as long as the marginal cost and marginal revenue curves intersect at a quantity of 20 000, Universal Motors will not change its price. Only if the marginal cost changed so dramatically that its curve and the marginal revenue curve no longer intersected at 20 000 (the vertical connection between the two segments) would Universal Motors change its price.

As in the case of monopolistic competitors, oligopolists achieve neither the minimum-cost nor the marginal-cost pricing conditions in either short-run or long-run equilibrium–but now with the possibility for quite large discrepancies. Because of limited competition created by entry barriers, an oligopolist that faces rivals can remain indefinitely at one price, such as $30 000 in Figure 6.10. At this price, the business is making a positive economic profit and fails to reach the output level where average cost is at its lowest value. So, the minimum-cost pricing condition is broken. The condition of marginal-cost pricing is also broken; as Figure 6.10 shows, the price of $30 000 is greater than marginal cost. The same conclusions apply for colluding oligopolists, as the prices they charge are even higher.

Game Theory

While the model of the kinked demand curve is useful in clarifying why oligopolists operating in conditions of rivalry are reluctant to change price, it cannot explain how the initial profit-maximizing price and quantity are established in such markets. Nor can it explain why a particular oligopolistic market is characterized by rivalry, or under what circumstances it might shift toward collusion.

In recent decades, economists have devised more powerful models to answer these questions. These models are part of a burgeoning area known as **game theory**, which analyzes how mutually interdependent actors try to

game theory: an analysis of how mutually interdependent actors try to achieve their goals through the use of strategy

achieve their goals through the use of strategy—in other words, by choosing actions that take account of possible responses of others, in the same way that players in games such as chess do.

Originally a field in mathematics, game theory has become a set of conceptual tools whose use has spread to all of the social sciences, with economists making especially extensive use of its insights. Among the range of possible situations it covers, we will look at one of its earliest and most famous applications.

THE PRISONER'S DILEMMA

The **prisoner's dilemma** is a valuable tool from game theory that shows how self-interested strategies can be self-defeating. Its name comes from a classic hypothetical example: two partners in crime, Peter and Paul, have been caught and put in separate jail cells. Each is considering the choice they are given by police: (a) confess to the crime and agree to implicate their partner, or (b) stay silent.

> **prisoner's dilemma:** a classic example of how players' self-interested actions can be self-defeating

Figure 6.11 outlines the possible strategies available to each prisoner, along with the jail time each will receive under different conditions. Peter's possible jail times are shown in the unshaded triangles along each row of this diagram, while Paul's are shown in the shaded triangles down each column. If both Peter and Paul confess, then, as shown in the upper left cell of Figure 6.11, each gets jail time of five years. If only one confesses, however, then the confessor is set free, while the other faces an extended jail term of ten years. This is shown in the lower left cell of the diagram, in the case where Paul confesses and gets no jail time, while Peter stays silent and receives a ten-year sentence. Likewise, in the upper right cell, Peter is the one who confesses and goes free, while Paul stays silent and gets ten years. Finally, as shown in the lower right cell, if both prisoners stay silent, they both get a reduced sentence of one year on a minor charge.

What strategy should each prisoner select? It depends on what each expects the other to do. If each could be assured that the other will not confess, then staying silent is the best strategy, with both prisoners serving just one year in jail. But as long as each prisoner has doubts about the other's trustworthiness, it makes sense to choose the strategy with the least harmful worst-case scenario.

FIGURE 6.11   The Prisoner's Dilemma

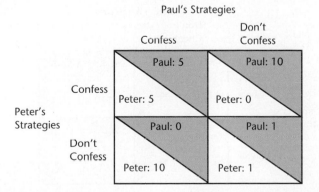

Peter's possible jail times are found in each row, and Paul's in each column. If both prisoners confess, each gets the five-year jail sentence depicted in the upper left cell. If just one confesses, then he is set free, while the other receives ten years, as shown in the lower left and upper right cells. If both stay silent, each gets a one-year sentence, as shown in the lower right cell.

For example, by looking at the unshaded triangles in each row of the diagram, Peter will see that if he confesses, the worst that could happen is that he receives a sentence of five years, which occurs if Paul confesses as well. But if he stays silent, the worst that could happen is a sentence of ten years if Paul confesses. Likewise, by focusing on the shaded triangles in each column, Paul will see that, if he confesses, again the worst-case scenario is a sentence of five years, while if he stays silent the worst-case scenario is a sentence of ten years. So the best for each appears to be to confess.

The reason why this situation is called a dilemma should be clear. By following a narrowly self-interested strategy that minimizes his own potential harm, each prisoner confesses–even though the best possible result would have been if both stayed silent. As a result, their strategies end up being self-defeating.

APPLYING THE PRISONER'S DILEMMA TO OLIGOPOLY

Situations like the prisoner's dilemma have many applications. For an oligopoly, it is most straightforward to look at a market with just two businesses, Gamma and Delta, that have signed an agreement to raise the prices they charge. (As we will see in more detail later in this chapter, such agreements are illegal in Canada.) This agreement provides each business with two possible strategies: to charge the high price they have agreed upon, or to break the agreement and, through cheating, charge the same lower price as before. The combined profit for Gamma and Delta is maximized when both refrain from cheating and charge the higher price, as depicted in the upper left cell in Figure 6.12, with an annual profit for each business of $20 million. But one of the businesses may sign the agreement and then, while the other charges the high price, cheat by shifting back to the low-price strategy to gain some of the other business's market share. Though the combined total profit for the two businesses is lower than it would be when both refrain from cheating, the individual profit for the cheater is higher than otherwise, and the other business's is lower. This is shown in the lower left and upper right cells in Figure 6.12, where the cheater's annual profit rises to $25 million, while the other's falls to $10 million. Finally, if both businesses cheat, their annual profits are each $15 million.

FIGURE 6.12 The Case of Oligopoly

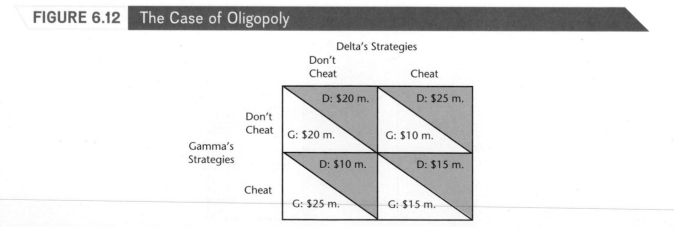

Profits for Gamma (G) appear in each row, and for Delta (D) in each column. When both businesses refrain from cheating, each makes $20 million in profit per year, as shown in the upper left cell. If just one cheats, then it receives $25 million annually, while the other gets $10 million, as found in the lower left and upper right cells. If both cheat, each makes $15 million, as shown in the lower right cell.

The strategies that each business chooses depend on a variety of factors—including how easy it is for either business to know what the other is doing. If cheating is soon discovered, both businesses have an incentive not to, meaning each receives the $20 million annually. But if price undercutting can be accomplished in an underhanded way, each business has an incentive to cheat, in which case each gets only $15 million in profits. As in the case of the classic prisoner's dilemma, when each business follows a narrowly self-interested strategy, the possible benefits of cooperation are sacrificed, and the market is characterized by rivalry.

This example makes clear that, while there are potential benefits to oligopolists (though not to consumers) from engaging in illegal forms of collusion, the agreements that are entered into are not necessarily long-lasting, given the incentives that always exist for individual businesses to cheat. Strategic considerations will therefore always be significant in oligopolies—just as they are in any other context in which game theory is used. Still, this case is only one of many possible results, with the range of possible outcomes for an individual business determined not just by the actions of competitors already in the market, but by the threat of entry from new competitors. **Contestable markets** are those in which the threat of new entrants is credible—a quite common situation that can significantly reduce the market power of businesses already in these markets.

contestable markets: those in which the threat of new entrants is credible

Applying game theory in oligopolistic contexts is not always easy, given the need to specify a market's distinctive attributes. But, as its principles and logic continue to be developed, game theory offers the greatest potential in improving our understanding of oligopolists and their behaviour.

Anti-Combines Legislation in Canada

Because of the inefficiencies that oligopolies can cause, their activities are subject to laws aimed at preventing industrial concentration and abuses of market power, which are known as **anti-combines legislation**. Canada's anti-combines laws date back to 1889, but until recent decades, were largely unsuccessful.

anti-combines legislation: laws aimed at preventing industrial concentration and abuses of market power

One reason for the lack of success was that violations were considered to be criminal offences. Criminal cases require that guilt be established beyond a reasonable doubt. This requirement does not easily make use of economic analysis—analysis that is so vital to considering anti-competitive behaviour. A second reason is that Canadian governments have traditionally been less opposed to industrial concentration than those in other countries, the United States in particular. Many Canadians have argued that domestic businesses need to be large in order to be internationally competitive, especially in sectors with significant increasing returns to scale. Canada's lawmakers, therefore, have typically given the goal of international competitiveness and efficiency greater weight than they have domestic competition.

The Competition Act of 1986 was a major reform of Canada's anti-combines legislation. It offered a combination of criminal and civil provisions, strengthened penalties, and built on the almost century-long experience of anti-combines legislation and prosecution. The Act covers business practices that prevent or lessen competition, including the practices described in the following sections. Of these, the first three are still criminal offences, with penalties ranging from fines to possible imprisonment of company executives, while the last two are considered civil matters, which are reviewed by a government-administered panel known as the Competition Tribunal.

CONSPIRACY

Businesses that conspire or agree to fix prices, allocate markets, or restrict entry to markets can be charged under the Competition Act. For a business to be found guilty, its actions must be proven to unduly restrain competition. Violators can face fines of up to $10 million or prison terms of up to five years. One case of conspiracy involved nine real estate boards in five provinces. After complaints from customers and some industry members about commissions, services, and other practices, an investigation began. The Canadian Real Estate Association came forward to settle the matter, which was resolved out of court, though investigations of the practices of real estate boards continue. Another case involved gas stations in the Eastern Townships region of Quebec fixing retail prices of gasoline. Complaints led the Competition Tribunal to investigate, resulting in criminal convictions that involved both fines and prison sentences.

BID-RIGGING

Companies that bid on contracts may arrange among themselves who will win each contract and at what price. By taking turns at winning bids and by inflating prices, all conspirators are winners. Unlike the more general conspiracy charge, bid-rigging is considered an automatic offence; undue restraint does not have to be proven. In one case, three heating equipment suppliers were convicted on six counts of sharing out the market, in part by rigging bids; each company was fined $1000 on each count. Penalties are at the courts' discretion, but reflect the seriousness with which the courts view the crime, and so can include, for example, $1 million fines and five-year prison terms.

PREDATORY PRICING

The policy and practice of temporarily dropping a price for a product below its average cost to drive a new competitor out of business is a criminal offence. In one case, a company provided free supplies of a drug to hospitals. Because the company's goal was to generate long-term sales after eliminating competition, the company was fined $50 000.

ABUSE OF DOMINANT POSITION

Companies that control most of the sales in a market are not allowed to use their dominant position to engage in anti-competitive behaviour. One case of abuse involved the Canadian maker of (and former patent-holder for) the artificial sweetener aspartame, known as NutraSweet. According to the findings of the Competition Tribunal, the company had used its power to have several major purchasers of aspartame sign long-term contracts to buy NutraSweet exclusively, rather than the products of the competition. The company was not allowed to enforce these old contracts or to negotiate new ones of the same sort. Typically, the Tribunal requires that the guilty company cease its anti-competitive behaviour. The Tribunal can also use stronger measures to restore competition in the market, for example by requiring partial break-up of a business into smaller units.

MERGERS

A merger is the combining of two companies into one. The Competition Tribunal has the power to prohibit a merger in Canada–no matter what the size or nationality of the companies involved–if the merger could prevent or substantially reduce competition. Exceptions are often made if a merger will increase efficiency and pass on savings to consumers. In practice, it is uncommon for the tribunal to disallow a merger.

Mergers can be of three sorts, depending on the connection between the companies involved. A **horizontal merger** combines former competitors. One example of a horizontal merger is the purchase over a decade ago of Canadian Airlines International by its rival, Air Canada. Horizontal mergers allow businesses to take advantage of the increasing returns to scale that arise from combining production. Horizontal mergers can also reduce the level of competition in the market, thereby giving the new combined company more market power and potential profit.

horizontal merger: a combination of former rivals

A **vertical merger** combines a business and its supplier. A steelmaker that purchases an iron ore mine is one example, as is a fashion design company merging with a clothing wholesaler. Vertical mergers can guarantee a supply of needed inputs or can ensure distribution of the product. For example, the Canadian restaurant company Cara has taken over many of its food suppliers, and PepsiCo's ownership of Pizza Hut ensures that PepsiCo soft drinks are sold in these restaurants.

vertical merger: a combination of a business and its supplier

A **conglomerate merger** combines businesses in unrelated industries. The main reason for such mergers is to help companies smooth out fluctuations in profit that occur during booms and recessions. A company whose profit plummets during a downturn in the economy–a manufacturer of luxury yachts, for example–might decide to purchase a chain of discount hardware stores, which are not affected in the same way.

conglomerate merger: a combination of businesses in unrelated industries

BRIEF REVIEW

1. A monopolistic competitor faces a marginal revenue curve that intersects with its corresponding demand curve only at their initial values. From that point, the marginal revenue curve falls faster than does the demand curve.

2. In the short run, a monopolistic competitor can make an economic profit or loss. In the long run, however, competitive forces drive monopolistic competitors to a breakeven point.

3. An oligopolist in a market that is characterized by rivalry faces a marginal revenue curve of two disconnected segments, one steeper than the other. These segments are associated with the two portions of the kinked demand curve.

4. Because of limited competition, oligopolists can make an economic profit even in the long run.

5. Imperfectly competitive businesses satisfy neither the minimum-cost nor the marginal-cost pricing conditions met by perfectly competitive businesses in the long run.

6. Game theory models, such as the prisoner's dilemma, can be used to analyze particular types of strategic behaviour in oligopolistic markets.

7. Governments in such countries as Canada use anti-combines legislation to prevent industrial concentration and abuses of market power.

6.3 | PRACTICE PROBLEMS

1. A photocopy shop in a monopolistically competitive market can sell 10 000 copies a day at a price of 4 cents, or it can sell 15 000 copies at a price of 3 cents.
   a. Identify the marginal revenue associated with this range of the business's demand curve.
   b. Because this business is a monopolistic competitor, how does marginal revenue compare with price?
   c. Draw the relevant range of this business's demand curve and identify a point on its marginal revenue curve. Plot two points of the demand curve and one point on the marginal revenue curve. Remember to plot marginal values such as marginal revenue halfway between the two relevant quantities on the horizontal axis.

2. A monopolistic competitor operates at its short run profit-maximizing point, with a weekly output of 100 000 units and a price of $5.
   a. If the business's average cost is initially $6, what happens in the long run if it stays in operation?
   b. If the business's average cost is initially $4 instead, then how will the long-run trends for this business differ?

3. An oligopolist in a market where rivalry prevails is operating at the kink in its demand curve, with a daily output of 400 units and a price of $5.
   a. At this output level, what is the shape of the business's marginal revenue curve?
   b. If costs for this business were to undergo a rise at every output level, would this business necessarily raise its price? Why?

4. Two prisoners, A and B, are being questioned by police. They may each confess to the crime they committed and thereby implicate their partner, or they may each remain silent. If A confesses and B does not confess, A is immediately set free and B gets 15 years in jail. In contrast, if B confesses and A stays silent, it is B who is set free and A who gets 15 years. If both confess, each gets eight years; if neither confesses, each gets two years.
   a. If A and B could decide together, would it be best for them to confess or stay silent? Why?
   b. If A and B cannot communicate with one another, are they likely to confess or stay silent? Why?

6.4 | Traits of Imperfect Competition

L04   Non-price Competition

non-price competition: efforts to increase demand through product differentiation, advertising, or both

In addition to changing product prices, imperfectly competitive firms can compete in another way. **Non-price competition** refers to the efforts of imperfectly competitive producers to increase demand for their products by swaying consumer preferences. The two strategies used are product differentiation and advertising.

PRODUCT DIFFERENTIATION

Product differentiation is a company's attempt to distinguish its product from competitors' products. Designer labels on a clothing manufacturer's jeans and an "exclusive" set of toppings on a restaurant's pizza are examples of product differentiation. The changes made to a product may be cosmetic—slick packaging, for example—or they may be substantial, such as providing the product at a more convenient location. Product differentiation has two goals: to increase demand (thus raising the quantity demanded at every price) and to decrease demand elasticity (so that prices can be increased without losing customers to competitors). Meeting both goals increases a business's profit and market power.

product differentiation: efforts to make a product distinct from competitors' products

ADVERTISING

Advertising can play two roles in imperfectly competitive markets. It can provide the consumer with information, as with online classified ads, and it can promote consumer preferences for a product, as is commonly the case for radio and television ads. Advertising has the same two goals as product differentiation: to increase demand for the product and to make the demand more inelastic. For example, a producer of athletic shoes, such as Nike, advertises to raise the quantity demanded of its shoes at every possible price. The producer also aims to make consumers less likely to switch brands if Nike shoes go up in price. Again, the company's profit and market power increase if its advertising strategy meets the two goals.

NON-PRICE COMPETITION AND BUSINESS

For a single imperfectly competitive business, product differentiation and advertising increase both revenues and costs. Total revenue increases when the demand for the business's product increases. In addition, total revenue is less subject to future declines when demand becomes more inelastic. However, the business's total costs increase because of the extra costs of undertaking non-price competition. If the long-term gain in total revenues outweighs the extra costs of product differentiation and advertising, profits are increased. Whether or not this extra profit can be made depends on how easy it is to influence consumer preferences. Businesses in oligopolies typically find advertising a profitable strategy, especially when large advertising budgets serve as an entry barrier.

NON-PRICE COMPETITION AND THE CONSUMER

For the consumer, product differentiation leads to higher prices by raising per-unit costs and enhancing individual businesses' market power. However, consumers will likely have more choices because of businesses' efforts to differentiate their products. So, for example, the fact that televisions produced by competing companies are distinctive raises the average price of televisions, but also gives consumers a wider selection of possible features than they would otherwise have.

The impact of advertising on the consumer is also mixed. In some cases, advertising is anti-competitive, leading to more market power for established firms. However, advertising can also increase competition. By giving new companies the chance to familiarize buyers with their products, advertising can offer consumers more choice. In this case, advertising lessens the market power of established businesses and leads to more industry flexibility. An example that portrays both possible effects is the Canadian soft-drink industry. This market is an oligopoly that for decades was dominated by two giant businesses, Coca-Cola and PepsiCo, whose market power was enhanced by their high levels of advertising. However, partly through the effects of advertising, smaller private-label producers (usually connected with supermarket chains) have been able to become major players in the Canadian market.

Industrial Concentration

It is usually fairly obvious when an industry is either perfectly competitive or monopolistic. Most industries, however, fall between the two extremes, and therefore represent some form of imperfect competition. It is not always easy to establish whether an imperfectly competitive industry is monopolistically competitive or an oligopoly. The most common indicator is a **concentration ratio**, which is the percentage of total sales revenue in a market earned by the largest business firms.

concentration ratio: the percentage of total sales revenue earned by the largest businesses in the market

Concentration ratios are commonly measured for the four largest business firms in any market, and are therefore known as four-firm ratios. An industry might be considered monopolistically competitive if its four-firm ratio is below 50 percent. If the four-firm ratio is above 50 percent, the industry is considered an oligopoly. So, for example, if a certain market has total annual sales revenues of $100 million, with the four largest companies having sales of $42 million, $27 million, $14 million, and $8 million, the four-firm ratio is 91 percent $\left(= \dfrac{42 + 27 + 14 + 8}{100} \times 100\%\right)$. In this case, the industry is considered an oligopoly. Figure 6.13 shows concentration ratios for selected Canadian industries.

In the late 1980s, about half of Canada's manufacturing industries had four-firm ratios of over 50 percent and could, therefore, be classified as oligopolies. Many Canadian service industries were concentrated as well. Compared with the United States, Canada had relatively small markets, each of which was more likely to be dominated by just one or a few businesses. It was estimated that,

---

FIGURE 6.13 | Concentration Ratios in Selected Canadian Industries (1988)

	Share of Industry Sales by Four Largest Businesses
Tobacco products	98.9
Petroleum and coal products	74.5
Transportation	68.4
Beverages	59.2
Metal mining	58.9
Paper and allied industries	38.9
Electrical products	32.1
Printing, publishing, and allied	25.7
Food	19.6
Finance	16.4
Machinery	11.3
Retail trade	9.7
Clothing industries	6.6
Construction	2.2

Sales in such industries as tobacco products, beverages, and transportation equipment were dominated by the four top businesses in each industry, indicating high levels of concentration. Meanwhile, in industries such as retail trade, clothing, and construction, the four top businesses in each industry had a much smaller proportion of industry sales, indicating low levels of concentration.

Source: Statistics Canada "Concentration Ratios in Selected Industries (1998)." Adapted from the Statistics Canada publication "Annual Report of the Minister of Industry, Science and Technology Under the Corporations and Labour Unions Returns Act, Part I, Corporations," 1988, Catalogue 61-210, October 1991, p. 94.

overall, about three-fifths of Canadian economic activity took place in concentrated markets that were either monopolies or oligopolies. In the American economy, the corresponding estimate was just over one-fifth.

Concentration ratios are becoming less useful indicators of market structure, since Statistics Canada includes only domestic businesses in its calculations. National concentration ratios can overestimate the level of competition in markets that are highly localized, with one or two businesses dominating certain regions. For example, while the many radio broadcasters in Canada would result in low official concentration ratios, the fact that most broadcasters operate in highly concentrated regional markets would not be reflected. But in markets where there is a significant international presence, official concentration ratios underestimate competition by ignoring the role of imports. So, for example, Canada's motor vehicle industry would appear less concentrated if foreign imports were taken into account.

Statistics Canada has not widely published industry concentration ratios since 1988, but it did calculate the proportion of operating revenue from all sources (not just sales) received by the largest five firms in a variety of Canadian industries up until 1999. In that year, these proportions ranged from a high of over 60 percent in banking to less than 10 percent in construction as well as in agriculture, forestry, fishing, and hunting. These proportions, though only rough indicators of market power, give a sense of the extent to which large businesses (both Canadian and foreign) have traditionally dominated some Canadian markets.

The Debate Over Industrial Concentration

The effect of market power on the economy can be studied in the context of **industrial concentration**, which refers to the domination of a market by one or a few large companies. Because of their small numbers and great sizes, these companies possess significant market power. Figure 6.14 gives an indication of how large some individual Canadian companies are in relation to Canadian business as a whole.

industrial concentration: market domination by one or a few large businesses

Can industrial concentration work to the advantage of consumers? To answer this question, we must weigh the costs and the benefits of huge companies dominating a given market.

INCREASING RETURNS TO SCALE VERSUS MARKET POWER

Defenders of industrial concentration emphasize the role of increasing returns to scale. They say this is especially important in a time when businesses are more likely than ever to compete in huge global markets. In many industries, only large

---

FIGURE 6.14   Concentration in the Canadian Economy (1999)

Share of Assets and Share of Revenues for Enterprises with $75 Million or More in Revenues		
	Assets	**Revenues**
Foreign	18.9	26.2
Canadian	57.8	30.5
	76.7	56.7

Enterprises with revenues of $75 million or more have traditionally controlled over three-quarters of total assets in Canadian industries. Of this, the bulk has been controlled by Canadian enterprises. In terms of sales revenue, these enterprises have had a less significant share.

Source: Statistics Canada "Concentration in the Canadian Economy (1999)." Adapted from the Statistics Canada publication "Corporations Returns Act (CRA)," 1999, Catalogue 61-220, June 2002, pp. 24–25.

businesses with a substantial market share can produce the quantity of output necessary to take advantage of increasing returns to scale. As a result, these big businesses have lower per-unit costs than would competitive businesses in the same market. These cost savings may then be passed on to consumers in the form of lower prices. Critics of industrial concentration say that the benefits of increasing returns to scale must be weighed against the market power held by large monopolists and oligopolists. This market power allows big companies to charge a higher price than would occur with more competition in the market.

INNOVATION

Some argue that "big business" is needed to promote innovation and technological advances. However, much evidence points to the opposite conclusion: companies in highly concentrated industries—either monopolies or oligopolies—tend not to innovate as rapidly as those in more competitive markets, where the continual jockeying for profit encourages improvements in products and production processes.

THINKING ABOUT ECONOMICS

How does the evolution in social media illustrate the benefits of competition as a driver of market innovation?

On the face of it, a large social media market should be a good thing, not just for the company that dominates the market, but also for consumers. When a user's friends and acquaintances are all customers of the same social media provider, it is easier to stay connected with them. Yet despite this clear advantage of size, strategic rivalry in the social media industry has been intense, with the market's dominant player Facebook fending off rivals such as Twitter and LinkedIn. As these companies jockey for position through innovative product differentiation, social media consumers benefit with imaginative new ways of communicating one-to-one, one-to-many, or group-to-group with their contacts. In addition, social media providers such as Facebook find new ways of making revenue through banner ads, acting as a host for online games, and selling online credits that consumers can apply to digital purchases. The results can be seen not just in the social media market itself, but in the ways that Internet use is being shaped for the future.

QUESTION   **How do Facebook, Twitter, and LinkedIn each differentiate their product in the social media market?**

BRIEF REVIEW

1. Product differentiation and advertising are forms of non-price competition common in imperfectly competitive markets. Their effect on the consumer is mixed.

2. Concentration ratios are measures of the percentage of total sales revenue in a market as earned by the biggest companies within the industry. These ratios suggest the degree of competition in an industry, although they do have some deficiencies.

3. Industrial concentration has its supporters and its critics. The arguments for and against concentration centre around increasing returns to scale, excess market power, and innovation.

6.4 | PRACTICE PROBLEMS

1. An industry is composed of 12 businesses, each with annual sales of $2 million.
   a. Calculate the industry's four-firm concentration ratio.
   b. How would you categorize this industry?
   c. If a business in this industry engages in non-price competition, what would be its reason?
   d. If two of the businesses in this market merged, what type of merger would it be classified as?
2. Will big businesses tend to have higher or lower average costs at higher outputs because of economies of scale? Does this represent a potential advantage or disadvantage of industrial concentration from the perspective of consumers?

LAST WORD

This chapter explored how the profit-maximizing procedure for businesses that operate as monopolists, monopolistic competitors, or oligopolists differs from that used by perfect competitors. At their profit-maximizing points, inefficiencies exist for businesses in all three market structures, since they break the minimum-cost and marginal-cost rules that indicate economic efficiency. Given the possible extent of these inefficiencies in monopolies and oligopolies, regulation and anti-combines legislation are applied in these markets. But these government controls are subject to debate, depending on how one views the potential costs and benefits of industrial concentration.

PROBLEMS

1. Biodata Software is the sole seller of a programming language with unique scientific applications. The company finds that it can sell 60 copies of the language each month at a price of $400 and 60 extra copies for each $100 reduction in price.
   a. Create a table showing the business's demand and marginal revenue schedules.
   b. Draw a graph showing the business's demand and marginal revenue curves. Plot only the two endpoints of the demand curve, and five points on the marginal revenue curve—the four points in the table as well as the point that extends the marginal revenue line to the vertical axis—for a total of seven points. Remember to plot marginal values such as marginal revenue halfway between the two relevant quantities on the horizontal axis.

2. Stan's Coffee Shop operates in a monopolistically competitive market. It sells 100 cups of coffee daily at a price of 95 cents per cup. For each 5-cent reduction in price, it sells 100 extra cups, until a minimum possible price of 80 cents is reached.
   a. Create a table showing the business's demand and marginal revenue schedules.
   b. Draw the business's demand and marginal revenue curves on one graph. Plot only the two endpoints of the demand curve and five points on the marginal revenue

curve—the four points in the table as well as a point that extends the marginal revenue line to the vertical axis—for a total of seven points. Remember to plot marginal values such as marginal revenue halfway between the two relevant quantities on the horizontal axis.

3. The Big Hair Company sells shampoo in an oligopoly characterized by rivalry. The business's daily sales are 2000 bottles at a price of $3, 4000 at $2.50, 5000 at $2, and 6000 at $1.50.
   a. Create a table showing the business's demand and marginal revenue schedules.
   b. Draw a graph showing the business's demand curve. Plot every point of the curve, five points in total.
   c. At what quantity does this business face a kink in its demand curve?
   d. Now draw the business's MR curve with its two downsloping segments connected by a vertical segment at the quantity highlighted in part c. Include a left endpoint of the first downsloping segment on the vertical axis. Also include a right endpoint of this same segment at the quantity highlighted in part c, and a left endpoint of the second downsloping segment at this same quantity. These last two points serve as the endpoints of the vertical segment. In total, your curve should have seven plotted points: four points on the first downsloping segment and three on the second.

4. Presto Cleaners, a small dry-cleaning shop, operates in a monopolistically competitive market, with revenues and costs as shown in the table below.

Profit-Maximization Table for Presto Cleaners

(1) Price ($ per shirt)	(2) Quantity (shirts per month)	(3) Total Revenue ($)	(4) Total Cost ($)	(5) Marginal Revenue ($ per shirt)	(6) Marginal Cost ($ per shirt)
$5.00	0	$_____	$3000	$_____	$_____
4.50	1000	_____	5000		
4.00	2000	_____	6250	_____	_____
3.50	3000	_____	8000	_____	_____
3.00	4000	_____	10 300	_____	_____
2.50	5000	_____	15 000	_____	_____

   a. Fill in the table.
   b. What is Presto's profit-maximizing or loss-minimizing quantity of output rounded to the nearest 1000 shirts, and what price does it charge?
   c. What is Presto's short-run profit or loss?
   d. What will happen to Presto's profit or loss in the long run?

5. A producer of fresh orange juice, Citrus Delight, operates in an oligopoly and has revenues and costs as shown in the table below.

Profit-Maximization Table for Citrus Delight

(1) Price ($ per carton)	(2) Quantity (thousands of cartons per day)	(3) Total Revenue ($ thousands)	(4) Total Cost ($ thousands)	(5) Marginal Revenue ($ per carton)	(6) Marginal Cost ($ per carton)
$2.20	0	$_____	$50	$_____	$_____
2.10	30	_____	90		
2.00	60	_____	110	_____	_____
1.90	90	_____	126	_____	_____
1.70	100	_____	143	_____	_____
1.50	110	_____	180	_____	_____

a. Fill in the table.

b. Identify Citrus Delight's profit-maximizing or loss-minimizing quantity of output rounded to the nearest 10 000 or 30 000 cartons and the price it charges. What is its short-run profit or loss?

c. At what quantity does the demand curve that Citrus Delight faces have a kink?

d. Will Citrus Delight's profit or loss necessarily disappear in the long run? Explain.

6. True North Railways, the sole provider of passenger rail service to a remote community, has revenues and costs shown in the table below.

Profit-Maximization Table for True North Railways

(1) Price ($ per passenger)	(2) Quantity (passengers per day)	(3) Total Revenue ($)	(4) Total Cost ($)	(5) Marginal Revenue ($ per passenger)	(6) Marginal Cost ($ per passenger)
	0	$_____	$24 750	$_____	$_____
350	50	_____	26 750	_____	_____
280	100	_____	27 750	_____	_____
210	150	_____	27 900	_____	_____
140	200	_____	28 000	_____	_____
70	250	_____	29 000	_____	_____
0	300	_____	34 500		

a. Fill in the table.

b. Identify True North's profit-maximizing quantity of output rounded to the nearest 50 passengers, and the price it charges.

c. At this quantity, what is True North's short-term profit or loss?

7. Two burglars, Harry and Marv, are being questioned separately by police. Each is now deciding whether or not to confess and implicate his partner, or to remain silent. The diagram below shows the jail times they will receive under different conditions.

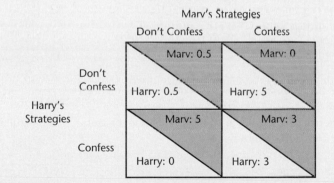

Marv's Strategies

	Don't Confess	Confess
Don't Confess	Marv: 0.5 / Harry: 0.5	Marv: 0 / Harry: 5
Confess	Marv: 5 / Harry: 0	Marv: 3 / Harry: 3

Harry's Strategies

a. If Harry and Marv can communicate, what action is each likely to take?

b. If Harry and Marv cannot communicate, what action is each likely to take?

8. Two businesses, Castor and Pollux, are the only two sellers in a particular market. They have just signed an agreement to raise their prices. Each firm is considering whether to charge the agreed-upon price or whether instead, through cheating, to charge the same price as before. If Castor cheats while Pollux refrains from doing so, then Castor makes an annual profit of $500 000 while Pollux makes a profit of $200 000. On the other hand, if Pollux cheats and Castor refrains from doing so, then Castor makes $200 000 and Pollux makes $500 000 annually. If both refrain from cheating, each makes $400 000, but if both cheat, each makes $300 000. The diagram on the next page shows the possible strategies for both Castor and Pollux.

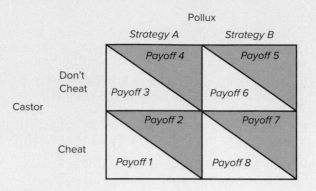

a. What are the monetary values of each of the eight payoffs? Which of the two strategies, A or B, involves the business cheating and which one does not?

b. If cheating by either seller is easily discovered, what strategy are Castor and Pollux likely to choose? What will be the profit of each?

c. If cheating is not easily discovered, what strategy are both of them likely to choose? What will be the profit of each?

9. An industry is made up of six firms with sales of $50 million, $55 million, $80 million, $30 million, $65 million, and $100 million.
   a. Calculate the industry's four-firm concentration ratio.
   b. How would you categorize this industry?

10. Identify whether official concentration ratios for the product in italics will tend to overestimate or underestimate the level of competition.
    a. *magazines*, which are sold in a market with a significant international presence
    b. *construction*, whose providers tend to operate in strictly regional markets

11. (Advanced Question)
    For each of the following cases of non-price competition, outline the likely effects on (i) the business undertaking the strategy, (ii) other businesses in the market, and (iii) consumers.
    a. A recording company is the first to produce recordings of a new style of popular music.
    b. A major corporation that makes laundry soap increases the amount it spends on advertising.
    c. A cosmetics firm changes the brand name of one of its perfumes to give it greater appeal to young buyers.
    d. A lawyer starting her practice decides to break with tradition by advertising the prices she charges.

12. (Advanced Question)
    In 2013, Google revamped its social networking service Google+ by introducing automatic enhancement to photos and videos uploaded on its members' home pages. Explain how this form of non-price competition was a response to Google's competitor Facebook and its photo-sharing service Instagram. Has Google's strategy succeeded in helping it to overturn Facebook's dominance in the global social media market? Explain.

THE GAMES PEOPLE PLAY

Thomas C. Schelling and Game Theory

SCHELLING AND HIS INFLUENCE

Thomas C. Schelling, an emeritus professor at the University of Maryland, is best known for his contributions to game theory, which won him and Israeli mathematician Robert Aumann the Nobel Prize in Economics in 2005. After studying economics at the University of California at Berkeley and at Harvard, Schelling carved out an academic career first at Yale and then at Harvard, while also being involved with government and research institutes.

At this time, game theory was still relatively new and largely confined to the mathematical sphere, thanks to its creators, mathematicians John von Neumann and Oskar Morgenstern, as well as others such as John Nash, subject of the Academy Award-winning movie *A Beautiful Mind*. Schelling transformed game theory by concerning himself less with mathematical details and more with the nuances of human perception and interaction. In doing so, he helped ensure that game theory became an integral part of economic thinking–not just in the analysis of oligopolistic behaviour, but wherever strategic game-playing occurs.

THOMAS C. SCHELLING
Photo courtesy of Thomas C. Schelling

THE CASE OF MILITARY STRATEGY

Schelling first became famous for employing game theory in the area of military strategy a field of study with more than a few similarities to the study of economic rivalry. While finishing his doctoral degree, he worked on the Marshall Plan, the far-sighted American program that helped rebuild war-ravaged Europe after 1945. This experience led to a stint as an adviser to American president Harry Truman in the early 1950s. Schelling was fascinated by the dynamics of the nuclear arms race that was being played out at that time between the United States and the Soviet Union. While most commentators were condemning the arms race as irrational, given that both nations were accumulating nuclear arsenals far in excess of the amounts needed to destroy one another, Schelling used game theory principles to delve into what he argued were the rational motivations of the two superpowers–motivations that involved not just rivalry, but also implicit cooperation between the two countries as well.

Until his analysis, outlined in his 1960 classic *The Strategy of Conflict*, the US military establishment focused its military spending on building the capacity to launch a nuclear attack, presuming it could do so before any nuclear attack by the Soviet Union. Schelling showed that the most effective deterrence came from something quite different: the capacity to retaliate effectively to an initial attack. To make the case for this second strike capability, he cited the example of two gunfighters in a threatened shootout: "if both were assured of living long enough to shoot back with unimpaired aim," he noted, "there would be no advantage in jumping the gun and little reason to fear that the other would try it."[1]

To deter a surprise attack by the other side, Schelling counselled an emphasis on "the safety of weapons rather than the safety of people."[2] As heartless as this strategy seems, it helped ensure that nuclear weapons were not used by either of the two superpowers during the entire Cold War. In other words, the nuclear standoff did reach a stable equilibrium of mutual deterrence for over 50 years. For this, Schelling deserves some of the credit.

THE CASE OF ELECTRICITY RATIONING

Schelling later used the very same sort of game theory logic that he had used in analyzing military strategy to examine a wide range of everyday social situations. Most of these cases were characterized by the "divergence between what people are individually motivated to do and what they might like to accomplish together,"[3] which, he argued, often called for the breaking of Adam Smith's laissez-faire principle.

This can be seen by studying one of Schelling's examples, the potential need for electricity rationing during summer heat waves. In many Canadian cities, electricity consumers are warned that, on particularly hot days, they should voluntarily cut down on electricity use to minimize the chance of system overload and resulting power outages. While all users would be better off if everyone engaged in rationing, each household and business knows that the impact of their own rationing is infinitesimal, so sees no individual benefit in doing so. Many users therefore continue with their customary electricity use, making it more likely that overloads will occur.

This dilemma may be overcome in several ways. Public authorities could appeal to each user's sense of civic virtue to encourage compliance. But while many users will change their behaviour as a result of these appeals, not all will, creating social discord. Much more effective, said Schelling, is a rule governing electricity consumption, complete with penalties (such as higher prices for excess usage) for those who break it. Electricity consumers are far more likely to cooperate knowing that, because of this formal rule, all others will cooperate as well. Schelling called this solution an enforceable social contract, and saw it as legitimate in cases where individual self-interest works against the incentive that people may have to cooperate with one another for the common good. As a result, he helped economists better understand exactly when and where government involvement in the economy can contribute to our collective welfare.

1. Schelling admits that his stress on second-strike nuclear capacity does not apply when dealing with threats from terrorism. Why not?

2. The dilemma that faces electricity consumers during periods of heavy usage can be interpreted in terms of the prisoner's dilemma. How?

Notes
[1] Thomas Schelling, *The Strategy of Conflict* (Cambridge MA.: Harvard University, 1960), pp. 232-233.
[2] Ibid., p. 233.
[3] Thomas Schelling, *Micromotives and Macrobehavior* (New York: W. W. Norton, 1978), p. 128.

CHAPTER 7

Economic Welfare and Income Distribution

In Canada today, many people enjoy all the luxuries of a consumer culture while others barely scrape by. Is this fair? If not, what could and should be done? We all strive to gain as much as we can from our participation in the economy. In this chapter we look at the ways economic welfare is generated within markets and some of the policies that governments use to affect this welfare creation: policies to minimize pollution and to forestall the harm caused by climate change, to intervene through taxes or regulations in particular markets, and to redistribute incomes throughout the economy to enhance income equity. This allows us to gain insight into some of the key economic functions of governments today.

> A decent provision for the poor is the true test of civilization.
>
> -SAMUEL JOHNSON, ENGLISH WRITER

LEARNING OBJECTIVES   After reading this chapter, you will be able to:

LO 1	LO 2	LO 3	LO 4	LO 5
Describe the concepts of consumer surplus, producer surplus, and deadweight loss, and explain how these concepts can further our understanding of the operation of markets	Distinguish between spillover costs and benefits, and identify the ways that government addresses these issues	Determine the impact of an excise tax on consumers and producers	Explain the effects of government price control programs on consumers and producers	Evaluate the effectiveness of government intervention to change the distribution of income

7.1 | Economic Welfare

LO1   Both consumers and producers gain from participating in markets–consumers through the satisfaction they gain from the products they consume, and producers through earning profit. In this chapter we look at both of these aspects of economic welfare, starting with the net benefits gained by consumers.

Consumer Surplus

An individual's demand for a certain item can be seen in two ways. Figure 7.1 shows the demand for pizza by an individual pizza consumer. Recall that an individual's demand curve tells us how much a person is willing to spend on each unit of the product–in other words, what her quantity demanded is at each price. The curve shows that this consumer will buy one pizza at a price of $14, two pizzas at a price of $12 each, and three pizzas at a price of $10 each. The demand curve can also be viewed in the opposite way. The height of the demand curve at each quantity is the maximum price the consumer is willing to pay for that unit. Therefore, in this example, the consumer is willing to pay up to $14 for her first pizza of the week, $12 for her second, and $10 for her third.

MARGINAL AND TOTAL BENEFIT

marginal benefit: the extra satisfaction, expressed in dollar terms, from consuming a certain unit of a product

total benefit: the total satisfaction, expressed in dollar terms, from consuming a product in a given time period

The maximum price that a consumer will pay for a certain unit of a product indicates that unit's **marginal benefit**, or the extra satisfaction, expressed in dollar terms, that the individual receives from consuming that unit. While our pizza consumer gains $14 worth of marginal benefit from her first pizza of the week, the second pizza gives her $12 in marginal benefit, and the third only $10, regardless of the actual price. To find a consumer's **total benefit**, or the total satisfaction from a product, with this satisfaction expressed in dollar terms, add together the marginal benefits of all units consumed during a given time period. In this case, our consumer receives marginal benefits of $14, $12, and $10 for the first three pizzas she eats each week. The sum of these three numbers–$36–gives the total benefit gained from pizza consumption. In Figure 7.1, this total benefit is shown as area AB under the demand curve–between zero and three pizzas.

CONSUMER SURPLUS DEFINED

consumer surplus: the net benefit, expressed in dollar terms, from buying a product at its market price

A consumer's expenditure on a product is simply the market price multiplied by the number of units purchased. With a price of $10, and a consumption of three pizzas per week, our consumer faces a weekly bill of $30. This dollar amount, which represents revenue to the seller, is shown as area B on the graph in Figure 7.1.

Consumers expect to receive more satisfaction from consuming a product than they actually pay for it. This **consumer surplus** is defined as the net benefit, expressed in dollar terms, from buying a product at its market price. It is found by subtracting the consumer's expenditure from the total benefit. In the case of our individual pizza-lover, her consumer surplus from pizzas is $6 (= $36 − $30). On the graph in Figure 7.1, consumer surplus is the difference between total benefit (area AB) and expenditure (area B), giving area A.

FIGURE 7.1   Consumer Surplus for an Individual

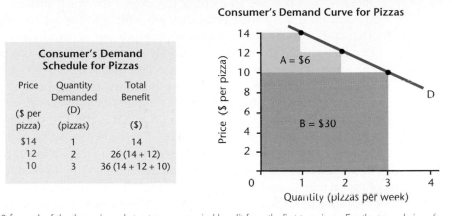

Consumer's Demand Schedule for Pizzas

Price	Quantity Demanded (D)	Total Benefit
($ per pizza)	(pizzas)	($)
$14	1	14
12	2	26 (14 + 12)
10	3	36 (14 + 12 + 10)

The consumer pays $10 for each of the three pizzas, but gets more marginal benefit from the first two pizzas. For the second pizza, for example, the $12 marginal benefit can be split into the $10 market price and the $2 surplus for that pizza. The consumer's total benefit from eating pizzas is area AB, and the total expenditure is area B. So, consumer surplus is area A

With the help of the market demand curve, the notion of consumer surplus can be extended to an entire market, as illustrated for the pizza market in Figure 7.2. The market demand curve shows that, at a price of $10, consumers buy 100 000 pizzas per week. By adding together the marginal benefits for each consumer, total benefit appears as the entire area AB beneath the demand curve, up to a quantity demanded of 100 000 pizzas. In contrast, total expenditure equals the rectangular area B. Because 100 000 pizzas are purchased at $10, area B equals $1 million (= $10 × 100 000). The consumer surplus for the entire market is the difference between the total benefit (area AB) and the total expenditure (area B), or the triangular area A. Because this triangle has a height of $8 (= $18 − $10) and a width of 100 000, its area equals $400 000 (= ($8 × 100 000) ÷ 2).

FIGURE 7.2   Consumer Surplus for a Market

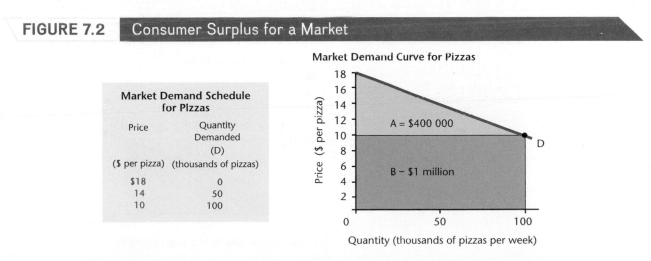

Market Demand Schedule for Pizzas

Price	Quantity Demanded (D)
($ per pizza)	(thousands of pizzas)
$18	0
14	50
10	100

When consumers in the pizza market are charged a price of $10, they consume 100 000 pizzas. Adding up consumers' marginal benefits for all these pizzas gives a total benefit in the market equal to area AB. At the same time, consumers' total expenditure on pizzas is area B. To find the total consumer surplus in the market, subtract area B from area AB, which is equal to area A.

Producer Surplus

Likewise, it is possible to identify the extent to which producers receive a price different from the lowest price they are willing to accept to sell a given unit of a product. Figure 7.3 shows a supply curve for our pizza market, presuming for the time being that this market is perfectly competitive. With the prevailing price of $10, the supply curve tells us that sellers provide 100 000 pizzas. This supply curve can also be viewed in the opposite way: the height of the supply curve at each quantity is the minimum price the relevant producer is willing to accept for that unit. For example, the producer who makes the 100 000th pizza receives the minimum price he is willing to accept if the price of pizzas is $10. But producers of the previous units would have been willing to accept a lower price. For example, the producer of the first pizza would have been willing to accept a minimum price of just above $2, and the producer of the 50 000th pizza would have been willing to accept a price as low as $6. In each of these cases, the minimum acceptable price for the producer is nothing but the marginal cost of producing that unit, as shown at the relevant quantity by the height of the supply curve.

PRODUCER SURPLUS DEFINED

In the aggregate, producers in a perfectly-competitive market gain more from selling the product than the minimum they would have been willing to accept. This **producer surplus** is defined as the difference between the price received from selling each unit of a product and the marginal cost of producing that unit. To find this surplus in an entire market, we must compare two amounts–the total revenue and the total area under the market supply curve at the prevailing price and quantity. In the case of our pizza market, the first is shown in Figure 7.3 by area CD. Meanwhile, the total area under the supply curve, or area D, gives the sum of the marginal costs of producing each unit of quantity. Producer surplus is the difference between these two amounts, the triangular area C. Because the height of this triangle is $8 and its width is 100 000, its area equals $400 000 (= ($8 × 100 000) ÷ 2).

producer surplus: the difference between the price received from selling each unit of a product and the marginal cost of producing it

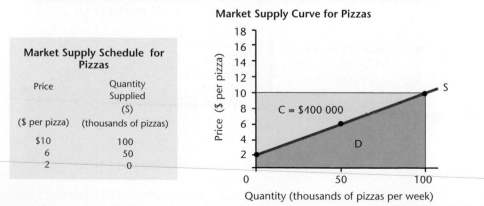

FIGURE 7.3   Producer Surplus for a Market

Market Supply Curve for Pizzas

Market Supply Schedule for Pizzas

Price	Quantity Supplied (S)
($ per pizza)	(thousands of pizzas)
$10	100
6	50
2	0

C = $400 000

At a market price of $10, producers in the pizza market supply 100 000 pizzas. Because market price and marginal cost are the same for the 100 000 pizzas, at this unit there is no producer surplus. But, for every previous pizza produced, price exceeds marginal cost, giving a total producer surplus equal to area C, found by subtracting the area under the supply curve, D, from the total revenue shown by area CD.

In terms of profit and costs, producer surplus includes both the economic profit and the fixed costs of all businesses in the market. The reason is that the area under the supply curve, which is not included in the calculation, can be interpreted as the sum of the marginal costs of making every single pizza. This sum gives the combined variable costs for all the businesses in the market. Since we subtract this amount from total revenue to derive producer surplus, what remains is fixed costs and profit.

The Case of Perfect Competition

Figure 7.4 shows the consumer surplus and the producer surplus for pizzas. When both amounts are depicted on the same graph, the graph confirms something we already know about perfectly-competitive markets. Recall from Chapter 5 that, in equilibrium, perfect competition meets the requirement of marginal-cost pricing, according to which a unit of an item should be produced if the price that consumers are willing to pay for the unit exceeds its marginal cost. If this condition is met in a market, then both the consumer surplus and the producer surplus are maximized.

First, consider why the consumer surplus is maximized when this condition is met. In Figure 7.4, if quantity falls short of the preferred level of 100 000 pizzas, as found using the marginal-cost pricing requirement, then the consumer surplus could be increased by producing those extra units for which the marginal benefit to consumers, as shown by the height of the demand curve, exceeds market price. In contrast, if quantity is greater than 100 000 pizzas, then excess units are being produced whose marginal benefit (the height of the demand curve) is less than market price. Because these units are detracting from the overall consumer surplus, output should be reduced. In each case, maximizing the consumer surplus means a return to the preferred point where the marginal-cost pricing condition is met.

Now, consider the producer surplus. In Figure 7.4, if quantity falls short of its preferred level of 100 000 pizzas, the producer surplus could be expanded

FIGURE 7.4 The Case of Perfect Competition

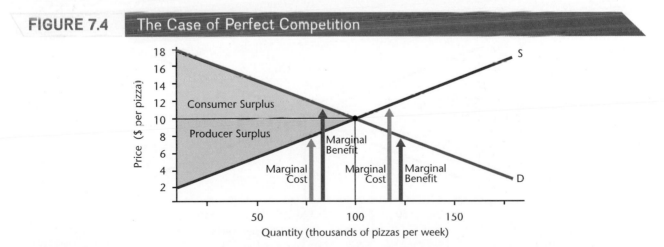

If the pizza market is perfectly competitive, then at the equilibrium price of $10 and output of 100 000 pizzas, the requirement of marginal-cost pricing is met, while the consumer surplus and producer surplus are both maximized, which means that excess benefit in the market is maximized as well. At quantities below 100 000 pizzas, marginal benefit exceeds marginal cost, which means economic welfare can be increased by raising quantity. At quantities above 100 000 pizzas, marginal cost exceeds marginal benefit, so that a reduction in quantity will bring about greater economic welfare.

by producing those units for which the price received exceeds marginal cost, as shown by the height of the supply curve. On the other hand, if quantity exceeds its equilibrium level, excess units are being produced for which the price received is less than marginal cost (the height of the supply curve). Given that these units reduce the overall producer surplus, output should be reduced. As in the case of the consumer surplus, this process leads us back to the preferred point where the producer surplus is maximized, and where the marginal-cost pricing condition is again satisfied. Producer surplus and consumer surplus are often treated together and referred to as **excess benefit**. This is the total difference between marginal benefit and marginal cost for all units produced and consumed in a market. For the preferred quantity of 100 000 pizzas in Figure 7.4, this is the total area of the consumer surplus and producer surplus.

excess benefit: the total difference between marginal benefit and marginal cost for all units that are produced and consumed in a market

When a Market Becomes Uncompetitive

What happens to the consumer surplus and producer surplus when the conditions of perfect competition no longer apply? Suppose that several producers are able to gain exclusive rights to operate in our pizza market, thanks to a new government licensing system. This means that all other producers are pushed out of the market. If the remaining pizza-makers are able to agree to restrict output to 75 000 pizzas, the new market price is $12. Profits are higher for the colluding pizza-makers than they were in a perfectly-competitive market. This gain, which is at the expense of consumers, is depicted in Figure 7.5 by the rectangular area E, which shows the amount of consumer surplus transformed into producer surplus. Reducing market output has another impact: it shrinks the consumer surplus by a further amount equal to the triangular area F. It also shrinks the producer surplus by the triangular area G–a loss borne by the producers who can no longer operate in the market. To summarize, area E is simply a transfer of benefits from consumers to producers. However, area FG depicts a net reduction in excess benefit in the market. This latter amount, known as the **deadweight loss**, represents the net loss in economic welfare

deadweight loss: the net loss in economic welfare that results from a government policy

| FIGURE 7.5 | When a Market Becomes Uncompetitive |

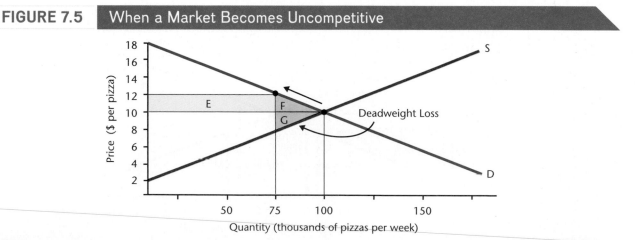

If some pizza-makers are allowed to collude, they might restrict output to 75 000 pizzas, raising the market price to $12. Area E represents the transfer of consumer surplus into producer surplus, which is gained by the colluding pizza-makers. Area FG represents the deadweight loss—combining a fall in both consumer surplus and producer surplus—as a result of the lower output. The loss of producer surplus is borne by producers who are no longer allowed to operate in the market.

that results from a government policy such as this decision to restrict entry into the pizza market.

The concepts of consumer surplus, producer surplus, excess benefit, and deadweight loss have a wide range of applications in evaluating government policy. Estimating changes in consumer and producer surpluses helps us understand how government actions influence both buyers and sellers, while estimating the deadweight loss gives us a sense of the net effect on overall economic welfare generated within a market. The fact that a government policy creates a deadweight loss does not mean that the policy is necessarily ill-conceived, because the policy might produce separate benefits that override this loss. But attempting to measure the deadweight loss, and then comparing it to any estimated benefits that a policy is expected to produce, helps ensure that government intervention has a net positive impact.

THINKING ABOUT ECONOMICS

Can imperfectly competitive businesses extract even more consumer surplus by charging different prices to different consumers?

Sometimes. For example, a municipal bus company may offer a discount to students rather than have them not ride the bus at all, a restaurant owner may lower the price of a meal for a lunch special and keep it high for dinner, or an airline may charge lower fares to tourists than to business travellers. This practice, known as "price discrimination," can be used to increase profits by any business with market power (either imperfectly competitive businesses or monopolists). Price discrimination can be used as long as the business can stop customers who pay different prices from exchanging the products between themselves. The business must also be able to distinguish between buyers willing to pay high and low prices, by using a condition such as the consumer's age or the time of day when the product is consumed.

QUESTION Are all consumers hurt when a business adopts a policy of price discrimination?

BRIEF REVIEW

1. The height of the demand curve at some quantity can be interpreted as the maximum price the consumer is willing to pay for that unit. This maximum price represents the extra satisfaction, expressed in dollar terms, that a consumer gains from that unit.

2. The consumer surplus in a market is the difference between the total benefit for consumers, expressed in dollars, and the amount of money that consumers spend on the product. The producer surplus is the difference between businesses' total revenue and the total area under the market supply curve at the prevailing price and quantity.

3. For a perfectly competitive market in equilibrium, the excess benefit, which is the sum of both consumer surplus and producer surplus, is maximized. This desirable result is due to the fact that perfectly competitive markets meet the requirement of marginal-cost pricing.

4. One of the common results of government policies, such as restricting competition, is a net reduction in consumer and producer surplus. This aggregate loss is known as the deadweight loss.

7.1 | PRACTICE PROBLEMS

1. The table below shows hypothetical market demand and supply schedules for maple syrup.

Market Demand and Supply Schedules for Maple Syrup

Price ($ per kg)	Quantity Demanded (millions of litres per year)	Quantity Supplied (millions of litres per year)	
	D	S_0	S_1
$5	0	12	6
4	3	9	3
3	6	6	0
2	9	3	-
1	12	0	-

a. Draw a graph showing the demand and supply curves D and S_0. Plot only the endpoints of the demand and supply curves.
b. What are the initial equilibrium price and quantity in this market?
c. Calculate the initial consumer surplus and producer surplus.
d. The supply curve in this market shifts to S_1. Draw the new supply curve on your graph, plotting only the endpoints of the curve. What are the new equilibrium price and quantity?
e. Calculate the new consumer surplus and producer surplus.
f. Have consumers become worse off or better off as a result of the supply shift? Have producers become worse off or better off?

7.2 | Spillover Effects and Market Failure

L02

spillover effects: external effects of economic activity, which have an impact on outsiders who are not producing or consuming a product

When intervening in particular markets, governments may be seeking to deal with the external effects of economic activity. These **spillover effects** arise whenever outsiders are affected by the production or consumption of a particular product. Spillover effects occur in even the ideal case of a perfectly-competitive market, simply because no market exists in isolation. Governments often step in to see that all costs and benefits–private and public–are accounted for, through the use of regulations, taxes, or subsidies.

Spillover Costs and Benefits

Spillover effects, also often referred to as externalities, may take the form of either costs or benefits.

SPILLOVER COSTS

spillover costs: negative external effects of producing or consuming a product

Spillover costs are the negative external effects of producing or consuming a product that fall on outsiders, not market participants. Environmental pollution is the most common example. Recall that some resources called free goods, such as air, can be used free of charge. Still other resources, such as water, have prices that do not reflect the resource's value. Any damage caused to these resources through market activity creates substantial costs for society as a whole.

Producers making products that have negative external effects focus only on their private costs as they make supply decisions. Consequently, the prices of these products are insufficient to cover both private and spillover costs. Figure 7.6 illustrates spillover costs with the example of gasoline used by motor vehicles. Assuming that the market for gasoline is competitive and free of government intervention, equilibrium occurs at point *b*, the intersection of the demand and supply curves D and S_0, with a price per litre of $1.50 and a quantity of 4 million litres.

Because of the environmental damage created by both the production and the consumption of gasoline, spillover costs are associated with this product. If these spillover costs are an extra $1 for each litre of gas, we can draw a new supply curve (S_1) that incorporates the additional cost per litre. Whereas the old supply curve (S_0) reflects the private costs of producing one more litre of gasoline, the new supply curve (S_1) reflects the *private* and *public* costs of each new

FIGURE 7.6 The Impact of Spillover Costs

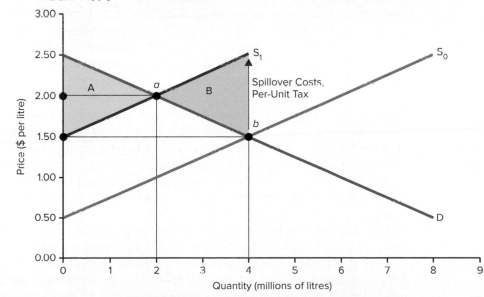

Demand and Supply Schedules for Gasoline

Price ($ per litre)	Quantity Demanded (D) (millions of litres)	Quantity Supplied (S_0) (millions of litres)	Quantity Supplied (S_1) (millions of litres)
$2.50	0	8	4
2.00	2	6	2
1.50	4	4	0
1.00	6	2	0
0.50	8	0	0

Demand and Supply Curves for Gasoline

Without government intervention, equilibrium occurs at point *b*. To account for spillover costs, the government may impose a tax of $1 per litre. As a result, the supply curve shifts from S_0 to S_1, moving equilibrium to point *a*.

litre. For example, at a quantity of 2 million litres, the private cost, as shown by the height of the old supply curve S_0 in Figure 7.6, equals $1. Meanwhile, once spillover costs are incorporated, the same quantity on the new supply curve S_1 is now associated with a total cost of $2–representing both the $1 private cost and the $1 spillover cost at this quantity level.

Where should the market operate? Recall the requirement of marginal-cost pricing, which states that the benefits of perfect competition are maximized when the price that consumers are willing to pay equals marginal cost, as long as marginal cost incorporates all possible costs to society. In this case, price should equal the height of the supply curve, once both private and spillover costs are accounted for. In other words, equilibrium should occur at point *a*, the intersection of D and S_1, at a price of $2 and a quantity of 2 million litres. Without government intervention, 2 million too many litres of gasoline are produced and consumed, given the environmental damage associated with both the production and consumption of gasoline. To achieve the preferred outcome, government can impose regulations on the use of gasoline or use its taxing powers. For example, it can levy a tax on gasoline equalling $1 per litre. This succeeds in shifting the supply curve from S_0 to S_1, and ensures that the oversupply of gasoline is corrected.

Before the tax, the excess benefit in this market is the area between the demand curve D and supply curve S_1, which incorporates the spillover costs, between 0 and 4 million litres. Triangle A in Figure 7.6 shows the excess benefit up to the preferred outcome of 2 million litres. Between 2 million and 4 million litres, S_1 is vertically higher than D, so triangle B represents a negative excess benefit. Area B is deducted from area A to find the initial excess benefit before the tax. Once the tax is implemented, quantity falls to the preferred level of 2 million litres and area B disappears. Therefore the excess benefit is the full amount of area A.

If taxes provide one way of dealing with spillover costs, then how are they actually being used in countries such as Canada? Taxes on motor fuels such as gasoline are just one example. Federal and provincial taxes on alcohol and cigarettes also serve this role. By reducing alcohol and tobacco consumption, these taxes lower spillover costs, such as the public danger created by impaired drivers in the case of alcohol, and the health-related effects of second-hand smoke in the case of tobacco. But the use of taxes to combat spillover costs is still in its infancy. Many economists foresee a marked expansion in the use of this tool in years to come–especially in dealing with environmental concerns.

To see how taxes on products might be extended, we return to the topic of climate change introduced in Chapter 1. To analyze possible policy on how global warming might be addressed, concentrate on its potential spillover costs. For economists who subscribe to the view that global warming is a serious problem, it is logical to add a monetary estimate of its harmful effects to the per-unit spillover costs we saw for gasoline in Figure 7.6. According to this argument, policymakers should calculate the future costs of higher global temperatures, viewed in terms of today's dollars, then apportion this monetary estimate to all goods and services that involve carbon emissions. To ensure that all these carbon emissions are incorporated fairly, it is necessary to employ a standardized *carbon equivalent* when gauging the future effects of various emissions on global temperatures. This measure is already being widely used by people and organizations interested in computing the carbon footprint of their consumption and production decisions.

In doing these calculations, it makes theoretical sense to tax every product at a dollar amount based on an estimate of total carbon emissions per product unit. Such a **carbon tax** would presumably be in addition to any other taxes already levied on products. Unlike product taxes such as the GST, the rate of the carbon tax rate imposed in each market would therefore differ, with products associated with heavy levels of carbon emissions taxed at higher rates than those for which carbon emissions are a relatively minor byproduct.

This new type of tax, whose effects on government revenue can be counteracted through reducing other types of taxes, is supported by many environmentally-minded economists. If applied correctly, carbon taxes would help ensure that any economic activity that contributes to global warming would be properly adjusted to account for these effects. Carbon tax supporters point out that the basket of products subject to this tax would be extremely large. Not only would obvious products such as gasoline or aircraft fuel be included, so too would any item whose production or consumption requires significant transportation of materials. Even many services–especially those that depend on electrical power, which is often generated through the burning of fossil fuels such as coal–would be affected.

Those suspicious of carbon taxes contend that the estimated spillover costs on which carbon tax rates would be based are too subjective to allow for a viable policy. These opponents often argue instead for laws that directly target producers through measures such as caps on the emissions that can be produced by new automobiles. Another policy often advocated by carbon tax opponents is the setting up of markets for carbon emissions. These markets can be either international or national. On the global stage, the most important of these markets is the Carbon Expo that takes place each year in Cologne, Germany. At this fair, buyers and sellers exchange *carbon credits* (rights to emit a certain amount of carbon equivalents). Buyers of these credits are primarily businesses and governments in rich countries interested in counteracting their own carbon emissions; sellers are businesses and governments in less rich countries that have implemented projects to cut their carbon emissions. Any event that causes increased concern over global warming causes a demand-led rise in the price of these credits. Supply factors also affect the market, with an expansion in the number of carbon-reduction projects causing a supply-led drop in price.

Some countries have set up their own markets for carbon emissions, commonly known as cap-and-trade systems, with domestic caps on emissions. In this case, a country's large emitters–mostly utility firms and companies involved in manufacturing and commodity processing–trade carbon credits among themselves. Again, the price of the credits is determined by demand and supply factors, this time in a national context.

Regardless of how emission caps are instituted, carbon tax supporters are not convinced they provide much benefit. All too often, companies are able to lobby political decision-makers to keep overall emission caps high, thereby minimizing the effect. Or, even more problematically, this lobbying might lead to entire sectors being excluded from the emissions guidelines. Moreover, while carbon taxes provide an explicit price signal for both consumer and producers, the prices derived from carbon emission trading are often unstable, complicating the incentive structure that such systems are supposed to provide. Only through a powerful market-based instrument such as carbon taxation, its supporters argue, can the full range of carbon emissions be constrained in a predictable, transparent manner. This debate is bound to continue for years to come.

carbon tax: tax levied on a wide range of products to counteract spillover costs associated with carbon emissions

Virtually the only point that all can agree on is that the economic study of environmental issues such as climate change is becoming one of the most exciting and innovative areas within the discipline of economics today.

SPILLOVER BENEFITS

spillover benefits: positive external effects of producing or consuming a product

Spillover benefits are positive external effects of producing or consuming a product. Education is an important example, since society as a whole gains from this service. From an economic perspective alone, education is considered beneficial because of the increased work and income-earning opportunities it affords each individual, and because it enriches the nation's human resources.

FIGURE 7.7   The Impact of Spillover Benefits

Demand and Supply Schedules for an Engineering Education			
Tuition ($ per year)	Enrolment Demanded (D_0) (thousands of students)	Enrolment Demanded (D_1) (thousands of students)	Enrolment Supplied (S) (thousands of students)
$6000	0	0	16
5000	0	4	12
4000	4	8	8
3500	6	10	6
3000	8	12	4
2000	12	16	0

Demand and Supply Curves for an Engineering Education

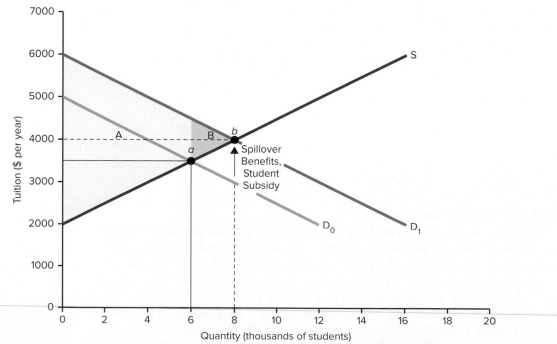

Without government intervention in the market for engineering education, equilibrium occurs at point *a*. If spillover benefits are determined to be $1000 per student, government can create a subsidy for students pursuing a career in engineering. As a result, the demand curve shifts from D_0 to D_1, and the new equilibrium is at point *b*, with $1000 of each student's tuition paid by government.

More generally, education is seen as a social good because it helps Canadians lead more informed, fulfilled, and productive lives.

Suppose that some students are considering an education in engineering. Figure 7.7 gives a hypothetical example. As in any education and career choice, the students would weigh the costs and benefits of obtaining an engineering degree. With the private market for an engineering education being competitive, the demand and supply curves D_0 and S have equilibrium point a, with a yearly tuition of $3500 per student and an enrolment of 6000 students.

Society as a whole benefits from having more trained engineers due to a faster pace of technological change. Hence there are spillover benefits. To see how much engineering education should be undertaken from society's perspective, we must estimate the spillover benefits of this education. Suppose the result is $1000 per student per year. As a result, we can draw a new demand curve (D_1) that incorporates the private and public benefits. For example, at an enrolment of 4000 students, the private benefit, as shown by the height of the old demand curve D_0, equals $4000. Meanwhile, once spillover benefits are incorporated, the same enrolment on the new demand curve D_1 is now associated with a total benefit of $5000—representing both the $4000 private benefit and the $1000 spillover benefit at this quantity level.

Again, the requirement of marginal-cost pricing is applicable. In this case, however, not only are consumers willing to pay a certain amount for each unit of the product—based on its private benefits—but society is willing to pay an extra amount to account for the spillover benefits. Therefore, price in this market should equal the height of the demand curve, once both private and spillover benefits are accounted for. In other words, equilibrium should occur at point b, at the intersection of S and D_1, with an annual tuition of $4000 and an enrolment of 8000 students. However, if private benefits alone were accounted for, only 6000 students (point a) would be enrolled, thereby creating a shortfall of 2000 students. To increase enrolment to the desired level, government itself could provide engineering education, or it could subsidize engineering education by giving prospective students vouchers to be turned in to the engineering school. The school would then turn in these vouchers to the government for $1000 per voucher. As a result, the demand curve for engineering education

THINKING ABOUT ECONOMICS

Is the Internet a public good?

For most businesses involved in e-commerce, the cost of accessing the Internet is so small as to be virtually negligible. And for many consumers—especially those who access the Internet from their place of work—the effective price is similar. This is because no one owns the Internet. Instead, its operation is overseen by various non-profit organizations, such as the National Science Foundation. The Internet, therefore, does have the features of a classic public good. As the price of access around the globe continues to fall, these features will become more prominent.

QUESTION   Given the ease of access to the Internet, how do the governing bodies that oversee it make sufficient revenues to cover their costs?

would shift to the right, thereby ensuring that society produces more engineers than would a fully private and competitive market. Before the voucher is implemented, excess benefit in this market is the difference between the demand curve D_1, which incorporates the spillover benefit, and the supply curve S between 0 and the initial enrolment of 6000 students. This is the shaded area A in the graph in Figure 7.7. With the voucher program, enrolment rises to 8000 and the excess benefit expands to the sum of areas A and B.

PUBLIC GOODS

public good: a product whose benefits cannot be restricted to certain individuals

At the extreme, there are some products for which private benefits and spillover benefits cannot be separated. A **public good** is a product whose benefits cannot be restricted to certain individuals. In other words, while some consumers pay for the product, others get a "free ride." Lighthouses are an example, since any ship that is navigated using a lighthouse benefits, whether or not the ship's owners help pay for the lighthouse's upkeep. In this situation, one option is to dispense with markets and have governments provide these products, which happens in the case of national defence. Since it is impossible to restrict the benefits of this service only to those citizens who are willing to pay for it, national defence must be financed through compulsory taxation.

But having governments provide public goods is not the only option. In some cases, governments can help turn public goods into private goods. For example, increasing elephant populations in African countries can be viewed as a public good. One option is to have governments finance policing measures to stop indiscriminate hunting. Another option that has been tried with some success in several African countries is to make elephants private property, so that the owners have an economic interest in maintaining a viable population for commercial hunting. In such cases, a government can prompt the formation of workable private markets.

In general, however, the challenges that arise in trying to organize a fair distribution of public goods remain extremely difficult to overcome. One succinct description of these challenges is the term *tragedy of the commons,*

THINKING ABOUT ECONOMICS

How is recycling affected by the fact that this activity is a public good?

Recycling is a public good due to its beneficial environmental effects. In recent decades, private markets have emerged for key recycled items such as paper, glass, and plastic. These markets can be analyzed using demand and supply. Demand for a recycled product flows largely from its potential use as an input in making other products—for example, when recycled paper is employed in producing newsprint. Following the law of demand, lower prices for a recycled product give users an incentive to increase their quantity demanded. The law of supply is similarly met in these markets, as a lower price for a particular recycled product reduces the incentive to engage in recycling, therefore decreasing quantity supplied. Hence equilibrium price and quantity are determined by demand and supply, with governments affecting these markets through various forms of subsidies.

QUESTION   What are two possible reasons—one demand-related and the other supply-related—why the equilibrium quantity in the market for a recycled product might rise?

which refers to the dilemma inherent in ensuring the fair exploitation of a public good. Take the case of a commonly-held plot of pasture land used by the inhabitants of a community. While it is not in the long-term interest of any member of the community that the pasture be over-exploited, each will have an incentive to let their animals use the pasture until it is over-grazed. A similar dilemma can be seen in the case of the fishing industry, with the maintenance of global fish stocks being potentially seen as a public good. For example, more than a decade ago the stock of Atlantic cod underwent a calamitous decline, with most commentators putting a large part of the blame on overfishing by both Canadian and international fishers. In practice, it is extremely difficult to establish government regulations that can adequately guard against such outcomes, as shown by the less precipitous but nonetheless highly worrisome drop in the population of Pacific salmon in recent years. Finding creative ways of overcoming the tragedy of the commons is one of the main goals of the field of environmental economics.

BRIEF REVIEW

1. Spillover effects are the external effects of economic activity that arise because no market exists in isolation.

2. Spillover effects can be negative or positive. Spillover costs, such as pollution, are the harmful effects of producing or consuming a product. Spillover benefits, such as those associated with education, are the positive effects of producing or consuming a product.

3. Governments often step in to see that public as well as private costs and benefits are accounted for. Governments might, for example, intervene with taxes to correct an oversupply in the case of spillover costs, or with subsidies to correct a shortfall in the case of spillover benefits.

4. Public goods are products whose benefits cannot be restricted to certain individuals. Governments often step in to provide these goods rather than leave them to private markets. Governments can also attempt to turn such goods into private goods by defining new types of property.

7.2 | PRACTICE PROBLEMS

1. In each case below, identify the situation as a spillover cost, spillover benefit, or tragedy of the commons.
   a. A late-night dance club in a suburban neighbourhood disturbs nearby residents.
   b. A new subway line reduces a city's traffic congestion.
   c. Poaching by hunters leads to the extinction of a certain animal species.
   d. The use of throw-away batteries adds to soil pollution.
   e. A recently invented electric light bulb uses far less electricity than conventional bulbs.
   f. A new high-speed jetliner uses more energy per passenger mile than existing aircraft.
   g. Proliferation of spam messages reduces the usefulness of email for many users.

2. The table below shows hypothetical demand and supply schedules for the flu vaccine.

Market Demand and Supply Schedules for the Flu Vaccine

Price ($ per vaccine)	Quantity Demanded (millions of vaccines per year)		Quantity Supplied (millions of vaccines per year)
	(D$_0$)	(D$_1$)	(S)
14	-	_____	8
12	0	_____	6
10	2	_____	4
8	4	_____	2
6	6	_____	0

a. Draw a graph showing the demand and supply curves D$_0$ and S. Plot only the endpoints of the demand and supply curves.

b. Before government intervention, what are the equilibrium price and quantity in this market?

c. It is estimated that the spillover benefits of vaccination are an extra $2 per vaccine. On the basis of this estimate, draw a new demand curve, D$_1$, on your graph that incorporates these spillover benefits, plotting only the endpoints of the new curve. Use your graph to fill in the empty column in the table. Based on the graph and the data in the table, what is the preferred quantity in this market?

d. What is the excess benefit in this market before government intervention?

e. If the government uses a subsidy to reach the preferred quantity, what dollar value per vaccine will the subsidy be set at? At this preferred quantity, what is the price as seen by consumers? as seen by producers?

f. How much money does the government spend on the subsidy?

g. After the subsidy, what is the new value of the excess benefit in this market? What is the excess benefit gained by imposing the subsidy?

7.3 | Excise Taxes

The Impact of an Excise Tax

excise tax: a tax on a particular product expressed as a dollar amount per unit of quantity

To illustrate how government could correct a spillover cost, we applied a type of tax known as an **excise tax**, which is a tax on a particular good or service expressed as a dollar amount per unit of quantity. In fact, excise taxes have a wide range of uses, not least as a way to raise revenue for government activities. Let's now explore their welfare impact in more detail. For example, a tax of $1 per kilogram may be imposed in the market for strawberries. Figure 7.8 shows its impact. The supply curve for producers remains at S$_0$ because the price producers see does not include the tax. But the supply curve facing consumers becomes S$_1$, since the price consumers see now includes an extra amount of $1 per kilogram at every possible quantity level. For example, at the initial quantity of 9 million kilograms, the price of strawberries seen by producers is $3, found at point c on S$_0$. Meanwhile, the price seen by consumers is $4, found at the corresponding point b on S$_1$.

The after-tax equilibrium is at point a, where the demand curve D crosses the new supply curve S$_1$ at a quantity of 7 million kilograms. The equilibrium

| **FIGURE 7.8** | The Impact of an Excise Tax |

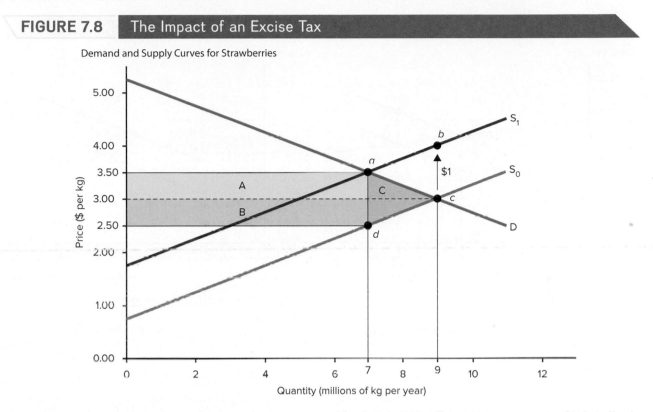

A $1 excise tax per kg causes the supply curve seen by strawberry consumers to shift to S_1. At the initial equilibrium, consumers pay a price of $4 (point b) and producers receive a price of $3 (point c). At the new equilibrium, consumers pay a price of $3.50, producers receive a price of $2.50, and the total tax payment is equally divided—area A paid by consumers and area B by producers.

quantity therefore drops because of the tax. For consumers, price is now $3.50, as shown by point a. For producers, price is $1 less at $2.50, shown by the corresponding point d on S_0.

The common myth is that excise taxes are always passed onto consumers. Figure 7.8 shows this myth to be untrue. Typically both consumers and producers pay a portion of any excise tax. In this market, half the tax is paid by consumers and half by producers. Graphically, the shaded area AB in Figure 7.8 shows the $7 million tax payment. Area A represents the $3.5 million payment by consumers, found by multiplying the tax-induced $0.50 price rise by the quantity of 7 million kilograms of strawberries. Likewise, area B represents the $3.5 million paid by producers, found by multiplying the corresponding $0.50 price drop by the quantity of 7 million kilograms. Meanwhile the tax causes a deadweight loss equal to area C, in this case equally shared by consumers and producers, showing the impact of the cutback in production of strawberries whose marginal benefit would have exceeded their marginal cost.

The Effect of Price Elasticity of Demand

The division of the tax burden is not always equal. One factor that affects this division is the price elasticity of the market demand curve. Figure 7.9 shows two

| FIGURE 7.9 | Excise Taxes and Demand Elasticity |

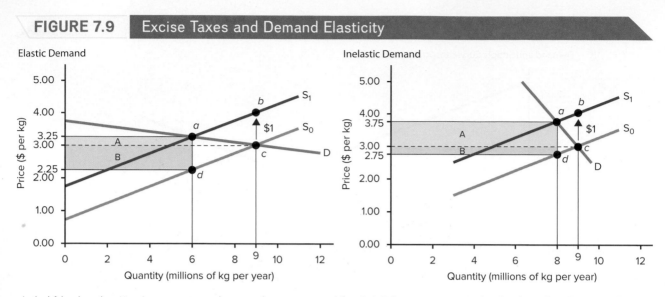

In the left-hand graph, a $1 excise tax causes supply as seen by consumers to shift to S_1. Initially consumers see a price of $4 (point b). At the new equilibrium, consumers pay a price of $3.25 (point a) while producers receive a price of $2.25. Because D is elastic, producers pay more of the tax (area B) than do consumers (area A). When D is inelastic, as in the right-hand graph, however, consumers pay more of the tax (area A) than do producers (area B).

possible demand curves for strawberries. In the left-hand graph, the relevant range of the demand curve is relatively elastic. In this case, the tax portion paid by consumers, as represented by area A, is smaller than that paid by producers, represented by area B. In contrast, the right-hand graph has a demand curve that is relatively inelastic in the relevant range. Consequently, the portion paid by consumers (area A) is larger than that paid by producers (area B). As a general rule, whenever supply is given, a more inelastic demand curve means a greater portion of an excise tax is paid by consumers.

The Effect of Price Elasticity of Supply

The division of the tax burden also depends on the price elasticity of supply, as shown in Figure 7.10. In the left-hand graph, supply is relatively elastic. Here the tax portion paid by consumers (area A) exceeds that paid by producers (area B). In the right-hand graph, the relatively inelastic supply curve means that the tax portion paid by consumers is now exceeded by that paid by producers. This is shown by the fact that area B exceeds area A. As a general rule, when demand is given, a more inelastic supply curve means a greater portion of an excise tax is paid by producers.

The Role of Elasticity in Tax Policy

These two general rules governing the relative burdens of an excise tax for consumers and producers explain why public authorities are so interested in estimating price elasticities of both demand and supply when considering an excise tax. The combined impact of the price elasticities of demand and supply determine which group ends up paying the bulk of the tax.

FIGURE 7.10   Excise Taxes and Supply Elasticity

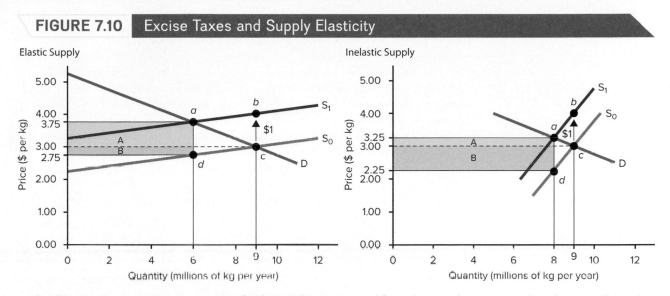

In the left-hand graph, consumers initially pay a price of $4 (point *b*) after an excise tax shifts supply as seen by consumers to S_1. At the new equilibrium, the price for consumers is $3.75 and for producers is $2.75. Because S is elastic, consumers pay more of the tax (area A) than do producers (area B). However, if S is inelastic, as in the right-hand graph, producers pay more of the tax (area B) than do consumers (area A).

BRIEF REVIEW

1. The division of the payment of an excise tax between consumers and producers depends on the extent to which the resulting price rise seen by consumers compares with the price drop seen by producers.

2. With supply given, a more inelastic demand means that a larger portion of an excise tax is paid by consumers.

3. With demand given, a more inelastic supply means that a larger portion of an excise tax is paid by producers.

7.3 | PRACTICE PROBLEMS

1. The table below shows hypothetical demand and supply schedules for chicken wings.

Market Demand and Supply Schedules for Chicken Wings

Price ($ per kg)	Quantity Demanded (millions of kg per year)	Quantity Supplied (millions of kg per year)	
	(D)	(So)	(S1)
$12	-	10	_____
11	0	8	_____
10	2	6	_____
9	4	4	_____
8	6	2	_____
7	8	0	_____

a. Draw a graph showing the demand and supply curves D and S_o. Plot only the endpoints of the demand and supply curves.

b. What are the equilibrium price and quantity in this market before government intervention?

c. In order to raise funds for the government, an excise tax of $2 per kilogram is imposed in this market. Draw the new supply curve S_1 facing consumers, plotting only the endpoints of the curve, and use your graph to fill in the empty column in the table.

d. What are the new equilibrium price faced by consumers and the new quantity? What is the price seen by producers?

e. What is the total tax payment? What amount falls on consumers? on producers?

f. Calculate the consumer surplus and producer surplus before the tax.

g. Calculate the consumer surplus and producer surplus after the tax.

h. Is the loss of welfare due to the tax greater for consumers or producers?

i. Calculate the total deadweight loss created by the tax.

7.4 | Price Controls

price floor: a legal minimum price

price ceiling: a legal maximum price

Sometimes governments see fit to control prices, thus overriding the forces of demand and supply and the "invisible hand" of competition. There are two types of price controls. A **price floor** is a legal minimum price. To be effective, such a floor must be set above the price that would otherwise exist in equilibrium. A **price ceiling** is a legal maximum price. This ceiling will be effective only if set below the equilibrium price. An example is rent controls. **Notice that "floor" and "ceiling" have special meanings in economics. Unless a price floor is higher than equilibrium, it will have no effect on the price prevailing in the market. Similarly, a price ceiling must be lower than equilibrium to be relevant.**

The concepts of consumer surplus, producer surplus, and deadweight loss can be used to analyze the effects of government programs to control prices. Because analyzing price controls also involves weighing one goal against another, the analysis depends on value judgments and so is part of normative economics.

Agricultural Price Supports

Agricultural markets provide a useful example. Unstable prices for many agricultural products cause large fluctuations in farmers' incomes. In the years when prices are high, farmers can make substantial revenues, but low prices cause revenues to plummet. As a result, farmers often request that governments intervene to stabilize prices at favourable levels. In the past, federal and provincial governments have often responded positively to these demands, not only out of a desire to stabilize prices and farm incomes, but also because the family farm represents a traditional institution that many Canadians wish to see maintained through government intervention.

One type of government program is price supports, illustrated by a hypothetical market for milk in Figure 7.11. Without government intervention, this market would reach an equilibrium price of $1.50 per litre and an associated quantity of 30 million litres sold per year. A government agency pays a minimum or floor price, such as $2, which is above the equilibrium level. The floor price has

FIGURE 7.11 | Effects of Price Supports

Market Demand and Supply Schedules for Milk		
Price ($ per litre)	Quantity Demanded (D) (millions of litres)	Quantity Supplied (S) (millions of litres)
$2.50	0	60
2.00	15	45
1.50	30	30
1.00	45	15
0.50	60	0

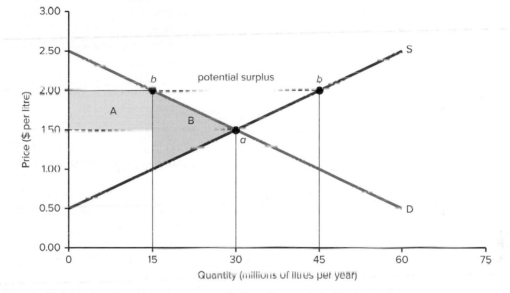

Market Demand and Supply Curves for Milk

Because the equilibrium price for milk (point *a*) is considered too low, the government agency imposes a price floor. If no output restriction is imposed, this creates a milk surplus at points *b*. As long as the demand and supply curves remain the same, this surplus will recur each year, and the government agency's stock of milk will increase. If an output restriction is imposed, then there is a transfer of consumer surplus to producer surplus equal to area A and a deadweight loss equal to area B.

two effects: quantity demanded decreases from 30 to 15 million litres, and quantity supplied increases from 30 to 45 million litres. Both effects lead to a surplus of the commodity of 30 million litres per year (= 45 million − 15 million), which, unless output restrictions are imposed, the government agency must purchase.

WINNERS AND LOSERS

Farmers are the obvious winners from price supports. In the absence of output restrictions, the program causes both price and quantity supplied to increase, and also raises farmers' revenues. Consumers lose because of the higher prices they pay, while taxpayers lose because they must foot the bill for the government agency's purchases of surplus products. Finally, by causing economic resources to be devoted to the production of unneeded agricultural surpluses, this program also works to the disadvantage of society as a whole. In order to forestall the expense of wasteful surpluses, governments sometimes also impose a restriction so that farmers can only produce the amount demanded in the market at the new higher price. If they do, then the impact of the price support program can be shown using the graph in Figure 7.11. The higher price leads to a transfer of consumer surplus to producer surplus equal to area A in the graph. The height of this area is the price increase and its width is the quantity of milk affected by the price change. There is also a deadweight loss. This equals area B in the graph, as some of the milk whose marginal benefit exceeds marginal cost is no longer produced.

THINKING ABOUT ECONOMICS

Are minimum wages another example of price supports?

Yes. Minimum wages apply in the markets for labour, which, like perfectly-competitive product markets, exhibit a downward-sloping demand curve and an upward-sloping supply curve. The negative slope of the demand curve reflects the fact that demanders of labour (i.e., employers) tend to cut back on the number of workers they hire at higher wage rates, while the positively-sloped supply curve shows that higher wage rates will tend to cause more workers to offer their labour in the market. As long as a particular labour market is competitive, then a minimum wage set above the equilibrium wage rate will tend to cause a surplus of labour at the prevailing minimum wage. In the case of labour markets, this surplus represents unemployed labour.

QUESTION   **In which sorts of labour markets do you think a set minimum wage will most likely exceed the equilibrium wage rate—a market for skilled labour or one for unskilled labour? Why?**

Rent Controls

Another way that governments override the "invisible hand" of competition is with price ceilings, which are upper limits to a price, such as rent. For example, a rent-control program was imposed on rental housing in Ontario in the 1970s due to pressure from tenant lobby groups, with capped rent increases kept below the rate of inflation. Figure 7.12 shows the effect of rent controls in a hypothetical large community with a competitive rental market, assuming that all rental units in this market are identical. Without a rent-control program, equilibrium in the market would occur at a monthly rent per unit of $750 and a total of 10 000 units rented per month. Controls push rents below the equilibrium level, to a value of $500. Consequently, quantity demanded increases from 10 000 to 15 000 units as more consumers enter the market. At the same time, quantity supplied falls from 10 000 to 5000 units as landlords find it less profitable to remain in the rental market and thus provide fewer units than before.

Quantity supplied is reduced in two ways: new rental construction is cut back, and some existing buildings are demolished or converted to other uses. The result of this artificially low rent is a shortage of 10 000 (= 15 000 − 5000) rental units. This shortage makes itself felt through a low vacancy rate for units. This means an unusually small percentage of units are available for rent at any given time.

As a rule, shortages foster underground markets. In the case of rental housing, some landlords and tenants who are subletting their apartments to other tenants charge a fee for preference among people on waiting lists. These fees, or bribes, are known as "key money" and are illegal. To get around the law, key

FIGURE 7.12	Effects of Rent Controls

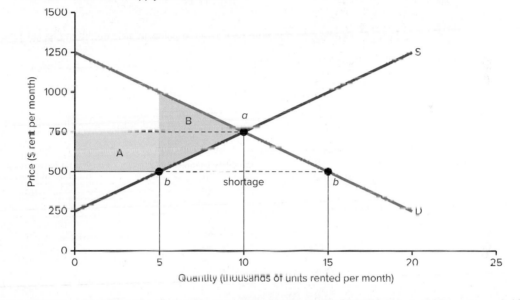

Market Demand and Supply Schedules for Units

Price ($ rent per month)	Quantity Demanded (D) (thousands of units)	Quantity Supplied (S) (thousands of units)
$1250	0	20
1000	5	15
750	10	10
500	15	5
250	20	0

Market Demand and Supply Curves for Units

Rent controls force price below the equilibrium level, from point *a* to points *b*. Quantity demanded rises at the new price, while quantity supplied falls. The price ceiling thus causes a shortage, a transfer of producer surplus to consumer surplus equal to area A, and a deadweight loss equal to area B.

money often takes imaginative forms, such as forced purchases of furnishings at exorbitant prices.

WINNERS AND LOSERS

As shown in Figure 7.12, the lower rent resulting from controls leads to a transfer of producer surplus to consumer surplus equal to area A in the graph, whose height is the drop in rental price and whose width is the quantity of rental units affected by the price drop. There is also a deadweight loss created equal to area B as some of the rental units whose marginal benefit exceeds marginal cost are no longer exchanged in the market. According to critics, even though rent controls may appear to offer tenants some short-run protection, in the long run they harm society as a whole by driving economic resources away from an important housing market and creating a shortage. Because of the restraints placed on landlords in setting their own price, they are particularly hurt by such controls. Some tenants gain from controls, especially middle-class tenants who have the connections and credentials to acquire the most desirable units. However, the shortage caused by controls pushes many poorer tenants into unregulated units, such as basement flats and rooming houses, with rents that are often higher than for units in the controlled market. Therefore, not only do rent controls lower the stock of rental housing, but they can affect different income groups unfairly.

BRIEF REVIEW

1. For various reasons, governments sometimes choose to intervene in markets to override the "invisible hand" of competition. Price controls are one form of intervention and take the form of price floors and price ceilings.

2. Setting a price floor, or a minimum allowable price, in a competitive market tends to cause surpluses.

3. Setting a price ceiling, or a maximum allowable price, in a competitive market tends to cause shortages.

7.4 | PRACTICE PROBLEMS

1. The table below shows hypothetical demand and supply schedules for milk.

Market Demand and Supply Schedules for Milk

Price ($ per litre)	Quantity Demanded (millions of litres per year)	Quantity Supplied (millions of litres per year)
	(D)	(S)
$1.00	40	80
0.90	50	70
0.80	60	60
0.70	70	50
0.60	80	40

a. Draw a graph showing the demand and supply curves, D and S. Plot only the endpoints of the demand and supply curves.
b. In the absence of government intervention, what are the equilibrium price and quantity? What are the consumers' total expenditure and producers' total revenue?
c. The government imposes a price support for milk of $0.90 per litre and agrees to purchase any unsold portion of the product at this price. Does the price support create an annual shortage or surplus? How large is this discrepancy?
d. Are consumers made worse off or better off by the price support program? Are producers made worse off or better off? What are the consumers' total expenditure and producers' total revenue?
e. How much does this program cost annually for taxpayers?
2. The table below shows hypothetical demand and supply schedules for apartments in a particular community.

Price ($ per month)	Quantity Demanded (thousands of units per month)	Quantity Supplied (thousands of units per month)
	(D)	(S)
$1400	35	45
1200	40	40
1000	45	35
800	50	30
600	55	25

a. Draw a graph showing the demand and supply curves, D and S. Plot only the endpoints of the demand and supply curves.
b. In the absence of government intervention, what are the equilibrium rent and quantity?
c. The government imposes an $800 maximum rent in this market. Does this create an annual shortage or surplus? How large is this discrepancy? Are tenants who are able to find units at the new rent made worse off or better off by this program? Are landlords made worse off or better off?
d. What is landlords' total revenue before and after the imposition of the policy?

7.5 | The Distribution of Income

So far, we have focused on how economic welfare is created within individual markets and the ways that governments can affect this process. We now turn to the broader issue of income equity—in particular, how household incomes are distributed within an entire economy.

Income Shares

To get an overview of who gets what in the economy, economists typically rank Canadian households by income and then categorize households into five groups of the same size on the basis of their income levels. Each group, therefore, represents 20 percent, or one fifth, of the total number of Canadian households. Figure 7.13 shows the pre-taxation income levels of the five groups for various years. In 2011, the fifth of Canadian households with the lowest incomes received a small proportion—a mere 4 percent—of all households' total pre-tax income, while the fifth of Canadian households with the highest incomes

---

FIGURE 7.13   Income Distribution in Selected Years

Percentage of Total Pre-Tax Income Received by Each Fifth of Households*

	1961	1971	1981	1991	2001	2011	Average Income (2011)
Lowest 20%	4	4	5	5	4	4	$ 15 500
Second 20%	12	11	11	10	10	10	35 900
Third 20%	18	18	18	17	16	15	57 500
Fourth 20%	25	25	25	25	24	24	89 100
Highest 20%	44	43	42	44	47	47	176 900
Average of total							75 000

*Percentages may not add to 100 due to rounding.

Income shares have varied since 1961, but consistently the group of households with the highest income received over 40 percent of the total income, while the group of households with the lowest income received less than 5 percent.

Sources: Statistics Canada "Income Distribution in Selected Years," adapted from the Statistics Canada publications "Incomes of Non-farm Families and Individuals in Canada" 1951-65, 1969, p. 78; "Income Distribution by Size in Canada," 1983, Catalogue 13-2307, March 1985; and Statistics Canada CANSIM database, http://www5.statcan.gc.ca/cansim/ Table 202-0701. Accessed January 31, 2014.

received 47 percent. The groups in-between the extremes received 10 percent, 15 percent, and 24 percent, respectively.

Looking at the figures for selected years, we can see that there has been some change in income distribution, especially since the 1970s and 1980s. For example, in 1981, the fifth of Canadian households with the highest incomes received 42 percent of all households' total pre-tax income, 5 percentage points lower than in 2011, with the increase in the percentage going to the highest fifth since 1981 coming at the expense of those in all four other categories.

The Lorenz Curve

Comparing distributions of income for different years can be a cumbersome task, given the amount of information included in Figure 7.13. Therefore, economists simplify matters by summarizing the results on a graph. However, rather than simply presenting the shares of each one-fifth of households, economists present the *cumulative* distribution of income. The **Lorenz curve**, as this graph is called, conveniently summarizes how equally or unequally income is distributed.

Lorenz curve: a graph showing the cumulative distribution of income among a country's households

To see how the Lorenz curve does this, take another look at the income distribution for 2011 given in Figure 7.13. Seen as separate shares of total pre-tax income, the figures–4 percent, 10 percent, 15 percent, 24 percent, and 47 percent–may not seem to say a lot. However, look at the first and second groups together; then the first, second, and third groups together; and so on. Figure 7.14 shows the results. For example, whereas the 20 percent of Canadian households with the lowest incomes receive 4 percent of the total income, the 40 percent of households with the lowest incomes receive 14 percent, and the 60 percent of households with the lowest incomes receive 29 percent. Plotted on a graph–with the variables being the percentage of households and the

FIGURE 7.14   The Lorenz Curve

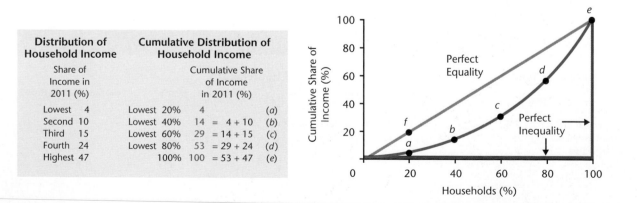

Distribution of Household Income		Cumulative Distribution of Household Income		
Share of Income in 2011 (%)		Cumulative Share of Income in 2011 (%)		
Lowest	4	Lowest 20%	4	(a)
Second	10	Lowest 40%	14 = 4 + 10	(b)
Third	15	Lowest 60%	29 = 14 + 15	(c)
Fourth	24	Lowest 80%	53 = 29 + 24	(d)
Highest	47	100%	100 = 53 + 47	(e)

Point *a* on the graph shows that the group with the lowest income received 4 percent of the total pre-tax income in 2011. Point *b* shows that the groups receiving the lowest 40 percent of pre-tax income in 2011 received 14 percent (= 4 + 10). Each subsequent point shows the cumulative income distribution; therefore, point *e* shows that 100 percent of households earned 100 percent of total incomes. Connecting all the points gives the Lorenz curve. To contrast, the extremes of perfect equality and perfect inequality are shown. The closer the Lorenz curve is to the curve representing perfect equality (and the farther from the curve of perfect inequality), the more equally incomes are distributed.

percentage of income—these figures give the Lorenz curve. The points *a*, *b*, *c*, *d*, and *e* represent the cumulative income shares.

Interpreting the Lorenz Curve

To see what this curve tells us about the distribution of income among Canadian households, compare it with Lorenz curves for two hypothetical economies with income distributions at the extremes: perfectly equal and perfectly unequal.

PERFECT EQUALITY

The first hypothetical Lorenz curve represents the case of *perfect equality,* where each household earns an identical amount. Therefore, 20 percent of households receive 20 percent of the total income (as shown at point *f* in Figure 7.14), 40 percent receive 40 percent, 60 percent receive 60 percent, and so on. The result is the 45-degree line shown in Figure 7.14. The closer the actual Lorenz curve is to this hypothetical case—in other words, the less bow-shaped it is—the more equal is the distribution of incomes in the economy.

PERFECT INEQUALITY

At the other extreme of income distribution is *perfect inequality,* with only one household receiving all of the economy's income, while all other households receive nothing. The hypothetical Lorenz curve in this circumstance would follow the horizontal and vertical axes of the graph, as shown by the two thick lines in Figure 7.14 forming a right angle at the bottom right-hand corner. The closer the Lorenz curve is to this hypothetical case—meaning, the more bow-shaped it is—the more unequal is the distribution of income.

BETWEEN THE EXTREMES

For Lorenz curves that show neither perfect equality nor perfect inequality, there exists a single numerical measure of income distribution. The **Gini coefficient** is defined as the area between a Lorenz curve and the 45-degree line of perfect equality divided by the entire triangular area under this same 45-degree line. The result is a value between 0 and 1, with 0 representing perfect equality and 1 representing perfect inequality. This coefficient is a useful tool when comparing income distributions across time or across countries.

Gini coefficient: a single numerical measure of income distribution

Reasons for Income Inequality: Wages

The differences in incomes of individual households can be attributed to a variety of causes. Wages and salaries make up about 70 percent of income earned in Canada. Hence, the factors that determine wages play an important role in income inequality.

Looking at the wider national labour market highlights the tremendous differences among Canadians' incomes gained from labour. Figure 7.15 shows the distribution of earnings (defined as wages and self-employed income) in the Canadian economy. In 2011, about three out of ten Canadian earners made less than $15 000 annually. At the other end of the scale, just under four in ten Canadian earners made $40 000 or more. (These figures are earnings before taxes.)

FIGURE 7.15   Distribution of Earnings (2011)

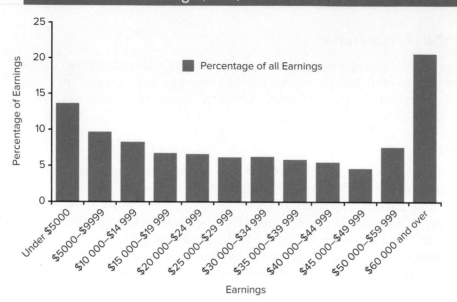

Earnings of Canadians varied widely in 2011, with about three out of ten Canadian earners making less than $15 000 annually. In contrast, just under four in ten Canadian earners made $40 000 or more annually.

Source: Statistics Canada "Distribution of Earnings (2011)," adapted from the Statistics Canada CANSIM database, http://www5.statcan.gc.ca/cansim/, Table 202-0101. Accessed March 16, 2014.

There are seven main determinants of wage levels in labour markets: labour productivity, education, experience, job conditions, regional disparities, market power, and discrimination.

THINKING ABOUT ECONOMICS

When making comparisons, shouldn't people's incomes over a lifetime be considered rather than focusing on yearly incomes?

Theoretically, yes. In any one year, someone's income may vary due to personal circumstances. For example, annual incomes of most full-time college and university students tend to be much lower than the yearly amounts they will earn later on in life. Similarly, someone undergoing a job change may see a sharp but temporary decline in annual income. Measures of income distribution using annual income miss these movements between income groups that people may make over time. But while it makes conceptual sense to measure income distribution using lifetime income, doing so in practice is extremely complicated. This is why Statistics Canada continues to use annual income when calculating Lorenz curves and Gini coefficients.

QUESTION   **Would using lifetime rather than annual incomes make the distribution of income appear more or less equal? Explain.**

LABOUR PRODUCTIVITY

labour productivity: the output per worker in a given time period

In a given job market, the level of **labour productivity**, or the output per worker in a given time, determines the wage of that worker. Among the determinants of wages, labour productivity is the most important. The output of each worker varies because of such factors as the worker's ability to do the job and the state of technology. With more capable workers or a technological innovation, labour productivity rises, pushing up the prevailing wage.

EDUCATION

In general, the more education a worker needs to perform a job, the higher the pay. As Figure 7.16 shows, using the example of income earners in management occupations, those with a university degree earn considerably more annual income than those with only up to eight years of school. The most significant differences in average annual incomes are between those with a post-secondary certificate or diploma and those with a university degree ($67 700 compared with $97 700, or a 44 percent increase for the university degree-holder), and for those with some high school education and those who graduated high school ($44 200 compared with $52 900, or a 20 percent increase for the high school graduate). Work that requires job-related training tends to produce more output per worker than does work that requires very little job-related training, so education is linked to labour productivity. Therefore, education has an impact on wages.

This relationship between education and wages is also affected by the fact that, as every student knows, education is costly and time-consuming. For example, students who undertake a full-time post-secondary program have not only out-of-pocket costs, such as tuition and books, but also an important opportunity cost: the income that could have been earned by entering the workforce immediately. Students who attend public post-secondary institutions do not bear the entire cost of their education—taxpayers, through government programs, pick up the remainder. Education provides benefits; acquiring skills and knowledge may itself be a reward for the work and effort involved. Just the same, a worker entering the labour force with a higher education tends to expect a return on his education investment.

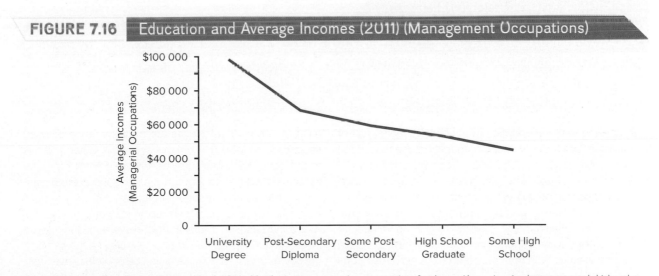

FIGURE 7.16   Education and Average Incomes (2011) (Management Occupations)

In general, incomes rise with the educational level achieved by the income earner. Average earnings for those with a university degree are much higher than those for income earners who have only completed some high school.

Source: Statistics Canada "Education and Average Family Income (2011)," adapted from the Statistics Canada, the Statistics Canada CANSIM database, http://www5.statcan.gc.ca/cansim/, Table 202-0106, Accessed January 31, 2014.

human capital: the income-earning potential of a person's skills and knowledge

Economists view work-related education as an investment in **human capital**, which is the income-earning potential of a person's skills and knowledge. According to this perspective, an educational program is worthwhile only if the expected rise in the individual's lifetime income outweighs the sum of that education's direct and indirect costs. **"Human capital" expresses the ways in which an individual's education choices correspond to businesses' investment decisions, but it is important not to let this term mask education's distinctive features. Education often has a consumption component, which is the pleasure associated with learning. This component may be especially significant in subject areas with little income-earning potential.**

EXPERIENCE

Experience is another determining factor of income levels. On-the-job experience increases a worker's productivity, pushing up the wage rate. In many industries, workers gain certain privileges the longer they work for a single employer. Because of these **seniority rights**, older workers are often paid higher wages and can apply first for promotions and overtime work, allowing them to earn higher incomes than their younger colleagues.

seniority rights: the workplace privileges provided to workers who have the longest experience with their employer

JOB CONDITIONS

Two occupations often provide very different earnings, even when productivity and education levels in each occupation are the same. One reason for this discrepancy is that working conditions in the two occupations can make one less appealing than the other. Employers must therefore offer higher wages to attract workers to less-appealing occupations. For example, garbage collectors

THINKING ABOUT ECONOMICS

Suppose three friends graduating from high school choose different career paths: the first enters the workforce directly as a clerical worker; the second enrolls in a university arts program for a major in English literature with a focus on medieval poetry, and the third pursues a degree in computer science. What do these decisions suggest about the friends' economic choices?

According to the economic view of human capital, by not making a further investment in education, the first friend sacrifices possible income gains later in life for immediate earnings. In other words, receiving a dollar in purchasing power now is worth much more to this individual than receiving greater purchasing power in the future. The English major is willing to give up immediate income for future benefit, and will likely have a future income greater than the first friend's, but perhaps not as much as he would if he pursued another type of postsecondary education. From this economic viewpoint, this friend sees the knowledge he will gain from his postsecondary education primarily as a consumption item rather than as an investment in human capital. The third friend is also willing to give up immediate income for future increases in welfare. She views education as an investment in her human capital to increase future earning power and, hopefully, as a source of pleasure as well.

QUESTION   **Is any one of these economic choices more rational than the others?**

receive higher wages than most other unskilled workers, in part because of this job's unattractive working conditions.

REGIONAL DISPARITIES

Wage differences often have a geographic dimension. In Canada, workers in the same occupation may earn different incomes depending on the region they live in. For example, a fish-plant worker in British Columbia may earn more than a worker doing the identical job in Newfoundland and Labrador. In a perfectly functioning labour market, workers in a single occupation would move from one part of the country to another until wage disparities in this occupation were eliminated. However, labour tends to be immobile.

Even when workers find moving to be economically feasible, they and their families may be reluctant to adjust to new jobs, schools, and surroundings. Labour immobility is especially pronounced for multiple-income families because of the added difficulty of two or more people changing jobs. Immobility is also common among older workers, who tend to be more settled in their jobs and communities.

MARKET POWER

The market power possessed by workers also affects their wages. As a rule, earnings in unionized labour markets tend to be higher than in non-unionized markets. Professional organizations for such groups as doctors and lawyers can also play a similar role in providing their members with market power. Unionized workers can use two main methods to increase their market power industrial unions and craft unions—each of which influences labour markets in different ways.

An **industrial union** includes workers in a certain industry, no matter what their occupations. These unions are also referred to as inclusive unions, and are most common in sectors that primarily use unskilled and semi-skilled labour. The automobile, steel, and forestry industries are examples.

industrial union: a labour union of workers in a certain industry, no matter what their occupations

A **craft union** includes workers in a particular occupation. Craft unions restrict whom they allow to be members, so they are also referred to as exclusive unions. They are common in skilled trades, such as printing, as well as in some parts of the construction industry, such as carpentry and bricklaying. Some professional organizations that limit numbers of newcomers in a particular occupation can also be viewed as being similar to craft unions. In any labour market dominated by a craft union, acquiring a union card is an essential first step in being allowed to work. To become a member of such a union, a worker often must complete an apprenticeship program and write a licensing examination. While craft unions' requirements attempt to ensure craft standards, they also allow unions to determine the supply of workers in the market and to negotiate higher wages for their members.

craft union: a labour union of workers in a particular occupation

DISCRIMINATION

Discrimination, too, can play a role in determining wages. **Job discrimination** occurs when decisions regarding hiring, wages, or promotion are based on some trait of the worker other than credentials or performance. Job discrimination stems from the prejudices of employers and may be based on a variety of factors,

job discrimination: hiring, wage, and promotion decisions based on criteria other than a worker's credentials or performance such as gender, race, age, or physical ability. While job discrimination in a variety of forms is illegal, it still exists.

Job discrimination is an important factor in explaining the wage gap between men and women, which in 2000 meant that women on average earned 71.7 percent of the average wage for men. Canadian studies suggest that while 40 percent of this gap is related to differences in hours worked by men and women, a third is due to a discriminatory division of jobs, and another 10 percent to direct job discrimination, which involves paying men and women different amounts for substantially the same work. The remainder of the gap is explained by a variety of factors, such as differing average levels of experience, education, and unionization for men and women.

Reasons for Income Inequality: Other Incomes

Not all income inequalities are related to factors that determine wages. Profit, rent, and interest also play a part. Three main factors determine these other types of income and can sometimes affect wages as well: risk-taking, ability, and wealth.

RISK-TAKING

Risk-taking in an economy can take a variety of forms. For example, workers in some occupations earn unstable incomes. More importantly, the risks that entrepreneurs take mean that their profit earnings fluctuate widely. While unsuccessful risk-takers often face the threat of hardship and bankruptcy, successful risk-takers reap significant rewards in the form of high profits.

ABILITY

Because of different abilities, some individuals may pursue careers in high-paying areas, while others make no earnings at all. Those individuals who find their talents are marketable and in short supply–star athletes or gifted computer programmers, for instance–can sometimes earn extravagantly high incomes due to their special abilities.

WEALTH

wealth: ownership of financial assets, such as stocks and bonds, or real assets, such as buildings and land

Most rent and interest incomes flow from the ownership of wealth. **Wealth** takes the form of financial assets, such as stocks and bonds, or real assets, such as buildings and land. There are two main ways to acquire wealth: through one's own saving, or by inheriting wealth from others.

Wealth tends to be much more unequally distributed than income. Figure 7.17 shows the share of wealth held by the top 10 percent and 50 percent of households in various years for five countries: Australia, Canada, South Korea, the United Kingdom, and the United States. In Canada in 1999, the top 10 percent owned 53 percent of the country's total wealth, while the top 50 percent owned 94 percent. While less equally distributed than in South Korea and Australia, wealth in Canada is distributed more evenly among households than it is in the United Kingdom or the United States.

FIGURE 7.17 | Distribution of Wealth in Selected Countries

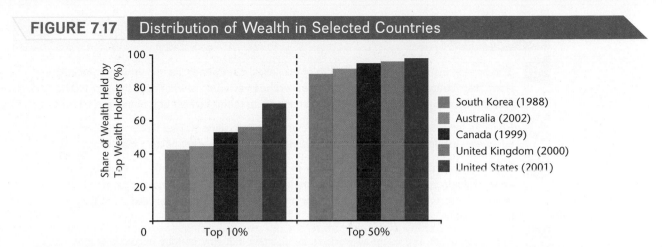

In 1999, the top 10 percent of Canadian households held 53 percent of Canada's wealth and the top 50 percent held 94 percent. In Canada, the distribution of wealth among households is more equal than it is in the United Kingdom or the United States, but less so than in South Korea or Australia.

Source: James B. Davies, Susanna Sandström, Anthony Shorrocks, and Edward N. Wolff, *The World Distribution of Household Wealth* (Helsinki: February 2008), p. 22.

THINKING ABOUT ECONOMICS

Is income inequality necessarily a bad thing?

While gross inequalities in income are undesirable, a perfect equality of incomes is not necessarily desirable because of the trade off between income equity and efficiency. Therefore, without differences in incomes, the incentive to undertake further education, to take unpleasant jobs for greater pay, to save one's earnings, and to take risks would be severely hampered. Without some degree of income inequality, an economy's total output would be below its highest possible level. The goal of income equity is, therefore, usually interpreted as reducing, rather than eliminating, the inequalities that would exist in a pure market economy, and, in particular, to ensure that income differences to not become entrenched from one generation to the next.

It is possible to gauge this entrenchment by looking at a factor called *intergenerational income mobility.* This is measured by the percentage income disadvantage that tends to be passed on through the generations. In Canada, for example, a household earning $10 000 less income than the average income in the entire economy will see its offspring earn $1900 less than the economy-wide average. In other words, 19 percent of an income shortfall is passed on to the next generation.

In the United States, the comparable figure is 47 percent, so that a household making $10 000 less than the economy-wide average will see its offspring make $4700 less than the average. In other countries, the extent of income entrenchment is far less—for example, just 15 percent in Denmark and 17 percent in Norway. But overall, Canada performs well with respect to this measure.

On the other hand, there are worrisome trends at work in many industrial countries, Canada included, in terms of the gap between the very rich—often defined as the top 1 percent of income earners—and all the rest. In 2011, for example, the top 1 percent received over 10 percent of total pre-tax income in Canada, a significant rise from the 7 percent they received in the early 1980s. Highly educated and concentrated in management and health-related careers, their average income in 2011 was just over $380 000, compared with the median income for the lowest 90 percent of under $30 000. They are part of a broader transnational elite whose share of the world's income may continue to increase in the years ahead as their skills and training are valued ever more highly in the global economy.

QUESTION Extremely unequal distributions of income can sometimes hamper rather than promote efficiency. Why?

BRIEF REVIEW

1. The pre-tax income share of each fifth of households in Canada, as shown using the cumulative distribution known as the Lorenz curve, has varied somewhat over the past 50 years, with a noticeable increase in the share going to the highest fifth of income earners.

2. Reasons for income inequality include factors that determine wages: labour productivity, education, experience, job conditions, regional disparities, market power, and discrimination.

3. Work-related education and training can be viewed as an investment in human capital, or an individual's earning power. Ignoring the consumption aspect of knowledge, an education is worthwhile when its returns, in the form of future income gains, exceed its direct and indirect costs.

4. Industrial unions represent all workers in a certain industry, so they negotiate wages across an industry. Craft unions represent workers in a particular occupation. Both types of unions affect the supply of labour in the market and negotiate wages.

5. Factors other than wages that are reasons for income inequality are risk-taking, ability, and wealth.

7.5 | PRACTICE PROBLEMS

1. In a hypothetical country called Libra, there are five households with annual incomes of $5000, $10 000, $15 000, $30 000, and $40 000.
    a. Calculate the shares of total income earned by each household.
    b. What are the cumulative shares of income earned by each household that would be used to draw this country's Lorenz curve, ranked from the lowest to highest?
    c. Draw a graph of the Lorenz curve for this economy. Plot a total of six points, including the origin point (0, 0).
2. In each of the following cases, which income earner is likely to be paid a higher income? Identify the primary reason for income inequality that is relevant in each case.
    a. a carpenter residing in Alberta or a carpenter residing in Quebec
    b. a truck driver or a cab driver
    c. a postal worker or an employee of a courier company
    d. a waitress or a warehouse clerk
    e. a lawyer or a paralegal consultant
    f. a retail store clerk who works on salary or a retail store clerk who works on commission
    g. a landowner or a tenant farmer

LAST WORD

In this capstone chapter on microeconomics, we covered important applications of our market models, looking at how perfectly-competitive markets maximize economic welfare when taking into account both consumer surplus and producer surplus. We also examined the ways that government can try to improve market outcomes in cases where spillover effects are relevant, extending the use of consumer and producer surplus to analyze the welfare impact of spillover effects and some of the government programs used to deal with them. We analyzed the distribution of income, exploring some of the controversies associated with this distribution, including the growing proportion of total income received by the top 1 percent of income earners. Having dealt with the microeconomic functions of government, in the next part of the text we will turn to government's actions in the macroeconomy as it attempts to stabilize the business cycle. In doing so, we will see that some of the government programs discussed in this chapter, which promote income equity, also have a role to play in stabilizing the economy over time.

PROBLEMS

1. The table below shows hypothetical market demand and supply schedules for cranberries.

Market Demand and Supply Schedules for Cranberries

Price ($ per kg)	Quantity Demanded (millions of kg per year)	Quantity Supplied (millions of kg per year)
	(D)	(S)
$2.50	0	4
2.00	1	3
1.50	2	2
1.00	3	1
.50	4	0

   a. Draw a graph showing the demand and supply curves, D and S. Plot only the endpoints of the demand and supply curves.
   b. What are the equilibrium price and quantity before government intervention?
   c. Calculate the initial consumer surplus and producer surplus.
   d. Certain producers in this market are given exclusive rights to sell cranberries, and they choose to restrict quantity supplied to 1 million kg per year. What are the new equilibrium price and quantity?
   e. Calculate the dollar amount of the transfer of consumer surplus to producer surplus and the size of the deadweight loss created by this policy.
   f. Are consumers worse off or better off as a result of this output restriction? What about producers still operating in the market?
   g. What does the deadweight loss created in this market represent in conceptual terms?

2. The table below shows hypothetical demand and supply schedules for cigarettes.

Market Demand and Supply Schedules for Cigarettes

Price ($ per pack)	Quantity Demanded (millions of packs per year)	Quantity Supplied (millions of packs per year)	
	(D)	(S_0)	(S_1)
$12	0	20	_____
10	4	16	_____
8	8	12	_____
6	12	8	_____
4	16	4	_____
2	20	0	_____

a. Draw a graph showing the demand and supply curves, D and S_0. Plot only the endpoints of the demand and supply curves.

b. What are the equilibrium price and quantity in the market before government intervention?

c. It is estimated that the spillover costs associated with cigarette smoking are an extra $2 for each pack sold. On the basis of this estimate, draw a new supply curve (S_1) on your graph, plotting only the endpoints of the curve, which incorporates the spillover costs of cigarettes. Using your graph, copy and complete the table accompanying the question. Based on the graph and the data in the table, identify the preferred quantity in this market.

d. What is the excess benefit in this market before government intervention?

e. If government uses a tax to reach the preferred outcome, what will be the dollar amount per pack of this tax? What will be the price as seen by consumers and by producers?

f. Calculate the total revenue raised by this tax.

g. After the tax is in place, what is the excess benefit in this market? What is the increase in excess benefit gained by imposing the tax?

3. The graph below shows hypothetical demand and supply curves for milkshakes, with S_0 representing the supply curve before and S_1 the supply curve after the imposition of an excise tax by the government to raise revenue.

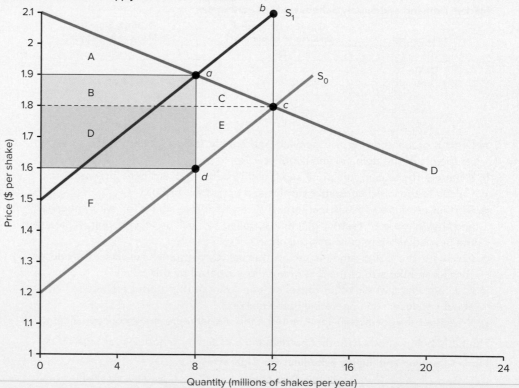

Market Demand and Supply Curves for Milkshakes

a. What are the equilibrium price and quantity before government intervention?

b. What is the per-unit amount of the excise tax per milkshake?

c. After the tax is imposed, what are the new equilibrium price as seen by consumers and the new quantity? What is the price as seen by producers?

d. What is the total tax payment and how much of this payment falls on consumers? on producers?

e. Calculate the consumer surplus and producer surplus before the tax.

f. Calculate the consumer surplus and producer surplus after the imposition of the tax.

g. How does the drop in consumer surplus compare with the drop in producer surplus? Who sees the bigger drop in welfare—consumers or producers?

h. Calculate the deadweight loss created by the tax.

4. **a.** Draw a graph without numbers (with P and Q as general labels instead) showing demand and supply in a perfectly competitive market with a perfectly elastic supply curve that is subject to an excise tax. Plot only the endpoints of the perfectly elastic market supply curves, S_0 and S_1, before and after the excise tax, and the market demand curve, D. How is the payment of this tax shared between consumers and producers?

b. Now draw another graph without numbers showing demand and supply in a perfectly competitive market with a perfectly elastic demand curve that is subject to an excise tax. Again, plot only the endpoints of the three curves—the market perfectly elastic demand curve, D, and the market supply curves, S_0 and S_1, before and after the tax. How is the payment of this tax shared between consumers and producers?

5. The table below shows hypothetical demand and supply schedules for cream cheese.

Market Demand and Supply Schedules for Cream Cheese

Price ($ per kilogram)	Quantity Demanded (millions of kilograms per year)	Quantity Supplied (millions of kilograms per year)		
	(D)	(S_0)		(S_1)
$10	0	4	→	6
8	1	3	→	4
6	2	2	)	2
4	3	1	)	0
2	4	0	→	0

a. Draw a graph showing the demand curve and supply curves, D and S_0. Plot only the endpoints of the demand and supply curves.

b. Identify the equilibrium price and quantity in the absence of government intervention.

c. The government imposes an $8 minimum price in this market. What is the new quantity demanded associated with this $8 minimum price? The new quantity supplied? Unless the government imposes additional policies, is a potential surplus or shortage created? How large is this discrepancy?

d. Calculate the consumer surplus and producer surplus before government intervention.

e. If along with the minimum price the government restricts output to cancel out the potential discrepancy in this market, at what quantity are quantity demanded and quantity supplied equal? What are the new consumer surplus and producer surplus?

f. Due to these combined policies, do the consumer surplus and producer surplus fall or rise? Are consumers worse off or better off? Producers?

g. Calculate the deadweight loss created by these combined policies.

h. In the long run, the annual supply curve for cream cheese becomes S_1, as shown in the table above. Draw S_1 on your graph. Without output restrictions, is a shortage or surplus created? How large is this discrepancy? Is this larger or smaller than the discrepancy that would result without output restrictions in the short run?

6. The table below shows hypothetical demand and supply schedules for apartments in a particular community.

Market Demand and Supply Schedules for Apartments

Price ($ per month)	Quantity Demanded (thousands of units rented per month)			Quantity Supplied (thousands of units rented per month)
	D_0		D_1	S
$1000	0	→	2	8
800	2	→	4	6
600	4	→	6	4
400	6	→	8	2
200	8	→	10	0

a. Draw a graph showing the demand and supply curves, D_0 and S. Plot only the endpoints of the demand and supply curves.

b. Identify the equilibrium price and quantity in the absence of government intervention.

c. If the government imposes a $400 rent ceiling, what is new quantity associated with this maximum rent? Is a shortage or surplus created? How large is this discrepancy?

d. Calculate the consumer surplus and producer surplus before controls.

e. What are the consumer surplus and producer surplus once the controls are in place?

f. Does this policy cause a rise or fall in the consumer surplus and producer surplus? Are tenants who are able to find units at the ceiling rent made better off or worse off? landlords?

g. Calculate the deadweight loss associated with this policy.

h. An increase in the price of single-family dwellings in the community causes the demand for apartments to shift from D_0 to D_1. Draw this demand curve on your graph, plotting only the endpoints of the new curve. With D_1, what happens to the discrepancy between quantity demanded and quantity supplied?

7. The table below shows the share of income received by each fifth of income earners, from lowest to highest, in three hypothetical countries.

Share of Income Received by Each Fifth of Income Earners

	1 (lowest)	2	3	4	5 (highest)
Country 1	7	11	17	24	41
Country 2	5	10	15	25	45
Country 3	9	14	18	23	36

a. Calculate the cumulative distribution of income among the five groups of income earners in each country.

b. Draw a graph showing the three countries' Lorenz curves. Plot six points for each curve, including the origin point (0, 0), for a total of 18 points.

c. Rank the countries from the most equal to the least equal income distribution.

8. The table on the next page shows the income shares going to each one-fifth of Canadian households before government transfer payments and after the receipt of transfer payments and the payment of personal income taxes.

Income Shares Going to Each One-fifth of Canadian Households

	Share of Income before Transfer Payments and Taxes (2008, %)	Share of Income after Transfer Payments and Taxes (2008, %)
Lowest 20%	1	5
Second 20%	7	11
Third 20%	15	16
Fourth 20%	25	24
Highest 20%	52	44

Source: Statistics Canada, the Statistics Canada CANSIM database, http://www5.statcan.gc.ca/cansim/, Table 202-0701. Accessed January 31, 2014.

a. Using the data above, create a graph giving two Lorenz curves: one using income shares prior to transfer payments and personal income taxes, and another after both transfer payments and personal income taxes. Plot six points for each curve, including the origin point (0, 0), for a total of 12 points.

b. Based on the Lorenz curves you have drawn in part a, do transfer payments and personal income taxes make Canada's distribution of income more or less equal?

9. **a.** The Gini coefficient for the distribution of total pre-tax income in Canada rose from .284 to .313 between 1981 and 2007. What does this suggest has happened to the equality of income distribution during this period?

b. Standardized Gini coefficients for the distribution of pre-tax income for 2007 are .373 in the United States, .302 in Japan, .286 in Germany, .280 in France, .357 in the United Kingdom, .327 in Italy, and .313 in Canada. What do these figures suggest about the comparative equality of income distribution in these seven countries?

10. **a.** With a system of carbon taxes, some products, which cause a net decrease in carbon emissions, would end up being subsidized. Give two illustrations.

b. If Canada were to introduce a system of carbon taxation that was designed to keep government revenue the same, some groups of Canadians would be hurt and others helped. Give two examples of a group that would end up paying more, and two examples of a group that would end up paying less tax.

11. (Policy Discussion Question)

In recent years, there has been rising concern over the spillover costs associated with "junk foods" such as hamburgers, hot dogs, and french fries, given their link to obesity and the prevalence of certain illnesses such as heart disease and diabetes. As a result, some commentators have proposed imposing excise taxes on such items.

a. In a country such as Canada, where health care costs are borne by taxpayers, explain how the spillover cost associated with a single serving of a food such as french fries would be calculated.

b. Assuming that french fries are bought and sold in a perfectly-competitive market, how could the imposition of an excise tax on this product address this spillover cost?

c. Critics of a junk food tax stress its possible practical shortcomings. Can you think of any?

ADVANCING ECONOMIC THOUGHT

THE DOOMSDAY PROPHET
Thomas Malthus and Population Growth

THOMAS MALTHUS

© National Portrait Gallery.
Reprinted by kind permission
of the Master of Haileybury.

MALTHUS AND HIS INFLUENCE

Known as the "doomsday prophet" for his gloomy predictions of the economic and social future, Thomas Malthus (1766-1834) was an economist as well as a clergyman. Malthus's theories and predictions sprang from an unlikely source: a reform-minded writer named William Godwin (1756-1836), who believed that future society would be transformed by science and human reason. Wars, disease, and crime would finally come to an end, Godwin thought, and the need for government would vanish. Malthus's *Essay on Population* (1798), in which he published his arguments against Godwin's vision, was destined to be one of the most influential economic works of the nineteenth century.

Malthus's basic point was that utopian visions of the future ignore the negative effects of population growth. According to Malthus, food production and population levels expand at different rates. At best, he said, food increases in what mathematicians call an algebraic progression (1, 2, 3, 4...) as more variable inputs are devoted to a certain amount of usable land. In contrast, population increases in a geometric progression (1, 2, 4, 8...), with levels doubling again and again in a set period. Malthus estimated this period to be 25 years.

Given these assumptions, it was easy for Malthus to predict a discrepancy between food production and the needs of the population. For example, assume that population and food stocks in Year 1 are set equal to 1 unit, and food production expands by 1 unit every 30 years as population doubles in the same period. After 30 years, food production and population would both equal 2 units, but after 120 years food production will be 5 units and population 8 units. After 270 years, population will have outstripped food by a factor of just over 50 (= 512 ÷ 10) to 1. Malthus warned of desperate circumstances if his predictions came true. He also outlined how population growth could be slowed by either a decrease in the birth rate or an increase in the mortality rate. He had little faith that the number of births would decrease; however, he did feel that at some point, if birth rates did not fall, a limited food supply would bring on misery, famine, plagues, or war, thereby decreasing the population.

IMPLICATIONS AND INFLUENCE OF MALTHUS'S THEORY

On the basis of his assumptions, Malthus believed that aid to those in need would be self-defeating, as it would encourage larger families and therefore more population growth. In the long run, he said, this population growth would result in starvation. During the nineteenth century, Malthus's views had a powerful effect on government policies. In Britain, for example, aid to people who were physically able to work was restricted to those willing to give up their possessions and move into a workhouse, where prolonged labour brought them virtually no pay—only room and board.

Social reformers attacked this "Malthusian" policy, calling it misguided and cruel. The appalling conditions in British workhouses were exposed in many books and pamphlets, Charles Dickens' fictional account *Oliver Twist* being the most famous. Not surprisingly, it was because of Malthus's work that economics was dubbed "the dismal science" by its critics.

RELEVANCE FOR TODAY

Fortunately, Malthus's dire predictions have proven to be wrong, at least in those countries with which he was directly concerned. While he later refined the logic of his arguments, their foundations were shaky. Malthus implied that the state of technology would remain fixed; however, the dramatic changes in technology since his day have increased food production in most countries. Malthus also overlooked the extent to which large families were the result of economic necessity. In his own day, high infant mortality rates and the lack of old age pensions meant that large families provided parents with security in old age. Also, during his time, child labour provided extra income to a family. Today, with social welfare programs, child labour laws, and the means to limit population growth, population growth rates in industrialized countries have been far below what Malthus imagined. In many of these nations, especially in Europe, the rate is close to zero, while some industrialized countries such as Japan and Russia have been experiencing population declines. Meanwhile, population growth is gradually declining in many emerging economies, though overall the world's population still continues to increase at just over 1 percent a year.

While population growth continues to be a *global* concern, the history of Malthus's theory has a valuable lesson: care must be taken in applying economic models to the real world and to government policy.

1. a. Briefly explain why Thomas Malthus believed the growth in living standards in such countries as Britain could eventually stagnate.
   b. Summarize two main reasons why the pessimistic warnings of Malthus proved to be unwarranted.

2. Critics of Malthus suggested that by assuming a set ratio between the growth rates of food and population, he was ignoring the role of food prices. Explain how this argument could be used against Malthus's theory.

In the long run, we are all dead. Economists set themselves too easy, too useless a task if in tempestuous seasons they can only tell us that when the storm is long past the ocean is flat again.

— JOHN MAYNARD KEYNES, ENGLISH ECONOMIST

Economic Stability

So far, we have focused on the microeconomic issues associated with efficiency, income equity, and the environment. Now we turn to macroeconomics, with its emphasis on economic stability. All of us feel the impact of fluctuations in the Canadian economy. For those who lose their jobs or see the purchasing power of their incomes drop, economic instability is far more than an abstraction. The next six chapters investigate the measurements of economic health, the nature and causes of fluctuations in the Canadian economy, and the ways in which these fluctuations can be reduced through government policy.

CHAPTER 8

Measures of Economic Activity

How much activity is occurring in the Canadian economy? Are incomes of Canadians rising or falling? How do the living standards in Canada compare with those in other countries? Just as you use a thermometer to check your temperature, nations must diagnose and understand their economic health before they can respond to questions such as these ones. This chapter examines various indicators of Canadian economic activity, especially the most prominent measure—Gross Domestic Product (GDP). In later chapters, we will consider GDP further and examine additional measures, what they indicate, and the economic realities of stability and instability.

> All progress is precarious, and the solution of one problem brings us face to face with another problem.
>
> —MARTIN LUTHER KING JR., AMERICAN CIVIL RIGHTS AND RELIGIOUS LEADER

LEARNING OBJECTIVES   After reading this chapter, you will be able to:

LO 1

Explain why economists choose to concentrate on Gross Domestic Product (GDP) and describe the two approaches to calculating it

LO 2

Identify real GDP and per capita GDP and their possible uses and limitations when comparing living standards in different years or different countries and distinguish GDP from other economic measures

8.1 | Gross Domestic Product

 National Income Accounts

national income accounts: accounts showing the levels of total income and spending in the Canadian economy

Keeping track of the Canadian economy is the task of Statistics Canada, a federal agency. This agency prepares the country's **national income accounts**, which give various measures of total income and spending in the Canadian economy. National income accounts play a role for the economy as a whole, comparable with the role of income statements in an individual business: they allow us to evaluate the performance of the Canadian economy and to compare it with other nations' economies.

Measuring Gross Domestic Product

Gross Domestic Product: the total dollar value at current prices of all final goods and services produced in Canada over a given period

A variety of measures of economic activity can be developed from the national income accounts. Of these, the most common measure in Canada is **Gross Domestic Product**, or GDP. GDP is the total dollar value of all final goods and services produced in the economy over a given period. The dollar value is calculated at current prices, and the period is typically a year. As Figure 8.1 shows, GDP uses dollar value because it effectively simplifies the picture; dollar value is a way to quantify and combine a wide range of goods and services.

TWO VIEWS OF GDP

income approach: a method of calculating Gross Domestic Product by adding together all incomes in the economy

expenditure approach: a method of calculating Gross Domestic Product by adding together all spending in the economy

Canada's GDP is calculated using two approaches, one measuring income and the other measuring spending. Figure 8.2, which illustrates the circular flow for a simple economy where only consumer products are sold, shows both approaches. The diagram depicts two economic sectors: households and businesses. Recall that whereas the inner (clockwise) loop represents the flow of payments, the outer (counterclockwise) loop represents the flow of products and resources. The upper portion of the diagram shows the economy's resource markets, in which natural and capital resources as well as human resources (labour and entrepreneurship) are sold by households for incomes. The **income approach** to GDP involves adding together all the incomes in the economy to give GDP. The lower portion of the diagram shows the economy's product markets, in which final consumer products are sold by businesses to households. The **expenditure approach** to GDP involves adding together all spending in the economy to give GDP.

FIGURE 8.1   Calculating Gross Domestic Product

Product	Current Price (P)	Annual Output (Q)	Total Dollar Value (P × Q)
Surgical lasers	$1000	3	$3000
Milkshakes	2	1000	2000
			GDP = $5000

It is impossible to add together the economy's annual output of surgical lasers and milkshakes without taking into account money values. If three surgical lasers and 1000 milkshakes are produced, then GDP is the sum of both outputs valued at their current prices.

THE GDP IDENTITY

In the simple economy shown in Figure 8.2, because all spending by someone is income for someone else, annual income equals annual spending. As a result, GDP found using the income approach and GDP found using the expenditure approach are the same.

This relationship between the two approaches is known as the **GDP identity**:

$$\text{GDP expressed as total income} \equiv \text{GDP expressed as total spending}$$

The triple-lined identity sign in this formula–a stronger version of the equals sign (=)–indicates that the expressions on both sides are by definition identical.

The GDP identity applies not only to the simplified economy shown in Figure 8.2, but also to the entire Canadian economy. Statistics Canada, therefore, uses both approaches–the income approach and the expenditure approach to calculate GDP. As we will see later in the chapter, the circular flows of income and spending in the Canadian economy incorporate not only the interaction of households and businesses in product and resource markets, but also flows relating to financial markets, government, and the rest of the world. This involves a wide range of goods and services. Therefore, Statistics Canada does not restrict itself to consumer products; instead, it considers incomes from and expenditures on all goods and services in Canada.

GDP identity: Gross Domestic Product calculated as total income is identical to Gross Domestic Product calculated as total spending

The Income Approach

As discussed in Chapter 1, wages, rent, profit, and interest make up Canadian incomes. These four payments form the basis of GDP calculated using the income approach. Because of practical difficulties in distinguishing resource earnings, Statistics Canada applies its own classification system which highlights wages and salaries, corporate income, and proprietors' incomes (including rent).

To these three classes of income, Statistics Canada adds three other classifications: indirect taxes, depreciation, and a statistical discrepancy account. These three categories help balance GDP that is calculated using the income approach

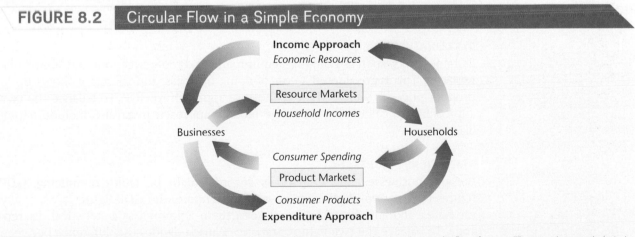

| FIGURE 8.2 | Circular Flow in a Simple Economy |

Income Approach
Economic Resources

Resource Markets

Household Incomes

Businesses   Households

Consumer Spending

Product Markets

Consumer Products
Expenditure Approach

Households and businesses meet in both resource and product markets. The inner (clockwise) loop represents the flow of money. The outer (counterclockwise) loop represents the flow of products and resources. The income approach to GDP measures the flow of incomes in the upper portion; the expenditure approach measures the flow of spending in the lower portion.

with GDP that is calculated using the expenditure approach. Using the income approach, GDP is the sum of all six categories.

WAGES AND SALARIES

Wages and salaries are the largest income category, representing about 50 percent of GDP. This category includes direct payments to workers in both business and government, as well as employee benefits, such as contributions to employee pension funds.

CORPORATE INCOME

Corporate income includes corporations' profits as well as interest paid out by corporations. In theory, all corporate profits are a payment to share-owning households. This category includes all corporate profits declared to government, including the profits paid as corporate income tax, the profits paid out to corporate shareholders as dividends, and the profits put back into the business. The final subcategory of profits put back into the business, or **retained earnings**, represents the funds that corporations keep for new investment. Also included in the category of corporate profits are adjustments to the value of businesses' unsold products.

retained earnings: profits kept by businesses for new investment

PROPRIETORS' INCOMES AND RENTS

Proprietors' incomes include the earnings of sole proprietorships and partnerships, including self-employed professionals and farmers. These incomes are received by owners for supplying various types of resources to their businesses. The income received by landlords from renting property is also included in this category.

INDIRECT TAXES

Indirect taxes, such as provincial sales taxes, are charged on products rather than levied against households or businesses. Because of this, their monetary value is not included in the main income components of GDP using the income approach. But this value is included in the expenditure approach. To balance the results from the two approaches, taxes (minus any subsidies businesses receive) are added to income-based GDP.

DEPRECIATION

Durable assets—such as buildings, equipment, and tools—wear out and need to be replaced. This is considered a cost of doing business, and therefore shows up in product prices as well as the expenditure approach to GDP. To balance the two approaches to calculating GDP, the income approach must also include depreciation.

STATISTICAL DISCREPANCY

Because businesses' and individuals' records might be faulty or missing, GDP figures for the two approaches do differ. Therefore, the GDP figures are actually estimates, and any discrepancy between them is known as a statistical discrepancy. To balance the two figures, Statistics Canada divides the difference between the two approaches. As shown in Figure 8.3, the discrepancy was $0.4 billion in 2013. Half the amount ($0.2 billion) is added to the lower estimate of GDP, and half ($0.2 billion) is deducted from the higher GDP estimate.

FIGURE 8.3 — Canada's Gross Domestic Product (2013)

Income Approach ($ billion)		Expenditure Approach ($ billion)	
Wages and salaries	956.9	Personal consumption (C)	1,045.9
Corporate income	239.5	Gross investment (I)	457.7
Proprietors' incomes and rents	167.7	Government purchases (G)	407.9
Indirect taxes	190.3	Net exports (X — M)	—31.9
Depreciation	324.9	Statistical discrepancy	—0.2
Statistical discrepancy	0.2		
Gross Domestic Product	1879.5	Gross Domestic Product	1879.5

With the income approach, GDP is the sum of incomes and balancing items, as shown on the left. With the expenditure approach, GDP is the sum of expenditures, as shown on the right. Both totals are reconciled with an equal amount for statistical discrepancy.

Sources: Statistics Canada "Canada's Gross Domestic Product (2013)," adapted from the Statistics Canada Summary Tables, http://www40.statcan.ca/l01/cst01/econ03-eng.htm and http://www40.statcan.ca/l01/cst01/econ04-eng.htm. Retrieved March 11, 2014.

The Expenditure Approach

GDP found using the expenditure approach is the sum of purchases in product markets. To explore this in greater detail, we must first distinguish between two categories of products on which expenditures can be made. Next we will examine several categories of purchases excluded from and included in the expenditure approach.

CATEGORIES OF PRODUCTS

Final products are those that will not be processed further and are purchased by the final or end user. How much the end user pays for the product determines the value of a final product. An example might be a pad of paper bought at the corner store. In contrast, **intermediate products** are those that will be processed further or will be resold. Creative advertising services bought by a soft-drink manufacturer or clothing bought by a wholesaler are examples. Something is a final product or an intermediate product on the basis of how it is used. For example, flour bought by a household for home baking is a final product; however, flour bought by a bakery to make bread to be sold is an intermediate product.

To understand why the distinction matters, consider that some products will be sold many times in product markets—first as intermediate products and then as final products. The products to make a pad of paper, for example, may be sold once by the logging company to the paper producer, a second time by the paper producer to the retailer, and a third time by the retailer to you. Since the cost of the wood may be $1 out of the retail price of $4, the value of the final product covers the value of the wood used to make it.

If the values of all products—final and intermediate—were included in the GDP calculations, we would have the problem of **double-counting**. Double-counting would cause estimates of GDP to be too high and not reflect the real activity in the economy. To avoid this problem, the concept of **value added** is applied to GDP. This concept helps quantify the extra worth of the product at each stage in its production. Figure 8.4 uses the example of the pad of paper to

final products: products that will not be processed further and will not be resold

intermediate products: products that will be processed further or will be resold

double-counting: the problem of adding to GDP the same item at different stages in its production

value added: the extra worth of a product at each stage in its production; a concept used to avoid double-counting in calculating GDP

FIGURE 8.4 — Value Added in Making Paper

Production Stage	Total Value Paid/Received	Value Added	Business That Adds Value
1. Wood is cut and transported to paper mill	$1.00	$1.00	logging company
2. Paper is processed and sold to retailer	2.75	1.75 (= 2.75 − 1.00)	paper company
3. Paper is sold by retailer to consumer	4.00	1.25 (= 4.00 − 2.75)	retailer
	$7.75	$4.00	

The value added by each business at each production stage is the value of the business's output, minus its cost of intermediate products. The sum of the values added at all stages of production represents the price of the pad of paper when it is finally sold.

show the results of double-counting and how the concept of value added deals with it. Statistics Canada subtracts the value of all purchases of intermediate goods and services by businesses from the value for which intermediate and final products are sold.

EXCLUDED PURCHASES

Expenditure-based GDP is calculated on the basis of almost all purchases in the Canadian economy. Note, once again, that figures for GDP calculated using this approach are adjusted for any statistical discrepancy. But before we examine the categories of purchases included in GDP, let us examine those that are excluded because they are not related to current production. There are two types: financial exchanges and second-hand purchases.

Financial Exchanges

A gift of money—between family members, for example—is not a transaction included in GDP for the simple reason that the transaction just shifts purchasing power from one party to another. Nor are interest payments on consumer loans included, for the same reason. Similarly, bank deposits and purchases of stocks are not included; however, payments for any financial service, such as bank service charges or a commission to a stockbroker, are included.

Second-Hand Purchases

Purchases of second-hand, or used, goods are also excluded from GDP because these products have already been counted at their first sale to a consumer. In other words, including second-hand purchases in GDP would double-count, or overestimate, the value of products sold.

INCLUDED PURCHASES

Purchases included in GDP calculations fall into four categories: personal consumption (C), gross investment (I), government purchases (G), and net exports (X − M). Each of these categories contributes to the circular flow of payments in the Canadian economy. The following **expenditure equation** shows that GDP is simply the sum of these four types of spending.

expenditure equation: the equation that states that GDP is the sum of personal consumption (C), gross investment (I), government purchases (G), and net exports (X − M)

$$GDP = C + I + G + (X - M)$$

THINKING ABOUT ECONOMICS

If exchanges of second-hand goods such as used cars are not included on the expenditure side of GDP, then how can the salaries of a sales force selling used cars be included on the income side?

When sales of second-hand goods are part of the formal economy—as they are when used cars are sold by an auto dealer—then the value added by the auto dealer in buying and selling the used car is included in the expenditure approach. This ensures that the expenditure and income sides of GDP are identical.

QUESTION   **Would the same value-added approach be needed if a used car were sold directly by its owner?**

Personal Consumption

Personal consumption (C) is spending on goods and services by households.[1] These purchases make up the largest component, about 56 percent, of GDP. Of the goods and services consumed, **non-durable goods**, such as food, are consumed just once. **Durable goods**, such as automobiles, are consumed over time.

personal consumption: household spending on goods and services

non-durable goods: goods that are consumed just once

durable goods: goods that are consumed over time

Gross Investment

The second component of expenditure in GDP is **gross investment** (I). This category includes purchases of assets that are intended to produce revenue. Gross investment varies—usually from between 15 and 25 percent of GDP—from year to year. The most important spending in this category is on equipment and machines used by businesses, for example, a carpenter's purchase of a lathe or a newspaper publisher's purchase of a printing press. Expenditures by government agencies and non-profit institutions on equipment and machines also fall into this category.

gross investment: purchases of assets that are intended to produce revenue

In addition, gross investment includes changes in the money value of unsold goods and materials, known as **inventories**. Businesses often keep inventories of inputs on hand so they can meet unexpected demand for particular products without stopping production to wait for deliveries of inputs. Because these inventories are income-producing assets, an increase in an economy's inventories over a given year is seen as positive investment spending. In contrast, a decrease in inventories is seen as negative investment spending.

inventories: stocks of unsold goods and materials

The construction of all buildings, including houses and apartments, is considered another part of gross investment. Owner-occupied housing is added here, rather than as part of personal consumption, because owner-occupied dwellings could be rented out by the owner to make an income. From an economic perspective, homeowners make an investment when they purchase their properties and then rent to themselves.

Gross investment is related to the economy's **capital stock**, which is the total value of productive assets that provide a flow of revenue. Recall that capital assets, such as machinery and equipment, wear out over time. The accompanying decrease in the value of these capital assets is known as **depreciation**. Subtracting annual depreciation of an entire economy's capital assets from new

capital stock: the total value of productive assets that provide a flow of revenue

depreciation: the decrease in value of durable real assets over time

---

[1] Besides direct spending by households, personal consumption also includes spending by non-profit institutions that serve households. These include entities such as trade unions, religious societies, and consumer associations.

FIGURE 8.5 Net Investment and Capital Stock

In a growing economy, the decline in the economy's capital stock during a year due to depreciation is outweighed by gross investment over the same period. The year-end capital stock is greater than the capital stock at the start of the year by the amount that gross investment exceeds depreciation. This increase, shown by the dark rectangle, represents the economy's net investment during the year.

net investment: gross investment minus depreciation

gross investment gives **net investment**. Net investment, therefore, represents the yearly change in the economy's stock of capital.

Consider the example in Figure 8.5. An economy has $200 billion of capital stock at the beginning of a year and depreciation of $40 billion during the year. If gross investment over the same period is $100 billion, then net investment equals $60 billion (= $100 billion − $40 billion). This $60 billion represents the amount by which the capital stock expands during the year. So, by the year's end, the value of the economy's capital stock is $260 billion (= $200 billion + $60 billion).

personal saving: funds saved by households

While they cannot be included in GDP, it is useful to highlight the sources of funds for investment. The funds used for capital investment come not only from businesses' retained earnings, but also from households' **personal saving** (S). By depositing funds in banks and by investing in stocks and bonds, households provide a flow of personal savings to businesses. Figure 8.6 shows this flow of funds for investment, as well as the flows of incomes and spending between businesses and households.

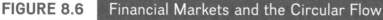

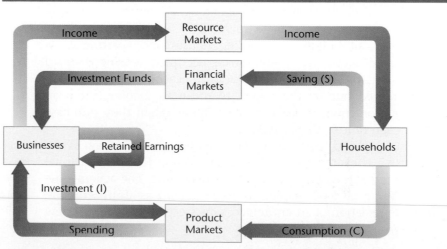

FIGURE 8.6 Financial Markets and the Circular Flow

Personal saving is transformed into investment funds for businesses by financial markets. Businesses then use these funds, plus their retained earnings, to make investment. Investment and personal consumption form part of total spending.

Government Purchases

Government purchases (G) include current spending by all levels of government on goods and services, and typically make up about 20 percent of GDP. The federal government buying a battleship for the armed forces and a municipality hiring a paving company to do road repairs are two examples of government purchases.

government purchases: current government spending on goods and services

Some types of government spending are not included in this category. Interest payments made by governments to bondholders are viewed simply as transfers of purchasing power. So too are **transfer payments**. These are payments from one level of government to another or to households. These are excluded from government purchases since they are simply a redistribution of purchasing power. For the same reason, government subsidies to businesses are also excluded. Both transfer payments and government subsidies are viewed, instead, as negative taxes, meaning they are tax payments in reverse. Expenditures by government-owned agencies on income-producing assets—for instance, hydro-electric dams built by a publicly-owned utility company, or post offices built by Canada Post—are also excluded from government purchases because these amounts are considered part of gross investment.

transfer payments: government payments to households or other levels of governments

Government spending is partly financed through taxes from both households and businesses. Governments also finance their spending through borrowing, which takes place in financial markets. Figure 8.7 shows the role of government in the economy's circular flow of incomes and spending.

Net Exports

This final category of purchase includes purchases of Canadian goods and services by the rest of the world, or **exports** (X). Suppose, for example, that a British consumer buys a Canadian cell phone, or an American tourist spends a night in a Canadian hotel. Because payments for these transactions remain in the Canadian circular flow of incomes and spending, exports contribute to GDP. This expenditure category also accounts for **imports** (M), or Canadian purchases of goods and services from the rest of the world. Such spending includes, for example, a

exports: foreign purchases of Canadian goods and services

imports: Canadian purchases of goods and services from the rest of the world

---

FIGURE 8.7   Government and the Circular Flow

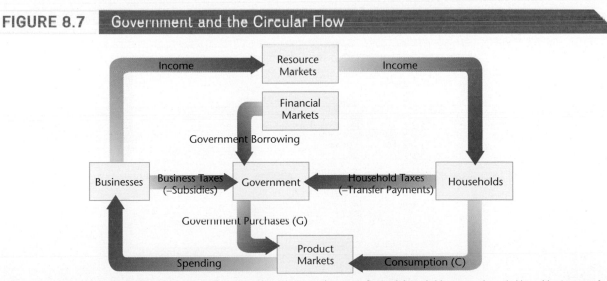

Government purchases of goods and services are part of total spending. These purchases are financed through (1) taxes on households and businesses after deducting transfer payments and business subsidies, and (2) government borrowing in financial markets.

THINKING ABOUT ECONOMICS

Does gross investment include spending on education and training?

As discussed in Chapter 7, education can be considered an investment in human capital, with knowledge and skills representing a vital part of an economy's productive assets. Some economists argue that Statistics Canada should include at least some spending on education as part of gross investment and add human capital to its estimate of Canada's total capital stock. Statistics Canada does not do this because of the difficulty in separating out the investment component of education. Instead, education appears either as part of personal consumption or government purchases.

QUESTION   **If spending on education were incorporated in Canada's gross investment, then how would the definition of Canada's total capital stock have to be adjusted?**

net exports: exports minus imports

Canadian cheese-lover buying French cheese, a Canadian steelmaker buying a Japanese-made casting machine, or a Canadian police force buying an American radar device. Because payments for these transactions leave the Canadian circular flow of incomes and spending, imports are subtracted from GDP.

To reconcile spending inside and outside the Canadian economy in calculating GDP, Statistics Canada uses the category of **net exports** $(X - M)$, or exports minus imports. When represented as net exports, these purchases represent a small fraction of GDP; however, the values of exports and imports, viewed separately, each accounts for about 30 percent of GDP.

Figure 8.8 shows the roles of exports and imports in the circular flow of the Canadian economy. Note that the rest of the world also plays a part in the Canadian economy by lending to and borrowing from financial markets. Loans from the rest of the world to the Canadian economy are flows into the economy, while Canadian loans to the rest of the world are flows out of the economy.

FIGURE 8.8   The Rest of the World and the Circular Flow

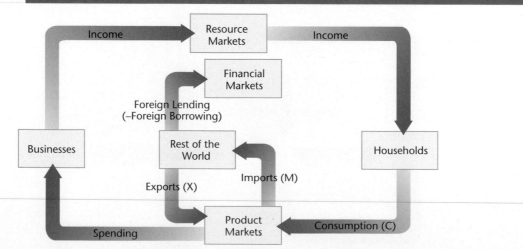

Whereas exports are part of total spending in product markets, imports are deductions from total spending. Lending by the rest of the world, after subtracting borrowing by the rest of the world, represents an inflow to Canadian financial markets.

BRIEF REVIEW

1. Statistics Canada prepares national income accounts to track various measures of income and spending in Canada.

2. The most prominent measure of economic activity is Gross Domestic Product (GDP), which is the total money value of all final goods and services produced in the economy over a given period.

3. GDP can be calculated by adding all incomes in resource markets or all expenditures in product markets. After taking into account several balancing items, including a statistical discrepancy, the two approaches give the same figure.

4. Using the income approach, GDP is the sum of three main income items—wages and salaries, corporate income, and proprietors' incomes (including rent)—plus indirect taxes and depreciation.

5. The expenditure approach depends on the concept of value added to avoid double-counting of purchases.

6. Using the expenditure approach, GDP is the sum of personal consumption, gross investment, government purchases, and net exports, but neither financial exchanges nor second-hand purchases.

8.1 | PRACTICE PROBLEMS

1. Identify whether or not each of the following transactions are included in GDP, and, if so, which expenditure or income component of GDP it is part of.
   a. a consumer purchases a used television
   b. a toy store adds to its stock of inventories
   c. a consumer buys a new car
   d. a Canadian corporation pays interest to owners of its bonds
   e. a provincial government repaves a highway
   f. a wealth-holder places $1000 in her bank account
   g. an unemployed worker receives an employment insurance payment from the government
   h. a French farmer purchases a Canadian-made piece of farm machinery

2. The table below shows the national accounts for a hypothetical economy, Macronia.

Macronia's National Accounts (2015)

	($ billions)
Government purchases	43
Proprietors' incomes and rents	29
Exports	14
Indirect taxes	25
Gross investment	35
Wages and salaries	76
Corporate income	55
Imports	15
Net investment	26
Personal consumption	85
Statistical discrepancy	?

Estimates of the size of Canada's underground economy vary widely. Some economists have tried to measure the underground economy by studying how much cash is held by the public, since underground transactions are commonly paid for with cash to escape detection. Using this method, it has been estimated that Canada's underground economy is equal to anywhere from 10 to 25 percent of GDP, meaning that it has an annual value of $190 billion or more. Statistics Canada's own studies suggest that Canada's underground economy is much smaller—between 1 and 5 percent of GDP. Because of the difficulty in gathering data, these are only "guesstimates."

PRODUCT QUALITY

Today's GDP includes purchases of products not available a few decades ago—flat screen televisions, smartphones, and digital music players, to name only a few. As well, many other products, such as photocopiers, cameras, and personal computers, have increased substantially in quality with little or no rise in price. GDP, which can only add up selling prices, cannot fully capture these quality improvements.

COMPOSITION OF OUTPUT

Another limitation related to the money-value basis of GDP is that it tells us nothing about what is produced and purchased. Suppose one country dedicates most of its GDP to military uses, but another country dedicates the same GDP to health care and education for its citizens. While the GDPs may be the same, the countries' living standards would differ considerably.

INCOME DISTRIBUTION

The fact that incomes may be distributed in a range of ways can have profound effects on the living standards of individuals. But GDP does not reflect how output is distributed among a country's citizens. So, for example, citizens in two countries with the same per capita GDP may have very different living standards if one country's income is widely distributed, while most of the other country's income is in the hands of a few.

LEISURE

Although we might be able to work every waking hour, most of us consider leisure as a requirement for a satisfactory standard of living. However, leisure is not bought and sold in the market, so it cannot be accounted for by GDP. Thus, although over time the average Canadian work week has gradually become shorter—to almost half of what it was a century ago—GDP has no way of representing this change. Because of this, GDP understates economic well-being.

THE ENVIRONMENT

Since GDP quantifies economic activity in terms of its money value, it does not adequately represent another factor: the environment. GDP does not differentiate between economic activities that are harmful to the environment and those that are not, and it may not effectively represent spillover costs and benefits. So, for example, while the clean-up following the 2010 Gulf of Mexico oil spill was added to GDP, the creation of a new nature preserve will not be added.

THINKING ABOUT ECONOMICS

Is it possible to overcome the problems associated with using GDP as an indicator of living standards by devising broader measures that include non-economic variables?

Some economists think so. One measure of living standards is the Human Development Index (HDI), outlined in the article on Mahbub ul Haq at the end of the chapter. Another is the Index of Economic Well-being, a relatively new indicator developed by an Ottawa-based research group known as Centre for Study of Living Standards. This index contains social, economic, and environmental components, including estimates of the value of unpaid work (both voluntary and housework); the value of natural capital, such as forests and the marine environment; and social indicators, such as income distribution and the level of job security. Values for this index are calculated annually for Canada, other rich industrial countries, as well for each Canadian province.

www.csls.ca/iwb.asp

QUESTION   Not all economists would agree with the philosophy behind the Index of Economic Well-being. Why not?

Statistics Canada uses the national income accounts to calculate other measures, which are employed in various ways.

Gross National Income

Gross National Income (GNI) is the total income acquired by Canadians both within Canada and elsewhere. Note that while GDP focuses on incomes made in Canada, GNI focuses on the earnings of *Canadians*.

Gross National Income: the total income acquired by Canadians both within Canada and elsewhere

To calculate GNI, two adjustments to GDP must be made. Income earned by the residents of other countries for their involvement in production in Canada—interest payments on a Canadian corporate bond held by a Japanese financial investor, for example, or compensation received by a British accountant who does work in Canada—is deducted from GDP to find GNI. Although included in GDP, such earnings are not part of the earnings of Canadians. Also, income earned by Canadian residents for their involvement in production in the rest of the world—a stock dividend from an American company paid to a Canadian shareholder, for example, or compensation received by a Canadian software designer in the United States—is added to GDP to find GNI. While not included in GDP, this income is part of Canadians' earnings.

These two adjustments can be made in a net international income account. Traditionally, involvement by the rest of the world in production in Canada (especially through financial investment) has been higher than involvement by Canadians in the rest of the world. As a result, the account gives net international income *to* the rest of the world, and is subtracted from GDP to give GNI. As Figure 8.9 shows, Canadian GNI is less than Canadian GDP.

This is the case in all countries, such as Canada, in which large parts of the nation's financial assets are owned by foreigners, so that each year there is a net

FIGURE 8.9 | Deriving Gross National Income (2013)

	($ billions)
Gross Domestic Product (GDP)	1879.5
Deduct: Net international income to rest of world	(−) 27.0
Gross National Income (GNI)	1852.5

Canadian GNI is less than GDP because income received by the rest of the world for involvement in production in Canada exceeds income received by Canadian residents for involvement in production in the rest of the world.

Sources: Statistics Canada "Gross Domestic Income, Gross National Income and Net National Income (2013)," adapted from the Statistics Canada CANSIM database, http://www5.statcan.gc.ca/cansim/, Tables 380-0082 and 380-0083. Retrieved March 12, 2014.

outflow of income. However, in other countries, such as the United Kingdom, the nation's citizens' foreign financial investments are greater than the amounts of the nation's assets owned by foreigners. For these countries, GNI is greater than GDP. In Canada, GNI is used primarily when comparisons are being made with countries that stress GNI rather than GDP in their national accounts.

Disposable Income

disposable income: household income, after payment of income taxes, which can be either consumed or saved

One other income measure that derives from the national accounts, and which we will make use of often in the chapters that follow, is **disposable income**, or DI, which is income, after the payment of income taxes, that households can either consume or save. As shown in Figure 8.10, this income measure is significantly lower than GDP and GNI.

FIGURE 8.10 | Deriving Other Income Measures (2013)

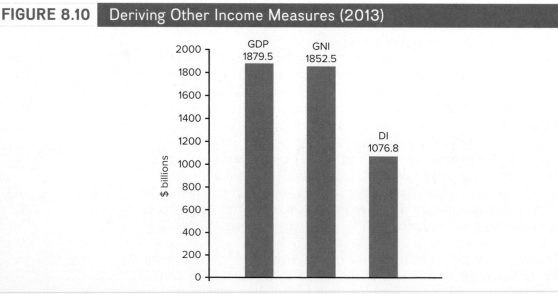

GNI is less than GDP, due to the importance of foreign financial investments in Canada. Disposable income (DI) is less than both GDP and GNI.

Sources: Statistics Canada "Gross Domestic Income, Gross National Income and Net National Income (2013)" and "Current and Capital Accounts - Households (2013)," adapted from the Statistics Canada CANSIM database, http://www5.statcan.gc.ca/cansim/, Tables 380-0083 and 380-0072. Retrieved March 12, 2014.

BRIEF REVIEW

1. To make comparisons among years and countries, GDP is expressed per capita, or per person. To compare GDP for different years, it is adjusted for inflation to derive real GDP, and then expressed per capita. To compare GDP among countries, a common currency must be used, usually US dollars.

2. GDP has its limitations as an indicator of living standards: it excludes non-market activities and the underground economy; it does not reflect changes in product quality or what specific products a country is producing; it cannot account for income distribution or leisure; and it cannot adequately account for environmental spillover costs and benefits.

3. Other measures of economic activity and income include Gross National Income and disposable income.

8.2 | PRACTICE PROBLEMS

1. In a given year, a country's GDP in terms of the country's own dollars is $235 billion.
   a. If the country's population is 6 million, then what is its per capita GDP?
   b. If each of the country's own dollars is worth US$0.56, then what is the country's per capita GDP in terms of US dollars?
   c. If each of the country's dollars is worth US$0.60 after adjusting for purchasing-power parity, then what is the country's per capita GDP in PPP-adjusted US dollars?
   d. Is the PPP-adjusted US dollar value of the country's currency higher or lower than the unadjusted US dollar value? What does this say about the prices in this country relative to those in the United States?
2. a. When is a country's GNI higher than its GDP?
   b. Do residents of a country benefit when GNI is higher than GDP?

LAST WORD

In this chapter, we examined how economists measure economic activity using a variety of statistics, in particular, GDP. And we have seen how GDP—adjusted for such factors as population, price changes, and differences in foreign currencies—is often used as an indicator of national well-being. In the follow following chapters, GDP will reappear as one of the main measures of economic fluctuations used by government policy-makers as they attempt to stabilize levels of economic activity. But first, in the next chapter, we will analyze the importance of two related statistics: the rates of inflation and unemployment.

PROBLEMS

1. The table below shows the national income accounts for a hypothetical country, Metrica.

   Metrica's National Accounts

	($ billions)
Corporate income	98
Exports	68
Wages and salaries	546
Net international income to the rest of the world	8
Gross investment	157
Government purchases	184
Indirect taxes	75
Personal consumption	490
Imports	27
Depreciation	79
Proprietors' incomes and rents	56
Statistical discrepancy	?

   a. What is the income-based estimate of Metrica's GDP?
   b. What is the expenditure-based estimate?
   c. What is the value of the statistical discrepancy that is added to the lower estimate and subtracted from the higher estimate to find a single GDP value?
   d. By how much is Metrica's capital stock expanding or contracting?
   e. What is Metrica's GNI? Is it higher or lower than its GDP? What does this suggest about income earned by residents of other countries for their involvement in production in Metrica relative to income earned by residents of Metrica for their involvement in production in the rest of the world?

2. The production of a kilogram of smoked salmon requires a fisher to catch salmon worth $1.40, which is prepared by a food processor and sold to a retailer for $2.20, who then sells it to a consumer for $2.75.
   a. What is the value added by the fisher? the food processor? the retailer?
   b. What is the total value added in all three stages of production?
   c. If final and intermediate products were double counted in GDP, what would be the total value of the salmon incorporated in GDP?

3. For each of the products below, identify whether it is a final product, an intermediate product, or potentially either.
   a. a ticket to a movie theatre
   b. a roll of newsprint
   c. electrical power

4. Identify whether or not each of the following transactions would be included in GDP, and, if it is included in GDP, which expenditure component it is part of.
   a. An accountant receives payment for preparing a client's personal income tax return.
   b. An owner of a Canada Savings Bond is paid interest on this bond.
   c. A business buys a new piece of production equipment.
   d. A student is paid for shovelling a neighbour's sidewalk.
   e. An unemployed carpenter receives an employment insurance payment.
   f. A town council hires a contractor to do paving work on the town's roads.
   g. A newspaper publisher buys newsprint to add to its inventories of supplies.
   h. An electronic hobbyist sells a used computer to a friend.
   i. A fisher receives a government subsidy to help relocate to a larger community.
   j. A Canadian business sells medical equipment to a Japanese hospital.
   k. A wealth-holder sells 1000 shares issued by a Canadian corporation.
   l. A homeowner repairs his own leaking roof.

5. Each of the following cases applies to a country whose per capita real GDP has been steadily rising at 1 percent a year. In each case, does GDP overstate or understate the change in living standards?
   a. The average amount of leisure time for workers has decreased.
   b. The relative importance of the non-market sector has risen.
   c. A larger proportion of the economy's resources are devoted to recycling and the introduction of environmentally sustainable production techniques.
   d. Incomes have become less equitably distributed.

6. The 2010 Gulf of Mexico oil spill was the worst ever recorded. Caused by a drilling accident at a well operated by the international oil company British Petroleum, it led to the release of almost 5 million barrels of oil, severely harming marine wildlife in the Gulf. It also caused long-term harm to the region's fisheries and tourism industry. The clean-up of the spill cost billions of dollars. What logic do economists use when arguing that the costs of this clean-up should be included in American GDP calculations? What logic do critics use when arguing that the costs should not be included in GDP?

7. (Advanced Problem)

   The figure below shows financial markets, government, and the rest of the world all integrated in the circular flow. Using the figures in the chapter, fill in the blanks in the diagram.

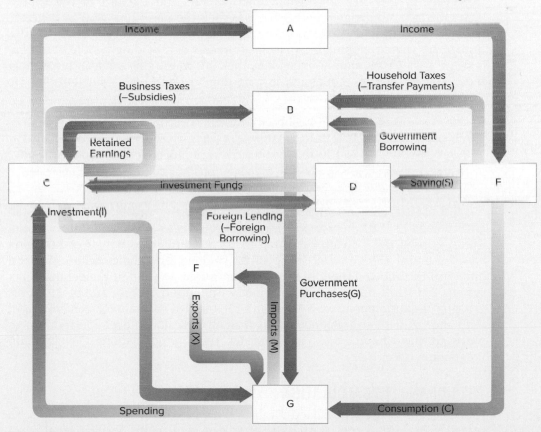

ADVANCING ECONOMIC THOUGHT

ADDING THE HUMAN DIMENSION
Mahbub ul Haq and the Human Development Index

MAHBUB UL HAQ

Photo courtesy of the United Nations Development Programme

Is the use of per capita GDP to compare national living standards inherently flawed? Some economists say it is. They point to such factors as access to education and to health care, which they argue are as vital as income in determining the quality of life. In recent decades, this view has led to the creation of more inclusive measures of national well-being. Most successful is the Human Development Index (HDI), published annually by the United Nations Development Programme, and the brainchild of economist Mahbub ul Haq (1934–1998), a leading figure in the field of development economics.

Haq grew up in Pakistan when it and neighbouring India were being established at the end of the British colonial period. The economic difficulties faced by both countries in their early years left Haq with an abiding interest in the issue of development. During his study of economics–first at Cambridge University in the United Kingdom, then at Yale and Harvard in the United States–he came to disagree with what was then the prevailing view of development, which stressed economic growth to the exclusion of all other factors. Instead, he saw development as a general process of providing people with new choices, rather than simply expanding their incomes. This perspective is now the dominant one in economics, in part due to Haq's own contributions. He described the change this way:

> Only 30 years ago, it would have been heresy to challenge the economic growth school's tacit assumption that the purpose of development is to increase national income. Today, it is widely accepted that the real purpose of development is to enlarge people's choices in all fields–economic, political, cultural. Seeking increases in income is one of many choices people make, but it is not the only one.[1]

Most of Haq's early career as an economist was spent working for the Pakistan government. In 1982, he was appointed the country's planning and finance minister and used this powerful position to try to curtail the power of Pakistan's wealthy feudal elite, a small group of 22 landowning families whose political influence had allowed them to maintain a favoured position in the country's tax system. But Haq's attempted reforms met with limited success, and by 1988, his growing disillusionment with Pakistan's regime (led by military general Zia ul Haq) and his wish to influence policy-making at a global level spurred him to move to the United States to work for the United Nations Development Programme (the UNDP).

THE HDI AND ITS CALCULATION

A charismatic figure who mixed idealism with powers of persuasion, Haq soon played a leadership role at the UNDP. It was due to his inspiration that, in 1990, the UNDP began publishing an annual Human Development Report, with detailed statistical estimates of the Human Development Index for countries across the globe. This index combines four separate statistics: each country's per capita gross national income adjusted for purchasing-power parity (PPP), the average of years of schooling of the country's adult citizens, the expected years of schooling for children of school-going age in the county, and life expectancy at birth. This gives an indicator of well-being that stresses the satisfaction of basic human needs.

The national rankings based on the HDI have some important differences from those based on per capita GDI alone. For example, in 2012, Canada had the eleventh highest HDI ranking of any country in the world, largely due to its high average length of schooling and life expectancy. But in terms of PPP-adjusted per capita GNI, Canada's position has gradually fallen so that the country is now in sixteenth place—not only behind traditionally rich countries such as Luxembourg and the United States, but also upstarts such as Singapore and Hong Kong.

THE DEBATE OVER THE HDI

How good is the HDI as a measure of living standards? While its inclusion of education and health-care indicators are easy to defend, some economists question the statistic's usefulness. In particular, the HDI rankings for rich countries are complicated by a close clustering of scores. For example, in 2012, second-ranked and third-ranked Australia and the United States were almost tied, with HDI rankings of 0.938 and 0.937. Given such minuscule numerical distinctions, is it meaningful to rank Australians' and Americans' living standards as being significantly different?

There is also controversy over the way income differences are treated in the HDI. Haq's insistence that human development is primarily an issue of satisfying basic human needs led him to downplay the importance of per capita income as a component in the index. A discounted version of per capita GNI (one based on the mathematical logarithm function) is used in calculating each country's HDI value. This means that for countries with relatively high per capita GNI values, extra income is discounted at higher and higher rates.

Another criticism relates to the HDI's use of life expectancy as a component. Changes in this statistic for any country are very gradual and difficult to estimate. Canada's current life expectancy of 81.1 years, for example, is one of the highest in the world. But is this statistic relevant for young Canadians today? Breakthroughs in medical research will probably mean that young people in Canada, as well as other rich industrialized countries, can expect to live much longer lives, and it is unclear in which countries this trend will be most pronounced.

REFINING THE HDI

Haq was aware of these objections: "The HDI is neither perfect nor fully developed," he admitted. "It requires continuous analysis and further refinement."[2] And there is no doubt that the index will be modified in the future as it has already been in the recent past. Haq was opposed to adding further components to the existing index because, "[m]ore variables will not necessarily improve the HDI," he argued. "They may confuse the picture and blur the main trends."[3] But in recent years, each new Human Development Report has included adjusted HDIs that highlight income disparities within particular countries, as well as disparities between men and women. The result has been a growing attention by economists to the crucial links between the distribution of incomes and economic development.

Despite debates over its composition, the HDI has gained ever greater prominence, and there is every indication that its importance will increase further.

By helping to make governments more accountable for the human dimensions of development, Haq has played an important role in broadening the conception of development to include notions of social justice and a practical concern for the world's poor.

1. Outline one possible problem with purchasing-power-adjusted GNI and a possible problem with life expectancy at birth given the way these two statistics are included in the Human Development Index.

2. Access the United Nations Development Programme's web site for the Human Development Index and its components (at **https://data.undp.org/dataset/Table-1-Human-Development-Index-and-its-components/wxub-qc5k**).

   a. Using HDI data for 2012, which were the countries with the 10 highest PPP-adjusted per capita GDP levels ranked from 1 to 10?

   b. Using the HDI date for 2012, which were the countries with the 10 highest life expectancies from birth ranked from 1 to 10?

   c. Based on your answers to parts a and b, can we conclude that country rankings for per capita GNI levels and life expectancy are closely aligned?

3. Using the information available at the UNDP's website (at **http://hdr.undp.org/sites/default/files/hdr_2013_en_technotes.pdf**), outline how the statistics included in the Human Development Index are measured in the HDI.

Notes

[1] Mahbub ul Haq, *Reflections on Human Development* (Oxford: Oxford University Press, 1995), p. xvii.

[2] *Ibid.*, p. 61

[3] *Ibid.*, p. 58

CHAPTER 9

Inflation and Unemployment

Ask a Canadian in the workforce what economic prospect concerns them most, and the answer will likely be unemployment. Ask a pensioner the same question, and chances are the answer will be inflation. Our anxiety over these two economic evils is not misplaced; in fact, price stability and full employment are among Canada's most important economic goals. This chapter explores the effects of a trend of rising prices, how the trend is measured, and how it often most hurts those who can afford it least. We will also examine unemployment: how it is measured and its costs not only for individuals, but for the entire economy.

> Unemployment and inflation still preoccupy and perplex economists . . . and everyone else.
>
> —JAMES TOBIN, AMERICAN ECONOMIST

LEARNING OBJECTIVES   After reading this chapter, you will be able to:

LO 1

Define inflation, describe how it is measured, and explain its effect on nominal and real incomes

LO 2

Identify the official unemployment rate and the different types of unemployment, and define full employment

9.1 | Inflation

Inflation, as introduced in Chapter 1, is a general increase in the prices of goods and services in an entire economy over time. **Suppose, for example, that Canada has an annual inflation rate of 3 percent this year. Inflation does not mean that all prices are rising. Some prices are rising, others are remaining constant, while still others may be falling; however, the overall rise in prices is 3 percent.** In exceptional cases–most notably during the 1930s–prices may remain constant, in which case the inflation rate is zero, or there may be a general decline in prices. A general decrease in the level of prices is called **deflation**. Finally, a situation in which inflation is out of control and prices increase rapidly–at double digits or even triple digits per month–is known as **hyperinflation**. A recent example occurred between 2007 and 2009 in the African country of Zimbabwe. During these years, the percentage rise in prices in Zimbabwean dollars rose into the millions. In April 2009, the country's currency was finally abandoned, which meant that the country had to turn to other currencies, such as the South African rand and US dollar, to use as money.

deflation: a general decrease in the level of prices

hyperinflation: a situation in which prices increase rapidly and inflation is out of control

To explain why Canadian governments stress the goal of price stability, let us first examine inflation in detail, how it is measured, and its implications for the economy. Inflation is one of the most talked-about economic concepts, and the analysis of exactly what causes it is a perennial source of discussion and debate. Is it mainly the result of demand factors related to the amount of spending in the economy, or is it primarily fuelled by rising costs? We will leave the discussion of its causes to a later chapter (Chapter 13), at which point we will explore both these possible causes of inflation–either through increases in demand for an economy's goods and services (known as demand-pull inflation), or through increases in costs (known as cost-push inflation).

The Consumer Price Index

The tool most commonly used to measure overall changes in prices is the **consumer price index** (CPI). This index monitors price changes in a representative "shopping basket" of consumer products. Statistics Canada surveys typical Canadian households' buying habits every few years so that it can determine what they buy.

consumer price index: a measure of price changes for a typical basket of consumer products

A simple illustration, as given by Figure 9.1, shows how the consumer price index indicates price changes. Suppose the shopping basket includes only two items–hamburgers and milkshakes. An investigator conducting a survey in 2014 finds that each month, an average consumer buys 10 hamburgers at $2 each and 30 milkshakes at $1 each. In other words, the typical consumer spends $20 on hamburgers and $30 on milkshakes, for a total of $50 per month. Therefore, two-fifths (0.4) of the consumer's total budget is spent on hamburgers and three-fifths (0.6) on milkshakes. These fractions represent the **item weights**, or proportions of each good in the total cost of the shopping basket.

item weights: the proportions of each good in the total cost of the basket of consumer goods used to calculate CPI

base year: the survey year used as a point of comparison in subsequent years

To give a point of comparison for prices in subsequent years, the year in which the survey is conducted acts as the **base year**. The combined price of the representative products in the base year is considered the reference point, and the index in the base year is set at 100. Suppose, in our example, that the prices of hamburgers and milkshakes rise to $2.20 and $1.05 in 2015. On the basis of the quantities determined by the 2014 survey, we can calculate the

FIGURE 9.1	Simple Consumer Price Index

		Result of 2014 Survey		
	Prices	Quantity Consumed per Month	Expenditure per Month	Weights
Hamburgers	$2.00	10	$20	$20 ÷ $50 = 0.4
Milkshakes	$1.00	30	$30	$30 ÷ $50 = 0.6
			$50	

	Prices in 2015		
	Prices		2015 Price 2014 Quantity
Hamburgers	$2.20		$2.20 × 10 = $22.00
Milkshakes	$1.05		$1.05 × 30 = $31.50
			$53.50

In this simplified economy, 10 hamburgers and 30 milkshakes fill the monthly shopping basket of an average consumer. If the value of this basket rises from $50 to $53.50 during the course of a year, the annual inflation rate is 7 percent, with the consumer price index moving from 100 to 107.

amount spent each month on hamburgers and milkshakes. In other words, the same quantity of hamburgers at the new hamburger price (= 10 × $2.20) and the same quantity of milkshakes at the new milkshake price (= 30 × $1.05) give a total cost of $53.50 (= $22 + $31.50). Compared with the 2014 total cost ($50) of the same products, prices have risen by $3.50 (= $53.50 − $50.00) or 7 percent from the base year [= (3.50 ÷ $50) × 100]. Hence, the 2015 consumer price index is 107.

While it includes many more items, Statistics Canada calculates the actual CPI in the same way. Figure 9.2 shows the item weights for the major components of the CPI. Every month, the prices of about 600 representative products included in the CPI shopping basket are measured in a variety of Canadian communities. The index is calculated from the results. In the typical case of rising prices, the percentage increase in the consumer price index represents the

FIGURE 9.2	Consumer Price Index Weights (2011)

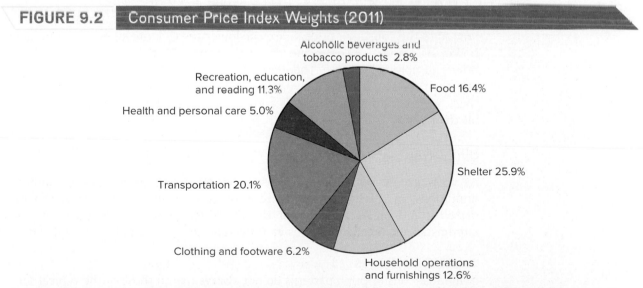

According to Statistics Canada's 2011 survey, a typical urban household's expenditures had the above weights. As shown, shelter was the biggest expenditure, followed by transportation and food.

Source: Statistics Canada "Consumer Price Index Weights (2011)," adapted from the Statistics Canada Database (Definitions, data sources, and methods), Record No. 2301, http://www23 .statcan.gc.ca/imdb-bmdi/document/2301_D48_T9_V2_eng.htm. Retrieved February 2, 2014.

inflation rate. For example, if the CPI has a value of 100 at the end of one year and a value of 110 at the end of the next year, the inflation rate over the year is 10 percent. In other words, the change in the index (= 110 − 100), expressed as a percentage [= (10 ÷ 100) × 100], is the inflation rate (10 percent).

NOMINAL VERSUS REAL INCOME

The consumer price index is useful in helping consumers determine the **cost of living**, or the amount they must spend on the entire range of goods and services they buy. In particular, the CPI allows consumers to judge how much better or worse off they are as a result of inflation. Suppose, for example, a consumer's monthly income increases from $1000 to $1050 during a year when the CPI rises from 100 to 110. If the consumer's own monthly purchases roughly correspond to those in the representative "shopping basket," he can evaluate the personal impact of inflation. To see how this consumer's purchasing power is affected by inflation, we can express his **nominal income**, or income valued in current dollars, as a **real income**, or income expressed in constant base-year dollars. To determine real income for a given year, divide the consumer's nominal income ($1050) by the value of the consumer price index for that year, expressed in hundredths (1.10):

$$\text{real income} = \frac{\text{nominal income}}{\text{CPI (in hundredths)}}$$

$$\$954.55 = \frac{\$1050}{1.10}$$

In other words, the consumer's monthly income of $1050 has a purchasing power of $954.55 when valued in constant base-year dollars. His income has not increased proportionally with the cost of living. For the consumer's purchasing power to keep up with inflation, his income would have to increase by the same percentage as the increase in prices–that is, by 10 percent, or $100 (= $1000 × 0.10), to $1100 (= $1000 + $100).

As our example shows, the purchasing power of a current dollar is inversely related to the consumer price index: the lower the CPI, the higher the purchasing power of nominal income; and the higher the CPI, the lower the purchasing power of nominal income. Therefore, those whose incomes increase at a higher rate than the rise in prices have a higher standard of living. On the other hand, those whose incomes increase at a lower rate than the rise in prices are worse off than before.

Limitations of the CPI

As with any economic indicator, the consumer price index has a number of limitations. In this case, they are: consumer differences, changes in spending patterns, and product quality or the introduction of new products. In some circumstances, these limitations can severely reduce the index's usefulness.

CONSUMER DIFFERENCES

Individual consumption patterns do not always match those of the typical urban household. Hence, the CPI may not apply to many consumers' individual cost of living. Consider, for example, a fashion-conscious reader of romance novels. This person tends to spend a larger proportion of her budget on clothing and books than the typical consumer, and consequently might travel less than the average

---

cost of living: the amount consumers must spend on the entire range of goods and services they buy

nominal income: income expressed in current dollars

real income: income expressed in constant base-year dollars

consumer. For this individual consumer, the official index understates the impact of price changes in clothing and books, but overstates the impact of price changes in travel fares.

CHANGES IN SPENDING PATTERNS

Statistics Canada periodically surveys households to update both the contents and the item weights of the "shopping basket." But these statistical changes occur relatively infrequently, while the changes in actual consumption patterns are ongoing and gradual. This can lead to an important bias in the stated inflation rate using the CPI. In the case of items whose prices rise very little, or even decrease, consumers will likely choose to buy more. For example, more smartphones were steadily purchased in the early 2010s as their prices fell. Over time, these products have too low a weight in the CPI basket, so that the index overstates the rate of inflation. In contrast, consumers tend to buy fewer items whose prices rise the most. Over time, these products have too high a weight in the CPI basket, meaning the index again overstates the rate of inflation.

PRODUCT QUALITY AND NEW PRODUCTS

The index cannot reflect changes in quality, or the introduction of new products, that are unmatched by changes in price. For example, items in the CPI shopping basket, such as medicines and flat screen TVs, may improve tremendously in quality, yet their prices may not increase proportionally with quality, and may even fall. Similarly, new products such as digital music players might replace older products that had higher prices. So, while the standard of living may increase because of increased product quality or new products, this will not be reflected in the CPI.

Over time, Statistics Canada tries to adjust the items in the index to account for these quality improvements, but it is difficult to do so completely. As with changes in spending patterns, the result is that the CPI overstates the rate of inflation—by a total amount of about 0.5 percent a year, according to Canadian estimates.

The GDP Deflator

Another indicator of price changes is the **GDP deflator**. Unlike the CPI, which focuses on a small number of consumer items, the GDP deflator measures price changes for all goods and services produced in the economy and weights them in terms of the economy's total output. The item weights in this index are altered yearly, depending on how goods and services are represented in current GDP. While this frequent updating increases the accuracy of the GDP deflator, it means that values for this index are not as quickly available as values for the consumer price index. Because of this drawback, the GDP deflator receives less publicity than the CPI. Given the difference in the way they are calculated, the two indicators give similar but not identical estimates of inflation.

Statistics Canada now uses an intricate mathematical method known as chaining to calculate the GDP deflator. This method can be approximated as outlined in Figure 9.3, which shows how a GDP deflator can be calculated in a simplified economy that produces only computer microchips. In 2014, which is the reference year, the GDP deflator is equal to 100. To calculate the value of the GDP deflator in each subsequent year, multiply the output of each year by

GDP deflator: an indicator of price changes for all goods and services produced in the economy

FIGURE 9.3	Simple GDP Deflator

(1) Year	(2) Output of Microchips	(3) Current Price	(4) Output at Current Price (2) × (3)	(5) Output at 2014 Price (2) × $0.20	(6) GDP Deflator [(4) ÷ (5)] × 100
2014	1000	$0.20	$200	$200	100
2015	2000	0.30	600	400	150
2016	2500	0.40	1000	500	200

To calculate the GDP deflator in any year, take the economy's annual output at current prices (column 4), divide by this same output valued in reference-year prices (column 5), and then multiply the result by 100. While the GDP deflator has a value of 100 in 2014, which is the reference year, it rises in proportion with the prices of the economy's output.

the current price per microchip, divide by the same output in reference-year prices, and then multiply by 100. For example, the 2015 output of microchips is 2000 and the price is 30 cents. Divide this $600 value of output (= 2000 × $0.30) by the same output in 2014 prices (= 2000 × $0.20), or $400, to give a GDP deflator of 150 [= (600 ÷ $400) × 100]. The result shows that the general price level has risen by one-half between 2014 and 2015. In other words, the inflation rate was 50 percent.

NOMINAL VERSUS REAL GDP

Just as nominal incomes for an individual household can be adjusted to take price changes into account, so can the value of the economy's entire output be adjusted for inflation. Recall that real GDP (or real output) is GDP expressed in constant dollars from a chosen reference year. In contrast, **nominal GDP** (or nominal output) is GDP expressed in current dollars. Recall also that real income for the individual household measures the purchasing power of that household over time. In the same way, real GDP gives an indication of the purchasing power of an entire economy. To find real GDP, economists and statisticians divide nominal GDP by the GDP deflator expressed in hundredths:

nominal GDP: Gross Domestic Product expressed in current dollars

$$\text{Real GDP} = \frac{\text{nominal GDP}}{\text{GDP deflator (in hundredths)}}$$

We can apply this formula to Canada's GDP, as Figure 9.4 shows, to give GDP in constant reference-year (2007) dollars. Canada's nominal GDP was $1879.5 billion in 2013. This amount divided by the GDP deflator expressed in hundredths, which was 1.10885 (= 110.885 ÷ 100), gives a real GDP of $1695.0 billion (= 1897.5 billion ÷ 1.108850). We can use the same approach for years prior to the reference year. For example, Canada's 2001 nominal GDP was $1134.8 billion. This amount divided by the GDP deflator expressed in hundredths, which is 0.84579 (= 84.579 ÷ 100), gives a real GDP for 2001 expressed in 2007 dollars, of $1341.7 billion (= $1134.8 billion ÷ 0.84579). Notice that when the adjusting number is more than 100, as in 2013, nominal GDP is reduced or deflated to find real GDP. In the opposite case, where the index falls short of 100, as in 2001, nominal GDP is expanded or inflated when this adjustment is made.

Inflation's Effects

Figure 9.5 shows Canada's inflation record since 1926. After a period of deflation during the Great Depression of the 1930s, significant inflation occurred during

FIGURE 9.4	Finding Real Gross Domestic Product

(1) Year	(2) Nominal GDP(current $ billions)	(3) GDP Deflator (2007 = 100)	(4) Real GDP (2007 $billions) [(2) ÷ (3)] × 100
2001	$1134.8	84.579	$1341.7
2007	1565.9	100.000	1565.9
2013	1879.5	110.885	1695.0

To find Canada's real GDP in any year, divide the economy's nominal GDP, which is expressed in current dollars, by the value of the GDP deflator. While Canada's nominal output rose from $1134.8 to $1879.5 billion between 2001 and 2013, the nation's real output in 2007 dollars increased by a much smaller amount, from $1341.7 to $1695.0 billion.

Sources: Statistics Canada "Finding Real Gross Domestic Product," adapted from the Statistics Canada CANSIM database, http://www5.statcan.gc.ca/cansim/, Table 380-0017, V3839799 and V3839800, and Table 380-0056, V3862688. Retrieved March 16, 2014.

and immediately after World War II. Relatively low rates of inflation during the 1950s and 1960s were then followed by gradually rising rates during the 1960s and 1970s. Since the mid-1980s, inflation rates have gradually fallen to low levels.

Why are high inflation rates, such as those experienced by Canadians during the 1970s and early 1980s, such a serious problem? Inflation redistributes purchasing power among different groups in ways that can be both economically harmful and unjust; in other words, purchasing power keeps pace with inflation for some individuals, but not for others. For this reason, Canada's central bank, the Bank of Canada, is committed to keeping annual inflation within a target range of between 1 and 3 percent, as we will see in more detail in Chapter 13. To see the effects of inflation, we will look at its effects on household incomes and on borrowing and lending.

FIGURE 9.5	The Inflation Rate

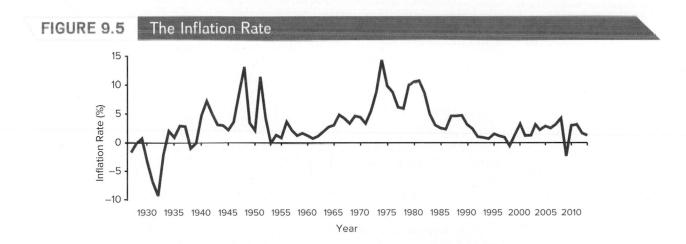

The graph shows annual inflation rates as measured by changes in the GDP price deflator. While deflation occurred during the early 1930s, inflation has been the dominant trend ever since. Inflation was most pronounced after World War II, during the 1970s, and in the early 1980s. In the late 1980s and early 1990s, the inflation rate dropped significantly and it has remained low since then.

Sources: Statistics Canada "The Inflation Rate," adapted from the Statistics Canada publication, *Canadian Economic Observer: Historical Statistical Supplement,* 2001/02, Catalogue 11-210, Vol. 16, July 2002; Statistics Canada CANSIM database, http://www5.statcan.gc.ca/cansim/, Table 380-0102. Retrieved March 17, 2014.

INCOMES

Inflation means not only increasing prices, but expanding nominal incomes as well. The effect on households' purchasing power depends on which is greater: inflation or the increase in nominal income. If a household's nominal income increases steadily every year but inflation is at a higher rate, the household loses purchasing power. So, for example, this year's dollars buy fewer items–such as groceries–than did last year's dollars, even with the expanding nominal income. If, in contrast, the same household has a nominal income that increases at roughly the same rate as inflation, the household maintains its purchasing power. In other words, each year's dollars buy about the same amount of items such as groceries. Therefore, whereas some households may feel the full impact of inflation on their living standards, others may have the impact cushioned by income adjustments, and others may even benefit from inflation because their nominal incomes rise more quickly than inflation. One of the most costly aspects of inflation for society is that this redistribution of purchasing power occurs in an arbitrary way. The winners are often those with substantial economic resources, while the losers are commonly those least able to withstand a drop in purchasing power.

cost-of-living-adjustment clauses: provisions for income adjustments to accommodate changes in price levels, which are included in wage contracts

Many labour unions negotiate income adjustments for their members. As a result, workers' wages are adjusted using the consumer price index, or cost of living, as it is popularly known. In collective agreements, provisions for these adjustments are called **cost-of-living-adjustment** (COLA) **clauses**. When workers' incomes automatically increase by the rate of inflation, they are called **fully indexed incomes**. In this case, nominal income rises at the same rate as prices, so real income stays the same. For example, if the inflation rate between 2014 and 2015 is 10 percent, a worker originally earning a monthly income of $1000 receives a new monthly income of $1100, thereby maintaining purchasing power. The worker's real income in 2014, using 2014 as the base year, is $1000 (= $1000 ÷ 1). In 2015, the same worker's real income, expressed in 2014 dollars, is again $1000 (= $1100 ÷ 1.10).

fully indexed incomes: nominal incomes that automatically increase by the rate of inflation

Other people may receive incomes that are only partially indexed or are fixed. These are the people–including, for example, pensioners, unskilled and non-unionized workers, and recipients of government transfer payments–who lose the most from inflation. **Partially indexed incomes** rise more slowly than the inflation rate, causing real incomes to fall. Suppose, for example, that a single parent has only welfare payments of $1000 per month as income. If the inflation rate is 10 percent between 2014 and 2015, the household needs a 10 percent rise, or an extra $100, in nominal income to maintain its purchasing power. If the payments increase by only 7 percent, they rise by $70, for a total of $1070 per month. Using 2014 as the base year, the household's real income falls from $1000 in 2014 to $972.73 (= $1070 ÷ 1.10) in 2015.

partially indexed incomes: nominal incomes that increase by less than the rate of inflation

fixed incomes: nominal incomes that remain fixed at some dollar amount regardless of the rate of inflation

In contrast to indexed and partially indexed incomes, **fixed incomes** stay at the same nominal dollar amount. In other words, these incomes do not change at all in response to inflation. Suppose, for example, that a pensioner receives a set monthly payment of $1000. Any increase in prices will cause purchasing power to decrease, and the pensioner's real income will be reduced. So, with the same hypothetical 10 percent inflation rate between 2014 and 2015, the pensioner's real income, expressed in 2014 dollars, drops from $1000 in 2014 to $909.09 (= $1000 ÷ 1.10) in 2015.

BORROWING AND LENDING

Whatever interest rate is established in financial markets, if the lender lends funds at an interest rate that is not adjusted for inflation, the lender may lose out. To illustrate, we need to distinguish between two types of interest rates. The **nominal interest rate** is the interest rate expressed in money terms. For example, Mariposa Vacations borrows $2000 at 7 percent per annum. At the end of the year, Mariposa Vacations will pay back the principal ($2000), plus interest ($0.07 \times \$2000 = \$140$), for a total of $2140 (= $2000 + $140).

In contrast, the **real interest rate** is the nominal interest rate minus the rate of inflation.

$$\text{Real interest rate} = \text{nominal interest rate} - \text{inflation rate}$$

nominal interest rate: the interest rate expressed in money terms

real interest rate: the nominal interest rate minus the rate of inflation

If the inflation rate is 3 percent in the year that Mariposa Vacations takes out the loan, then the loan's real interest rate is 4 percent–the 7 percent nominal interest rate minus the 3 percent rate of inflation. The real interest rate reflects the fact that because of inflation, the funds lent (the principal) have less purchasing power at the end of the one-year term than they did at the time the loan was made. Thus, the bank lending to Mariposa Vacations receives $140 (7 percent) in nominal interest at the end of the year, but only $80 (4 percent) in real interest.

Once the nominal interest rate has been agreed upon, it is fixed. So, lenders try to anticipate the rate of inflation for the loan period and build it into the nominal interest rate. This rate built into the nominal interest rate is known as the **inflation premium**. Lenders, therefore, determine what real interest rate they desire and add an inflation premium to determine the nominal interest rate:

inflation premium: a percentage built into a nominal interest rate to anticipate the rate of inflation for the loan period

$$\text{Nominal interest rate} = \text{desired real interest rate} + \text{inflation premium}$$

For example, the manager at Mariposa Vacations' bank may have anticipated a 2 percent inflation rate and wanted a real interest rate of 5 percent. So, on the $2000 one-year loan, she expected the bank would receive real interest of $100 (= $2000 × 0.05) and an inflation premium of $40 (= $2000 × 0.02) to compensate for the reduced purchasing power of the original $2000 principal.

What happens if the inflation rate turns out to be higher than lenders anticipated? Suppose, in our example, the inflation rate is actually 4 percent instead of 2 percent. As a result, the bank actually receives only 3 percent real interest–that is, the 7 percent nominal rate minus the 4 percent inflation rate. This is less than the 5 percent real interest rate the bank manager anticipated. Because the inflation rate is higher than anticipated, the real interest rate is lower than the desired real interest rate, and lenders are worse off, while borrowers are better off. On the other hand, if the inflation rate is less than anticipated, the real interest rate is higher than the desired real interest rate, and lenders are better off, while borrowers are worse off. Only when the inflation rate is exactly as anticipated will the real interest rate be the same as the desired real interest rate, so that lenders and borrowers are unaffected by inflation.

THINKING ABOUT ECONOMICS

Why is inflation much more common than deflation?

Like inflation, deflation arbitrarily redistributes purchasing power—though in ways opposite to inflation. More importantly, deflation can feed on itself. When the general price level falls, households may delay purchases as they expect further price declines. With less spending in the economy, prices tend to fall an extra amount. As a result, households postpone spending even longer, which risks causing a potentially sharp and painful downturn in economic activity. To forestall such self-building cycles of delayed spending, central bankers generally do all they can to avoid even small amounts of deflation. As well, even deflation restricted to certain important markets—such as real estate or financial assets—tends to be monitored closely by policy-makers to ensure that such trends do not cause a more general deflationary spiral. In the aftermath of the credit crunch in 2008, for example, fears of deflation became pronounced—especially in those countries where spending shrank the most. In the United States and parts of Europe, which faced significant slumps in both real estate and financial markets, the world's main central banks made it clear that they were on the lookout for deflation and were prepared to fight it with all the policy tools at their disposal.

QUESTION   **Who is helped and who is harmed by deflation?**

BRIEF REVIEW

1. Inflation is a general increase in the prices of goods and services in the entire economy. A general fall in prices is known as deflation.

2. The consumer price index (CPI) is one indicator of inflation, or changes in the cost of living. The CPI measures price changes in a typical "shopping basket" of consumer products.

3. Whereas nominal income is expressed in current dollars, real income is expressed in constant base-year dollars. Real income equals nominal income divided by the current value of the CPI (expressed in hundredths).

4. The GDP deflator measures price changes for all goods and services produced in the economy and weights them in terms of the economy's total output. Nominal GDP divided by the current value of the GDP deflator (expressed in hundredths) gives the economy's real GDP, or real output in terms of dollars from some reference year.

5. The extent to which inflation affects individuals' purchasing power varies. Those people whose incomes are fully indexed to inflation rates maintain purchasing power. However, those with partially indexed or fixed incomes lose purchasing power.

6. Lenders also lose from inflation if inflation is higher than they anticipated with the inflation premium.

9.1 | PRACTICE PROBLEMS

1. The table below shows a consumer's weekly purchases during 2014 and 2015.
   a. Calculate the value of the consumer's 2014 shopping basket using first 2014 and then 2015 prices.
   b. If 2014 is used as the base year, what is the 2014 value of the consumer's price index? the 2015 value?
   c. Using 2014 as the base year, what is the inflation rate between 2014 and 2015?

Consumer's Weekly Purchases

	Prices		Quantities Consumed per Week	
	(2014)	**(2015)**	**(2014)**	**(2015)**
Hamburgers	$2.50	$2.75	5	4
Bottles of cola	1.25	1.30	10	11

2. Fill in the blanks in the table below for a hypothetical economy. Note that 2013 is the reference year.

Year	Nominal GDP (current $ billion)	GDP Deflator	Real GDP (2013 $ billions)
2012	$___	97.458	$210.7
2013	234.3	___	___
2014	245.9	101.340	___
2015	258.7	___	251.3
2016	___	105.438	261.4

9.2 | Unemployment

Recall from Chapter 1 that another economic goal of Canada is full employment. Of all economic statistics, the unemployment rate is the one most often highlighted in the media, discussed by politicians, and noticed by Canadians. For most people, the prospect of involuntary unemployment provokes considerable anxiety. To see why, we must understand unemployment, how it is measured, and its implications for individuals and for the economy as a whole.

The Labour Force Survey

Statistics Canada keeps track of the Canadian workforce through a monthly survey of about 54 000 households. These households are a random sample of the **labour force population**, which includes all residents of Canada 15 years of age and over, except those living on First Nations reserves in provinces (as opposed to those on reserves in the three northern territories, who are included) and in institutions (for example, jails and psychiatric hospitals), as well as full-time members of the armed forces.[1] The **labour force** is made up of those people in the labour force population who either have jobs or are actively seeking employment. By its definition, the labour force leaves out such groups as pensioners who do not have jobs and are not looking for work. It also excludes those who have given up looking for a job, as well as full-time homemakers who, while they work, do not do so in the formal job market.

The **participation rate** is the percentage of the entire labour force population that makes up the labour force. For example, in 2013, Canada's labour force was 19.0794 million, and the labour force population was 28.6732 million, so the participation rate was 67 percent. In other words, of the defined labour force population, 67 percent was participating in the labour market.

labour force population: the population, with specific exclusions, from which Statistics Canada takes a random sample for the labour force survey

labour force: all people who either have a job or are actively seeking employment

participation rate: the percentage of the entire labour force population that makes up the labour force

[1]For the rationale underlying these exemptions, see the explanation in the Statistics Canada publication *Guide to the Labour Force Survey* (Catalogue 71-543 GIE), available at the Statistics Canada website www.statcan.gc.ca.

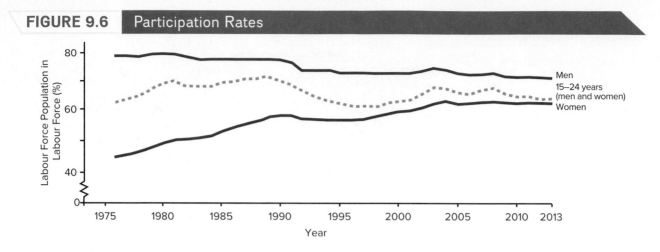

| FIGURE 9.6 | Participation Rates |

Since the 1970s, participation in the labour force by women has increased. In contrast, participation rates for men have fallen. Participation rates for young people have fluctuated widely.

Sources: Statistics Canada "Labour Force Characteristics by Sex and Age Group (2013)," adapted from the Statistics Canada Summary Table, http://www.statcan.gc.ca/tables-tableaux/sum-som/l01/cst01/labor05-eng.htm. Retrieved January 10, 2014.

Statistics Canada also examines the participation rates of specific groups of people. Figure 9.6 shows recent trends in labour force participation for women and men overall, as well as for young people. As shown, the participation rate for women increased steadily until a lull in the early 1990s, and has gradually continued rising since. In contrast, the participation rate for men has decreased. One important reason is the growing popularity of early retirement. Overall, the participation of young people in the labour force is at a value similar to that in 1975, but it has fluctuated as young people respond to shifts in the business cycle by moving in and out of the labour force.

The Official Unemployment Rate

Once the labour force has been defined, its members can be divided into those who are employed and those who are unemployed. The official unemployment rate is the number of unemployed people in the labour force as a percentage of the entire labour force. For example, Canada's 2013 labour force of 19.0794 million people was composed of 17.7312 million people who were employed and 1.3482 million who were not. Therefore, the unemployment rate was 7.1 percent. Figure 9.7 summarizes the relationships among Canada's population, labour force, labour force population, and unemployed labour force.

Drawbacks of the Official Unemployment Rate

Because of the way the official unemployment rate is calculated, it may either understate or overstate the true level of unemployment in the Canadian economy. Critics of this official rate point to the following factors: underemployment, discouraged workers, and dishonesty.

UNDEREMPLOYMENT

The official unemployment rate makes no distinction between part-time and full-time employment, nor does it reflect the appropriateness of the work. While some

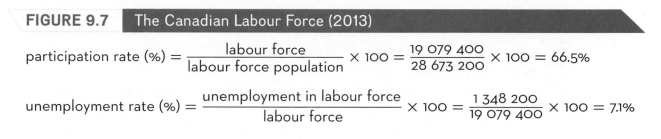

| FIGURE 9.7 | The Canadian Labour Force (2013) |

$$\text{participation rate (\%)} = \frac{\text{labour force}}{\text{labour force population}} \times 100 = \frac{19\ 079\ 400}{28\ 673\ 200} \times 100 = 66.5\%$$

$$\text{unemployment rate (\%)} = \frac{\text{unemployment in labour force}}{\text{labour force}} \times 100 = \frac{1\ 348\ 200}{19\ 079\ 400} \times 100 = 7.1\%$$

In 2013, Canada's total population was about 35 million. Of this number, 28 673 200 were considered part of the labour force population. The labour force constituted 66.5 percent of the labour force population, or 19.0794 million. Of this labour force, 92.9 percent, or 17.7312 million, were employed. The remaining 1.3482 million in the labour force were unemployed, giving an unemployment rate of 7.1 percent.

Source: Statistics Canada "Labour Force Characteristics (2013)," adapted from the Statistics Canada Summary Table, http://www.statcan.gc.ca/tables-tableaux/sum-som/l01/cst01/econ10-eng.htm. Retrieved January 10, 2014.

part-time workers prefer part-time work, others would want full-time work if it were available. Also, some workers work at jobs that do not fully use their skills and education. Thus, we have the problem of **underemployment**. Some argue that the official rate understates unemployment by ignoring underemployed workers. This is of particular concern to those younger workers who find it difficult to gain suitable entry jobs that fully use their education and skills. How significant is this type of underemployment? Are young job entrants, especially those who have attained post-secondary credentials at university or community college, in a more difficult position than their parents or grandparents were at the same point in their lives?

underemployment: the problem of workers being underused, either as part-time workers or by working at jobs not appropriate to their skills or education

This is controversial topic, with economists and other experts voicing a range of views. Some focus on the fact that demand is not as robust in many desirable occupations as in the past, with potential entrants facing hiring barriers as they compete with more senior market participants. This may push new entrants into occupations in which their training and skills are not adequately used. Commentators who stress the relevance of these trends argue that the result is a *dual labour market*, divided into two sectors: one comprising attractive high-paying occupations characterized by considerable barriers to entry, and the other made up of less attractive occupations with lower pay and more rapid turnover. Other commentators—a group that includes many, if not most, economists—view such trends as being limited in scope, with greatest relevance to high-paying jobs in the public sector where entry barriers are strongest. In the private sector, these commentators contend, such anti-competitive forces are far less pronounced, and if they are prevalent they will be addressed over time by the impact of shifting demand and supply on wages. Even in highly regulated public sector occupations, competitive forces will tend to have an impact on wages and other job aspects over time, though potentially at such a slow pace that the career aspirations of some entrants are stymied.

DISCOURAGED WORKERS

Unemployment statistics also do not take into account people who, after searching for a job without luck, give up looking. Because they are not actively seeking employment, these **discouraged workers** are not considered part of the labour force. Again, it is sometimes argued that this causes the official rate to understate unemployment.

discouraged workers: unemployed workers who have given up looking for work

The number of underemployed and discouraged workers rises during an economic downturn, since job prospects—especially for full-time work—are at their bleakest. During the 2008-09 economic downturn, for example, estimates suggested that adding underemployed and discouraged workers would have added up to 3 percent to the official unemployment rate. At other times, adding these groups to the official rate would result in a smaller increase.

DISHONESTY

People responding to Statistics Canada's labour market survey may state that they are actively looking for work when, in fact, they are not. While the extent to which such dishonesty affects the unemployment rate is difficult to measure, it does make it possible for the official rate to overstate unemployment.

Types of Unemployment

When examining unemployment, we should distinguish among four types: frictional, structural, cyclical, and seasonal unemployment.

FRICTIONAL UNEMPLOYMENT

frictional unemployment: unemployment due to being temporarily between jobs or looking for a first job

Workers who are temporarily between jobs or have begun looking for their first jobs are experiencing **frictional unemployment**. A dental assistant who has left one job voluntarily to look for another and a recent college graduate looking for career-related work are examples. Frictional unemployment is a permanent feature of labour markets and represents about 3 percent of the labour force at any given time.

STRUCTURAL UNEMPLOYMENT

structural unemployment: unemployment due to a mismatch between people and jobs

Another type of unemployment is closely connected to structural trends in the economy. **Structural unemployment** is due to a mismatch between people and jobs—unemployed workers cannot fill the sorts of jobs that are available. This type of unemployment occurs primarily because of gradual changes in the economy. Long-term adjustments in what items are produced (for example, the current shift from goods to services), how they are produced (largely due to technological change), and where they are produced cause such unemployment.

Because of these changes, workers lose out; they are displaced. Consider a worker who loses her job in manufacturing because of automation. She might not yet have the skills for the expanding service sector. In the same way, an unemployed fisherman living in a remote village cannot easily take advantage of employment opportunities elsewhere. Because gaining new skills, moving to obtain work elsewhere, and developing new industries in a region all take time, structural unemployment can persist for long periods.

CYCLICAL UNEMPLOYMENT

cyclical unemployment: unemployment due to fluctuations in output and spending

Economies and businesses must cope with fluctuations in output and spending, causing unemployment to rise and fall. This type of unemployment is called **cyclical unemployment**. An auto worker, for example, may work overtime in periods of strong consumer demand for cars, but be laid off in leaner times.

SEASONAL UNEMPLOYMENT

seasonal unemployment: unemployment due to the seasonal nature of some occupations and industries

In some Canadian industries—agriculture, construction, and tourism, for example—work is seasonal, with lower employment in the winter months. As a result, some workers experience **seasonal unemployment**. Compared with many other countries, seasonal unemployment is significant in Canada, given its climate and the importance of its primary resource industries. So that month-to-month comparisons can be made without the influence of seasonal unemployment, Statistics Canada calculates seasonal changes and adjusts the official unemployment rate accordingly.

Full Employment

Defining **full employment** is a tricky task. In effect, full employment is the highest reasonable expectation of employment for the economy as a whole, and is defined in terms of a **natural unemployment rate**. This rate includes frictional unemployment, but traditionally excludes cyclical unemployment. This rate also excludes seasonal unemployment, which is already omitted from the official unemployment rate using seasonal adjustment.

In the 1950s and 1960s, full employment in the Canadian economy was defined by the Economic Council of Canada as a natural unemployment rate of 3 percent. In other words, full employment was 100 percent labour force employment minus 3 percent frictional unemployment. As Figure 9.8 shows, the unemployment rate, which reached almost 20 percent during the Great Depression of the 1930s, decreased considerably over the following decades. However, full employment—as it was then defined—was only occasionally achieved.

Since the 1970s, the unemployment rate has been well over 3 percent. In light of recent economic trends and thinking, many economists argue that in addition to frictional unemployment—which will always exist—the definition of full employment should also accommodate at least some structural unemployment. This, they say, is because structural unemployment *can* be reduced, but only very gradually. While definitions of full employment in the 2010s vary, most include a natural unemployment rate of between 6 and 7 percent. **Because of this, full employment does not mean what it would seem to—that everyone who wants a job has one. Indeed, a significant proportion of the labour force (6 to 7 percent) is unemployed.**

The gradual increase that took place over recent decades in both the actual and the natural unemployment rates represents a worrisome trend. Several factors are often highlighted in explaining this trend.

full employment: the highest reasonable expectation of employment for the economy as a whole

natural unemployment rate: the unemployment rate that defines full employment

STRUCTURAL CHANGE

Recall that structural adjustments in an economy occur whenever there are changes regarding what products are produced, as well as in how and where they are produced. Over the past few decades, the pace of structural change in the

---

FIGURE 9.8 | The Unemployment Rate

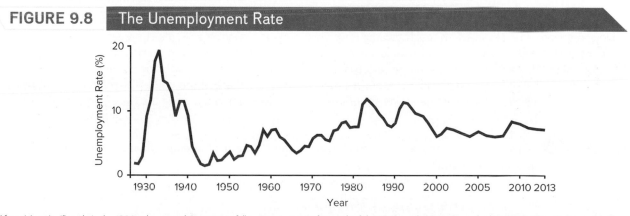

After rising significantly in the 1930s, the unemployment rate fell to 2 to 4 percent for much of the 1940s and 1950s. Since the late 1950s, the rate has gradually risen. Much of this increase can be attributed to a rise in natural unemployment.

Sources: Statistics Canada "Labour Force Characteristics (2013)," adapted from the Statistics Canada Summary Table, www.statcan.gc.ca/tables-tableaux/sum-som/l01/cst01/econ10-eng. htm. Retrieved January 14, 2014.

Canadian economy has accelerated. The growth of the service sector and shrinking of the traditional manufacturing sector, the rise of the new economy, and the removal of many international trade barriers have each led to the displacement of workers and, therefore, pushed up long-term structural unemployment.

UNEMPLOYMENT INSURANCE

Most unemployed workers today have a significant advantage over those in previous generations. The financial cushion provided by unemployment insurance allows job seekers to devote more time and effort to searching for employment than in the past, which increases frictional unemployment. Reforms to unemployment insurance in the early 1970s also made it easier for those experiencing seasonal and structural unemployment to claim benefits. Thus, unemployment insurance can be a factor in increasing the unemployment rate. Overall, it is estimated that this factor has added between 0.5 percent and 2 percent to the unemployment rate since the 1970s. However, more recent changes to the unemployment insurance system (now called Employment Insurance) have made it more difficult to claim benefits, reducing this effect.

MINIMUM WAGES

Minimum wage levels set by the provinces have increased a great deal in the past few decades. For young people in particular–who are more likely than others to be affected by minimum wage laws–this has meant an increase in the number of people looking for work. For example, one Canadian study suggested that a 10 percent increase in the minimum wage reduces employment by 1 percent for male teenagers and 2.7 percent for female teenagers. As we saw in Chapter 5, minimum wages cause unemployment in the market for unskilled labour by creating a wage floor above equilibrium. The minimum wage, therefore, creates a surplus, with a greater number of workers wishing to work than there are available jobs at that wage.

THINKING ABOUT ECONOMICS

Are the Canadian and US unemployment rates directly comparable?

There are important differences in the way the unemployment rate is calculated in each country, which means that the Canadian rate would be lower if computed using US definitions. For example, a job-seeker who consults just one job ad a month would be classified as actively seeking employment (and hence officially unemployed) in Canada, but not in the US. Statistics Canada takes these measurement differences into account by occasionally publishing a Canadian unemployment rate calculated using US definitions. The resulting figure is anywhere up to a percentage point below the rate determined using the Canadian definitions.

QUESTION **Given these measurement differences, is the US natural unemployment rate likely to be above or below that in Canada?**

The Costs of Unemployment

High unemployment rates hurt both individuals and the Canadian economy as a whole. As Figure 9.9 shows, the rates vary from province to province and among groups of people. To jobless workers and their families, unemployment, especially for extended periods, can create stress and discouragement, disrupt family life,

| FIGURE 9.9 | Unemployment Rates by Province, Gender, and Age (2013) |

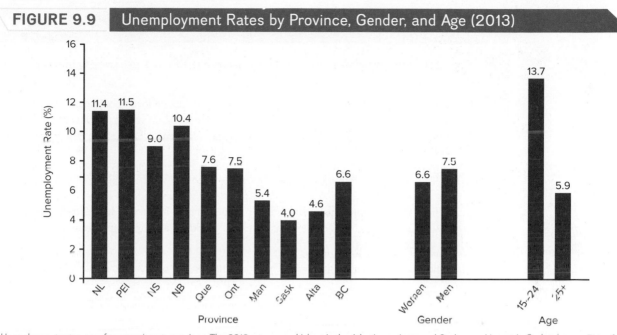

Unemployment rates vary from province to province. The 2013 rates were highest in the Atlantic provinces and Quebec, and lowest in Saskatchewan. Rates for women were lower than for men, and young people were more likely to be unemployed than those 25 years and over.

Sources: Statistics Canada "Labour Force, Employment and Unemployment, Levels and Rates, by Province (2013)," and "Labour Force Characteristics by Age and Sex (Rates) (2013)," adapted from the Statistics Canada websites, www.statcan.gc.ca/tables-tableaux/sum-som/l01/cst01/labor07a-eng.htm and www.statcan.gc.ca/tables-tableaux/sum-som/l01/cst01/labor20b-eng.htm. Retrieved January 10, 2014.

lower self-esteem, and cause financial hardship. In addition, the economy as a whole loses the output the unemployed workers could have produced.

One way to measure the cost of unemployment for the entire economy is by calculating the extent to which **potential output**, or the real output associated with full employment, exceeds actual output. According to Okun's Law— named after the American economist Arthur Okun—for every percentage point that the unemployment rate exceeds the natural unemployment rate, the gap between potential output and actual output is 2.5 percent.

In 2013, for example, real GDP in (constant) 2007 dollars was $1695.0 billion, while the unemployment rate was 7.1 percent, or 0.6 percent above an assumed natural unemployment rate of 6.5 percent. According to Okun's Law, real output could have been 1.5 percent (= 0.6 × 2.5) higher if unemployment equalled the natural rate. In other words, in 2007 dollars, 2013 real GDP could have been $25.4 billion (= $1695.0 billion × 0.015) higher.

This method of measuring the costs of unemployment is difficult to apply, both because of disagreements over the natural unemployment rate and because it can be argued that there are costs of unemployment even if actual output equals or exceeds potential output. There are also indications, more so in the US than in Canada, that the numerical relationship of 2.5 that underlies Okun's Law may be undergoing a gradual, but significant, reduction. Automation and the increased use of computers mean that extra output can be created by adding fewer jobs than before. But as an approximation, it gives a good indication of the substantial cost of unemployment, not just to those workers who are directly affected, but also to the economy as a whole.

potential output: the real output, or Gross Domestic Product, associated with full employment

BRIEF REVIEW

1. The labour force population is Canada's population age 15 years and over, with some exclusions.

2. The participation rate is the percentage of those in the labour force population who make up the labour force, which includes all those who are employed or who are actively seeking work within the formal economy. Participation rates for women have risen considerably in the last few decades.

3. The official unemployment rate is the percentage of the labour force that is unemployed.

4. The official unemployment rate, which has gradually risen in the last few decades, does not take into account underemployment, discouraged workers, and dishonest answers given in labour market surveys.

5. Unemployment can be categorized as frictional, structural, cyclical, or seasonal.

6. Full employment is the highest reasonable expectation of employment for the economy as a whole, and is defined in terms of a natural unemployment rate. Traditionally, the natural unemployment rate only accommodated frictional unemployment; now, however, many economists believe it should include at least some structural unemployment.

7. The costs of unemployment are profound and numerous for unemployed workers and their families. Unemployment costs to the economy as a whole are indicated by the extent to which potential output exceeds actual output.

9.2 | PRACTICE PROBLEM

1. The information below applies to a hypothetical economy.

Unemployed members of the labour force	2.3 million
Total population 15 years of age and over	58.9 million
Participation rate	64 percent
Workers with full-time jobs	21.4 million
Part-time workers who do not wish to have full-time jobs	4.2 million
Part-time workers who wish to have full-time jobs	3.5 million
Total population less than 15 years of age	14.6 million

Use the information to find the following:
a. the size of the labour force
b. the size of the labour force population
c. the official unemployment rate
d. an estimate of the unemployment rate that includes underemployment

LAST WORD

In this chapter, we explored how inflation and unemployment are measured and examined the economic problems caused by each. While we looked at some of the causes of both problems, it is necessary to build a model of macroeconomic activity to fully understand the factors that determine them and to analyze the relationship that exists between them. In the next chapter, we devise a model that serves this role.

PROBLEMS

1. The table below gives data on Student A's monthly purchases during 2014 and 2015.

Student A's Monthly Purchases

	Prices		Quantities Consumed per month	
	(2014)	(2015)	(2014)	(2015)
Hotdogs	$1.50	$1.60	3	2
Cans of cola	.75	.70	16	18
Chocolate bars	1.00	1.00	7	7
Magazines	3.50	4.50	3	2
Movies	3.00	2.75	2	3

   a. Calculate the value of Student A's 2014 shopping basket using 2014 prices. What are the item weights associated with this shopping basket?
   b. Calculate the value of Student A's 2014 shopping basket using 2015 prices. If 2014 is used as the base year, what is the 2015 value of Student A's price index? What is the 2014 value of this index? By what percentage has this index changed between 2014 and 2015?

2. The table below shows output and prices during 2015 in a hypothetical economy that produces only two goods—sweatshirts and bags of chips.

Finding the GDP Deflator

	Output In 2015	Prices in 2015	Prices in 2014
Sweatshirts	4	$22.00	$16.00
Bags of chips	50	1.80	1.50

   a. What is the total value of the economy's output in 2015 valued in 2015 prices?
   b. What is the total value of the economy's output in 2015 valued in 2014 prices?
   c. On the basis of your answers to parts a and b, calculate the value of the GDP Deflator In 2015 If 2014 is treated as the reference year
   d. In what ways does the calculation of the GDP deflator differ from the calculation of the consumer price index?

3. Fill in the table below for a hypothetical economy.

Finding Real Gross Domestic Product

Year	Nominal GDP (current $ billion)	GDP Deflator	Real GDP (2013 $ billions)
2012	$____	91.691	$913.4
2013	982.4	98.923	____
2014	1152.9	____	____
2015	1373.8	110.187	____
2016	1589.6	____	1318.1

4. Identify how each of the following individuals is influenced by unexpected inflation:
   a. a lawyer whose costs and revenues both rise by the inflation rate
   b. the owner of a heavily indebted restaurant
   c. a worker with a union contract that includes a COLA clause
   d. an injured worker who lives on a partially indexed pension

5. For each of the following years, determine the real interest rate. Find the difference between this rate and the desired real interest rate, and explain how any difference affects borrowers and lenders.
   a. In year 1, the nominal interest rate is 9 percent, the inflation premium on loans is 3 percent, and actual rate of inflation is 4 percent.

    b. In year 2, the nominal interest rate is 10 percent, the inflation premium is 4 percent, and the actual rate of inflation is 2 percent.

    c. In year 3, the nominal interest rate is 8 percent, the inflation premium is 2 percent, and the actual rate of inflation is 2 percent.

6. The relationship between nominal and real interest rates continues to hold when there is deflation rather than inflation, except that the overall change in prices is now negative. For example, take the case where the desired real interest rate is 3 percent, the expected deflation rate is 2 percent (i.e., the inflation rate is −2 percent), and the actual deflation rate is 3 percent (i.e., the inflation rate is −3 percent).

    a. What is the nominal interest rate?

    b. What is the actual real interest rate?

    c. If the reduction in prices is greater than expected, do borrowers or lenders benefit? Which is made worse off?

7. The table below shows labour force information for a hypothetical economy.

Finding Participation and Unemployment Rates

	2014	2015
Total population 15 years and over	4.2 million	4.2 million
Those 15 years and over not in the labour force population	1.4 million	1.4 million
Part-time workers who wish to have full-time jobs	100 000	125 000
Part-time workers who do not wish to have full-time jobs	300 000	375 000
Discouraged workers	400 000	500 000
Workers with full-time jobs	1.2 million	1.3 million
Unemployed members of the labour force	150 000	160 000

    a. Calculate the labour force population, labour force, participation rate, and official unemployment rate in 2014. Then, calculate values for the same variables in 2015.

    b. Has the official unemployment rate risen or fallen between 2014 and 2015? Has the number of unemployed members of the labour force increased or decreased?

    c. Calculate, for both 2014 and 2015, what the unemployment rate would be if it included underemployed and discouraged workers.

8. Identify which labour market condition best describes the situation of each of the following individuals, where the official unemployment rate refers to the rate before seasonal adjustment.

    a. a laid-off typesetter who so far has had no success finding a similar job due to the replacement of typesetters by computers

    b. a former cod fisherman who has given up looking for work and has gone on welfare

    c. a farm labourer who is unemployed during the winter months

    d. a graphic artist who loses her job during an economic downturn

    e. a store clerk who is currently working part-time and looking for a full-time position in the same occupation

    g. a recent business school graduate who searches for her first career-related position

9. Using Okun's Law, calculate the gap between potential output and actual output in a hypothetical economy in 2014 and 2015. In your answers, assume a natural unemployment rate of 6.5 percent.

    a. In 2014, the unemployment rate was 7.2 percent and real GDP in 2012 dollars was $1543.2 billion.

    b. In 2015, the unemployment rate was 8.3 percent and real GDP in 2012 dollars was $1612.8 billion.

10. (Advanced Problem)

    a. Using the table accompanying Problem 1, calculate the value of Student A's 2015 shopping basket using 2015 prices, as well as the item weights associated with this basket.

    b. What would the value of the 2015 shopping basket have been in 2014? If 2015 is used as the base year, what is the 2014 value of Student A's price index? What is the 2015 value? By what percentage has this index changed between 2014 and 2015?

ADVANCING ECONOMIC THOUGHT

BOOM, BUST & ECHO
David K. Foot and the Economics of Age Distribution

DAVID K. FOOT
© Footwork Consulting Inc./D'arcy Glionna, photographer

What economic indicators can we apply to our personal lives? David K. Foot, a well-known Canadian economist and demographer, suggests that our ages can give us insights into our economic futures. In the following excerpt from his book *Boom, Bust & Echo 2000* (written with Daniel Stoffman), Foot outlines some of the effects of Canada's huge "baby-boom generation" (people born from 1947 to 1966), its smaller "baby-bust generation" (people born from 1967 to 1979), and its "baby-boom echo generation" (people born from 1980 to 1995).

Demography, the study of human populations, is the most powerful—and most underutilized—tool we have to understand the past and to foretell the future. Demographics affect every one of us as individuals, far more than most of us have ever imagined. They also play a pivotal role in the economic and social life of our country.

What kinds of foods will people buy, and what kinds of cars will they drive? Where will they choose to live? Which investments will they favour? These and many other things can be confidently predicted, simply on the basis of readily available data on the age of Canadians. The two keys to these forecasts are the number of people in each age group and the probability that each person will participate in a given behaviour.

Canada's population pyramid (see Figure A) contains a massive bulge, representing the huge generation of baby-boomers born in the 20 years from 1947 to 1966. By comparison, the Depression and World War II generations that preceded the baby boom are small, as is the baby bust that followed it. But the most recently arrived group, the offspring of the boomers—or the baby-boom echo—is comparatively large.

FIGURE A   Canada's Population Projections, 2009, 2036, 2061

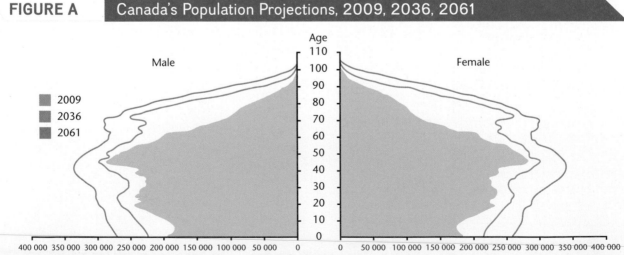

Source: "Age Pyramids (in number) of the Canadian Population, 2009, 2036, and 2061 (scenario M1)," adapted from the Statistics Canada publication, *Population Projections for Canada, Provinces and Territories, 2009 to 2036*, Catalogue 91-520-XIE2010001, page 45, www.statcan.gc.ca/pub/91-520-x/91-520-x2010001-eng.pdf.

THE BABY BOOM (1947 TO 1966)

Why did the baby boom happen? A likely explanation is that during these 20 years, Canadians knew they could afford large families. The post-war economy was robust, the future seemed full of promise, and young couples wanted to share that bright future with a big family. The second reason was the high immigration levels that prevailed during the 1950s; immigrants tend to be people of childbearing age, and they made an important contribution to the boom.

The front-end boomers have done pretty well for themselves. There are a lot of them, so they had to compete for jobs when they entered the workforce in the 1960s. But the entry of vast numbers of young baby-boomers into the marketplace through the 1970s and 1980s created wonderful opportunities for the front-enders already entrenched in business and government.

Those born toward the end of the 1950s also understand the baby boom but, unlike the front-enders, they are less well positioned to profit from that knowledge. Most members of this boomer subgroup have a house and are in a career, but that career seems to be going nowhere because the rungs ahead of them are clogged with older boomers who are still 15 to 20 years from retirement.

Things are tough for the late-1950s group, but not nearly as bad as they are for the back end that arrived just after them. These are the 3.1 million people born from 1961 to 1966. They are the same age as the characters in Douglas Coupland's novel *Generation X*, which gave the early-1960s group its name. Many of them were still living at home with their parents at their 30th birthday because, faced with horrendous obstacles in the labour market, they have not been able to get their careers on track. That is why, while front-end boomers were earning 30 percent more than their fathers by age 30, back-enders were making 10 percent less than their fathers at the same age.

One of the worst things the Gen-Xers have to cope with is their parents—the Depression generation. These are the 60-year-olds sitting at the top of the corporate ladder, approaching the end of very successful careers, and unable to fathom why their 30-year-old offspring are living at home. Tension is tremendous in these families. Often, the father is certain that his own success is based solely on his own merit, while he sees his son's failure as a result of lack of drive and ambition.

THE BABY BUST (1967 TO 1979)

The commercial introduction of the birth control pill in 1961 and the rising participation of women in the labour market led to declining fertility over the 1960s. The result was a decline in births and a smaller cohort, often called the baby bust. The baby-busters have done pretty well so far, especially the younger ones. They had no difficulty finding part-time jobs in high school, unlike their older brothers and sisters who had less opportunity to earn money in high school because they had so many competitors. During the 1990s, university entry standards fell, making it easier for busters to get into the school of their choice.

THE BABY-BOOM ECHO (1980 TO 1995)

What is the outlook for the echo kids? It will not be quite as smooth sailing as the baby-busters have had, but it will not be as disastrous as for Generation X either. Like

Breakdown of Generations in Canada – A Summary

Birthdates	Generation
1947–1966	Baby-Boom Generation
1967–1979	The Baby Bust
1980–1995	The Baby-Boom Echo
1996–2010	Children of the Baby Bust (Millennials)
2011–2025*	Children of the Baby-Boom Echo

*projected

the baby boom, the echo has a front end, born in the 1980s, that will have an easier ride than its back end, born in the first half of the 1990s. The latter group, Generation X-II, will experience the familiar disadvantages of arriving at the rear of a large cohort. Generation X-II will have a life experience similar to that of its parents, the first Generation X. Just as the first Gen-Xers have done, Gen X-II will have to scramble.

However, Gen X-II should be better prepared than its parents were to cope with high youth unemployment and other difficulties associated with a large cohort. That is because these kids have their Gen-X parents to teach them. By contrast, the original Generation X was the offspring of a small cohort that was not equipped to prepare them for the difficult world they encountered when they left home in the early 1980s.

1. On the basis of the demographic factors outlined in this article, predict whether, everything else remaining the same, the following variables will rise or fall between 2016 and 2026. In each case, explain your answer.
   a. unemployment rates for youth aged 15–24
   b. interest rates
   c. sales of housing
   d. stock market prices
   e. premiums paid by working Canadians to fund retirement pensions

Economic Fluctuations

For decades, real output and average living standards in Canada have gradually increased, but economies such as Canada's rarely grow steadily. Sometimes, production and incomes increase sharply; at other times, they inch up or even fall, occasionally with devastating results. During the Great Depression of the 1930s, for example, real output in Canada dropped by over 25 percent, while unemployment soared. In the late 1960s, the opposite happened: an overheated economy led to accelerating inflation, which significantly reduced some Canadians' living standards. More recently, the financial turmoil of the late 2000s led to layoffs and plant closings, leaving a legacy of displaced workers and lost production. This chapter analyzes the causes of these types of instability.

> It's a recession when your neighbor loses his job; it's a depression when you lose yours.
>
> **-HARRY TRUMAN, AMERICAN PRESIDENT**

LEARNING OBJECTIVES   After reading this chapter, you will be able to:

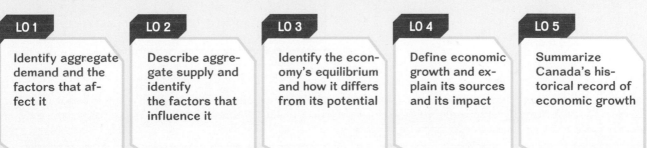

LO 1	LO 2	LO 3	LO 4	LO 5
Identify aggregate demand and the factors that affect it	Describe aggregate supply and identify the factors that influence it	Identify the economy's equilibrium and how it differs from its potential	Define economic growth and explain its sources and its impact	Summarize Canada's historical record of economic growth

10.1 | Aggregate Demand

What determines the connections among inflation, unemployment, levels of spending, and real output in the Canadian economy? As in the case of individual markets, the explanation can be given in terms of demand and supply. First, we will look at how the concept of demand can be applied to the economy as a whole to see the relationship between the general price level and total spending in the economy, which is known as **aggregate demand** (AD).

Recall that total spending on an economy's goods and services is the sum of four components: consumption, investment, government purchases, and net exports. The primary groups responsible for this spending are households, businesses, governments, and the rest of the world. Total spending in an economy, adjusted for changes in the general price level, is referred to as **real expenditures** and is calculated using the GDP price deflator. Suppose, for example, that $1080 billion in nominal dollars is spent in Canada in a year, in which the GDP deflator has a value of 120. Therefore, real expenditures, or total output purchases, equal $900 billion (= $1080 billion ÷ 1.2) in constant dollars.

Economists attempt to identify the factors that influence real expenditures. One of the most important factors is the price level, since changes in prices cause changes in spending. In other words, not only is the price level used to calculate real expenditures, it also affects real expenditures.

aggregate demand: the relationship between the general price level and total spending in the economy

real expenditures: total spending in an economy, adjusted for changes in the general price level

aggregate demand schedule: the relationship between the general price level and total spending in the economy expressed in a table

aggregate demand curve: the relationship between the general price level and total spending in the economy expressed on a graph

The Aggregate Demand Curve

We can express aggregate demand in a table, known as the **aggregate demand schedule**, or on a graph, known as the **aggregate demand curve** (AD). Figure 10.1 shows an aggregate demand schedule and an aggregate demand

---

FIGURE 10.1   Aggregate Demand

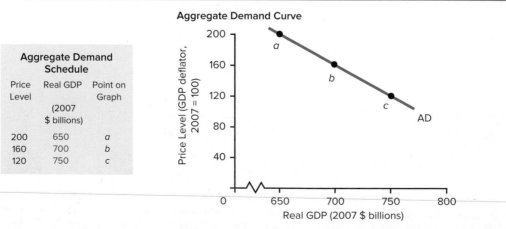

Aggregate Demand Schedule		
Price Level	Real GDP (2007 $ billions)	Point on Graph
200	650	a
160	700	b
120	750	c

As the general level of prices increases, less real output is bought for two reasons. (1) The real value of financial assets, such as bank accounts and bonds, decreases. As a result, households feel less wealthy, so they reduce their consumption spending. (2) Net export spending is reduced, as both foreigners spend less on Canadian exports and Canadian residents spend more on imports.

curve. Just as with a demand curve for a single product, the price variable is placed on the vertical axis of the graph, and the output variable is placed on the horizontal axis.

Recall that price and quantity demanded of a single product almost always have an inverse relationship: as price rises, quantity demanded decreases, and vice versa. The same can be said for the general price level and real expenditures, although for different reasons. Whereas the quantity demanded of a certain product can be explained by the law of diminishing marginal utility, the amount spent in the entire economy is determined by two entirely different factors: the wealth and foreign trade effects. Note that the response to a change in the price level is a movement along the aggregate demand curve. For example, if the GDP price deflator rises from 160 to 200, then real expenditures on this particular AD curve fall from $700 billion to $650 billion in terms of 2007 dollars.

WEALTH EFFECT

A household may have wealth in the form of financial assets as well as real assets. The nominal values of these financial assets—such as bank accounts and retirement savings plans—may stay the same, no matter what the price level; however, their real values change with any rise or fall in the price level. To find the real value of financial assets, divide their nominal value by the price level:

$$\text{Real value of financial assets} = \frac{\text{nominal value of financial assets}}{\text{price level}}$$

When the price level rises, the real value of households' financial assets decreases. Because consumers feel they have less wealth, they spend less on consumption items. As a result of this **wealth effect**, real expenditures drop.

wealth effect: with changes in the price level, the real value of households' financial assets changes, causing households to adjust their spending

FOREIGN TRADE EFFECT

Changes in the price level also influence foreign trade. When the price level in Canada rises, Canadian exports become more expensive for foreigners. As a result, sales in foreign markets fall, causing a decrease in export expenditures. At the same time, products imported into Canada become cheaper relative to higher-priced domestic products. Therefore, import expenditures by Canadians rise. The **foreign trade effect** as this combination of effects is known—involves a decrease in net exports $(X - M)$, and thus a decline in real expenditures.

foreign trade effect: with changes in the price level, expenditures on imports change in the same direction, while expenditures on exports change in the opposite direction

Changes in Aggregate Demand

In addition to the price level, other factors can influence total spending. However, these factors, called **aggregate demand factors**, change total spending at all price levels. In other words, they shift the aggregate demand curve. Recall that spending has four components: consumption, investment, government purchases, and net exports. When factors other than the price level affect any of these components, they, in turn, affect total real expenditures.

Suppose, for example, that due to an increase in government purchases, the aggregate demand curve shifts to the right by $50 billion, as shown in Figure 10.2, from AD_0 to AD_1. This change is known as an **increase in aggregate demand**. Similarly, a decrease in another component of real expenditures, such as consumption spending, would cause a decrease in total expenditures. This **decrease in aggregate demand** would be represented by a shift in the aggregate demand curve to the left.

aggregate demand factors: variables that cause changes in total expenditures at all price levels

increase in aggregate demand: an increase in total expenditures at all price levels

decrease in aggregate demand: a decrease in total expenditures at all price levels

| FIGURE 10.2 | Changes in Aggregate Demand |

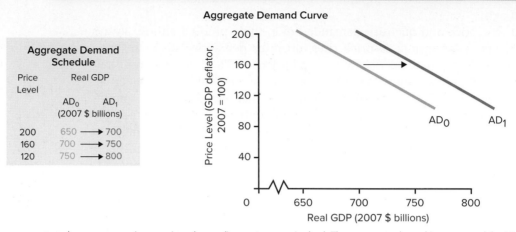

Aggregate Demand Curve

Aggregate Demand Schedule		
Price Level	Real GDP	
	AD_0 AD_1 (2007 $ billions)	
200	650 → 700	
160	700 → 750	
120	750 → 800	

An increase in government purchases causes an increase in real expenditures at every price level. Thus, aggregate demand increases, and the AD curve shifts to the right from AD_0 to AD_1.

Aggregate demand factors can be categorized by the spending component they immediately affect. As we consider each in turn, we must assume that all other aggregate demand factors and the price level remain constant.

CONSUMPTION

Recall that personal consumption and saving are the two uses of disposable income. Thus, consumer spending is decided when households determine how much to spend or save. Changes in disposable income, wealth, consumer expectations, and interest rates can all affect consumer spending. With any change in consumer spending, total expenditure also changes, thereby shifting the aggregate demand curve.

Disposable Income

The most significant determinant of consumer spending is the level of disposable income (DI) in the entire economy. The economy's total DI may change as a result of changes in population or changes in DI per household. Higher income taxes, for example, decrease household DI. Disposable income and consumer spending have a direct relationship. So, when DI rises, there is a rise in consumer spending, thereby adding to total expenditures and shifting the aggregate demand curve to the right.

Wealth

Wealth and income are quite different. Whereas income consists of earnings received over time, wealth is made up of financial and real assets. Real assets (such as houses and appliances) and financial assets (such as stocks and bonds) are measured at a particular point in time. We have already considered the wealth effect—the effect of the price level on the value of wealth, which then influences consumer spending. Factors other than the price level can affect wealth, however, and in turn affect consumer spending. For example, if stock prices jump, households owning stocks enjoy increased wealth; as a result, these households will likely spend more of their disposable income. Aggregate demand will increase, and the aggregate demand curve will shift to the right. Conversely, an increase in consumer debt means that households lose wealth. Households reduce their spending as a result, and aggregate demand decreases.

Consumer Expectations

Consumer expectations influence the demand for a single product. Similarly, these expectations can affect aggregate demand by changing general consumption patterns. If consumers expect prices to rise–for example, because of a calamity, such as war or a flood–they will spend more now and save less. As a result of this higher consumer spending, aggregate demand increases, and the aggregate demand curve shifts to the right. In the same way, if consumers expect their incomes to rise soon, they again spend more and save less, causing an increase in aggregate demand.

Interest Rates

Because households often borrow to purchase durable goods, such as cars and furniture, changes in real interest rates can affect their purchasing decisions. If the real interest rate falls, consumers are more likely to borrow to buy big-ticket items. As a result, consumer spending rises, and the aggregate demand curve shifts to the right. Conversely, a jump in the real interest rate has the opposite effect: because consumer spending falls, aggregate demand decreases, and the aggregate demand curve shifts to the left.

INVESTMENT

Investment represents spending on projects where earning a profit is anticipated. The investment component of aggregate demand is limited to planned investment, which excludes unintended changes in inventories.

How does a business decide whether or not to make an investment? The business first calculates all the expected revenues and costs of the project in constant dollars. Then it calculates the project's **real rate of return**, which is the constant-dollar extra profit provided by the project each year, stated as a percentage of the project's initial cost. For example, consider a T-shirt maker, Pure 'n' Simple T-Shirts. As its owner, you are deciding whether to buy a $100 sewing machine, which is expected to last for one year. After its effects on day-to-day operating costs are taken into account, the machine is expected to add $112 in constant dollars to your business's net revenue. The extra profit gained from purchasing the machine is, therefore, $12 (= $112 − $100). Thus, the machine's real rate of return, as a percentage of its $100 price, is 12 percent (= ($12 ÷ $100) × 100%).

Because most businesses borrow money to finance their investment projects, they will pursue projects for which the return on the project exceeds, or at least equals, the real interest rate they will be charged. In other words, any project is undertaken if its annual benefit is greater than or at least equal to its annual cost.

We have focused on a single business; now let us turn our attention to the entire economy. Suppose that businesses in the economy are considering four possible investment projects. Projects A, B, C, and D each have a cost of $15 billion; however, their real rates of return differ. Project A has a real rate of return of 10 percent, B a rate of 8 percent, C a rate of 6 percent, and D a rate of 4 percent. Figure 10.3 shows the projects' respective profits as rectangles. While each rectangle has the same width, representing the projects' uniform $15 billion cost, the heights differ to reflect the different rates of return.

To see how interest rates affect investment in the economy, let us incorporate the real interest rate in Figure 10.3, also on the vertical axis. Recall that only

real rate of return: constant-dollar extra profit provided by a project each year, stated as a percentage of the project's initial cost

FIGURE 10.3 Investment Demand

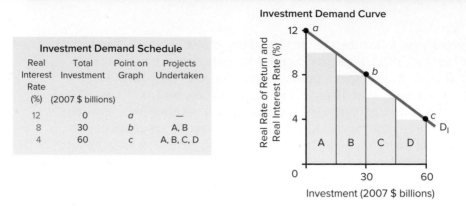

Investment Demand Schedule

Real Interest Rate (%)	Total Investment (2007 $ billions)	Point on Graph	Projects Undertaken
12	0	a	—
8	30	b	A, B
4	60	c	A, B, C, D

As the real interest rate decreases, more investment projects are undertaken. When the interest rate is 8 percent, only Projects A and B are carried out, since their estimated real rates of return are greater or equal. If the interest rate falls to 4 percent, Projects C and D can be pursued as well.

investment projects with a real rate of return equal to or greater than the prevailing real interest rate will be undertaken. So, if the real interest rate is 12 percent, businesses in the economy would not invest in any project, since none provides a sufficient real rate of return to cover the cost of borrowing. This is shown as point *a* in Figure 10.3. If the real interest rate falls to 8 percent, businesses in the economy will invest in Projects A and B, as shown by point *b*, because their real rates of return equal or exceed the costs of borrowing. As a result, investment in the economy rises to $30 billion. Finally, if interest rates drop even further, to 4 percent, businesses in the economy will invest in Projects A, B, C, and D, as shown by point *c*, thereby increasing investment in the economy to $60 billion. This relationship between interest rates and investment is known as **investment demand**. Investment demand can be expressed in a table, called the **investment demand schedule**, or on a graph, called the **investment demand curve** (D_I).

Now that we have seen how total investment in the economy is determined, it is easier to recognize the various aggregate demand factors related to investment. A rise in investment causes an increase in aggregate demand, thereby shifting the aggregate demand curve to the right. Conversely, a fall in investment causes a decrease in aggregate demand, thereby shifting the aggregate demand curve to the left. Investment not only changes because of interest rates, as we have seen, but also because of business expectations.

investment demand: the relationship between interest rates and investment

investment demand schedule: the relationship between interest rates and investment expressed in a table

investment demand curve: the relationship between interest rates and investment expressed on a graph

Interest Rates

As shown by the investment demand curve in Figure 10.3, real interest rates and investment have an inverse relationship. Hence, a rise in real interest rates causes a decrease in aggregate demand, and a fall in real interest rates causes an increase in aggregate demand.

Business Expectations

Business expectations—whether optimistic or pessimistic—can affect the position of the investment demand curve. If businesses anticipate that profits will increase, the investment demand curve shifts to the right, causing an increase in aggregate demand. Conversely, if businesses anticipate that profits will drop, the investment demand curve shifts to the left, leading to a decrease in aggregate demand.

GOVERNMENT PURCHASES

A rise in government purchases–such as highway construction, for example–causes an increase in aggregate demand, while a fall in government purchases causes a decrease in aggregate demand. Recall that this component of spending does not include government transfer payments. Seniors' benefit payments, for example, are classified as negative taxes, which flow *from* rather than *to* governments.

NET EXPORTS

As seen earlier, net exports can vary due to changes in the price level. For example, a drop in the Canadian price level increases net exports because Canadian exports are cheaper in the rest of the world and imports are made more expensive in Canada. As a result of this foreign trade effect, a change in the price level influences total spending in the economy, which is expressed as a movement along the aggregate demand curve.

Other factors that affect net exports and that cause a *change* in aggregate demand–include incomes in foreign countries and foreign exchange rates. The effect of changes in these factors is represented by a shift in the aggregate demand curve.

Foreign Incomes

Suppose incomes rise in a foreign country, such as France. French citizens will be able to buy more products as a result. Not only will they purchase French products, but also those of other countries. As a result, Canadian net exports to France will rise, thereby increasing Canada's aggregate demand. Conversely, a fall in foreign incomes will reduce Canadian net exports, thereby decreasing Canada's aggregate demand.

Exchange Rates

An **exchange rate** is the value of one nation's currency in terms of another currency. The value of the Canadian dollar can be expressed in any other currency, but is usually compared with US dollars. One way to express the exchange rate is to state how many US cents are needed to buy one Canadian dollar. A rise in the value of the Canadian dollar–for example, from 90 to 95 cents–means more US currency is needed to purchase Canadian funds. In this example, Canada's currency becomes more expensive for Americans to purchase. At the same time, US currency becomes cheaper for Canadians to purchase, since we get more of it–95 cents as opposed to 90 cents–in exchange for one Canadian dollar.

If the Canadian dollar goes up in value, exports from Canada become more expensive for Americans. So, a product priced at $1 in Canada costs not 90 cents in US funds, but 95 cents. At the same time, American products imported into Canada fall in price when expressed in Canadian currency. One Canadian dollar now buys American products with a US price of 95 cents, whereas earlier the same dollar could buy American products with a US price of only 90 cents.

Because of the impact of exchange rates on prices, net exports fall when the Canadian dollar goes up in value, causing aggregate demand to decrease. A drop in the value of the Canadian dollar has the opposite effect: net exports rise, thereby increasing aggregate demand. Figure 10.4 summarizes the effects of this and other aggregate demand factors.

exchange rate: the value of one nation's currency in terms of another currency

FIGURE 10.4	Shifts in the Aggregate Demand Curve

Aggregate demand increases and the AD curve shifts to the right, with the following:	Aggregate demand decreases and the AD curve shifts to the left, with the following:
(1) An increase in consumption due to	(1) A decrease in consumption due to
(a) a rise in disposable income	(a) a fall in disposable income
(b) a rise in wealth unrelated to a change in the price level	(b) a fall in wealth unrelated to a change in the price level
(c) an expected rise in prices or incomes	(c) an expected fall in prices or incomes
(d) a fall in interest rates	(d) a rise in interest rates
(2) An increase in investment due to	(2) A decrease in investment due to
(a) a fall in interest rates	(a) a rise in interest rates
(b) an expected rise in profits	(b) an expected fall in profits
(3) An increase in government purchases	(3) A decrease in government purchases
(4) An increase in net exports due to	(4) A decrease in net exports due to
(a) a rise in foreign incomes	(a) a fall in foreign incomes
(b) a fall in value of the Canadian dollar	(b) a rise in the value of the Canadian dollar

THINKING ABOUT ECONOMICS

Which of the components of aggregate demand is most likely to vary?

While consumption, government purchases, and net exports all vary substantially, investment is the most unstable element in aggregate demand. This is because investment depends so heavily on business expectations, which can be subject to volatile swings as perceptions of the future change.

QUESTION   **Which component of aggregate demand is the most stable?**

BRIEF REVIEW

1. Aggregate demand is the relationship between the price level and total spending in the economy. This relationship can be expressed in an aggregate demand schedule or on an aggregate demand curve (AD).

2. Total spending in the economy, adjusted for inflation, is known as real expenditures, and includes the spending of households, businesses, governments, and the rest of the world.

3. The general price level and total spending in the economy have an inverse relationship, thereby giving the aggregate demand curve a negative slope.

4. Both the wealth effect and the foreign trade effect, which arise from price level changes, cause movements *along* the aggregate demand curve.

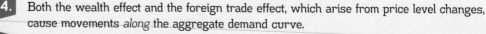

5. In contrast, aggregate demand factors cause a change in total spending at all price levels, thereby *shifting* the aggregate demand curve. Anything other than the price level that changes consumption spending, investment, government purchases, or net exports shifts the aggregate demand curve.

10.1 | PRACTICE PROBLEM

1. Identify the impact of each of the following trends on the aggregate demand curve.
    a. The federal government cuts taxes for low-income households.
    b. There is a slump in share prices on Canadian stock markets.
    c. The price level in Canada rises.
    d. Canadian interest rates fall.
    e. The Canadian dollar rises in value against the US dollar.
    f. Canadian businesses become less confident about the future.

10.2 | Aggregate Supply

So far in this chapter, we have focused on the role of spending in the economy. Now, let us turn our attention to the role of production. **Aggregate supply** is the relationship between the general price level and real output produced in the economy. Figure 10.5 shows aggregate supply expressed in a table, called the **aggregate supply schedule**, and on a graph, called the **aggregate supply curve** (AS).

The Aggregate Supply Curve

As Figure 10.5 shows, the price level and real output are directly related, giving the aggregate supply curve a positive slope. At higher price levels in the economy, businesses are encouraged to produce more; at lower price levels, businesses may not be able to make a profit or break even in the short run, so they reduce output. Variations in an economy's output caused by changes in the price level result in movements *along* the aggregate supply curve.

LO2

aggregate supply: the relationship between the general price level and real output produced in the economy

aggregate supply schedule: the relationship between the general price level and real output expressed in a table

aggregate supply curve: the relationship between the general price level and real output expressed on a graph

FIGURE 10.5   Aggregate Supply

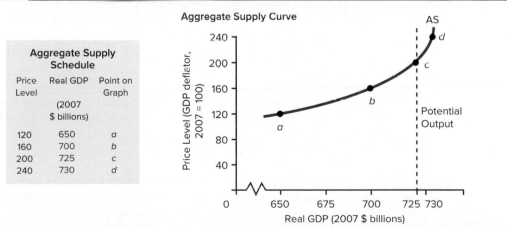

Aggregate Supply Schedule		
Price Level	Real GDP	Point on Graph
	(2007 $ billions)	
120	650	*a*
160	700	*b*
200	725	*c*
240	730	*d*

Businesses respond to increasing prices by producing more real output. At low output levels (such as point *a*), businesses produce significantly below capacity, and the AS curve is relatively flat. As output increases above the potential output level of $725 billion (point *c*), businesses produce above their normal capacity, and the AS curve is steep.

Recall from Chapter 9 that unemployment reduces real output from what it could be. If full employment were achieved—in other words, if only natural unemployment occurred—the economy would reach its potential output. If, as sometimes happens, the unemployment rate temporarily falls below the natural unemployment rate, real output rises temporarily above potential output.

Let us consider the hypothetical example in Figure 10.5. Potential output—the real output associated with full employment—has a value of $725 billion. The real output level, as shown by the aggregate supply curve (AS), is much lower than its potential at point *a*, but greater than the potential output at point *d*. Note that above the potential output level, the aggregate supply curve becomes very steep. This shows that businesses are producing above their normal capacity, which is possible in the short run only if businesses employ overtime labour and temporarily rent new machinery. These temporary measures mean that any expansion in real output—for example, from $725 billion (point *c*) to $730 billion (point *d*)—requires a relatively large increase in the price level to cover businesses' additional per unit costs. Conversely, at real output levels below the potential output, the production capacity of businesses is underutilized, with some labour and capital equipment either working part-time or sitting idle. A rise in real output, as from $650 billion (point *a*) to $700 billion (point *b*), can be made with a relatively small increase in the price level to cover additional per unit costs.

Changes in Aggregate Supply

aggregate supply factors: variables that change total output at all price levels

Other factors, in addition to the price level, can influence real output. However, these factors, known as **aggregate supply factors**, change real output at *all* price levels. In other words, they *shift* the aggregate supply curve. Once again, as we examine each factor in turn, we must assume that all other aggregate supply factors and the price level remain constant.

INPUT PRICES

Aggregate supply assumes steady input prices for the businesses that are producing the output. Changes in input prices—an increase in wages, for example, or decreased prices for imported raw materials due to a rise in the value of the Canadian dollar—alter production costs. These changes can occur frequently over brief periods of time. When a rise in the price of an input pushes up production costs, businesses reduce their real output and the aggregate supply curve shifts to the left. Note, however, that nothing happens to change the economy's potential output. Conversely, if the price of an input decreases, production costs fall. Businesses then raise their real output, causing the aggregate supply curve to shift to the right, while the economy's potential output stays the same. These changes apply to the short run, so they are called a **short-run decrease in aggregate supply** and a **short-run increase in aggregate supply**, respectively. Figure 10.6 shows an example.

short-run decrease in aggregate supply: a decrease in total output at all price levels, with no change in potential output

short-run increase in aggregate supply: an increase in total output at all price levels, with no change in potential output

RESOURCE SUPPLIES

long-run increase in aggregate supply: an increase in total and potential output at all price levels

Over the long term, supplies of resources in an economy—especially human and capital resources—tend to grow. With any such increase, businesses produce more real output at every price level. In other words, more inputs over the long run increase aggregate supply, as well as the economy's potential output. Figure 10.7 shows the outcome—a **long-run increase in aggregate supply**. The reverse is also possible. With a long-run reduction in the amounts of any resource, businesses will produce lower real output at all prices, thereby causing

FIGURE 10.6   A Short-Run Change in Aggregate Supply

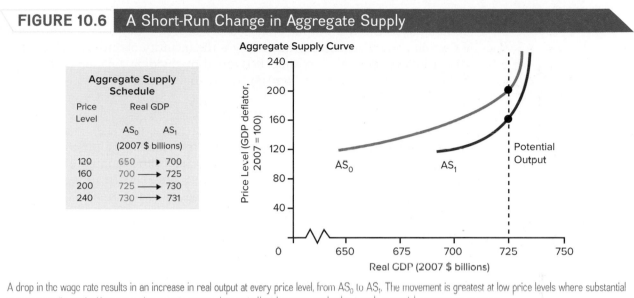

Aggregate Supply Schedule

Price Level	Real GDP	
	AS$_0$	AS$_1$
	(2007 $ billions)	
120	650	▶ 700
160	700 ⟶	725
200	725 ⟶	730
240	730 ⟶	731

A drop in the wage rate results in an increase in real output at every price level, from AS$_0$ to AS$_1$. The movement is greatest at low price levels where substantial excess capacity exists. Because a decrease in wages does not affect long-run production trends, potential output stays constant.

a **long-run decrease in aggregate supply**, which is accompanied by a reduction in the economy's potential output.

Because production tends to adjust less rapidly than spending, changes in aggregate supply tend to be slower to occur than changes in aggregate demand. Input prices, which may change quickly, often take time to affect real output. Changes in resource supplies and the other long-run determinants of aggregate supply tend to occur even more gradually. Though aggregate supply is more stable than aggregate demand over the short run, the long-run effect of aggregate supply on the economy can be profound.

long-run decrease in aggregate supply: a decrease in total and potential output at all price levels

FIGURE 10.7   A Long-Run Change in Aggregate Supply

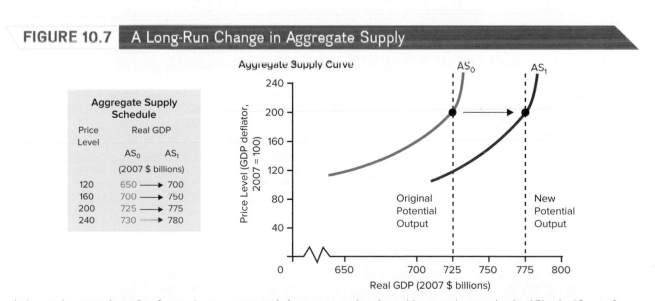

Aggregate Supply Schedule

Price Level	Real GDP	
	AS$_0$	AS$_1$
	(2007 $ billions)	
120	650 ⟶	700
160	700 ⟶	750
200	725 ⟶	775
240	730 ⟶	780

An increase in a country's supplies of economic resources causes both aggregate supply and potential output to increase, thereby shifting the AS curve from AS$_0$ to AS$_1$ and raising potential output.

PRODUCTIVITY

Productivity is the real output produced per unit of input over a given period of time. In particular, labour productivity is the quantity of output produced per worker in a certain period of time. It is found by dividing a nation's real output by the total number of hours worked by its labour force:

$$\text{Labur productivity} = \frac{\text{real output}}{\text{total hours worked}}$$

Increases in productivity are due largely to technological progress. A technological innovation raises productivity when the same amount of economic resources can produce more real output at every price level, causing a long-run increase in aggregate supply similar to that shown in Figure 10.7. Likewise, a technological decline reduces the real output produced with the same resources, resulting in a long-run decrease in aggregate supply.

GOVERNMENT POLICIES

Government policies can also influence aggregate supply through their effects on the business environment in an economy. For example, suppose that taxes rise for businesses and households. Because the after-tax returns on supplying economic resources are pushed down, businesses and households may reduce the resources they supply at every price level. As a result, real output falls, causing a long-run decrease in aggregate supply. Conversely, lower taxes may encourage businesses and households to expand their supply of economic resources, leading to a rise in real output and a long-run increase in aggregate supply.

Government regulations, such as environmental and safety standards, typically raise per unit costs for businesses. Hence, more regulation causes businesses to produce less real output at every price level, causing a long-run decrease in aggregate supply. Similarly, less regulation stimulates production, leading to a long-run increase in aggregate supply. Figure 10.8 summarizes the effects of these and other aggregate supply factors.

FIGURE 10.8   Shifts in the Aggregate Supply Curve

Aggregate supply increases, with the AS curve shifting to the right, and potential output staying the same with the following:	Aggregate supply decreases, with the AS curve shifting to the left, and potential output staying the same with the following:
(1) A decrease in input prices due to	(1) An increase in input prices due to
(a) a fall in wages	(a) a rise in wages
(b) a fall in raw material prices	(b) a rise in raw material prices
Aggregate supply increases, with the AS curve shifting to the right, and potential output increasing with the following:	**Aggregate supply decreases, with the AS curve shifting to the left, and potential output decreasing with the following:**
(2) An increase in supplies of economic resources due to	(2) A decrease in supplies of economic resources due to
(a) more labour supply	(a) less labour supply
(b) more capital stock	(b) less capital stock
(c) more land	(c) less land
(d) more entrepreneurship	(d) less entrepreneurship
(3) An increase in productivity due to technological progress	(3) A decrease in productivity due to technological decline
(4) A change in government policies:	(4) A change in government policies:
(a) lower taxes	(a) higher taxes
(b) less government regulation	(b) more government regulation

THINKING ABOUT ECONOMICS

Is the information revolution having a significant effect on the position of Canada's aggregate supply curve?

According to some economists, the aggregate supply curve in countries such as Canada is being significantly affected by the advances in information technology (IT)—not so much because of the rise of the new economy, but rather due to the way that IT is improving efficiency in the old economy. According to these economists, the result is an improvement in labour productivity and a gradual shift to the right of the aggregate supply curve. There is a good deal of evidence that this trend occurred in the American economy, especially during the late 1990s, given its high growth rates in labour productivity. Evidence for this trend in Canada, however, is less compelling.

QUESTION   **How does the information revolution improve efficiency among old-economy businesses?**

BRIEF REVIEW

1. Aggregate supply is the relationship between the price level and real output produced in the economy. This relationship can be expressed in an aggregate supply schedule or on an aggregate supply curve.

2. Because higher prices encourage increased real output and vice versa, the price level and real output have a direct relationship, thereby giving the aggregate supply curve a positive slope.

3. Since real output may not reflect the full use of all resources—for example, labour—an economy may not reach its potential output.

4. While changes in the price level cause movement *along* the aggregate supply curve, aggregate supply factors—changes in input prices, supplies of economic resources, productivity, and government policies—*shift* the curve and so change real output of an economy and aggregate supply.

5. Short-run changes in aggregate supply, caused by varying input prices, do not change an economy's potential output. However, long-run changes in aggregate supply do change an economy's potential output in the same direction.

10.2 | PRACTICE PROBLEM

1. Identify the impact of each of the following trends on aggregate supply.
   a. The capital stock available to the Canadian economy undergoes a significant expansion.
   b. The federal government introduces tough new environmental regulations on Canadian business.
   c. The price of electricity increases.
   d. Wages for Canadian workers are reduced.
   e. Global warming causes a rise in ocean levels, affecting Canadian coastal areas.
   f. Due to a fall in immigration, the size of the Canadian labour force declines.
   g. The rate of adoption of new technologies by Canadian firms increases.

10.3 | Equilibrium

 Aggregate Demand and Supply

So far, we have looked at aggregate demand and aggregate supply separately. Now we will consider them together. What happens if real output at a certain price level exceeds real expenditures? Alternatively, what happens if real output at a certain price level falls short of what participants in the economy wish to spend? Figure 10.9 presents the answers to these questions. As with demand and supply in a competitive market for an individual product, the forces underlying aggregate demand and aggregate supply push the economy to an equilibrium point. An economy's equilibrium price level and real output occur at the intersection of the aggregate demand and aggregate supply curves.

INVENTORY CHANGES

Unintended changes in inventories cause the price level and real output to reach equilibrium. We will look at the two possibilities: the results of an inventory increase and of an inventory decrease.

Results of an Inventory Increase

Suppose the general price level is above the equilibrium price level, at 200 (points *a* in Figure 10.9). At this price level, real output exceeds real expenditures, meaning more is produced than is purchased in the economy. Businesses

---

FIGURE 10.9 | An Economy in Equilibrium

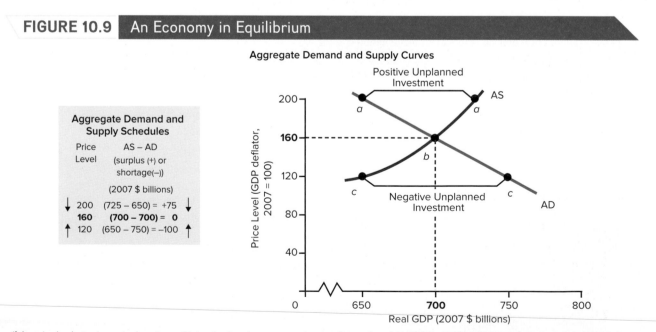

Aggregate Demand and Supply Curves

Aggregate Demand and Supply Schedules		
Price Level	AS – AD (surplus (+) or shortage(–))	
	(2007 $ billions)	
↓ 200	(725 – 650) = +75	↓
160	**(700 – 700) = 0**	
↑ 120	(650 – 750) = –100	↑

If the price level, at points *a*, is above its equilibrium level, real output exceeds expenditures. An unintended rise in inventories causes businesses to lower prices until output and expenditures are the same (point *b*). When the price level is below its equilibrium value (points *c*), there is an unintended fall in inventories. Businesses increase prices until equilibrium is reached (point *b*).

have an unintended increase in inventories–in other words, a surplus–which represents **positive unplanned investment**. As a result of this surplus, prices of individual products decrease, pushing down the general price level.

positive unplanned investment: an unintended increase in inventories; a surplus

The general decrease in prices influences both households and businesses. Because of the wealth and foreign trade effects, the response of buyers is to increase spending. So, real expenditures in our example increase toward point b. Meanwhile, lower prices cause businesses to decrease real output, and since real output and unemployment are inversely related, this causes a rise in the unemployment rate. These trends continue until real output and real expenditures are equal at the equilibrium point (point b).

Results of an Inventory Decrease

Suppose, on the other hand, that the price level is below its equilibrium value, at 120 (points c). Expenditures exceed production, creating a shortage. This leads to an unintended decrease in inventories, known as **negative unplanned investment**. Because particular products are in short supply, prices rise. The response of buyers is to decrease spending. Meanwhile, the higher price level causes businesses to raise real output, resulting in a fall in unemployment. These trends continue until real output and real expenditures are equal at the equilibrium point (point b).

negative unplanned investment: an unintended decrease in inventories; a shortage

The Role of Unplanned Investment

Note that in the case of either an unintended increase or decrease in inventories, unplanned investment plays a central role in stabilizing the economy. Unplanned investment is positive when the price level is above its equilibrium value and negative when the price level is below its equilibrium value. In each case, unplanned investment is identical to the discrepancy between aggregate demand and aggregate supply.

This is illustrated by the aggregate demand and supply schedules in Figure 10.9. The $75 billion discrepancy between aggregate demand and aggregate supply at a price level of 200 means there is an unintended $75 billion increase in inventories. Hence, there is unplanned investment of $75 billion. Likewise, the shortage of $100 billion that appears at the 120 price level translates into an unintended $100 billion drop in inventories. Unplanned investment is, therefore, −$100 billion.

Injections and Withdrawals

The tendency of an economy to move toward equilibrium can also be outlined by looking at the flows of income payments and purchases that connect resource and product markets.

There are three flows, known as **injections**, that add to the main income-spending stream in any economy: investment (I), government purchases (G), and exports (X). Corresponding to these injections are three outward flows of funds, known as **withdrawals**. Withdrawals, which divert funds from the income-spending stream in any economy, are saving (S), taxes (T), and imports (M).

injections: additions to an economy's income-spending stream

withdrawals: deductions from an economy's income-spending stream

There is no need for these individual injections and withdrawals to be equal. Even those injections and withdrawals related to the same sector can have different values. To see why, we will look at each related pair of injections and withdrawals in turn.

INVESTMENT AND SAVING

Recall that personal savings from households provide the bulk of funds in financial markets. Most funds are borrowed by businesses for investment. However, the amount saved and the amount invested in an economy are not equal for three reasons. First, recall that companies keep a portion of their profits to reinvest. These retained earnings supplement personal savings in financing investment. Second, governments also borrow money. The more governments borrow, the less personal savings end up in the hands of businesses. Third, we must also consider the international flows we have already discussed in Chapter 8. Because lending by the rest of the world has usually exceeded borrowing by the rest of the world, foreign funds have typically added to savings available for investment in Canada.

GOVERNMENT PURCHASES AND TAXES

Recall that transfer payments and business subsidies are viewed as negative taxes. In the past, government purchases have usually exceeded taxes. To make up for the discrepancy, governments have borrowed funds in financial markets. At times, taxes exceed government purchases. Governments use these excess revenues to pay off some of their outstanding debt.

EXPORTS AND IMPORTS

Canada's imports of both goods and services have typically been greater than its exports. In other words, Canadians spend more on products from the rest of the world than they receive in revenues from selling products to the rest of the world. At the same time, foreign lenders have typically provided funds to Canadian financial markets, with lending by foreigners being greater than borrowing by foreigners. So, the surplus of lending by foreigners has helped make up for the shortfall in net exports.

TOTAL INJECTIONS AND WITHDRAWALS

While individual injections and withdrawals are not necessarily equal, there is an important connection between them that applies when an economy is at equilibrium. If the circular income-spending stream is thought of as a flow of water–a water ride at an amusement park, for example–then it is easy to see what will happen if the amount of water flowing into this stream is either more or less than the water flowing out. If inward flows exceed outward flows, the amount of water circulating in the stream must be increasing. Conversely, if inward flows are less than outward flows, the amount of water must be decreasing. Only if inward and outward flows are equal will the water ride function well. Viewed in this way, comparing total injections and withdrawals provides a way of explaining macroeconomic equilibrium that complements the approach using aggregate demand and aggregate supply.

Total injections are the sum of investment, government purchases, and exports $(I + G + X)$. Total withdrawals are the sum of saving, taxes, and imports $(S + T + M)$. Just as only the planned portion of investment is included in real expenditures to find aggregate demand, only planned investment is included in total injections.

Total injections $(I + G + X)$ and total withdrawals $(S + T + M)$ may be equal or unequal. When total injections exceed total withdrawals, flows into the income-spending stream are greater than flows out. Hence, the income-spending stream rises and speeds up. In other words, real output and spending in the economy expand. On the other hand, if total withdrawals exceed total injections, flows into the income-spending stream are less than outflows. As a result, the income-spending stream falls and slows down. In other words, real output and spending in the economy contract. Finally, in the case of equilibrium, total injections equal total withdrawals. Because inward and outward flows match, the income-spending stream circulates at a steady rate so that real output and spending in the economy stay constant.

Equilibrium versus Potential Output

An economy's equilibrium point can occur at its potential output, as illustrated in Figure 10.10. If so, then unemployment at equilibrium equals the natural unemployment rate.

RECESSIONARY GAPS

While the situation shown in Figure 10.10 is possible, an economy's real output rarely equals its potential output. If equilibrium output is below its potential level, unemployment is above the natural unemployment rate. In this case, the difference between equilibrium output and potential output is known as a **recessionary gap**. Figure 10.11 shows, on the left, an economy with a recessionary gap of $25 billion. This is the amount by which real output would have to increase from its equilibrium value of $700 billion to attain its potential level of $725 billion.

recessionary gap: the amount by which equilibrium output falls short of potential output

INFLATIONARY GAPS

If equilibrium output is above its potential output, unemployment is temporarily below the natural unemployment rate. Inflation will accelerate if this situation persists. When equilibrium output exceeds potential output, therefore, the discrepancy is called an inflationary gap. Figure 10.11 shows, on the right, an economy with an **inflationary gap** of $5 billion. In this case, the equilibrium output of $730 billion would have to fall by $5 billion to achieve the potential output of $725 billion.

inflationary gap: the amount by which equilibrium output exceeds potential output

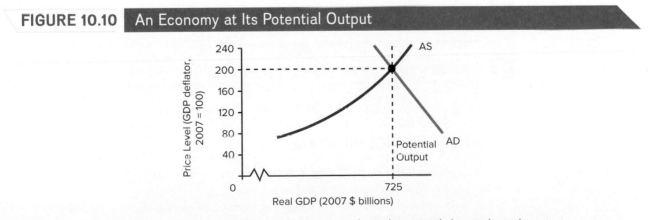

FIGURE 10.10   An Economy at Its Potential Output

It is possible for equilibrium to occur at the economy's potential output. In this case, actual unemployment equals the natural unemployment rate.

FIGURE 10.11 | Recessionary and Inflationary Gaps

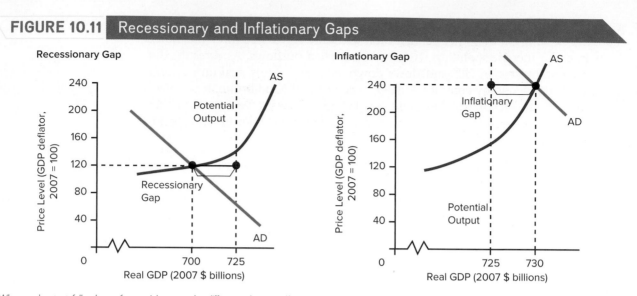

When real output falls short of potential output, the difference between the two is a recessionary gap, as shown on the left. In contrast, when real output temporarily exceeds its potential level, the difference between the two is an inflationary gap, as shown on the right.

A recession differs from the notion of a recessionary gap. As we will soon see, during a recession, real output moves from above to below its potential level, with an inflationary gap transformed into a recessionary gap. On the other hand, a recessionary gap occurs whenever real output is below its potential level–in the latter stage of a recession as well as the first stage of an expansion or recovery.

BRIEF REVIEW

1. An economy's equilibrium price level and real output occur at the intersection of the aggregate demand and aggregate supply curves.

2. The economy moves toward equilibrium through the workings of positive and negative unplanned investment—in other words, surpluses and shortages.

3. When an economy is at equilibrium, total injections (I + G + X) equal total withdrawals (S + T + M). If total injections exceed total withdrawals, real output rises, and the economy expands; if the reverse is true, real output falls, and the economy contracts.

4. If equilibrium output is less than potential output, the difference between the two is a recessionary gap. When equilibrium output exceeds potential output, the discrepancy in the output levels is an inflationary gap.

10.3 | PRACTICE PROBLEM

1. a. For each injection I, G, and X, there is a related withdrawal. Identify the three pairs of related injections and withdrawals.
   b. When the economy is in equilibrium, does each injection have to be in balance with its related withdrawal?

10.4 | Economic Growth

Economic Growth and Its Impact

Recall from Chapter 1 that economic growth is an increase in the total output of goods and services. The term can refer to the percentage increase in an economy's total output, usually measured by real GDP, or it can refer to a percentage increase in the per capita real GDP. For example, Canada's real GDP, valued in 2007 dollars, was $1661.559 billion in 2012 and $1694.941 billion in 2013. During the same period, the country's population expanded from 34 754.3 to 35 158.3 million.

Using the first definition, Canada's annual rate of economic growth was 2.0 percent [= ($1694.941 billion − $1661.559 billion) ÷ $1661.559 billion]. Since per capita real GDP rose from $47 809 (= $1661.559 billion ÷ 34 754.3 million) to $48 209 (= $1694.941 billion ÷ 35 158.3 million), economic growth using the second definition was 0.8 percent. Use of each definition depends on the context. **The first definition of economic growth is most appropriate when measuring an economy's overall productive capacity, while the second definition better indicates long-term changes in living standards, since more output per capita means an average individual is better off than before.**

Economic growth can be caused by a long-run increase in aggregate supply (which is accompanied by a rise in an economy's potential output) or by short-run changes in aggregate demand or aggregate supply. Economic growth can also be portrayed using the production possibilities curve. In Chapter 1, we saw that this curve demonstrates the combination of outputs that an economy can produce, assuming constant economic resources and technology. Economic growth occurs either when there is an outward shift in the production possibilities curve (due to technological change or an increase in economic resources), or when there is movement toward the curve (in the case where the economy is inside the curve because all resources are not employed or used to their full capacity)

Consider the hypothetical economy illustrated in Figure 10.12. This economy produces consumer goods (hamburgers) and capital goods (lasers). Initially, its production is limited to the combinations of consumer goods and capital goods demonstrated by the curve PPC$_0$. The economy chooses to produce 40 hamburgers and two lasers (point a).

FIGURE 10.12   The Process of Economic Growth

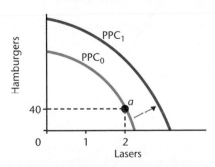

Initially, the economy has production possibilities as shown by the curve PPC$_0$ and chooses to produce at point a. Only by increasing economic resources and/or improving the productivity of these resources can the economy grow. By doing so, the economy can expand the production possibilities from PPC$_0$ to PPC$_1$.

Because the curve represents all production combinations that are attainable, this hypothetical economy is producing the most it can, given its preferences for hamburgers and lasers. Only by increasing economic resources and/or improving the state of technology to use the resources more efficiently can production possibilities be increased. In Figure 10.12, the shift from PPC$_0$ to PPC$_1$ demonstrates an increase in production possibilities. Now, the economy is able to produce more of either good, and economic growth can take place.

Note that the production possibilities model highlights not only the limits of any economy, but also the tradeoffs between various goods. Expanding our example in Figure 10.13, a country can choose to produce 40 hamburgers and two lasers (point *a*) on the left graph. Alternatively, it can choose to produce 100 hamburgers and one laser (point *c*) on the right graph.

Although a simplification, the two options demonstrate that economies can focus their resources on the production of consumer goods (hamburgers) or the production of capital goods (lasers). In contrast to consumer goods, which are simply consumed, capital goods can be used to produce more products. As such, capital goods are an investment in further production. Because of this, the choices that an economy makes between the production possibilities affect its future growth.

To demonstrate this, consider the hypothetical Countries A and B in Figure 10.13, which initially have identical production possibilities curves. By producing 40 hamburgers and two lasers (point *a* on the left graph), Country A adds to its economic resources, which, in turn, fuels economic growth and can mean that more of both consumer and capital goods will be produced in the future. As shown on the left, the production possibilities curve shifts from PPC to PPC$_A$. While the opportunity cost of focusing on capital goods is fewer consumer goods, production of both consumer and capital goods is enhanced in a year. So, for example, Country A can have an output of 250 hamburgers and two lasers (point *b*).

FIGURE 10.13   Production Options and Their Implications

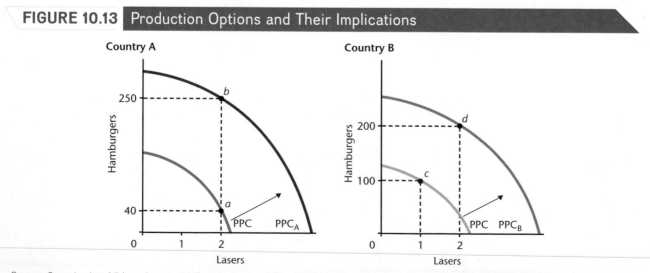

Suppose Countries A and B have the same initial production possibilities (PPC). However, Country A chooses point *a* on the left and Country B chooses point *c* on the right. Because Country A focuses more of its resources on producing a capital good (lasers) than does Country B, which focuses on a consumer good (hamburgers), Country A encourages greater growth. Within the same time period, Country A's production possibilities expand to PPC$_A$ so that it may choose point *b*. Country B's production possibilities expand less so, to PPC$_B$, so that it may choose point *d*.

In contrast, Country B produces 100 hamburgers and one laser (point *c* on the right graph). Because of this choice, the country has more consumer goods for its citizens immediately. However, the opportunity cost of more consumer goods is fewer capital goods, which means that Country B's economy grows considerably less than Country A's. As shown on the right, the production possibilities curve shifts–from PPC to PPC$_B$–but less so than Country A's curve. So, for example, Country B can have an output of 200 hamburgers and two lasers (point *d*).

By consuming fewer hamburgers in the first year, Country A's citizens have gained an advantage in the second year. If they wish, they can now consume more hamburgers and match the production of lasers in Country B. Moreover, Country A now starts from a position of even greater production possibilities as it seeks further economic growth in future years. The benefits of a high-growth strategy multiply over time. To see why, imagine what happens if, instead of choosing point *b*, the citizens of Country A continue their emphasis on capital goods by again choosing a point on PPC$_A$ with fewer hamburgers and more lasers produced. The longer they follow this policy, the more their production possibilities curve expands and the greater is their future potential consumption, compared with consumption in Country B. With the passage of time, Country A reaps increasing benefits from a high-growth strategy, while Country B's policy of favouring current over future consumption has an increasing opportunity cost in terms of sacrificed economic growth.

Even small differences in growth rates can have a major long-run effect on a country's prosperity and living standards. This is because economic growth, like population growth, builds on itself, thereby showing a pattern of **exponential growth**. To see the effects, we can use a handy mathematical rule, the **rule of 72**, which states that the number of years it takes a variable to double can be estimated by dividing 72 by the variable's annual percentage growth rate. A variable that grows exponentially at 4 percent a year, therefore, doubles its value in 18 years:

$$\text{Rule of 72 : Number of years} = \frac{72}{\text{annual percentage growth rate}}$$

$$\text{for variable to double}$$

$$18 \text{ years} = \frac{72}{4\%}$$

Because of their long-term impact, small discrepancies in growth rates are treated seriously by economists and government policy-makers. Consider the hypothetical example in Figure 10.14. Both countries have a Year 1 output of $100 billion, but each has a different growth rate (2 and 4 percent). After only 10 years, the difference between Country X's and Country Y's outputs is over $20 billion.

exponential growth: growth that is based on a percentage change and that builds on itself

rule of 72: states that the number of years it takes a variable to double can be estimated by dividing 72 by the variable's annual percentage growth rate

Sources of Economic Growth

The production possibilities model shows that the main causes of growth in an economy's total real output are the stock of economic resources and how productively these resources are used. One of the most important causes of growth in Canada's total output–accounting for an estimated 35 percent of the growth in Canada's real GDP in the last two decades of the twentieth century–has been the increase in the quantity of labour. Some of this increase is due to higher participation rates of women in the labour force. However, most of it arises from population growth, which now runs at just over 1 percent annually.

FIGURE 10.14   GDP and Growth Rates

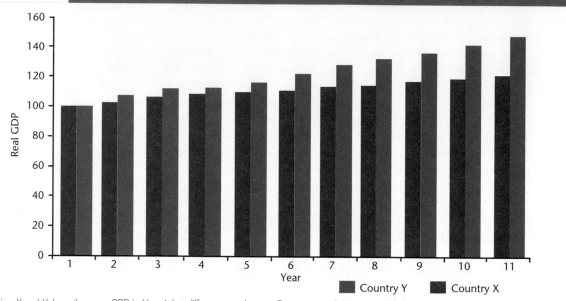

Two countries, X and Y, have the same GDP in Year 1, but different growth rates. Because growth is exponential, Country X's GDP falls behind Country Y's by an increasing margin. For example, Country X's GDP rises from $100 billion to $102 billion (= $100 billion × 0.02) in Year 2. Meanwhile, Country Y's rises from $100 billion to $104 billion (= $100 billion × 0.04).

The long-term growth in Canada's living standards, as measured by per capita real output, is determined by the other main source of growth, labour productivity, or the quantity of output produced per worker in a certain period of time.

Economic Growth and Productivity

To see how labour productivity can be applied to countries' economies, consider a hypothetical economy with a labour force of five workers who are employed for 2000 hours annually. In other words, the economy uses 10 000 hours of labour per year (= 5 × 2000). If real GDP in the economy is $200 000, labour productivity is $20 (= $200 000 ÷ 10 000):

$$\text{Labour productivity} = \frac{\text{real output}}{\text{total hours worked}}$$

$$\$20 = \frac{\$200\ 000}{10\ 000}$$

If real GDP in this economy rises to $202 000 in the following year and the number of labour hours remains constant, then the new level of labour productivity is $20.20 (= $202 000 ÷ 10 000), representing an increase of 1 percent [(= $20.20 − $20.00) ÷ 20) × 100%].

Given the close association between changes in labour productivity and per capita real output, increases in Canadian labour productivity closely follow Canada's record of economic growth. From a long-term perspective, there was a significant slowdown in Canadian labour productivity growth after 1973, and this slowdown has become worse since 2007. As shown in Figure 10.15, Canada's annual rate of productivity growth between 1995 and 2012 has

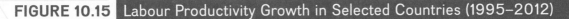

FIGURE 10.15   Labour Productivity Growth in Selected Countries (1995–2012)

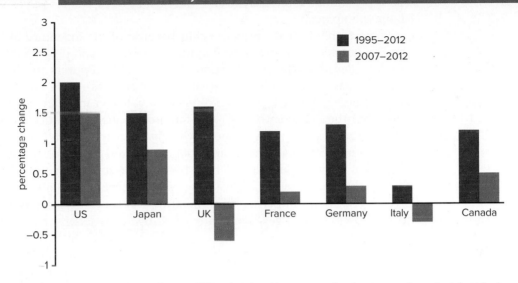

Canada's average annual growth in labour productivity between 1995 and 2012, at 1.2 percent, was less than in most other major industrialized countries, except for Italy and France. Between 2007 and 2012, Canada's performance deteriorated significantly to 0.5 percent, in line with deteriorating performance in other industrial economies. Canada's annual growth during this period exceeded that of France, Germany, the United Kingdom, and Italy, but was less than that of the United States and Japan.

Source: "Labour Productivity Growth in the Total Economy," *OECD Stat Extracts* at http://stats.oecd.org/Index.aspx?DataSetCode=PDYGTH. Retrieved February 1, 2014.

surpassed only that of Italy and France among the industrial economies cited in the chart. Growth in labour productivity is dependent on the quantity of capital, technological progress, the quality of labour, efficiency in production, the quantity of natural resources, and social and political factors.

QUANTITY OF CAPITAL

As indicated by the production possibilities model, an economy's supply of capital resources plays a central role in enhancing economic growth. By saving a higher proportion of their disposable incomes, Canadians can increase net investment, which accelerates the accumulation of capital resources, which, in turn, pushes out the production possibilities curve and fuels economic growth. On average, the rates of Canadian saving and investment as a proportion of GDP have been higher than in the US, but lower than in high-growth countries, such as China and South Korea.

Nonetheless, increases in the quantity of capital goods in Canada were high enough to account for an estimated 40 percent of total growth in its real GDP during the 1980s and 1990s. Because capital inputs have risen more quickly than labour inputs in the Canadian economy, each Canadian worker is employed with a gradually increasing amount of capital. Since 1961, for example, it is estimated that the ratio of capital to labour in Canada has risen by over 80 percent.

TECHNOLOGICAL PROGRESS

Technological progress is a broad term that encompasses scientific discoveries and their application, advances in production methods, and the development of new types of products. Technological progress–in all its forms–can cause

technological progress:
consists of scientific discoveries and their application, advances in production methods, and the development of new types of products

economic growth. Over the long term, it plays an important role in increasing labour productivity, often by raising the quality of capital resources with which labour is employed.

Some technological advances occur because of the ingenuity of individuals. Think of notable innovations in computer technology and programming over the past few decades. The introduction of personal computers in the 1970s, for example, was due to independent innovators such as Apple co-founders Steve Jobs and Steve Wozniak. The more recent revolution in online search methods arose from the collaboration of two Stanford graduate students, Larry Page and Sergey Brin, who went on to found Google. Similarly, Mark Zuckerberg, along with several of his roommates and friends, created Facebook while they were students at Harvard. Such stories have become the stuff of legend, but they mask the fact that much technological progress still occurs through the initiative of large organizations, in particular corporations. This evolutionary type of innovation is closely tied to **research and development (R&D) expenditures**, or spending whose purpose is to accelerate the pace of technological progress.

research and development (R&D) expenditures: spending that is meant to accelerate the pace of technological progress

Canadians have been somewhat successful in adopting the fruits of international innovation, but Canada's own R&D expenditures have historically been relatively low compared with those of similar countries. For example, R&D expenditures in 2009 represented an average of 2.3 percent of GDP in OECD countries and 2.8 percent in the United States, but only 1.9 percent in Canada. In the past, it was argued that the potential benefits of Canadian R&D were relatively insignificant because of a small national market. But with free trade creating global product markets, this argument has lost much of its relevance.

Innovative Canadian companies such as Bombardier have shown that domestic business can compete effectively in technologically sophisticated global markets, but arguably there are not enough of these types of companies in Canada. Several other relatively small countries on the world stage—including Sweden, Finland, and Switzerland—have fostered far more dynamic cultures of research and innovation than Canada has.

What accounts for Canada's relatively poor performance? Most economists who study the issue cite a lack of coordination among Canadian corporations, universities, and research hospitals (whose contribution is especially crucial in the growing biomedical area). Other possible reasons include the relatively high prevalence of foreign ownership in Canada, given that companies often centralize R&D initiatives at their global headquarters. Finally, Canadians have often seemed satisfied to depend on healthy international demand for natural resources, such as energy and minerals, rather than branching out into other products more dependent on continual innovation. Whatever the cause, Canadian policymakers continue to make considerable efforts to improve this lacklustre record.

QUALITY OF LABOUR

The productivity of labour is tied not only to investment in capital goods, but also to investment in human capital through education and training. Since the 1950s, a growing proportion of young people have been completing high school and then pursuing post-secondary education, and this proportion is expected to continue to rise. Between 1990/91 and 2016/17, for example, it is expected that the proportion of those between the ages of 20 and 24 years enrolled full-time in universities and community colleges will have increased from under a quarter to about 40 percent. To the extent that these trends augment the quality of Canada's labour force, they are also raising its productivity as well as the economy's rate of growth.

EFFICIENCY IN PRODUCTION

Economic growth is also influenced by changes in the efficiency of production through increasing returns to scale and the reallocation of resources among different sectors. Canadian businesses—especially those in manufacturing—have traditionally been unable to take full advantage of increasing returns to scale due to the small size of the Canadian market. Freer trade is gradually removing this disadvantage, stimulating both labour productivity and the rate of economic growth. However, the shift of Canadian workers from the higher-productivity manufacturing sector to the lower-productivity service sector has, at least in the past, dampened the rate of economic growth.

QUANTITY OF NATURAL RESOURCES

Canada's rich supplies of natural resources have doubtless contributed to its past economic growth. This occurred during the boom period of rapidly expanding western settlement between 1896 and 1914, and again during the commodity boom of the mid-2000s when supplies of profitably exploitable resources (especially oil-related) increased markedly. During many periods, however, the stock of exploitable natural resources in a country has remained constant, so that their impact on economic growth in these periods has been minimal.

SOCIAL, POLITICAL, AND LEGAL FACTORS

A variety of social, political, and legal factors can affect economic growth. Growth will be enhanced in a society that promotes competition, innovation, and entrepreneurship, and by social institutions geared toward enterprise and profit-making. In the political sphere, government regulations and taxes sometimes inhibit economic growth, especially through their impact on levels of saving and investment in the economy. Finally, a stable legal framework of property rights is an essential prerequisite to private investment and capital accumulation.

The Debate over Growth

Is economic growth necessarily desirable? There are arguments both for and against the emphasis placed on economic growth.

ARGUMENTS FOR ECONOMIC GROWTH

Supporters of economic growth point to three main advantages: its effect on living standards, the opportunities it provides for social improvements, and its psychological benefits.

Living Standards

The main benefit of economic growth is its positive effect on living standards. With rising incomes and output, more wants can be satisfied, both for individuals and for society as a whole. Indeed, the main reason life for most Canadians today is more pleasant than for Canadians of three or four generations ago is due to the tremendous material benefits that economic growth has provided. The same applies in even more dramatic fashion to many citizens of fast-growing emerging economies such as China, India, and Brazil, whose lives have been transformed by the protracted high economic growth rates in these countries.

Social Improvements

Economic growth can be channelled not only into more consumption and investment by private households and businesses, but also into higher government spending, allowing for greater expenditures in such areas as health, education, and the promotion of income equity. Such programs are easier to implement when they can be funded from the proceeds of growth rather than through reductions in existing incomes.

Supporters of growth, and its potential connection with social improvements, stress that the supposed tradeoff between income equity and economic growth has often been broken in recent decades. Examples include Singapore, whose relatively equal distribution of income has been associated with high long-term growth rates, and various Latin American countries, such as Argentina and Bolivia, whose highly unequal distributions of income have been accompanied by lacklustre growth records.

Psychological Benefits

Some people suggest that there are also intangible psychological benefits of economic growth. A growing economy helps create a mood of optimism and a sense of expanding opportunities.

ARGUMENTS AGAINST ECONOMIC GROWTH

Critics of the emphasis on economic growth point to its direct opportunity cost and to its indirect environmental and social costs.

Opportunity Cost of Growth

Economic growth has a direct opportunity cost, as indicated by the production possibilities model. To promote growth, a country must devote more of its scarce resources to investment in capital goods, rather than to current consumption. While this cost is not an overwhelming one for a rich country such as Canada, it is far more significant for citizens of poor countries as they choose an appropriate growth strategy.

THINKING ABOUT ECONOMICS

The growth in Canadian per capita incomes was lower between the mid-1970s and the mid-1990s than in previous decades. Why?

The main reason was lacklustre growth in labour productivity. Partly to blame for this poor productivity were Canada's low rates of investment and technological progress (due, in part, to contractionary government policies to combat inflation during much of this period) and the shift of workers from the manufacturing to the service sectors. In manufacturing, Canadian productivity growth continued to be high in certain "old economy" industries, such as textiles, clothing, leather goods, and furniture.

But Canada's record in "new economy" manufacturing industries, such as those producing electrical and electronic machinery, as well as industrial and commercial machinery, was less healthy. By the late 1990s and early 2000s, Canadian productivity growth rates began to improve, arguably due to the advances in information technology that have been occurring throughout industrialized economies. This rise in productivity growth was not as pronounced as in the US, and it is yet to be determined whether this improvement will be long-lasting.

QUESTION   What have been the long-term consequences of Canada's relatively poor productivity performance in recent decades?

Environmental Costs

One of the main indirect costs of economic growth is damage to the environment—especially in an era when the potential costs of global climate change have become an ever greater concern. Higher levels of economic activity lead to greater exploitation of the world's limited supply of natural resources, as well as higher levels of various forms of pollution and waste. Supporters of growth suggest that environmental damage is the result of flaws in private markets rather than of economic growth itself. They also argue that, when moving from middle-income to high-income status, countries can actually improve their environmental performance, especially when moving from a manufacturing-based to a service-based economy. According to these growth supporters, proper government programs—for example, a broadly-based system of carbon taxes to deal with the threat of climate change—can create the conditions for sustainable growth in the future.

Critics argue that the dynamics of growth tend to swamp the impact of government regulations and controls. China's recent emergence as the world's largest carbon emitter, thanks to its high-powered growth rates, is a prime example. Environmental damage cannot be corrected through tinkering with the market system, they say, but only by a shift in values to end the quest for never-ending increases in living standards.

Social Costs

The social costs of growth are related to the insecurity and risks that come with technological progress. While the general quality of life may be enhanced by technological advances, some resource suppliers will be hurt, and these individuals are often the members of society who are least able to adapt easily to change. At the same time, the pursuit of economic growth may not allow for traditional methods and lifestyles to be maintained. For some economic participants, therefore, the losses that stem from economic growth may far outweigh any economic benefits.

BRIEF REVIEW

1. Economic growth refers to either increases in an economy's real output or increases in its real output per capita.

2. When economic growth expands production possibilities, it can be expressed as a shift to the right of the production possibilities curve. Such growth is caused by an increase in economic resources or by technological progress. Economic growth also occurs when an economy moves toward the production possibilities curve from a point within it.

3. An economy might choose to focus on producing consumer or capital goods. A high-growth strategy involves focusing production on capital goods at the short-run expense of consumer goods.

4. Because economic growth is exponential growth, the rule of 72 applies. Even small differences in percentage rates of growth make a significant difference over time.

5. Population growth and labour productivity have been the main sources of Canada's economic growth. Labour productivity is determined by the quantity and quality of capital, technological progress, efficiency, and social and political factors.

6. Arguments for growth concern living standards, social improvements, and psychological benefits. Arguments against growth concern its direct opportunity cost and the indirect environmental and social costs.

10.4 | PRACTICE PROBLEM

1. Calculate the following values using the rule of 72:
   a. the number of years it will take a country's population to double if the annual growth rate is 0.5 percent
   b. the average annual rate of growth in per capita real GDP, if it takes this variable 27 years to double
   c. the approximate number of times a country's capital stock will double in 24 years if the annual growth rate in the capital stock is 6 percent

---

10.5 | Economic Growth and Business Cycles

LO5   Economic Growth in Canada

In the past, Canada has had comparatively high rates of economic growth. As a result, Canada had the sixteenth highest per capita output of the rich industrialized countries (after adjusting for purchasing power differences) in 2012. However, while Canada's long-term growth has been impressive, Figure 10.16 shows that increases in per capita real output have varied widely since Confederation.

FIGURE 10.16 | Canada's Economic Growth

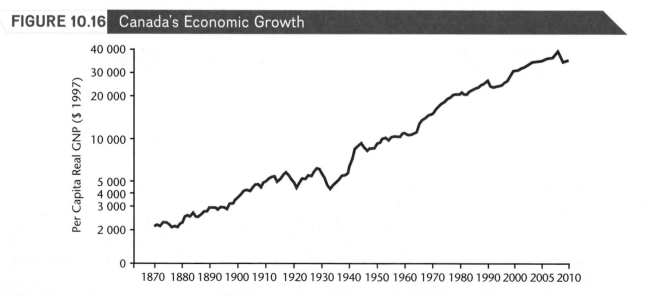

In terms of real output per capita, Canada's growth was gradual between 1870 and 1914. There were steep upswings in both the 1920s and early 1940s, but an abrupt decline in the early 1930s. Until 1973, there was steady growth in per capita income, averaging about 2 percent per year. Until the mid-1990s, the average rate of growth was less. Note that the scale on the vertical axis is *logarithmic* to highlight change.

Sources: Adapted from A.G. Green and M.C. Urquhart, "New Estimates of Output Growth in Canada: Measurement and Interpretation," in Douglas McCalla and Michael Huberman (eds.), *Perspectives on Canadian Economic History* (Toronto: Copp Clark Longman, 1994), pp. 160–61; Adapted from the Statistics Canada publications, *Canadian Economic Observer; Historical Statistical Supplement,* 2001/02, Catalogue 11-210, Vol. 16, July 2002, pp. 6, 7, 42, and from the Statistics Canada CANSIM II database, http://cansim2.statcan.ca, Tables 380-0030 and 051-000. Retrieved April 2, 2011.

BEFORE WORLD WAR I (1870–1914)

In the 44 years from just after Confederation to World War I, Canada's per capita output, measured in 1997 dollars, rose from $2312 to $5283. The economy's lacklustre growth record in the 1870s was followed by a more rapid rise in per capita real output in the 1880s and 1890s–sometimes attributed to Prime Minister John A. Macdonald's National Policy, which stimulated Canadian manufacturing through high tariffs on imports. The gradual increase in growth rates during these decades was also a part of the worldwide trend toward greater prosperity, as well as a rapid expansion of staple exports, such as wheat, that accompanied the settlement of the Canadian West.

THE INTERWAR PERIOD (1914–1945)

World War I ushered in a period of more unstable growth, with a lower long term growth trend than in the previous era. After a period of negative growth just after World War I, Canada's per capita real output rose and then fell sharply during the 1920s and early 1930s, before increasing rapidly during the latter part of the 1930s and World War II. Overall, between 1914 and 1945, per capita real output almost doubled from $5283 to $9660.

THE POSTWAR PERIOD (1945–PRESENT)

Between 1945 and 1973, Canada shared in the worldwide rise in prosperity, achieving a fairly steady growth in living standards of about 2 percent annually. After the OPEC-spurred oil crisis of 1973, however, there was a worrisome decrease in the rate of Canadian growth, except between 1983 and 1989, between 1997 and 1999, and during the first half of the 2000s, when annual growth in per capita real output again exceeded 2 percent. Overall, since 1945, per capita real output in Canada has increased by over four times to $35 194 by 2010.

Business Cycles

In terms of aggregate demand and aggregate supply, economic growth can be caused by a long-run increase in aggregate supply (which is accompanied by a rise in an economy's potential output) or by short-run changes in aggregate demand and aggregate supply. As Figure 10.17 shows, the growth of actual output rarely follows the gradually rising long run trend in the economy's potential output. Usually, the growth in actual real output is accompanied by recessionary and inflationary gaps, and these gaps do not happen at random. Instead, they occur on the basis of a pattern of short-run changes in aggregate demand and aggregate supply.

As a rule, a sustained rise in real output, known as a period of **expansion** or recovery, is followed by an extended period of falling real output, known as a **contraction**. These rises and falls in real output constitute a pattern known as the **business cycle**.

Figure 10.17 shows the business cycle in a simplified form. The long-run trend of potential output to rise is shown by a dashed line. Actual output moves toward and away from this potential output in a cycle of successive contractions and expansions.

ACTUAL VERSUS POTENTIAL OUTPUT

When actual output exceeds potential output, the resulting inflationary gap is the difference between real output (point *a*) and potential output (point *b*), as

expansion: a sustained rise in the real output of an economy

contraction: a sustained fall in the real output of an economy

business cycle: the cycle of expansions and contractions in the economy

FIGURE 10.17   The Business Cycle

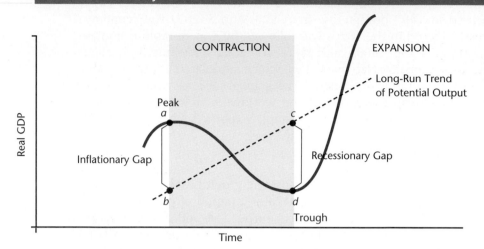

Real GDP rises and falls in a cycle of expansion and contraction. These fluctuations can be compared with a trend line that represents long-run growth potential. The distance between actual output and the trend line represents the size of either the economy's inflationary gap (as in the case of points *a* and *b*) or the economy's recessionary gap (as in the case of points *c* and *d*).

shown in Figure 10.17. Real output then falls below its potential level shown by the trend line. In this case, the recessionary gap is the amount by which real output falls short of its potential—in other words, the difference between potential output (point *c*) and real output (point *d*).

Contraction

peak: the point in the business cycle at which real output at its highest

Consider the case of an economy that has reached its **peak**. At this point (point *a*), the economy is said to be experiencing a boom, which occurs when real GDP is at its highest value in the business cycle. The inflationary gap has reached its maximum width, unemployment is at its lowest possible level, and real output can grow no larger in the short run. From this point, the economy contracts.

THE ROLE OF EXPECTATIONS

Any decrease in aggregate demand can be magnified by the reactions of both households and businesses to initial reductions in spending and output. To understand how this occurs, recall that spending by both households and businesses is influenced by expectations of the future. Households vary consumption expenditures depending on their anticipation of future prices and incomes, while businesses decide how much to invest on the basis of estimates of future profit.

Expectations of the future are often made simply by extending current trends. Sometimes this can create a self-fulfilling prophecy—that is, if the economy is experiencing reductions in real output and spending, then many households and businesses assume that income and spending will drop further. As a result, there will likely be decreases in three types of spending: consumption, investment, and exports. The prospect of lower future incomes causes households to spend less, especially on durable items. Similarly, the decline in spending that businesses expect causes a drop in real rates of return for investment projects, leading to further declines in investment. The effect on exports occurs because periods of contraction usually arrive in various countries simultaneously. Therefore, it is probable that foreign consumers and businesses are reacting in the same way as their domestic counterparts, thus reducing exports. In other words, the expectations of businesses and households create a downward spiral in which declines in real output lead to further declines in spending and in output. Enough pessimism creates the very economic conditions people fear.

EFFECTS OF A CONTRACTION

Figure 10.18 shows the effects of a decrease in aggregate demand from AD_0 to AD_1. Equilibrium output declines from its initial value of $730 billion (point f) to a final value of $700 billion (point e). As a result, unemployment gradually rises above its natural rate, with the initial inflationary gap of $5 billion turning into a recessionary gap of $25 billion. At the same time, there is downward pressure on prices. If inflation is originally zero, as in Figure 10.17, then the price level falls from 240 to 160, causing deflation.

RECESSIONS AND DEPRESSIONS

In general, the longer the period of declining real output, the more serious are its effects. A decline in real output that lasts for six months or more is known as a **recession**. For example, the Canadian economy followed global trends in experiencing a recession in 2008–2009, with previous recessions occurring in 1981–1982 and 1990–1991. The latest recession lasted for a total of nine months (the last quarter of 2008 and the first two quarters of 2009), and saw real output decline by over 3 percent and unemployment rise by 2.5 percent. A **depression** occurs if the reduction in real output is particularly long and harsh, as happened

recession: a decline in real output that lasts for six months or more

depression: a particularly long and harsh period of reduced real output

FIGURE 10.18 Expansion and Contraction

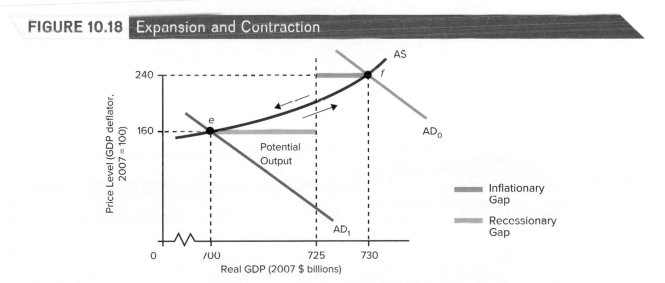

Periods of contraction lead to a decrease in aggregate demand, shifting the curve from AD_0 to AD_1. This leads to a fall in equilibrium output from $730 to $700 billion (points f to e). As a result, the initial inflationary gap of $5 billion turns into a recessionary gap of $25 billion. Periods of expansion reverse the change, causing the curve to shift from AD_1 to AD_0 and increasing equilibrium output (points e to f).

during the early 1930s. Other more informal terms are often used to describe the path of real GDP during contractionary periods. A "V-shaped recession" is the case where a recession is relatively short-lived, with a steep increase in real GDP after the trough, as shown in Figure 10.17. With a "double-dip recession," two troughs occur in quick succession, so that the initial recovery from the first is relatively short-lived.

Expansion

trough: the point in the business cycle at which real output is at its lowest

The spiral of worsening expectations and declining real output does not last indefinitely. Sooner or later, the economy reaches a **trough**, where real output is at its lowest possible value in the business cycle. In Figure 10.17, this occurs at point *d*. At this point, not only is the economy's recessionary gap at its widest, but unemployment is at its highest level. After this turning point, the dampening effect of expectations is counteracted by other factors, and the economy enters a phase of expansion.

THE ROLE OF EXPECTATIONS

As in periods of contraction, expectations play a role in maintaining a recovery. Initial increases in real output and spending lead to optimistic forecasts of continuing growth, therefore, consumption, investment, and exports all increase. Consumers react to the prospect of higher incomes by spending more, especially on durable goods. At the same time, businesses increase their investment because optimism causes further rises in estimated real rates of return. Finally, in the case where other countries are experiencing similar trends, foreign buyers also increase their spending and buy more exports. Increased consumer spending, business investment, and exports lead to continual increases in aggregate demand, until a new peak is reached and the stage is set for another period of contraction.

EFFECTS OF AN EXPANSION

Figure 10.18 also shows the effects of an expansion. In this case, the aggregate demand curve shifts to the right, from AD_1 to AD_0. Because of the rise in equilibrium output, the original recessionary gap is turned into an inflationary gap. Corresponding to this movement, the unemployment rate goes from above to below its natural rate, while the accompanying rise in the general price level causes inflation.

THINKING ABOUT ECONOMICS

Which sectors of the economy are most affected by a downturn?

While a recession or a depression is felt in every sector, those industries that make capital goods or durable consumer goods, such as automobiles and appliances, are the hardest hit. This is because purchases of these products can be postponed until after the downturn has ended.

QUESTION **What sectors are least affected by a downturn?**

BRIEF REVIEW

1. Overall, Canada's rate of economic growth has been comparatively high, giving Canada the sixteenth highest per capita output of the rich industrialized countries in 2012.

2. Real output rarely equals potential output. Instead, output and expenditures generally follow a cycle of expansions and contractions, which together make up the business cycle.

3. The highest output occurs at a peak in the business cycle. From this point, the economy contracts, so aggregate demand decreases. Consumer and business expectations magnify the downward trend.

4. The lowest output occurs at a trough in the business cycle. From this point, the economy expands, so aggregate demand increases. Again, expectations magnify the upward trend.

10.5 | PRACTICE PROBLEM

1. Identify how each of the following will tend to move during economic expansions and economic contractions.
   a. consumption of durable goods
   b. planned investment
   c. exports
   d. wage rates
   e. unplanned investment

LAST WORD

In this chapter, we developed a model to show how an economy's real output is determined, and we examined the factors that cause the growth in real output to veer from the long-run trend of potential output. In the next chapter, we begin our discussion of how government policy-makers can intervene in this process to reduce the instability of economic growth—first by focusing on the use of fiscal policy, and then on money and the application of monetary policy. We will see that the macroeconomic role of governments in conducting stabilization policy is an area in which disagreement is quite common—not just in the political sphere, but also among different groups of economists.

PROBLEMS

1. In a hypothetical economy, no investment projects are undertaken when the real interest rate is 12 percent or above, 50 projects worth $1 million each are undertaken when the real interest rate is 10 percent, and 50 more projects worth $1 million each are undertaken every time the real interest rate falls by 2 percent until it reaches a value of zero.
   a. Draw a graph showing the investment demand curve. Plot seven points in total.
   b. If the interest rate is 4 percent, how much investment will take place in the economy?
   c. If the interest rate rises to 6 percent, what is the new value of investment?

2. Identify the impact of each of the following trends on aggregate demand, the equilibrium price level, and equilibrium real output.
   a. Consumers become more confident about the prospects for the Canadian economy.
   b. Canadian interest rates rise.
   c. Political pressure causes an increase in tax rates on households earning high incomes.
   d. A newly-elected federal government increases its purchases of goods and services.
   e. The Chinese economy experiences a boom.
   f. The Canadian dollar falls in value against the US dollar.
   g. A tumble in the economies of Canada's major trading partners takes place.

3. Identify the impact of each of the following trends on aggregate supply, the equilibrium price level, equilibrium real output, and potential output.
   a. Canadian workers receive higher wages.
   b. A cheap new source of energy raises labour productivity in the Canadian economy.
   c. The federal government reduces corporate income tax rates.
   d. Due to a global environmental crisis, there is a reduction in the amount of available land.
   e. The price of oil decreases.
   f. The Canadian dollar rises in value against the American dollar.

4. The table below shows aggregate demand and aggregate supply schedules in a hypothetical economy.

Aggregate Demand and Aggregate Supply Schedules

Price Level (2007 = 100)	Real GDP			
	(AD0)	(AD1)	(AS0)	(AS1)
	(2007 $ billions)			
140	190	240	270	320
130	210	260	260	310
120	230	280	230	280
110	250	300	200	250
100	270	320	160	210

   a. Draw a graph showing AD_0, AD_1, AS_0, and AS_1. Plot only the endpoints of the two aggregate demand curves and all five points for each of the two aggregate supply curves.
   b. If initially AD_0 and AS_0 are the relevant schedules, what are the equilibrium price level and real output? What happens if the price level is 140? 110?
   c. If aggregate demand shifts from AD_0 to AD_1 while aggregate supply remains at AS_0, what are the new equilibrium price level and real output? Describe this change in aggregate demand.
   d. If aggregate supply shifts from AS_0 to AS_1 while aggregate demand remains at AD_0, what are the new equilibrium price level and real output? Describe this change in aggregate supply. Is it a short-run or long-run change?

5. Calculate the following values using the rule of 72.
   a. the number of years it will take a country's real GDP to double if the annual growth rate of real GDP is 1.5 percent

b. the average annual rate of inflation if the general price level doubles each 27 years

c. the approximate number of times a country's population will double in 96 years if the annual growth rate is 3 percent

6. In Ergonia, 8 million workers produce a real output of $500 billion in 2014 and the same number of workers produce $540 billion in 2015.
   a. Calculate Ergonia's labour productivity in each year.
   b. What is Ergonia's rate of productivity growth between 2014 and 2015?

7. Study the table below and identify the following:
   a. years in which the economy expanded
   b. years in which the economy contracted
   c. peaks
   d. troughs

Year	Annual Percentage Change in Real GDP (2007 $)	Year	Annual Percentage Change in Real GDP (2007 $)
1982	−3.1	1998	4.1
1983	2.6	1999	5.4
1984	5.7	2000	5.4
1985	5.2	2001	1.4
1986	2.8	2002	2.7
1987	4.6	2003	2.0
1988	4.6	2004	3.1
1989	2.5	2005	3.2
1990	0.0	2006	2.4
1991	−2.0	2007	2.2
1992	0.9	2008	1.1
1993	2.4	2009	−2.9
1994	4.9	2010	3.3
1995	2.7	2011	2.4
1996	1.6	2012	1.7
1997	4.5		

Sources: Statistics Canada "Finding Real Gross Domestic Product," adapted from the Statistics Canada CANSIM database, www5.statcan.gc.ca/cansim/, Table 380-0106. Retrieved March 18, 2014.

8. Because of the time it takes for official GDP statistics to be released, economists sometimes look at some creative statistics that have been shown to foreshadow the business cycle. For each of the following statistics, state whether they are likely to vary in the same direction or opposite direction to the business cycle.
   a. sales of romance novels
   b. registrations with online dating services
   c. cosmetic surgery bookings

9. Identify in which direction the following variables would have to change to reduce either an inflationary gap or a recessionary gap through shifts in aggregate demand.
   a. personal and corporate tax rates
   b. government purchases
   c. interest rates
   d. the Canadian dollar's value in American dollars

10. Binomia produces milkshakes (a consumer good) and computers (a capital good) as shown in the table below.
    a. Draw a graph showing Binomia's initial production possibilities curve, PPC_0. Plot a total of four points.

Production Possibilities Schedule

Production Scenario	Milkshakes	Computers
A	400	0
B	350	1
C	225	2
D	0	3

b. If Binomia initially produces 350 milkshakes and one computer and the country's citizens decide to increase computer production by one unit, while keeping all resources fully employed, what happens to Binomia's milkshake output? What happens to the future stock of economic resources and to the production possibilities curve in Binomia?

c. If a technological innovation occurs in the production of computers, but not the production of milkshakes, what happens to Binomia's production possibilities curve?

11. Outline how a fall in injections will affect the income-spending stream and equilibrium real output. Discuss how the same result can be found using aggregate demand and aggregate supply.

12. Why does a $100 million decrease in aggregate demand have a greater impact on real output when the economy is below its potential output than when it is above its potential output?

ADVANCING ECONOMIC THOUGHT

MAKING AN ECONOMY GROW
Paul Romer and New Growth Theory

Paul Romer
Photo courtesy of Paul Romer

Recently, the role of knowledge has been highlighted in theories of economic growth. Part of this new emphasis is due to the contemporary American economist Paul Romer.

The knowledge economy. Knowledge workers. Knowledge-based industries. Ideas-driven growth. The words trip off the tongue with ease, not just in academic circles, but in the mainstream population as well.

These new economic buzzwords reflect the fact that knowledge and ideas have become the vital engines of economic growth. The boom in such fields as computer software, telecommunications, pharmaceuticals, and bio-technology clearly shows that the jobs of the future, and Canada's overall prosperity, depend on wise investments in the new knowledge based economy.

The brain behind the buzzwords is Paul Romer, an intense, 59-year-old economist who has had a revolutionary impact on economic thinking and, in the process, upset the apple cart of traditional economic theories of growth.

Romer is a professor of economics at the University of California at Berkeley, a visiting fellow at the Hoover Institution, and the Royal Bank Fellow at the Canadian Institute for Advanced Research (CIAR). The praise for Romer's work is lavish and, to him, slightly embarrassing. *The Economist* has said that historians will date the revival of Growth Theory in economics to Romer. The effect of his work has been likened to the intellectual upheavals caused by Adam Smith and John Maynard Keynes.

Romer's New Growth Theory is now widely accepted, but back in 1979, when he was a 25-year old graduate student at Queen's University in Kingston, Ontario, it was tantamount to claiming that the emperor had no clothes. Romer was at Queen's because his wife, Virginia Langmuir of Toronto, was returning there to complete her residency as a physician. Left alone, with little academic supervision, Romer began to ponder the question that has intrigued economists for decades: what are the causes of long-term growth?

"One of the features of that year at Queen's was that there was no one to tell me that this is how you have to think about growth," Romer recalls. "So I started, in a sense, from a clean piece of paper and said: 'Gee! How should I try to go about understanding this really interesting phenomenon?'

"Economists had built up a relatively sophisticated and productive way of thinking about growth, but we weren't learning much more from that framework. So, as much by trial and error as by chance, I started out on a new path."

Traditional economic theory held that growth is the result of two factors of production: labour and capital. But there was a nagging problem with this so-called neoclassical theory: it could not explain why developing countries, given liberal amounts of labour and capital, fail to grow as fast as developed nations.

Romer had the answer: knowledge. He made it the third—and most important—factor of production. By knowledge, he meant new and better ways of doing things, as well as ideas, innovation, invention, and discovery. Knowledge entails taking objects that are relatively worthless and rearranging them in new combinations to create value. For example, the sand on a beach has little value, but turn it into a silicon chip, and it becomes immensely valuable. Another compelling example is Bill Gates. He can walk through a customs barrier anywhere in the world and swear he has nothing to declare, when, in fact, his brain carries the multi-billion-dollar secrets of Microsoft, which have made him the wealthiest man on earth.

"The key issue is to understand knowledge or ideas as economic goods," Romer explains. "Ideas are very different from things. When you're dealing with things, the best institutions to use are prices, free markets, and strong property rights."

But you cannot just transfer these same governing principles to the marketplace of ideas, Romer says. Objects tend to have relatively fixed costs per unit, while ideas have high upfront costs but low reproduction costs. Developing an idea–say a new piece of software–might take $100 million, while producing a copy of it on a floppy disk can cost less than 50 cents.

This raises the question of how to set the right price for the discovery of an idea. Romer cites the example of polymerase chain reaction (PCR)–a way of getting tiny amounts of DNA to multiply–which won the Nobel Prize in chemistry for Kary Mullis in 1993.

"At the start, we put a very high price on PCR because it's extremely valuable," Romer says. "But after the idea has been produced, the most efficient thing for society as a whole is to let that idea be freely used by other scientists and researchers in the hope that it will lead to the discovery of more new ideas."

Romer's New Growth Theory seems to have struck a chord with academia and the general public alike, because it carries with it the message of optimism. Traditional economic theory held that since the way of doing things is relatively constant, no matter the capital and labour expended, over time, society will get smaller and smaller returns. This is known as the law of diminishing returns. New Growth Theory, by contrast, embraces a law of increasing returns.

To illustrate the mind-boggling opportunities that ideas can generate, Romer uses the example of a manufacturing process in which 20 different parts must be attached to a frame. You could attach them in a given order: part one first, part two second, part three third, and so on. Or you may attach them in another order: part one first, then part 20, then part seven, and so on. If you calculate all the possible sequences for attaching those parts, you get 10 to the 18th power, a number that is larger than the total number of seconds that have elapsed since the Big Bang created the universe. So the possibilities out there are virtually limitless.

What lies ahead for Paul Romer? Plenty of different things. At the CIAR, he is descending from the ivory tower and examining practical policy questions about restructuring financial incentives for universities so that graduates can find better niches in the knowledge economy. But this influential economist is, at heart, a loner: "People like me don't work very well in structured environments. A colleague of mine says that trying to work with us (economists) is like trying to herd cats."

Asked about leisure time, he replies with a laugh, "What's that?" And the future? "Oh, more of the same," Romer says. "I'll continue to be an intellectual bomb-thrower."

Indeed.

Source: Gillian Cosgrove, "Knowing about Growing," *Canadian Banker* (May/June, 1996), pp. 20-22.

1. **a.** Give an example of a Canadian idea that has been subject to the increasing returns associated with knowledge.
   b. Summarize how the company that invented it can benefit from these increasing returns.
2. Does Romer's theory provide an argument for or against strong patent protection for new ideas? Explain.

CHAPTER 11

Fiscal Policy

Should governments sit idly through the upheavals caused by the business cycle? Certainly not, according to John Maynard Keynes, the founder of modern macroeconomics, as well as his present-day followers. Governments can do plenty to stabilize the economy — not only during downturns when unemployment is high, but also during inflationary upswings. Governments can use certain policies to achieve economic stability; for example, they can spend more money or reduce taxes to cause changes in total spending and aggregate demand. This chapter examines the theory behind such policies and their outcomes.

> Democracy will defeat the economist at every turn at its own game.
>
> -HAROLD INNIS, CANADIAN ECONOMIST AND HISTORIAN

LEARNING OBJECTIVES   After reading this chapter, you will be able to:

LO 1

Identify expansionary and contractionary fiscal policies, which are used by governments seeking economic stability

LO 2

Outline the multiplier effect of fiscal policy, as determined by the marginal propensities to consume and withdraw

LO 3

Distinguish between budget surpluses and deficits and describe their impact on public debt and public debt charges

11.1 | Fiscal Policy

 The Goal of Stabilization

stabilization policy:
government policy designed to lessen the effects of the business cycle

To lessen the effects of ups and downs in the business cycle–particularly inflation and unemployment–governments use stabilization policies. A **stabilization policy** attempts to influence the amounts spent and produced in an economy. The goal of such a policy is to keep the economy as close as possible to its potential output. At this point, only natural unemployment exists, and inflation is restrained.

Stabilization policies fall into two categories, depending on the state of the economy and the effect the policy is meant to have on the economy. When total output is below its potential, policy-makers want to eliminate the recessionary gap–in other words, reduce unemployment and stimulate total output. Policies with these goals are called **expansionary policies**.

expansionary policies:
government policies designed to reduce unemployment and stimulate output

contractionary policies:
government policies designed to stabilize prices and reduce output

In contrast, if the economy is booming, policy-makers want to cut the inflationary gap–in other words, stabilize prices and bring the economy back down to its potential output. Policies with these goals are called **contractionary policies**.

STABILIZING THE BUSINESS CYCLE

Assuming that it can be applied quickly and effectively, stabilization policy may be used to smooth out the business cycle. Figure 11.1 shows how stabilization policy can reduce the severity of economic troughs and peaks and the recessionary and inflationary gaps associated with them. The closer the economy stays to the long-run trend of potential output, the lower will be the social costs of unemployment and inflation to the country's citizens.

In general, governments can affect spending and output levels in an economy through two sets of instruments. First, recall that governments have an extensive impact on the economy through taxation and government purchases. Because a government's annual budget sets out what the government will tax and spend,

---

FIGURE 11.1   Stabilization Policy and the Business Cycle

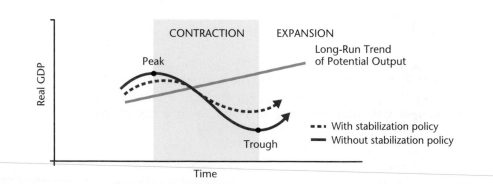

Effective stabilization policy minimizes the severity of the peaks and troughs in the business cycle. Differences between actual output and the long-run trend of potential output are therefore smaller, thus reducing recessionary and inflationary gaps.

the budget becomes an instrument of stabilization policy. Such a policy is called **fiscal policy**, where "fiscal" means "budgetary." The 12-month period to which the budget applies is called the **fiscal year**. Governments can also exert their influence on interest rates and the economy's money supply. A policy that uses these tools is called **monetary policy**. We will focus on fiscal policy in this chapter and turn our attention to monetary policy in later chapters.

Use of Fiscal Policy

Governments apply fiscal policy during any part of the business cycle. So, during a recession or depression, government action is geared toward increasing spending and output in the economy. Such **expansionary fiscal policy** involves increasing government purchases, decreasing taxes, or both. In contrast, during an inflationary boom, government policy-makers concentrate on restraining output and spending. Such **contractionary fiscal policy** involves decreasing government spending, increasing taxes, or both.

INJECTIONS AND WITHDRAWALS
One way to see how fiscal policy works is to look at injections and withdrawals. Recall from Chapter 10 that investment, government purchases, and exports make up injections to the income-spending stream; saving, taxes, and imports are withdrawals from the stream.

With expansionary fiscal policy, governments increase their purchases, and thus raise injections to the circular flow. As a result, injections rise relative to withdrawals, and the total flow increases. Reducing taxes has the same effect. By withdrawing less from the income-spending stream, withdrawals decrease relative to injections, and the total flow increases. As the total flow rises, equilibrium output is pushed up.

Contractionary fiscal policies have the opposite effect. Governments that decrease their purchases reduce injections to the circular flow. As a result, injections fall relative to withdrawals, and the total flow decreases. Raising taxes has the same effect; withdrawals rise relative to injections, and the total flow decreases. As the total flow falls, equilibrium output is pushed down.

AGGREGATE DEMAND
Another way to look at fiscal policy is through its effects on aggregate demand and aggregate supply. To increase aggregate demand so that the economy expands to its potential, policy-makers raise government purchases, cut taxes, or both. Increasing government purchases has an immediate effect on aggregate demand since government purchases are a component of real expenditures. As Figure 11.2 demonstrates, the equilibrium price level and output are pushed up as a result.

The effect of tax cuts is less immediate because there is no guarantee that households and businesses will alter spending in response to a tax change. Cutting taxes enables households and businesses to spend more, so both consumption and investment should increase, thereby shifting the aggregate demand curve to the right. Again, Figure 11.2 illustrates the results.

If a government has a contractionary fiscal policy—in other words, if it wants to decrease aggregate demand so that the economy contracts to its potential—policy-makers will reduce government purchases, raise taxes, or both. As with expansionary fiscal policy, the effect of decreasing government purchases is immediate, while the effect of increasing taxes is less so. Figure 11.3 illustrates both cases. A fall in

fiscal policy: government stabilization policy that uses taxes and government purchases as its tools; budgetary policy

fiscal year: the 12-month period to which a budget applies

monetary policy: government stabilization policy that uses interest rates and the money supply as its tools

expansionary fiscal policy: government policy that involves increasing government purchases, decreasing taxes, or both to stimulate spending and output

contractionary fiscal policy: government policy that involves decreasing government purchases, increasing taxes, or both to restrain spending and output

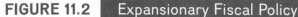

| FIGURE 11.2 | Expansionary Fiscal Policy |

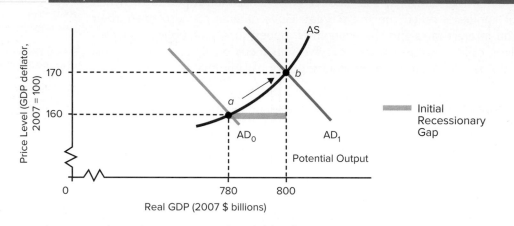

A rise in government purchases or a cut in taxes increases aggregate demand, shifting the aggregate demand curve from AD$_0$ to AD$_1$. This causes a rise in the equilibrium price level, and output rises to its potential level (from point *a* to point *b*). As a result, the economy's $20 billion recessionary gap is eliminated.

government purchases reduces aggregate demand, thereby shifting the aggregate demand curve to the left. Higher taxes reduce households' disposable income and businesses' profits. Consumption and investment both decline, thereby reducing aggregate demand and shifting the aggregate demand curve to the left.

AUTOMATIC STABILIZERS

As we have seen, fiscal policy involves adjusting government purchases or taxes. These actions are intentional; laws must be passed and budgets brought down. Because it is up to a government's discretion to take these actions, fiscal policy is known as **discretionary policy**. In contrast, some stabilizing forces are automatic— that is, they do not involve the direct involvement of government decision-makers.

Established taxation and transfer payment programs, such as progressive income taxes, Employment Insurance, welfare payments, and some agricultural

discretionary policy:
intentional government intervention in the economy, such as budgeted changes in spending or taxation

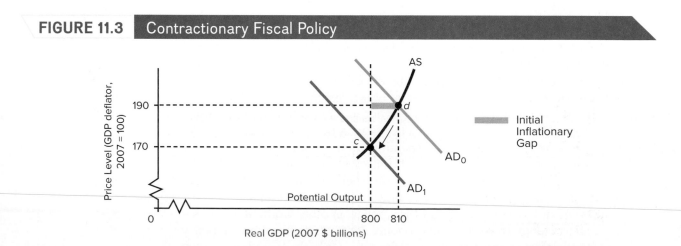

| FIGURE 11.3 | Contractionary Fiscal Policy |

A fall in government purchases or a rise in taxes decreases aggregate demand, shifting the aggregate demand curve to the left from AD$_0$ to AD$_1$. This causes a fall in the equilibrium price level, and output falls to its potential level (from point *d* to point *c*). As a result, the economy's inflationary gap is eliminated.

How significant are automatic stabilizers in the Canadian economy?

The expanding role of Canadian governments since World War II has led to a substantial increase in rates of taxation, as well as rising expenditures on transfer payments. Higher tax rates and more generous transfer payments have both served as important automatic stabilizers in the Canadian economy during recent decades—a point stressed by economists who support greater government involvement in the economy.

QUESTION   How would tax cuts by federal and provincial governments affect the significance of automatic stabilizers?

subsidies, act as **automatic stabilizers** in the business cycle. In a period of contraction, **net tax revenues** (taxes minus transfers and subsidies) decrease; during a period of expansion, net tax revenues increase. As a result, spending and aggregate demand are stimulated in a downturn and suppressed in an upswing, thereby helping to smooth out the business cycle.

To see how automatic stabilizers work, first consider an economy that is contracting. Because household incomes and business profits fall, the taxes that a government can collect from households and businesses also fall. As jobs are lost and businesses suffer, government transfer payments and subsidies increase. Both trends cause a decline in net tax revenues. Because incomes are bolstered by one program and taxes are reduced by the other, spending increases over what it would have been, helping to push the economy back up toward its potential output.

When the economy expands, the opposite happens: personal incomes and business profits increase. As a result, governments collect more in taxes. Because the nation is more prosperous and the employment rate is high, transfer payments and subsidies are reduced. Both trends cause a rise in net tax revenues. Because taxes have risen, spending and aggregate demand decrease, helping to push the economy back down to its potential output.

automatic stabilizers: built-in measures, such as taxation and transfer payment programs, that loosen the effects of the business cycle

net tax revenues: taxes collected minus transfers and subsidies

BRIEF REVIEW

1. Governments use stabilization policies to minimize ups and downs in the business cycle. Such policies are categorized as expansionary or contractionary policies, depending on the state of the economy and the effect of the policy on the economy.

2. Fiscal policy affects spending and output through taxes and government purchases. Monetary policy affects spending and output through interest rates and the economy's money supply.

3. Expansionary fiscal policy involves increasing government purchases, decreasing taxes, or both. Such a policy increases aggregate demand and pushes up the equilibrium price level and output.

4. Contractionary fiscal policy involves decreasing government purchases, increasing taxes, or both. Such a policy decreases aggregate demand and pushes down the equilibrium price level and output.

5. In contrast to discretionary policies, automatic stabilizers are built-in factors that affect aggregate demand and minimize the impact of inflationary and recessionary gaps.

11.1 | PRACTICE PROBLEMS

1. In each of the following cases, state what types of fiscal policy, if any, should be applied.
    a. Real output is less than its potential level.
    b. Unemployment is below its natural rate.
    c. Real output equals its potential level and unemployment is at its natural rate.
2. Explain how automatic stabilizers work during the following periods.
    a. The economy is experiencing a recession, with shrinking incomes and spending.
    b. The economy is in a period of growth, with rising incomes and spending.

11.2 | The Spending Multiplier

L02

Government decision-makers must have some way of estimating, in terms of money values, the impact that their policies will have on the economy. In general, a certain money change in government purchases or taxation does not cause the same money change in total real output. Like a pebble dropped in a pond causes ripples, fiscal policy has a multiplier effect.

The Multiplier Effect

multiplier effect: the magnified impact of a spending change on aggregate demand

The **multiplier effect** is the magnified impact of any spending change on aggregate demand. It assumes that the price level stays constant. So, the multiplier effect is the change in spending at one price level, multiplied by a certain value to give the resulting change in aggregate demand.

Consider an example. Suppose government institutes an expansionary fiscal policy. As part of this policy, government pays Spender A, a trade consultant, $1000 for her services. The economy's output rises by $1000, and the consultant's revenues rise by $1000. (Assume that the consultant incurs only negligible costs.) This consultant spends half the amount she earns on a Canadian product and uses the rest for saving, imports, and taxes. In other words, she pays $500 to the supplier of a Canadian product, Spender B, thereby increasing Spender B's income (assuming that B also has negligible costs). The economy's total output has been expanded again by $500, with the remaining $500 withdrawn from the income-spending stream by Spender A in the form of saving, imports, and taxes. Spender B, with his $500 in new income, spends $250 on Canadian products and uses the other $250 on saving, imports, and taxes. His $250 purchase also has an impact on the Canadian economy and provides income to someone else. And it goes on. Any given purchase made by government has an initial effect, a secondary effect, and so on.

As the example illustrates, the inclination to spend and the inclination to save or otherwise withdraw funds from the economy both determine the multiplier effect. These factors are summarized by the concepts of marginal propensity to consume and marginal propensity to withdraw.

Marginal Propensity to Consume

The **marginal propensity to consume** (MPC) is the effect on domestic consumption of a change in income, and applies to individual households and the economy as a whole. In effect, MPC answers the question: "If income increases this amount, how much extra will be spent on domestic goods and services?" MPC is defined as the change in consumption on domestic products as a proportion of the change in income.

marginal propensity to consume: the effect on domestic consumption of a change in income

$$MPC = \frac{\text{change in consumption on domestic items}}{\text{change in income}}$$

Marginal Propensity to Withdraw

As the earlier example illustrated, not all income is spent, and what is spent may not be spent on domestic products. As a result, some income does not reappear in the circular flow. Recall from Chapter 10 that there are three types of withdrawals: saving, taxes, and imports. Part of income is saved, part is paid out in taxes, and part is used to buy imports. The **marginal propensity to withdraw** (MPW) is the effect of a change in income on withdrawals. It is defined as the change in total withdrawals as a proportion of the change in income.

marginal propensity to withdraw: the effect on withdrawals—saving, imports, and taxes—of a change in income

$$MPW = \frac{\text{change in total withdrawals}}{\text{change income}}$$

Next, consider the concepts of MPC and MPW together. Suppose a person's income rises by \$1000. Of that, the consumer spends \$300 on domestic products, but uses the rest on savings, taxes, and imports. In this case, the marginal propensity to consume is 0.3 (= \$300 ÷ \$1000), while the marginal propensity to withdraw is 0.7 (= \$700 ÷ \$1000). Note the relationship between the values of the marginal propensities to consume and withdraw: their sum equals 1. This is always the case because income is either spent on domestic consumption or withdrawn from the circular flow as saving, imports, or taxes.

$$1 = MPC + MPW$$
$$1 = 0.3 + 0.7$$

To see in detail how the multiplier effect works, consider again the trade consultant example. The marginal propensities to consume and withdraw in each round, or stage, of spending help to determine the multiplier effect. Figure 11.4 illustrates the example.

FIRST ROUND
Recall that the government pays Spender A, the trade consultant, \$1000. Not only does her income rise, but the economy's output also rises by \$1000. The effect is illustrated on the left in Figure 11.4.

SECOND ROUND
Spender A starts the second round of spending by using the extra \$1000 in income. Because her marginal propensity to consume is 0.5 (= \$500 ÷ \$1000) and her marginal propensity to withdraw is also 0.5 (= \$500 ÷ \$1000), she puts an extra \$500 into the circular flow but withdraws \$500 in the form of saving, imports, and taxes. As a result, the economy's real output undergoes a further rise of \$500.

FIGURE 11.4 | The Effect of a Rise in Government Purchases

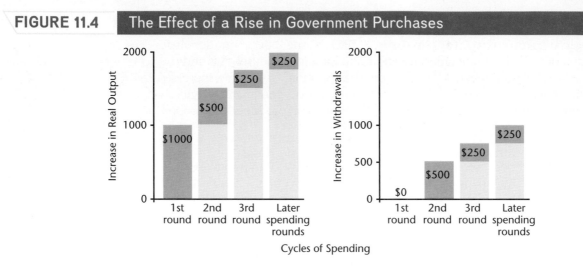

On the left, a $1000 rise in government purchases gradually pushes up real output by $2000, with each round of spending adding successively smaller amounts (as indicated by the darker rectangles). On the right, each successive round of spending involves a greater amount of total withdrawals, until new withdrawals equal the initial rise in spending.

THIRD ROUND

Recall that Spender B spends $250 of his $500 in income on domestic products and an equal amount on saving, imports, and taxes. Therefore, Spender B's marginal propensity to consume is 0.5 (= $250 ÷ $500), and his marginal propensity to withdraw is also 0.5 (= $250 ÷ $500). Figure 11.4 shows that he adds another $250 to the economy's real output.

LATER SPENDING ROUNDS

The same process of spending providing income—which is then spent domestically or withdrawn—repeats, with expenditures and withdrawals getting smaller in each round. For example, if the spender in the fourth round also has a marginal propensity to consume of 0.5, another $125 (= $250 × 0.5) will be added to the economy's real output. This process finally ends when real output has risen by a total of $2000.

INJECTIONS AND WITHDRAWALS

To see why total output grows by $2000, let us turn our attention to the withdrawals that occur with each spending round, shown on the right in Figure 11.4. Note that with each subsequent round of spending, there are new withdrawals. Eventually, total withdrawals equal $1000. This result can be interpreted in terms of injections and withdrawals.

Before the expansionary fiscal policy, the economy was in equilibrium, with injections and withdrawals being equal. As a result of the government's discretionary policy—that is, its $1000 planned increase in government purchases—total injections exceed total withdrawals, causing output to rise. In each round of spending, withdrawals increase. This expansion continues until withdrawals equal the initial discretionary injection. At this point, injections and withdrawals are both $1000 higher than they were before government purchases were increased.

Spending Multiplier

Now that we have seen the multiplier effect in action, we will give it a numerical value. The **spending multiplier** is the value by which the initial spending change is multiplied to give the total change in output–in other words, the shift in the aggregate demand curve.

spending multiplier: the value by which an initial spending change is multiplied to give the total change in real output

$$\text{Total change in output (shift in AD curve)} = \text{initial change in spending} \times \text{spending multiplier}$$

In our example, because initial spending rose by \$1000 and total output increased by \$2000, the spending multiplier equals 2. This figure can be found by rearranging the above equation to isolate the multiplier:

$$\text{Spending multiplier} = \frac{\text{total change in output}}{\text{shift in AD curve}}$$

$$2 = \frac{\$2000}{\$1000}$$

If total output increased instead by \$3000 as a result of a \$1000 rise in government purchases, then the multiplier would be 3 (= \$3000 ÷ \$1000).

To see what determines the value of the spending multiplier, recall that the economy's total output expands until new withdrawals equal the initial government purchase–the new injection. In our original example, the marginal propensity to withdraw was 0.5, meaning that 50 cents were withdrawn for every \$1 of new output in the economy. Output, therefore, had to expand by \$2000 to create the needed \$1000 in new withdrawals, giving a spending multiplier of 2. If the marginal propensity to withdraw had been 0.33, then 33 cents would have been withdrawn for each dollar of new output. Hence, output would have had to increase by \$3000 to create \$1000 in extra withdrawals, giving a spending multiplier equal to 3.

These examples point to the inverse relationship between the marginal propensity to withdraw and the spending multiplier. If MPW is 0.5, the multiplier equals 2. If MPW is 0.33, the multiplier is 3. Therefore, the spending multiplier is the reciprocal of the marginal propensity to withdraw.

$$\text{Spending multiplier} = \frac{1}{\text{MPW}}$$

$$2 = \frac{1}{0.5}$$

EFFECT OF A TAX CUT

The multiplier effect can be applied to the other stimulus that governments use: tax cuts. Recall that tax cuts can be used to expand the economy. Lower taxes leave households and businesses with more funds to spend and invest. In this case, the initial spending stimulus of the tax cut is multiplied by the spending multiplier, or the reciprocal of MPW. The result is an increase in total output, shown as a shift in the aggregate demand curve.

In contrast to government purchases, however, a tax adjustment has a smaller initial effect on spending. Recall our example of a \$1000 government purchase from Spender A. Spender A's initial transaction with the government was added directly to real output before taking into account further rounds of spending. In contrast, if a reduction in taxes increases Spender A's disposable income by $1000, some of this amount would be withdrawn from the circular flow before its first effect on real output. Only that amount used to buy domestic products represents the initial spending increase. For example, if the marginal propensity to consume is 0.5, then the initial change in spending on domestic items is $500 (= $1000 × 0.5). This $500 spending increase is then multiplied by the spending multiplier, or 2 (= 1 ÷ 0.5). As a result, the aggregate demand increases by $1000 (= $500 × 2), which is less than the $2000 increase caused by an initial $1000 government purchase.

The effect of a tax change can be summarized in mathematical terms. To find the initial change in spending on domestic items that results from a change in taxes (T), multiply the economy's marginal propensity to consume by the size of the tax change, and then multiply this product by the economy's spending multiplier (= 1 ÷ MPW) to derive the overall shift in the aggregate demand curve. Since this spending change is in the opposite direction to the tax change itself, the expression is preceded by a minus sign.

$$\begin{array}{c} \text{Total change in output} \\ \text{(shift in AD curve)} \end{array} = \begin{array}{c} \text{initial change} \\ \text{in spending} \end{array} \times \begin{array}{c} \text{spending} \\ \text{multiplier} \end{array}$$

$$\$1000 = -(\text{MPC} \times \text{change in T}) \times \frac{1}{\text{MPW}}$$

$$\$1000 = -(0.5 \times \$1000) \times \frac{1}{0.5}$$

$$\$1000 = \$500 \times 2$$

RELEVANCE OF THE SPENDING MULTIPLIER

Recall that throughout our discussion of the multiplier effect, we have assumed that the price level is constant. However, what happens to the spending multiplier if price levels vary?

As shown in Figure 11.5, fiscal policy affects the price level as well as output. Recall from Chapter 10 that the slope of the aggregate supply curve is steep as it reaches or surpasses the potential output level. So, as shown in Figure 11.5, when the aggregate demand curve shifts to the right from AD_0 to AD_1, it moves to a steep portion of the aggregate supply curve. In this case, the change in the equilibrium point, from point a to point c, means that while both price levels and output rise, the price level rises proportionally more than output does. So, in general, when the economy is close to its potential level, the increase in aggregate demand translates into higher price levels more than into expanded production. In other words, with the stated goal being a stable economy and expanded output, expansionary fiscal policy is less effective the closer the economy is to its potential. This same dominance of increasing price levels is even more pronounced if government policy-makers overshoot their target and, through the use of expansionary fiscal policy, push the economy above its potential output level. Similar reasoning applies to contractionary fiscal policy. When the economy is above its potential, a decrease in aggregate demand means that both the price level and total output fall. However, the price level falls proportionally more than total output does.

In summary, because of possible changes in the price level, the multiplier effect is less definite than the use of a simple formula would indicate. The multiplier calculation is, nonetheless, useful in indicating the *maximum* change in equilibrium output following a certain fiscal policy.

FIGURE 11.5   The Multiplier Effect and Price Changes

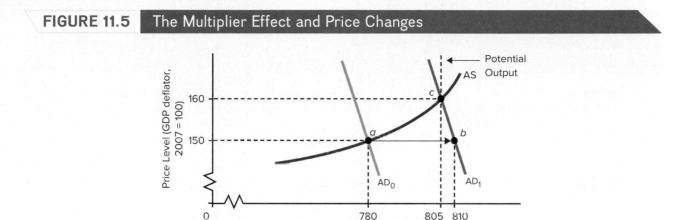

If spending affected output alone, with a spending multiplier of 1.5, a $20 billion rise in government purchases would push output from point *a* to point *b*. However, since the price level is also affected, the shift from AD₀ to AD₁ causes equilibrium to move to point *c*. Because of the slope of the AS curve, the closer an economy is to its potential, the greater will be the impact of a change in aggregate demand on the price level instead of output.

Benefits of Fiscal Policy

Fiscal policy has two benefits as a stabilization tool: its regional focus and its direct impact on spending.

REGIONAL FOCUS

Some parts of Canada may be more affected than others by the business cycle. Fortunately, discretionary fiscal policy can focus on particular regions. For example, during a recession, new government purchases or programs to reduce the amount of tax paid can be targeted to regions where unemployment rates are highest. In a boom, spending cuts and tax hikes can be concentrated on the regions where inflation is at its worst. Similarly, automatic stabilizers have the greatest effect in regions that need them the most. During recessions, net tax revenues drop most in regions hardest hit by unemployment and falling output. For example, the greatest rise in Employment Insurance payments is in areas with the highest growth in unemployment. During booms, the largest increase in net tax revenues occurs in regions where the economy is most overheated. For example, revenues from personal income tax expand most quickly in areas where employment and incomes are most buoyant.

IMPACT ON SPENDING

As indicated by the previous discussion of the multiplier effect, the influence of a stabilization policy is tied to its initial effect on spending. Monetary policy influences spending through a fairly elaborate chain of events. In contrast, fiscal policy has a more straightforward impact—at least when altering government purchases. The first spending adjustment is then assured, since the government itself initiates the change.

How large is the spending multiplier in the Canadian economy?

Several estimates of the Canadian spending multiplier have been made. The average value is about 1.5. If this figure is correct, then, as Figure 11.5 illustrates, a $20 billion jump in government purchases shifts the aggregate demand curve to the right by $30 billion. However, given the positive slope of the aggregate supply curve, this change means a rise in the price level as well as in total output. In this case, output would rise by $25 billion.

QUESTION   **Why has the value of Canada's spending multiplier fallen in recent decades?**

Drawbacks of Fiscal Policy

Offsetting the benefits of fiscal policy are three main drawbacks: policy delays, the political visibility of this policy, and its effects on public debt.

DELAYS

While automatic stabilizers work promptly to stabilize the economy, discretionary measures are sometimes delayed. Three time lags can slow down fiscal policy-makers: the recognition lag, the decision lag, and the impact lag.

recognition lag: the amount of time it takes policy-makers to realize that a policy is needed

The **recognition lag** is the amount of time it takes policy-makers to realize that a policy is needed. Suppose that economic growth suddenly slows. A few months may pass before statistical evidence of this becomes available. It may then take several more months for policy-makers to decide whether this represents a minor fluctuation or the start of a recession.

decision lag: the amount of time needed to formulate and implement an appropriate policy

The **decision lag** is the period that passes while an appropriate response is formulated and implemented. Suppose policy-makers decide that, indeed, the economy is entering a recession. They must then decide what to do about it. Should they increase government purchases, reduce taxes, or use some combination of the two measures? Once they decide, the policy must be passed into law and included in a budget.

impact lag: the amount of time between a policy's implementation and it having an effect on the economy

Finally, once the policy is implemented, there is an **impact lag**—the time that elapses between implementing the policy and it having an effect on the economy. In the case of government spending to combat a recession, for example, many rounds of spending must take place before the economy feels the full multiplier effect.

As a result of these time lags, a year or more may pass between the cause and the effect of a fiscal policy. Meanwhile, the economy may already have moved to a completely different point in the business cycle. In the extreme case, the use of fiscal policy may worsen the business cycle by stimulating output during upswings and suppressing it during downturns.

POLITICAL VISIBILITY

Discretionary fiscal policy is a highly visible element of government activity. Not surprisingly, therefore, it is often affected by political as well as economic considerations. Voters are likely to respond more favourably to increases in government purchases and cuts in taxes than they are to spending decreases and tax hikes, regardless of the appropriateness of these policies for the economy. As a result, political parties understandably favour expansionary fiscal policy, especially when an election is coming up. Moreover, parties in power often attempt to push through any planned cuts in government purchases or tax increases—leading to a contractionary fiscal effect—early in their term in office, while leaving expansionary spending increases and tax cuts to near the end. This pattern is referred to as the *political business cycle.*

PUBLIC DEBT

While there remains a political bias toward expansionary policy, the federal government has used stimulative measures more sparingly in recent recessions—the 2008-2009 recession being an important exception. This reluctance to increase government purchases or decrease taxes is related to Canada's **public debt**, which is the total amount owed by the federal government as a result of its past borrowing. This differs from total government debt, which includes the debts of individual provinces and territories—and sometimes incorporates local governments and hospitals as well. Given the substantial size of provincial debt (it totalled $509.3 billion at the end of the 2012-2013 fiscal year), this distinction can be important. Public debt, which is owed by Canadian taxpayers to owners of Canadian government bonds, totalled $602.4 billion at the end of the 2012-2013 fiscal year.

public debt: the total amount owed by the federal government as a result of its past borrowing

The federal government spends large sums related to its debt. **Public debt charges** are the amounts paid out each year by the federal government to cover the interest charges on its public debt. Just as payments of interest on a bank loan do not reduce the principal of the loan, public debt charges do not reduce the overall size of the public debt.

public debt charges: the amounts paid out each year by the federal government to cover the interest charges on its public debt

In 2012-2013, for example, the federal government's public debt charges were $29.2 billion. This figure represented an average interest rate of about 5.0 percent [(− $29.2 billion ÷ $583.6 billion) × 100%] that the federal government paid to the bondholders who owned its $583.6 billion debt.

Given the growth in public debt during recent decades, public debt charges are by far the largest single expenditure made by the federal government. In 2012-2013, for example, just over 11 cents of every federal tax dollar went to pay interest on Canada's public debt. Usually when an individual bondholder cashes in a Canadian government bond, the government replaces the funds by selling more bonds. It is therefore taxation and government spending levels, rather than the actions of individual bondholders, which ultimately determine the size of public debt.

BRIEF REVIEW

1. The multiplier effect—the magnified impact of fiscal policy on aggregate demand—is determined by the marginal propensity to consume and the marginal propensity to withdraw.

2. Assuming a constant price level, the spending multiplier is the value by which an initial spending change is multiplied to give the total change in real output.

3. Because a new injection brings about new withdrawals that equal the initial injection, the spending multiplier is the reciprocal of the marginal propensity to withdraw.

4. In the case of a tax cut, the initial spending adjustment is less than the change in taxes because a portion of the tax cut represents withdrawals from the circular flow of spending and income.

5. While fiscal policy can target certain regions and have a direct impact on spending, it also suffers from delays, problems associated with political visibility, and its impact on public debt.

11.2 | PRACTICE PROBLEMS

1. a. If an economy is initially in equilibrium and injections rise by $1 million, then by how much will withdrawals have to rise to bring injections and withdrawals back in balance?
   b. If the economy's MPW is 0.67, then by how much will incomes and output have to rise to create the required additional expenditures?
2. In each of the following cases, identify the direction and size of the shift in the AD curve.
   a. Government purchases fall by $10 billion in an economy with an MPW of 0.60.
   b. A tax cut causes an initial $25 billion rise in spending in an economy with an MPW of 0.80.
   c. Government purchases rise by $15 billion in an economy with an MPC of 0.25.
   d. A $30 billion tax rise occurs in an economy with an MPC of 0.4.

11.3 | Impact of Fiscal Policy

Budget Surpluses and Deficits

Government expenditures and revenues are affected both by discretionary fiscal policy and by the workings of automatic stabilizers. In the rare case where a government's expenditures and revenues are equal, the government is running a **balanced budget**.

balanced budget: a government's expenditures and revenues are equal

budget surplus: a government's revenues exceed its expenditures

In general, government expenditures and revenues are not equal. When a government's revenues exceed its expenditures, there is a **budget surplus**. For example, in 2007–2008, the federal government's total expenditures were $232.8 billion, and its total revenues were $242.4 billion. Therefore, the budget surplus was $9.6 billion.

Budget surplus = government revenues − government expenditures
$9.6 billion = $242.4 billion − $232.8 billion

budget deficit: a government's expenditures exceed its revenues

In contrast, when a government's expenditures exceed its revenues, there is a **budget deficit**. For example, in 2012–2013, the federal government's total expenditures were $275.6 billion and its total revenues were $256.6 billion. Therefore, the budget deficit (with a slight difference due to rounding) was $18.9 billion:

Budget deficit = government revenues − government expenditures
−$18.9 billion = $256.6 billion − $275.6 billion

The size of a government's surplus or deficit in relation to the economy's overall GDP gives an indication of what type of discretionary fiscal policy is in operation, as well as the built-in effects of automatic stabilizers.

For example, the federal government's $9.6 billion budget surplus in the 2007–2008 fiscal year was 0.6 percent (= $9.6 billion ÷ $1535.6 billion) of the

2007 nominal GDP of $1535.6 billion. In contrast, the (−)$18.9 billion budget deficit in the 2012-2013 fiscal year was −1.0 percent (= −$18.9 billion ÷ $1180.0 billion) of the 2012 nominal GDP of $1820.0 billion.

A government's deficit should not be confused with its debt. A budget deficit occurs when a government's expenditures exceed its revenue during a given period. The government's debt, on the other hand, represents the sum of all its past budget deficits minus any budget surpluses.

SURPLUSES

In some unusual cases, budget surpluses are related to discretionary fiscal policy. For example, a government might decide to suppress the inflationary effects of an economic boom by cutting defence spending and raising income taxes. However, it is more likely that budget surpluses are the result of built-in factors. During a boom, for example, rising tax revenues that outweigh transfer payments can cause provincial budgets to show a surplus.

DEFICITS

Budget deficits sometimes indicate active expansionary policies that increase government expenditures or reduce revenues. During an economic downturn, for example, the federal government may increase its spending on roads and bridges, or it may institute a temporary sales-tax cut to stimulate household spending. Budget deficits more often come about as a result of automatic stabilizers. For instance, fewer jobs and less spending during a recession lead to rising Employment Insurance benefits and sagging income tax revenues. Both these trends push the federal budget into a deficit position.

IMPACT ON PUBLIC DEBT

Because federal surpluses and deficits in Canada have not balanced each other in the long run, they have had a tremendous impact on the size of the country's public debt. When the federal government has a budget deficit, which in the past has been most common, the public debt increases by the same amount. For example, Canada's public debt at the start of the 2012-2013 fiscal year was $583.5 billion. Because the federal government ran a budget deficit of $18.9 billion in 2012-2013, its public debt at the start of the 2013-2014 fiscal year increased to $602.4 billion (= $583.5 billion + $18.9 billion). In the case of a federal budget surplus, the public debt can be reduced by the same amount. For example, when the federal government ran a $9.6 billion budget surplus in 2007-2008, its public debt was reduced from $467.3 billion at the beginning of the fiscal year to $457.7 billion (= $467.3 billion − $9.6 billion) at the beginning of the next fiscal year.

Fiscal Policy Guidelines

Three principles guide government fiscal policy: annually balanced budgets, cyclically balanced budgets, and functional finance.

ANNUALLY BALANCED BUDGETS

Those who criticize government intervention in the economy tend not to support fiscal policy. In general, these critics suggest that any fiscal policy that is used must be guided by the principle of an **annually balanced budget.** In

annually balanced budget: the principle that government revenues and expenditures should balance each year

other words, revenues and expenditures should balance every year. So, for example, new spending programs must be matched with higher taxes. In essence, by advocating an annually balanced budget, these critics dismiss active fiscal policy as an option.

Opponents of this principle suggest that it is based on faulty reasoning. While an annually balanced budget might make sense for a particular household, it is not necessarily appropriate for society as a whole. After all, the business cycle does not span one year, but several. During an economic contraction, for example, tax revenues decrease. To balance the budget, a government would have to reduce government purchases, thereby worsening the slump in spending. This problem occurred during the early years of the Great Depression in Canada.

CYCLICALLY BALANCED BUDGETS

cyclically balanced budget:
the principle that government revenues and expenditures should balance over the course of one business cycle

A less stringent principle—and one that has more supporters—is that of a **cyclically balanced budget**. In other words, government revenues and expenditures need not be balanced every year, but they should balance over one business cycle. The deficits from periods of contraction should roughly equal the surpluses from periods of expansion.

FUNCTIONAL FINANCE

functional finance: the principle that government budgets should be geared to the yearly needs of the economy

The principle of **functional finance** stems from the view that policy-makers should concern themselves primarily with correcting fluctuations caused by the business cycle. Rather than trying to balance budgets either annually or over the business cycle, governments should base a year's fiscal policy on the needs of the economy.

In practice, the choice of fiscal policy guidelines depends on the government's belief in fiscal policy as an effective tool for stabilizing the economy. The defenders of functional finance see fiscal policy as a powerful stabilization tool, while economists who back a cyclically or annually balanced budget tend to be less convinced of fiscal policy's effectiveness.

Recent Fiscal Policy

The predominant view of fiscal policy in Canada has undergone a profound change since the mid-1980s. Similar changes have taken place in other developed economies. In the 1970s and early 1980s, functional finance was the guiding principle behind fiscal policy in Canada and many other countries. Since then, there have been attempts to move toward cyclically balanced budgets.

In Canada, this change in view resulted primarily from past budget deficits and their impact on the economy as a whole. Figure 11.6 shows the combined budget balance of the federal, provincial, and territorial governments as a proportion of Canada's nominal GDP for the years 1980-1981 to 2012-2013. For example, in relation to Canada's 2012 nominal GDP of $1820.0 billion, the federal government's budget deficit of (−)$18.9 billion in 2012-2013 was −1.0 percent [(= −$18.9 billion ÷ $1820.0 billion) × 100%]. Similarly, the provincial and territorial governments, when viewed as a single unit, had a combined budget deficit in 2012-2013 of (−)$17.3 billion, which as a share of

| FIGURE 11.6 | Budget Balances Relative to GDP |

Federal and Combined Provincial Budget Balances (% of nominal GDP)

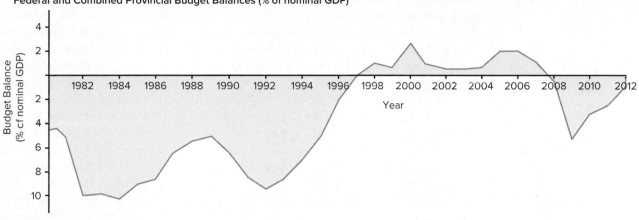

The combined budget balances for the federal, provincial, and territorial governments are shown as percentages of Canada's nominal GDP. Recessions in the early 1980s and early 1990s each caused an increase in combined budget deficits. During the long economic expansion of the 1990s, these deficits gradually declined and turned to a combined surplus, only to return to a deficit in the aftermath of the 2008–2009 recession.

Source: Department of Finance Canada, *Fiscal Reference Tables* (October 2013), pp. 10, 34. Reproduced with the permission of the Minister of Finance Canada, 2014.

nominal GDP was 0.9 percent [(= −$17.3 billion ÷ $1820.0 billion) × 100%]. Therefore, the sum for both levels of government was −1.9 percent of nominal GDP. Because this period spans three recessions and two periods of expansion, it illustrates the changing view of fiscal policy.

Total government deficits were highest during the periods corresponding to the recessions of the early 1980s and early 1990s. However, there were significant differences in fiscal policy. During and just after the slump of the early 1980s, the overall budget deficits of Canadian governments were about 10 percent of Canada's nominal GDP. The budget deficits of the lower levels of government, which were relatively small, came about largely because of automatic stabilizers as tax revenues fell with slumping output and incomes. The large federal deficits were due not only to automatic stabilizers, but also to the use of discretionary expansionary policy by government policy-makers. In particular, the federal government increased purchases of goods and services to counteract the effects of sagging output and incomes.

Following the recession of the early 1980s, the Canadian economy experienced a prolonged period of economic growth, with first a recovery and then a boom occurring in the later years of the decade. By 1988, the Canadian economy was near its potential output. Despite these boom conditions, budgets did not show an overall surplus. In fact, the combined deficits of the federal, provincial, and territorial governments were still about 5 percent of nominal GDP in 1988 and 1989.

During and just after the downturn of the early 1990s, the combined deficits of the lower levels of government were much more significant in comparison with the size of the federal deficit. As a result, the overall budget deficits of all levels of government were again nearly 10 percent of Canada's nominal GDP. However, these deficits were less a result of discretionary policy than of automatic stabilizers. This difference resulted from worry over the increased government debt and reduced confidence in the effectiveness of discretionary fiscal policies to counteract a recession. As the economy expanded during the mid- and late-1990s, the impact of automatic stabilizers, falling interest rates, and spending cuts by all levels of government led to the emergence of an overall budget surplus for Canadian governments. Only with the faltering economic growth rates of the late 2000s, due to the financial crisis of 2008, was this surplus eradicated, with both the federal and provincial governments again incurring significant deficits during and after the 2008-2009 recession. This time, due to fears over the recession's potential seriousness, discretionary fiscal policy was applied at both the federal and provincial levels. As a proportion of each province's GDP, the rise in deficits was most marked in Quebec and Ontario, given the extent to which the economic slump affected these provinces' exports of manufactured products to the US market. Meanwhile, overall budget deficits of all levels of government continued to rise in the recession's aftermath, reaching 5.6 percent of nominal GDP by 2009. Again, concerns over rising government debt caused policy-makers to respond with a round of spending cuts and tax increases, despite lingering worries that their austerity would dampen an already tepid economic recovery.

To minimize this unwanted dampening effect, policy-makers stressed expenditure cuts over tax increases. Several recent economic studies have shown that, when comparing a tax rise and expenditure cut of the same dollar amount, the expenditure drop has a less long-term contractionary effect on economic output because of the way tax increases tend to decrease aggregate supply. There are other compelling reasons to limit discretionary public spending in the near future. As in many other countries, Canadian health care expenditures continue a seemingly unstoppable year-over-year rise, while the costs of public pensions and other government-subsidized benefits to the elderly keep expanding as more and more baby boomers retire. These trends are making it more difficult for Canadian governments, especially provincial governments responsible for such high-growth areas as health care, to return to the virtuous cycle of surplus budgets last seen in the early and mid-2000s. The regional shifts in economic power within the country are also having an effect, as some provincial governments–such as those in Alberta, Saskatchewan, and Newfoundland–take advantage of expanding resource-based revenues to help achieve budgetary balance, something that is far less easy for other provinces to do.

Despite these considerable challenges, the overall fiscal policy record of Canadian governments in the past few decades has been relatively successful. Most recently, the use of fiscal policy during and after the 2008 financial crisis meant that Canada was able to weather this global storm with minimal long-term damage. More generally over the past few decades, Canadian fiscal policy has succeeded in smoothing out the business cycle, and has done so without causing government debt levels to become unsustainable. To see just how damaging such unsustainable debt levels can be, look no further than the recent history of European countries such as Ireland and Greece, whose spiralling government debts have caused close brushes with national bankruptcy and

FIGURE 11.7   Government Debt Relative to GDP: International Comparison

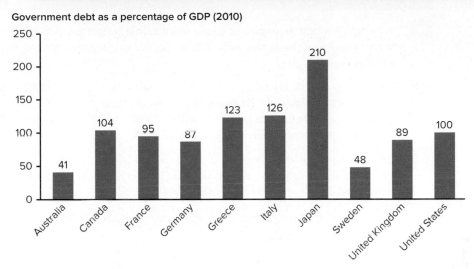

Government debt as a percentage of GDP (2010)

When comparing general government debt (including all levels of government, including other obligations such as estimated pension payouts for government workers) as a percentage of GDP in each country, Canada's debt, at just over 100 percent, is lower than for countries such as Japan, Italy, and Greece, but is higher than for several others, including Germany, France, the United Kingdom, and the United States.

Source: OECD (2013), "Government debt", in OECD Factbook 2013: Economic, Environmental and Social Statistics, OECD Publishing, http://dx.doi.org/10.1787/factbook-2013-82-en, January 2013.

have created an overriding need for budget austerity that will last for years to come. As shown in Figure 11.7, Canada's general government debt (which includes the debts of all three levels of government) as a percentage of GDP is significantly lower than for some other industrial countries, such as Italy and Japan, but is a good deal higher than for some others, such as Australia, Sweden, and Germany.

THINKING ABOUT ECONOMICS

Why, until recently, have budget deficits been so common for Canadian governments through all phases of the business cycle?

Many observers believe that Canada entered a harmful deficit–debt spiral in the early 1990s. Large federal budget deficits expanded Canada's public debt, which, in turn, raised annual interest payments on the public debt. The same trend was also noticeable for provincial governments. Greater debt charges for all levels of government increased their spending, which, in turn, raised deficits even more. Without the deficit-cutting measures pursued by all levels of government in the mid-1990s, this trend could have led to even higher government deficits and debt levels in the future. It has yet to be seen how quickly federal and provincial governments will be able reduce budget deficits in the aftermath of the latest recession.

QUESTION   **What benefits can arise from a protracted period of budget surpluses?**

BRIEF REVIEW

1. When government expenditures equal revenues, the budget is balanced. Budget surpluses occur when revenues exceed expenditures. When expenditures exceed revenues, there is a budget deficit.

2. Fiscal policy may be based on three possible guidelines: annually balanced budgets, cyclically balanced budgets, or functional finance. At the federal level, functional finance was the guiding principle in Canada between the 1970s and early 1980s, although cyclically balanced budgets are now increasingly favoured.

3. Between the early 1980s and mid-1990s, repeated budget deficits—in periods of both expansion and contraction—caused Canada's government debt to balloon. Sizeable deficits reappeared during and after the 2008–2009 recession.

11.3   PRACTICE PROBLEM

1. A government has an outstanding debt of $100 billion.
    a. If, in a given year, the government spends $10 billion and brings in $15 billion in taxes, then what is the government's budget deficit or surplus, and what happens to its debt?
    b. If, instead, the government's expenditures are $12.5 billion and its tax revenues are $10 billion, then what is the government's budget deficit or surplus, and what happens to its debt?

LAST WORD

In this chapter, we saw how governments can use their own spending and taxation decisions to affect the price level or real output in the entire economy. We saw how such discretionary actions can have an amplified impact through the workings of the spending multiplier, and how established government spending and taxation programs, such as Employment Insurance and welfare, help stabilize economic activity, even without the use of discretionary fiscal policy. In the next chapter, we begin our analysis of the monetary and financial components of the economy to see how these elements offer government policy-makers another set of tools in pursuing stabilization policy.

PROBLEMS

1. In each of the following cases, state whether the economy faces a recessionary or inflationary gap and outline possible fiscal policies.
   a. The unemployment rate is 5.5 percent, and inflation is rising.
   b. The unemployment rate is 6.5 percent, and prices are stable.
   c. Real output is falling, and the unemployment rate is 9.5 percent.

2. In each of the following cases, calculate the values of MPC, MPW, and the spending multiplier.
   a. A $1 million increase in income leads to a $350 000 rise in consumption on domestic items.
   b. A $4 million decrease in income results in a $1 million drop in consumption on domestic items.
   c. A $5 million decrease in income causes a $3 million drop in withdrawals.

3. Assume that Canadian government taxes away 40 cents of each dollar of new income, that 30 percent of the remaining 60 cents of disposable income is spent on imports, and that 5 percent of disposable income is saved.
   a. What is the value of the marginal propensity to withdraw?
   b. How much from each new dollar of income is spent on domestic consumption items?
   c. What is the value of the Canadian spending multiplier?

4. In each of the following cases, a particular fiscal policy affects an economy's AD curve via the spending multiplier. Calculate the spending multiplier and find the direction and size of the shift in the AD curve.
   a. Government purchases increase by $2 billion in an economy with an MPW of 0.65.
   b. Government purchases decrease by $5 billion in an economy with an MPC of 0.45.
   c. A $3 billion tax rise occurs in an economy with an MPW of 0.7.
   d. A $4 billion tax cut causes an initial $1.5 billion increase in spending on domestic items.

5. A decrease in government purchases of $8 billion leads to an initial $4.4 billion decrease in withdrawals.
   a. Find the values of MPW, MPC, and the spending multiplier in this economy.
   b. State the direction and size of the shift in the AD curve.
   c. In which direction does the equilibrium price level change? equilibrium real output?

6. "The more regressive Canada's tax system, the less effective automatic stabilizers become." Explain why this statement is true.

7. With the aid of aggregate demand/aggregate supply graphs, outline how the principle of an annually balanced budget can increase the severity of recessionary and inflationary gaps through the business cycle.

8. Explain how a series of federal budget surpluses can lead to a spiral of larger surpluses and rapidly decreasing public debt.

connect   **LEARNSMART**   **SMARTBOOK**

ADVANCING ECONOMIC THOUGHT

ECONOMIST EXTRAORDINAIRE

John Maynard Keynes and the Transformation
of Macroeconomics

**JOHN MAYNARD
KEYNES**
©Bettmann/CORBIS

KEYNES AND HIS INFLUENCE

The best blueprint for a model economist comes from the past century's most
illustrious one–John Maynard Keynes (1883-1946). An Englishman, he was a well-
rounded and energetic individual who wrote on mathematics, formulated economic policy as an adviser to the British government and a director of its central
bank, and served as a representative at international conferences, such as the Paris
Peace Conference that ended World War I. On top of all this, Keynes found time
to be a college administrator, edit a major economics journal, produce theatre,
chair an insurance company, and serve as an investment trust manager, while
accumulating a considerable personal fortune through his own investments.[1]

Keynes came from a privileged background–his father was an economist and his
mother was a city politician. After attending the exclusive boarding school Eton,
Keynes studied mathematics at Cambridge University. While there, he began a lifelong association with the Bloomsbury Group, an influential circle of English writers
and artists with a shared taste for the unconventional and a reputation for snobbery.

In response to the Great Depression plaguing North America and Europe,
Keynes published his book *The General Theory of Employment, Interest, and
Money*. By 1936, when the book was published, millions of jobless people had
given up hopes of finding work, and capitalism seemed to many to be on the
verge of self-destruction, just as Karl Marx had predicted decades earlier. There
was a widespread call for government intervention to combat the Depression.
Keynes, however, went one step further: he supported the call for government
intervention with a coherent theory, which stressed the role played by aggregate demand in determining output in the macroeconomy.

Keynes and his followers were able to convince most politicians and economists that action was needed. The government programs they advocated were
later viewed as crucial in hastening the end of the Depression. Keynesian ideas
dominated macroeconomics from after World War II to the 1970s, when events
brought about a new period of questioning and debate.

NEOCLASSICAL THEORY

Prior to Keynes' influence, most economists held the opinion that economic
slowdowns–even those as severe as the Great Depression–were self-correcting.
This view of the economy, referred to as neoclassical theory, is based on two
major assumptions: flexible labour markets and Say's Law.

Flexible Labour Markets According to neoclassical economists, both the
demand and supply of labour depend on the real wage rate, or wages expressed
in constant base-year dollars, rather than the nominal wage rate, which is valued
in current dollars. Neither workers nor employers are fooled by price changes;

[1]D.E. Moggridge, *Keynes* (London: Macmillan, 1976), p. 12.

therefore, they adjust their behaviour only when the purchasing power of wages changes. Employers demand less labour at higher real wage rates, while workers choose to supply more. As Figure A illustrates, the labour market can be shown using the demand and supply curves D_L and S_L.

Neoclassical economists distinguished between two types of unemployment: voluntary and involuntary. Voluntary unemployment exists whenever workers decide that real wages are not high enough to make work worthwhile. In contrast, involuntary unemployment–when someone wants to work at the current real wage rate but cannot find a job–is of much greater concern to policy-makers. According to neoclassical economics, involuntary unemployment occurs when market demand and supply create a surplus–for example, at a $6 real wage rate, as shown in Figure A. As long as labour markets are flexible, the market forces of demand and supply eradicate the surplus–for example, when market forces push wages toward an equilibrium point of $5. Because markets are flexible, involuntary unemployment is no more than a short run problem.

Say's Law Neoclassical economists also assumed that periods of underspending in the economy are short-lived. Their view was based on a principle known as Say's Law, first outlined by the French economist Jean-Baptiste Say. Using the circular flow of money in the economy, Say argued that supply automatically creates its own demand; that is, we produce goods and services in order to purchase others. A tailor makes clothes, for example, to have funds to buy other products.

Even if some of these funds are withdrawn from the circular flow, the production of goods and services generates enough funds to purchase them, as long as total withdrawals and total injections are equal. Neoclassical economists believed that this occurred because total withdrawals and injections can be equal *at any output*. According to their view, interest rates charged in financial markets will vary until withdrawals leaving the circular flow are matched by injections. Therefore,

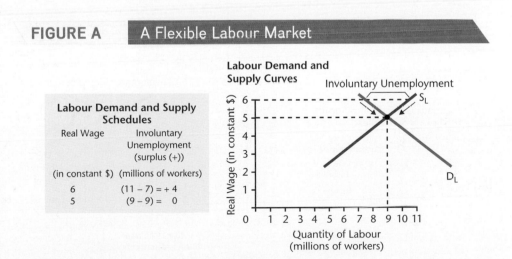

FIGURE A   A Flexible Labour Market

If the real wage is $6 per hour, the quantity supplied of labour exceeds the quantity demanded, resulting in 4 million workers involuntarily unemployed. According to neoclassical economics, the forces of demand and supply push the wage to the equilibrium level, eliminating the surplus.

reduced spending is only temporary; total expenditures and production soon balance each other out.

KEYNESIAN THEORY

Keynes challenged both assumptions of the neoclassical economists. Having done so, he provided a theory that explained how involuntary unemployment and underspending had become chronic problems during the Depression.

Challenge to Flexible Labour Markets Unlike the neoclassical economists, Keynes believed that workers are influenced by money illusion. By this, he meant that workers respond to changes in nominal wages rather than in real wages and purchasing power.

Consider a case in which prices fall, as they did during the Great Depression. If the price level drops by 10 percent, workers should not mind if their nominal wages are cut by 10 percent as well because real wages and purchasing power are not affected. However, workers do mind, according to Keynes. Workers see a decrease in nominal income as a drop in living standards, and trade unions tend to reject nominal wage cuts. Therefore, the nominal wage rate does not move despite downward pressure.

Figure B illustrates Keynes' view of labour markets. The quantity demanded and supplied of labour both vary with the nominal wage rate. Because the nominal wage will not decrease despite market pressure, the involuntary unemployment caused by a nominal wage, such as $8, can last indefinitely. Only if there is an increase in spending, shifting demand to the right, will this unemployment be reduced.

Challenge to Say's Law Keynes proved that despite its superficial appeal, Say's Law is not always valid. Output levels–not interest rates–adjust to bring about a balance between total injections and withdrawals. When injections are less than

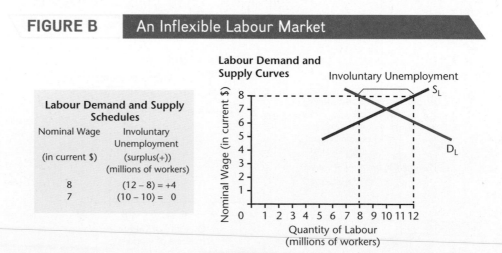

FIGURE B   An Inflexible Labour Market

Labour Demand and Supply Schedules

Nominal Wage (in current $)	Involuntary Unemployment (surplus(+)) (millions of workers)
8	(12 − 8) = +4
7	(10 − 10) = 0

At a nominal wage of $8 per hour, 4 million workers are involuntarily unemployed. According to Keynesian economics, because these nominal wages will not respond to downward pressure, the market does not move toward the equilibrium wage of $7 per hour. Instead, involuntary unemployment persists.

withdrawals, output falls until a new equilibrium level is reached. It is only at this equilibrium output that Say's Law is true, with injections and withdrawals the same. Also, this output is quite possibly associated with high unemployment. Keynes therefore concluded that underspending is not necessarily self-correcting, so governments must step in to create the needed jobs.

Keynesian Theory Today Despite the debates over Keynes's theory in the decades since his death, few economists today would dispute his profound impact on mainstream economic thinking. The model of aggregate demand and aggregate supply introduced in Chapter 10 owes its underlying principles to Keynesian thinking, especially in its focus on the possibility of protracted discrepancies between equilibrium and potential output, and the resulting need for government stabilization policy. Especially during the 2008 credit meltdown and the recession that ensued, Keynes was the figure from the past most often cited by contemporary economists who sought historical inspiration to help understand the unsettling challenges of that period, which mirrored economic conditions last seen during the 1930s. Indeed, most economists would agree that the ability of the world economy to escape a second Great Depression was due to the rapid response of government policy-makers keenly aware of the dangers that Keynes had highlighted over seven decades before in *The General Theory*. Thanks to this recent experience, Keynesian ideas remain alive and well today.

1. Outline how the neoclassical economists and Keynes differed in their answers to the following questions:
   a. Can a drop in wages lead to underspending in the economy?
   b. Will an increase in injections have its primary effect on interest rates or equilibrium output?

2. a. Why did neoclassical economists believe government intervention to be unnecessary during periods of low output and high unemployment?
   b. Why did Keynes disagree with neoclassical economists on this issue?

Mountain or Mirage

THE DEBATE OVER PUBLIC DEBT

At first sight, the figures are astounding: in 1982, public debt was under $5000 per Canadian; by 2013, the federal government's debt rose to about $17 100 per capita. And supplementing this 2013 figure is another amount of just over $14 500 that each Canadian owes because of the debts of the provincial and territorial governments—making a total of just over $31 600 a head.

Is public debt too high? Are the potential costs of this debt exaggerated by those who want less government involvement in the economy? Or does the truth lie somewhere in-between? Because the costs are great, whatever the truth—huge debt at one extreme, potentially reduced government programs at the other—this is a question not only for economists and policy-makers, but also for the public as a whole. Let us take a look at the opposing perceptions.

Debt Problems Are Overemphasized

People who believe that the negative aspects of public debt have been exaggerated give four main arguments: public debt can increase current output; most of this debt is owed to ourselves; we should take into account the assets created by this debt; and as a percentage of GDP, the debt is still lower than it has sometimes been in the past.

Benefits of Public Debt

As discussed in Chapter 9, the amount by which real output falls short of its potential level represents the permanent loss of output due to high unemployment. To the extent that expansionary fiscal policy minimizes this gap, it provides a significant benefit, both by supplementing the economy's output and by reducing the human costs of unemployment. According to this argument, any disadvantages caused by the increases in federal debt are minor compared with its positive contribution to economic growth.

Debt to Ourselves

The federal government issues bonds to deal with the debt. However, most federal bonds—just over 82 percent of the total value—are actually a liability Canada owes to Canadian bondholders. Supporters of fiscal policy stress this number's significance. They argue that when interest is paid on Canadian-owned public debt, funds are simply taken from one group of Canadians in the form of taxes or new borrowing and given to another group of Canadians. In other words, the total "economic pie" does not get bigger or smaller—just the sizes of the slices.

Assets versus Liabilities

When debt is used to create productive assets, it can be defended in the same way as the debt acquired by businesses for investment purposes. While Canadian government investment in capital goods—at least as defined in the national accounts—has fallen in recent decades as a percentage of GDP, supporters of fiscal policy suggest that the problem lies in the definitions. They believe that we should define productive assets more widely to include the country's human resources, whose worth is promoted through such expenditures as education. Unfortunately, it is difficult to put a value on a country's stock of productive assets when they are broadly defined in this way.

Comparisons with the Past

Because of substantial inflation and economic growth over the years, debt trends expressed in current-year dollars are inadequate. A much better indication of the economy's ability to bear public debt is to express the debt as a percentage of nominal GDP, as shown in Figure A. For example, the $602.4 billion public debt at the end of the 2012–2013 year equalled 33 percent of the 2012 nominal GDP of $1820.0 billion [= ($602.4 b. ÷ $1820.0 b.) × 100%]. In contrast, the federal government's debt charges of $29.2 billion equalled 1.6 percent [= $29.2 b. ÷ $1820.0 b.) × 100%]. It is interesting to note that, when measured in this way (column 3), public debt has sometimes been at higher levels in the past. For example, Canada's public debt in 1936–1937, while only $3.1 billion in nominal dollars, was 67 percent of that year's GDP. By 1946–1947, after federal borrowing to help finance Canada's involvement in World War II, public debt was over 100 percent of that year's GDP—a figure much higher than today.

Public Debt Is a Major Problem

People who are concerned about levels of public debt concentrate on a different set of arguments: the trend of public debt charges in relation to the size of the economy, the recent significance of provincial and territorial government debts, the apparent limits to future tax increases, and the potential future burdens that government debt may place on Canadians.

FIGURE A — Public Debt and GDP (billions of current dollars)

(1) Year	(2) Public Debt (billions of current-year $)	(3) Public Debt (% of nominal GDP)	(4) Public Debt Charges (% of nominal GDP)
1926–1927	2.3	46	2.5
1936–1937	3.1	67	3.0
1946–1947	12.7	107	3.9
1956–1957	11.4	35	1.5
1966–1967	17.7	27	1.8
1976–1977	41.5	21	2.4
1986–1987	257.7	50	5.6
1996–1997	562.9	67	5.6
2006–2007	467.3	32	2.3
2012–2013	602.4	33	1.6

As a percentage of nominal GDP, public debt rose between the 1920s and 1940s, and then fell until the 1970s, before rising somewhat until the mid-1990s. However, high interest rates during the 1980s and the first part of the 1990s meant that as a percentage of nominal GDP, public debt charges were higher than before. After falling during the early and mid-2000s, by the early 2010s, public debt had risen to levels last seen in the late 1990s, with public debt charges still relatively manageable thanks to very low interest rates

Sources: Department of Finance Canada, *Quarterly Economic Review: Special Report* (March 1992), pp. 33–34; Fiscal Reference Tables (October 2013), pp. 9–10; Reproduced with the permission of the Minister of Finance Canada, 2014.

Public Debt Charges

Although public debt as a proportion of GDP is lower today than during some other periods in Canada's history, public debt charges—or the annual interest payments on this debt—rose substantially during the 1970s and 1980s. As shown in column 4 of Figure A, public debt charges as a percentage of GDP were much higher in the 1980s and 1990s than in any previous decade since the 1920s, with public debt charges reaching almost 6 percent of nominal GDP in the mid-1990s. This trend was due to high real interest rates during the 1980s and the first part of the 1990s. A subsequent drop in real interest rates has eased the problem, especially the very low interest rates in the aftermath of the 2008–2009 recession.

Provincial and Territorial Debts

The comparison of public debt and nominal GDP shown in Figure A underestimates the overall expansion of debt for all levels of government in Canada. In former decades, the debts of the provincial and territorial governments in Canada tended to be relatively minor. At the end of the 1981–1982 fiscal year, for example, the combined net debts of the provincial and territorial governments represented only 4 percent of Canada's GDP. By the end of the 2012–2013 fiscal year, however, this combined debt stood at $509.2 billion, or 28 percent of the country's GDP. Adding this debt to the federal debt means that the total debt of both levels of government was over to 60 percent of GDP—even before adding in local government debt and other government obligations incorporated in debt-to-GDP numbers such as those found in Figure 11.7.

Tax Limits

When total government debt charges rise, Canadian governments can keep their budget deficits in check either by increasing taxes or by reducing other expenditures, known as program spending. In the past, tax increases have commonly been used as a way of limiting budget deficits. However, Canadians have grown more reluctant to shoulder further tax burdens, making it less likely that tax rates can rise much beyond present levels. In the 1990s, for example, governments were forced to engage in unpopular cuts in program spending given the lack of popular support for deficit reduction via higher taxes.

Potential Future Burdens

Many economists argue that government debt imposes future burdens on the entire Canadian economy. According to the *crowding-out effect*, higher levels of government borrowing raise the demand for loans. This leads to an increase in interest rates, causing businesses to reduce their investment spending. The result is a lower future stock of real capital in the economy, and therefore a lower rate of economic growth.

Another potential burden of government debt is the portion owed to foreigners. Especially because of the attractiveness of provincial bonds to foreign financial investors (largely because of the relatively high interest rates on these bonds), almost one-third of Canada's combined federal and provincial debt is now foreign-held, and, until recently, this proportion had risen considerably. Unlike the case of domestically-held debt, the interest payments on this debt represent a transfer of purchasing power from Canadians to foreigners. The higher the proportion of public debt owed to foreigners, therefore, the greater this transfer will be in the future.

1. During a certain fiscal year, federal spending excluding public debt charges is $180 billion, and federal tax revenues are $200 billion.

   a. What is the federal government's budget deficit if the interest rate is 6 percent and public debt at the start of the year is $500 billion? If the interest rate is still 6 percent but public debt at the start of the year is $600 billion? What conclusions can you draw concerning the relationship between budget deficits and the size of the public debt?

   b. What is the federal government's budget deficit if the interest rate is 5 percent while public debt at the start of the year is $500 billion? If public debt at the start of the year is still $500 billion but the interest rate is 6 percent? What conclusions can you draw concerning the relationship between budget deficits and interest rates?

2. "A reduction in public debt should cause an increase in investment." Evaluate this statement making reference to the crowding-out effect.

CHAPTER 12

Money

Money talks, and, depending on who is listening, it can say a variety of things. Money's allure is undeniable. However, it is neither static nor easy to define; it has taken many forms and continues to evolve today. This chapter highlights four main issues: the functions money performs in modern economies; the connection between money and interest rates; how banks help create money; and why governments choose to so closely oversee the financial system.

> The two greatest inventions of the human mind are writing and money—the common language of intelligence and the common language of self-interest.
>
> —HONORÉ-GABRIEL MIRABEAU, FRENCH STATESMAN AND ORATOR

LEARNING OBJECTIVES   After reading this chapter, you will be able to:

LO 1

Outline the functions of money, its components, and the various definitions of money

LO 2

Identify the demand for and supply of money and describe equilibrium in the money market

LO 3

Explain how money is created and define the money multiplier

12.1 | Money and Its Uses

The Functions of Money

Money serves three separate functions in any economy: it provides a means of exchange, a store of purchasing power, and a measure of value.

MEANS OF EXCHANGE

The most important function of money is that it acts as a means of payment whenever items are bought and sold. Without money, market participants must trade one product for another product, a transaction known as **barter**.

Barter is an unwieldy method of exchanging products. Someone purchasing an item must find a seller who wants what the purchaser is offering in return. In other words, there must be a **coincidence of wants** between both parties. For example, a barber who wants to buy a clock must find a clockmaker who wants a haircut. Because a coincidence of wants is usually difficult to achieve, trade is discouraged, so most people living in a barter system produce many items for themselves.

Money overcomes these problems. The barber can deal with any clockmaker and pay in money, which the clockmaker can then use to purchase a wide range of items.

The benefits of money as a means of exchange are far-reaching. People can minimize the time they spend finding others with whom they can buy and sell. They can also focus their productive activity by devoting themselves to economic pursuits in which they are most adept: the barber can stick to cutting hair and the clockmaker to making clocks. Specialization promotes the division of labour and allows an economy to achieve higher levels of output. Therefore, the use of money not only facilitates transactions of goods and services–it also raises living standards.

STORE OF PURCHASING POWER

Money's second function is providing a safe and accessible store of wealth. Money is an attractive store of purchasing power during the period between the time it is earned and the time it is spent.

There are both benefits and drawbacks associated with holding wealth as money. Money's major advantage is its **liquidity**, or the ease with which it can be turned into a means of payment. Assets are most liquid when they can be quickly turned into money with little loss in value. All financial assets are liquid to some degree, but none as much as money, which is perfectly liquid by its very nature.

Recall, however, that for any economic choice, there is an opportunity cost. In this case, the cost of holding wealth in the form of money is the income sacrificed by not holding it in some other form. For example, someone who holds wealth by stashing a stack of $100 bills in a cookie jar is sacrificing the income the wealth could earn if it were converted into a stock or bond. As a result, people hold wealth as money when the benefits of liquidity outweigh the income that could be earned by holding it in another form.

barter: a system of trading one product for another

coincidence of wants: the situation where someone purchasing an item finds a seller who wants what the purchaser is offering in return

liquidity: the ease with which an asset can be converted into a means of payment

MEASURE OF VALUE

Money also provides buyers and sellers with a **unit of account**, or pricing standard. The unit of account allows all products to be valued consistently against a common measure–in other words, it provides a point of comparison between, for example, apples and oranges. So, if apples cost $2 per kilogram and oranges cost $4 per kilogram, it is easy to see that oranges cost twice as much as apples. Recall from Chapter 8 that the unit of account does the same on a grander scale; expressing Gross Domestic Product (GDP) as a money value simplifies the picture by allowing a wide range of products to be quantified and combined.

In contrast, a barter economy requires many measures of value. The question, "How much does this cost?" would bring the inevitable reply, "It depends on what you've got." A clock, for example, might be exchanged for 100 apples, 50 oranges, 20 loaves of bread, two haircuts, or some number of any other product a market participant is offering. As well as creating a confusion of prices, a barter economy is difficult to measure as an entire entity.

unit of account: a pricing standard that allows all products to be valued consistently

THE CANADIAN FINANCIAL SYSTEM

Now that we have defined the functions money serves, we will consider the system in which it operates, as well as the supply of money. The supply of money is closely associated with institutions known as **deposit-takers**, which accept funds provided by savers and lend these funds to borrowers. For the deposit-taker, the deposits it accepts and owes back to savers are its liabilities; the funds it lends to borrowers and which borrowers owe the deposit-taker are its assets. These institutions make a profit by paying lower interest rates on deposits than they charge on loans.

deposit-takers: institutions or businesses that accept funds provided by savers and lend these funds to borrowers

Not all funds flowing into the institution flow out. Deposit-takers also keep on hand some amount, known as **cash reserves**, so that depositors can withdraw funds when they request them. Because deposit-takers make little or no income from cash reserves, they hold only the minimum of their assets in this form.

cash reserves: funds kept on hand by deposit-takers to meet the needs of depositors withdrawing funds

Deposit-takers fall into two categories: chartered banks and near banks.

CHARTERED BANKS

Chartered banks form the backbone of Canada's financial system. Unlike other deposit-takers, these institutions are allowed to sell a wide range of financial services through a charter they receive from the federal government.

chartered banks: deposit-takers allowed by federal charter to offer a wide range of financial services

While 80 chartered banks operate in Canada, six big banks dominate the sector: RBC (Royal Bank), TD (Toronto-Dominion) Canada Trust Bank, Scotiabank, BMO (Bank of Montreal), CIBC (Canadian Imperial Bank of Commerce), and the National Bank of Canada. Each of these banks has many branches, following what is known as a branch banking system. Together, the "big six" control the bulk of Canadian chartered banks' assets, as shown in Figure 12.1. Most of the remaining chartered banks are relatively small foreign-owned banks. Apart from American and Mexican banks, which are exempt because of recent trade agreements, these banks are limited by law to 12 percent of Canadian chartered bank assets.

The Canadian chartered banking system is, therefore, an oligopoly. While the reduced competition may lead to some market inefficiencies, it also enhances the financial soundness of the Canadian system. By comparison, there are over 7000 commercial banks in the United States. About a third of them operate under federal law and are known as national banks. The others, called state banks, are controlled by state governments. Many of these state banks are

FIGURE 12.1 Canadian Chartered Banks and Near Banks

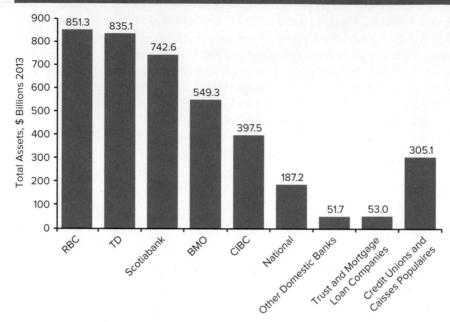

The "big six" chartered banks hold the lion's share of Canadian chartered bank assets, which include funds given out as loans as well as other forms of financial holdings. Their combined assets are over 10 times those of Canadian near banks.

Sources: Bank of Canada, *Bank of Canada Banking and Financial Statistics* (December 2013), Tables D1–D2; Canadian Bankers Association, *Financial Results 2012–13 Fiscal Year,* Third Quarter ended July 31 (July 2013), p. 2.

relatively small and have few branches. While competition is enhanced by the number of players, the modest size of each bank can increase the chance of financial difficulties.

NEAR BANKS

near banks: deposit-takers that are not chartered and have more specialized services; mainly trust companies, mortgage loan companies, and credit unions

In contrast to chartered banks, **near banks** are not chartered and have more specialized services. The most important are trust companies, mortgage loan companies, and credit unions.

Trust companies administer various types of accounts, including estates and trust funds. They also compete with chartered banks by taking deposits and granting loans, mainly to households. As their name suggests, mortgage loan companies specialize in granting mortgages and raise some of their funds through deposit-taking. A mortgage is a loan whose collateral is in the form of land and buildings. Credit unions (called caisses populaires in Québec, where they are particularly prevalent) are non-profit institutions that take deposits and grant loans to their members.

OTHER FINANCIAL INSTITUTIONS

In addition to deposit-takers–especially chartered banks–there are other types of financial institutions: insurance companies and investment dealers. Insurance companies offer insurance policies to their clients and use the funds to buy various types of income-producing financial assets. Investment dealers buy and sell financial securities, such as stocks and bonds, for their customers.

THE FINANCIAL SYSTEM

Traditionally, chartered banks, trust companies, insurance companies, and investment dealers formed the four pillars of the financial system. Each group had its specialized functions. In the 1980s, however, regulations governing financial institutions in Canada and in other countries were loosened. Financial deregulation, as it is called, has allowed each institution to perform a wider range of functions.

For example, chartered banks have taken on some of the functions of other financial institutions. "Financial supermarkets" have sprung up to give a complete range of financial services under one corporate roof. While deregulation has promoted competition and efficiency, it has led to several giant companies (primarily chartered banks) controlling most of the Canadian financial system.

The Supply of Money

The supply of money is made up of currency and some deposits.

CURRENCY

Currency includes paper notes, such as 20-dollar bills, issued by Canada's central bank, the Bank of Canada. It also includes coinage produced by the Royal Mint. Except in highly unusual circumstances, currency serves exclusively as a means of exchange. Even in the automated economies of today, it continues to be an attractive way to pay in many types of transactions. Not only is currency convenient and universally accepted, sometimes (especially in transactions involving illegal activities or tax avoidance) it provides users with the added benefit of anonymity.

currency: paper money and coins

DEPOSITS

Recall that deposits are given to deposit-takers and lent out to borrowers, who pay interest. In this way, chartered banks and near banks make their profits. Deposits can be classified according to the conditions of their use. In general, the access depositors have to their funds determines the interest rates paid on deposits. The longer a deposit-taker can make use of the funds and the fewer the services the deposit-taker provides, the higher the interest rate.

Demand Deposits

In some cases, depositors can demand immediate access to their money. Such deposits are called **demand deposits** and take the form of current and personal chequing accounts. Depositors can withdraw money directly from the bank or can write cheques, which are a convenient way for depositors to authorize banks to pay a certain sum to a named person or institution. In return for easy access to their deposits and because processing cheques is a relatively expensive operation, depositors receive a lower interest rate, or no interest, on their money. Traditionally, only chartered banks accept demand deposits.

demand deposits: accounts of funds to which depositors have immediate access

Notice Deposits

Deposit-takers can require notice before depositors withdraw funds in certain cases. **Notice deposits**, as these are called, pay substantial rates of interest but limit or exclude cheque-writing. Traditionally, both chartered banks and near banks accept notice deposits. Notice deposits may have chequing privileges, in which case they are called chequable notice deposits, while those without chequing privileges are referred to as non-chequable.

notice deposits: accounts of funds for which deposit-takers may require notice before withdrawals can be made

Term Deposits

term deposits: accounts of funds to which depositors have no access for a fixed period of time

When depositors guarantee that they will not withdraw their funds for a fixed period of time, deposit-takers can pay a higher interest rate. **Term deposits** are traditionally accepted by chartered banks and near banks. Term deposits made by households are called personal term deposits, and those made by businesses are known as non-personal term deposits.

Foreign Currency Deposits

foreign currency deposits: accounts of funds held by Canadian residents that are valued in foreign currency

Some deposits provided by chartered banks in Canada are valued in terms of a foreign currency–usually the American dollar. These **foreign currency deposits**, which are held by Canadian residents, are treated as a separate class of deposit.

Money Defined

What is money? The definitions range from the very narrow to the broad. In the following sections and in Figure 12.2, we will examine the four most common definitions used by economists and government decision-makers: M1+, M2, M3, and M2+.

| FIGURE 12.2 | The Canadian Money Supply |

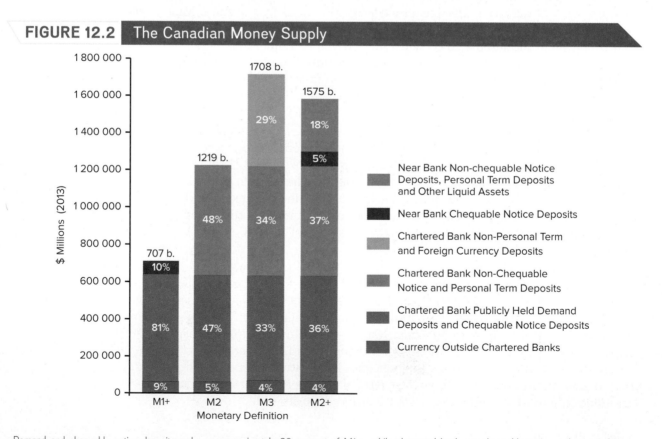

Demand and chequable notice deposits make up approximately 90 percent of M1+, while chartered bank non-chequable notice and personal term deposits make up almost half of M2. These deposits are less dominant in M3. M2+ includes deposits made in near banks (as well as other liquid assets) as well as similar deposits made in chartered banks.

Source: Bank of Canada, *Bank of Canada Banking and Financial Statistics*, (December 2013), Table E1.

M1+

The narrowest definition of money now used in Canada is **M1+**. Its components–currency outside chartered banks, publicly-held demand deposits at chartered banks, chequable notice deposits at chartered banks, and chequable notice deposits at near banks–are the most intensively used forms of money. Note that only currency circulating outside chartered banks is part of M1+; cash reserves held by chartered banks are not included. Also note that only demand deposits held by the public at chartered banks are included; government-owned deposits are left out. Currency outside chartered banks and chequable deposits at chartered banks (both demand and chequable notice deposits) also appears in all other money definitions.

M1+: the narrowest definition of money, consisting of currency outside chartered banks, publicly-held demand deposits at chartered banks, and chequable notice deposits at chartered banks and near banks

M2

M2 is a broader definition of money that includes not only currency outside chartered banks, publicly-held demand deposits at chartered banks, and chequable notice deposits at chartered banks, but also funds from non-chequable notice deposits and personal term deposits at chartered banks. While currency and chequable deposits are perfectly liquid, non-chequable notice deposits and personal term deposits are often converted into another form before being used as a means of payment.

M2: a broader definition of money, consisting of currency outside chartered banks, plus the following chartered bank deposits: publicly-held demand deposits, notice deposits (both chequable and non-chequable), and personal term deposits

M3

An even broader definition of the money supply is **M3**. M3 includes the components of M2 (currency outside chartered banks plus publicly-held demand deposits, notice deposits, and personal term deposits at chartered banks), as well as non-personal term deposits and foreign currency deposits at chartered banks. These additional types of deposits are relatively liquid, although less so than those included in M2.

M3: the definition of money consisting of M2 plus non-personal term deposits and foreign currency deposits at chartered banks

M2+

The growing similarity between chartered banks and near banks in the Canadian financial system means that economists have been paying more attention to a fourth definition of the money supply. **M2+** includes currency outside chartered banks plus publicly-held demand deposits, notice deposits, and personal term deposits at both chartered banks and near banks. Some similar assets issued by other financial institutions are also included. It does not, however, include any non-personal term deposits or foreign currency deposits.

M2+: the definition of money consisting of M2 plus corresponding deposits at near banks and some other liquid assets

Note how the definitions of M2 and M3 build on one another, and how the definitions of M1+ and M2+ also build on one another. In contrast to M1+, other definitions of money include what is sometimes called **near money**. Near money includes all deposits at chartered banks and near banks except publicly-held demand deposits at chartered banks and chequable notice deposits at chartered banks and near banks (which are included in M1+). It also includes some other highly liquid assets, such as Canada Savings Bonds. While relatively easily converted to a means of payment, near money is less frequently used than money as defined by M1+.

near money: all deposits not included in M1+ along with some other highly liquid assets

Choosing a Definition

Since currency, demand deposits, and chequable notice deposits are used almost solely as means of payment, they seem to fit best the definition of money. Therefore, many economists view M1+ as the most accurate measure of the money supply. Others believe that M1+ is too narrow; these economists prefer broader definitions, especially M2+. They point to recent innovations in payment methods that have made the accounts included in M2+ more liquid.

THE ROLE OF CREDIT CARDS

credit card: a means of payment that provides instantly borrowed funds

One of the main causes of the increasing liquidity of M2+ is the ability many consumers now have to pay with "plastic." A **credit card** provides its holder with the opportunity to buy goods and services with instantly borrowed funds. **When a credit card is used for a purchase, the lending institution makes a loan or "credit" to the user equal to the amount of the sale. This loan lasts as long as it takes the credit card user to pay off the monthly bill.**

Contrary to popular perception, credit cards are not money; they are simply an easy way for buyers to borrow funds for short periods. However, credit cards do have an indirect effect on the money supply by altering the way depositors use their deposit accounts.

Well-timed purchases made with credit cards do not have to be settled for over a month. So, for example, a person making a $50 purchase with a credit card is essentially taking out a short-term loan for the same amount. As long as this loan is paid back promptly, the purchaser is charged no interest. If credit card balances are not cleared monthly, however, the interest rate charged is higher than on most other consumer loans.

About half of all credit card users pay off their outstanding balances each month. Rather than paying currency for purchases throughout a month, card users can keep their funds in their deposit accounts until credit card payments are due. Because they can maintain their deposit accounts longer, they can accumulate more interest. If card users pay off their balance monthly (and so incur no interest charges), they can profit by using credit cards effectively. This trend to use deposit accounts in combination with credit cards has led some economists to suggest that M2+ is increasingly the most accurate measure of the money supply.

THE ROLE OF DEBIT CARDS

debit card: a means of payment that instantaneously transfers funds from buyer to seller

Buyers have one more way of paying with plastic. A **debit card** allows a payment to be made through an instantaneous transfer of funds. While similar in appearance to credit cards, debit cards represent a different type of transaction because the buyer's account is instantly reduced or "debited" by the amount of the purchase. Like credit cards and cheques, debit cards are not money. They are simply a convenient way for holders to access monetary balances in the same way that cheques are.

Unlike credit cards, which are issued only to people who have an acceptable credit history, debit cards can be employed by virtually any depositor. They can be of particular benefit to people who are tempted to overuse the instant spending power provided by credit cards. There are costs associated with debit cards, however. Retailers who use them must pay for access to a sophisticated computer system that tracks these transactions. These retailers tend to pass on this cost by charging higher prices to the consumer. However, in the long term, there is a downward pressure on prices as business costs associated with handling cash are reduced.

THINKING ABOUT ECONOMICS

Will cash eventually disappear?

Because everyone with a deposit account can use a debit card, it is possible that paper currency may one day be phased out. A cashless society would bring with it some significant benefits. Conceivably, consumers would face lower prices as the costs associated with handling cash fall, while the problems of conventional theft would be reduced. Also, since records would exist for all transactions, it would be easier for governments to collect taxes and stamp out illegal activities.

However, a cashless society also has potential drawbacks. Critics point out that governments may intervene unduly. Computer records of citizens' transactions and activities would also mean a loss of privacy—not just to governments, but potentially to computer hackers engaged in fraud and other illegal activities. In addition, the expense and complexities of cashless business would shut down some businesses and deter others from starting. And, of course, many of those involved in the underground economy, which depends on cash, would not welcome its demise.

A widespread desire for the benefits associated with traditional cash is leading to new forms of electronic currency. "E-currency," whose worth is measured in digital value units (DVUs), uses encryption technology and digital signatures to make anonymous payments possible. Interestingly, it is private institutions, rather than governments, which are issuing these new forms of currency.

QUESTION **How is the creation of new e-currencies affecting the ability of national governments to control the money supply?**

BRIEF REVIEW

1. Money serves as a means of exchange, a store of purchasing power, and a measure of value. In contrast, barter is a cumbersome system of exchange.

2. Canada's financial system includes chartered banks, near banks, insurance companies, and investment dealers. Until recently, increasing deregulation changed the functions of financial institutions, though the 2008–2009 recession has led governments to tighten regulation of the financial system.

3. Deposit-takers accept deposits and grant loans. Deposits vary according to their conditions of use and the interest rates they provide.

4. Money may be defined narrowly as currency outside chartered banks, publicly-held demand deposits at chartered banks, and chequable notice deposits at chartered banks and near banks (M1+), or it may be defined more broadly to include other assets.

5. Credit and debit cards are not directly part of the money supply, but are gradually changing the use of money.

12.1 | PRACTICE PROBLEM

1. The table below provides data for a hypothetical economy. Use this data to find:
   a. M1+
   b. M2
   c. M2+

Currency outside chartered banks	$25 billion
Chequable notice deposits at near banks	$17 billion
Personal term deposits at near banks	$18 billion
Non-chequable notice deposits at chartered banks	$36 billion
Personal term deposits at chartered banks	$45 billion
Other liquid assets included in M2+	$20 billion
Publicly-held deposits at chartered banks	$12 billion
Currency inside chartered banks	$15 billion
Chequable notice deposits at chartered banks	$28 billion
Non-chequable notice deposits at near banks	$32 billion

12.2 | The Money Market

The Demand for Money

Recall that money functions as a means of exchange, a store of purchasing power, and a measure of value. In the economy as a whole, money is demanded for reasons related to the first two functions.

TRANSACTIONS DEMAND

If there is a rise in an economy's real output or price level, the total value of transactions expands. This increases the demand for money. Conversely, a fall in real output or the price level decreases the total value of transactions and the demand for money. In other words, changes in the total value of transactions affect the **transactions demand** for money, which is connected to money's use as a means of exchange.

transactions demand: the demand for money related to its use as a means of exchange

ASSET DEMAND

In contrast, the **asset demand** for money is associated with money's function as a store of purchasing power. As discussed earlier, the main cost of holding money is the added income that could have been earned by converting it into a higher-paying asset, such as a bond.

asset demand: the demand for money related to its use as a store of purchasing power

Bonds are formal contracts that set out the amount borrowed, by whom, for what period of time, and at what interest rate. Most bonds can be bought and sold among lenders on the open market. When bonds "mature," or reach the end of their term, the bond issuer pays the principal to the bondholder.

On the bond market, prices for bonds are inversely related to the prevailing interest rate. To see why, suppose you purchased a $1000 bond with an interest rate specified as 6 percent per annum. In other words, you are guaranteed an annual interest payment of $60 until the bond matures, at which time you, or whoever else holds the bond, will be repaid the $1000 principal. Two years later, you want to sell the bond, but the prevailing interest rate is 12 percent. In other words, newly issued $1000 bonds are promising annual interest payments of $120, while the bond you own promises only a $60 annual interest payment. Because its annual payment is half that of new bonds, your bond will fall in price to about $500, or half the value of a newly issued $1000 bond. Similarly, if the interest rate declines from its initial value of 6 percent to 3 percent, the price of your bond will double from its original value of $1000 to about $2000, since it provides twice the annual interest payment ($60) than the payment found on a newly issued $1000 bond ($30).

Bonds are the most popular way for governments and large businesses to raise funds. They are also attractive assets. Because they can be easily bought and sold before their term has ended, they offer liquidity as well as relatively high rates of return in exchange for the risk associated with changes in bond prices. For individuals who hold wealth, therefore, bonds offer the likeliest alternative to holding money—depending on how individuals view the trade off between bonds' higher rates of return and higher risk.

For these reasons, the asset demand for money is inversely related to the nominal interest rate on bonds. When this interest rate increases, the prices of bonds fall. Lower bond prices cause some individuals to convert their money into bonds, reducing the asset demand for money. Similarly, a reduction in the nominal interest rate means that the prices of bonds rise. Higher-priced bonds become a less attractive option for wealth holders, causing more of them to hold money rather than bonds, thus pushing up the asset demand for money.

Money demand represents the amounts of money demanded, unadjusted for inflation, at all possible interest rates at a given real output and price level. Money demand expressed in a table gives the **money demand schedule**; expressed on a graph, it gives the **money demand curve** (D_m). As Figure 12.3 shows, the money demand curve has a negative slope. This slope is determined by the asset demand for money, which is inversely related to interest rates. As we have just seen, a rise in the nominal interest rate on bonds reduces the asset demand for money, while a fall in the nominal interest rate increases the asset demand. Therefore, a change in the asset demand causes a change in the quantity of money demanded, or a movement along the money demand curve.

In contrast, a change in transactions demand changes the amounts demanded at all interest rates—that is, it causes a shift in the money demand curve. An increase in either real output or the price level raises the transactions demand

money demand: the amounts of money demanded at all possible interest rates

money demand schedule: money demand expressed in a table

money demand curve: money demand expressed on a graph

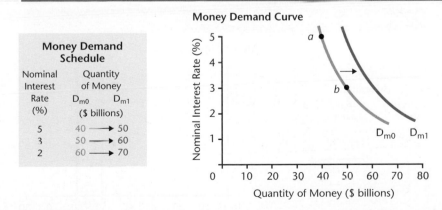

FIGURE 12.3   The Demand for Money

Because a greater quantity of money is demanded at lower nominal interest rates, the money demand curve has a negative slope. A change in the interest rate causes a change in the asset demand for money, which is shown as a movement along the money demand curve. For example, a rise in the interest rate causes a decrease in the quantity of money demanded (from point b to point a). An increase in real output or the price level causes money demand to increase at all interest rates, as shown by the shift from D_m0 to D_m1.

for money at every possible interest rate. Hence, the money demand curve shifts to the right, from D_{m0} to D_{m1}, as shown in Figure 12.3. Conversely, a decrease in either real output or the price level shifts the money demand curve to the left.

The Supply of Money

money supply: a set amount of money in the economy, as determined by government decision-makers

money supply schedule: money supply expressed in a table

money supply curve: money supply expressed on a graph

While money demanded is inversely related to interest rates, the **money supply** is a set amount, unadjusted for inflation, determined by government decision-makers. As Figure 12.4 shows, money supply can be expressed in a table, giving the **money supply schedule**, or on a graph, giving the **money supply curve** (S_m). No matter what the nominal interest rate, the amount of money supplied is a constant value, as depicted by the vertical supply curve (S_{m0}). Only when government decision-makers decide to change the money supply does the supply curve shift. Therefore, the supply curve shifts to the right, from S_{m0} to S_{m1}, only when the government increases the money supply. Likewise, the money supply curve shifts to the left only when the government decreases the money supply.

Equilibrium in the Money Market

The demand and supply of money interact in the money market to bring about a state of equilibrium. As shown in Figure 12.5, the equilibrium level of the nominal interest rate is found at the intersection of the money demand and money supply curves. As usual, surpluses and shortages help bring about equilibrium in the market.

When the interest rate is above its equilibrium level–for example, at 5 percent as opposed to 3 percent in Figure 12.5–there is a surplus of money. In other words, more money is supplied than is demanded. As people try to rid themselves of money and buy assets, such as bonds, that will provide high earnings, the demand for these assets rises, pushing up their price and causing the nominal interest rate to fall. This trend of falling interest rates continues until the discrepancy between the demand and supply of money is eliminated.

In the opposite case, the interest rate falls short of the equilibrium value, as at 2 percent on the graph, causing a shortage of money. In other words, more money is demanded than is supplied. As people try to sell assets, such as bonds, to acquire money, the price of these assets falls, causing the nominal interest rate to rise until the equilibrium point is attained.

FIGURE 12.4 The Supply of Money

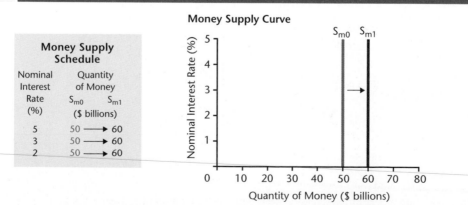

Because government policy-makers determine the supply of money at any given time, the money supply curve is a vertical line at that amount. Any change in the money supply results in a shift of the vertical line, as shown, for example, by the shift from S_{m0} to S_{m1}.

FIGURE 12.5 Equilibrium in the Money Market

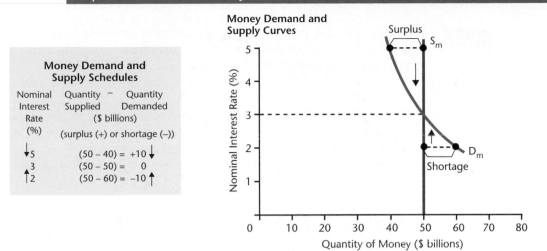

Money Demand and Supply Curves

Money Demand and Supply Schedules

Nominal Interest Rate (%)	Quantity Supplied	–	Quantity Demanded
		($ billions)	
		(surplus (+) or shortage (−))	
↓5	(50 − 40) =	+10 ↓	
3	(50 − 50) =	0	
↑2	(50 − 60) =	−10 ↑	

When the nominal interest rate exceeds its equilibrium value, the quantity of money supplied exceeds quantity demanded. This surplus leads to more buying of bonds, forcing bond prices up and the nominal interest rate down until the quantity of money demanded and supplied are the same. When the nominal interest rate is below its equilibrium value, the opposite occurs. A shortage of money pushes the interest rate up until the equilibrium point is reached.

BRIEF REVIEW

1. Demand for money is of two types, each of which is related to a function of money. Transactions demand relates to the function of money as a means of exchange; asset demand relates to the function of money as a store of purchasing power.

2. Money demand is the amount of money demanded at all possible interest rates, which can be expressed in a table or on a graph. The money demand curve has a negative slope because of the inverse relationship of money demanded to interest rates.

3. Money supply is a set amount that is determined by government decision-makers. The money supply curve is a vertical line at this set amount.

4 The economy's equilibrium interest rate and money supply occur at the intersection of the money demand and money supply curves.

12.2 | PRACTICE PROBLEMS

1. Explain what happens in the money market in the following situations:
   a. The nominal interest rate is above its equilibrium level.
   b. The nominal interest rate is below its equilibrium level.
2. A $20 000 bond provides an interest rate specified as 5 percent of the bond's initial face value per annum.
   a. What is the annual interest payment on this bond?
   b. What would happen to the price of this bond if the prevailing interest rate moves to 2 percent?
   c. What would happen to the price of this bond if the prevailing interest rate moves to 10 percent?

12.3 | Money Creation

When setting the money supply, government policy-makers must take into account the actions of deposit-takers. This is because a substantial portion of money in the economy is held in the form of deposits.

Recall that deposit-takers receive deposits from savers and lend to borrowers, while keeping some cash reserves on hand for withdrawals by depositors. By charging higher interest rates to borrowers than they pay to depositors, deposit-takers make profits. In a sense, through this process of receiving deposits and lending funds, chartered banks and near banks create deposit money. This is not by some trick of magic, but by the roles played by cash reserves and the profit motive.

Desired Reserves

Until 1994, chartered banks were legally required to hold certain levels of cash reserves, more than near banks were required to hold. Since then, both chartered banks and near banks have kept only **desired reserves**, which are the minimum amounts of cash necessary to satisfy anticipated withdrawal demands.

desired reserves: minimum cash reserves that deposit-takers hold to satisfy anticipated withdrawal demands

The Reserve Ratio

In general, the more money a deposit-taker holds in deposits, the greater the withdrawals it can expect. Therefore, the best way to deal with anticipated withdrawals is for the deposit-taker to hold a certain portion of deposits in the form of cash reserves. This portion, which can be expressed as a percentage or in decimal terms, is the **reserve ratio**. Suppose, for example, that a bank has a reserve ratio of 0.10. If the bank has deposits of $100 million, then it will hold 10 percent of this dollar value as desired reserves (=$100 million × 0.10):

reserve ratio: desired reserves expressed as a percentage of deposits or as a decimal

$$\text{Reserve ratio} = \frac{\text{desired reserves}}{\text{deposits}}$$

$$0.10 = \frac{\$10 \text{ million}}{\$100 \text{ million}}$$

Different types of deposits have different reserve ratios. For example, banks hold higher reserves against demand deposits than against notice deposits. However, to examine the process of money creation, we will simplify matters by assuming a uniform reserve ratio.

Excess Reserves

At times, deposit-takers find that their cash reserves exceed desired levels, or they have **excess reserves**. For example, a chartered bank with deposits of $100 million and desired reserves of $10 million may find itself holding $14 million in actual cash reserves:

excess reserves: cash reserves that are in excess of desired reserves

$$\text{Excess reserves} = \text{cash reserves} - \text{desired reserves}$$

$$\$4 \text{ million} = \$14 \text{ million} - \$10 \text{ million}$$

Because idle cash reserves earn no profit, deposit-takers will try to transform any excess reserves into income-producing assets as quickly as possible. Therefore, they lend out the full amount of excess reserves. In our example, the bank will lend out the $4 million excess to borrowers.

The Money Creation Process

To see how lending out excess reserves "creates" money, consider an example. For the time being, we will make two key assumptions. First, the public holds money in the form of deposits and uses only cheques for transactions. Second, all deposits are made to one sort of deposit-taker, which we will simply call banks, and all deposits are of one type, which allows cheques to be written against them. We will also assume the banks' reserve ratio for their deposits to be 0.10, or 10 percent.

As we look at the money creation process, keep in mind that the main assets of a bank (found in the left column of its balance sheet) are its cash reserves and its loans. A bank's main liabilities (found in the right column of its balance sheet) are its customers' deposits.

FIRST TRANSACTION

At the outset, Cabot Bank has cash reserves equal to desired reserves. However, Saver A receives $1000 in currency and immediately deposits it in Cabot Bank. As shown in Figure 12.6, Cabot Bank has a new cash asset as well as a new deposit liability to Saver A, each equalling $1000. So far, there has been no change in the amount of money in the economy, only in who holds it. Because the $1000 in currency is transformed into $1000 held in a deposit, no money is added to the money supply. (Recall that the $1000 in currency sitting in the vault of Cabot Bank is not considered part of the money supply.)

SECOND TRANSACTION

Because of Saver A's deposit, Cabot Bank's total deposits increase by $1000. At the same time, the actual cash reserves increase by $1000 as well. However, with a reserve ratio of 0.10, Cabot Bank really only wants to keep $100 (= $1000 × 0.10) of the newly deposited $1000 on hand as desired reserves. As a result of this new deposit, Cabot Bank has excess reserves of $900 (= $1000 − $100).

The bank responds by lending $900 to Borrower X. As Figure 12.7 demonstrates, the new loan increases Cabot Bank's deposit liabilities by $900. In other words, by lending out its excess reserves, Cabot Bank creates $900 in new money.

FIGURE 12.6   Opening a Deposit

Cabot Bank

Assets		Liabilities	
Cash Reserves	+ $1000	Saver A's Deposit	+ $1000

Saver A deposits $1000 at Cabot Bank. As a result, Cabot Bank has new cash assets and deposit liabilities of $1000.

FIGURE 12.7   Granting a Loan

Cabot Bank

Assets		Liabilities	
Cash Reserves	$1000	Saver A's Deposit	$1000
Loan to Borrower X	+$900	Borrowers X's Deposit	+$900

Cabot Bank lends out its $900 in excess reserves to Borrower X, creating new loan assets and deposit liabilities of $900. Since Borrower X's new deposit is money, the money supply has risen by $900.

THIRD TRANSACTION

Now that he has the money, Borrower X uses his $900 loan to purchase goods or services. Figure 12.8 shows the resulting changes in both Cabot Bank's cash assets and the new deposit to Borrower X–they are both reduced by $900.

FOURTH TRANSACTION

So, does reducing Cabot Bank's deposits mean the newly created money suddenly disappears? It does not, if we take Borrower X's $900 purchase into account. Suppose Borrower X bought something for $900 from Saver B. Saver B, in turn, deposits the $900 from the sale in her account at Fraser Bank. As a result, Fraser Bank's cash assets and deposit liabilities increase by $900, as shown in Figure 12.9. This means that the $900 deposit originally created by Cabot Bank has simply moved to Fraser Bank. As a result of this transaction, there is no change in the money supply.

FIFTH TRANSACTION

Now, let us consider Fraser Bank. Because Saver B's deposit to Fraser Bank increases the total deposits of the bank, desired reserves should increase by $90 (= $900 × 0.10). Once again, however, the deposit of $900 also increases the cash reserves, thereby giving excess reserves of $810 (= $900 − $90).

Because the excess reserves can be put to use to earn profits, Fraser Bank lends the $810 to Borrower Y. As a result, Fraser Bank's loan assets and deposit liabilities have jumped by $810, as shown in Figure 12.10. Because of this rise in deposits, more new money has been created, so the money supply has been boosted by another $810.

The Money Multiplier

The possible transactions are endless. However, we can see the process of money creation in the few transactions outlined. Recall that the quantity of money increased once, when Cabot Bank lent out its $900 in excess reserves to Borrower X, and again, when Fraser Bank lent out its excess reserves of $810 to Borrower Y. In other words, the money supply increased by $1710 in these few

FIGURE 12.8   Withdrawing a Deposit

Cabot Bank

Assets		Liabilities	
Cash Reserves	$100 (−$1000 − $900)	Saver A's Deposit	$1000
Loan to Borrower X	$900	Borrowers X's Deposit	$0 (=$900 − $900)

When Borrower X withdraws the $900 from his deposit, Cabot Bank's cash assets and deposit liabilities each fall by $900.

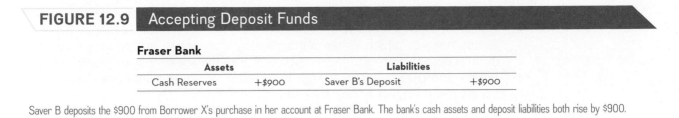

FIGURE 12.9 | Accepting Deposit Funds

Fraser Bank

Assets		Liabilities	
Cash Reserves	+$900	Saver B's Deposit	+$900

Saver B deposits the $900 from Borrower X's purchase in her account at Fraser Bank. The bank's cash assets and deposit liabilities both rise by $900.

transactions. Money will continue to be created as long as banks find they have excess cash reserves to lend out.

Note how the process of money creation is similar to the process of the spending multiplier, as outlined in Chapter 11. In this money creation process, an initial change in money has a magnified effect on the money supply. The **money multiplier** is the value by which the initial change is multiplied to give the maximum total change in money supply. Suppose, for example, that the initial change in excess reserves is $900 and the final change in the money supply is $4500; the money multiplier, therefore, has a value of 5:

money multiplier: the value by which the amount of excess reserves is multiplied to give the maximum total change in money supply

$$\text{Change in money supply} = \text{change in excess reserves} \times \text{money multiplier}$$
$$\$4500 = \$900 \times 5$$

The Multiplier Formula

The value of the money multiplier is determined in the same way as the size of the spending multiplier. Recall that the spending multiplier is the reciprocal of the marginal propensity to withdraw (MPW), which indicates how much is taken out of the income-spending stream with each spending cycle.

In the case of the money creation process, deposit-takers hold back a certain portion of the funds in each lending cycle. As we have seen, this portion is determined by the reserve ratio. So, in money creation, the multiplier is the reciprocal of the reserve ratio. In our example, with banks reserving 10 percent (or 0.10) of deposits, the money multiplier is 10 (= 1.00 ÷ 0.10). In other words, the initial change in excess reserves ($900) eventually causes an increase in the money supply of $9000:

$$\text{Money multiplier} = \frac{1}{\text{reserve ratio}}$$
$$10 = \frac{1}{0.10}$$

$$\text{Change in money supply} = \text{change in excess reserves} \times \text{money multiplier}$$
$$\$9000 = \$900 \times 10$$

FIGURE 12.10 | Withdrawing a Deposit

Fraser Bank

Assets		Liabilities	
Cash Reserves	$900	Saver B's Deposit	$900
Loan to Borrower Y	+$810	Borrowers Y's Deposit	+$810

Fraser Bank lends out its $810 in excess reserves to Borrower Y. This creates added loan assets and deposit liabilities of $810. Since Borrower Y's new deposit is money, the money supply increases by $810.

Therefore, when government decision-makers wish to change the money supply by a given amount, as seen earlier in Figure 12.4, they cause a change in excess reserves which, when multiplied by the money multiplier, creates the desired change. For example, if they wish the money supply to change by $10 billion, and the money multiplier has a value of 10, then the initial change in excess reserves is $1 billion (= $10 billion ÷ 10).

Adjustments to the Money Multiplier

To see how money is created, we temporarily assumed that all money is in the form of deposits, and all deposits are made to one sort of deposit-taker offering only a single type of deposit. However, these assumptions do not hold true in reality. Consider the implications in turn.

PUBLICLY-HELD CURRENCY

The public, of course, does use currency, and currency is a part of all definitions of money. So, rather than all money going to deposit-takers, who then keep some as reserves and lend the rest, some money does circulate and is unaffected by the money multiplier. Thus, in our example, the money supply would not increase by $9000, but by a lesser amount.

DIFFERENCES IN DEPOSITS

As we have noted, there is a wide range of deposit types, and not all types are represented in the narrowest definition of money, M1+. Therefore, as deposit money expands in the succession of transactions, not all of it will be reflected as an increase in money supply defined as M1+. So, the money supply in our example would increase by an amount less than $9000.

THINKING ABOUT ECONOMICS

How relevant is the money multiplier in the Canadian monetary system?

The money multiplier represents the maximum possible effect of money creation. Returning to our example, the money multiplier formula allows us to specify the maximum amount of $9000 by which the quantity of money rises as a result of the infusion of $900 in new excess cash reserves into the economy. Because of the various factors that influence this increase, the exact size of the money multiplier can vary significantly.

QUESTION When Canada moved to voluntary from legally required cash reserves, what happened to the size of the money multiplier?

BRIEF REVIEW

1. Deposit-takers reserve a certain percentage of deposits to satisfy withdrawal requests from depositors. This percentage is known as the reserve ratio, and the resulting dollar amount equals the desired reserves.

2. Cash reserves in excess of desired reserves are lent out to borrowers to create profit.

3. In the same way that spending is magnified, lending excess reserves magnifies deposits.

4. The money multiplier is the reciprocal of the reserve ratio and the maximum value by which an initial change in excess reserves changes the money supply.

12.3 | PRACTICE PROBLEMS

1. A chartered bank has $1 million in deposits and $40 000 in desired reserves. Its excess reserves are initially zero.
   a. What is the reserve ratio in this banking system?
   b. If a further $100 000 is deposited in the bank, by how much do the bank's desired reserves increase? the bank's excess reserves?
   c. Calculate the money multiplier in this case and identify the final increase in the money supply in the banking system due to this bank's increase in excess reserves.
2. A depositor places $200 in cash in her bank. The reserve ratio in the banking system is 6 percent.
   a. By how much do excess reserves initially change in the depositor's own bank? Do they increase or decrease?
   b. Calculate the money multiplier in this banking system and identify the maximum amount by which the money supply changes once the process of money creation in the banking system is complete.

LAST WORD

In this chapter, we examined the relationship between the money supply and the financial system and the factors that affect the demand and supply of money. Money demand results from the public's desire to hold money for transactions and as an asset. Money supply is determined by government decision-makers, who can change the amount of excess reserves in the banking system, which then has an amplified effect on the money supply through the workings of the money multiplier. In the next chapter, we analyze the monetary role of government decision-makers in more detail by focusing on the Bank of Canada and the way it conducts monetary policy to stabilize the economy.

PROBLEMS

1. Identify which of the three functions of money is most relevant in the following situations:
   a. A consumer compares prices on various brands of clothing.
   b. A restaurant-owner writes a cheque to pay for food purchases.
   c. A wealth-holder temporarily keeps part of her financial assets in a chartered bank deposit.
   d. A borrower deposits currency in his chartered bank to pay off a loan.
   e. An item receives a series of bids before being sold on an online auction.
   f. A bank withdraws monthly service charges from a deposit-holder's account.

2. Use the data in the table below to calculate (a) M1+, (b) M2, (c) M3, and (d) M2+.

Total value of corporate shares	$500 billion
Currency outside chartered banks	$28 billion
Chequable notice deposits at chartered banks	$88 billion
Publicly-held demand deposits at chartered banks	$31 billion
Federal government bonds	$623 billion
Other liquid assets included in M2 +	$18 billion
Non-personal term and foreign currency deposits at chartered banks	$254 billion
Personal term deposits at chartered banks	$120 billion
Non-chequable notice deposits at chartered banks	$80 billion
Chequable notice deposits at near banks	$75 billion
Personal term deposits at near banks	$100 billion
Non-chequable notice deposits at near banks	$60 billion

3. The table below shows money demand and supply schedules for a hypothetical economy.

Money Demand and Supply Schedules

Nominal Interest Rate (%)	Quantity Demanded (D_{mo}) ($ billions)	Quantity Supplied (S_{mo})
4	2.5	10
3	10	10
2	20	10
1	40	10
0		10

   a. Draw a graph showing D_{mo} and S_{mo}. Plot all four points for the money demand curve. For the money supply curve, plot only the two endpoints when the interest rate is 4 percent and 0 percent.
   b. Identify the initial equilibrium interest rate and equilibrium quantity of money.
   c. What happens in this market if the prevailing interest rate is initially 4 percent? 1 percent?
   d. Outline the effects of a $10 billion increase in the money supply at every interest rate and show the new money supply curve S_{m1} on your graph. Plot only the two endpoints of the new curve, when the interest rate is 4 percent and 0 percent.
   e. If the money supply stays at S_{m1}, outline the effects of a $10 billion increase in money demand at every interest rate and show the new money demand curve D_{m1} on your graph. Plot all four points of the new curve.
   f. In which direction will the equilibrium interest rate move if real output in the economy increases? if the price level decreases?

4. A bond is initially worth $10 000 and provides an interest rate of 4 percent.
   a. Explain how this bond's price changes if the prevailing interest rate falls to 2 percent.
   b. What happens to the bond's price if the prevailing interest rate rises to 6 percent?

5. Hudson Bank has a reserve ratio of 5 percent and $10 million issued in deposits.
   a. If the bank's actual reserves are $600 000, what are its excess reserves?
   b. Calculate the money multiplier in this banking system.
   c. What is the final amount by which the money supply increases once the process of money creation in the banking system is complete?

6. Champlain Bank has a reserve ratio of 4 percent, $5 million issued in deposits, and $200 000 in actual reserves.
   a. Identify this bank's initial desired reserves and initial excess reserves.
   b. What is the effect on the bank's excess reserves if $15 000 in currency is deposited in the bank?
   c. Calculate the money multiplier in this banking system.
   d. What is the final amount by which the money supply can change once the process of money creation in the banking system is complete?

7. A wealth-holder withdraws $200 from her bank and stashes this currency in a cookie jar. Assume that other economic participants hold their money in one type of deposit in a financial system with a single type of deposit-taker with a reserve ratio of 5 percent.
   a. Outline the first two transactions that occur as a result of this withdrawal.
   b. What is the final decrease in the money supply? Explain.

8. (Policy Discussion Question)
   In the latter half of 2008, financial institutions in many countries, especially in the United States and the United Kingdom, were battered by a financial crisis, with falling real and financial asset values and a spate of bankruptcies resulting in a domino effect. Canada's financial system was less affected by these gyrations than financial systems in many other industrial countries. Could the fact that Canadian deposit-takers are dominated by the "big six" chartered banks have played a role? What other factors might have been at play? Discuss using the concepts introduced in this chapter.

9. (Advanced Question)
   a. How can the value of deposit-takers' assets, such as the loans they made, be negatively affected during economic downturns?
   b. How might the reactions of depositors to the threat of a negative impact on deposit-takers' assets intensify the problems outlined in part a?
   c. Suggest some ways these financial risks faced by deposit-takers can be minimized either by government policy-makers or by deposit-takers themselves.

MONEY MATTERS
Milton Friedman and Monetarism

Milton Friedman
© Bettmann/CORBIS

FRIEDMAN AND HIS INFLUENCE

One of the most influential figures in the discipline of economics during recent decades has been the American economist Milton Friedman (1912–2006). He was both a student and a long-time professor at the University of Chicago, an institution where the ideas of the neoclassical economists lived on during the Keynesian revolution of the 1930s and 1940s.

Friedman is perhaps most famous as a promoter of laissez-faire capitalism in the tradition of Adam Smith. He popularized his views in his books *Capitalism and Freedom* (1962) and *Free to Choose* (1980), as well as in numerous magazine articles and TV appearances. Friedman's pro-market outlook stemmed from his belief that wages and prices in private markets are fairly close to their most efficient, perfectly competitive values, while such spillover effects as pollution can best be dealt with through private lobbying and negotiation, rather than through government intervention. Since governments are inefficient by their very nature, said Friedman, and because they hinder individual freedom, their intervention in private markets should be minimized.

Friedman suggested replacing income-support programs, such as welfare and Employment Insurance, with a single, guaranteed annual income system. He also argued that many functions currently performed by governments could be performed more efficiently by the private sector, if businesses are chosen to fulfill each specified task at the lowest possible cost.

THE ROLE OF MONEY

Friedman contributed to various aspects of economics, but his most wide-ranging work was associated with the economic perspective known as "monetarism," which emphasizes the influence of money in the economy.

Monetarism is an extension of theories that dominated macroeconomics before John Maynard Keynes. Like neoclassical economists such as William Stanley Jevons, monetarists believe that the economy is able to adjust to shocks without government intervention. While admitting that the economy can be temporarily set off course, monetarists argue that misguided government intervention usually just makes economic fluctuations worse. Because they stress the importance of money, monetarists blame unwise use of monetary policies in particular.

Central to monetarism is the concept known as the velocity of money (V), or the number of times, on average, that money is spent on final goods and services during a given year. For the economy as a whole, the velocity of money can be calculated by dividing nominal GDP by the money supply (M). Suppose, for example, that Canada's nominal GDP is $1 trillion and M1+ is $50 billion. Each of the dollars in the stock of money must then have been used 20 times to finance this level of activity:

$$\text{Velocity of money (V)} = \frac{\text{nominal GDP}}{\text{M}}$$

$$20 = \frac{\$1 \text{ trillion}}{\$50 \text{ billion}}$$

These calculations lead us to another cornerstone of monetarism. Recall that nominal GDP is the total money value of all final goods and services produced in the economy over a given period. So GDP expresses both the price level (P) and real output (Q). In other words, the $1 trillion in nominal GDP may be broken down into a price level of 2.0 and a real output of $500 billion:

$$\text{Nominal GDP} = P \times Q$$

$$\$1 \text{ trillion} = 2.0 \times \$500 \text{ billion}$$

The two formulas above can be combined to derive the equation of exchange, which was central to Friedman's views. The equation states that the money supply multiplied by the velocity of money (= M × V) equals the price level multiplied by real output (= P × Q):

$$M \times V = P \times Q$$

$$\$50 \text{ billion} \times 20 = 2.0 \times \$500 \text{ billion}$$

THE QUANTITY THEORY OF MONEY

According to the quantity theory of money, which was accepted by Friedman and is still subscribed to by current monetarists, both the velocity of money and real output are relatively stable. Changes in velocity, monetarists say, are primarily due to long-run factors, such as the move to credit and debit cards, while real output varies only slightly from its potential level. Friedman accommodated Keynesian theory by recognizing that wages can be inflexible, but he believed that this inflexibility is short-lived, with economic participants soon adjusting to any changes in prices or unemployment.

If both the velocity of money and real output are fairly stable, as is assumed in the quantity theory of money, then there is a straightforward relationship between money and prices. This is shown by the equation of exchange, when both velocity and real output are set at constant values, V^* and Q^*:

$$M \times V^* = P \times Q^*$$

Adjustments in the price level (P) must then be due to changes in the money supply (M), keeping in mind that the money supply is defined in nominal terms. In other words, according to Friedman, inflation is primarily caused by too much money chasing the products available for purchase in an economy.

MONETARIST POLICIES

Unlike other economists who treat money as only one element that determines output and inflation levels, monetarists consider variations in the money supply to be the most significant factor in the economy. In mainstream theory, the process through which money influences the economy is a lengthy one. An expansion in the money supply, for example, must first reduce interest rates, then boost investment and consumer spending on durable goods, and finally change aggregate demand, thereby shifting the aggregate demand curve to the right. If any of these links in the chain is weak, then the process of change breaks down. In contrast, monetarists view the impact of monetary changes as being more straightforward and predictable. In this perspective, an assumed stable velocity of money means that adjustments in the money supply translate immediately into higher nominal GDP and increased prices.

Because monetarists consider monetary policy to be a powerful instrument, most judge it too strong for central banks to apply wisely. Fluctuations in real output will be lessened, they suggest, if no discretionary policy is used at all. Instead, governments should impose a monetary rule that forces the central bank to increase the money supply by a constant rate each year. The rate that monetarists recommend–usually in the range of 3 percent–is based on long-term real growth in the economy.

But the experience in Canada and other countries during the 1970s through to the 1990s–and even more so during the major boom and bust of the 2000s–has not provided convincing evidence for the overriding importance of money in influencing the economy or in the usefulness of a set monetary rule. As a result, most economists do not support monetarist theory and its recommendations in its entirety. However, monetarist thinking has caused an increased focus in contemporary macroeconomics on the possible links between money and other central economic variables, such as the price level and real output.

1. In a hypothetical economy, the annual velocity of money is 10 and level of real output is $800 billion. In year 1, the economy's money supply is $100 billion, and in year 2 it is $112 billion. Calculate the rate of inflation between years 1 and 2 in each of the following cases:

   a. The velocity of money and the economy's real output stay constant.
   b. The velocity of money in year 2 rises to 12, and the level of real output stays constant.
   c. The velocity of money stays constant at 10, and the level of real output rises 3 percent.

2. If the pace of technological change in an economy increases, then what problems does this create for central banks following the monetary rule?

3. If money is defined in real terms as the money supply divided by the price level, rather than in nominal terms, then how would it behave according to the monetarist interpretation of the equation of exchange?

CHAPTER 13

Monetary Policy

Economists, like any social scientists, do disagree, and very often their disagreements revolve around stabilization policy—especially monetary policy. Since the 2008 credit meltdown, these differing ideas have been publicized in ways rarely seen before, which means that debates over monetary policy are increasingly common in a host of public contexts, including the mainstream media. In this chapter, we explore the workings of monetary policy and why the banking system is so involved in monetary policy movements. We then study some of the issues that are key to the use of both fiscal and monetary policies.

> There were warnings of apprehension from economists. There always are: apprehension is their business.
>
> **-STEPHEN LEACOCK, CANADIAN WRITER AND ECONOMIST**

LEARNING OBJECTIVES   After reading this chapter, you will be able to:

LO 1

Explain the Bank of Canada's function and the role of monetary policy

LO 2

Outline the tools the Bank of Canada uses to conduct monetary policy

LO 3

Identify the trade off between inflation and unemployment

13.1 | The Bank of Canada and Monetary Policy

L01

The moving force behind Canada's monetary policy is the Bank of Canada, which has served as Canada's central bank since 1935. A wholly government-owned institution, the "Bank," as it is known, has a mandate to perform four basic functions relating to money and the financial system: managing the money supply; acting as "the bankers' bank"; acting as the federal government's fiscal agent; and ensuring the stable operation of financial markets.

Managing the Money Supply

The most important role of the Bank of Canada is to conduct monetary policy by controlling the amount of money circulating in the economy. Not only does it issue paper currency, but more importantly, it affects the activities of chartered banks and near banks so that it can vary the supply of money and interest rates. In managing the money supply, the Bank is concerned with three goals: minimizing inflation to preserve the purchasing power of the dollar; maintaining real output as close as possible to its potential level; and regulating the external value of the Canadian dollar on foreign exchange markets.

Acting as the Bankers' Bank

The Bank of Canada holds the deposits of financial institutions that are members of the Canadian Payments Association (CPA). The association includes the chartered banks and some near banks—in particular, the larger trust companies and representatives of credit unions and *caisses populaires*.

The CPA acts as a clearing house for cheques for both chartered banks and near banks. Suppose, for example, that Depositor A has a chequing account with Tecumseh Trust. He writes a $50 cheque to Depositor B, who deposits this cheque in her account at Elgin Bank, increasing her deposit balance by $50. Elgin Bank delivers the cheque to Tecumseh Trust and receives $50 in return. This payment between the two banks is actually made by using the accounts kept by both institutions (or larger banks acting as their representatives) at the Bank of Canada. The $50 is transferred from Tecumseh Trust's account to Elgin Bank's account at the Bank of Canada. To complete the entire exchange, Tecumseh then cancels the cheque it has received and reduces Depositor A's deposit account by $50. Each day, every cheque transaction like this is added up, and the accounts of CPA members are all "cleared" at once. This procedure vastly simplifies the transactions that are made necessary by the use of cheques among various deposit-takers.

The accounts of CPA members at the Bank of Canada, which are known as settlement balances and are part of the CPA members' cash reserves, are kept so that funds are available to meet the daily clearing of payments. When a CPA member finds that its account is too low, it can borrow from the Bank of Canada. The Bank provides an overnight loan, or an "advance," as it is usually known, by depositing the required funds in the CPA member's account. The interest rate charged on these advances is called the **bank rate**. Because the bank rate is usually higher than interest rates on other overnight loans, CPA members try to minimize their advances from the Bank of Canada. Nonetheless, they are a necessary backup to guarantee that CPA members always have sufficient funds in their accounts at the Bank of Canada.

bank rate: the interest rate CPA members are charged on advances from the Bank of Canada

Acting as the Federal Government's Fiscal Agent

In Chapter 11, we discussed the fiscal, or budgetary, policy that the Canadian government institutes to level out the business cycle. To conduct the business of spending, taxing, and so on, the federal government needs a bank to manage its transactions and financial assets. In its role as the government's fiscal agent, the Bank of Canada engages in three main tasks: the Bank holds some of the government's bank deposits and decides where the other deposits should be held; it acts as the government's banker by clearing federal government cheques; and it handles the financing of the federal government's debt by issuing bonds. Government bonds fall into various categories, the most notable being Canada Savings Bonds and treasury bills.

Canada Savings Bonds are popular with household savers. These bonds differ from others in that they are not bought and sold after they have first been issued. Instead, holders of Canada Savings Bonds who want their funds back before the bonds have matured must cash in the bonds with the Bank of Canada at a set price. Since savers are guaranteed a minimum rate of interest on their bonds, this feature of Canada Savings Bonds increases their attractiveness. Recall that ordinary bonds, in contrast, fluctuate in price before their maturity date, depending on the value of interest rates in the economy. Hence, they are somewhat riskier than Canada Savings Bonds.

Canada Savings Bonds: federal government bonds that have a set value throughout their term

Treasury bills are an important type of short-term federal government bond. They have terms of three months to a year and are usually issued in large denominations. Unlike other government bonds, treasury bills provide no interest payments. Rather, they are sold at a marked down price. For example, a one-year treasury bill worth $100 000 might be bought—usually by banks and other financial institutions—for $95 000. Once the treasury bill matures, the holder receives the face value of $100 000, thereby earning an income of $5000 (= $100 000 − $95 000). Viewed in another way, the $5000 earned at maturity can be seen as interest on the original purchase price, or as a nominal rate of interest of 5.3 percent [= ($5000 ÷ $95 000) × 100%].

treasury bills: short-term federal government bonds that provide no interest, but are sold at a discount

The price for federal treasury bills is decided at an auction conducted every second Tuesday by the Bank of Canada. The main buyers in the treasury bill market are the chartered banks, the large near banks, and investment dealers. The Bank of Canada also buys treasury bills to become part of its bond holdings. Buyers provide written bids that outline the price they are willing to pay and the number of bills they want. As in any auction, the bills go to the highest bidders; those who bid highest have their orders filled first.

Ensuring the Stability of Financial Markets

In tandem with other agencies, the Bank of Canada supervises the operation of financial markets to ensure their stability. The Bank has a particular responsibility in overseeing the activity of chartered banks. By doing so, it helps protect the safety of depositors' funds and the soundness of the financial system. In this supervisory task, the Bank works in tandem with the Office of the Superintendent of Financial Institutions, currently headed by economist Julie Dickinson. Canada's supervision of its financial system, and in particular its chartered banks, has received considerable international attention, especially in the aftermath of the 2008 global credit meltdown when several major financial institutions in the United States and parts of Europe—but not Canada—faced the threat of collapse.

As a result of the international financial crisis, Canada's big banks will soon face heavier regulation, as the federal government falls in line with updated international banking rules overseen by the Basel Committee on Banking Supervision, named after the Swiss city where this committee is based. The new Basel rules involve constraints on the sorts of financial markets that large global banks can enter, and limit the extent to which these banks can make certain types of loans or trade particular assets. Also, large banks will have to raise a larger portion of their overall assets from shares, rather than from deposits and bonds. By increasing the extent to which they are financed through shares, banks will thereby expand the safety cushion against losses for their depositors and bondholders. In the United States, new regulations have been instituted to limit American banks' engagement in investment dealing, and to force banks to issue more shares. In addition, the United States' central bank, the Federal Reserve, is gaining the power to oversee large US-based financial firms, and to take over and dismantle any of these firms if they are at risk of imminent failure.

As the world economy recovers from the effects of the 2008 crisis and financial regulations are re-introduced, recent examples of national policy-making provide important lessons on what to avoid. The most interesting case is the experience in Japan since its own credit crunch two decades ago. After an extended bubble in real estate values, the Japanese economy tumbled during the early 1990s, with many of its largest banks kept from insolvency only through government aid. Instead of responding quickly to this crisis, the country's financial regulators allowed Japanese banks to maintain non-paying business loans on their books. This meant that the Japanese companies that had taken out these loans were being kept afloat only through new bank lending. Because of the need to prop up these borrowers, Japanese banks were limited in the loans they could make to companies intent on making new investments, which contributed to the extended economic slump that Japan has faced ever since. As this experience shows, allowing national banking problems to fester in the vain hope that they will correct themselves is not a viable option. Instead, regulators must respond decisively to any signs of spreading turmoil in their country's banking system.

The Japanese lesson is one that international financial regulators have taken to heart. The response to the 2008 credit meltdown in most large economies was a tightening of financial regulations. In some countries, this has included the use of so-called stress tests that measure the extent of non-paying loans on the books of individual banks. In many cases, these "bad loans" have also been consolidated so that they can be administered by government authorities. While not all countries have been equally quick to identify the problems in their national banking sectors revealed by the 2008 crisis, overall the response has been substantial. The sideline article "A Crisis Too Far" at the end of the chapter provides further details on the 2008 meltdown, its causes, and how regulators have responded.

Monetary Policy

Recall that monetary policy involves the Bank of Canada changing interest rates, altering the money supply, or both, to stabilize the economy. Our analysis of money and deposit-takers allows us to examine the way in which monetary policy is conducted.

EXPANSIONARY MONETARY POLICY

expansionary monetary policy: a policy of increasing the money supply and reducing interest rates to stimulate the economy

When real output falls short of its potential level, a recessionary gap is created. To stimulate output and increase employment, the Bank of Canada can use **expansionary monetary policy**. Such action is referred to informally as "easy money policy."

THINKING ABOUT ECONOMICS

What factors accounted for the ability of Canada's big banks to weather the 2008 credit meltdown so successfully?

Starting in the 1980s, the global financial industry underwent a remarkable expansion during which the world's large chartered banks and near banks enjoyed a long span of stable growth and high profits. All this changed during the autumn of 2008, with a sudden meltdown in financial markets. As outlined in "A Crisis Too Far" at the end of the chapter, some of the blame for the meltdown rests with a number of global financial institutions, especially those based in the United States and parts of Europe. These institutions engaged in risky forms of lending and splurged on new financial products whose properties were little understood. Their actions were made worse by the reluctance of financial regulators to clamp down on such activity until it was too late.

Like their American and European counterparts, Canada's biggest banks specialize not just in conventional banking activities, but also in the riskier area of investment dealing through short-term trading of financial securities. Yet despite the close financial ties between banks in Canada and elsewhere, Canada's big six were able to escape the worst effects of the meltdown.

The most important reason for this favourable performance was that Canadian banks engaged in far less risky behaviour than many of their international counterparts. In their investment dealing, Canada's big six showed restraint by largely avoiding what turned out to be the most toxic new types of financial securities: mortgage-backed collateralized debt obligations and credit default swaps. This restraint was due partly to close regulation and supervision, and partly to Canadian banks' own decisions.

In their main banking operations, Canada's big six maintained a high proportion of shareholders' equity relative to their overall liabilities, helping ensure that any reduction in the value of their assets could be covered by shareholders. This was shown by their average leverage ratio, which is defined as the multiple by which a company's liabilities exceed its shareholders' equity. For Canadian banks, before the meltdown this ratio was 18 to 1, in contrast to 35 to 1 in the United States and 45 to 1 in Europe.[1] Again, part of this difference was due to stricter financial regulations within Canada, and part was due to the relatively risk-averse nature of the big six, which maintained leverage ratios well below the regulatory maximum. Also, the Canadian property market had not succumbed to the same bubble conditions as existed in some other countries, which meant a gentler decline in real estate values and a far lower rate of mortgage foreclosures as a result of the meltdown and the ensuing recession.

Given all these factors, Canadian banks were less affected by the meltdown, and are having to adjust their operations far less than banks in many other countries as a result of the new global regulations that have arisen. But given Canada's close integration in the global economy, the meltdown nonetheless had a considerable domestic impact, especially in the short run.

Like other central banks, the Bank of Canada responded by making loans available to a wide range of financial institutions, for the first time including pension funds and other major financial players as possible recipients of these loans. In addition, the Bank promised intervention if necessary to prop up struggling financial institutions. The Bank also loosened its monetary policy by pumping reserves into the banking system and reducing interest rates. Because interest rates were driven so low, the only way to engage in expansionary policy in the meltdown's immediate aftermath was through quantitative easing, whereby the Bank increased the money supply by using its own reserves to buy extensive holdings of government bonds and other assets.

QUESTION Why would a bank choose to increase its leverage ratio even though it increases the bank's risks?

---

[1] See John Lanchester, *I.O.U.: Why Everyone Owes Everyone and No One Can Pay* (Toronto: McClelland & Stewart, 2010), p. 37.

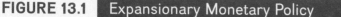

FIGURE 13.1 Expansionary Monetary Policy

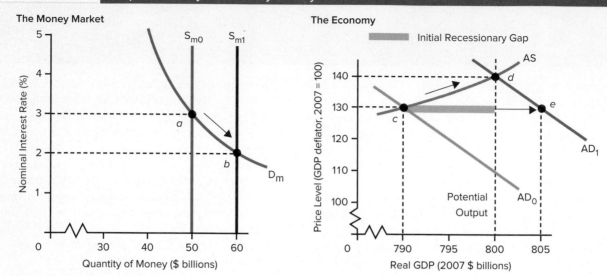

When the economy is in a recession, the Bank of Canada can increase the supply of money, shown by the shift from S_{m0} to S_{m1} on the left, thereby pushing down the interest rate (point a to point b). Because of the initial spending increase and the spending multiplier, the result in the economy as a whole is an increase in aggregate demand, as shown on the right as the $15 billion shift from AD_0 to AD_1. Output does not rise by $15 billion (from point c to point e); rather, the price level and output both rise to give a new equilibrium at point d, with output at the potential level of $800 billion and the recessionary gap eliminated.

The Bank of Canada applies easy money policy by expanding the money supply. As shown on the left in Figure 13.1, increasing the money supply shifts the money supply curve (S_m) to the right, causing a drop in the equilibrium interest rate.

To see how this lower interest rate affects aggregate demand, remember that a fall in interest rates makes borrowing funds cheaper. With a decline in the nominal interest rate, the real rate of interest falls as well. Businesses respond by increasing their investment spending, and households purchase more durable goods, raising consumption. Both adjustments spur an initial increase in spending that is then magnified by the same successive cycles of new spending, as seen in the case of an expansionary fiscal policy (discussed in Chapter 11).

The effect is the same as when government purchases increase. The change in aggregate demand, or total spending, is found by calculating the product of the spending multiplier and the initial spending change. Suppose, for example, that the initial increase in investment and consumption totalled $9 billion and the value of the economy's spending multiplier is 1.67. The total change in aggregate demand is then $15 billion:

$$\begin{array}{c} \text{Total change in output} \\ \text{(shift in AD curve)} \end{array} = \begin{array}{c} \text{initial change} \\ \text{in spending} \end{array} \times \begin{array}{c} \text{spending} \\ \text{multiplier} \end{array}$$

$$\$15 \text{ billion} = \$9 \text{ billion} \times 1.67$$

As shown on the right in Figure 13.1, the $15 billion shift in the aggregate demand curve causes equilibrium output to rise by a smaller amount—$10 billion—because of the accompanying price level rise.

FIGURE 13.2   Contractionary Monetary Policy

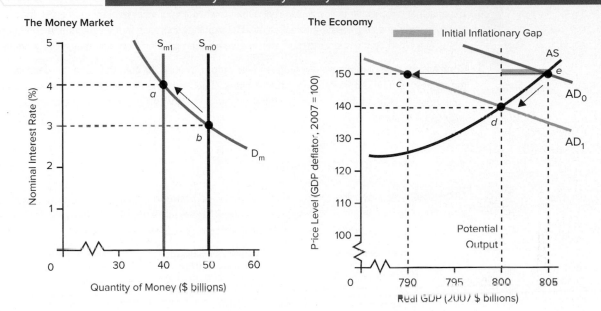

During an economic boom, the Bank of Canada can decrease the supply of money, shown by the shift from S_{m0} to S_{m1} on the left, thereby pushing up the interest rate (point b to point a). Because of the initial spending decrease and the spending multiplier, the result in the economy as a whole is a decrease in aggregate demand, as shown on the right as the $15 billion shift from AD_0 to AD_1. Output does not fall by $15 billion (from point e to point c); rather, the price level and output both fall to give a new equilibrium at point d, with output at the potential level of $800 billion and the inflationary gap eliminated.

CONTRACTIONARY MONETARY POLICY

Conversely, during an economic boom, the Bank of Canada can inhibit spending and inflation with **contractionary monetary policy**. Such action, also known as "tight money policy," decreases the money supply. The result, as shown on the left in Figure 13.2, is that the money supply curve (S_m) shifts to the left, driving up the equilibrium interest rate.

The higher nominal interest rate results in a higher real interest rate as well. This discourages investment spending by businesses as well as consumption spending on durable items by households, so it influences aggregate demand. Both trends cause an initial reduction of spending that is then magnified by the spending multiplier. Suppose, for example, that investment and consumption spending decline initially by $9 billion, and the spending multiplier is 1.67. As a result, the total decrease in aggregate demand is $15 billion.

Once again, the change in output causes a lesser change in actual spending because of the change in price level at the same time. In this case, as shown on the right in Figure 13.2, the $15 billion decrease in aggregate demand causes a $5 billion decrease in equilibrium output.

contractionary monetary policy: a policy of decreasing the money supply and increasing interest rates to dampen the economy

BRIEF REVIEW

1. Canada's central bank—the Bank of Canada—manages the money supply, serves as a bank for chartered banks and some near banks, acts as the federal government's fiscal agent, and helps to ensure the stability of financial markets.

2. Expansionary monetary policy raises real output toward its potential level by increasing the money supply and decreasing interest rates. The resulting increase in investment and consumption is magnified by the spending multiplier to give an even greater increase in aggregate demand.

3. Contractionary monetary policy reduces real output toward its potential level by decreasing the money supply and increasing interest rates. The resulting decrease in investment and consumption is magnified by the spending multiplier to give an even greater decrease in aggregate demand.

13.1 │ PRACTICE PROBLEM

1. The tables below show hypothetical money demand and supply schedules as well as aggregate demand and aggregate supply schedules for an economy whose natural unemployment rate is estimated to be 7 percent.

Nominal Interest Rate (%)	Quantity Demanded ($ billions) (D_m)	Quantity Supplied ($ billions) (S_{mo})
4	150	200
3	200	200
2	300	200
1	500	200
0	–	200

Price Level (2007 = 100)	AD_o (2007 $ billions)	AS (2007 $ billions)
140	100	450
130	200	400
120	300	300
110	400	100
100	500	–

a. Suppose the economy is facing an unemployment rate of 8.5 percent and a declining rate of inflation. Is this economy facing a recessionary or inflationary gap? Should its central bank use a contractionary or expansionary monetary policy?

b. Identify the steps by which this monetary policy will affect the economy.

c. Draw one graph showing the demand and supply curves D_m and S_{mo} in the money market and another showing the aggregate demand and aggregate supply curves AD_o and AS in the economy. Plot four points for the demand curve D_m and four points for the aggregate supply curve AS. Plot only the two endpoints for the supply curve S_{mo} and the aggregate demand curve AD_o. What is the initial equilibrium interest rate in the money market? What are the initial equilibrium price level and real GDP?

d. If the monetary policy applied in part b leads to a $100 billion change in the money supply, then what is the new equilibrium interest rate? Add the new money supply curve S_{m1} to your graph. Plot only the endpoints of this new curve.

e. If the change in the interest rate in part d causes a $200 billion change in real expenditures at every price level, then what are the new equilibrium price level and real GDP? Add the new aggregate demand curve AD_1 to your graph. Plot only the endpoints of this new curve.

2. a. What is the nominal interest rate on a one-year treasury bill with a face value of $1 million if its purchase price is $980 000?

b. If the Bank of Canada wishes to move the nominal interest rate on one-year treasury bills to 3 percent, should it increase or decrease the supply of these bills it sells in its auction?

13.2 | Tools of Monetary Policy

The Bank of Canada uses two different tools to conduct monetary policy: open market operations and (as a signal of its intentions) the target overnight rate.

Open Market Operations

Recall that the Bank of Canada sells and buys back federal government bonds. Its role in the bond market is a major tool with which the Bank of Canada conducts monetary policy. Through selling and buying back federal and other bonds, the Bank of Canada can use deposit-takers' cash reserves as a lever to influence both the money supply and interest rates. Because transactions of existing bonds take place in the open bond market—for example, when the Bank enters the market to sell to or repurchase existing federal bonds from a chartered bank or investment dealer—they are called **open market operations**.

open market operations: the buying and selling of bonds by the Bank of Canada in the open market

BOND SALES

Consider the sale by the Bank of Canada of a $1000 bond to Bondholder A. When the sale takes place, Bondholder A pays for the bond with a cheque written against his deposit account at Cartier Bank. The Bank of Canada sends the cheque to Cartier Bank, which then cancels the cheque and reduces Bondholder A's account by $1000. Most importantly, Cartier Bank pays the Bank of Canada for the cheque by having $1000 taken out of its Bank of Canada account, as shown in Figure 13.3.

The money supply immediately falls by $1000 due to the loss of the deposit previously held by Bondholder A. Assuming that the reserve ratio is 0.10, Cartier Bank's excess reserves are cut by $900, causing a multiple reduction of the money supply. Cartier Bank has less money available to lend. With a reserve ratio of 0.10 and a maximum money multiplier of 10, the further decline in the supply of money could be as much as $9000 (= $900 × 10).

Therefore, the sale of bonds reduces the cash reserves of deposit-takers, which, in turn, cuts back on lending and finally decreases the supply of money. By selling bonds, the Bank of Canada engages in contractionary monetary policy.

FIGURE 13.3   A Bond Sale

Bank of Canada

Assets		Liabilities	
Bonds	−$1000	Cartier Bank's Deposit	−$1000

Cartier Bank

Assets		Liabilities	
Reserves at Bank of Canada	−$1000	Bondholder A's Deposit	−$1000

When the Bank of Canada sells a bond to Bondholder A, its bond assets fall, as do its deposit liabilities to Cartier Bank. Meanwhile, Cartier Bank's cash assets at the Bank of Canada decrease, as do its deposit liabilities to Bondholder A. The drop in Bondholder A's deposit immediately reduces the money supply by $1000. With a reserve ratio of 10 percent, Cartier Bank's excess reserves fall by $900 and the money multiplier has a value of 10. Because reductions to deposits are magnified, the money supply drops by as much as an extra $9000 (the $900 decrease in excess reserves multiplied by the money multiplier).

BOND PURCHASES

Now, consider the implications of the Bank of Canada buying back bonds from members of the public in the open market. Suppose the Bank of Canada buys back a $1000 bond from Bondholder B. Bondholder B receives a cheque from the Bank of Canada, which she deposits in her account at Cartier Bank. On acquiring the cheque, Cartier Bank delivers it to the Bank of Canada and receives in return a $1000 addition to its Bank of Canada deposit.

As Figure 13.4 shows, both the money supply and Cartier Bank's cash reserves increase by $1000 due to the new deposit held by Bondholder B. However, the bank, with a reserve ratio of 0.10, need only hold back $100. Therefore, the bank has excess reserves of $900 (= $1000 − $100). Cartier Bank will lend this money, which, in turn, will increase the money supply in a series of transactions similar to those outlined earlier in this chapter. Assuming a uniform reserve ratio of 0.10, we can see that the money multiplier (10, or the reciprocal of 0.10), creates a further increase in the money supply of up to $9000 (= $900 × 10).

Therefore, buying back bonds allows the Bank of Canada to practise expansionary monetary policy. Cash reserves increase, resulting in increased lending, which causes the money supply to expand.

The Target Overnight Rate

overnight rate: the interest rate on overnight loans between chartered banks and other financial institutions

The **overnight rate** is the interest rate on overnight loans between chartered banks and other financial institutions. At any given time, the Bank makes sure that the overnight rate stays within a publicized range of 50 basis points (a basis point is one-hundredth of a percentage point), with the target overnight rate at the midpoint of this range. The Bank keeps the overnight rate near the target overnight rate by using its main monetary policy tool. When the Bank buys bonds on the open market, the accounts of CPA members at the Bank increase in value, which reduces the need for overnight borrowing and pushes down the overnight rate. On the other hand, when the Bank engages in an open-market sale of bonds, the accounts of CPA members at the Bank are reduced, raising the need for overnight borrowing as well as the overnight rate.

The bank rate is set at the ceiling of the 50-basis-point range for the overnight rate. Whenever the Bank changes the target overnight rate, the 50-basis-

FIGURE 13.4   A Bond Purchase

Bank of Canada

Assets		Liabilities	
Bonds	+$1000	Cartier Bank's Deposit	+$1000

Cartier Bank

Assets		Liabilities	
Reserves at Bank of Canada	+$1000	Bondholder A's Deposit	+$1000

If the Bank of Canada purchases a bond from Bondholder B, its bond assets rise, as do its deposit liabilities to Cartier Bank. From Cartier Bank's perspective, its cash assets at the Bank of Canada increase, as do its deposit liabilities to Bondholder B. The new deposit from Bondholder B immediately adds $1000 to the money supply. With a reserve ratio of 0.10, Cartier Bank's excess reserves increase by $900, while the money multiplier has a value of 10. Because deposits expand, the money supply increases as much as an extra $9000 (the $900 increase in excess reserves multiplied by the money multiplier).

point range and the bank rate change as well. This signifies where monetary policy is heading in the near future.

If the change in the target overnight rate is substantial, deposit-takers may decide to alter their own interest rates in the same direction. In particular, they adjust their **prime rate**, which is the lowest possible rate charged by deposit-takers on loans to their best corporate customers. When the prime rate varies, so do all other rates for depositors and borrowers.

prime rate: the lowest possible interest rate charged by deposit-takers on loans to their best corporate customers

Benefits of Monetary Policy

Monetary policy has two main benefits: its separation from politics, and the speed with which it can be applied. These benefits have made monetary policy the most important stabilization tool in recent years.

SEPARATION FROM DAY-TO-DAY POLITICS

Unlike fiscal policy, which is a well-publicized element of the political process, monetary policy is detached from immediate political influence. While the Bank of Canada is under the control of parliament, as represented by the prime minister and cabinet, in practice the Bank of Canada is controlled by appointed officials—the most important being its governor (Stephen Poloz, as of 2013), who serves a seven-year term. This structure is intended to help focus monetary policy on economic rather than political goals.

SPEED

Recall that fiscal policy suffers from recognition, decision, and impact lags. While recognizing a problem can also cause a delay in monetary policy and the impact of any policy may also be delayed (by anywhere between 12 and 18 months), decisions regarding monetary policy can be made speedily.

Drawbacks of Monetary Policy

Monetary policy does have three major drawbacks: its relative weakness as an expansionary tool, its broad impact, and its potential conflict with the goal of financial stability.

WEAKNESS AS AN EXPANSIONARY TOOL

The Bank of Canada is quite capable of restraining an overheated economy during a boom period. By squeezing deposit-takers' excess reserves through open-market sales of bonds, it can be assured that the money supply will fall, pushing up interest rates and reducing spending and output.

However, matters are not necessarily so straightforward during a severe recession or depression. While the Bank can increase deposit-takers' cash reserves through open-market purchases of bonds, there is no guarantee that this will translate into more bank loans and an expansion of the money supply. If deposit-takers hold on to their extra cash reserves, the desired increase in the money supply will not occur, which can make the use of expansionary monetary policy seem like "pushing a string."

BROAD IMPACT

Unlike fiscal policy, which can be focused on particular regions, monetary policy affects every region of the country uniformly. When the Bank of Canada raises interest rates during a boom, for example, the impact is felt not only in those areas with overheated economic conditions, but also in areas that have been relatively unaffected by the upswing. As a result, regions already enduring high rates of unemployment experience even more.

POTENTIAL CONFLICT WITH FINANCIAL STABILITY

One lesson from the 2008 credit meltdown is that extended periods of low interest rates—such as during the decade preceding the recent crisis—can have serious effects on the financial sector's stability. Over time, low interest rates may promote risky lending practices, with borrowers and lenders growing complacent over the risks posed by interest rate spikes and the higher loan default rate such spikes bring. It was just such a global spike in interest rates that made the 2008 credit meltdown so dangerous, with financial intermediaries in many countries finding sizeable portions of their loans tumbling in value due to widespread defaults. In the future, policy-makers are bound to take this possibility seriously.

BRIEF REVIEW

1. One major way in which the Bank of Canada pursues monetary policy is through open-market operations. Buying bonds from the public is expansionary policy that increases chartered bank reserves, leading to a magnified increase in the money supply. In contrast, selling bonds reduces the money supply.

2. The Bank of Canada signals its intentions by setting the target overnight rate, which, in turn, influences the prime rate. A rise in the target overnight rate signals contractionary policy. A fall in the target overnight rate signals expansionary policy.

3. While monetary policy has the benefits of its isolation from politics and the speed with which decisions can be made, it is less effective for expansion than for contraction, it can sometimes conflict with the goal of financial stability, and it cannot be focused on particular regions as can fiscal policy.

13.2 | PRACTICE PROBLEM

1. The Bank of Canada buys a $10 000 bond from a member of the public when the reserve ratio in the banking system is 5 percent. Outline the effects on this bond purchase on each of the following variables:
   a. the bond seller's bank deposit
   b. desired reserves at the bond seller's bank
   c. excess reserves at the bond seller's bank
   d. the maximum change in the money supply
2. The Bank of Canada sells a $2000 bond to a member of the public when the reserve ratio in the banking system is 10 percent. Outline the effects of this bond sale on each of the following variables:
   a. the bond buyer's bank deposit
   b. desired reserves at the bond buyer's bank
   c. excess reserves at the bond buyer's bank
   d. the maximum change in the money supply

13.3 | Inflation and Unemployment

Stabilization policies—both fiscal and monetary—are usually applied to affect inflation and unemployment. The task of policy-makers is complicated by the fact that the relationship between inflation and unemployment is usually an inverse one. So, for example, an increase in aggregate demand during an economic expansion means that equilibrium between aggregate demand and aggregate supply is found at a higher price level and higher output, as Figure 13.5 shows. The increase in price level translates into inflation, and the increase in output translates into lower unemployment. In other words, there is a trade off: higher prices for more jobs. Because increased demand pulls up prices, economic expansion that causes inflation is known as **demand-pull inflation**.

LO3

demand-pull inflation: inflation that occurs as increased aggregate demand pulls up prices

The Phillips Curve

Recall from Chapters 10 and 11 that Keynesian economics stresses the inverse relationship between inflation and unemployment as found in demand-pull inflation. On the basis of the assumption that there is a fixed and predictable inverse relationship between unemployment and inflation, one Keynesian economist—A.W.H. Phillips—created a curve that expresses this relationship. Figure 13.6 shows this **Phillips curve**.

According to the Keynesian perspective, if an economy with an inflation rate of 2 percent and an unemployment rate of 8 percent (point *b* in Figure 13.6) experiences demand-pull inflation, the inflation rate will rise at the same time that unemployment decreases to, for example, point *a*. Increased aggregate demand creates shortages in labour markets, which put upward pressure on wages, thereby boosting inflation. In the same way, decreased aggregate demand increases unemployment, which puts downward pressure on wages, thereby reducing the rate of inflation. We see this in the shift from point *b* to point *c*.

In the past, the Phillips curve was often treated by governments as a "policy menu." Governments using expansionary fiscal or monetary policies would anticipate a move up the curve, for example, from point *b* to point *a*; governments using contractionary fiscal or monetary policies would expect a move

Phillips curve: a curve expressing the assumed fixed and predictable inverse relationship between unemployment and inflation

---

FIGURE 13.5 | Demand-Pull Inflation

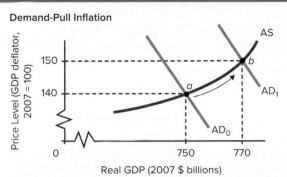

Demand-Pull Inflation

During expansionary times, aggregate demand increases, shown by a shift of the aggregate demand curve from AD_0 to AD_1. The result is that the price level rises from point *a* to point *b*. In other words, increased demand *pulls* up prices.

FIGURE 13.6 The Phillips Curve

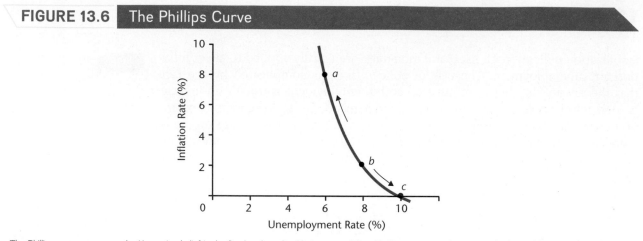

The Phillips curve expresses the Keynesian belief in the fixed and predictable inverse relationship between unemployment and inflation that occurs with demand-pull inflation. When the economy moves from point *b* to point *a*—which may happen as a result of expansionary stabilization policies—inflation increases and unemployment decreases. In contrast, contractionary policies cause the economy to move from point *b* to point *c*.

down the curve, for example, from point *b* to point *c*. The curve is no longer used in such a blunt manner, for reasons that can be seen by examining historical data for Canada. Figure 13.7 plots annual unemployment and inflation rates for 1960 to 2013. To get a sense Canada's experience with inflation and unemployment, it is useful to break down this data into three distinct periods.

FIGURE 13.7 Shifts in the Phillips Curve

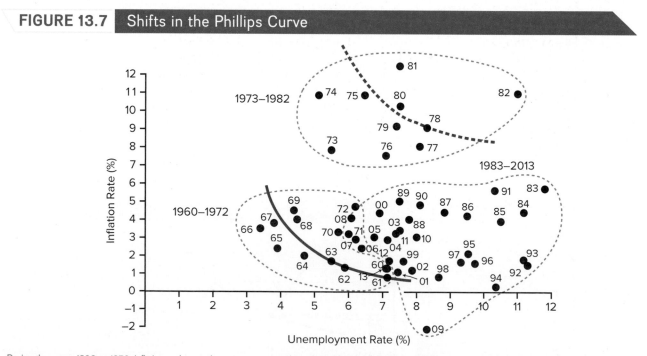

During the years 1960 to 1972, inflation and unemployment rates stayed in a broad band, from which a Phillips curve can be drawn (shown as a solid line). In the period from 1973 to 1982, the predictable relationship broke down. However, it seems that the Phillips curve moved to the right (shown as a dashed line) as both inflation rates and unemployment rates were above those in the previous period. In the period from 1983 to 2013, the trend was to lower inflation, but unemployment rates remained high until just before the 2008–2009 recession. As a result, the new position of the Phillips curve was not clear.

Sources: Statistics Canada "Shifts in the Phillips Curve." Adapted from the Statistics Canada publication "National Income and Expenditure Accounts: Annual Estimates," 1926–1986, Catalogue 13-531, April 1989, pp. 214–215 and from the Statistics Canada CANSIM database, http://www5.statcan.gc.ca/cansim/, Tables 380-0102 and 282-0002. Retrieved March 18, 2014.

FROM 1960 TO 1972

For the years 1960 to 1972, in general, higher inflation accompanied lower unemployment, and vice versa. In other words, inflation during this period was of the demand-pull variety. Therefore, the points indicating inflation and unemployment rates fall in a broad band from which we can draw a Phillips curve, shown in Figure 13.7 with a solid line. Because inflation and unemployment had a predictable inverse relationship, Canadian federal governments were able to use the curve when trying to foresee how their stabilization policies would affect the economy.

FROM 1973 TO 1982

In the years between 1973 and 1982, the previously predictable relationship between inflation and unemployment in Canada broke down. Most notably, inflation rose from 1973 to 1974, while unemployment remained about the same. This trend was repeated in the years 1979 to 1981. The Phillips curve for the Canadian economy during this period, shown as a dashed line in Figure 13.7, demonstrates that inflation and unemployment overall were greater in this period than in the last.

As this period illustrates, sometimes unemployment and inflation have a direct relationship rather than an inverse relationship. A rising rate of inflation associated with constant or expanding unemployment—that is, consistently low output—is known as **stagflation**. **This name refers to the combination of stagnation and inflation.**

A decrease in aggregate supply can cause stagflation. During the period from 1973 to 1982, for example, businesses faced rising prices for inputs, largely due to rising oil prices. Oil prices were 10 times higher in 1981 than they were at the start of 1973 because of the cartel behaviour of OPEC—the Organization of Petroleum Exporting Countries. In response to increases in input prices, businesses decrease their output, thus reducing aggregate supply. The result, shown in Figure 13.8, is a fall in equilibrium output and a rise in the price level. Because the increased costs push price levels up, this situation is known as **cost-push inflation**. During the 1970s, demands for increased wages further decreased aggregate supply and worsened cost-push inflation.

stagflation: a combination of consistently low output (and so constant or expanding unemployment) and rising inflation

cost-push inflation: occurs as increased production costs decrease aggregate supply, which then pushes up prices

---

FIGURE 13.8   Cost-Push Inflation

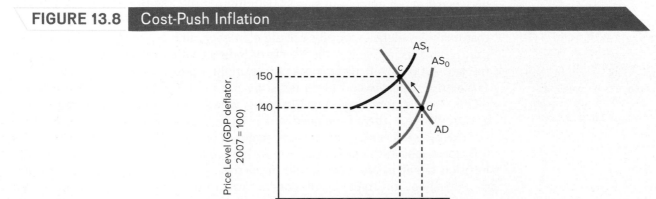

Increased input prices cause businesses to decrease output. The resulting decrease in aggregate supply means a shift in the aggregate supply curve from AS_0 to AS_1. The result is that the price level is pushed up from point d to point c. In other words, increased costs *push* up prices.

FROM 1983 TO 2013

From 1983 to 2013, the stagflation of the previous period was gradually reversed. While unemployment rates remained stubbornly high in Canada through most of the 1980s and 1990s, by the mid-1990s inflation had fallen to levels not seen since the early 1970s. Note, however, that there was no consistent relationship between inflation and unemployment during this period. While the new Phillips curve was presumably below the Phillips curve for the previous period, its position was not apparent from the behaviour of the economy between 1983 and 2013, as illustrated in Figure 13.7.

Even though the curve's position is no longer stationary, the short-run trade-off between unemployment and inflation that it encapsulates is still relevant and a powerful determinant of how stabilization policy is actually used, though this may be impossible to tell by simply a visual inspection of the constellation of points in Figure 13.7. For example, Bank of Canada researchers estimate that if policy-makers want to bring inflation down by one percentage point, unemployment will need to exceed its natural rate by two-thirds of a percentage point for at least a year.[2] It was just this type of trade off, for example, that was behind controversies in the early 1980s and then again in the early 1990s when the Bank of Canada chose to institute highly anti-inflationary policies in ways that critics of the Bank believed worsened unemployment just at the time when the economy was already facing recessionary pressures. If there comes a time when inflation again becomes a significant problem, similar controversies could easily erupt.

Three main factors account for Canada's lower inflation since 1983. Oil prices fell dramatically in the mid-1980s and the pace of technological change accelerated after the mid-1990s, increasing aggregate supply and restraining increases in the price level. In addition, the recessions of 1981–1982, 1990–1991, and 2008–2009 had a major impact on reducing inflation rates by decreasing aggregate demand, even causing a rare case of deflation during the recessionary year 2009.

inflation targeting: a monetary policy program that requires a central bank to keep annual inflation within a given range

core inflation: based on a CPI definition excluding eight volatile elements, as well as effects of indirect taxes

price-level targeting: a monetary policy program that requires a central bank to keep the price level on a desired path

In recent years, the Bank has also engaged in **inflation targeting**, a monetary policy program now used in many countries, which commits a central bank to keeping annual inflation within a given range—in the Bank of Canada's case, between 1 and 3 percent. A special definition of the inflation rate is used by the Bank in targeting inflation. **Core inflation** is based on a definition of the CPI that excludes eight especially volatile elements, such as energy costs and mortgage payments, as well as the effects of indirect taxes, in the index. Starting in the late 2000s, the Bank also began to plan for a possible switch to **price-level targeting**, which would mean targeting the price level directly. Such a policy differs from inflation targeting. Currently, when an inflation target is not met in a particular year, there is no need for the Bank to change its policy in later years. For example, exceeding the inflation target in one year does not affect the Bank's inflation target in the next year. But with price-level targeting, overshooting the inflation target in one year would mean that the Bank would have to attempt to undershoot its targets in subsequent years until it had returned to its desired

---

[2] See Pierre Duguay, "Empirical Evidence on the Strength of the Monetary Transmission Mechanism in Canada: An Aggregate Approach," in *The Transmission of Monetary Policy in Canada* (Bank of Canada, 1996), p. 102.

path of gradual price level increases. If price-level targeting is introduced, the Bank is likely to commit to keeping the price level rising annually at a rate comparable to the current 1 to 3 percent range.

The Economy's Self-Stabilizing Tendency

Another reason for shifts in the AS curve relates to the economy's capacity to stabilize itself in the long run, as forces push the economy toward its potential output where unemployment is at its natural level. While the economy may rarely reach this long-run equilibrium, economic fluctuations can be fully understood only if this self-stabilizing tendency is taken into account.

Figure 13.9 illustrates a simplified version of this process for a hypothetical economy. The short-run tradeoff between output and the price level is shown by the aggregate supply curve. But only at point *b*, which is associated with the economy's potential output, is the economy stationary in the long run. At any other point on the curve, the economy will sooner or later display its built-in tendency to stabilize.

During an economic boom, the economy's equilibrium may be at a point, such as *c*, where output is above its potential level. Because unemployment is below its natural rate, tight labour markets allow workers to bargain for higher nominal wages. These wage hikes raise business costs, leading to a decrease in aggregate supply. Equilibrium, therefore, moves back toward the economy's potential output, and unemployment rises toward its natural rate.

The opposite occurs when an economy's equilibrium is below its potential output, as at point *a* on Figure 13.9, with a high unemployment rate. Workers initially resist any attempts to reduce their nominal wages, as was pointed out originally by Keynes. However, over time, unemployment puts downward pressure on nominal wages. This causes an increase in aggregate supply, boosting output back toward its potential level and lowering unemployment toward its natural rate.

FIGURE 13.9   The Self-Stabilizing Economy

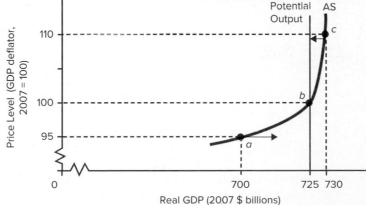

At point *b*, the economy could remain indefinitely at its potential output. However, when equilibrium is at point *c* in a boom, the economy's self-stabilizing tendency will push the aggregate supply curve to the left so that the potential output can be resumed. The same is true if the economy's equilibrium is at point *a* in a recession; the self-stabilizing tendency will push the aggregate supply curve to the right.

The Long-Run Supply Curve

long-run aggregate supply curve: the vertical AS curve at the potential output level

In either case, the vertical line shown on the graph at the potential output level can be interpreted as this hypothetical economy's **long-run aggregate supply curve**, since it shows all those points consistent with stable equilibrium in the long run.

The existence of this curve, and the self-stabilizing process that underlies it, represents a partial return to the perspective of neoclassical economics before John Maynard Keynes. It is now accepted by most economists, though its importance is disputed. Those economists who see little need for government stabilization policy believe the economy adjusts quickly by itself toward its potential output level. In contrast, many economists see the self-adjusting process as a slow one, which means that government stabilization policy can still play an important role in reducing the severity of the ups and downs in the business cycle.

BRIEF REVIEW

1. Inflation and unemployment have often had an inverse relationship. In periods of expansion, the result is demand-pull inflation.

2. The Phillips curve represents the Keynesian assumption of an inverse and predictable relationship between inflation and unemployment. While the Phillips curve applied to Canada in the period from 1960 to 1972, it has been less relevant since.

3. Since the 1970s, inflation and unemployment in Canada have frequently had a direct relationship. Stagflation has been caused largely by decreases in aggregate supply due to price increases of inputs. The result is cost-push inflation.

4. Overall inflation and unemployment rates in Canada increased from 1973 to 1982, shifting the Phillips curve to the right. From 1983 to the 2008–2009 recession, unemployment exhibited a downward trend, but declined much more gradually than inflation.

5. In the long run, changes in wage rates and the resulting movement in the aggregate supply curve mean that equilibrium is driven toward the long-run aggregate supply curve, which is at the economy's potential output.

13.3 | PRACTICE PROBLEM

1. Identify the effect of the following trends on an economy's position on its Phillips curve:
   a. a bout of cost-push inflation
   b. a bout of demand-pull inflation
   c. a contractionary monetary policy

2. a. If an economy is initially at an equilibrium point to the right of its long-run aggregate supply curve, then what will be the long-run process whereby the economy will reach this curve?
   b. In the opposite case where an economy is initially at an equilibrium point to the left of its long-run aggregate supply curve, how will the economy reach this curve in the long run?

LAST WORD

In this chapter, we saw how the Bank of Canada uses its available tools of monetary policy to affect inflation and unemployment, as well as to stabilize the economy over the business cycle. Next, we turn to the Bank of Canada's possible influence on the international value of the Canadian dollar, as well as examine the balance of payments accounts that help determine it. This discussion introduces the topic of Canada's role in the global economy, which is the theme of Part IV. In this final section, we examine not only the foreign sector, but also international trade, as well as some of the contentious issues connected with economic growth and Canada's role in the global economy.

PROBLEMS

1. **a.** What is the nominal rate of interest on a one-year $1 million treasury bill if its purchase price is $975 000? if its purchase price is $960 000?
   b. How can the Bank of Canada adjust supply in the auction of treasury bills to raise the nominal rate of interest on treasury bills?
   c. How can the Bank of Canada adjust its own purchases in the auction of treasury bills to raise the nominal rate of interest on treasury bills?

2. The Bank of Canada purchases $1 million of government bonds from Bondholder X, who has a deposit at Frontenac Bank.
   a. How will this transaction affect the balance sheets of the Bank of Canada and Frontenac Bank?
   b. If the reserve ratio is 5 percent, how will this affect Frontenac Bank's excess reserves?
   c. What is the final maximum effect of this purchase on the money supply?

3. What is the maximum amount by which the following policies will change the money supply?
   a. The Bank of Canada buys $100 million of bonds when the reserve ratio is 5 percent.
   b. The Bank of Canada sells $50 million of bonds when the reserve ratio is 7.5 percent.

4. The table below shows inflation and unemployment data for Macronia.

   Inflation and Unemployment in Macronia

Year	Inflation Rate	Unemployment Rate
2013	4	5
2014	2	8
2015	3	6

   a. Would expansionary or contraction stabilization policies have caused the change that takes place between 2013 and 2014? What type of stabilization policies would have caused the change between 2014 and 2015?
   b. Suppose that in 2016, the inflation rate is 5 percent and the unemployment rate is 10 percent. What has happened to the Phillips curve? What could explain this change? Give an example of a factor that might have caused it.
   d. Draw a graph showing the Philips curve based on the values for inflation and unemployment in this economy from 2013 to 2015. Plot three points for this curve.

5. When would it be more advantageous to hold Canada Savings Bonds than to hold regular bonds, when nominal interest rates are rising or falling?

6. "Changes in the target overnight rate can affect the money supply only if backed up by the use of open market operations." Discuss, using either expansionary or contractionary monetary policy as an example.

7. If one part of Canada (e.g., Saskatchewan) is experiencing an inflationary boom, while another part (e.g., Ontario) is facing a downturn in spending and rising unemployment, what problems does the Bank of Canada face in trying to fashion an appropriate monetary policy for the nation as a whole?

8. Given the economy's self-stabilizing trends that determine the long-run aggregate supply curve, what shape does the Phillips curve have in the long run? Explain.

9. (Advanced Question)
   American economist Alan Blinder has popularized what he calls Murphy's Law of Economic Policy: "Economists have the least influence where they know the most and are most agreed; they have the most influence on policy where they know the least and disagree most vehemently." Using evidence from this chapter, state whether you agree or disagree with Blinder's statement.

connect **LEARNSMART** **SMARTBOOK**

For more information on the resources available from McGraw-Hill Ryerson, go to **www.mcgrawhill.ca/he/solutions**.

BREAKING THE MOULD

Mark Carney and Monetary Policy in the Aftermath of the 2008 Crisis

THE CANADIAN PRESS/
Adrian Wyld

Central banking can seem a sealed world, dominated by specialists who spend lifetimes rising through government ranks or who are drafted from academic economics. So when in 2008, when the Bank of Canada found itself with a 42-year-old governor who had spent most of his career in the private sector, people took notice.

Upending tradition has been a Mark Carney trademark. Born in the Northwest Territories hamlet of Fort Smith and growing up in Yellowknife and Edmonton, he left Canada to study economics at Harvard. After graduating he was hired by the international investment firm Goldman Sachs and started in the firm's Tokyo and London offices. Then came a four-year stay at Oxford University where he completed an MA and doctorate with a final thesis that focused on the interplay between competition in national and global markets.

Carney returned to Goldman and Sachs, posted again to London and later New York and Toronto. He rose to be managing director of the firm's Canadian operations, and along the way earned another degree in international relations from the University of Pennsylvania. Once he had returned to Canada, opportunities beckoned to jump into government. He left Goldman Sachs to take on a series of jobs at the Department of Finance and the Bank of Canada, culminating in his appointment as Bank governor early in 2008. As it happened, he took the reins just as rumblings of major problems in the international financial system were beginning. Within a month he boldly slashed Canada's bank rate at a time when many other central banks were still keeping interest rates high. When the full crisis hit during early autumn of that year, he was ready.

Carney's primary task was to ensure that the Canadian economy was insulated from the worst impact of the crisis. Aligning the Bank's monetary stance with the expansionary fiscal measures initiated by the federal government, he oversaw an extremely expansionary quantitative easing, as the Bank injected new money into the Canadian economy through purchases of various types of government bonds to raise their prices and push down interest rates. As the Bank's main spokesperson, he took care to clearly signal its intentions and plans, while ensuring that Canada's banking system had the resources to weather the storm. He was also thrust into behind-the-scenes discussions on fixing the regulation of international banking to ensure that such turmoil could never happen again. His years of direct industry experience proved invaluable in this role, allowing Canada to have a major say in the search for long-term solutions.

Carney exhibited another talent behind closed doors: a combative streak that had its roots in his keen passion for hockey, first displayed when playing for his high school team, then as backup goalie at Harvard. While he was a graduate student, it led to a memorable stint with the Oxford Blues, the university's varsity team. Joining what, on his arrival, was a lacklustre group of student players, he quickly became their chief strategist and taskmaster. During his time as team-member, the Blues improved to the point that they trounced their Cambridge University archrivals in the annual varsity match with a humiliating 19 to 0 win, a notable entry in Oxford's sports records that ensured Carney's years at the university were not forgotten. Now as governor, he showed a similar willingness to do both public and private battle–this time in strongly worded disagreements–with several executives from the global banking industry who were strongly opposed to the sorts of strict new regulations that Carney was known to be advocating.

Again, this brought him wider notice. In 2011 he was asked to chair a committee based in Switzerland, known as the Financial Stability Board, which is tasked with implementing improvements in national regulatory regimes, a part-time role he took on while remaining governor. But in 2013 came a much larger assignment. After much speculation, Carney announced he was leaving the Bank and heading for Britain to become governor of the Bank of England. The Old Lady of Threadneedle Street, as it is affectionately known, is the oldest central bank in the world. Never before in its 320-year history had it been headed by someone from outside the United Kingdom. Still, Carney's links with Britain run deep thanks to his previous extended stays in the country and the fact that his wife Diana Carney, an economist whom he met while at Oxford, is originally British.

The Bank of England's reputation stems not just from its long history, but from the fact that just steps away from its front portico is the world's most important financial centre. London's City district is headquarters for many of the largest international banking and investment firms. That means that whatever regulations the British government implements, with the Bank of England's active collaboration, have global repercussions. So too do any problems with these regulations, as became evident when major scandals erupted over the uncompetitive–and in the view of many commentators, illegal–price-fixing practices of several London-based banks. These scandals involved the setting of important international wholesale interest rates, as well as the banks' role in overseeing price adjustments in exchange rate markets. Just as importantly, at least from a domestic British perspective, is the fact that the nation has been heavily harmed by the crisis due to its close ties to the financial industry. The more immediate impact of the severe problems encountered by British chartered banks led to the largest government bank bailout in history.

It has not taken Carney long to make his mark as he addresses these challenges with characteristic vigour. Reorganizing the Bank's internal structure, he has announced his intention to strengthen the links between the short-term stabilization goals of monetary policy and the longer term needs to ensure financial stability. This means shifting away an overriding stress on minimizing inflation, something he sees as having driven monetary policy worldwide for the past decade and a half. "[W]hile there were enormous innovations of enduring value during this period," he has said referring to this fifteen-year span, "the reductionist vision of a central bank's role that was adopted around the world was fatally flawed. In particular, it failed to recognize that financial stability is as important an objective of macroeconomic policy as price stability. . . "[1] He has also promised to take active steps to counter the financial industry long-entrenched lack of transparency: "The age of informal responsibilities, nods, winks, secrecy and instinct is long past."[2] Changing age-old practices that involve some of the most

---

[1] "One Mission. One Bank. Promoting the Good of the People of the United Kingdom," Mais Lecture at Cass Business School, March 18, 2014, p. 4.

[2] Ibid, p. 11.

powerful private interests in today's global economy will be not be easy, but few doubt that Carney is up to the task.

As for what comes next once his time at the Bank of England is over, there is already considerable speculation. Some believe he will stay in the world of global finance in a regulatory position–for example, his name is often mentioned as a future head of the International Monetary Fund. Others think he will return to Canada, with a career in federal politics a possibility. Whatever he ends up choosing, there is little doubt he will keep on an unconventional path as he continues to find innovative ways to mesh theoretical insights with the practical needs of real-world economics and their financial systems.

1. Given the importance of the financial industry to the British economy, briefly explain why the financial problems associated with the 2008 financial crisis caused a particularly deep recession in the United Kingdom.

2. Summarize the likely reasoning behind Carney's contention that central banks need to be concerned with financial stability to ensure that monetary policy operates as they intend.

A Crisis Too Far

The 2008 Crisis and its Causes

The financial crisis of 2008 was the most serious in global finance since the 1929 stock market crash. After an extended boom in the world's large economies, the first signs of trouble arose in 2007 as mortgage borrowers in several countries began defaulting on their debts. Not until the following year did the systemic nature of these events become evident. In September 2008, two government sponsored agencies in the United States—the Federal Home Loan Mortgage Corporation (commonly known as Freddie Mac), and the Federal National Mortgage Association (Fannie Mae)—were taken over by the government, as American mortgage foreclosures reached alarming levels. Days later, the giant investment dealer Lehman Brothers faced bankruptcy and the American government took over the bankrupt mega-insurance company AIG. By October, stock markets were tumbling worldwide. Meanwhile, sources of credit in the United States and large parts of Europe dried up as financial intermediaries desperately cut back on their lending. The entire banking system in Iceland imploded, and there were fears that the British system might as well. Only with forced mergers involving banks and investment dealers in several countries, as well as breathtakingly large infusions of public funds in both North America and Europe, was the nightmare of total collapse averted.

Though the world's economy gradually rebounded and the global financial industry reconsolidated, the effects of the crisis are still being felt today with elevated unemployment rates, high levels of government debt, and extremely low interest rates as central banks continue to stimulate their economies. Meanwhile, a consensus has emerged regarding the lessons for policy-makers. First, those in charge of stabilization policy must guard against speculative bubbles in asset markets. Second, the need to regulate financial markets has not been lessened by global financial integration and increasingly sophistication of financial instruments. Third, economists need to maintain a healthy skepticism over the extent to which their insights can ever completely eradicate the business cycle. We'll look at each of these lessons in turn.

Guarding Against Speculative Bubbles

Starting in the 1990s, property prices in many countries began rising year after year. This unsustainable trend was driven by easy financing and low interest rates. As long as buyers believed there were others willing to pay even more for over-inflated property assets, it was expected that high returns from real estate would continue: the classic conditions for what is known as a speculative bubble.

In the United States, the bubble was intensified by the availability of *subprime mortgages*—mortgage loans incorporating a high risk premium and made to borrowers with weak credit ratings. Many of these mortgages were backed by the public agencies Freddie Mac and Fannie Mae, whose mandate was to encourage more Americans to own their own homes. At the height of the property boom, it was possible for Americans to receive high-interest mortgages with minimal checks on their credit worthiness, and without investing more than a nominal amount as a down payment. As more risky mortgages were issued, the chances of mass default by mortgage borrowers grew.

Regulating Financial Markets

At the same time, a dazzling array of new financial products was introduced, fueled by a loosening of regulations in the world's major banking centres, especially London and New York. These products, which still exist, are examples of *derivatives*, financial instruments directly tied to other items such as commodities, shares, bonds, and international currencies. The most basic types of derivatives are futures and options, which have a long history. These instruments provide ways for two parties to exchange an underlying item at a set price in the future—a required exchange at an established time in the case of a futures contract, and an optional exchange before some expiration date in the case of an option. Futures and options are used by risk-avoiding hedgers to reduce risk in trading the underlying item, and by speculators who wish to take on risk in the hopes of making gains.

Futures and options were originally created to expedite the trading of commodities such as wheat, gold, and oil. Beginning in the 1970s and 1980s, their use expanded so that the underlying items included financial securities. It became possible to buy and sell futures and options tied to individual shares, bonds, and international currencies, or even financial indexes such as those found in stock markets.

The 1990s brought more specialized derivatives, such as collateralized debt obligations (CDOs). These are collections of a certain class of security such as bonds or mortgages sold in packages. Intended to help financial investors manage risk by making it possible to average out the chances of default on individual securities, these new products began to be used in dangerous ways. In the United States, financial intermediaries began packaging collections of mortgages—in particular the risky subprime variety—and selling them to private investors as well as to Freddie Mac and Fannie Mae.

Another new derivative was the credit default swap. This instrument requires its holder to pay an annual premium to the supplier in return for a guarantee that, if the issuer of underlying security can't pay and defaults on their debt, the supplier will pay the full value of the swap's underlying financial security. In the early 2000s, risk-averse investors began using credit default swaps as insurance on the financial securities they held. By paying the swap's annual premium, they were assured that they would not suffer a major loss in the event their securities defaulted. To meet this demand, some financial firms began underwriting credit default swaps, including ones built on the shaky foundation of subprime mortgages. These firms were liable to make huge payments if there were extensive defaults on the underlying securities.

Unfortunately, the characteristics of such new financial products were so elusive that even financial experts were at a loss to predict how their prices might behave under different market conditions. For their part, government regulators did little to limit these products, not only because their complexity made them difficult to regulate, but because they spanned national borders. Once the crisis hit, firms and government agencies with large holdings of collateralized debt obligations, as well as issuers of credit default swaps, faced crippling losses. This experience led to a new consensus among economists that stronger regulation of complex financial instruments is essential in the future.

In many countries, Canada included, there has been a long-term reaction in terms of tighter financial regulations on banks and other lenders to ensure that the investment business of these institutions is kept separate from other functions. Thanks to tightened global regulations, they are also being required to hold a higher proportion of assets in relatively liquid form to deal with various types of financial risk, including those associated with financial instruments such as derivatives. Whether these new policies will be sufficient to forestall a repetition of another such crisis in the future is uncertain. Just as importantly, it will take years for some countries to recover fully from the profound effects on their economies in the crisis's wake.

Appreciating the Limits of Stabilization Policy

Just as investors, financial firms, and their regulators learned from the crisis, so too did macroeconomic policy-makers. First, the crisis proved that speculative bubbles and

the business cycle are by no means things of the past. Second, it showed that more emphasis must be placed on policy coordination at the international level, as well as possible new global regulatory agencies. Third, as the global economy recovered, it became clear that government budget deficits still have a part to play in countercyclical fiscal policy.

All this is something of a departure from what observers call the overconfidence of policy-makers during the lead-up to the crisis. In 2004, for example, Ben S. Bernanke, former chairman of the Federal Reserve, voiced the notion that industrial economies had achieved "The Great Moderation,"[1] having successfully overcome severe bouts of macroeconomic volatility. Such thinking is now definitely passé. The consensus that is gradually taking its place is eloquently expressed by noted American economist Paul Krugman:

> [E]conomists will have to learn to live with messiness. That is, they will have to acknowledge the importance of irrational and often unpredictable behavior, face up to the often idiosyncratic imperfections of markets and accept that an elegant economic 'theory of everything' is a long way off. In practical terms, this will translate into more cautious policy advice—and a reduced willingness to dismantle economic safeguards in the faith that markets will solve all problems.[3]

1. Some financial investors purchased credit default swaps tied to particularly risky collateralized debt obligations with no intention of using these swaps as an insurance on CDOs they were holding, but rather as standalone speculative investments. Briefly explain why this small group of investors made spectacular gains during the depths of the 2008 credit meltdown.

2. In *The General Theory of Employment, Interest and Money*, John Maynard Keynes noted: "When the capital development of a country becomes the by-product of a casino, the job is likely to be ill-done." Some observers have suggested this statement was relevant to the financial crisis and its causes. Explain.

Notes

[1] "Remarks at the meetings of the Eastern Economic Association," February 20, 2004 (www.federalreserve.gov/Boarddocs/Speeches/2004/20040220/default.htm).

[2] Paul Krugman, "How Did Economists Get It So Wrong?" *The New York Times*, September 2, 2009 (www.nytimes.com/2009/09/06/magazine/06Economic-t.html).

Like other animals, we find and pick up what we can use, and appropriate territories. But unlike the other animals, we also trade and produce for trade.

— JANE JACOBS, AMERICAN URBAN
AFFAIRS EXPERT AND AUTHOR

Canada in the Global Economy

Products used to move relatively slowly in the world—Canadian lumber was transported by sailing ships to Britain, for example. Now goods are often flown by aircraft, and services are provided by satellite or optical cable. Just as innovations in telecommunications have broken down barriers of geographical distance to create a "global village"—a term coined by Canadian communications theorist Marshall McLuhan—a unified world marketplace is gradually coming into being, with significant ramifications for us all. These last two chapters consider Canada in the global economy, first looking at the foreign sector in Canada, and then examining international trade.

CHAPTER 14
The Foreign Sector

CHAPTER 15
The Foreign Trade

The Foreign Sector

For all nations, including Canada, the move toward a global economy is bringing about changes in living standards, employment patterns, and prospects for growth, sometimes with dizzying speed. In this chapter, we examine how foreign transactions are summarized in the balance-of-payments accounts, and we study the influence of currency exchange rates. We also see how international financial investment has affected Canada's external debt and levels of foreign ownership in the Canadian economy.

That knowledge has become the key resource means that there is a world economy, and that the world economy, rather than the national economy, is in control.
—PETER F. DRUCKER, AMERICAN SOCIAL PHILOSOPHER

LEARNING OBJECTIVES After reading this chapter, you will be able to:

LO 1

Explain the balance-of-payments accounts, which include the current account and the capital and financial accounts

LO 2

Define exchange rates and describe how they are determined

LO 3

Summarize exchange rate systems and their evolution

14.1 | The Balance of Payments

LO1 As seen in earlier chapters, the rest of the world is linked with the Canadian economy through trade. Foreigners enter Canadian product markets by buying Canadian exports. In turn, Canadians buy foreign imports. Foreign spending on Canadian exports represents a monetary inflow for Canada's product markets, while Canadian spending on imports represents a monetary outflow from the Canadian economy.

Recall also that the same principles apply to trading financial assets, such as stocks and bonds. Foreigners enter Canadian financial markets by buying Canadian stocks and bonds, thereby creating an inflow of funds to Canadian financial markets. Of course, foreigners also sell foreign stocks and bonds to Canadians, thereby creating an outflow of funds from Canadian financial markets.

The Balance-of-Payments Accounts

The connections between the Canadian economy and the rest of the world are shown in detail using Canada's balance-of-payments accounts. Recall from Chapter 1 that these accounts provide a summary of all international transactions between residents of Canada and those of foreign countries that involve exchanging Canadian dollars for some other international currency. At any given time, a statement of the accounts shows how the inflows and outflows "balance."

RECEIPTS AND PAYMENTS

Transactions in the accounts are divided into receipts and payments. The receipts represent monetary inflows to the Canadian economy, including both foreign purchases of Canadian exports and inflows from foreigners when they buy Canadian financial assets. Receipts are considered positive, so they are given a plus sign (+) in the accounts.

Payments, on the other hand, represent monetary outflows from the Canadian economy. They include outlays by Canadians for foreign imports and foreign financial assets. Payments are considered negative, so they are given a minus sign (−) in the accounts.

The Current Account

current account: the summary of all international transactions associated with current economic activity in Canada and involving Canadian dollars

Figure 14.1 shows the portion of the balance-of-payments statement that is called the **current account**. This account summarizes all international transactions associated with current economic activity in Canada and involving Canadian dollars. The current account includes four types of transactions: trade in merchandise (in other words, tangible goods), as well as in three "invisible" items—trade in services, flows of investment income, and transfers.

TRADE IN MERCHANDISE

merchandise balance of trade: merchandise export receipts minus merchandise import payments

The most significant and obvious components of the current account are Canadian exports and imports of goods, or "visibles," as they are known. Canadians sell a broad range of merchandise exports and buy an equally broad range of merchandise imports. In years when the dollar value of Canadian exports of visibles are outweighed by that of Canadian imports of visibles, the current account shows a negative **merchandise balance of trade**. For example, in

	Receipts (+) (Canadian $ inflows)		(Canadian $ billions) Payments (−) (Canadian $ outflows)		Balance (net) (Canadian $ inflows − $ outflows)
Merchandise trade	479.0	−	486.3	=	−7.3
Trade in services	86.8	−	111.3	=	−24.5
Balance of trade (net exports)					−31.8
Investment income	70.7	−	94.5	=	−23.8
Transfers	12.1	−	17.1	=	−5.0
Current account surplus (+) or deficit (−)					−60.7

FIGURE 14.1   Canada's Current Account (2013)

The current account details receipts (Canadian dollar inflows) and payments (Canadian dollar outflows) for merchandise trade and non-merchandise transactions (trade in services, investment income, and transfers). In contrast to the small deficit in the 2013 merchandise balance of trade, Canada had a larger deficit in its 2013 balance of trade (net exports). Overall for 2013, the difference between total receipts and total payments gave a current account deficit of $60.7 billion.

Source: Statistics Canada "Canada's Current Account (2013)." Adapted from the Statistics Canada website, Summary Table, www.statcan.gc.ca/tables-tableaux/sum-som/l01/cst01/econ01a-eng.htm. Retrieved March 8, 2014.

2013, payments for Canadian exports of merchandise were $479.0 billion and payments for Canadian imports of merchandise were $486.3 billion, giving a negative merchandise balance of trade of $7.3 billion. In contrast, in years when exports of goods outweigh imports, the current account shows a positive merchandise balance of trade.

NON-MERCHANDISE TRANSACTIONS

The three remaining "invisible" components of the current account—trade in services, investment income, and transfers—are known collectively as non-merchandise transactions.

Services

Not only do Canadians import and export goods, they also exchange services with foreigners. One important type of traded service is tourism. Spending by foreign tourists travelling in Canada represents a service export that creates an inflow of funds from foreign countries. Conversely, when Canadians travel outside Canada, their spending in foreign countries is considered a service import that causes an outflow of Canadian funds to foreign hands.

Canadians also import services when they pay foreigners to provide freight and shipping for goods. Likewise, Canadians export services when they transport goods on behalf of foreigners. In addition, a host of other invisible service items, such as insurance and telecommunications, are traded between Canadians and other countries. In 2013, the service account had a net balance of −$24.5 billion, showing that more services were imported by Canadians than were exported.

Investment Income

Dividends to owners of company stocks appear as investment income in the current account, as do interest payments to owners of bonds. A US company's dividends received by a Canadian stockholder, for example, are treated as a receipt in the current account, or a positive figure. In contrast, payments to a German owner of a Canadian government bond are shown as a payment in the accounts, or a negative figure.

Because of extensive foreign ownership of Canadian stocks and bonds, payments of investment income usually overwhelm receipts, giving Canada a negative balance on its investment income account. This is illustrated by the 2013 balance of −$23.8 billion.

Transfers

Transfers are funds entering and leaving Canada through payments, either by individuals or government, that do not involve shifts in financial assets. Private gifts that involve cash rather than financial assets and that are either to or from Canada, pension payments to and from Canada, as well as government development assistance to low-income countries, are all considered to be transfers. When an immigrant to Canada receives pension payments from a foreign source, these funds are considered an inflow to the Canadian economy. In contrast, federal government spending on development assistance is considered an outflow. In 2013, transfers showed a net balance of −$5.0 billion.

Current Account Balance

current account deficit: a negative net balance in the current account resulting from lower receipts than payments for merchandise and non-merchandise transactions

current account surplus: a positive net balance in the current account resulting from higher receipts than payments for merchandise and non-merchandise transactions

When the receipts represented in Canada's current account are lower than the payments, this results in a negative net balance, which is known as a **current account deficit**. In 2013, this totalled −$60.7 billion. On the other hand, when receipts on the current account outweigh payments, Canada has a **current account surplus**.

The Balance of Trade

balance of trade: for both goods and services, receipts (inflows of Canadian dollars) less payments (outflows of Canadian dollars)

Two of the four components of the current accounts can be viewed in another way. Canada's **balance of trade** represents both goods and services, so it is identical to net exports (X − M), which was discussed in previous chapters. In most recent years (though not in 2013), Canada has had a surplus in merchandise trade greater than the deficit in trade in services, giving a surplus in the balance of trade of all products. **Note that the two terms "balance of trade" and "merchandise balance of trade" are quite different; despite this, the terms are frequently and inaccurately interchanged by the media, leading to some confusion.**

The Capital and Financial Accounts

capital account: the summary of international transfers of intangible assets and savings involving Canadian dollars

Figure 14.2 shows another portion of the balance-of-payments statement called the capital and financial accounts. The **capital account** summarizes a fairly narrow range of inflows and outflows involving Canadian dollars–those linked to transfers either of intangible assets, such as patents or trademarks, or of savings. For example, if a Canadian acquires a patent owned by a company in India, this is considered a negative payment on the capital account. In contrast, when a recent newcomer to Canada receives a bequest from a relative in China or moves financial assets to Canada, this is a positive receipt on the capital account.

financial account: the summary of all international transactions of financial assets involving Canadian dollars

The **financial account** summarizes all international transactions of financial assets involving Canadian dollars. Suppose a foreigner buys a Canadian government bond and holds bank deposits valued in Canadian dollars. This ownership of financial assets is being *exported* from Canada, so an inflow of receipts is shown on the financial account. Note, however, that the interest paid on bonds or deposits appears as an outflow on the current account.

| FIGURE 14.2 | Canada's Capital and Financial Accounts (2013) | | | | |

	Receipts (+) (Canadian $ inflows)		(Canadian $ billions) Payments (−) (Canadian $ outflows)		Balance (net) (Canadian $ inflows − outflows)
Capital Account	0.3	−	0.4	=	−0.1
Financial Account					
Direct investment	64.2	−	43.9	=	20.3
Portfolio investment	42.8	−	27.2	=	15.6
Other financial investments					27.3
Total capital and financial account surplus (1) or deficit (2) (excl. official reserves)					63.1

The capital and financial accounts detail net flows for financial investment (portfolio and direct investment) and other financial transactions. In 2013, the large positive balances for other financial investments, direct investment, and portfolio investment more than offset the tiny negative balance in the capital account, giving a capital and financial accounts surplus.

Source: Statistics Canada "Canada's Financial Accounts (2013)" and "Canada's Current and Capital Accounts (2013)." Adapted from the Statistics Canada website, Summary Table, www.statcan.gc.ca/tables-tableaux/sum-som/l01/cst01/econ01b-eng.htm and CANSIM Table 376-0101. Retrieved March 8, 2014.

Suppose also that a Canadian purchases stock in a foreign company. In this case, the Canadian's ownership is seen as an import of ownership, so the transaction is considered to be an outflow from the financial account. Once again, note that any payment on the financial asset–in this case, a dividend–would appear as an inflow on the current account.

DIRECT AND PORTFOLIO INVESTMENT

The most significant transactions on the financial account are associated with the buying and selling of stocks and bonds. These flows are often referred to as financial investment and can be divided into portfolio investment and direct investment. **Note that financial investment differs from investment, as defined by economists. While investment refers to businesses' purchases of real assets, financial investment refers to the buying of stocks and bonds.**

Direct investment is financial investment that gives the buyer of the financial assets a significant influence in a company. In the case of a corporation, Statistics Canada defines this as occurring when the buyer has 10 percent of the company's voting shares. For example, an inflow of direct investment would occur if an Australian financier gained control of a Canadian gold mining company. An outflow would arise if a Canadian retailer acquired significant ownership of a British competitor.

Canada's net balance of direct investment varies widely from year to year. If Canada is viewed as an attractive place in which to do business, heavy inflows of direct investment lead to an overall positive balance as was the case in 2013, when direct investment totalled +$20.3 billion. If other countries seem more appealing to foreign and Canadian investors, there can be an overall negative balance.

In contrast to direct investment, when the financial investment does not give the buyer a significant interest in the institution issuing the assets, it is called **portfolio investment**. Suppose, for example, a Japanese resident buys a Canadian federal government bond. This would be shown as a receipt, or positive entry, on the financial account. Conversely, if a Canadian purchases a few hundred shares in a large US corporation that trades on the New York Stock

direct investment: financial investment (purchases of stocks) that gives the buyer of the financial assets a significant influence in the institution issuing the assets

portfolio investment: financial investment (purchases of stocks and bonds) that does not give the buyer a significant interest in the institution issuing the assets

Exchange, the transaction would be shown as a payment, or negative entry, on the financial account. Portfolio investment in and out of Canada may produce either a positive or negative balance. In 2013, for example, there was a net balance of +$15.6 billion.

OTHER FINANCIAL INVESTMENTS

Most of the remaining transactions on the financial account are connected with day-to-day fluctuations in bank deposits. If, for example, a foreigner puts funds into a Canadian-dollar bank account, a positive receipt is created in Canada's financial account. Likewise, a negative payment on the account can be caused by a Canadian adding more to a US-dollar bank account.

CAPITAL AND FINANCIAL ACCOUNT BALANCES

When receipts on Canada's capital and financial accounts exceed payments, this results in a positive net balance known as a **capital and financial accounts surplus**. In 2013, for example, this balance was +$63.1 billion. Such a surplus means that there are lower investments by Canadians in foreign markets than by foreigners in the Canadian economy. It is also possible to show a **capital and financial accounts deficit**, with a negative net balance and outflows exceeding inflows. Such a deficit means that there are higher investments by Canadians in foreign markets than by foreigners in the Canadian economy.

Balance-of-Payments Surpluses and Deficits

Adding Canada's current and capital and financial accounts balances (as well as a statistical discrepancy, which accounts for hidden transactions that are impossible to measure) gives a relatively small figure known as a **balance-of-payments surplus** if it is positive and a **balance-of-payments deficit** if it is negative. This surplus or deficit shows whether or not inflows are higher than outflows on all foreign transactions involving trade and financial assets. In 2013, for example, Canada had a balance-of-payments surplus of +$4.9 billion, as shown by the positive balance in Figure 14.3. In other words, for that year, inflows exceeded outflows on the combined current and capital and financial accounts.

CHANGES IN OFFICIAL RESERVES

To influence the international value of the Canadian dollar (as we will discuss later), the Bank of Canada sometimes buys and sells foreign currencies using government's reserves of foreign currency. The effect of these operations on the flow of Canadian dollars is known as the **change in official reserves**. As shown in Figure 14.3, the change in official reserves is equal in value (and opposite in sign) to the surplus or deficit noted in the balance of payments. In 2013, for example, the −$4.9 billion change in reserves matches the +$4.9 billion balance-of-payments surplus. This negative change in official reserves indicates that the Bank of Canada sold Canadian dollars (creating an outflow) by buying foreign currency for the government's official reserves. In the same way, if there were a balance-of-payments deficit, there would be a positive change in official reserves equal to that amount. This positive change in official reserves would indicate that the Bank of Canada bought Canadian dollars (causing an inflow) and sold foreign currency.

Once the change in official reserves is added to the balance-of-payments surplus or deficit, the balance-of-payments accounts sum to zero. In other words, the inflow of funds from foreigners matches the outflow of funds from Canadians,

capital and financial accounts surplus: a positive net balance in the capital and financial accounts, demonstrating lower investments by Canadians in foreign markets than by foreigners in the Canadian economy

capital and financial accounts deficit: a negative net balance in the capital and financial accounts, demonstrating higher investments by Canadians in foreign markets than by foreigners in the Canadian economy

balance-of-payments surplus: a positive net balance on the balance-of-payments statement, demonstrating greater receipts than payments for the current and capital and financial accounts combined; balanced with changes in official reserves

balance-of-payments deficit: a negative net balance on the balance-of-payments statement, demonstrating lower receipts than payments for the current and capital and financial accounts combined; balanced with changes in official reserves

change in official reserves: use of government's reserves of foreign currency to influence the international value of the Canadian dollar, as shown on the balance-of-payments statement

FIGURE 14.3	Canada's Balance of Payments (2013)

	(Canadian $ billions)	Balance (net)
1.	Current account	−60.7
2.	Capital and financial accounts	63.1
	Statistical discrepancy	2.4
3.	Balance-of-payments surplus (+) or deficit (−)	+4.9
4.	Change in official reserves	−4.9

The sum of the current and capital and financial accounts, adjusted for the statistical discrepancy, gives Canada's balance of payments. In 2013, the result was a balance-of-payments surplus of +$4.9 billion. Because there must be change in the official reserves of foreign currency to balance any deficit or surplus, the 2013 balance of payments shows a negative change in reserves.

Source. Statistics Canada "Canada's Balance of Payments (2013)." Adapted from the Statistics Canada website, Summary Table, www.statcan.gc.ca/tables-tableaux/sum-som/l01/cst01/econ01b-eng.htm. Retrieved March 8, 2014.

ensuring that the accounts balance. This balance occurs because holders of Canadian dollars who buy foreign currency must engage in transactions of equal value with holders of foreign currency buying Canadian dollars. For example, $1 in Canadian currency can be sold for Japanese yen only if someone is willing to purchase this Canadian dollar in return for yen.

The fact that the balance-of-payments account sum to zero provides Statistics Canada with the means of estimating the size of the statistical discrepancy. As seen in Figure 14.3, this discrepancy is significant when compared to the size of the balance of payments surplus. This relates to the fact that there are considerable international flows that government authorities are unable to directly measure. Funds that either enter or leave the country due to the smuggling of goods or because of undeclared financial investments are the largest part of these unrecorded foreign transactions. Studies suggest that other major sources of this discrepancy include government authorities overlooking investment income payments, especially those associated with offshore banking centres, and the overlooking of much maritime freight, particularly by countries with large shipping industries.

THINKING ABOUT ECONOMICS

Very often in the past, and now habitually since the 2008 financial crisis, Canada has run a deficit on its current account and a surplus on its combined capital and financial accounts. Why?

The frequency of deficits in Canada's current account has been closely tied to the high degree of foreign ownership in the Canadian economy. To compensate for this outflow of interest and dividend payments, there has to be a sizable inflow of investment funds from foreigners on the financial account, which means even more foreign ownership of Canadian financial assets. Financial account inflows are assured whenever Canadian bonds are seen as being especially attractive to foreign buyers. Traditionally, this was accomplished through higher real interest rates than in other countries—particularly the United States—though this is no longer necessarily the case.

QUESTION   Because of Canada's relative attractiveness to financial investors since the **2008** financial crisis, the interest rate on Canadian bonds is often below rates on foreign bonds. Why?

BRIEF REVIEW

1. Because products and financial assets are exchanged between Canadians and foreigners, foreigners participate in the Canadian economy.

2. The current account summarizes all receipts and payments from international trade in merchandise, trade in services, flows of investment income, and transfers of funds. The current account has typically shown payments exceeding receipts, giving a current account deficit.

3. Because Canada's balance of trade is the exports of goods and services less imports of goods and services, it is the same as net exports $(X - M)$.

4. The capital and financial accounts summarize all foreign transactions related to the buying and selling of assets. Large inflows of funds from foreigners buying Canadian bonds has meant that Canada has typically shown a capital and financial accounts surplus.

5. The current account and the capital and financial accounts are adjusted for statistical discrepancy but balanced by changes in the official reserves. The Bank of Canada either sells or buys Canadian dollars to adjust monetary flows.

14.1 | PRACTICE PROBLEM

1. For each of the following transactions, identify where it appears on Canada's current account and whether it is classified as a receipt or a payment.
   a. A Canadian movie chain purchases the rights to screen an Italian film in Canada.
   b. An American family purchases a Canadian-made trailer for their summer vacation.
   c. A Canadian sends a monetary gift to relatives in India.
   d. A Canadian shareholder receives dividends from a Japanese corporation.
2. For each of the following transactions, identify where it appears on Canada's capital and financial accounts and whether it is classified as a receipt or a payment.
   a. A British wealth-holder purchases bonds issued by a Canadian provincial government.
   b. An Australian mining company is purchased by a Canadian-owned corporation.
   c. A Canadian receives a monetary bequest from a Spanish relative.
   d. A Norwegian shipping company opens a bank deposit in Canada.

14.2 | Exchange Rates

LO2   Any transaction that appears in the balance-of-payments accounts involves trading Canadian dollars for another currency. Transactions that are classified as receipts involve foreign currency being sold to buy Canadian dollars. For example, a French company that purchases Canadian paper sold in France trades European euros for Canadian dollars to pay the Canadian paper company. In contrast, transactions that are classified as payments involve Canadian dollars being sold to buy foreign currency. A Canadian buying the services of a Japanese architect, for example, exchanges Canadian dollars for Japanese yen to pay the architect.

Currencies are traded in the global **foreign exchange market**. In the Canadian sector of this market, which is run by the chartered banks, Canadian dollars are exchanged for US dollars, Japanese yen, European euros, and other international currencies. Thanks to communications technology, the foreign exchange market is a truly global one, with currency prices internationally consistent and immediately available. For example, if the Canadian dollar is trading at a price of 95 US cents in Toronto, then the same price applies in London and Tokyo.

Recall from Chapter 10 that the exchange rate is the value of one nation's currency in terms of another currency, and it becomes the price at any location where the two currencies are being exchanged. There are many exchange rates for a certain currency. For example, at any given moment, one Canadian dollar may trade for 90 US cents, 130 Japanese yen, or 0.70 European euros. Because most of Canada's trade is with the United States, the price of the Canadian dollar is commonly related to US dollars. We will be using the example of Canadian and US dollars in the rest of the chapter, although the same principles apply to all currencies.

Two exchange rates can be used to compare any two currencies—for example, a Canadian dollar with its US counterpart. The first tells us how many US dollars it takes to buy one Canadian dollar—for example, one Canadian dollar may cost 90 US cents. The other way to express the exchange rate is to ask how many Canadian dollars are needed to purchase one US dollar. This amount can be calculated from the first exchange rate by using the following formula:

$$\text{Canadian dollars to buy US\$1} = \frac{1}{\text{US dollars to buy CDN\$1}}$$
$$\text{CDN\$1.11} = \frac{1}{\text{US\$0.90}}$$

In other words, the second exchange rate—CDN$1.11 buys US$1—is the reciprocal of the first exchange rate.

Exchange Rates and Prices

One important application of exchange rates is to determine prices of products in terms of a foreign currency—either the US dollar price of a Canadian product, for example, or the Canadian dollar price of a US item.

Foreign prices of Canadian products are calculated by applying the exchange rate to the goods' Canadian dollar prices. For example, when a Canadian export with a Canadian price of $20 is sold in the United States, find its US dollar price by multiplying its Canadian price by the exchange rate expressed as the number of US dollars it takes to buy one Canadian dollar. When the exchange rate has a value of US$0.90 for each Canadian dollar, the US price of this product is, therefore, US$18:

$$\text{US dollar price} = \text{Canadian dollar price} \times \text{US dollars to buy CDN\$1}$$

$$\text{US\$18.00} = \text{CDN\$20.00} \times \text{US\$0.90/CDN\$}$$

Canadian prices of foreign goods are calculated in reverse. For example, suppose a US product imported to Canada has a US price of $40. To find the import's Canadian dollar price, multiply the US price by the exchange rate expressed as the number of Canadian dollars it takes to buy one US dollar. When the exchange rate has a value of CDN$1.11 for each US dollar, the item's Canadian price is CDN$44.40:

Canadian dollar price = US dollar price × Canadian dollars to buy US$1

CDN$44.40 = US$40.00 × CDN$1.11/US$

Foreign Exchange Markets

To see how exchange rates are set, we must look at the demand for and supply of Canadian currency in foreign exchange markets. In doing so, we concentrate on the number of US dollars needed to purchase a Canadian dollar.

DEMAND FOR CANADIAN DOLLARS

demand for Canadian dollars: the relationship between the price of a Canadian dollar and the quantity demanded in exchange for another currency

The **demand for Canadian dollars** is the relationship between the price of a Canadian dollar and the quantity of Canadian dollars demanded in exchange for another currency during a given time period. The relationship can be expressed in a schedule and a curve. As Figure 14.4 shows, this relationship is inverse, so the curve has a negative slope. For example, a jump in the price of the Canadian dollar in terms of the US dollar reduces the quantity of Canadian dollars demanded.

Canadian dollars are demanded on foreign exchange markets to finance foreign purchases of either Canadian exports or Canadian financial assets. Foreigners buying Canadian exports of goods and services exchange their own currencies for Canadian dollars to pay Canadian producers. Likewise, foreigners acquiring Canadian financial assets buy Canadian dollars to settle their purchases.

FIGURE 14.4 A Foreign Exchange Market

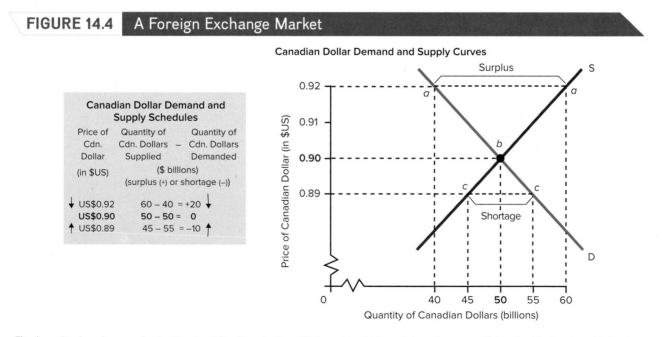

Canadian Dollar Demand and Supply Schedules		
Price of Cdn. Dollar (in $US)	Quantity of Cdn. Dollars Supplied	Quantity of Cdn. Dollars Demanded
	($ billions) (surplus (+) or shortage (−))	
↓ US$0.92	60 − 40 = +20 ↓	
US$0.90	50 − 50 = 0	
↑ US$0.89	45 − 55 = −10 ↑	

The demand and supply curves for the Canadian dollar determine its equilibrium value, which equals its exchange rate. If the price falls (to points *c*) below the equilibrium value (point *b*), a shortage of Canadian dollars results. Without government intervention, the forces of demand and supply push the price up to equilibrium (point *b*), causing the Canadian dollar to appreciate. A price above the equilibrium value (at points *a*) causes a surplus of Canadian dollars. Without government intervention, the Canadian dollar would depreciate, returning to its equilibrium value.

The negative slope of the demand curve is determined by the first of these two groups–foreign export buyers. A higher Canadian dollar means that Canadian goods and services have higher US prices. Suppose, for example, the exchange rate for Canadian dollars is US$0.90. As a result, a Canadian export with a price of CDN$2 originally has an US price of US$1.80 (= $2 × $0.90). If the value of the Canadian dollar increases from US$0.90 to US$0.95, the US price of this export rises to US$1.90 (= $2 × $0.95). Because US buyers find Canadian exports more expensive, they purchase fewer of them, decreasing both Canadian export receipts and the quantity of Canadian dollars demanded in exchange for US dollars.

SUPPLY OF CANADIAN DOLLARS

In contrast, the **supply of Canadian dollars** is the relationship between the price of the Canadian dollar and the quantity of Canadian dollars supplied in exchange for another currency during a given time period. Once again, the relationship can be expressed in a schedule or a curve. As Figure 14.4 shows, the relationship is direct, as is typical in supply relationships. A rise in the price of the Canadian dollar causes an increase in the quantity supplied of Canadian dollars.

Canadian dollars are supplied in foreign exchange markets for Canadian purchases of foreign products and financial assets. Canadians buying imported products or foreign financial assets sell Canadian dollars for another currency to complete their transactions.

The first of these two groups, Canadian import buyers, determines the positive slope of the supply curve. For example, a higher Canadian dollar lowers domestic prices of imported goods and services from the United States. If the Canadian dollar rises from US$0.90 to US$0.95, the US dollar falls in terms of the Canadian dollar from CDN$1.11 (= $1 ÷ $0.90) to CDN$1.05 (= $1 ÷ $0.95). A US import that costs $3 in the United States, therefore, drops from CDN$3.33 (= $3 × $1.11) to CDN$3.15 (= $3 × $1.05). Canadians respond to these lower prices by purchasing more imports, increasing both Canadian import payments and the quantity of Canadian dollars supplied in exchange for US dollars.

MARKET EQUILIBRIUM

Recall that in competitive markets, the forces of demand and supply bring the market to an equilibrium point, where demand and supply intersect. The same is true of foreign exchange markets. So, when a government allows the value of its currency to vary, foreign exchange markets will move toward an equilibrium point where any discrepancy between amounts demanded and supplied is eliminated. Figure 14.4 provides a hypothetical example.

If the Canadian dollar exchange rate (points *c*) is below its equilibrium price of US$0.90 (point *b*), the quantity demanded of Canadian dollars on this foreign exchange market is greater than the quantity supplied of Canadian dollars. This causes a $10 billion shortage of Canadian currency, as shown at the exchange rate of US$0.89 (= $55 billion − $45 billion). When exchange rates are allowed to vary, the price of the Canadian dollar is forced up to its equilibrium value. In this case, when one currency's price increases against another, the increased currency is said to **appreciate**. The movement to equilibrium is very rapid because foreign exchange markets are highly competitive and involve large numbers of price-conscious buyers and sellers.

In contrast, if the Canadian dollar is above its equilibrium price (points *a*), the quantity supplied of Canadian dollars exceeds the quantity demanded on

supply of Canadian dollars: the relationship between the price of a Canadian dollar and the quantity supplied in exchange for another currency

appreciate: to increase, as when a currency's price rises in comparison with the price of another currency

this foreign exchange market. The result is a $20 billion surplus of Canadian currency, as shown at the exchange rate of US$0.92 (= $60 billion − $40 billion). When exchange rates are allowed to vary, this excess soon pushes down the price of the Canadian dollar until it reaches its equilibrium value. In this case, the Canadian dollar is said to **depreciate**, compared with the US dollar. Again, the movement toward equilibrium happens very quickly.

depreciate: to decrease, as when a currency's price falls in comparison with the price of another currency

Note that both the preceding examples involve the variations in exchange rates that bring about changes in quantities demanded or supplied. In other words, the examples demonstrate movements *along* the Canadian dollar demand and supply curves.

Changes in Demand and Supply

Of course, other factors can cause the Canadian dollar demand and supply curves to shift. Demand and supply shifts in foreign exchange markets are related either to trade or to financial conditions. As a result of shifts in the curves, the equilibrium exchange rate changes. Four main factors affect the equilibrium value of the exchange rate: price differences, product demand, interest rates, and speculation.

PRICE DIFFERENCES

A country's price level may rise more rapidly than the price levels in other countries so that its own products become more expensive than foreign products. The left graph in Figure 14.5 illustrates a hypothetical example of what happens when Canada's rate of inflation outpaces inflation in the United States.

At any given exchange rate between the two currencies, increases in the prices of Canadian products mean that Americans will purchase fewer Canadian exports, reducing the amount of Canadian currency demanded on this foreign exchange market. This reduces the demand for Canadian dollars, shown as a shift in the demand curve for Canadian dollars from D_0 to D_1. A lower US inflation rate also means that American products become cheaper relative to Canadian products. As a result, Canadian buyers purchase more American imports at any given exchange rate. This increases the supply of Canadian dollars, thereby shifting the supply curve from S_0 to S_1. As a result of these demand and supply changes, the Canadian dollar depreciates, or falls in value, from point *a* to point *b*.

PRODUCT DEMAND

The appeal of a country's products to prospective buyers can also affect exchange rates. Suppose, for example, the quality of Canadian products improves. As a result, the demand for Canadian products in both foreign and domestic markets increases. The result is illustrated on the right graph in Figure 14.5.

In this case, Americans increase their purchases of Canadian products, thereby shifting the demand curve for Canadian dollars from D_2 to D_3 in this foreign exchange market. Also, Canadians buy more domestic products and fewer US imports. This reduces the sale of Canadian dollars on this foreign exchange market and so shifts the supply curve to the left, from S_2 to S_3. Both trends cause the Canadian dollar to appreciate, or rise in value, from point *c* to point *d*.

INTEREST RATES

Suppose that the Bank of Canada implements expansionary monetary policy, causing Canadian interest rates to fall in comparison with corresponding US rates. As shown in Figure 14.5 on the left, this has implications for the Canadian dollar.

FIGURE 14.5   Exchange Rate Changes

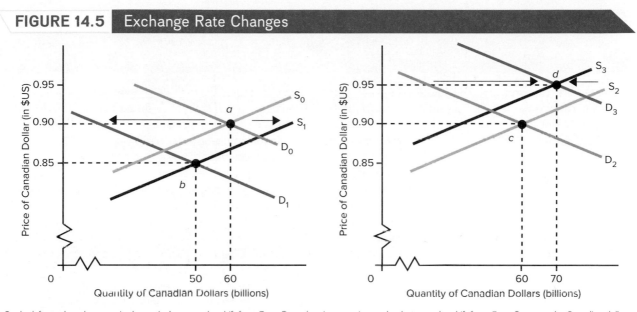

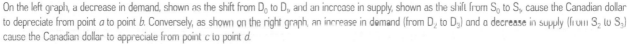

On the left graph, a decrease in demand, shown as the shift from D_0 to D_1, and an increase in supply, shown as the shift from S_0 to S_1, cause the Canadian dollar to depreciate from point *a* to point *b*. Conversely, as shown on the right graph, an increase in demand (from D_2 to D_3) and a decrease in supply (from S_2 to S_3) cause the Canadian dollar to appreciate from point *c* to point *d*.

With the drop in the Canadian interest rate, Canadian bonds become less appealing to financial investors in both Canada and the United States. Fewer American purchases of Canadian bonds mean that the demand for Canadian dollars decreases, thereby shifting the demand curve from D_0 to D_1. Meanwhile, Canadians also reduce their purchases of domestic bonds and are more likely to buy foreign financial assets. To buy the foreign financial assets, Canadians must sell additional Canadian dollars on foreign exchange markets. The result is an increase in the supply of Canadian dollars, shown as a shift to the right of the supply curve from S_0 to S_1. The movements in demand and supply both cause the Canadian dollar to depreciate.

SPECULATION

Some individuals, but more often financial institutions, buy and sell on foreign exchange markets simply to profit from short-run changes in currency values. The activities of these profit-seekers, known as **speculators**, affect the demand and supply of particular currencies, and so lead to changes in exchange rates.

For example, if there are signs that the Canadian dollar will soon rise in value against the US dollar, speculators enter the market in such a way as to make this expectation a reality. The graph on the right in Figure 14.5 shows the effects. Lured by potential profits, American speculators demand the currency that is expected to rise in value, so they purchase Canadian dollars by selling their holdings of US dollars. As a result, the demand curve for Canadian dollars shifts from D_2 to D_3. At the same time, Canadian speculators hold onto and perhaps buy more Canadian dollars, rather than buying US dollars. As a result, the supply curve for Canadian dollars shifts from S_2 to S_3. Due to both trends, the Canadian dollar appreciates and speculators make a tidy profit.

speculators: individuals or organizations that buy and sell currencies for profit

THINKING ABOUT ECONOMICS

What factors prompt speculators to enter foreign exchange markets?

Speculators respond to three factors: interest rates, inflation rates, and the political climate. Because of the influence of interest rates on exchange rates, speculators pay particular attention to monetary policy. Any indication that the Bank of Canada is following contractionary policy, for example, leads speculators to forecast a rise in Canadian interest rates and a resulting increase in the value of the Canadian dollar. Speculation, therefore, hastens the Canadian dollar's appreciation in the foreign currency market.

Speculators also act on the basis of expectations about inflation. For example, they may expect that the Canadian inflation rate will fall, compared with inflation rates in other countries. As a result, speculators expect a future rise in the Canadian dollar's value. This prediction again causes intervention in the foreign exchange market that immediately raises the value of the Canadian dollar.

Finally, speculators pay attention to political factors—especially their possible impact on foreign-held debt. Suppose, for example, there is a risk that Canada will become politically unstable. Speculators will expect that instability to make Canadian bonds less attractive to foreign investors, thereby reducing the demand for Canadian dollars on the foreign exchange market. In anticipation of the possible fall in the Canadian dollar's value, speculators will sell Canadian dollars immediately, thus hastening the change they predict.

QUESTION   **How would speculators react to a tax cut in Canada that is expected to increase foreign-held Canadian debt?**

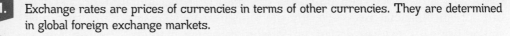

BRIEF REVIEW

1. Exchange rates are prices of currencies in terms of other currencies. They are determined in global foreign exchange markets.

2. The demand for Canadian dollars is the relationship between the price of a Canadian dollar and the quantity of Canadian dollars demanded in exchange for another currency. The relationship is inverse; for example, an increase in price causes a decrease in quantity demanded. This is shown as a movement along the demand curve. Demand for Canadian dollars in foreign exchange markets is created by foreigners' purchases of Canadian exports and financial assets.

3. The supply of Canadian dollars is the relationship between the price of the Canadian dollar and the quantity of Canadian dollars supplied in exchange for another currency. The relationship is direct; for example, an increase in price causes an increase in quantity supplied. This is shown as a movement along the supply curve. Canadian dollars are supplied in foreign exchange markets for Canadian purchases of foreign products and financial assets.

4. When currency values are allowed to vary, a currency's exchange rate will move toward its equilibrium value, the point of intersection of the demand and supply curves for the currency.

5. Factors that shift the demand and supply curves for a particular currency, and so the equilibrium point as well, are price differences, product demand, interest rates, and speculation.

14.2 | PRACTICE PROBLEM

1. The table below shows hypothetical demand and supply schedules for the Canadian dollar in terms of the US dollar.

Price of Cdn. Dollar (in $US)	Quantity of Cdn. Dollars Demanded (D_0) ($ billions)	Quantity of Cdn. Dollars Supplied (S_0) ($ billions)
1.10	2	10
1.05	4	8
1.00	6	6
0.95	8	4
0.90	10	2

  a. Draw a graph showing the initial demand and curves D_0 and S_0. Plot only the endpoints of each curve. What is the initial equilibrium price of the Canadian dollar in terms of the US dollar and the initial quantity of Canadian dollars traded in this market?

  b. Due to a change in Canadian interest rates, the quantity demanded of Canadian dollars in this market increases by $2 billion and the quantity supplied of Canadian dollars decreases by $2 billion at every possible price of the Canadian dollar in terms of US dollars. Draw the new demand and supply curves D_1 and S_1 on your graph. Plot only the endpoints of the two new curves. What is the new equilibrium price of the Canadian dollar in terms of the US dollar and the new quantity of Canadian dollars traded in this market?

  c. Were the shifts in demand and supply outlined in part b due to a decrease or increase in the Canadian interest rate?

2. Cross border shopping by Canadians in the United States and by Americans in Canada varies with the exchange rate in terms of the US dollar. How?

14.3 | Exchange Rate Systems

Flexible Exchange Rates

L03

Governments that allow the exchange rate of their currency to vary freely, as assumed in Figures 14.4 and 14.5, are following a system of **flexible exchange rates**, or floating rates, as they are sometimes known.

flexible exchange rates: currency exchange rates that are allowed to move freely to their equilibrium levels; also called floating rates

Flexible exchange rates offer one main advantage: market forces quickly eliminate shortages or surpluses so that inflows and outflows soon match each other. However, flexible rates also have an important disadvantage. Dramatic changes in exchange rates mean considerable risks for businesses involved in importing or exporting.

Consider, for example, a Canadian importer of US-made products. If the Canadian dollar depreciates suddenly, the price of the products is pushed up to the point that the products become too expensive for Canadian consumers, and quantity demanded decreases. Canadian exporters and their suppliers face similar uncertainty. Suppose, for example, the Canadian dollar jumps in value in relation to the US dollar. The exporter who exports Canadian products to the US market finds that the products become too expensive for the US market, and quantity demanded decreases. Because of these fluctuations, incomes and employment in the import and export industries are harmed.

Fixed Exchange Rates

fixed exchange rates:
currency exchange rates set or "pegged" to a certain value by each country's government

To avoid the uncertainty caused by flexible exchange rates, governments often intervene directly in foreign exchange markets. **Fixed exchange rates** offer the most striking alternative to floating rates. When a government establishes a fixed exchange rate, it sets or "pegs" the value of the country's currency at a certain price in terms of another currency.

IMPACT OF MARKET INTERVENTION

The hypothetical example in Figure 14.6 illustrates the effects of fixed exchange rates on a foreign exchange market. This shows that whenever the government's target rate differs from the equilibrium level, either a balance-of-payments surplus or deficit is created.

Suppose the federal government sets a target exchange rate of 89 cents in US currency (at points *c*). Because this rate is below its equilibrium level of 91 cents (point *b*), it creates excess demand for Canadian dollars, with more sought than are available on the market. This means that the inflows represented on the current and capital and financial accounts, which are associated with buying Canadian dollars, exceed the outflows represented on these accounts, which are tied to sales of Canadian dollars. This shortage leads to a balance-of-payments surplus of CDN$20 billion.

To make up for the excess demand of Canadian currency in the foreign exchange market, the Bank of Canada intervenes by selling CDN$20 billion and purchasing US currency in return. In doing so, the Bank is able to curb any rise in the value of the Canadian dollar above the desired level of US$0.89.

FIGURE 14.6	Fixed Exchange Rates

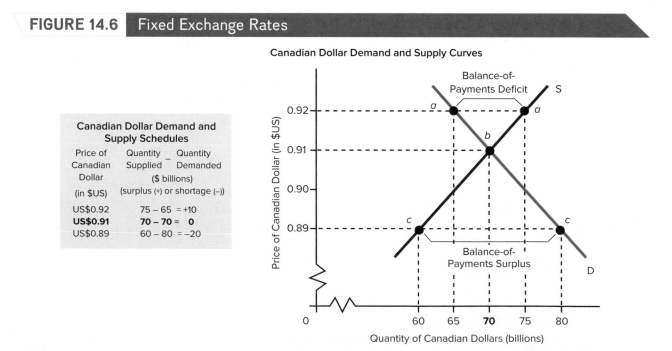

Canadian Dollar Demand and Supply Schedules

Price of Canadian Dollar (in $US)	Quantity Supplied	Quantity Demanded ($ billions) (surplus (+) or shortage (−))
US$0.92	75 − 65	= +10
US$0.91	**70 − 70**	**= 0**
US$0.89	60 − 80	= −20

With fixed rates, the target value of the Canadian dollar can differ from the equilibrium determined by the market demand and supply curves. A target level above (at points *a*) the equilibrium value (point *b*) produces a balance-of-payments deficit. A target level below (at points *c*) the equilibrium value (point *b*) results in a balance-of-payments surplus.

Suppose, instead, the federal government sets the target level of the Canadian dollar at 92 cents in US currency (points *a*), above the market equilibrium price (point *b*). As a result, a $10 billion surplus of Canadian dollars translates into a $10 billion balance-of-payments deficit. To prop up the Canadian dollar at this preferred rate of US$0.92, the Bank of Canada intervenes by buying CDN$10 billion and selling US currency in return. In this way, it eliminates the excess supply of Canadian dollars.

Exchange Rate Policy

Sometimes governments use fixed exchange rates to affect domestic output and prices. To see how policy-makers can use exchange rate policy to different ends, consider the impact of low exchange rates, high exchange rates, and monetary policy.

LOW EXCHANGE RATES

A low target rate for the Canadian dollar, such as US$0.89 in Figure 14.6, makes Canadian exports cheap and imports of US products expensive. This policy stimulates export revenues and inhibits import spending, thereby increasing net exports. Recall from the discussion of aggregate demand and supply in Chapter 10 that a rise in net exports increases aggregate demand. Hence, lowering the exchange rate serves as expansionary policy. Both real output and employment are boosted, and any recessionary gap that exists is reduced.

However, there are several problems in setting a low exchange rate. First, there is the danger of inflation. This hazard is especially acute if the economy is near its potential output, when shifts in the aggregate demand curve primarily affect prices. Second, there is a chance that a country's trading partners may respond by reducing *their* exchange rates to maintain their own export markets. When this happens, currencies return to their original relative values, and the original policy achieves nothing.

Despite these risks, a policy of low exchange rates has sometimes been pursued with success. For example, countries such as Singapore, South Korea, and Taiwan typically depress the values of their currencies as a way of encouraging export-driven growth. Evidence of this strategy is found in their large holdings of foreign currency, which result from the balance-of-payments surpluses associated with a low exchange rate policy.

At present, China is following a similar policy with respect to its own currency. The relatively low value of China's yuan against the US dollar has led to a large Chinese balance-of-payments surplus, and has allowed China to pursue a protracted expansionary policy by maintaining a large surplus in its balance of trade with the United States. In recent years, there have been repeated demands by US policy-makers that China end this policy, though when seen in relation the size of its overall economy, China's use of this policy is far less significant than in South Korea and Taiwan, as well as other emerging economies such as Peru. But as long as China's positive balance of trade remains so large—and is matched by an equally large negative balance of trade for its major trading partner, the United States—the controversy over the use of this policy will continue.

HIGH EXCHANGE RATES

Setting a high target for the Canadian dollar, such as US$0.92 in Figure 14.6, has the opposite effect: high exchange rates make imports cheaper and push up the prices of Canadian exports. Therefore, raising the exchange rate serves as contractionary policy by reducing net exports and decreasing aggregate demand. This puts downward pressure on inflation as well as on real output and employment.

Using a high exchange rate as an anti-inflationary tool has its problems, however. Not only is there a reduction in output and employment—especially in exporting industries—but there is also a reduction in the government's foreign currency holdings. Sooner or later, through continual balance-of-payments deficits, the holdings are depleted. In this situation, countries sometimes attempt to bolster their currency reserves by such measures as forcing citizens to sell their foreign currency to the government rather than allowing them to trade it privately. These laws produce underground foreign exchange markets, with prices set at equilibrium levels determined by demand and supply.

MONETARY POLICY AND EXCHANGE RATES

The Bank of Canada can use monetary policy to back its intervention in the foreign exchange market. Recall that interest rates and the price of the Canadian dollar move in the same direction. If the Bank wishes to raise the exchange rate without incurring a balance-of-payments deficit, it can force up interest rates using contractionary monetary policy. Conversely, an easy money policy of low interest rates can be applied to depreciate the exchange rate. In either case, the Bank of Canada influences the Canadian dollar by adjusting its equilibrium value.

Unfortunately, applying monetary policy in this way can complicate stabilization policy. If the Bank of Canada focuses its monetary policy excessively on maintaining a certain target exchange rate, it may end up worsening the business cycle. Therefore, the Bank must make sure its target value for the Canadian dollar allows the economy to move toward its potential output.

Evolution of Exchange Rate Systems

During the past century, industrialized countries have used three major exchange rate systems: a fixed gold standard, a structure of adjustable fixed rates, and the widespread use of the managed float, which offers a middle ground between the extremes of fully flexible and fixed exchange rates.

THE GOLD STANDARD (1879–1934)

Except for a brief time during the financial turmoil caused by World War I, the international gold standard was in place for over five decades. With this system, each country set the value of its currency in terms of an amount of gold. (For example, the Canadian dollar traded for 23.22 grains of gold.) Because these standards were not adjustable, maintaining a constant exchange rate took precedence over stabilization policy. The gold standard finally broke down under the strains of the Great Depression of the 1930s, as governments unsuccessfully attempted to stimulate their exports and domestic employment levels by depreciating their currencies.

THE BRETTON WOODS SYSTEM (1945–1971)

The disarray caused by exchange rate movements in the latter half of the 1930s led to the creation of the Bretton Woods system after World War II. (Bretton Woods is the name of the town in the United States where the conference to establish an international monetary system was held.) This system was based on adjustable fixed exchange rates. Rather than letting currencies appreciate and depreciate of their own accord, governments set an official exchange rate for their currency until persistent surpluses or shortages in the foreign exchange market forced an adjustment.

A currency underwent a **devaluation** (a reduction in value) when a government was reacting to persistent surpluses in the foreign exchange market, or a **revaluation** (an increase in value) when the response was to persistent shortages.

The organization known as the International Monetary Fund (IMF) was also established at this time. Among other tasks, it promotes the stability of exchange rates through loans to countries that are running out of foreign currency reserves to stabilize their currencies.

From 1950 to 1962, the Canadian government chose to diverge from the international Bretton Woods system and adopted floating rates instead. Substantial inflows of foreign financial investment kept the value of the Canadian dollar high during these years. During most of this period, the Canadian dollar traded above the price of US$1.

Canada returned to a fixed exchange rate system from 1962 to 1970, pegging its dollar at a relatively low value of US$0.925. This action was prompted by speculators who were driving down the Canadian dollar's value. The Canadian experience in the 1960s points out an interesting problem with fixed exchange rates: it is difficult for a country to shield itself from foreign inflation with this system. In Canada's case, rising inflation experienced by the United States during this period was automatically "imported" to Canada as prices for US items sold in Canada increased.

MANAGED FLOAT (1971 TO THE PRESENT)

The stability provided by the Bretton Woods system helped promote the high growth rates experienced by most countries in the postwar period. However, the system fell apart in 1971 when the United States—whose dollar had come to serve as an "international currency"—was forced to adopt a **managed float**. Under this system, the foreign value of a currency is allowed to vary over time. However, the effects of short-run demand and supply movements in the foreign exchange market are sometimes lessened through government intervention. The move to a partially floating exchange rate provided the United States government with the leeway needed to deal with imbalances in the foreign exchange market. By 1974, most other major economies had also switched away from fixed exchange rates.

Canada preceded most other countries in adopting a managed float in 1970. During the early 1970s, high prices for many of Canada's resource exports boosted the demand for Canadian currency. As a result, the Canadian dollar traded above US$1. Relatively rapid inflation in Canada during the late 1970s and early 1980s, however, caused the Canadian dollar to decline to an all-time annual low of US$0.72 by 1986. In the late 1980s and the first half of the 1990s, the dollar rose and then fell in response to interest rate adjustments by the Bank of Canada. It fell even further during the latter part of the 1990s until the early 2000s, due in part to a slump in the prices of many of Canada's resource exports. By the mid-2000s, however, it had regained much of its value, thanks in large part to a significant rise in the global demand for natural resources—a major Canadian export. This rise had a range of effects for Canadians. It reduced the prices of imports at the same time as it has adversely affected Canadian producers of manufactured goods and of services, by pushing up export prices. Figure 14.7 shows the behaviour of the US price of the Canadian dollar in the last few decades.

At the international level, what are the contemporary trends in exchange rate systems? Because of two factors—the uncertainty of fluctuating currency prices and multinational trade arrangements—some countries started moving back to pegged exchange rates in the 1990s. For example, various member nations of the

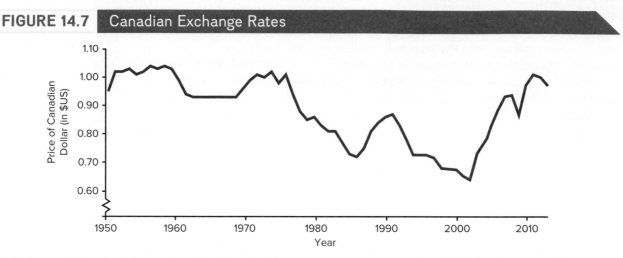

FIGURE 14.7   Canadian Exchange Rates

With floating rates, the Canadian dollar rose above US$1 in the 1950s. Between 1962 and 1970, it remained at its fixed value of US$0.925. With a managed float in place since 1970, the Canadian dollar has fluctuated widely.

Source: Bank of Canada.

European Union (EU), including Germany and France, synchronized their currencies through a system of adjustable fixed exchange rates before adopting a single currency, the euro. With the growing integration of national economies, these types of regional arrangements will probably become more common. However, the debt crises faced by several members of the so-called "euro zone" in the aftermath of the 2008–2009 global recession has revealed weaknesses of regional currency agreements that do not include effective limits on different members' fiscal policies. Many economists have predicted that the integration of national economies may one day bring about a single international currency. But in the meantime, the partial return of pegged exchange rates has led to the appearance of international tensions over currency value movements.

THINKING ABOUT ECONOMICS

How has the partial return of pegged exchange rates affected global trade and financial movements in recent years?

As the role of emerging economies in the global economy increases, the use of low exchange-rate policies by some of these countries is coming under increased scrutiny. This applies in particular to China's use of capital controls to keep the value of the yuan low relative to the US dollar. For rich countries—the United States in particular—China's exchange-rate policy is seen as an important reason for the imbalance that currently exists in global trade, as a large net flow of Chinese manufactured exports to rich Western countries is accompanied by reductions in these nations' domestic output and employment levels in manufacturing. Whether China's exchange-rate policy or other factors account for this imbalance is a matter of serious contention. Regardless, the political tensions that have resulted are increasing fears of a trade war between China and the United States. If such a trade war were to happen, each country would use various policy tools at its disposal to try to manipulate the size of the net flow of manufactured exports from China, with damaging consequences for the entire global economy.

QUESTION   **What would be the benefits to American companies and workers if China were to allow the value of the yuan to rise against the US dollar?**

BRIEF REVIEW

1. While flexible exchange rates allow the foreign exchange market to correct imbalances automatically, this system can create instability in the domestic economy, especially for businesses involved in importing or exporting.

2. By fixing, or pegging, an exchange rate, a government can create balance-of-payments surpluses or deficits.

3. Governments can use exchange rate policy as a means of influencing output and price levels. A lower exchange rate fosters more domestic output and employment, while a higher exchange rate reduces inflation. Governments can also use monetary policy to influence exchange rates by adjusting interest rates.

4. Three main exchange rate systems have prevailed worldwide over the past century: the fixed gold standard, the Bretton Woods system of adjustable fixed rates, and the recent preference for the managed float.

14.3 | PRACTICE PROBLEM

1. The table below shows hypothetical demand and supply schedules for the Canadian dollar in terms of the US dollar. Assume the US dollar is the only foreign currency traded with the Canadian dollar and that the Canadian dollar sets a target exchange rate of US$0.90 when the equilibrium value of the Canadian dollar would otherwise be US$1.00.

Canadian Dollar Demand and Supply Schedules

Price of Cdn. Dollar (in $US)	Quantity of Cdn. Dollars Demanded (D) ($ billions per year)	Quantity of Cdn. Dollars Supplied (S) ($ billions per year)
1.15	5	35
0.85	35	5

a. Will the Bank of Canada need to buy or sell Canadian dollars? buy or sell US dollars? Will doing so create a balance-of-payments deficit or a balance-of-payments surplus?

b. As a result of this intervention, will the "changes in official reserves" in Canada's balance-of-payments accounts be positive or negative?

c. Draw a graph showing the effects on the foreign exchange market of the target exchange rate. Plot the endpoints of the demand and supply curves and in your graph highlight the resulting balance-of-payments deficit or surplus.

LAST WORD

In this chapter, we examined what the balance-of-payments accounts reveal about the international aspects of the Canadian economy, and we also saw how foreign exchange rates for national currencies, such as the Canadian dollar, are determined. In the next chapter, we extend this analysis by taking an in-depth look at foreign trade—the reasons why countries engage in trade, how governments sometimes seek to encourage or to block it, and why it is that, in recent decades, there has been a move toward freer trade, both within certain regions and on a global scale.

1. How will the following situations affect Canada's exports, imports, and balance of trade?
   a. a boom in the US economy
   b. a rise in the value of the Canadian dollar in terms of US dollars
   c. an expansion of transnational corporations' processing of Canadian resources in Canada
   d. a "made-in-Canada" recession

2. For each transaction below, identify where it appears on Canada's current account and whether it is classified as a receipt or payment:
   a. A Canadian furniture dealer buys an antique clock in France.
   b. A German bondholder is paid interest by the Canadian government.
   c. A Canadian shareholder receives dividends from a Mexican company.
   d. A Canadian spends her holidays in Switzerland.
   e. An Australian television network buys a weekly series from a Canadian program producer.
   f. A Canadian sends funds to relatives living in Somalia.
   g. An Israeli consumer buys paper stationery produced in Canada.

3. For each transaction below, identify where it appears in Canada's capital and financial accounts and whether it is classified as a receipt or payment.
   a. A British retailer opens a chain of stores in Canada.
   b. A Canadian buys 1000 IBM shares on the New York Stock Exchange.
   c. A Japanese investment company adds funds to its Canadian bank account.
   d. A financial investor in China purchases a bond issued by a Canadian provincial government.
   e. A Canadian media company takes over a chain of newspapers in India.
   f. A Canadian mining firm opens a bank account in Chile.
   g. An Italian immigrant to Canada transfers funds from his Italian bank to his Canadian bank account.
   h. A resident of Pakistan receives a financial bequest from a Canadian relative.
   i. A Saudi Arabian entrepreneur purchases a patent from a Canadian firm.

4. **a.** Copy and fill out the table below.
   b. What is Delphi's balance of trade?
   c. Calculate the surplus or deficit on Delphi's current account and the surplus or deficit on its capital and financial accounts.

Delphi's Balance-of-Payments Accounts (Delphi $ millions)

	Receipts	Payments	Balance
Current Account			
Merchandise trade	183.4	323.6	_____
Trade in services	187.9	_____	90.5
Investment income	192.3	157.9	
Transfers	_____	24.5	32.3
Capital and Financial Accounts			
Capital Account	4.7	3.5	_____
Financial Account			
Direct investment	65.9	_____	−20.2
Portfolio investment	32.7	45.8	_____
Other financial investments	_____	15.2	22.9

   d. If the statistical discrepancy in Delphi's balance-of-payments accounts is $4.5 million, is Delphi running a balance-of-payments surplus or deficit? How large is this surplus or deficit?

   e. Calculate the "change in official reserves" that appears in Delphi's balance-of-payments accounts. Is this figure positive or negative? Why?

5. Calculate the following:

   a. the US dollar price of an item priced at $520 in Canadian currency when the exchange rate is CDN$1 = US$0.91

   b. the Canadian dollar price of an item priced at $24 000 in US currency if the exchange rate is US$1 = CDN$1.03

   c. the US dollar price of an item priced at $3 in Canadian currency when the exchange rate is US$1 = CDN$1.06

   d. the Canadian dollar price of an item priced at $82 in US currency when the exchange rate is CDN $1 = US$0.97

6. a. The table below shows hypothetical Canadian dollar demand and supply schedules. Draw demand and supply curves for the Canadian dollar in exchange for US dollars. Plot the endpoints of each curve for a total of four points.

Canadian Dollar Demand and Supply Schedules

Price of Cdn. Dollar (in $US)	Quantity of Cdn. Dollars Demanded	Quantity of Cdn. Dollars Supplied
	($ billions per year)	
0.97	30	70
0.96	40	60
0.95	50	50
0.94	60	40
0.93	70	30

   b. With a flexible exchange rate, what will the value of the Canadian dollar be?

   c. If the Canadian government sets a target exchange rate of US$0.96, will the result be a balance-of-payments surplus or deficit? How large will this surplus or deficit be? Calculate the "change in official reserves" that would appear in Canada's balance-of-payments accounts, presuming that the US dollar is the only foreign currency traded with the Canadian dollar.

   d. If instead the Canadian government sets a target exchange rate of US$0.93, will a balance-of-payments surplus or deficit result? Again calculate the "change in official reserves" that would appear in Canada's balance-of-payments accounts, still presuming that the US dollar is the only foreign currency traded with the Canadian dollar.

7. For each of the following situations, outline the effect on the price of the Canadian dollar in terms of US dollars and draw a demand and supply graph that illustrates the changes that occur in the foreign exchange market for the Canadian dollar.

   a. A contractionary monetary policy initiated by the Bank of Canada raises Canadian interest rates.

   b. Canada's real output rises at a time when real output in the United States is falling.

   c. Americans (but not Canadians) find Canada a more attractive place to make financial investments.

   d. Given Canada's aging population, more Canadian "snowbirds" travel to the United States each winter.

   e. Due to a credit crisis that affects US financial institutions more than it does Canadian ones, Canada's attractiveness as a destination for direct and portfolio investment increases.

   f. The Bank of Canada initiates an expansionary monetary policy that reduces Canadian interest rates.

g. Canada is viewed as a less attractive place to make financial investments by Americans but not by Canadians.

h. Canada's real output falls at the same time as real output in the United States is staying constant.

8. a. Access the Bank of Canada online document *How Monetary Policy Works* (at www.bankofcanada.ca/monetary-policy-introduction/why-monetary-policy-matters/4-monetary-policy/), which explains how an adjustment in the exchange rate fits into the chain of events that follows the Bank's increase in the target range for the overnight rate. When the Bank of Canada raises its target range for the overnight rate, raising other interest rates, how does this affect (i) investment and consumption spending on durables, (ii) aggregate demand, and (iii) inflationary pressures in the Canadian economy? Meanwhile, how does the change in interest rates affect (i) the value of the Canadian dollar, (ii) net exports, (iii) aggregate demand, and (iv) inflationary pressures in the Canadian economy?

b. Does this exchange rate adjustment outlined in part counteract or reinforce the Bank's policy and make monetary policy more or less effective?

c. On the basis of your answer to part b, is monetary policy likely to be more effective under a system of flexible exchange rates or fixed exchange rates?

9. In recent years, there has been a growing net flow of direct and portfolio investment from rich Western countries, such as the United States, to emerging economies in Asia, Africa, and Latin America. If this growth continues, what effect will it have on the value of the currencies of these emerging economies in relation to the US dollar?

10. (Advanced Question)

Given the close links between the Canadian and US economies, some commentators suggest that the Canadian dollar should be fixed against the US dollar. What would be the main advantages and disadvantages of this arrangement to Canadians?

11. (Policy Discussion Question)

Before the financial crisis of 2008, the governments of several euro zone countries were able to run continual high budget deficits. This was due to foreign lenders' confidence in the stability of the euro relative to other major currencies, and the low interest rates that these euro zone governments were able to offer on their bonds. Briefly explain why this trend of continual expansionary fiscal policy was ultimately harmful.

ADVANCING ECONOMIC THOUGHT

CITIES, CREATIVITY, AND DIVERSITY

Jane Jacobs and a New View of Economics

Jane Jacobs (1916–2006) was a thinker known for her wide ranging interests and startlingly original economic ideas. These ideas resonated powerfully in Canada, especially once she made this country her adopted home. Born in Pennsylvania during World War I, she started work as a freelance journalist and secretary, first in her hometown of Scranton and later in New York City. Her move to New York had a major effect on her outlook, giving her a lifelong fascination with cities and their place in human life. After World War II, she gained fame as a critic of prevailing notions of urban renewal. Her first book, *The Death and Life of American Cities* (1961), made the case for urban diversity. After she and her family moved to Toronto, she led a successful movement to block plans for a modern expressway through the city's central districts in the early 1970s, and her name became the byword for a view of cities that highlights vibrant neighbourhoods shaped by residents rather than by outside planners.

Jane Jacobs
Photo courtesy of Mark Trusz, photographer

CITIES AT CENTRE STAGE

Meanwhile, Jacobs was turning her attention to economics. "[P]overty has no causes," she observed. "Only prosperity has causes."[1] In three books–*The Economy of Cities* (1969), *Cities and the Wealth of Nations* (1984), and *The Nature of Economies* (2000)–she sought to pinpoint exactly what these causes of prosperity are. For Jacobs, small-scale creativity and productive diversity are the main drivers of economic growth, and these factors are inextricably tied to cities:

> Once we . . . try looking at the real economic world in its own right rather than as a dependent artifact of politics, we can't avoid seeing that most nations are composed of collections or grab bags of very different economies, rich regions and poor ones within the same nation. We can't avoid seeing, too, that among all the various types of economies, cities are unique in their abilities to shape and reshape the economies of other settlements.[2]

How, in practice, does a city achieve prosperity? Through finding ways to produce items previously imported from outside the city's boundaries, said Jacobs. As businesses improvise ways of making these items, economic output gradually increases, and costs of production fall. Through this process, a city creates new export industries as well.

Using these ideas, Jacobs was able to trace ties of economic influence from age to age and continent to continent, as new cities expand thanks to their trade with older ones. A Canadian city such as Toronto, she argued, owes the origins of its present-day prosperity to nineteenth-century trade links with British cities, such as London. London was similarly indebted to its medieval trade with Venice, which, in turn, was indebted to even older cities such as the Byzantine

---

[1] *The Economy of Cities* (New York, Random House, 1969), p. 121.

[2] *Cities and the Wealth of Nations: Principles of Economic Life* (New York: Random House, 1964), p. 32.

Empire's capital, Constantinople, whose own economic origins can be traced back, with just a few more iterations, to the earliest cities of the Near East.

Jacobs' analysis is just as easily applied to the present day. The main way a country gains long-term wealth, she contended, is not by finding just one or two items to export internationally—since growth is then far too dependent on conditions in specific markets—but by fostering vigorous import-replacing cities within its borders. For example, it is primarily through the establishment of innovative cities that relatively resource-poor countries such as Japan, South Korea, and, more recently, China, have been so successful when compared with resource-rich countries that have experienced brief spurts of resource-led growth. All countries, she said, are better off giving their cities the tools needed for small-scale improvisation, rather than trying to manage growth through large public subsidies, especially to businesses in areas disconnected from major cities. The latter sort of subsidies, in her view, tend to privilege short-term exports over the long-term replacement of imports, and focus too heavily on investment in a narrow range of products.

A MODEL OF ETHICS

At mid-career, Jacobs chose to extend her thinking to an entirely new setting. In *Systems of Survival* (1992), she devised a model of social and economic ethics in which the concept of diversity is again key. Societies thrive and prosper only if the rules that underlie commerce and politics remain distinct. Businesspeople, she argued, typically subscribe to an outlook that touts honesty, personal initiative, and inventiveness. Participants in business have to understand the benefits of efficiency and voluntary contracts, know when it is best to collaborate or when to compete, and understand the potential costs of ostentatious consumption and excessive pessimism about the future. The same virtues, Jacobs argued, do not necessarily apply in politics. Indeed, there are good reasons why rulers honour loyalty, discipline, and respect for hierarchy over the sorts of traits respected in business. It is therefore important to ensure that rulers do not start acting like businesspeople, or businesspeople like rulers. If their roles do get mixed, then trouble ensues.

For Jacobs, one of the most harmful examples of this type of "monstrous hybrid" is the mania for corporate mergers and acquisitions, which started in North America during the 1980s and recurred intermittently up to the late 2000s. During these periods, corporate executives, aided by compliant investment dealers and auditing companies, stopped acting like businesspeople and became more like battlefield generals as they attempted to vanquish competitors by buying up other companies' shares. "Entire organizations, in the end an entire system composed of many organizations," Jacobs argued, "had slid by degrees across the commercial syndrome barriers, into taking."[3]

In her last book, *Dark Age Ahead* (2004), Jacobs predicted that any further loosening of accounting rules could create the conditions for social collapse:

> [C]ertified public accountants (in Canada called chartered accountants), have been trusted to oversee and guarantee honest financial reporting by business,

---

[3] *Systems of Survival: A Dialogue on the Moral Foundations of Commerce and Politics* (New York: Random House, 1992), p. 142.

which is why business at large is trusted. . . . When a profession with responsibilities like that goes rotten, it is a cultural and economic nightmare.[4]

Though she is no longer alive to analyze how recent events might relate to her predictions, some present-day commentators suggest that Jacobs' predictions were uncanny. For these observers, moral corruption was a primary cause of the worldwide financial rout that occurred in 2008–though how much of this was due to corrupt accounting practices and how much due to government regulations that ignored the risks associated with complicated new financial instruments is difficult to resolve. Whatever the detailed causes of the 2008 collapse, Jacobs' main question is still highly pertinent: was the crisis spurred by a systemic moral lapse? Economists and others who study this event will be forced to grapple with her provocative insights.

1. The term "Jane Jacobs externality" is now used in economics to refer to the positive effects on efficiency and productivity that come from the clustering of production within a given local area. Taking a hypothetical example, explain how such a trend might work.

2. Jacobs' views on the 2008 financial crisis parallel in many ways those of John Kenneth Galbraith. Using the ideas of both, explain how it is possible for a corporation's managers to engage in merger and takeover activity that ends up being to the long-run detriment of their own business and its shareholders.

---

[4] *Dark Age Ahead* (Toronto: Random House, 1992), pp. 132-3.

CHAPTER 15

Foreign Trade

Foreign trade is an everyday part of our lives. Consider, for example, what you are wearing or what you ate today. It is likely that many of these products come from outside Canada's borders. The role of exports in our lives is less obvious, but still significant, through the effect that export industries have on Canada's economic activity and employment. In this chapter, we will see why nations exchange goods and services and how governments influence foreign trade. We will also study how the trend toward freer trade is affecting Canada's economy and look at various ways it is influencing the well-being of individual Canadians.

> It is very odd that, enjoying one of the highest living standards in the world, Canadians in all walks of life should nevertheless believe that their economy is a frail, hothouse creation.
>
> -JOHN H. DALES, CANADIAN ECONOMIC HISTORIAN

LEARNING OBJECTIVES After reading this chapter, you will be able to:

LO 1

Identify Canada's trade relationships and the case for trade, based on absolute and comparative advantage

LO 2

Analyze the impact of trade protection and identify the arguments for and against it

LO 3

Summarize Canada's trade policies from its beginnings as a country, including recent international trade arrangements

15.1 | The Case for Trade

The Importance of Trade

The rapid growth of foreign trade and investment flows and the resulting spread of international businesses and markets are all part of a trend known as **globalization**. In recent decades, reductions in transportation costs have helped increase the worldwide importance of foreign trade. Between 1950 and 2013, for example, world trade grew from under 10 percent of world GDP to over 30 percent. There has been an even more rapid increase in foreign investment flows. For example, transactions in foreign exchange markets have soared and now total over US$5 trillion per day. This trend, too, has been driven by lower costs. The costs of computing power have undergone a precipitous decline over the past few decades, as have the costs of long-distance communication. For example, the cost of a three-minute transatlantic telephone call in 1930 was about $500 in current Canadian dollars. It is now less than 30 cents for a regular phone hookup, and virtually zero if Internet-based phoning software is used. Such innovations have changed the way businesses are organized and have made global procurement and outsourcing more economically feasible than ever before—especially in the case of services that can be exchanged electronically.

globalization: the trend of growing foreign trade and investment and the spread of international businesses and markets

The 2008–2009 global recession reduced the pace of globalization—in particular the increase in trade flows. For example, while global real GDP dropped by just 0.6 percent in 2009, the volume of global exports fell by just over 12 percent. But the expansion in trade and investment flows is now a well-entrenched long term trend. Emerging economies are playing a central role in these changes, with rates of economic growth that are allowing them to play roles in the world trading system as significant as that of the major Western economies. As shown in Figure 15.1, the shares of global GDP (allowing for differences in the purchasing power of different currencies) provided by the rich economies of the West is projected to fall from two-thirds in 2011 to well under half by 2060 as the shares provided by emerging economies—in particular China, especially between 2011 and 2030, and India, especially between 2030 and 2060—undergo a counteracting increase. This means that at some point within the coming decade, the countries of the emerging world will, for the first time, control more than half of global output. Much of this trend is associated with the shift of manufacturing from rich to emerging economies. Most notably, China has become the world's manufacturing powerhouse. During the two decades beginning in the mid-1990s, the demands of China's growing manufacturing sector led to an appreciable rise in the prices of primary commodities, which had a major benefit for resource-rich countries such as Canada.

The effects of the globalization trend have been profound since the early 1950s. Most significantly, markets are no longer contained within national boundaries, and businesses are more likely to buy resources and sell products internationally. For example, a business with its headquarters in Canada may choose to borrow from Japanese savers, purchase German-made machinery, employ Mexican workers, and sell the bulk of its output in the United States. In both its resource markets and product markets, this Canadian company probably competes with businesses from all over the world.

Within this international trend, Canada has shown a heavy reliance on trade. Figure 15.2 compares the value of exports of various countries as a percentage

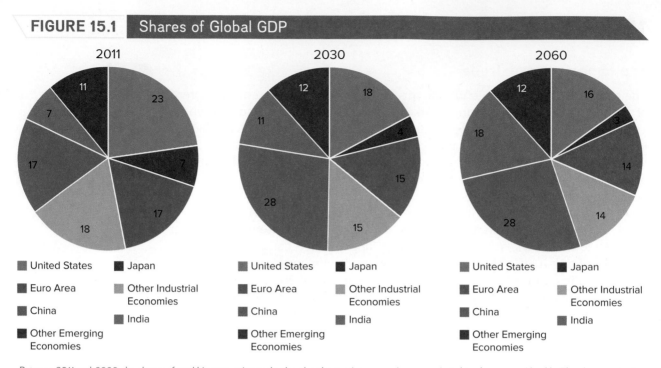

FIGURE 15.1 | Shares of Global GDP

2011

2030

2060

■ United States   ■ Japan
■ Euro Area   ■ Other Industrial
■ China   Economies
■ Other Emerging ■ India
   Economies

■ United States   ■ Japan
■ Euro Area   ■ Other Industrial
■ China   Economies
■ Other Emerging ■ India
   Economies

■ United States   ■ Japan
■ Euro Area   ■ Other Industrial
■ China   Economies
■ Other Emerging ■ India
   Economies

Between 2011 and 2060, the shares of world income going to developed and emerging economies are projected to change considerably. The shares going to China and India are forecast to rise significantly, while the portion going to other emerging economies is projected to stay relatively constant. The shares going to the United States, the European Union countries that use the euro as their currency, Japan, and other industrial economies are forecast to decrease.

Source: "Looking to 2060: Long-Term Global Growth Prospects," OECD Economic Policy Paper 3, at www.oecd-ilibrary.org/economics/looking-to-2060-long-term-global-growth-prospects_5k8zxpjsggf0-en, November 2012, p. 23.

of their GDP. Canada's exports have a value equal to 30 percent of its GDP, approximately the same as the world average of 31 percent and considerably higher than the United States' 14 percent and Japan's 15 percent, whose large and diversified economies allow them to be less dependent on exports and imports. However, Canada's reliance on foreign trade is not as great as that of some small industrialized countries, such as Belgium (85 percent).

Canada's Trading Partners

With whom is Canada trading? As Figure 15.3 demonstrates, the United States is Canada's principal trading partner. In 2013, 75 percent of Canada's merchandise exports went to the United States and 65 percent of its merchandise imports came from the United States. The remaining merchandise trade was shared among nations that are part of the European Union (a group of European nations we will discuss later in the chapter), Japan, other countries in the Organisation for Economic Co-operation and Development (OECD), and all other nations.

While Canada's trade with individual emerging economies (included in the final category) is relatively modest, this segment of our trade is expanding, though not as rapidly as might be expected. For example, between 1990 and 2013, the value of Canadian merchandise exports to non-OECD countries increased from 10 to 12 percent of the total, while imports to Canada from these countries increased from 11 to 17 percent. But these modest growth rates in Canada's trade with the emerging world tell only part of the tale. The economic rise of emerging economies, especially China, *has* had a profound effect on

FIGURE 15.2 Importance of Trade

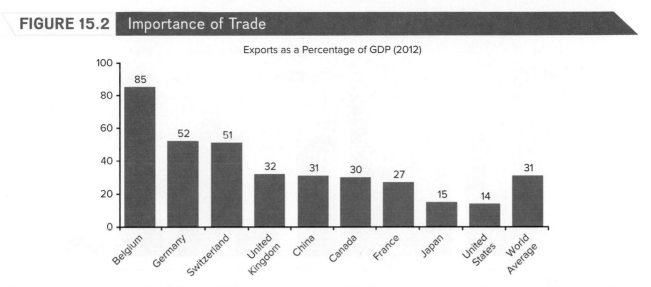

The exports of small countries, such as Belgium, are high in comparison to their level of GDP. In contrast, the exports of most large countries, such as Japan and the United States, are lower as a proportion of overall economic activity. When compared with the world average of 31 percent, Canada's exports are comparable as a proportion of its GDP.

Source: International Bank for Reconstruction and Development/The World Bank. Adapted from World Development Indicators, 2013. "Data and Statistics," Table 4.8. Retrieved March 18, 2014.

Canadian trade, but much of this impact has been indirect by affecting world prices of many of the commodities that Canada tends to export.

Canada's Trade Patterns

Canada's merchandise trade is made up of exports and imports of both natural resources and manufactured products. As Figure 15.4 shows, Canada's 2013 merchandise exports included almost equal portions of raw or processed natural resources (agricultural and fish products, energy products, forest products, and

FIGURE 15.3 Canada's Merchandise Trade by Region (2013)

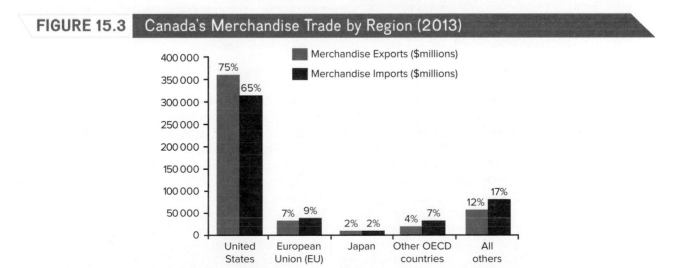

The bulk of Canada's merchandise trade is with the United States. The remaining merchandise trade is shared among the member countries of the European Union, Japan, other countries in the OECD, and all other nations.

Source: Statistics Canada "Canada's Merchandise Trade by Region (2013)." Adapted from the Statistics Canada website, Summary Table, www40.statcan.gc.ca/l01/cst01/gblec02a-eng.htm. Retrieved March 18, 2014.

| FIGURE 15.4 | Canada's Merchandise Trade by Type of Product (2013) |

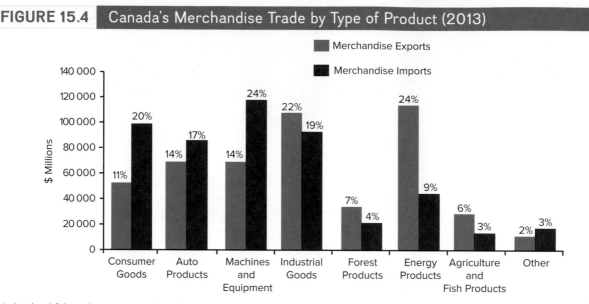

Agricultural and fish products, energy products, forest products, and industrial goods such as minerals and metals, together accounted for just over half of Canada's 2013 merchandise exports. Machines and equipment, automobile products, consumer goods, and other products made up the rest. In terms of merchandise imports, natural resources formed just over a third of the total, whereas manufactured goods formed about two-thirds.

Source: Statistics Canada, "Canada's Merchandise Trade by Type of Product (2013)." Adapted from the Statistics Canada website, Summary Tables, www40.statcan.gc.ca/l01/cst01/gblec04-eng.htm and www40.statcan.gc.ca/l01/cst01/gblec05-eng.htm. Retrieved March 18, 2014.

industrial goods, such as minerals and metals) and manufactured products (machines and equipment, automobile products, consumer goods, and other). In contrast, merchandise imports of manufactured goods are almost double that of natural resources. In total, Canada had merchandise exports of about $480 billion and merchandise imports of $487 billion.

THINKING ABOUT ECONOMICS

How has the worldwide financial crisis of 2008 affected globalization?

The financial turmoil of 2008 temporarily reversed the forces of globalization, especially in Europe and North America. The trend of economic integration has since resumed, but with noticeable differences. Financial institutions in many countries are now more heavily regulated than before, which has constrained these institutions' intervention in international markets. This regulation has not lessened the opposition to their power in some quarters, as evidenced most dramatically by the protests that have accompanied recent international meetings, such as in Seattle and Toronto. The driving force of globalization has also shifted from industrialized Western countries to emerging economies, which were able to bounce back from the 2008 financial crisis far more quickly than their rich world counterparts. One of the main reasons for this shift in economic power is the growth of a massive pool of savings in the emerging world. As a sizeable portion of these savings is finding its way into the international arena, emerging economies have gained significant clout in the management of global integration. This has often occurred through takeovers made by publicly-owned companies and financial investments made by so-called sovereign funds controlled by emerging economy governments—a changed reality that Canadians, among others in the West, are having to learn to accept.

QUESTION **What were some of the problems with the old model of globalization that the financial crisis exposed?**

However, this is not the whole picture. Canada trades not only in merchandise, but also in services. Of these–including travel, transportation, and commercial and government services–Canada exported about $87 billion and imported $111 billion in 2013.

Historically, Canada has been a significant exporter of natural resources. Despite the boom in commodity exports which began in the mid-2000s, the proportion of natural resources in Canada's merchandise exports has gradually decreased, while the proportion of manufactured goods has increased. For example, compared with the roughly equal proportions of manufactured and natural resource exports in 2013, just over a third of Canada's merchandise exports were manufactured goods in 1971. In the same period, the ratio of natural resources to manufactured goods in Canada's imports has varied only slightly, with manufactured goods expanding.

Within Canada's service trade, business services such as insurance, management services, and research and development, have increased most quickly as a proportion of both imports and exports. Overall, growth in Canada's trade in services has not outpaced growth in its merchandise trade. Between 1971 and 2013, service exports as a percentage of total exports stayed at 15 percent, while service imports fell from 21 to 19 percent of total imports. These figures are surprising, given the recent growth in Canada's service sector. Between 1967 and 2013, for example, Canada's service sector grew from 55 to 70 percent of Canada's real GDP, while the goods sector fell from 45 to 30 percent.

What Is Traded

In general, countries export the commodities they produce most efficiently and import those they would produce least efficiently. Whether or not a country can produce a particular product efficiently is determined by the country's resources, market size, climate, and sometimes by chance as well.

RESOURCES

A country's pool of resources is the main factor affecting what it exports and imports. For example, Canada has been endowed with plentiful and rich natural resources that have allowed it to be a major exporter of such products as paper, wheat, and natural gas. As well, Canada has developed its human resources and

THINKING ABOUT ECONOMICS

Why has the rise of a service-based economy not been reflected in Canada's international trade?

One reason is that services are usually bought and sold within national borders. For example, in 1989, less than 10 percent of services produced in Canada were exported. In comparison, over a third of all Canadian-made goods were destined for foreign markets. Another reason for the apparent slow growth in service trade relates to measurement problems. Because services are intangible, foreign trade in these products often escapes detection, especially in the common case where services are traded within a single company. Furthermore, goods and services are often sold in "bundles," and it is the merchandise part of the bundle that is counted. For example, new computer software may be exchanged in physical form and is therefore counted as a good rather than as a service. These problems make it difficult to collect trade statistics that adequately reflect the importance of services.

QUESTION   **Is the expansion of e-commerce making it more or less difficult to measure trade in services?**

capital resources in such a way that it can export capital-intensive goods. In contrast, countries with less abundant natural resources, such as Belgium, tend to be major importers of unprocessed products, and countries with a huge pool of labour and relatively few capital resources, such as Bangladesh, tend to be major exporters of labour-intensive goods. For example, a large portion of Bangladesh's exports consist of textiles and clothing, whose production tends to be labour-intensive.

MARKET SIZE

Recall that the production of some items exhibits increasing returns to scale–that is, the cost of inputs per unit of output decreases as production increases. Such items tend to be produced in settings where businesses can take advantage of increasing returns to scale. So, for example, cars tend to be produced in countries with large markets of car buyers, rather than in small countries or in those where few people own cars.

CLIMATE

Climate plays a key role in determining where some items, especially agricultural goods, are produced. While tropical fruit could be grown in Canada–in climate-controlled greenhouses, for example–it makes little sense to do so, since these goods can be imported cheaply from countries that are internationally competitive in producing them.

Gains from Trade

Having determined what Canada trades and with whom, the question "Why trade?" still remains. International trade brings significant economic gains: it increases product variety for consumers, promotes competition in each country's markets, and adds to output by allowing countries to specialize in commodities in which they are internationally competitive.

PRODUCT VARIETY

When countries trade, the number of products available to consumers expands. Consider a category of products that you purchase regularly–for example, clothing, online music, or magazines. You will probably notice that many of your purchases were supplied from other countries. Adding imports to domestic products gives you greater choice.

COMPETITION

International trade increases the number of businesses selling in a country's product markets. Added competition encourages all businesses to produce goods as efficiently as possible. This results in lower prices for consumers.

SPECIALIZATION

The most important gain from international trade comes from specialization. Without international trade, a country would have to produce everything its citizens need. With international trade, however, a country can use its resources to specialize in the products it makes most efficiently, allowing it to compete in the expanded market. The income from exporting the products that the country has made so efficiently can then pay for imported products that would be more expensive to make domestically. By increasing the output gained from various countries' resources, specialization raises world living standards. In the next sections, we will see how these gains from specialization can be quantified using two related economic concepts: absolute advantage and comparative advantage.

FIGURE 15.5	Gains from Trade Based on Absolute Advantage

	Time Spent Building Furniture	Time Spent Preparing a Will	Time Saved through Specialization
Lawyer	20 hours	2 hours	20 − 2 = 18 hours
Carpenter	5 hours	10 hours	10 − 5 = 5 hours

A carpenter can build furniture in less time than it would take a lawyer, while the lawyer can draw up a will in less time than it would take the carpenter. Each has an absolute advantage in one task. To use the resources most efficiently, the carpenter should specialize in building the furniture, while the lawyer should specialize in preparing the will.

Absolute Advantage

Specialization is easiest to see in the case of two trading partners, each of whom is better than the other at one activity. Suppose a lawyer wants custom-made wooden furniture. At the same time, a carpenter wants to prepare a will. As shown in Figure 15.5, the lawyer could build the furniture herself in 20 hours, or she could hire the carpenter to do the job in 5 hours. Similarly, the carpenter could prepare the will for himself in 10 hours, or hire the lawyer to do it for him in 2 hours. If the two were to trade their products, each product would be produced in the most efficient way possible.

In the example, the lawyer and the carpenter each has an **absolute advantage**; that is, each trading partner is able to produce one product using fewer resources than would other producers. The third column of Figure 15.4 summarizes the resources in this case, time–saved by trading partners specializing in what they each do most efficiently.

The same principle applies to countries that engage in trade. For example, Canada may be more efficient than Japan in producing wheat, while Japan is more efficient than Canada in producing stereos. Canadians should, therefore, specialize in wheat production, leaving the Japanese to concentrate on stereo production. Through trade, both Canada and Japan can use their economic resources to produce the greatest possible output of each commodity. As a result, living standards in both countries increase.

absolute advantage: the benefit enjoyed by a producer who can supply a certain quantity of an item more efficiently than can other producers

Comparative Advantage

Because of the varying strengths of countries, trade advantages are some-times not as clear-cut as in the case of absolute advantage. Consider a hypo-thetical case: both Canada and Mexico can produce paper and computers, but Canada has an absolute advantage over Mexico in both products. As shown in Figure 15.6, using equal resources, Canada can produce 12 tonnes

FIGURE 15.6	Gains from Trade Based on Comparative Advantage

	Hypothetical Output per Worker		Opportunity Cost	
	Paper	Computers	of 1 tonne of paper	of 1 computer
Canada	12 tonnes	12 computers	1.0 computer	1.0 tonnes paper
Mexico	3 tonnes	9 computers	3.0 computers	0.33 tonnes paper

Paper has a lower opportunity cost in Canada. Thus, Canadians have a comparative advantage in producing paper, while Mexicans have a comparative advantage in making computers. In other words, each has the lower opportunity cost of producing one product.

of paper, compared with Mexico's 3 tonnes, or 12 computers to Mexico's 9 computers.

For the sake of efficiency, it might seem that both paper products and computers should be produced in Canada. But if we explore the possibility of trade between the two countries, we get a surprising result—one with profound consequences in any discussion of free trade. As we will now see, as long as trade is carried out in a way that minimizes each product's opportunity cost, then both countries are made better off. To determine what each trading partner should supply, they must therefore determine the opportunity cost of each product, and then supply the product for which they have the lowest opportunity cost. The trading partner with the lowest opportunity cost for a given product has the **comparative advantage**. **This name reflects the fact that this benefit can be determined only after comparing opportunity costs in both countries.**

In our example, the opportunity cost of producing 12 tonnes of paper in Canada is 12 computers, and the opportunity cost of 12 computers is 12 tonnes of paper. This gives a cost ratio of one to one between paper and computers, so that the opportunity cost of 1 tonne of paper is 1 computer. In Mexico, the cost of producing 3 tonnes of paper is 9 computers, and the opportunity cost of producing 9 computers is 3 tonnes of paper. This gives a cost ratio of one to three between paper and computers in Mexico, so that the opportunity cost of 1 tonne of paper is 3 computers and the opportunity cost of 1 computer is only 0.33 tonnes of paper. Because paper has a lower opportunity cost in Canada than in Mexico, Canada has a comparative advantage in paper production. Conversely, since each computer has a lower opportunity cost in Mexico than in Canada, Mexico has a comparative advantage in computer production.

Given the comparative advantages in our hypothetical example, the opportunity costs would be lowest if Canada produced paper and Mexico produced computers. This conclusion follows the **law of comparative advantage**, which states that output is maximized when producers specialize in what they can make at a lower opportunity cost than can other producers.

Let us assume that there are twice as many workers in Mexico as in Canada. Figure 15.7 shows the gains from each country fully specializing in the product in which it has a comparative advantage. If there are 10 workers in Canada and 20 workers in Mexico, then before trade, each country may devote half its

comparative advantage: the benefit enjoyed by a producer who can supply a certain item with a lower opportunity cost than can other producers

law of comparative advantage: states that maximum output is achieved when producers specialize in what they can make at a lower opportunity cost than can other producers

---

FIGURE 15.7   Total Gains from Specialization

	Before Trade		After Trade	
	Paper	**Computers**	**Paper**	**Computers**
Canada	60 tonnes	60 computers	120 tonnes	0 computers
Mexico	30 tonnes	90 computers	0 tonnes	180 computers
	90 tonnes	150 computers	120 tonnes	180 computers

Suppose that production in both Mexico and Canada were equally split between paper and computers before they began to trade. The combined countries would produce 90 tonnes of paper and 150 computers. By specializing through trade, combined production would rise to 120 tonnes of paper and 180 computers.

labour force to each product. The combined paper output of both countries is therefore 90 tonnes – 60 tonnes from Canada (= 5 workers × 12 tonnes per worker) and 30 tonnes from Mexico (= 10 workers × 3 tonnes per worker). At the same time, the combined computer production of both countries is 150 computers, with 60 from Canada (= 5 workers × 12 computers per worker) and 90 from Mexico (= 10 workers × 9 computers per worker).

When both countries specialize completely in the product in which they have a comparative advantage, Canada produces 120 tonnes of paper (= 10 workers × 12 tonnes per worker) and Mexico makes 180 computers (= 20 workers × 9 computers per worker). Thus, world paper production has risen by 30 tonnes, and world computer production by 30 computers. By specializing on the basis of comparative advantage, the two countries are, therefore, able to raise their total output of both items, with this added production being shared through trade.

TERMS OF TRADE

The benefits of specialization are distributed between trading partners on the basis of the **terms of trade**, or the international price of one product in terms of another product. This price depends partly on the opportunity costs of the products in each country, since producers must get at least the opportunity cost that applies in domestic transactions if they are to engage in foreign trade.

terms of trade: the international price of one product in terms of another

Returning to our hypothetical example, recall that in Canada, tonnes of paper and units of computers have a cost ratio of one to one. To make trading with Mexico worthwhile, Canadian paper producers demand one or more computers for each unit of paper they sell to Mexico. At the same time, in Mexico the cost ratio of tonnes of paper and units of computers is one to three. To make trading with Canada worthwhile, Mexican computer producers demand 1 tonne of paper for every 3 or fewer computers they sell to Canada. As a result, the international price of one product in terms of the other must fall somewhere between these limits in order for the two countries to trade:

> Limits to terms of trade   1 tonne of paper: 1 computer
> 1 tonne of paper: 3 computer

The actual terms of trade are then set by the international demand for each product. So, for example, when the demand for paper is high in both countries, the international price of paper in terms of computers will be close to the limit of 3 computers for 1 tonne of paper. If, instead, the demand for computers is high in both countries, the international price of computers will be pushed toward the limit of 1 computer for 1 tonne of paper.

Since Canadians export paper to purchase Mexican computers, they will be best off when paper has the highest possible international price in terms of computers—in other words, when 1 tonne of paper has its maximum value of 3 computers. In contrast, Mexicans are best off when the terms of trade have reached their lowest limit. In this case, each 1 tonne of paper imported by Mexicans has an international price of 1 computer, which is the minimum possible value for paper in terms of computers.

BRIEF REVIEW

1. With the trend toward globalization, over time there has been substantial growth in foreign trade and investment and international businesses and markets, despite temporary downturns caused by such events as the 2008 financial crisis.

2. In comparison with other countries, Canada depends extensively on international trade. Its most significant trading partner is the United States.

3. Canada's merchandise exports include almost equal portions of natural resources and manufactured products. In contrast, its merchandise imports of manufactured products are double that of natural resources. In addition to merchandise, Canada also has significant trade in services.

4. Canada's exports of natural resources are becoming less significant than they used to be. Since the early 1970s, manufactured goods have grown considerably as a proportion of merchandise exports and slightly as a proportion of merchandise imports. While the service sector has been growing in Canada, international trade in services has not grown as much as international trade in merchandise. This is because services tend to be bought and sold within national economies, and because of problems in measuring service trade.

5. Which specific products a country produces for trade depends on what it produces most efficiently. Three factors affect efficiency: resources, market size, and climate.

6. Trade among nations brings significant gains: product variety, increased competition, and specialization.

7. The gains of specialization can best be seen in the cases of absolute advantage and comparative advantage. The law of comparative advantage states that output is maximized when producers specialize in what they can make at a lower opportunity cost than can other producers.

8. The terms of trade are the international price of a product in terms of another product. The terms of trade are determined by both the opportunity costs of the products for the trading partners and the international demand for the products.

15.1 | PRACTICE PROBLEMS

1. Approximately what proportion of Canada's merchandise exports go to the United States?
2. Approximately what proportion of Canada's merchandise imports come from the United States?
3. The table below shows how many Blu-ray discs or Blu-ray players can be produced daily by one worker in Pisces and Aries.

Daily Output per Worker

	Blu-ray Discs	Blu-ray Players
Pisces	20	4
Aries	25	1

a. Which country is more efficient at producing discs? players?
b. What are the opportunity costs of the two goods in each country?

   c. On the basis of absolute advantage, which country should specialize in the production of each good? Explain.
   d. Identify the limits of the terms of trade for these two goods.
4. The table below shows how many computer monitors or digital TVs can be produced daily by one worker in Taurus and Virgo.

Daily Output per Worker

	Computer Monitors	Digital TVs
Taurus	1	2
Virgo	2	6

   a. Which country is more efficient at producing computer monitors? digital TVs?
   b. What are the opportunity costs of the two goods in each country?
   c. On the basis of comparative advantage, which country should specialize in the production of each good? Explain.
   d. Identify the limits of the terms of trade for these two goods.

15.2 | The Impact of Trade Protection

Despite the benefits of international trade, countries often try to block imports or subsidize domestic industries. First, we will examine how governments intervene in international trade. Later, we will consider the arguments against trade that motivate such intervention.

Tariffs

To see the role that foreign trade plays in markets for a specific product, consider a hypothetical competitive market for bicycles in Canada. The left graph in Figure 15.8 shows the demand (D) and domestic supply curves (S_{do}) for bicycles in the unlikely case where there is no foreign trade. Market equilibrium would occur at a price of $150 and a quantity of 90 000 (point c).

   If international trade in bicycles existed and this trade were unrestricted, then Canadian consumers would have the opportunity to buy either domestic or imported bicycles. Assuming for our example that the cost of transporting the product is zero, Canadians would be able to purchase foreign-made bicycles for $100, which is the prevailing world price. Since Canadian consumers make up a small proportion of the world bicycle market, their purchases do not affect equilibrium in this market. Hence, an unlimited quantity supplied is available from foreign bicycle producers at $100, as shown by the horizontal line (S_{i0}) at this price.

   As shown on the left in Figure 15.8, at a price of $100, Canadian consumers would demand 130 000 bicycles (point e). However, Canadian suppliers are willing to supply only 50 000 bicycles at this price (point a). The 80 000 difference between domestic supply (S_{do}) and domestic demand (D) represents the quantity foreign producers could sell in this market. As a result of the international trade, the price has fallen and a significant number of consumers are buying foreign-produced bicycles.

FIGURE 15.8   The Impact of Import Barriers

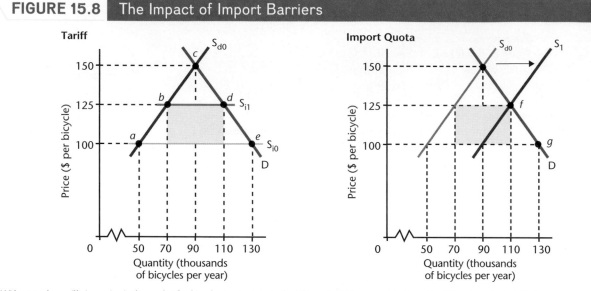

Without trade, equilibrium price in the market for bicycles is at point *c* in the left graph. With unrestricted imports of bicycles priced at $100, consumers demand more bicycles (point *e*), but domestic producers will supply fewer bicycles (point *a*). Imports make up the difference. With a $25 tariff, the price rises to $125 (shown by S_{i1}), imports fall (points *b* to *d*), and the government gains extra revenue shown by the shaded rectangle. With an import quota of 40 000 bicycles, as shown in the right graph, supply shifts from S_{d0} to S_1. Compared with the case of unrestricted trade, the change in price and the quantity of imports (from point *g* to point *f*) is identical to those resulting from tariffs, but now the shaded rectangle indicates extra revenue to foreign producers. This extra revenue from a higher price at least partially offsets the loss due to fewer sales.

tariff: an excise tax on imported goods

Governments may respond to such a situation by imposing a **tariff**, which is an excise tax on imported goods. Until recent years, tariffs were a major tool of trade protection in Canada as well as in many other countries, especially against foreign manufactured goods. In our example, if a $25 tariff is applied on foreign-made bicycles, Canadian consumers must pay an additional $25–or a total price of $125. The result of this price increase is again shown on the left in Figure 15.8. The supply of imported bicycles is now depicted by a horizontal line (S_{i1}) at a price of $125. At this price, Canadian consumers demand 110 000 bicycles (point *d*). Since Canadian suppliers are willing to supply 70 000 bicycles at this price (point *b*), the difference between domestic demand and domestic supply at this price is 40 000, which foreign producers supply.

When compared with the case of unrestricted trade, tariffs affect consumers and the government in opposite ways. Consumers pay a higher price ($125 instead of $100) and buy fewer bicycles (110 000 instead of 130 000) than they did before the tariff was introduced. However, the government benefits from the tariff through the additional tax revenue it is able to raise. With a $25 tariff per bicycle and 40 000 bicycles imported, the government's extra revenue is $1 million (= $25 × 40 000). This is shown in Figure 15.8 on the left graph by the area of the shaded rectangle, whose height represents the tariff per bicycle and whose width indicates the quantity of imports once the tariff is in place.

Domestic and foreign producers are also affected in opposite ways by the tariff. Canadian bicycle producers and their resource suppliers benefit because of the extra earnings tied to the increase in price from $100 to $125 and the rise in domestic production from 50 000 to 70 000 bicycles. Foreign bicycle producers, however, are harmed by the tariff. They face an unchanged after-tax price for each bicycle they sell ($100) while accepting a reduction in imports–from 80 000 to 40 000 bicycles.

Import Quotas

If tariffs are not an option, a government may use other trade restrictions, known as **non-tariff barriers (NTBs)**, to limit imports. Recently, these barriers have become more popular, since governments find it harder to levy tariffs because of international trade agreements.

The most common non-tariff barrier is an **import quota**, which is a set limit on the quantity of a good that can be imported in a certain year. Import quotas can work in two ways. A government can impose an import quota itself, or it can use the threat of trade restrictions to force foreign producers to set their own "voluntary" quotas, which are known as **voluntary export restraints (VERs)**. One well-known illustration of a voluntary export restraint involves Canada's imports of Japanese cars. In 1981, an agreement limiting annual Japanese exports of automobiles to Canada was worked out between the two countries. In 1986, when the agreement expired, Japanese automakers continued to limit their exports to Canada voluntarily to stop the Canadian government from taking other types of trade action.

More recent examples include agreements in 1998 and 1999 between the United States government and steel producers in Japan and South Korea to reduce US-bound exports. Because these agreements have become illegal under world trade law, they are now made informally, rather than being set out in writing.

Generally, foreign producers find import quotas preferable to tariffs. To see why, we return to our hypothetical example of the bicycle market in Figure 15.8. The impact of an import quota on this market is portrayed on the right graph, in which the domestic demand and supply curves, D and S_{d0}, as well as the prevailing world price, are identical to those on the left graph. As before, a situation of unrestricted trade (point y) leads to an original $100 price, with consumption exceeding domestic production by 80 000, which represents the initial amount of bicycles imported.

By imposing a maximum level of imports of 40 000, this number of bicycles is added to the domestic supply (S_{d0}) at every price, thereby giving the combined domestic and foreign supply curve S_1. Domestic demand (D) and the new supply (S_1) intersect at the new equilibrium price of $125 and quantity of 110 000 (point f). Again, production is split between domestic and foreign producers. Canadian businesses produce 70 000 bicycles, leaving 40 000 for foreign businesses, shown along the shaded area.

The policy's effect on consumers and domestic producers is the same as with a tariff. The results for the government and foreign producers are different, however. With an import quota, the government no longer receives tax revenue. Instead, the extra revenue indicated by the shaded rectangle on the graph on the right flows to foreign producers in the form of higher prices on the bicycles they still sell in Canada. This extra revenue partly counteracts the loss that foreign producers bear because of the lower quantity they supply in the Canadian market.

Domestic Regulations

Regulations in particular markets can make trade within them expensive for foreign producers, therefore acting as obstacles to trade. For example, Canada has certain licensing procedures and imposes relatively high safety and environmental

non-tariff barriers (NTBs): trade barriers other than tariffs that are used to restrict imports; include import quotas, voluntary export restraints, and domestic regulations

import quota: a set limit on the quantity of a good that can be imported in a given year

voluntary export restraints (VERs): import quotas that are voluntarily put in place by the exporting country

standards. Also, rules controlling government purchases–known as government procurement policies–may require that whenever possible, governments should buy domestic rather than foreign items. If imports are successfully restricted through these practices, the results are the same as in the case of an import quota.

Export Subsidies

export subsidies: payments by a government to domestic exporters so that these exporters can reduce the prices they charge in foreign markets

Export subsidies are payments by a government to domestic exporters so that they can reduce the prices they charge in foreign markets. These programs are intended to raise the amount of exports, thus increasing output and employment in the domestic economy. Besides helping domestic exporters and foreign consumers, an export subsidy imposes a cost on foreign producers, who lose sales to the new low-priced competition, and on the exporting country's own taxpayers, who must foot the bill for the program. Many countries, including Canada, have used such subsidies, especially in agricultural markets.

The Case for Trade Protection

The gains in economic welfare associated with specialization and the law of comparative advantage are generally large enough to make a compelling case for free trade. Consequently, it is common for economists to oppose government policies that protect trade. Nonetheless, particular cases of trade protection can be defended with either economic or non-economic arguments. We will look at each of these arguments in turn.

ECONOMIC ARGUMENTS

Five economic arguments can be applied to support various types of trade protection. According to these arguments, trade barriers help stimulate domestic employment, foster infant industries, improve a country's terms of trade, protect a country's environmental and safety standards, and shield domestic workers from imports produced with cheap foreign labour.

Domestic Employment

Because imports are a withdrawal from an economy's circular flow, they have a dampening effect on total spending and output. Thus, a reduction in the level of imports through trade barriers can potentially increase the level of economic activity in the country and provide more jobs for domestic workers.

This argument is legitimate only in certain circumstances, however. Because a strategy of import reduction causes foreign countries' exports to diminish, output and employment levels in these foreign nations will fall. Hence, the new domestic employment in the country imposing trade barriers comes at the expense of jobs elsewhere. The threat of foreign retaliation means that this policy can easily backfire–other nations may try to recapture some of their lost exports and jobs by imposing new trade barriers of their own. Such behaviour makes everyone worse off by limiting the opportunities for each country to specialize on the basis of comparative advantage.

Infant Industries

infant industry: a domestic industry that is young in comparison to its foreign competitors

An **infant industry** is made up of domestic producers that are young compared with competitors in foreign countries. Because of their recent origin and small size, domestic producers are not able to take full advantage of increasing returns to scale. Until they are able to, according to supporters, lower-priced foreign imports must be blocked.

This type of protection is often used by countries whose prosperity is closely tied to just a few export products and where there is a wish to develop new industries in which there is no immediate comparative advantage.

But the argument for protecting infant industries is valid only if other countries do not retaliate with their own trade barriers. Even if retaliation does not occur, the argument is open to abuse. Once imposed, trade barriers in a given industry are difficult to eliminate. Industry groups–representing both business and labour–tend to fight any reduction in barriers, even after their industry has fully matured. In addition, industries created in this fashion often represent an inefficient employment of resources. In the absence of international competition in protected markets, domestic consumers pay high prices for what may be substandard goods.

Terms of Trade

If a country's volume of trade is large enough to affect prices in a world product market, then it can use trade barriers to improve its terms of trade. For example, the United States could impose a tariff on its imports of Canadian lumber. This would decrease the global demand for lumber, pushing down lumber's international price. As a result, Americans would be able to acquire the same amount of Canadian lumber with a smaller quantity of American products. As long as Canada does not retaliate with its own trade barriers, the terms of trade move in the United States' favour.

Environmental and Safety Standards

To address spillover costs, in particular those related to the environment and safety, many governments impose standards that can be quite costly to certain businesses.

However, standards vary. While some countries may regulate industry either to reduce or to compensate for spillover costs, other countries–especially those with low per capita GDP–may have very lax environmental and safety regulations to allow exporters there to reduce their expenses and product prices.

THINKING ABOUT ECONOMICS

In what industries is the infant industry argument currently relevant?

In recent years, the argument relating to infant industries has gained new importance in high-technology markets, such as the aircraft and semiconductor industries. In these markets, a few large businesses are able to take advantage of increasing returns to scale, and the flourishing of one high-tech industry can act as a magnet for firms in other high-tech industries as well. Strategic trade policy is the use of tariffs and export subsidies to help domestic producers gain a foothold in these industries.

QUESTION   **What are some arguments that could be made for and against the use of strategic trade policy?**

Critics of lax environmental standards suggest that without trade protection, increased globalization will be accompanied by an increase in environmental damage. Similarly, critics of lax safety standards believe that without trade protection, workers in all countries are hurt. Those in countries with low safety standards face increased risks of injury on the job, while those in countries with strict standards face a reduction in the demand for labour, and therefore fewer available jobs.

According to critics of low environmental and safety standards, countries should maintain high standards and set up trade barriers against exports from countries with lower standards. They argue that without these two measures, businesses operating in countries with lax standards will continue to profit, other businesses will move their operations to such countries to gain a competitive edge, and spillover costs will increase internationally.

Low-Wage Foreign Labour

A related argument has gained much political force in recent years with the new competitiveness of emerging economies such as China and India. It suggests that imports produced by low-wage foreign labour need to be blocked from entering an industrialized country to protect the jobs of domestic workers. In its basic form, this argument is flawed because it ignores the key reason for the differences among wage rates in various countries. Workers in countries with a higher per capita GDP tend to earn more than workers elsewhere because of their higher productivity, as explored in Chapter 7. Workers in industrialized countries tend to be highly skilled and are employed along with larger amounts of capital per worker. Once average wages in various countries are compared with these different productivity levels, workers in industrialized nations still possess a comparative advantage over low-wage foreign labour in many types of production. Nonetheless, it is likely that certain groups of workers in industrialized countries will be hurt by increased trade with emerging economies.

THINKING ABOUT ECONOMICS

Wages for Canadian unskilled and semi-skilled workers have not kept up with wages for skilled workers and returns on capital in recent years. Why?

These trends are common to most industrialized countries. Economists point to two factors as explanations, one related to technology and the other to trade. First, as technological progress takes place, production processes, especially in manufacturing, are using ever more capital relative to labour, especially in the completion of simple and highly repetitive tasks. This causes demand for unskilled and semi-skilled labour to fall relative to skilled labour and capital. Second, freer trade, combined with rapid industrialization in emerging economies, means that labour productivity is rapidly rising in key export sectors within these economies, even though their overall productivity levels remain significantly lower than in countries such as Canada. As long as wages being paid to unskilled and semi-skilled workers in emerging economies are lower than in industrialized countries, the demand for these types of labour in Canada will be dampened by growing trade, even as overall incomes in rich countries are buoyed by globalization. Most economists agree that both factors are at play, though there are strong differences of opinion concerning the relative importance of technological progress and globalization as causes of this shift in the pattern of wages.

QUESTION   Do reductions in wages for unskilled and semi-skilled workers mean that freer trade is harmful overall for Canada?

NON-ECONOMIC ARGUMENTS

The two remaining arguments in favour of trade barriers are based on non-economic factors: national security and cultural sovereignty.

National Security

The oldest argument for trade barriers relates to national security. A country's citizens may wish to be self-sufficient in producing certain strategic commodities, such as energy, basic food items, and military equipment. In periods of political instability, or even outright armed conflict, a country will then be guaranteed supplies of these commodities. The way to ensure that domestic industries can develop in these sectors is to insulate them from foreign competition. This argument has been applied in such countries as Israel, where military threats to national security have been a major concern, but its relevance to Canada seems limited.

Cultural Sovereignty

Another non-economic argument for certain types of trade protection relates to culture. Some countries, including Canada, feel the need to protect and nurture their own cultural industries by, for example, restricting the imported content of radio and TV programming, limiting broadcast licences, subsidizing "home-grown" authors and visual artists, or purchasing only domestically produced textbooks. In one recent incident, to help the French movie industry withstand foreign competition—especially from Hollywood—France blocked US attempts to liberalize international trade in movies. However, critics suggest that in an age of satellite communications and the Internet, trade barriers relating to many cultural industries can no longer be enforced.

BRIEF REVIEW

1. Governments may intervene in international markets through a variety of means, including tariffs, non-tariff barriers (import quotas, voluntary export restraints, and domestic regulations), and export subsidies.

2. Tariffs are excise taxes on imported goods. In contrast, import quotas and voluntary export restraints are limits on the quantity of a product that can be imported in a certain year. These barriers result in higher prices, lower consumption, fewer imports, and more domestic production of the item affected. With a tariff, governments gain extra tax revenue; with an import quota or voluntary export restraint, revenues from the resulting higher prices flow to the foreign producers, partly offsetting the effect of the decrease in sales.

3. Domestic regulations can present obstacles to trade. When successful, the results parallel the effects of an import quota.

4. Export subsidies are another form of trade intervention. In this case, governments make payments to domestic exporters so that exporters can lower the prices they charge in foreign markets. The results are lower sales of foreign products and higher domestic taxes.

5. The economic arguments in favour of trade barriers relate to domestic employment, infant industries, the terms of trade, environmental and safety standards, and low-wage foreign labour.

6. The non-economic arguments in favour of trade barriers relate to maintaining national security and cultural sovereignty.

15.2 | PRACTICE PROBLEMS

1. A tariff is imposed on a good sold in a perfectly competitive market in which a portion of domestic demand is met by imports. The following questions refer to the case where the tariff is imposed when compared with the case of freely available imports with no tariff.
   a. How do (i) equilibrium price, (ii) quantity demanded, (iii) domestic quantity supplied, and (iv) the quantity imported compare with the case of freely available imports?
   b. Do consumers benefit or lose due to the tariff? Why?
   c. How are domestic producers affected? Why?
   d. Do foreign producers benefit or lose? Why?
   e. How is the country's government affected? Why?

2. An import quota is imposed on a good sold in a perfectly competitive market in which a portion of domestic demand is met by imports. The following questions refer to the case where the import quota is imposed when compared with the case of freely available imports with no quota.
   a. How do (i) equilibrium price, (ii) quantity demanded, (iii) domestic quantity supplied, and (iv) the quantity imported compare with the case of freely available imports?
   b. Do consumers benefit or lose due to the quota? Why?
   c. How are domestic producers affected? Why?
   d. Do foreign producers benefit or lose? Why?
   e. How is the country's government affected? Why?

15.3 | Trade Policies

Recall that Canada's most significant trading partner now and throughout much of its history is the United States. As a result, trade between the two countries has played an important role in determining Canadian trade policy.

Early Canadian Trade Policy

THE NATIONAL POLICY

As portrayed in Figure 15.9, the average Canadian tariff rate as a percentage of total merchandise imports rose in the years after Confederation.

In 1879, Canada's first prime minister, Sir John A. Macdonald, instituted a wide-ranging tariff policy based on the infant industry argument for trade protection. The **National Policy** led to high tariffs on manufactured imports to stimulate the development of a domestic manufacturing sector. Without this policy, supporters argued, Canadian manufacturers would be swamped by low-priced American competition produced with the benefits of increasing returns to scale. Due to the National Policy, many US manufacturers chose to "jump the tariff wall" by setting up branch plants in Canada to allow them to continue selling in Canadian markets.

National Policy: a Canadian policy initiated in 1879 that included high Canadian tariffs on manufactured imports to stimulate a domestic manufacturing sector

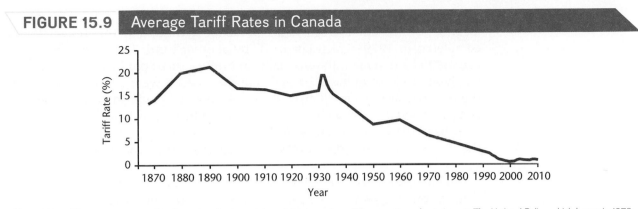

FIGURE 15.9   Average Tariff Rates in Canada

Since 1868, tariffs as a percentage of total merchandise imports have fallen from above 20 percent to under 1 percent. The National Policy, which began in 1879, pushed up the average tariff rate. While the rate gradually fell from the early 1890s, it rose again during the Great Depression. Since the early 1930s, the rate has declined considerably due to the effects of various GATT and WTO agreements, as well as regional agreements, that Canada has signed.

Sources: Statistics Canada "Average Tariff Rates in Canada." Adapted from "Historical Statistics of Canada," Catalogue 11-516, 1983, Series G473-487 and from the Statistics Canada CANSIM database www5.statcan.gc.ca/cansim/, Tables 384-0001 and 228-0003. Retrieved February 2, 2014.

THE GREAT DEPRESSION

The Great Depression sparked a new round of protectionism. Such a trend is common during economic downturns. With falling output and employment, domestic producers see trade barriers as a way of maintaining their sales despite shrinking markets. In the early 1930s, governments in most industrialized countries raised tariffs—partly for domestic reasons and partly to retaliate against foreign trade barriers placed on their own exports. Not surprisingly, all countries were made worse off by this move because of the resulting decline in world trade.

Once the damaging effects of this protectionism became evident, Canada signed trade liberalizing agreements, reducing Canada's average tariff rate to below its pre-Depression level. And the lessons learned from this harmful protectionism live on to this day. The 1930s example is one important reason that countries did not respond with another round of protectionism in the aftermath of the 2008 financial crisis.

General Agreement on Tariffs and Trade

The liberalizing trend in global trade continued after World War II. In 1947, Canada was one of 22 nations that signed the **General Agreement on Tariffs and Trade (GATT)**, which until recently was the most important example of a "multilateral" trade agreement involving many countries. In 1995, GATT was replaced by the **World Trade Organization (WTO)**. This organization, with almost 150 members, continues GATT's task of lessening trade protection among member countries, including Canada.

The WTO is based on the principle that trade policies of member countries should treat all other members equally. Complaints by one country against the trade policies of another are subject to formal rules and judged by impartial panels. If a settlement cannot be reached through compromise, then the complainant country has recourse to limited forms of trade retaliation.

Through rounds of negotiation, first among GATT members and then among WTO members, both tariff and non-tariff barriers have been gradually reduced.

General Agreement on Tariffs and Trade (GATT): a multilateral trade agreement that lessened the degree of trade protection among member countries, including Canada

World Trade Organization (WTO): a multilateral trade organization that has replaced GATT

The most important of these negotiations was the Kennedy Round, completed in 1967, which cut average tariffs by about a third, and the Tokyo Round, completed in 1979, which cut tariffs by another third. The result has been a marked reduction of tariffs–especially on manufactured products. Average tariffs for these products in industrialized countries, which were above 50 percent in the 1930s, have since fallen to below 5 percent. Trade in services, such as computer software, as well as agricultural products, continues to be gradually liberalized thanks to current WTO negotiations, despite recent setbacks such as the limited success of the WTO's most recent Doha Round, which emphasizes agricultural trade and farm subsidies.

While gradual, the long-run impact of WTO-induced regulatory changes for Canada could be profound–especially in relation to countries such as China and India, whose trade with Canada is likely to continue increasing at a significant pace. The rise of these nations as major players in the international economy provides significant opportunities, as well as challenges, for Canadian producers. For example, the rapid expansion of manufacturing in emerging economies is one reason for the boom in commodity prices benefiting Canadian natural resource suppliers from the mid-2000s onwards. But countries such as China and India are gaining a comparative advantage in the production of many manufactured goods as well as services. This is providing a keen new source of international competition for Canadian businesses. The overall results should be highly beneficial for the world economy as a whole, but there will be short-run and sometimes painful adjustment costs as established economies such as Canada are forced to respond to these competitive challenges. Recent layoffs in the North American auto industry during the 2008–2009 global recession, as production continues to move to other parts of the world including China and India, represent one significant example for Canada.

Recent Trading Blocs

trading bloc: a relatively small number of countries involved in a trade agreement

A wish to pursue closer economic ties has led some groups of countries to liberalize trade among themselves. A **trading bloc** is a relatively small group of countries involved in a trade agreement. There are three types: free trade area, customs union, and common market. Each type involves increased integration of trade policies.

FREE TRADE AREA

free trade area: an area in which trade is tariff-free, although member countries are able to impose separate trade barriers on outside countries

Trade within a **free trade area** is tariff-free, although member countries are able to impose separate trade barriers on outside countries. Contemporary examples of free trade areas are the North American Free Trade Agreement among Canada, the United States, and Mexico, and the free trade area established in 2010 between China and the ten-nation Association of South-East Asian Nations. This latter trading bloc is the now the largest in the world, with its member nations including almost 2 billion people.

CUSTOMS UNION

customs union: a group of countries with common trade barriers with outside countries as well as a free trade area

A **customs union** is a stronger form of regional integration that includes not only free trade among member countries, but also common trade barriers with the rest of the world. An example of an emerging customs union is Mercosur, which has six member countries, including Brazil and Argentina.

COMMON MARKET

A **common market** is a customs union that allows for the free movement of labour and capital among member nations. The best-known example of a common market is the previously mentioned **European Union (EU)**, formerly known as the European Economic Community (EEC), which was first formed in 1956 by six countries: Germany, France, Italy, the Netherlands, Belgium, and Luxembourg. Since then, the European Union has expanded to include a majority of countries in Europe. In 1992, a treaty was signed among member countries that set them on a path to close economic and political integration. Though the pace of integration has slowed in recent years, the result has been relatively free movement of economic resources, standardized economic regulations, and a common currency, the euro, for many, though not all, EU members.

Supporters of the EU suggest that the gains from past trade liberalization among members have helped boost recent living standards in European countries. Critics point out the loss of national sovereignty that has accompanied the EU's evolution and argue that European living standards would have risen with or without freer trade.

common market: a group of countries with not only a free trade area and common trade barriers with outside countries, but also free movement of labour and capital

European Union (EU): an expanding common market of European countries first formed in 1956, formerly known as the European Economic Community (EEC)

The Free Trade Agreement

The Canada–US **Free Trade Agreement (FTA)** is an example of a bilateral free trade agreement, which involves two partners and includes trade in virtually all products between the two countries. It was signed by Canada and the United States in 1988 and came into effect in 1989. Under the terms of the agreement, all remaining tariffs on trade between the two countries were phased out by 1998, and non-tariff barriers were reduced. Services were also included, with a national treatment principle being adopted so that service industries in either country could compete in both national markets. Licensing procedures in the two countries have been standardized to help ease this liberalization of services. Canada's ability to screen foreign direct investment has been reduced, while non-North American car companies can trade autos and auto parts freely across the Canada–United States border if they meet a revised 50 percent North American manufacturing content rule. There is also greater access for American wine and liquor producers—and, more gradually, for American brewers—in the Canadian market. A continental market for energy has been created. While Canada may still limit its energy exports to the United States during a period of global shortages, Canadians will have to limit their own energy consumption by the same proportion. Of particular note, Canadian cultural policies are largely exempted from the agreement, allowing Canada to impose policies that affect the trade and ownership of its cultural industries. Finally, a dispute settlement procedure is in place so that when either country retaliates against the other's trade policies, the dispute is judged by an impartial panel using the trade legislation of the retaliating country.

Free Trade Agreement (FTA): the 1988 pact between Canada and the United States to form a free trade area

As usual, supporters of free trade point out the economic benefits that have occurred from increased specialization and trade between the two countries. Canadian advocates of the agreement also suggest that it has reduced the risk of US protectionist measures directed against Canadian exports. Critics of the deal focus on the loss of political sovereignty for Canada, especially because of the restrictions placed on government attempts to screen foreign investment and restrict energy exports. While either country can end the agreement with six months' warning, the gradual strengthening of trade ties between the two countries has made it practically impossible for any Canadian government to do so. Critics also stress that Canadian jobs were lost in previously protected manufacturing industries as foreign companies closed their remaining branch plants so they could centralize their production and take advantage of increasing returns to scale.

Finally, in recent years critics point to the fact that the United States has been willing to circumvent some panel rulings that go against American interests by reintroducing tariffs on certain goods and then using the delay in dispute resolution as an informal trade barrier. Such actions often reflect compromises by US presidential administrations to take into account protectionist-minded sentiments within Congress. However, it is argued, these actions nonetheless go against the spirit of the agreement.

A good example is the long-running dispute over trade in softwood lumber, which is used primarily for construction. Because of complaints by American lumber producers that provincial governments in Canada charge domestic companies artificially low prices to harvest timber on Crown lands, the US government imposed tariffs on lumber exports to the United States–most recently in 2002. Canada took this issue to NAFTA dispute resolution panels and won the majority of the rulings, but the US government refused to abide by the panel decisions. Only in 2006 was an agreement finally worked out between the two countries, and even then the result does not represent true free trade. The United States is returning most of the tariff duties collected since 2002. However, Canada has agreed to cap its share of the US softwood lumber market and to impose an export tax if the Canadian lumber price falls below a certain level. Such illustrations show the difficulties in maintaining a free trade agreement unless there is a strong will on the part of all participating governments to abide by the spirit of the agreement.

EFFECTS OF THE FREE TRADE AGREEMENT

As expected, in the early years of the Free Trade Agreement both Canada and the United States experienced expanding trade flows. From 1989 to 1992, for example, Canadian merchandise exports in sectors liberalized by the agreement increased by 33 percent, while Canadian merchandise imports in the same sectors rose by 28 percent. The increase in Canada's exports was most pronounced in manufacturing industries, such as office and telecommunications equipment, as well as in resource-based industries, such as chemical products and paper. Meanwhile, Canada's merchandise imports grew most in such industries as processed food, clothing, and furniture. In the following decade, Canada's total exports to the United States continued to expand faster than did US imports into Canada. However, there has been some fallback in exports to the US as a proportion of both total Canadian exports and Canadian GDP in recent years, as shown in Figure 15.10. So far, the impartial dispute settlement procedure has often worked in Canada's favour, despite the US government's tendency to reintroduce trade complaints if a panel decision goes against its perceived interests.

There were also short-term adjustment costs associated with the agreement. The bulk of these costs fell on workers who lost their jobs in formerly protected industries. It is important to remember that other factors also caused unemployment

| FIGURE 15.10 | Exports to the US Relative to Total Exports and GDP (1988–2013) |

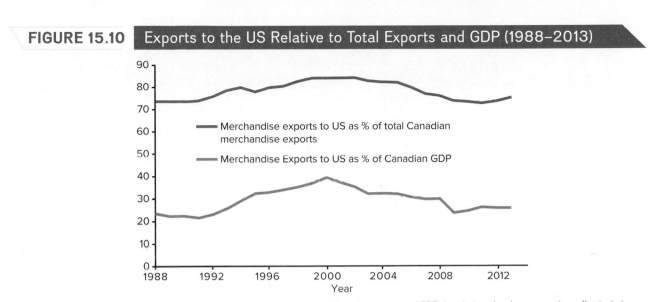

Since 1988, Canada's exports to the US have risen both as a percentage of total Canadian exports and GDP, though there has been some drop-off in both these proportions since the year 2000.

Source: Statistics Canada "Exports to the US Relative to Total Exports and GDP (1988–2013)." Adapted from the Statistics Canada CANSIM database www5.statcan.gc.ca/cansim/, Tables 228-0058, and 384-0038. Retrieved March 18, 2014.

to rise during the years immediately after the FTA took effect. The first was the continuing shift of Canadian jobs away from manufacturing and toward the service sector. Second, the agreement came into effect just before the start of a significant global recession. And, in the long run, trade theory suggests, jobs lost in declining industries hurt by free trade have been replaced by employment in expanding export industries—one of the main reasons for the significant decline in Canada's unemployment rate during the latter part of the 1990s and early 2000s.

The North American Free Trade Agreement

The **North American Free Trade Agreement (NAFTA)**, which was settled in 1993 and came into effect in 1994, is an illustration of a trilateral trade accord, which is among three countries. It extends most of the provisions of the Free Trade Agreement to include Mexico. If we consider only trade with this new partner, NAFTA has not had a significant impact on either Canada or Mexico because their trade relationship has never been significant, and much of this trade was virtually tariff-free even before NAFTA.

However, critics of NAFTA suggest there are possible problems with including a country with a lower GDP per capita in the same free trade area as wealthier, more industrialized countries. They point to the loss of Canadian jobs that occur when businesses move to Mexico to take advantage of low-wage labour. Concern has also been expressed over Mexico's lax enforcement of labour and environmental standards. This last concern prompted the addition of two side-agreements to NAFTA. Under the side-agreements, two NAFTA members can set penalties on the third member if that country does not enforce its labour and

North American Free Trade Agreement (NAFTA): the 1993 pact among Canada, the United States, and Mexico to form a free trade area

THINKING ABOUT ECONOMICS

How could Canada's trade be further liberalized in the future?

Canada has signed bilateral trade agreements with a range of countries, and is participating in current WTO negotiations on agricultural trade and on services. It is also a member of the Asia-Pacific Economic Cooperation forum (APEC), whose goal is to liberalize trade with Asian countries, and it is involved in Pan-American talks, whose aim is to form a Free Trade Agreement of the Americas (FTAA). In addition, it has signed a Comprehensive Economic and Trade Agreement (CETA) with the European Union. Some Canadians are also calling for the formation of a European-style common market with the United States, which would allow for the free movement of goods, services, and people across the Canada–US border. However, such a common market arrangement would be problematic from a political standpoint, given the reduction in national sovereignty that such a common market arrangement would cause.

QUESTION   **What are the main economic arguments for and against forming a common market with the US?**

environmental laws. So far, these provisions have not been invoked, and it is difficult to judge the relevance of the criticisms made against NAFTA, at least from a Canadian perspective.

From a Mexican perspective, the impact of NAFTA on economic growth has been inconclusive, though it has tied the country's trade ever closer with the United states and to a far lesser extent with Canada. Still, because of ongoing economic reforms and its recent success in raising exports, especially of manufactured goods such as automobiles, the country is being tagged as a potential economic giant–along with other emerging economies such as Indonesia, Nigeria, and Turkey–in the decades to come.

BRIEF REVIEW

1. Canadian trade policy became increasingly restrictive after 1867, particularly with the adoption of the National Policy in 1879. The National Policy raised tariffs to stimulate Canada's own manufacturing sector.

2. High tariff rates continued until after the Great Depression, at which point this approach to trade was reassessed.

3. The General Agreement on Tariffs and Trade (GATT) was a multilateral trade agreement created in 1947, based on the principle that member countries should treat all other members equally. Until its replacement in 1995 by the World Trade Organization (WTO), GATT was a major force in liberalizing international trade.

4. Trading blocs, which are trade agreements among a small number of countries, take a variety of forms: free trade areas, customs unions, and common markets.

5. Trade within a free trade area is tariff-free, although member countries can impose separate trade barriers on outside countries. The Free Trade Agreement (FTA) and its extension, the North American Free Trade Agreement (NAFTA), are examples.

6. A customs union is a stronger form of regional integration. Not only is the free trade area tariff-free, but members have common trade barriers with the rest of the world. An example is Mercosur.

7. A common market is a customs union that allows for the free movement of labour and capital. The European Union (EU) is an example of a common market, which since the early 1990s has moved toward closer economic and political integration.

15.3 | PRACTICE PROBLEMS

1. Which of the following is (i) a free trade area, (ii) a customs union, or (iii) a common market?
   a. Mercosur
   b. NAFTA
   c. The European Union
2. Between the late 1980s and early 2010s, how did Canada's merchandise exports to the United States and merchandise imports from the United States vary as proportions of Canada's overall merchandise exports and imports?

LAST WORD

This chapter focused on foreign trade—the economic case for trade, the special cases in which trade protection can be defended, and the regional and global trade agreements that have arisen over the past few decades. We determined that the main purpose behind the recent moves toward freer trade is its potential effect on real output. How we evaluate the relative success of these recent global trends is subject to significant debate. While global GDP has grown at a relatively high rate in the past two decades, the distribution of this growth has arguably been less than equitable. On the whole, rich economies such as Canada's and the United States' have performed well within this new global setting, as have major developing economies such as China's and India's. However, for many of the world's poor, such as those in countries like Sudan and Ethiopia, the benefits of freer trade are still a distant mirage.

PROBLEMS

1. Ada can prepare a tax return in 4 hours and paint a kitchen in 10 hours, while it takes Paulo 12 hours to prepare a tax return and 2 hours to paint a kitchen.
   a. Who is more efficient at preparing a tax return? at painting a kitchen?
   b. What are the opportunity costs for the two activities for Ada? for Paulo?
   c. Who should specialize in each activity? Why?

2. The table below shows how many video games or digital cameras can be produced daily by one worker in Atlantica and Pacifica.

   Daily Output per Worker

	Video Games	Digital Cameras
Atlantica	8	4
Pacifica	10	2

   a. Which country is more efficient at producing games? cameras?
   b. What are the opportunity costs of the two goods in each country?
   c. On the basis of absolute advantage, which country should specialize in the production of each good?
   d. Identify the limits of the terms of trade for these two goods.
   e. Suppose there are 3 million workers in Atlantica and 4 million workers in Pacifica. Before trade, half of each country's labour force makes each good. Outline how specialization and trade lead to a gain in the two countries' total output of both goods.

3. The table below shows how many T-shirts or jeans can be made daily by one worker in Aquarius and Capricorn.

   Daily Output per Worker

	T-Shirts	Jeans
Aquarius	40	4
Capricorn	30	2

   a. Which country is more efficient at producing T-shirts? jeans?
   b. What are the opportunity costs for the two goods in each country?
   c. On the basis of comparative advantage, which country should specialize in the production of each good?
   d. Identify the limits of the terms of trade for these two goods.
   e. Suppose there are 200 000 workers in Aquarius and 300 000 workers in Capricorn, and before trade, half of each country's labour force makes each good. Outline how specialization and trade lead to a gain in the total output of both goods.

4. Suppose that one digital music player has an opportunity cost of 10 smartphones in Canada and an opportunity cost of 5 smartphones in South Korea.
   a. Which country should export each good?
   b. Identify the limits of terms of trade for these two goods.
   c. What international price would be preferred by Canadians? by the South Koreans? Explain each of your answers.

5. The table below shows hypothetical data for the Canadian market for watches, presuming this market is perfectly competitive.

Domestic Demand and Supply Schedules

Price ($)	Quantity Demanded (D_d) (millions per year)	Quantity Supplied (S_d) (millions per year)
80	1.4	1.8
70	1.6	1.6
60	1.8	1.4
50	2.0	1.2
40	2.2	1.0

a. Draw a graph showing the domestic demand and supply curves for watches, D and S. Plot only the endpoints of the two curves. Identify the equilibrium point in the absence of foreign imports.

b. If unrestricted foreign imports of watches are allowed at a constant world price of $50, then what are the (i) equilibrium price, (ii) quantity demanded, (iii) domestic quantity supplied and (iv) quantity imported?

c. If a $10 tariff on imported watches is imposed, then what are the new (i) equilibrium price, (ii) quantity demanded, (iii) domestic quantity supplied and (iv) quantity imported? Show the result of this tariff in your graph.

d. When comparing the $10 tariff with the case of freely available imports with no tariff, do (i) consumers, (ii) domestic producers, (iii) foreign producers and (iv) the Canadian government benefit or lose?

e. If rather than using a tariff the government imposes an import quota of 400 000 watches a year, then with the import quota, what are the (i) equilibrium price, (ii) quantity demanded, (iii) domestic quantity supplied, and (iv) quantity imported? Show the result of this tariff in your graph.

f. When comparing the import quota with the case of freely available imports with no tariff, do (i) consumers, (ii) domestic producers, and (iii) foreign producers benefit or lose?

g. If given the choice of the $10 tariff or the 400 000 import quota, which would foreign producers prefer?

6. Explain how the requirement by the Canadian government that there be English and French labelling of products sometimes operates as an "invisible" non-tariff barrier and give a possible example.

7. Participants in so-called infant industries are like Peter Pan—they do not want their industry to be seen as "grown up." Why?

8. "Incorporating more countries within NAFTA is in Canada's best long-term interests." Discuss.

9. What are the special advantages and disadvantages of trade agreements between countries with significantly different levels of per capita GDP?

10. (Advanced Question)
In many cases, countries import and export the same products. For example, automobiles and auto parts are traded back and forth between Canada, the US, and Mexico. Why?

11. (Policy Discussion Question)

"Due to the job losses associated with previous trade agreements, the need to maintain Canadian agricultural subsidies, as well as many other aspects of Canadian economic policy-making, Canada's decision to participate in the World Trade Organization, and its negotiations over further trade agreements, has been harmful to the Canadian economy." Discuss.

12. Access the website of the World Trade Organization (at www.wto.org/). Use information at this site to explain the following principles of the WTO's multilateral trading system:

   a. MFN (most-favoured-nation) status
   b. national treatment
   c. dumping
   d. plurilateral agreements

BRAVE NEW WORLD

Tyler Cowen on the Information Revolution

Tyler Cowen
*Photo courtesy of
Tyler Cowen*

Machine intelligence is all around us—at home, at work, and commuting between the two—and its ever-expanding powers affect our lives in myriad ways. Economists have much to say about its impact; few more so than Tyler Cowen. Ever since he was a student at George Mason University, where he now teaches, and at Harvard, where he worked with game theorist Thomas Schelling (see Chapter 6's Advancing Economic Thought article), he has studied the information revolution and its economic implications. With the aid of a popular blog, co-authored with Canadian-born colleague Alex Tabarrok, and through books and newspaper columns, he explains the economic ramifications of the digital transformation we are witnessing and makes bold predictions on where this transformation is taking us.

As he notes in his book, *Average is Over,* "every time you use Google you are relying on machine intelligence." This also applies "[e]very time Facebook recommends a new friend for you or sends an ad your way. Every time you use GPS to find your way to a party."[1] Machine intelligence has even intruded into our love lives, as millions use dating site algorithms to select who they will meet. These changes bring major benefits for consumers, but what of the effects on the world of work? Cowen's answers are disturbing. Though he concentrates on US data, his argument is applicable to Canada. In the past decade, global youth unemployment has surged. Of the jobs that are available, especially for recent graduates, average wages paid have declined. But incomes accruing to top earners, both young and old, keep rising, so that the gap separating the top 1 percent from everyone else continues to widen.

THE 2000s: STRUCTURAL OR CYCLICAL CHANGE?

Cowen identifies the information revolution, and to a lesser extent globalization, as important drivers of these trends. Few economists would disagree. More distinctive is the extent to which he downplays other factors, especially the 2008 financial crisis and its associated economic downturn as independent causes. While Keynesian economists argue that the damage to wages and employment since 2008 will reverse as the business cycle turns, Cowen is not so sure. Instead, he views the labour market trends that accompanied the recent recession as a delayed reaction to pressures building for a decade or more.

He emphasizes that, for the first time since the Great Depression, the initial decade of 2000s saw no new job creation in the US. And continuing a trend dating back to the 1980s, real wages of unskilled workers kept tumbling. What rich economies saw during the recession of 2008–2009, says Cowen, was the impact of the growing productivity of intelligent machines relative to low-skilled workers. With the arrival of the economic downturn, companies were forced into wrenching restructuring they had put off for years. Now that companies are rehiring, the lost jobs that paid relatively good wages for unskilled and

---

[1] *Average is Over: Powering America Beyond the Age of the Great Stagnation* (New York: Penguin, 2013), p. 7.

semi-skilled work are not going to return. In their place is a more polarized labour market based on the nature of workers' skills. The few who strategically complement the role of computers are being hired at high wages; those doing jobs that machine intelligence still cannot handle are thrown into a part of the labour market where the demand and supply are relentlessly pushing average wages lower.

Who, in Cowen's view, will benefit from these trends for the foreseeable future? Labour market entrants with quantitative and critical thinking skills, those at ease with computers and their operation, and those who can apply machine intelligence to new areas of work. Those with the skills to become managers, marketers, and providers of high-return personal services will also reap high-paying jobs. The rest will likely not fare anywhere near so well. In particular, Cowen sees no end to the phenomenon of young threshold earners, sometimes known as the limbo generation, delaying entry into full-time careers through living at home and working in temporary and part-time jobs:

> I do not presume the limbo generation consists entirely or even mostly of unhappy individuals. They have freedoms and flexibilities older generations might have envied, and they have a chance to spend lots of time with friends and family. Sex and parties and good ethnic food seem to be everywhere, if Facebook is any kind of guide. Still, the longer-run job prospects for many of this crop of twenty-somethings may not turn out to be so great.[2]

CHESS AS A WINDOW ON THE FUTURE

In fleshing out this prediction, Cowen examines the transformation that has occurred in a pursuit he has closely followed since his youth: the playing of chess. Becoming a chess champion when he was 15, he had a ringside seat as the chess world morphed through the application of sophisticated machine intelligence. Chess is a famously subtle game. When Cowen began playing in the 1970s, the clunky computer programs of that era were a long way from beating the world's best players. But in 1997, IBM's Deep Blue beat the reigning world champion Garry Kasparov. Since then, the chess programs have continued to grow in processing power.

Competitive chess players are numerically ranked based on their record of wins and losses. Today's most challenging games are no longer those played by humans unaided with computers, or even computers unaided by humans. They involve humans, each working with their own bank of computers at lightning speed. The players of these games, known as Freestylers, are not necessarily superlative at play in the absence of computer aid. Instead, they are experts at the rapid processing of computer generated information.

What computers have wrought in the chess world, Cowen argues, will appear in a multitude of other settings. In health care, for example, image searching software can already match, and in many cases exceed, the ability of doctors alone to diagnose particularly complicated illnesses. And similar trends are visible in fields such as law, business management, education, and even academic research. In education, for example, intelligent teaching software is increasingly providing an array of educational paths geared to individual students' needs.

---

[2] Ibid, p. 62.

Similarly, academic research, particularly in the physical and social sciences and in mathematics, is often driven by data-rich models so huge and complex they are beyond the capacity of any single person to fully comprehend.

PREPARING FOR UPCOMING TRENDS

Will Cowen's brave new world unfold as he forecasts? Critics say his pro-market libertarian views have heavily affected the political shading he gives to the future. Like other commentators on technological progress, Cowen presumes that machine intelligence is capable of continuing refinements that transform the way we live. The next great hurdle is computers' acquisition of abilities to interact with humans via natural speech. It is a process that is already underway with the introduction of intelligent personal assistants such as Apple's popular Siri. It is possible that there are impregnable barriers to computers' acquisition of full facility in natural speech, in which case there may be a limit to the extent that age-old human professions can continue to be made redundant. Or there may be economic or social shifts—a popular revolt against the attitudes and values that are pushing the information revolution, for example—that may slow or stop such further innovations from happening in the first place.

But there is no doubt that Cowen's predictions deserve attention, especially by young people. Students today must keep up with the economic signals provided by labour markets—not necessarily to shift their aspirations based simply on what these signals say, but to have a clear-headed sense of what these signals augur for their own future personal satisfaction and success.

1. Why, in Cowen's analysis, will decreased future demand for workers in highly skilled professions, such law and education, affect the wages paid to workers in other less skilled occupations, such as servers in the hospitality industry?

2. If Cowen's predictions are accurate, why is it likely that incomes received by the highest 1 percent of income earners in countries such as the United States will continue to rise?

Glossary

absolute advantage: the benefit enjoyed by a producer who can supply a certain quantity of an item more efficiently than can other producers

accounting profit: the excess of a business's total revenue over its explicit costs

accounting-profit rate: a measure of a business's profitability, calculated as its accounting profit divided by owner's equity

aggregate demand: the relationship between the general price level and total spending in the economy

aggregate demand curve: the relationship between the general price level and total spending in the economy expressed on a graph

aggregate demand factors: variables that cause changes in total expenditures at all price levels

aggregate demand schedule: the relationship between the general price level and total spending in the economy expressed in a table

aggregate supply: the relationship between the general price level and real output produced in the economy

aggregate supply curve: the relationship between the general price level and real output expressed on a graph

aggregate supply factors: variables that change total output at all price levels

aggregate supply schedule: the relationship between the general price level and real output expressed in a table

annually balanced budget: the principle that government revenues and expenditures should balance each year

anti-combines legislation: laws aimed at preventing industrial concentration and abuses of market power

appreciate: to increase, as when a currency's price rises in comparison with the price of another currency

asset demand: the demand for money that is related to its use as a store of purchasing power

automatic stabilizers: built-in measures, such as taxation and transfer payment programs, that lessen the effects of the business cycle

average cost: the sum of average fixed cost and average variable cost at each quantity of output

average-cost pricing: the practice of setting price where it equals average cost

average fixed cost: the fixed cost per unit of output

average product: the quantity of output produced per worker

average revenue: a business's total revenue per unit of output

average variable cost: the variable cost per unit of output

balance-of-payments accounts: a summary of all transactions between Canadians and foreigners that involve exchanging Canadian dollars for other currencies

balance-of-payments deficit: a negative net balance on the balance-of-payments statement, demonstrating lower receipts than payments for the current and capital and financial accounts combined; balanced with changes in official reserves

balance-of-payments surplus: a positive net balance on the balance-of-payments statement, demonstrating greater receipts than payments for the current and capital and financial accounts combined; balanced with changes in official reserves

balance of trade: for both goods and services, receipts (inflows of Canadian dollars) less payments (outflows of Canadian dollars)

balanced budget: a government's expenditures and revenues are equal

bank rate: the interest rate CPA members are charged on advances from the Bank of Canada

barter: a system of trading one product for another

base year: the survey year used as a point of comparison in subsequent years

breakeven point: the profit-maximizing output where price (or average revenue) equals average cost

budget deficit: a government's expenditures exceed its revenues

budget surplus: a government's revenues exceed its expenditures

business: an enterprise that brings individuals, financial resources, and economic resources together to produce a good or service for economic gain

business cycle: the cycle of expansions and contractions in the economy

business's demand curve: the demand curve faced by an individual business, as opposed to an entire market

business's labour demand curve: a graph showing the possible combinations of workers demanded by a business at each possible wage

business's labour supply curve: a graph showing the possible combinations of workers supplied to a business at each possible wage

business's supply curve: a curve that shows the quantity of output supplied by a business at every possible price

Canada Savings Bonds: federal government bonds that have a set value throughout their term

capital account: the summary of international transfers of intangible assets and savings involving Canadian dollars

capital and financial accounts deficit: a negative net balance in the capital and financial accounts, demonstrating higher investments by Canadians in foreign markets than by foreigners in the Canadian economy

capital and financial accounts surplus: a positive net balance in the capital and financial accounts, demonstrating lower investments by Canadians in foreign markets than by foreigners in the Canadian economy

capital-intensive process: a production process that employs more capital and less labour

capital resources: the processed materials, equipment, and buildings used in production; also known as capital

capital stock: the total value of productive assets that provide a flow of revenue

carbon tax: excise tax levied on a wide range of products to counteract spillover costs associated with carbon emissions

cartel: a union of oligopolists who have a formal market-sharing agreement

cash reserves: funds kept on hand by deposit-takers to meet the needs of depositors withdrawing funds

ceteris paribus: the assumption that all other things remain the same

change in official reserves: use of government's reserves of foreign currency to influence the international value of the Canadian dollar, as shown on the balance-of-payments statement

change in quantity demanded: the effect of a price change on quantity demanded

change in quantity supplied: the effect of a price change on quantity supplied

chartered banks: deposit-takers allowed by federal charter to offer a wide range of financial services

coincidence of wants: the situation where someone purchasing an item finds a seller who wants what the purchaser is offering in return

collusion: oligopolists acting together as if they are a monopoly

command economy: an economic system based on public ownership and central planning

common market: a group of countries with not only a free trade area and common trade barriers with outside countries, but also free movement of labour and capital

comparative advantage: the benefit enjoyed by a producer who can supply a certain item with a lower opportunity cost than can other producers

complementary products: products that are consumed together

concentration ratio: the percentage of total sales revenue earned by the largest businesses in the market

conglomerate merger: a combination of businesses in unrelated industries

constant-cost industry: an industry that is not a major user of any single resource

constant returns to scale: a situation in which a percentage increase in all inputs results in an equal percentage increase in output

consumer price index: a measure of price changes for a typical basket of consumer products

consumer sovereignty: the effect of consumer needs and wants on production decisions

consumer surplus: the net benefit, expressed in dollar terms, from buying a product at its market price

contestable markets: those in which the threat of new entrants is credible

contraction: a sustained fall in the real output of an economy

contractionary fiscal policy: government policy that involves decreasing government purchases, increasing taxes, or both to restrain spending and output

contractionary monetary policy: a policy of decreasing the money supply and increasing interest rates to dampen the economy

contractionary policies: government policies designed to stabilize prices and reduce output

core inflation: inflation based on a CPI definition excluding eight volatile elements, as well as effects of indirect taxes

cost of living: the amount consumers must spend on the entire range of goods and services they buy

cost-of-living-adjustment clauses: provisions for income adjustments to accommodate changes in price levels, which are included in wage contracts

cost-push inflation: inflation that occurs as increased production costs decrease aggregate supply, which then pushes up prices

craft union: a labour union of workers in a particular occupation

credit card: a means of payment that provides instantly borrowed funds

cross-price elasticity: the responsiveness of a product's quantity demanded to a change in the price of another product

currency: paper money and coins

current account: the summary of all international transactions associated with current economic activity in Canada and involving Canadian dollars

current account deficit: a negative net balance in the current account resulting from lower receipts than payments for merchandise and non-merchandise transactions

current account surplus: a positive net balance in the current account resulting from higher receipts than payments for merchandise and non-merchandise transactions

customs union: a group of countries with common trade barriers with outside countries as well as a free trade area

cyclical unemployment: unemployment due to fluctuations in output and spending

cyclically balanced budget: the principle that government revenues and expenditures should balance over the course of one business cycle

deadweight loss: the net loss in economic welfare that results from a government policy

debit card: a means of payment that instantaneously transfers funds from buyer to seller

decision lag: the amount of time needed to formulate and implement an appropriate policy

decrease in aggregate demand: a decrease in total expenditures at all price levels

decrease in demand: a decrease in the quantity demanded of a product at all prices

decrease in supply: a decrease in the quantity supplied of a product at all prices

decreasing returns to scale: a situation in which a percentage increase in all inputs causes a smaller percentage increase in output

deflation: a general decrease in the level of prices

demand: the relationship between the various possible prices of a product and the quantities of that product consumers are willing to purchase

demand curve: a graph that expresses possible combinations of prices and quantities demanded of a product

demand deposits: accounts of funds to which depositors have immediate access

demand factors: factors that can cause an increase or a decrease in a product's demand

demand for Canadian dollars: the relationship between the price of a Canadian dollar and the quantity demanded in exchange for another currency

demand-pull inflation: inflation that occurs as increased aggregate demand pulls up prices

demand schedule: a table that shows possible combinations of prices and quantities demanded of a product

dependent variable: the variable in a causal relationship that is affected by another variable

deposit-takers: institutions or businesses that accept funds provided by savers and lend these funds to borrowers

depreciate: to decrease, as when a currency's price falls in comparison with the price of another currency

depreciation: the decrease in value of durable real assets over time

depression: a particularly long and harsh period of reduced real output

desired reserves: minimum cash reserves that deposit-takers hold to satisfy anticipated withdrawal demands

devaluation: a reduction in the value of a currency by the government that sets the exchange rate

direct investment: financial investment (purchases of stocks) that gives the buyer of the financial assets a significant interest in the institution issuing the assets

direct relationship: a change in the independent variable causes a change in the same direction of the dependent variable

discouraged workers: unemployed workers who have given up looking for work

discretionary policy: intentional government intervention in the economy, such as budgeted changes in spending or taxation

disposable income: household income, after payment of income taxes, which can be either consumed or saved

double-counting: the problem of adding to GDP the same item at different stages in its production

durable goods: goods that are consumed over time

economic costs: a business's total explicit and implicit costs

economic efficiency: employing scarce resources in a way that derives the highest benefit

economic growth: an increase in an economy's total output of goods and services

economic models: generalizations about or simplifications of economic reality; also known as laws, principles, or theories

economic problem: having unlimited wants but limited resources with which to satisfy them

economic profit: the excess of a business's total revenue over its economic costs

economic resources: basic items that are used in all types of production, including natural, capital, and human resources

economic system: the organization of an economy, which represents a country's distinct set of social customs, political institutions, and economic practices

economics: the study of how to distribute scarce resources to make choices

economies of scope: the cost advantage related to a single business producing different products

elastic demand: demand for which a percentage change in a product's price causes a larger percentage change in quantity demanded

elastic supply: supply for which a percentage change in a product's price causes a larger percentage change in quantity supplied

emerging economies: economies that have recently exhibited high rates of economic growth and rising average incomes

entrepreneurship: initiative, risk-taking, and innovation necessary for production

entry barriers: economic or institutional obstacles to businesses entering an industry

European Union (EU): an expanding common market of European countries first formed in 1956, formerly known as the European Economic Community (EEC)

excess benefit: the total difference between marginal benefit and marginal cost for all units that are produced and consumed in a market

excess reserves: cash reserves that are in excess of desired reserves

exchange rate: the value of one nation's currency in terms of another currency

excise tax: a tax on a particular product expressed as a dollar amount per unit of quantity

expansion: a sustained rise in the real output of an economy

expansionary fiscal policy: government policy that involves increasing government purchases, decreasing taxes, or both to stimulate spending and output

expansionary monetary policy: a policy of increasing the money supply and reducing interest rates to stimulate the economy

expansionary policies: government policies designed to reduce unemployment and stimulate output

expenditure approach: a method of calculating Gross Domestic Product by adding together all spending in the economy

expenditure equation: the equation that states that GDP is the sum of personal consumption (C), gross investment (I), government purchases (G), and net exports (X − M)

explicit costs: payments made by a business to businesses or people outside of it

exponential growth: growth that is based on a percentage change and that builds on itself

export subsidies: payments by a government to domestic exporters so that these exporters can reduce the prices they charge in foreign markets

exports: foreign purchases of Canadian goods and services

fair rate of return: the maximum accounting-profit rate allowed for a regulated monopoly

final products: products that will not be processed further and will not be resold

financial account: the summary of all international transactions of financial assets involving Canadian dollars

fiscal policy: government stabilization policy that uses taxes and government purchases as its tools; budgetary policy

fiscal year: the 12-month period to which a budget applies

fixed costs: economic costs for inputs that remain fixed at all quantities of output

fixed exchange rates: currency exchange rates set or "pegged" to a certain value by each country's government

fixed incomes: nominal incomes that remain fixed at some dollar amount regardless of the rate of inflation

fixed inputs: inputs whose quantities cannot be adjusted in the short run

flexible exchange rates: currency exchange rates that are allowed to move freely to their equilibrium levels; also called floating rates

foreign currency deposits: accounts of funds held by Canadian residents that are valued in foreign currency

foreign exchange market: the global market in which national currencies are traded

foreign trade effect: with changes in the price level, expenditures on imports change in the same direction, while expenditures on exports change in the opposite direction

Free Trade Agreement (FTA): the 1988 pact between Canada and the United States to form a free trade area

free trade area: an area in which trade is tariff-free, although member countries are able to impose separate trade barriers on outside countries

frictional unemployment: unemployment due to being temporarily between jobs or looking for a first job

full employment: the highest reasonable expectation of employment for the economy as a whole

fully indexed incomes: nominal incomes that automatically increase by the rate of inflation

functional finance: the principle that government budgets should be geared to the yearly needs of the economy

game theory: an analysis of how mutually interdependent actors try to achieve their goals through the use of strategy

GDP deflator: an indicator of price changes for all goods and services produced in the economy

GDP identity: Gross Domestic Product calculated as total income is identical to Gross Domestic Product calculated as total spending

General Agreement on Tariffs and Trade (GATT): a multilateral trade agreement that lessened the degree of trade protection among member countries, including Canada

Gini coefficient: a single numerical measure of income distribution

globalization: the trend of growing foreign trade and investment and the spread of international businesses and markets

government purchases: current government spending on goods and services

Gross Domestic Product: the total dollar value at current prices of all final goods and services produced in Canada over a given period

gross investment: purchases of assets that are intended to produce revenue

Gross National Income: the total income acquired by Canadians both within Canada and elsewhere

horizontal merger: a combination of former rivals

human capital: the income-earning potential of a person's skills and knowledge

hyperinflation: a situation in which prices increase rapidly and inflation is out of control

immediate run: the production period during which none of the resources required to make a product can be varied

impact lag: the amount of time between a policy's implementation and it having an effect on the economy

implicit costs: the owner's opportunity costs of being involved with a business

import quota: a set limit on the quantity of a good that can be imported in a given year

imports: Canadian purchases of goods and services from the rest of the world

income approach: a method of calculating Gross Domestic Product by adding together all incomes in the economy

income elasticity: the responsiveness of a product's quantity demanded to a change in average consumer income

increase in aggregate demand: an increase in total expenditures at all price levels

increase in demand: an increase in the quantity demanded of a product at all prices

increase in supply: an increase in the quantity supplied of a product at all prices

increasing-cost industry: an industry that is a major user of at least one resource

increasing returns to scale: a situation in which a percentage increase in all inputs causes a larger percentage increase in output

independent variable: the variable in a causal relationship that causes change in another variable

industrial concentration: market domination by one or a few large businesses

industrial union: a labour union of workers in a certain industry, no matter what their occupations

inelastic demand: demand for which a percentage change in a product's price causes a smaller percentage change in quantity demanded

inelastic supply: supply for which a percentage change in a product's price causes a smaller percentage change in quantity supplied

infant industry: a domestic industry that is young in comparison to its foreign competitors

inferior products: products whose demand changes inversely with income

inflation: a rise in the general level of prices

inflation premium: a percentage built into a nominal interest rate to anticipate the rate of inflation for the loan period

inflation targeting: a monetary policy program that requires a central bank to keep annual inflation within a given range

inflationary gap: the amount by which equilibrium output exceeds potential output

injections: additions to an economy's income-spending stream

inputs: the resources used in production

intermediate products: products that will be processed further or will be resold

inventories: stocks of unsold goods and materials

inverse relationship: a change in the independent variable causes a change in the opposite direction of the dependent variable

investment demand: the relationship between interest rates and investment

investment demand curve: the relationship between interest rates and investment expressed on a graph

investment demand schedule: the relationship between interest rates and investment expressed in a table

item weights: the proportions of each good in the total cost of the basket of consumer goods used to calculate CPI

job discrimination: hiring, wage, and promotion decisions based on criteria other than a worker's credentials or performance

kinked demand curve: a demand curve with two segments, one fairly flat and one steep, that is typical of rival oligopolists

labour: human effort employed directly in production

labour force: all people who either have a job or are actively seeking employment

labour force population: the population, with specific exclusions, from which Statistics Canada takes a random sample for the labour force survey

labour-intensive process: a production process that employs more labour and less capital

labour market demand curve: a graph showing the possible combinations of workers demanded in a certain labour market at each possible wage

labour market supply curve: a graph showing the possible combinations of workers supplying their labour in a certain labour market at each possible wage

labour productivity: the output per worker in a given time period

law of comparative advantage: states that maximum output is achieved when producers specialize in what they can make at a lower opportunity cost than can other producers

law of demand: states that there is an inverse relationship between a product's quantity demanded and its price

law of diminishing marginal returns: at some point, as more units of a variable input are added to a fixed input, the marginal product will start to decrease

law of increasing opportunity costs: the concept that as more of one item is produced by an economy, the opportunity cost of additional units of that product rises

law of supply: states that there is a direct relationship between a product's quantity supplied and its price

liquidity: the ease with which an asset can be converted into a means of payment

long run: the production period during which all resources required to make a product can be varied, and businesses may either enter or leave the industry

long-run aggregate supply curve: the vertical AS curve at the potential output level

long-run average cost: the minimum short-run average cost at each possible level of output

long-run decrease in aggregate supply: a decrease in total and potential output at all price levels

long-run increase in aggregate supply: an increase in total and potential output at all price levels

Lorenz curve: a graph showing the cumulative distribution of income among a country's households

M1+: the narrowest definition of money, consisting of currency outside chartered banks, publicly held demand deposits at chartered banks, and chequable notice deposits at chartered banks and near banks

M2: a broader definition of money, consisting of currency outside chartered banks, plus the following chartered bank deposits: publicly-held demand deposits, notice deposits (both chequable and non-chequable), and personal term deposits

M2+: the definition of money consisting of M2 plus corresponding deposits at near banks and some other liquid assets

M3: the definition of money consisting of M2 plus non-personal term deposits and foreign currency deposits at chartered banks

macroeconomics: the branch of economics that takes a wide-ranging view of the economy, studying the behaviour of economic sectors

managed float: a flexible exchange rate system that sometimes involves short-term government intervention

marginal benefit: the extra satisfaction, expressed in dollar terms, from consuming a certain unit of a product

marginal cost: the extra cost of producing an additional unit of output

marginal-cost pricing: the practice of setting the price that consumers are willing to pay equal to marginal cost

marginal product: the extra output produced by an additional worker

marginal productivity theory: the theory that businesses use resources on the basis of how much extra profit these resources provide

marginal propensity to consume: the effect on domestic consumption of a change in income

marginal propensity to withdraw: the effect on withdrawals—saving, imports, and taxes—of a change in income

marginal resource cost: the extra cost of each additional unit of a resource

marginal revenue: the extra total revenue earned from an additional unit of output

marginal revenue product: the change in total revenue associated with employing each new unit of a resource

market: a set of arrangements between buyers and sellers of a certain item

market demand: the sum of all consumers' quantity demanded for a product at each price

market economy: an economic system based on private ownership and the use of markets in economic decision-making

market equilibrium: the stable point at which demand and supply curves intersect

market power: a business's ability to affect the price of the product it sells

market share: a business's proportion of total market sales

market supply: the sum of all producers' quantity supplied at each price

merchandise balance of trade: merchandise export receipts minus merchandise import payments

microeconomics: the branch of economics that focuses on the behaviour of individual participants in various markets

minimum-cost pricing: the practice of setting price where it equals minimum average cost

modern mixed economy: an economic system that combines aspects of a market economy and a command economy; production decisions are made both in private markets and by government

monetary policy: government stabilization policy that uses interest rates and the money supply as its tools

money demand: the amounts of money demanded at all possible interest rates

money demand curve: money demand expressed on a graph

money demand schedule: money demand expressed in a table

money multiplier: the value by which the amount of excess reserves is multiplied to give the maximum total change in money supply

money supply: a set amount of money in the economy, as determined by government decision-makers

money supply curve: money supply expressed on a graph

money supply schedule: money supply expressed in a table

monopolistic competition: a market structure characterized by many buyers and sellers of slightly different products and easy entry to and exit from the industry

monopoly: a market structure characterized by only one business supplying a product with no close substitutes and restricted entry to the industry

multiplier effect: the magnified impact of a spending change on aggregate demand

mutual interdependence: the relationship among oligopolists in which the actions of each business affect the other businesses

national income accounts: accounts showing the levels of total income and spending in the Canadian economy

National Policy: a Canadian policy initiated in 1879 that included high Canadian tariffs on manufactured imports in order to stimulate a domestic manufacturing sector

natural monopoly: a market in which only one business is economically viable because of increasing returns to scale

natural resources: the resources from nature that are used in production, including land, raw materials, and natural processes

natural unemployment rate: the unemployment rate that defines full employment

near banks: deposit-takers that are not chartered and have more specialized services; mainly trust companies, mortgage loan companies, and credit unions

near money: all deposits not included in M1+ plus some other highly liquid assets

negative unplanned investment: an unintended decrease in inventories; a shortage

net exports: exports minus imports

net investment: gross investment minus depreciation

net tax revenues: taxes collected, minus transfers and subsidies

nominal GDP: Gross Domestic Product expressed in current dollars

nominal income: income expressed in current dollars

nominal interest rate: the interest rate expressed in money terms

non-durable goods: goods that are consumed just once

non-market activities: productive activities that take place outside the marketplace

non-price competition: efforts to increase demand through product differentiation, advertising, or both

non-tariff barriers (NTBs): trade barriers other than tariffs that are used to restrict imports; include import quotas, voluntary export restraints, and domestic regulations

normal products: products whose demand changes directly with income

normal profit: the minimum return necessary for owners to keep funds and their entrepreneurial skills in their business

normative economics: the study of how the economy ought to operate

North American Free Trade Agreement (NAFTA): the 1993 pact among Canada, the United States, and Mexico to form a free trade area

notice deposits: accounts of funds for which deposit-takers may require notice before withdrawals can be made

oligopoly: a market structure characterized by only a few businesses offering standard or similar products and restricted entry to the industry

open market operations: the buying and selling of bonds by the Bank of Canada in the open market

opportunity cost: the utility that could have been gained by choosing an action's best alternative

output: the quantity of a good or service that results from production

overnight rate: the interest rate on overnight loans between chartered banks and other financial institutions

partially indexed incomes: nominal incomes that increase by less than the rate of inflation

participation rate: the percentage of the entire labour force population that makes up the labour force

peak: the point in the business cycle at which real output is at its highest

per capita GDP: GDP per person, calculated as GDP divided by population

per capita real GDP: GDP per person, expressed in constant dollars from a given year

perfect competition: a market structure characterized by many buyers and sellers of a standard product and easy entry to and exit from the industry

perfectly elastic demand: demand for which a product's price remains constant regardless of quantity demanded

perfectly elastic supply: supply for which a product's price remains constant regardless of quantity supplied

perfectly inelastic demand: demand for which a product's quantity demanded remains constant regardless of price

perfectly inelastic supply: supply for which a product's quantity supplied remains constant regardless of price

personal consumption: household spending on goods and services

personal saving: funds saved by households

Phillips curve: a curve expressing the assumed fixed and predictable inverse relationship between unemployment and inflation

portfolio investment: financial investment (purchases of stocks and bonds) that does not give the buyer a significant interest in the institution issuing the assets

positive economics: the study of economic facts and why the economy operates as it does

positive unplanned investment: an unintended increase in inventories; a surplus

potential output: the real output, or Gross Domestic Product, associated with full employment

predatory pricing: an unfair business practice of temporarily lowering prices to drive out competitors in an industry

price ceiling: a legal maximum price

price elasticity of demand: the responsiveness of a product's quantity demanded to a change in its price

price elasticity of supply: the responsiveness of a product's quantity supplied to a change in price

price floor: a legal minimum price

price leadership: an understanding among oligopolists that one business will initiate all price changes in the market and the others will follow by adjusting their prices and output accordingly

price-level targeting: a monetary policy program that requires a central bank to keep the price level on a desired path

prime rate: the lowest possible interest rate charged by deposit-takers on loans to their best corporate customers

prisoner's dilemma: a classic example of how players' self-interested actions can be self-defeating

producer surplus: the difference between the price received from selling each unit of a product and the marginal cost of producing it

product markets: markets in which consumer products are traded

production: the process of transforming a set of resources into a good or service that has economic value

production possibilities curve: a graph that illustrates the possible output combinations for an economy

production possibilities schedule: a table that shows the possible output combinations for an economy

productive efficiency: making a given quantity of output at the lowest cost

profit-maximizing employment rule: a business should use a resource up to the point where the resource's marginal revenue product equals its marginal resource cost

public debt: the total amount owed by the federal government as a result of its past borrowing

public debt charges: the amounts paid out each year by the federal government to cover the interest charges on its public debt

public good: a product whose benefits cannot be restricted to certain individuals

quantity demanded: the amount of a product consumers are willing to purchase at each price

quantity supplied: the amount of a product businesses are willing to supply at each price

rational behaviour: making choices by logically weighing the personal benefits and costs of available actions, then selecting the most attractive option

real expenditures: total spending in an economy, adjusted for changes in the general price level

real GDP: GDP expressed in constant dollars from a given year

real income: income expressed in constant base-year dollars

real interest rate: the nominal interest rate minus the rate of inflation

real rate of return: constant-dollar extra profit provided by a project each year, stated as a percentage of the project's initial cost

recession: a decline in real output that lasts for six months or more

recessionary gap: the amount by which equilibrium output falls short of potential output

recognition lag: the amount of time it takes policy-makers to realize that a policy is needed

research and development (R&D) expenditures: spending that is meant to accelerate the pace of technological progress

reserve ratio: desired reserves expressed as a percentage of deposits or as a decimal

resource markets: markets in which economic resources are traded

retained earnings: profits kept by businesses for new investment

revaluation: an increase in the value of a currency by the government that sets the exchange rate

rule of 72: states that the number of years it takes a variable to double can be estimated by dividing 72 by the variable's annual percentage growth rate

seasonal unemployment: unemployment due to the seasonal nature of some occupations and industries

self-interest motive: the assumption that people act to maximize their own welfare

seniority rights: the workplace privileges provided to workers who have the longest experience with their employer

short run: the production period during which at least one of the resources required to make a product cannot be varied

short-run decrease in aggregate supply: a decrease in total output at all price levels, with no change in potential output

short-run increase in aggregate supply: an increase in total output at all price levels, with no change in potential output

shortage: an excess of quantity demanded over quantity supplied

shutdown point: the level of output where price (or average revenue) equals minimum average variable cost

speculators: individuals or organizations that buy and sell currencies for profit

spending multiplier: the value by which an initial spending change is multiplied to give the total change in real output

spillover benefits: positive external effects of producing or consuming a product

spillover costs: negative external effects of producing or consuming a product

spillover effects: external effects of economic activity, which have an impact on outsiders who are not producing or consuming a product

stabilization policy: government policy designed to lessen the effects of the business cycle

stagflation: a combination of consistently low output (and so constant or expanding unemployment) and rising inflation

structural unemployment: unemployment due to a mismatch between people and jobs

substitute products: products that can be consumed in place of one another

supply: the relationship between the various possible prices of a product and the quantities of the product that businesses are willing to supply

supply curve: a graph that expresses possible combinations of prices and quantities supplied of a product

supply factors: factors that can cause an increase or a decrease in a product's supply

supply of Canadian dollars: the relationship between the price of a Canadian dollar and the quantity supplied in exchange for another currency

supply schedule: a table that shows possible combinations of prices and quantities supplied of a product

surplus: an excess of quantity supplied over quantity demanded

tariff: an excise tax on imported goods

technological progress: consists of scientific discoveries and their application, advances in production methods, and the development of new types of products

term deposits: accounts of funds to which depositors have no access for a fixed period of time

terms of trade: the international price of one product in terms of another

total benefit: the total satisfaction, expressed in dollar terms, from consuming a product in a given time period

total cost: the sum of all fixed and variable costs at each quantity of output

total product: the overall quantity of output produced with a given workforce

total revenue: the total income earned from a product, calculated by multiplying the product's price by its quantity demanded

trading bloc: a relatively small number of countries involved in a trade agreement

traditional economy: an economic system in which economic decisions are made on the basis of custom

traditional mixed economies: economic systems in which a traditional sector co-exists with modern sectors

transactions demand: the demand for money that is related to its use as a means of exchange

transfer payments: government payments to households or other levels of government

treasury bills: short-term federal government bonds that provide no interest, but are sold at a discount

trough: the point in the business cycle at which real output is at its lowest

underemployment: the problem of workers being underutilized, either as part-time workers or by working at jobs not appropriate to their skills or education

underground economy: all the market transactions that go unreported

unemployment rate: the percentage of a labour force that is involuntarily unemployed

unit-elastic demand: demand for which a percentage change in price causes an equal change in quantity demanded

unit of account: a pricing standard that allows all products to be valued consistently

utility: the satisfaction gained from any action

value added: the extra worth of a product at each stage in its production; a concept used to avoid double-counting in calculating GDP

variable costs: economic costs for inputs that vary at each quantity of output

variable inputs: inputs whose quantities can be adjusted in the short run

variables: factors that have measurable values

vertical merger: a combination of a business and its supplier

voluntary export restraints (VERs): import quotas that are voluntarily put in place by the exporting country

wealth: ownership of financial assets, such as stocks and bonds, or real assets, such as buildings and land

wealth effect: with changes in the price level, the real value of households' financial assets changes, causing households to adjust their spending

withdrawals: deductions from an economy's income-spending stream

World Trade Organization (WTO): a multilateral trade organization that has replaced GATT

Index